Criteria of adequacy'
explain what
we mean

DOING PHILOSOPHY

An Introduction through Thought Experiments

Third Edition

THEODORE SCHICK, JR.
Muhlenberg College

LEWIS VAUGHN

Boston   Burr Ridge, IL   Dubuque, IA   Madison, WI   New York
San Francisco   St. Louis   Bangkok   Bogotá   Caracas   Kuala Lumpur
Lisbon   London   Madrid   Mexico City   Milan   Montreal   New Delhi
Santiago   Seoul   Singapore   Sydney   Taipei   Toronto

Higher Education

Published by McGraw-Hill, an imprint of The McGraw-Hill Companies, Inc., 1221 Avenue of the Americas, New York, NY 10020. Copyright © 2006. All rights reserved. No part of this publication may be reproduced or distributed in any form or by any means, or stored in a database or retrieval system, without the prior written consent of The McGraw-Hill Companies, Inc., including, but not limited to, in any network or other electronic storage or transmission, or broadcast for distance learning.

This book is printed on acid-free paper.

1 2 3 4 5 6 7 8 9 0 DOC / DOC 0 9 8 7 6 5

ISBN-13: 978-0-07-299197-0
ISBN-10: 0-07-299197-6

Editor in Chief: Emily Barrosse
Publisher: Lyn Uhl
Sponsoring Editor: Jon-David Hague
Editorial Coordinator: Allison Rona
Marketing Manager: Suzanna Ellison
Project Manager: Brett Coker
Manuscript Editor: Darlene Bledsoe
Design Manager: Preston Thomas
Cover Designer: DiAnna VanEycke
Text Designer: Ellen Pettengell
Art Editor: Ayelet Arbel

Illustrator: Larry Daste
Photo Research Coordinator:
   Nora Agbayani
Photo Researcher: David Tietz
Production Supervisor: Tandra Jorgensen
Media Producer: Christie Ling
Composition: 10.5/12 Goudy
   by TBH Typecast, Inc.
Printing: 45# New Era Matte
   by R. R. Donnelley & Sons

Cover: Homero Aguilar. ART-IMAGE © 2004. Oil on canvas. 29 × 23".
www.homero-aguilar.com.

Credits: The credits section for this book begins on page C-1 and is considered an extension of the copyright page.

Library of Congress Cataloging-in-Publication Data

Schick, Theodore.
   Doing philosophy: an introduction through thought experiments /
   Theodore Schick, Jr., Lewis Vaughn.—3rd ed.
      p. cm.
   Includes bibliographical references and index.
   ISBN 978-0-07-299197-0   ISBN 0-07-299197-6 (alk. paper)
   1. Philosophy—Introductions.   I. Vaughn, Lewis.   II. Title.
BD21.S34 2005
100—dc22
                                                    2005052238

The Internet addresses listed in the text were accurate at the time of publication. The inclusion of a Web site does not indicate an endorsement by the authors or McGraw-Hill, and McGraw-Hill does not guarantee the accuracy of the information presented at these sites.

www.mhhe.com

Preface

Teaching an introductory philosophy course is one of the most difficult tasks a philosophy instructor faces. Because philosophy isn't usually taught in secondary schools, most entering college students have no idea what philosophy is or why they should be studying it. Any notions they do have about philosophy generally have little to do with the practice of professional philosophers. To help students understand the nature and purpose of philosophical inquiry, *Doing Philosophy: An Introduction through Thought Experiments* explains how philosophical problems arise and why searching for solutions is important.

It is essential for beginning students to read primary sources, but if that is all they are exposed to, the instructor must bear the burden of interpreting, explaining, and providing context for the selections. This burden can be a heavy one, for most articles in introductory anthologies were written for professional philosophers. After reading a number of these articles, students are often left with the impression that philosophy is a collection of incompatible views on a number of unrelated subjects. To pass the course, they end up memorizing who said what and do not develop the critical thinking skills often considered the most important benefit of studying philosophy. By exploring the interrelationships among philosophical problems and by providing a framework for evaluating their solutions, *Doing Philosophy* overcomes the problem of fragmentation encountered in smorgasbord approaches to philosophy.

One can know a great deal about what philosophers have said without knowing what philosophy is because philosophy is as much an activity as it is a body of knowledge. So knowing how philosophers arrive at their conclusions is at least as important as knowing what conclusions they've arrived at. This text acquaints students with both the process and the product of philosophical inquiry by focusing on one of the most widely used philosophical techniques: the method of thought experiment or counterexample. Thought experiments test philosophical theories by determining whether they hold in all possible situations. They make the abstract concrete and highlight important issues in a way that no amount of exegesis can. By encouraging students to evaluate and perform thought experiments, *Doing Philosophy* fosters active learning and creative thinking.

Good critical thinkers are adept at testing claims by asking the question "What if . . . ?" and following the answer through to its logical conclusion. Thought experiments are particularly useful in testing philosophical theories because they often reveal hidden assumptions and unexpected conceptual complications. Given the central role that thought experiments have played in philosophical inquiry, there is reason to believe that knowing classic thought experiments is as important to understanding philosophy as knowing classic physical experiments is to understanding science. By tracing the historical and logical development of thinking on a number of classic philosophical problems, we hope to provide students with a solid grounding in the discipline and prepare them for more advanced study.

Students sometimes express surprise that philosophy is still being done. They have the idea that it's merely a historical curiosity, of no contemporary relevance. Purely historical survey courses often perpetuate that idea. *Doing Philosophy* attempts to show that philosophy is a vibrant, thriving discipline actively engaged in some of the most important intellectual inquiries being conducted today.

In order to give instructors maximum flexibility in designing their course, the text is divided into self-contained chapters, each of which explores a philosophical problem. The introduction to each chapter explains the problem, defines some key concepts, and identifies the intellectual objectives students should try to achieve as they read the chapter. Classic arguments and thought experiments are highlighted in the text, and numerous "thought probes" or leading questions are placed throughout to encourage students to think more deeply about the material covered. Various boxes and quotations are also included that relate the material to recent discoveries or broader cultural issues. Each section concludes with study and discussion questions. Classic and contemporary readings are included at the end of each chapter so that students can see some of the more important theories and thought experiments in context. Each set of readings contains a piece of fiction—an extended thought experiment—which raises many of the questions dealt with in the chapter. The goal throughout is not only to present students with the best philosophical thinking on each topic but to challenge them to examine their own philosophical beliefs. Only through active engagement with the issues can real philosophical understanding arise.

The third edition of *Doing Philosophy* features new readings by Russell, Bisson, Lamont, MacIntyre, and Swinburne and new or expanded sections on the pre-Socratics, Socrates, Plato's cave, the causal exclusion problem, emergentism, mental causation, the consequence argument, the principle of alternative possibilities, libertarianism, the narrative view of the self, the ethics of care, virtue ethics, evidentialism, existentialism, skepticism, rationalism, and empiricism. In addition, many new "In the News" boxes report on current developments that demonstate the relevance of philosophy to contemporary issues.

Acknowledgments

Many people have offered us their wisdom and insight on this project. Although we have not always heeded it, we would especially like to thank Wayne Alt, Community College of Baltimore County; Gordon Barnes, SUNY Brockport; Jack DeBellis, Lehigh University; Nori Geary, New York Hospital–Cornell Medical Center; Stuart Goldberg; James Hall, Kutztown University; Dale Jacquette, Pennsylvania State University; Robert Charles Jones, Stanford University; Jonathan Levinson; Jeffrey Nicholas, Bridgewater State College; Nick Oweyssi, North Harris College; Abram Samuels; Ludwig

Schlecht, Muhlenberg College; Thomas Theis, Thomas J. Watson Research Center; Vivian Walsh, Muhlenberg College; Robert Wind, Muhlenberg College; and James Yerkes, Moravian College. We would also like to thank the following reviewers for their suggestions: David Chalmers, University of Arizona, Tucson; Alfred A. Decker, Bowling Green State University; Rev. Ronald DesRosiers, SM, Madonna University; Kevin E. Dodson, Lamar University; Jeremiah Hackett, University of South Carolina; David L. Haugen, Western Illinois University; Douglas E. Henslee, San Jose State University; Charles Hinkley, Texas State University, San Marcos; Karen L. Hornsby, North Carolina A&T State University; Margaret C. Huff, Northeastern University; John Knight, University of Wisconsin Centers–Waukesha; Richard Lee, University of Arkansas; Thomas F. MacMillan, Mendocino College; Mark A. Michael, Austin Peay State University; Dr. Luisa Moon, Mira Costa College; David M. Parry, Penn State Altoona; Leonard Shulte, North West Arkansas Community College; Robert T. Sweet, Clark State Community College; Ron Wilburn, University of Nevada, Las Vegas; and David Wisdo, Columbus State University. We also wish to thank Muhlenberg College and the staff of the Trexler Library for their unflagging support.

Contents

Chapter 2 The Mind-Body Problem 65

Chapter 5   The Problem of Relativism and Morality   325

Chapter 7　The Problem of Skepticism and Knowledge   529

Readings

To Erin, Kathy, Katie, Marci, Patrick, and T. J.
for their patience, understanding, and encouragement

Chapter 1
The Philosophical Enterprise

*P*hilosophy, Plato tells us, "begins in wonder"—wonder about the universe, its contents, and our place in it. What is the universe? Is it composed solely of matter, or does it contain immaterial things like spirits? How can we tell? Is sense experience the only source of knowledge, or are there other ways of knowing? Why are we here? Were we created by God as part of a divine plan, or did we come into being as the result of purely natural processes? Is there a God? If so, what sort of being is he (she) (it)? What kind of creatures are we? Do we have a soul that will survive the death of our bodies, or will we cease to exist when our bodies die? Are we masters of our destiny, or are our actions determined by forces beyond our control? What are our obligations to other people? Do we have a duty to help others, or is our only obligation to not harm them? Such questions are at once both familiar and strange: familiar because most of us have had to face them at some point in our lives; strange because it's unclear how we should go about answering them. Unlike most questions, they can't be answered by scientific investigation. Some would say that that makes the answers unknowable. But to say that something is unknowable is to have already answered the question about the nature of knowledge. You can't claim that something is unknowable without assuming a particular theory of knowledge. Philosophical questions are unavoidable because any attempt to avoid them requires taking a stand on them. As Pascal put it, "To ridicule philosophy is to philosophize."

Whether you know it or not, you assume that certain answers to the foregoing questions are true. These assumptions constitute your philosophy. The discipline of philosophy critically examines such assumptions in an attempt to determine whether they are true. The word "philosophy" means "love of wisdom." It's derived from the Greek *philo* meaning "love" and *sophia* meaning "wisdom." The desire to know the truth—the love of wisdom—is only one motivation for doing philosophy, however. The desire to lead a good life is another. Actions are based on beliefs, and actions based on true beliefs have a better chance of succeeding than those based on false ones. So it's in your best interest to have true philosophical beliefs. This text is designed to help you achieve that goal. By describing, explaining, and encouraging you to do philosophy, it attempts to provide you with the intellectual tools necessary to develop your own philosophy.

"An expert," says physicist Werner Heisenberg, "is someone who knows some of the worst mistakes that can be made in his subject and how to avoid them."[1] In philosophy, knowing the major theories and the problems they face is particularly important. As you construct your own philosophy, you don't want to commit the same mistakes made by others, and as you study the problems faced by various philosophical theories, you may discover that some of your philosophical beliefs are mistaken. To help you avoid making philosophical errors, this text traces both the logical and historical development of philosophical thinking on a number of central philosophical problems. After reading each chapter, you should have a good sense of the strength and weaknesses of past theories, as well as the most promising avenues for future research.

Philosophy is a search for the truth about the world and our place in it. By doing philosophy, you'll learn to distinguish good reasons from bad ones, strong arguments from weak ones, and plausible theories from implausible ones. You'll find that every view is not as good as every other. Whereas everyone may have a right to an opinion, not every opinion is right. Acquiring such critical thinking skills will improve your ability to make sound judgments and lessen the chance that you'll be taken in by frauds, swindlers, and charlatans.

Doing philosophy involves reflecting on the beliefs and values you use to organize your experience and guide your decisions. It entails questioning assumptions, analyzing concepts, and drawing inferences. In the process, you'll come to see connections, relationships, and meanings that you were previously unaware of. As a result, doing philosophy will refine your worldview, enrich your experience, and broaden your horizons.

We will begin our philosophical explorations by examining the nature and import of a number of central philosophical problems. We will then take a look at the methods philosophers use to solve these problems. Philosophical thinking is nothing if not logical. To distinguish between plausible and implausible philosophical claims, you must know the difference between logical and illogical arguments. The second section of this chapter provides an overview of the different types of arguments people use to make their points. The final section examines one of the most useful techniques for testing philosophical theories: thought experiments. Philosophical problems are conceptual problems, and conceptual problems can be most effectively solved in the laboratory of the mind.

Objectives

After reading this chapter, you should be able to

- identify the various branches of philosophy.
- describe a number of basic philosophical problems.
- distinguish necessary from sufficient conditions and logical from causal possibility.
- identify and evaluate different types of arguments.
- summarize the criteria of adequacy used to evaluate hypotheses.
- explain the nature and function of thought experiments.

Explaining the Possibility of the Impossible
Philosophical Problems and Theories

Philosophy is the art and law of life, and it teaches us what to do in all cases, and, like good marksmen, to hit the white at any distance.

— SENECA

*T*he extent to which our thoughts and actions are influenced by our philosophy becomes most evident when we examine the lives of those who don't share our philosophy. For example, many in the West believe that the world contains physical objects, that our senses give us knowledge of those objects, and that our selves are legitimate objects of concern. Many in the Orient, however, deny all three of these claims. For them, consciousness is the only reality, mystical experience is the only source of knowledge, and belief in the existence of the self is the root of all evil. As a result, they lead very different lives than we do. (Compare the life of a Hindu monk with that of a Wall Street tycoon.) Because the kind of lives we lead is determined by the philosophical beliefs we hold, we ignore philosophy at our peril. If our philosophy is flawed, we may well spend our lives pursuing false ideals, worshipping false gods, and nurturing false hopes. That is why the ancient Greek philosopher Socrates maintained that the unexamined life is not worth living.

If we have not examined our philosophy, not only may the quality of our lives suffer, but so may our freedom. Every society, every religion, and every ideology provides answers to philosophical questions. We internalize those answers in the process of growing up. But if we never question those answers—if we never critically evaluate them in light of the alternatives—then our beliefs aren't truly our own. If we haven't freely chosen the principles on which our thoughts and actions are based, our thoughts and actions aren't truly free. By replacing the blind acceptance of authority with a reasoned consideration of the evidence, philosophical inquiry liberates us from preconceived ideas and prejudices.

Man is made by his belief. As he believes, so he is.

— BHAGAVAD GITA

Because our lives are shaped by our philosophy, many have been willing to die for their philosophy. Revolutions, for example, are often inspired by a philosophy. The American, Russian, and Iranian revolutions, for example, were fueled, respectively, by the philosophies of democratic capitalism, Marxist communism, and Islamic fundamentalism. Whether a revolution ultimately succeeds is determined not by force of arms but by the strength of its philosophy. As Napoleon realized, "There are two powers in the world, the sword and the mind. In the long run, the sword is always beaten by the mind." But the mind can overcome the sword only if it is armed with viable ideas. The goal of philosophical inquiry is to determine whether our philosophical beliefs are, in fact, viable.

Philosophical Problems

Philosophical beliefs fall into four broad categories, which correspond to the major fields of philosophy: (1) *metaphysics*, the study of ultimate reality, (2) *epistemology*, the study of knowledge, (3) *axiology*, the study of value, and (4) *logic*, the study of correct reasoning. Some of the questions explored by the various branches of philosophy include the following:

> *Science without epistemology is—insofar as it is thinkable at all— primitive and muddled.*
> —ALBERT EINSTEIN

Metaphysics

- What is the world made of?
- Does the world contain only one basic type of substance (e.g., matter), or are there other types (e.g., mind)?
- What is the mind?
- How is the mind related to the body?
- Can the mind survive the death of the body?
- Do we have free will, or is every action determined by prior causes?
- What is a person?
- Under what conditions is a person at one time identical with a person at another time?
- Is there a God?

Epistemology

- What is knowledge?
- What are the sources of knowledge?
- What is truth?
- Can we acquire knowledge of the external world?
- Under what conditions are we justified in believing something?

Axiology

- What is value?
- What are the sources of value?
- What makes an action right or wrong?
- What makes a person good or bad?

- What makes a work of art beautiful?
- Are value judgments objective or subjective?
- Does morality require God?
- Are there universal human rights?
- What is the best form of government?
- Is civil disobedience ever justified?

Logic

- What is an argument?
- What kinds of arguments are there?
- What distinguishes a good argument from a bad one?
- When are we justified in believing the conclusion of an argument?

Each of these fields has various subfields. For example, *ethics* is the branch of axiology that deals with the study of moral value, and *aesthetics* is the branch of axiology that focuses on the study of artistic value. We all have beliefs about what is real, what is valuable, and how we come to know what is real and valuable. Philosophy examines these beliefs in an attempt to develop a way of looking at the world that makes sense of it.

Metaphysics is the anatomy of the soul.
—Stanislas Boufflers

Philosophical beliefs affect how we conduct our inquiries as well as how we lead our lives. What we look for is determined by our theory of reality, how we look for something is determined by our theory of knowledge, and what we do with what we find is determined by our theory of value. In science, as in everyday life, having a good philosophy is important, for as English philosopher Alfred North Whitehead observed, "No science can be more secure than the unconscious metaphysics which it tacitly presupposes." The philosophical assumptions underlying various endeavors are studied by such additional subfields of philosophy as the philosophy of science, philosophy of religion, philosophy of art, philosophy of history, philosophy of education, and philosophy of law. Even though every intellectual pursuit takes certain answers to philosophical questions for granted, the correct answer to those questions is by no means obvious. What makes definitive answers to philosophical questions so hard to come by is that conflicting views of reality, knowledge, and value often appear equally plausible.

Consider, for example, the beliefs that the universe contains only material objects and that we have minds. The success of science lends credence to the former, whereas our personal experience supports the latter. It also seems that both of these beliefs can't be true, for minds do not appear to be material objects. Material objects have properties like mass, spin, and electric charge; minds, apparently, do not. Take, for example, your thought that you're reading a book right now. How much does that thought weigh? How long is that thought? What is its electric charge? Such questions seem absurd because thoughts do not seem to be the type of things that can have physical properties. Does that mean that the mind is immaterial? If so, how can the mind affect the body (and vice versa)? Such are the issues raised by the **mind-body problem.**

The **problem of personal identity** arises from the beliefs that we change in many ways throughout our lives and that these changes happen to the same person. But if we change, we're different. So how is it possible for a person to change and yet remain the same?

The **problem of free will** arises from the beliefs that every event has a cause and that humans have free will. Yet if every event is caused by some prior event, how can anything we do be up to us?

The **problem of evil** arises from the beliefs that there is an all-powerful, all-knowing, and all-good being (namely, God) and that there is evil in the world. If God is all-knowing, he knows that evil exists; if he is all-good, he doesn't want evil to exist; and if he is all-powerful, he can prevent evil from existing. So how can there be evil in a world created by such a being?

The **problem of moral relativism** arises from the beliefs that certain actions are objectively right or wrong and that all moral judgments are relative. If all moral judgments are relative (to individuals, societies, religions, etc.), then no actions are objectively right or wrong. But if no actions are objectively right or wrong, how is moral disagreement possible? If believing something to be right makes it right, how can anyone legitimately claim that what another did was wrong?

The **problem of skepticism** arises from the beliefs that knowledge requires certainty and that we have knowledge of the external world. Our knowledge of the external world is based on sense experience. But our senses sometimes deceive us. Given that we can't be certain of what we've learned through our senses, how can we have knowledge of the external world?

Philosophical problems arise from the realization that some of our most fundamental beliefs seem to be inconsistent with one another. To anyone who wants to understand the world and our place in it, these inconsistencies should be disturbing. If the beliefs in question really are inconsistent with one another, at least one of them must be false. And any view of the world that is based on false beliefs must be mistaken. In an attempt to arrive at a comprehensive and coherent worldview, philosophical inquiry tries to eliminate these inconsistencies from our belief system.

The Stakes in Philosophical Inquiry

Making our belief system consistent is no idle task, for not only do our individual thoughts and actions depend on the truth of certain philosophical beliefs, but so do many of our social institutions. If those beliefs turned out to be false, the institutions that rely on them would have to be radically altered or even abolished. To get an idea of what's at stake in philosophical inquiry, let's examine the implications of accepting or rejecting some of the beliefs just mentioned.

The Mind-Body Problem

Many philosophers and scientists have held that the mind is nothing but the brain. Francis Crick, the Nobel Prize–winning codiscoverer of the structure of

Philosophy is an attempt to see how things, in the broadest possible sense of the term, hang together, in the broadest possible sense of the term.
— WILFRED SELLERS

mind-body problem The philosophical problem of explaining how it is possible for a material object to have a mind.

problem of personal identity The philosophical problem of explaining how it is possible for a person to change and yet remain the same person.

problem of free will The philosophical problem of explaining how it is possible for a causally determined action to be free.

problem of evil The philosophical problem of explaining how it is possible for there to be evil in a world created by an all-powerful, all-knowing, and all-good being.

problem of moral relativism The philosophical problem of explaining how it is possible for there to be absolute moral standards.

problem of skepticism The philosophical problem of explaining how it is possible for there to be knowledge.

DNA, has defended this view. In his book *The Astonishing Hypothesis*, Crick claims, "The astonishing hypothesis is that you, your joys and your sorrows, your memories and ambitions, your sense of personal identity and free will, are in fact no more than the behavior of a vast assembly of nerve cells and their associated molecules. As Lewis Carroll's Alice might have phrased it, 'You're nothing but a pack of neurons.'"[2] Although Crick's hypothesis may be astonishing, it is by no means new. The idea that we are purely material beings was proposed more than twenty-five hundred years ago by the ancient Greek philosophers Leucippus and Democritus. In their view, we are nothing but a pack of atoms—indivisible material particles that are in constant random motion. If Crick and Leucippus are right, then most religious believers are wrong—we can't survive the death of our bodies. When our bodies die, we cease to exist.

What's more, if the mind is a physical thing, it should be possible to construct one. Many working in the field of artificial intelligence believe that it's only a matter of time before we produce a robot that is as intelligent as we are. Because computers evolve much more rapidly than we do, intelligent robots could quickly become much smarter than us. Of such robots, Marvin Minsky, head of MIT's artificial-intelligence laboratory, has reportedly said, "If we're lucky, maybe they'll want to keep us around as pets."

The Problem of Free Will

It is commonly believed that we can be held responsible only for those actions that we freely perform. If we are forced to do something against our will, we aren't to blame. But if every event has a cause, then it would seem that nothing we do is up to us, for all of our actions are determined by forces beyond our control. The principle of universal causation, then, seems to be inconsistent with the notion of free will.

The view that we have no free will has long been thought to follow from materialism. The ancient Greeks realized that if everything happens as the result of a collision between atoms, then we are powerless to change the future. Whatever will be, will be. We may seem to be masters of our destiny, but that is just an illusion.

In recent years, this view has been most forcefully argued by the late Harvard psychologist B. F. Skinner. Skinner claims that the belief in free will is a prescientific belief left over from animist days when we believed that every object contained a spirit. Physics, chemistry, and biology advanced only after they had given up that notion. Similarly, he says, psychology can become a science only if it gives up the belief that human behavior is caused by an indwelling agent. According to Skinner, we are robots that are programmed by our environment. What we do as adults is the result of what happened to us as children. Consequently, we should not be held responsible for our actions and should not be given credit for our achievements. A truly enlightened society would have no use for the notions of freedom and dignity.[3]

Although Skinner believes that our behavior is determined primarily by how we are brought up or nurtured, other scientists believe that it is determined primarily by our genetic endowment or nature. According to these scientists, the information encoded in our genes determines not only what proteins our bodies manufacture but also how we respond to our environment. As biologist Richard Dawkins puts it, "We are survival machines—robot vehicles blindly programmed to preserve the selfish molecules known as genes."[4] So Dawkins shares Skinner's belief that we are robots. He simply has a different view about where our dominant program comes from.

If either of these scientists is right, then a good number of our social institutions need to be overhauled. Skinner recognized this and wrote a novel, *Walden II*, depicting what life would be like in a world where the idea of free will had been abolished. In such a world, there would be no lawyers, for lawyers determine responsibility, and, according to Skinner, individuals are not responsible for their actions. There would also be no jails, for if individuals are not responsible for their actions, no one should be punished for what he or she does. Those who engage in antisocial behavior have simply been programmed improperly and thus need to be reprogrammed at a behavioral reconditioning center.

Some psychologists have argued that the use of behavioral reconditioning techniques should be much more widespread than it currently is. Psychologist James McConnell, for example, writes,

> . . . the day has come when . . . it should be possible . . . to achieve a very rapid and highly effective type of positive brainwashing that would allow us to make dramatic changes in a person's behavior and personality. . . .
>
> We should reshape our society so that we all would be trained from birth to want to do what society wants us to do. We have the techniques now to do it. . . . No one owns his own personality. . . . You had no say about what kind of personality you acquired, and there is no reason to believe you should have the right to refuse to acquire a new personality if your old one is antisocial. . . . Today's behavioral psychologists are the architects and engineers of the Brave New World.[5]

A world in which these techniques were the norm would indeed be a brave new world.

The Problem of Personal Identity

The belief that people retain their identity over time is a cornerstone of our legal system. If you sign a thirty-year mortgage contract, for example, you will normally be expected to honor the terms of that contract even though your body and your memories will change considerably during that time. The law recognizes, however, that under certain circumstances people change enough to alter their legal responsibilities. At parole hearings, for example, it isn't uncommon to hear the following sort of argument: "He isn't the same person he was ten years ago. He has realized the error of his ways and has completely reformed. Therefore, he should be granted parole." But how much and in what ways must someone change in order to be considered a different person?

Some maintain that any change, no matter how slight, makes us a different person. Buddhists, for example, maintain that because everything in the world is constantly changing, so are we. For them, the self is created anew each instant. Others maintain that only certain types of changes can alter our personal identity. Who we are seems to be closely tied to our memories. If we suffered from total amnesia and were unable to remember anything about ourselves, there would be grounds for saying that we had ceased to exist. Does that mean that we are our memories? If we have no memory of doing something, can we legitimately claim that we didn't do it? Would it be wrong to punish us for something that we had no recollection of doing? What if there were a way to transfer our memories from our present body to another, say through a brain transplant? (Partial brain transplants have already been performed.) Would we survive such a transfer? What if our memories were transferred into a body of a different sex? A number of computer scientists believe that it will soon be possible to transfer our memories from our brains into a computer. Could we exist inside a computer? What if we uploaded our memories into two different computers? Would there then be two of us? Although these questions may seem far-fetched, some believe that we will have to face them in the not-too-distant future. How we answer them will be determined by our notion of personal identity.

The Problem of Moral Relativism

All of us make moral judgments. Sometimes we even get into heated arguments about the morality of an action or policy. But the widespread disagreement about what is moral—as for example in discussions over abortion, capital punishment, and drug use—has led many to believe that there are no objective moral standards. If morality is just a matter of personal opinion, however, then there is no more reason to argue about what is right or wrong than there is to argue about what tastes better—chocolate or vanilla. There is no accounting for taste.

Furthermore, if there were nothing more to something's being right than our believing it to be right, we would be morally infallible. As long as we did what we thought was right, we could do no wrong. But that, too, seems implausible. Our believing something to be right doesn't make it right. If it did, we would have to say that what Hitler did was right (provided, of course, that he believed in what he was doing). Doing the right thing seems to involve more than simply doing what you believe in.

The notion that morality is subjective faces serious difficulties. But so does the notion that morality is objective. Resolving these difficulties is of the highest importance, for many of the problems we face as individuals and as a society are moral ones. When we ask, "What should we do about . . . ?" we are asking a moral question. How we answer such questions will be determined by what we consider our moral obligations to be. So it's important to be clear about just what those obligations are.

The Problem of Evil

We have seen that the existence of an all-powerful, all-knowing, and all-good being seems to be incompatible with the existence of evil. If God possessed only two of these three attributes, however, there would be no problem. For example, if God were all-knowing and all-good but not all-powerful, we could account for the existence of evil by claiming that God is powerless to prevent it. If God were all-powerful and all-good but not all-knowing, we could account for the existence of evil by claiming that God is ignorant of its existence. If God were all-powerful and all-knowing but not all-good, we could account for the existence of evil by claiming that God isn't opposed to it. To many, however, a being that is limited in any of these ways would not be God. So unless a solution to this problem can be found, the traditional conception of God must be revised.

The Problem of Skepticism

We claim to know many things about the world around us. We claim to know, for example, that snow is white, that the earth orbits the sun, and that $E = mc^2$. If we really know something, however, it seems that we must be certain of it, for any possibility of error appears to undercut our claim to know. The problem is that most of our information about the external world comes to us through our senses, and we can't be certain of anything we have learned through our senses. There is always the possibility that we've misidentified or misinterpreted our sense experience. Because we can't rule out these possibilities, some claim that we can't have knowledge of the external world.

Skeptics in the Western intellectual tradition usually don't claim that our sense experience is illusory, only that it could be. As long as knowledge requires certainty, all the skeptics need to make their claim is the possibility that our sense experience misleads us. Many Oriental thinkers, however, go farther than the Western skeptics and claim that our sense experience is illusory. This doesn't mean that we cannot have knowledge of reality, however, because, for them, knowledge can be acquired through mystical experience. Mystical experience, they claim, puts us in direct contact with reality and reveals that our ordinary waking consciousness is just a dream. Because what the mystics tell us about reality seems similar to the claims of some modern physicists, some Western thinkers have endorsed the claim that mystical experience is a source of knowledge. If knowledge of the external world is impossible or if there are other sources of knowledge than those traditionally recognized in the West, our conception of education and intellectual inquiry would have to be radically altered.

It should now be clear that a lot hangs on our philosophy. The structure of our belief system can be compared to that of a tree. Just as certain branches support other branches, so certain beliefs support other beliefs. And just as bigger branches support more branches than little ones, so fundamental beliefs support more beliefs than secondary ones. Our philosophical beliefs are among our most fundamental because their truth is assumed by so many of our other beliefs. Consequently, rejecting a philosophical belief is like cutting off a large branch or even part of the tree's trunk: all the beliefs that depend on that fundamental belief must be rejected as well.

Philosophical inquiry attempts to arrive at a belief system or worldview that is both comprehensive and coherent: comprehensive in the sense that it can account for every aspect of our experience, coherent in the sense that

What we know here is very little, but what we are ignorant of is immense.

—PIERRE-SIMON LAPLACE

It may well be doubted whether human ingenuity can construct an enigma of the kind which human ingenuity may not, by proper application, resolve.

—EDGAR ALLAN POE

Where do you stand on these issues? What are your philosophical beliefs? You can indicate your views by writing the appropriate number in the space provided at the end of each question. Use the following scale: 5 = true; 4 = probably true; 3 = neither probable nor improbable; 2 = probably false; and 1 = false.

1. The mind (soul) can exist independently of the body. _____

2. The mind is the brain or a by-product of the brain. _____

3. Humans have free will. _____

4. All of our actions are determined by forces beyond our control. _____

5. Persons retain their identity over time so that a seventy-year-old and a five-year-old can be one and the same person. _____

6. Persons do not retain their identity over time because they are constantly changing. _____

7. There are universal moral principles that apply to everyone everywhere. _____

8. Morality is relative to the individual or to society. _____

9. An all-powerful, all-knowing, all-good God exists. _____

10. There is no God. _____

11. We can have definite knowledge about the external world. _____

12. Real knowledge is impossible; all we can have are opinions. _____

Are your views consistent? After you've finished the book, you might want to take the survey again to see if your views have changed.

none of the beliefs contradict one another. Such a worldview would not only give us a better understanding of the world, it would also help us deal more effectively with it.

Necessary and Sufficient Conditions

Philosophical problems arise because the belief that certain concepts apply to certain things seems to conflict with other beliefs we have. For example, the belief that we have minds seems to conflict with the belief that we are purely physical organisms; the belief that we have free will seems to conflict with the belief that every event has a cause; the belief that we retain our identities over time seems to conflict with the belief that we are constantly changing; the belief that there are universal moral principles seems to conflict with the belief that different people make different moral judgments; the belief that God exists seems to conflict with the belief that there is evil in the world; and the belief that we have knowledge seems to conflict with the belief that nothing is certain. In each of these cases, it seems that a certain concept can't apply because the conditions required for its proper application are not present. To solve these problems, then, we have to explain how it's possible or why it's impossible for these concepts to apply. And to do that, we have to identify the conditions under which they apply.

The conditions that need to be met in order for something to occur or exist are known as **necessary conditions.** For example, being unmarried is a necessary condition for being a bachelor because it's impossible to be a bachelor without being unmarried. A necessary condition, then, is a requirement—it's a condition that must be fulfilled whenever the thing in question occurs or exists.

The conditions that suffice for the application of a concept are known as **sufficient conditions.** For example, being an unmarried adult male is a sufficient condition for being a bachelor because it's impossible to be an unmarried adult male without being a bachelor. A sufficient condition, then, is a guarantee—it's a condition that, if met, ensures that the thing in question occurs or exists.

The relationship between necessary and sufficient conditions is a logical one. In general, if X is a necessary condition for Y, then Y implies X. For example, being three-sided is a necessary condition for being a triangle because being a triangle implies being three-sided. The words "only if" are often used to indicate that something is a necessary condition. For example, being three-sided is a necessary condition for being a triangle because something is a triangle *only if* it is three-sided.

If X is a sufficient condition for Y, then X implies Y. For example, being a closed three-sided plane figure is a sufficient condition for being a triangle because being a closed three-sided plane figure implies being a triangle. The word "if" is often used to indicate that something is a sufficient condition. For example, being a closed three-sided plane figure is a sufficient condition for being a triangle because something is a triangle *if* it's a closed three-sided plane figure.

Logicians use the phrase "if and only if" to indicate that a condition is both necessary and sufficient. For example, something is a noun *if and only if* it is a word used as a name or designation. A condition can be necessary without being sufficient, however. Completing the required number of courses is a necessary condition for graduating from college, but it's not sufficient, because if you haven't also paid all your college bills, you won't graduate. Similarly, a condition can be sufficient without being necessary. Getting your head cut off is a sufficient condition for dying, but it's not a necessary condition because you can die in many other ways.

Determining whether a proposed condition is necessary or sufficient for the application of a concept involves determining whether it's possible for the concept to apply without the condition being met or vice versa. If a concept can apply without the condition being met, then the condition is not necessary for the application of the concept. For example, suppose that someone claimed that being less than ten feet tall is a necessary condition for being a bachelor. Now it may well be that all bachelors who have ever lived—and all bachelors who ever will live—are less than ten feet tall. Nevertheless, being less than ten feet tall is not a necessary condition for being a bachelor because it's possible for someone to be a bachelor and be over ten feet tall. Conversely, if it's possible for a condition to be met without the concept applying, then the condition is not sufficient for the application of a concept. For example, being a closed four-sided plane figure is not a sufficient condition for being a square, because it's possible for something to be a closed four-sided plane figure and not be a square—it might be a

necessary condition
Something X is a necessary condition for something Y if and only if it is impossible for Y to exist without X.

sufficient condition
Something X is a sufficient condition for something Y if and only if it is impossible for X to exist without Y.

rectangle. Determining whether a proposed condition for the application of a concept is either necessary or sufficient is one of the most important tasks of philosophical inquiry.

Philosophical problems arise because, on reflection, it seems that certain concepts can't apply to the things we normally apply them to. To solve these problems, we have to get clear about the conditions under which they apply. Ideally, we would like to know both the necessary and sufficient conditions for their application, because if we knew only a necessary condition, we could identify some of the things to which the concept doesn't apply, but we couldn't be sure in any particular case whether it does apply. For example, if all we knew about bachelors was that they are unmarried, we wouldn't be able to tell whether an unmarried woman was a bachelor. Similarly, if we knew only a sufficient condition, we could identify some of the things to which the concept does apply, but we couldn't be sure in any particular case whether it doesn't apply. For example, if all we knew about bachelors was that priests are bachelors, we wouldn't be able to tell whether someone who wasn't a priest was a bachelor. It may not always be possible to specify complete, necessary, and sufficient conditions for a concept because it may not have precise boundaries. Nevertheless, it's usually possible to specify some necessary or sufficient conditions, and that may be all that's needed to solve a philosophical problem. In many cases, we can explain how it's possible for a concept to apply by showing that a condition is *not* necessary or sufficient.

Identifying necessary and sufficient conditions can be difficult because we can have a concept without being able to state the conditions for applying it. For example, we can have the concept of a joke without being able to say what it is that makes something a joke. When the conditions for applying concepts are unclear, clarifying them usually requires taking a hypothetical approach. This involves formulating a hypothesis about the conditions for applying a concept and testing that hypothesis to determine whether the conditions specified are necessary or sufficient. If you can identify a situation where the concept applies but the conditions do not, you've shown that the conditions specified are not necessary. If you can identify a situation where the conditions apply but the concept does not, you've shown that the conditions specified are not sufficient. This method of conceptual inquiry was pioneered by the celebrated Greek philosopher Socrates (470?–399 B.C.).

Socrates and the Socratic Method

Socrates is the pivotal figure in the history of Western philosophy. Not only was he the first to ask many of the questions that are central to the discipline, but he also pioneered a method of answering them that is still in use today. There were philosophers before Socrates, but they are known collectively as "pre-Socratics," again indicating his importance to the discipline. The pre-Socratics were concerned primarily with questions about the nature of reality. Socrates, too, was originally interested in such questions. He studied under Anaxagoras, who was charged with the crime of impiety for teaching that the sun was a molten mass of rock. Socrates eventually gave up the study of na-

The men of action are, after all, only the unconscious instruments of the men of thought.

—HEINRICH HEINE

It was a saying of the ancients, that "truth lies in a well"; and to carry on the metaphor, we may justly say that logic supplies us with steps whereby we may go down to reach the water.

—ISAAC WATTS

In the News: The Oracle at Delphi

The Oracle at Delphi was one of the most revered and powerful people in ancient Greece. She advised farmers when to plant their crops and generals when to wage war. No great project was undertaken without the blessings of the Oracle. The oracle in the movie *The Matrix* was modeled after the Oracle at Delphi. Both foretold the future, and both had the saying "Know Thyself" hanging over the entrance to their chambers (although one was in Greek and the other in Latin). Who was this enigmatic figure? It turns out that the Oracle at Delphi was not any one person, but a succession of older women of impeccable virtue who served as the mouthpiece of the god Apollo.

Delphi, which is situated at the foot of Mt. Parnassus, was considered sacred to Apollo because it was there, according to Homer, that he slew the dragon Python. The dragon's body allegedly fell into a fissure in the floor of a cave on the side of Mt. Parnassus. As it decomposed, it gave off fumes. The Oracle, also known as the Pythia, would sit on a tripod over the fissure in the cave, breathe in the fumes, and become possessed by the spirit of Apollo. In this intoxicated state, she gave her prophecies. They were often incoherent, but the Greek priests would make them more intelligible by translating them into hexameter verse.

Before Alexander the Great set out on his first military campaign, he traveled to Delphi to seek the Oracle's counsel. When he arrived, legend has it that the Oracle was unavailable. Anxious to know his prospects for success, he tracked down the Oracle and forced her to make a prediction. She is reported to have cried out in exasperation, "Oh, child, you are invincible." Alexander took this as a favorable omen and went on to conquer the world.

Recent geological research has identified a possible source of the fumes.

Several years ago, Greek researchers found a fault running east to west beneath the oracle's temple. De Boer [a geologist at Wesleyan University] and his colleagues discovered a second fault, which runs north to south. "Those two faults do cross each other, and therefore interact with each other, below the site," said De Boer. . . .

About every 100 years a major earthquake rattles the faults, the faults are heated by adjacent rocks and the hydrocarbon deposits stored in them are vaporized. These gases mix with ground water and emerge around springs.

De Boer conducted an analysis of these hydrocarbon gases in spring water near the site of the Delphi temple. He found that one is ethylene, which has a sweet smell and produces a narcotic effect described as a floating or disembodied euphoria.

"Ethylene inhalation is a serious contender for explaining the trance and behavior of the Pythia," said Diane Harris-Cline, a classics professor at The George Washington University in Washington, D.C.

"Combined with social expectations, a woman in a confined space could be induced to spout off oracles," she said.[6]

When the fissure at Delphi stopped producing gas, the Greek priests purportedly started burning belladonna and jimson weed in the cave and found that they could get some pretty good oracular declamations from the smoke that produced as well.

---

ture, perhaps because there seemed to be no way to decide among competing theories. (The experimental method that we associate with scientific investigation had not yet been invented.) Instead, he focused his considerable intellectual talents on the study of problems more directly relevant to human life. He sought answers to such questions as "What is justice?" "What is virtue?" "What is knowledge?" Because our lives are guided by what we take to be the correct answers to such questions, Socrates claimed that only those who had considered such questions could lead a good life.

Socrates was a native of Athens, Greece, and a stonecutter by trade. Like most able-bodied Athenian men at that time, he served in the army. But unlike most of them, he distinguished himself on the battlefield. In the battle of Delium, he reportedly saved the life of Xenophon and retreated with dignity when the other Athenians were running for their lives. In the battle of Potideaea, he won a citation for valor for holding his ground throughout the night. He is most famous, however, for the public conversations he had with the leading figures of Athens.

Socrates' strength of character and force of mind were widely known. So much so, that when his friend Chaerophon asked the Oracle at Delphi whether anyone was wiser than Socrates, the priestess replied, "Of all men living, Socrates is the wisest." When word of this got back to Socrates, he thought the Oracle must have made a mistake. So he set out to prove the Oracle wrong. He reasoned that if he could find at least one person who was wiser than himself, he would have shown the Oracle to be in error. He sought out the greatest politicians, poets, and craftsmen of his day in an attempt to determine whether any of them possessed true wisdom. Socrates describes his search this way:

> I went to one who had the reputation of wisdom, and observed him. When I began to talk with him, I could not help thinking that he was not really wise, although he was thought wise by many, and wiser still by himself; and I went and tried to explain to him that he thought himself wise, but was not really wise; and the consequence was that he hated me, and his enmity was shared by several who were present and heard me. So I left him, saying to myself, as I went away: Well, although I do not suppose that either of us knows anything really beautiful and good, I am better off than he is—for he knows nothing, and thinks that he knows. I neither know nor think that I know. In this latter particular, then, I seem to have slightly the advantage of him.[7]

Although Socrates was unable to find anyone wiser than himself, he did not conclude that he had any substantive knowledge that they lacked. What made him wiser than them, he claimed, was that, unlike them, he knew that he didn't have any wisdom.

Socrates liked to conduct his inquiries in the marketplace, and he often drew a large crowd. No one likes to be made a fool of in public, however, and eventually some of those who felt the sting of his sharp tongue brought charges against him. His accusers were Miletus the poet, Anytus the tanner, and Lycon the orator. They claimed that he was guilty of worshipping false gods and corrupting the youth. The penalty they sought was death. Socrates was tried before the Athenian Council of 500, and the proceedings were recorded by his pupil Plato. (Socrates never committed his thoughts to paper, so most of what we know about Socrates' philosophy comes from the dialogues of Plato in which Socrates always appears as the main character.) Socrates argued that the charges were false; that he was guilty of nothing more than seeking the truth. The council wasn't convinced, however, and by a vote of 280 to 220 found him guilty as charged. When asked, as was the custom, what an appropriate penalty would be, Socrates defiantly replied that he should be kept in the Pyrtaneum (the dining hall of Olympic and military heroes) at the public expense in recognition of the service he had performed for the people of Athens. Outraged by his impudence, the council took another vote and by a vote of 360 to 140 sentenced him to death.

Normally, convicted criminals were executed the day after the trial. Socrates' execution was delayed for thirty days, however, because the sacred ship sent to Delos every year to celebrate Theseus's victory over the minotaur had just set sail. In honor of the god Apollo, no one was allowed to be executed while the ship was at sea. During that time, Socrates had a number of remarkable philosophical discussions with his disciples.

Socrates' friends knew that the charges brought against him were false and the conviction unjust, so they tried to help him escape. They prepared a ship for him and convinced the guard to unlock the door to his cell. Socrates refused to leave, however, arguing that because he had enjoyed the benefits of Athenian citizenship throughout his life, he owed it to the people of Athens to abide by their decision. When the sacred ship returned from Delos, Socrates drank a cup of hemlock and died.

According to the biographer, Diogenes Laertius, the citizens of Athens soon recognized the error of their judgment. He writes,

> Not long afterward, the Athenians felt such remorse that they closed the training grounds and gymnasiums. They put Meletus to death and banished his other accusers. They erected a bronze statue of Socrates to honor him; it was the work of Lysippus and was placed in the hall of processions.[8]

Apparently the Athenians came to agree with Socrates that he had indeed performed a valuable public service in teaching them to seek virtue and wisdom.

When Socrates asked questions like "What is justice?" "What is virtue?" "What is knowledge?" those he interrogated often responded by citing instances of the concept in question. Socrates wouldn't accept such responses, however, for they didn't answer his question. He wanted to know what made a concept apply, and listing examples didn't give him that knowledge. Once he got his interlocutors to specify the conditions under which a concept applied, he would examine those conditions to determine whether they were necessary or sufficient.

For example, in Plato's dialogue *Euthyphro*, Socrates tries to determine what makes something holy. Believing that a theologian should know something about this, he questions the young theologian Euthyphro, who at the time was prosecuting his own father on a charge of murder. It seems that one of the father's hired laborers had killed one of his house slaves in a fit of drunken rage. Euthyphro's father captured the laborer, tied his hands and feet, and threw him into a ditch. He then sent a messenger to Athens to consult a religious authority to determine what should be done with the culprit. In the meantime, he neglected the laborer, figuring that it would not matter if he died, because he was a murderer. The laborer did die before the messenger returned, and Euthyphro alleged that his father was guilty of murdering the laborer. Socrates meets Euthyphro on the steps of the courthouse:

Pre-Socratic Philosophers

Philosophy and science have a common origin in ancient Greece. There, on the banks of the Aegean Sea around 600 B.C., Thales (ca. 624–547 B.C.) asked—and answered—a question that philosophers and scientists are struggling with to this day: "What is the world made of?" Two important assumptions underlie Thales' question: (1) that the nature of a thing is determined by the stuff out of which it is made, and (2) that everything is made out of the same kind of stuff. These assumptions lie behind our most advanced physical theory: string theory. According to that theory, everything in the world is made out of infinitesimally small, multidimensional strings that vibrate at different frequencies. Thales' basic stuff is not so arcane. According to him, the world is made of water. Although that theory may not seem very plausible, it should be noted that water can exist in a number of different states: solid, liquid, and gas. Thales apparently believed that everything in the world was a different state of water.

The Greeks traditionally recognized four different substances: earth, air, fire, and water. Thales claimed that there was only one—water—and that everything else was a modification of it. Thales' pupil Anaximander (ca. 610–546 B.C.) didn't find Thales' explanation convincing, however, because it couldn't account for fire. Earth and air may be types of water, but fire cannot be made out of water because water puts out fire. Furthermore, he argued that Thales' theory couldn't account for change. Water may exist in many different forms, but Thales doesn't explain what causes it to assume all those forms.

Anaximander sought to improve on Thales' theory by postulating a mechanism for change. He argued that change was the result of a war between opposites that he called "the hot," "the cold," "the wet," and "the dry." Because each of these forces is struggling for dominance, none of them can be basic. So the original stuff, Anaximander reasoned, must be utterly different from anything that currently exists. He referred to this stuff as "the Apeiron," meaning the indefinite or the unbounded. The four forces precipitated out of this basic stuff and gave rise to the world as we know it.

Echoes of Anaximander can also be found in current scientific theories. Modern physics recognizes four basic forces—electromagnetism, gravity, the strong nuclear force, and the weak nuclear force—as the causes of change. It also teaches that the original stuff out of which everything came is no longer present. That stuff existed at the moment of the big bang (the explosion that brought our universe into existence), but as it cooled, it turned into the particles we are familiar with.

Anaximines (d. 528 B.C.), another student of Thales, thought that Anaximander's theory was no better than Thales' because it couldn't explain how the four forces emerged out of the Apeiron. He thought that Thales had the right idea but the wrong substance. According to Anaximines, the basic stuff is air. Unlike Thales, however, he was able to explain how air could take on so many different forms: through the processes of condensation and rarefaction. Condense air, he claimed, and you get water. Condense water, and you get earth.

SOCRATES: Then tell me. How do you define the holy and the unholy?

EUTHYPHRO: Well then, I say that the holy is what I am now doing, prosecuting the wrongdoer who commits a murder or a sacrilegious robbery, or sins in any point like that, whether it be your father, or your mother, or whoever it may be. And not to prosecute would be unholy. . . .

SOCRATES: . . . my friend, you were not explicit enough before when I put the question. What is holiness? You merely said that what you are now doing is a holy deed—namely, prosecuting your father on a charge of murder.

EUTHYPHRO: And, Socrates, I told the truth.

Rarefy air, and you get fire. Thus, Anaximines could account for all four elements in terms of one basic substance.

Pythagoras (fl. 530 B.C.) is the only pre-Socratic philosopher whose name is still widely known. We recognize him as the discoverer of the Pythagorean theorem. But he also pioneered a novel approach to understanding the world. According to Pythagoras, what makes something what it is, is not the stuff out of which it is made but the form that it possesses. What's more, Pythagoras claimed, that form can be represented mathematically. Pythagoras made a number of important mathematical discoveries, including square numbers, cube numbers, and irrational numbers. Modern science shares Pythagoras's insight that the underlying form of nature can be represented mathematically. (That's why all science students have to take math courses.)

Other pre-Socratics focused on the problem of change and developed radically different theories to deal with it. The problem is, How can something change and yet remain the same thing? If it has changed, it's different, and if it's different, it's no longer the same. Heraclitus (ca. 540–480 B.C.) took change to be an undeniable fact and concluded that we must give up the notion that things remain the same through change. "The only constant is change," he paradoxically proclaimed. "You can never step into the same river twice." Parmenides (b. 515 B.C.), on the other hand, believed that only that which is unchanging is real, so he denied that change occurred. For him, change was an illusion.

Parmenides' view is important because it was backed by a logical argument. He recognized that anything that involves a logical contradiction cannot exist. So he concluded that nonexistence cannot exist. What's more, he reasoned that if there is no place where there is nothing—if every place is occupied—there is no place to move to. So motion, and thus change, is impossible. It may seem that we can move from one place to another, but that is just an illusion. For Parmenides, the world is a solid ball of matter that never changes.

This view did not sit well with most Greek thinkers, although Parmenides' pupil Zeno of Elea (ca. 490–435 B.C.), provided a number of additional arguments to support his claim. To resolve the impasse, Democritus (ca. 460–370 B.C.) combined the insights of both Heraclitus and Parmenides. He affirmed the existence of empty space and claimed that the world is made of particles that are constantly moving through space. These particles are like Parmenidean worlds: they have no internal structure and cannot be broken down into any smaller constituents. Democritus called them "atoms," which comes from the Greek *atomon*, meaning "uncuttable." What we call atoms are not indivisible, but we do recognize the existence of indivisible particles, such as electrons and quarks, out of which everything is made. What's important about the pre-Socratics is not the details of their theories but the type of questions they asked and the type of answers they gave to them, for they have shaped Western intellectual history for more than two thousand years.

SOCRATES: Possibly. But, Euthyphro, there are many other things that you will say are holy.

EUTHYPHRO: Because they are.

SOCRATES: Well, bear in mind that what I asked of you was not to tell me one or two out of all the numerous actions that are holy; I wanted you to tell me what is the essential form of holiness which makes all holy actions holy. I believe you held that there is one ideal form by which unholy things are all unholy, and by which all holy things are holy. Do you remember that?

EUTHYPHRO: I do.

SOCRATES: Well then, tell me what, precisely, this ideal is, so that, with my eye on it, and using it as a standard, I can say that any action done by you or anybody else is holy if it resembles this ideal, or, if it does not, can deny that it is holy.

EUTHYPHRO: Well, Socrates, if that is what you want, I certainly can tell you.

SOCRATES: It is precisely what I want.

EUTHYPHRO: Well then, what is pleasing to the gods is holy, and what is not pleasing to them is unholy.

SOCRATES: Perfect Euthyphro! Now you give me just the answer that I asked for. Meanwhile, whether it is right I do not know, but obviously you will go on to prove your statement true.

EUTHYPHRO: Indeed I will.[9]

Socrates has now received an answer to his question. Euthyphro has finally proposed necessary and sufficient conditions for something's being holy. Socrates proceeds to test this proposal by trying to determine whether the conditions identified really are necessary and sufficient.

SOCRATES: Come now, let us scrutinize what we are saying. What is pleasing to the gods, and the man that pleases them, are holy; what is hateful to the gods, and the man they hate, unholy. But the holy and unholy are not the same; the holy is directly opposite to the unholy. Isn't it so?

EUTHYPHRO: It is. . . .

SOCRATES: Accordingly, my noble Euthyphro, by your account some gods take one thing to be right, and others take another and similarly with the honorable and the base, and good and bad. They would hardly be at variance with each other, if they did not differ on these questions. Would they?

EUTHYPHRO: You are right.

SOCRATES: And what each one of them thinks noble, good and just, is what he loves and the opposite is what he hates?

EUTHYPHRO: Yes, certainly.

SOCRATES: But it is the same things, so you say, that some of them think right, and others wrong, and through disputing about these they are at variance, and make war on one another. Isn't it so?

EUTHYPHRO: Yes it is.

SOCRATES: Accordingly, so it would seem the same things will be hated by the gods and loved by them; the same things would alike displease and please them.

EUTHYPHRO: It would seem so.

SOCRATES: And so, according to this argument, the same things, Euthyphro, will be holy and unholy.

EUTHYPHRO: That may be.

SOCRATES: In that case, admirable friend, you have not answered what I asked you. I did not ask you to tell me what at once is holy and unholy, but it seems that what is pleasing to the gods is also hateful to them. Thus, Euthyphro, it would not be strange at all if what you now are doing in punishing your father were pleasing to Zeus, but hateful to Cronus and Uranus, and welcome to Hephaestus, but odious to Hera, and if any other of the gods disagree about the matter, satisfactory to some of them and odious to others.[10]

Euthyphro suggests that holiness is what is pleasing to the gods. Socrates puts this suggestion to the test by exploring its implications. He points out that what is pleasing to one of the gods may not be pleasing to the others—for example, what is pleasing to Zeus may not be pleasing to Hera. So if being pleasing to the gods is what makes something holy, something could be holy and unholy at the same time. But that's impossible. Nothing can have a property and lack it at the same time. Consequently, the conditions proposed can't be correct. Being pleasing to the gods can be neither a necessary nor a sufficient condition for being holy.

The Socratic Method for analyzing a concept, then, involves the following steps:

1. *Identify a problem or pose a question.* Ask, "How is it possible for concept X to apply?" "What makes X apply?" "What is the logical relationship between X and Y?"

2. *Propose a hypothesis.* Specify the necessary or sufficient conditions for applying the concept in question. Try to identify the features shared by all and only those things to which the concept applies.

3. *Derive a test implication.* Ask, "What if the hypothesis were true?" "What does it imply?" "What does it commit us to?" Test implications have the following form: If hypothesis H is true, then concept X should apply in this situation.

4. *Perform the test.* Determine whether the concept applies in the situation envisioned.

5. *Accept or reject the hypothesis.* If the concept applies in the situation envisioned, there is reason to believe that it is true. If it doesn't apply, there is reason to believe that it is false. In that case, you should either reject the hypothesis or go back to step 2 and revise it.

Science and the Scientific Method

While philosophers are in the business of trying to identify the necessary or sufficient conditions for the application of concepts, scientists are in the business of trying to identify the necessary or sufficient conditions for the occurrence of events. Consider, for example, the problem of Uranus's orbit. By 1844, it was known that there was a wobble in Uranus's orbit that couldn't be explained by Newton's theories of gravity and motion. The observed orbit differed from the predicted orbit by two minutes of arc, a discrepancy much greater than that of any other known planet. If astronomers couldn't explain how this was possible, Newton's theory would be in trouble because it would be inconsistent with the data. In 1845, astronomer Urbain Leverrier explained how the wobble was possible by postulating the existence of an unknown planet. Using Newton's theories of gravity and motion, he calculated the mass and trajectory a planet would need to have in order to affect Uranus's orbit in the way observed. On the basis of those calculations, he requested astronomer Johann Galle to search a particular region of the sky for such a planet. Less than an hour after Galle began his search, he noticed something that was not on his charts. When he checked again the next night, the object had moved a considerable distance. Galle had discovered Neptune.

Uranus's orbit seemed impossible because it conflicted with Newton's laws of gravity and motion. Leverrier explained how it was possible by identifying sufficient conditions for Uranus having the orbit it did that were consistent with Newton's laws of gravity and motion. Because Leverrier's claim turned out to be true, Newton's laws did not have to be revised or abandoned.

The scientific method, then, involves the following steps:

1. *Identify a problem or pose a question.* Ask, "How is it possible for event X to occur?" "What makes X occur?" "What is the causal relationship between X and Y?"

2. *Propose a hypothesis.* Specify the necessary or sufficient conditions for the event's occurring. Try to identify the features shared by all and only those things that cause X.

3. *Derive a test implication.* Ask, "What if the hypothesis were true?" "What does it imply?" "To what does it commit us?" Test implications have the following form: If hypothesis H is true, then event X should occur in this situation.

4. *Perform the test.* Produce the situation in the laboratory or look for it in the field.

5. *Accept or reject the hypothesis.* If the event occurs in the situation specified, there is reason to believe that the hypothesis is true. If it doesn't apply, there is reason to believe that it is false. In that case, you should either reject the hypothesis or go back to step 2 and revise it.

Philosophy, like science, aims at solving problems and getting at the truth. Unlike science, however, philosophy explains how it's possible for concepts to apply rather than how it's possible for events to occur. Jerry Fodor illuminates the difference between these two types of inquiry with the following example:

> Consider the question: 'What makes Wheaties the breakfast of champions?' (Wheaties, in case anyone hasn't heard, is, or are, a sort of packaged cereal. The details are very inessential.) There are, it will be noticed, at least two kinds of answers that one might give. A sketch of one answer, which belongs to what I shall call the 'causal story' might be: 'What make Wheaties the breakfast of champions are the health-giving vitamins and minerals that it contains'; or 'It's the carbohydrates in Wheaties, which give the energy one needs for hard days on the high

hurdle'; or 'It's the special springiness of all the molecules in Wheaties, which gives Wheaties eaters their unusually high coefficient or restitution', etc.

. . . I suggested that there is another kind of answer that 'What makes Wheaties the breakfast of champions?' may appropriately receive. I will say that answers of this second kind belong to the 'conceptual story'. In the present case, we can tell the conceptual story with some precision: What makes Wheaties the breakfast of champions is the fact that it is eaten (for breakfast) by nonnegligible numbers of champions. This is, I take it, a conceptually necessary and sufficient condition for anything to be the breakfast of champions; as such, it pretty much exhausts the conceptual story about Wheaties.

The point to notice is that answers that belong to the conceptual story typically do not belong to the causal story and vice versa.[11]

Scientists explain how it's possible for an event to occur by specifying the *causally* necessary or sufficient conditions for its occurrence. Philosophers, on the other hand, explain how it's possible for a concept to apply by identifying the *logically* necessary or sufficient conditions for its application. In other words, scientists try to explain the causal relations among events while philosophers try to explain the logical relations among concepts. To understand the difference between philosophy and science, then, it's important to understand the difference between logical and causal (or physical) possibility.

Logical versus Causal Possibility

Something is **logically impossible** if and only if it violates a law of logic known as the **law of noncontradiction,** which says that nothing can have a property and lack it at the same time. For example, a round square is logically impossible because nothing can be both round and square at the same time. Anything that is logically impossible cannot exist. We know, for example, that there are no round squares, no married bachelors, and no largest number because these notions involve a contradiction. The laws of logic, then, not only determine the bounds of the rational, they also determine the bounds of the real. That is why the great German logician Gottlob Frege called logic "the study of the laws of the laws of science."

The laws of science must obey the laws of logic. But the laws of logic need not obey the laws of science. In other words, something can be logically possible even though it's causally impossible. Something is **causally impossible** if and only if it violates a law of nature. A cow's jumping over the moon, for example, is causally impossible because it violates natural laws concerning mass, force, acceleration, and gravity, among others. But such a feat isn't logically impossible, for the notion of a moon-jumping cow doesn't involve a logical contradiction, so the notion of logical possibility is more inclusive than that of causal possibility.

Because scientific theories try to explain how it's causally possible for an event to occur, they can often be tested by means of physical experiments in the laboratory. If a scientific theory is true, then certain events should occur under certain conditions. Scientists test their theories by constructing artificial

logical impossibility Something is logically impossible if and only if it violates the law of noncontradiction.

law of noncontradiction The principle that nothing can both have and lack a property at the same time and in the same respect.

causal impossibility Something is causally impossible if and only if it violates a law of nature.

The Laws of Thought

The laws of logic are often called the laws of thought because, just as social laws make society possible, so logical laws make thought possible. Aristotle (384–322 B.C.) was the first to codify these laws. They include

The law of noncontradiction: Nothing can both have a property and lack it at the same time. (No statement can be both true and false at the same time.)

The law of identity: Everything is identical to itself. (Everything is what it is and not another thing.)

The law of excluded middle: For any property, everything either has it or lacks it. (Every statement is either true or false.)

In order to think or communicate, our thoughts and sentences must have a specific content; they must assert one thing rather than another. In other words, they must be either true or false but not both. But if the laws of thought didn't hold, this wouldn't be the case. No thought or sentence could be considered to be any more true than any other because they would all be equally true and false. In such a situation, as Aristotle notes, thinking would be impossible:

. . . if all are alike both wrong and right, one who is in this condition will not be able either to speak or to say anything intelligible; for he says at the same time both "yes" and "no." And if he makes no judgment but "thinks" and "does not think" indifferently, what difference will there be between him and a vegetable?[12]

What difference, indeed? Without the law of noncontradiction, we can't believe things to be one way rather than another. But if we can't believe things to be one way rather than another, we can't think at all.

Because the laws of thought are the basis for all logical proofs, they can't be directly proven by means of a logical demonstration. But they can be indirectly proven by showing that you cannot deny them without assuming them! Aristotle puts the point this way:

The starting point for all such proofs is that our opponent shall say something which is significant both for himself and for another; for this is necessary if he really is to say anything. For if he means nothing, such a man will not be capable of reasoning, either with himself or with another. But if any one says something that is significant, demonstration will be possible; for we shall already have something definite. The person responsible for the proof, however, is not he who demonstrates but he who listens; for while disowning reason he listens to reason. And again he who admits this has admitted that something is true apart from demonstration.[13]

The law of noncontradiction can't be demonstrated to someone who won't say something definite, for demonstration requires that our words mean one thing rather than another. On the other hand, the law of noncontradiction need not be demonstrated to someone who will say something definite, for in saying something definite, the speaker has already assumed its truth.

situations in which those conditions are met. If the events occur as predicted, the test is successful. If not, it's unsuccessful. Suppose, for example, that you wanted to test the effectiveness of a new antibacterial drug. You could grow some bacteria in a culture and then apply the drug to them. If most of the bacteria died, you would have reason to believe that the drug was effective.

Because philosophical theories explain how it's logically possible for a concept to apply, they cannot be tested by physical experiments in a scientist's laboratory. But they can be tested by thought experiments in the laboratory of the mind. If a philosophical theory is true, then certain concepts should apply under certain conditions. Philosophers test their theories by constructing imaginary situations in which those conditions are met. If the concepts apply as predicted, the test is successful. If not, it's unsuccessful. So even though philosophy deals with abstract concepts rather than concrete events, its theories can be tested, and the results of these tests can be used to judge the plausibility of these theories.

Thought Probe

Possibilities

Are the following situations causally possible? Are they logically possible? A human with feathers. Traveling faster than the speed of light. A cat speaking English. A bowling ball speaking English. A rabbit laying multicolored eggs. A soft-shelled prime number. A thinking machine. A computer with a soul.

Summary

We all have a philosophy, for we all have beliefs about what is real, what is valuable, and how we come to know what is real and valuable. The quality of our lives is determined by the nature of our philosophy, for every decision we make is influenced by our views of reality, value, and knowledge. The goal of philosophical inquiry is to determine whether these views are viable.

Philosophical problems arise from the realization that some of our most fundamental beliefs seem to be inconsistent with one another. Apparent inconsistencies among some of our central beliefs give rise to the mind-body problem, the problem of personal identity, the problem of free will, the problem of evil, the problem of moral relativism, and the problem of skepticism. Philosophical theories try to resolve such conflicts by explaining how it is possible (or why it is impossible) for a concept to apply to something.

Philosophy differs from science in that it tries to explain how it's possible for a concept to apply rather than how it's possible for an event to occur. Philosophical theories provide the logically necessary and sufficient conditions for a concept's applying whereas scientific theories provide the physically necessary and sufficient conditions for an event's occurring. Because scientific theories explain the causal relations between events, they can be tested by means of physical experiments in the laboratory. Because philosophical theories explain the logical relations between concepts, they can be tested by means of thought experiments in the laboratory of the mind.

Study Questions

1. What are the four main branches of philosophy?
2. How do philosophical problems arise?
3. How can philosophical problems be solved?

4. What is a necessary condition?

5. What is a sufficient condition?

6. What do philosophical theories try to explain?

7. What do scientific theories try to explain?

8. What makes something logically impossible?

9. What makes something causally impossible?

10. How can scientific theories be tested?

11. How can philosophical theories be tested?

Discussion Questions

1. How does your philosophy affect your decisions? Give specific examples.

2. Are philosophical beliefs the only beliefs worth dying for? Illustrate your answer by means of examples.

3. What if Crick were able to demonstrate convincingly that we are "nothing but a pack of neurons"? What effect, if any, should this have on our legal system? On our religious beliefs?

4. What if it were convincingly demonstrated that we do not have free will? What effect, if any, should this have on our legal system? On our religious beliefs?

5. What if it were convincingly demonstrated that knowledge is impossible? What effect, if any, should this have on our educational system? On government support for research?

6. Is being a resident of Iowa a necessary or a sufficient condition for being a resident of the United States?

7. Is being a citizen of the United States a necessary or a sufficient condition for being president of the United States?

8. Is it logically possible for a human to grow feathers instead of hair? Is such a thing causally possible?

9. Is it logically possible for a cow to jump over the moon? Is such a thing causally possible?

Evidence and Inference
Proving Your Point

To arrive at the truth, we have to reason correctly. Philosophers have always appreciated that fact and have made the study of correct reasoning—logic—one of their central concerns. Logic doesn't attempt to determine how people in fact reason. Rather, it attempts to determine how people should reason if they want to avoid error and falsehood. Logical thinking is rational thinking, and rational thinking is that which is most likely to lead us to the truth.

To make an inference is to draw a conclusion on the basis of certain evidence. We are justified in making an inference, however, only if the evidence is related to the conclusion in the right way. To help us distinguish legitimate from illegitimate inferences, logic identifies the ways in which evidence and conclusion must be related in order for the evidence to justify the conclusion. To present your reasons for believing something is to make an **argument.** From a logical point of view, then, an argument is a group of statements that attempts to justify a claim. The claim that the statements attempt to justify is known as the **conclusion** of the argument, and the statements that supposedly justify it are known as **premises.** For example, consider the classic argument:

1. All men are mortal.
2. Socrates is a man.
3. Therefore, Socrates is mortal.

In this argument, statements 1 and 2 are premises, and statement 3 is the conclusion.

The premises and conclusion of an argument are not always easy to identify. Often, however, they are preceded by certain indicator words. For example, words such as "thus," "therefore," "and hence," "so," "then," "consequently," "as a result," "shows that," "means that," and "implies that" serve as conclusion indicators, while words such as "because," "for," "if," "as," "follows from,"

Our reason must be considered as a kind of cause, of which truth is the natural effect.

—DAVID HUME

argument A group of statements consisting of one or more premises and a conclusion that purportedly follows from the premises.

conclusion The claim that an argument is trying to establish.

premise A reason given for accepting the conclusion of an argument.

"given that," "provided that," and "assuming that" serve as premise indicators. Writers and speakers do not always explicitly state their premises or their conclusions, however. Learning to identify arguments with unstated premises or conclusions (known as "enthymemes") is a skill that can be acquired only through practice.

Arguments come in two basic varieties: deductive and inductive. Good deductive arguments differ from good inductive ones in that they are valid. In a **valid argument,** the conclusion logically follows from its premises. In other words, in a valid argument, it's logically impossible for the premises to be true and the conclusion false because the conclusion expresses what is implied by the combination of premises. Consider, for example, this argument:

1. If all that exists is matter in motion, then there are no disembodied spirits.

2. All that exists is matter in motion.

3. Therefore, there are no immaterial spirits.

This argument is valid because if the premises are true, the conclusion must be true. There's no way that the premises can be true and the conclusion false. So deductive arguments are said to be "truth preserving" because the truth of their premises guarantees the truth of their conclusions.

Inductive arguments, on the other hand, are not truth preserving because the truth of their premises doesn't guarantee the truth of their conclusions. Consider, for example, this argument:

1. Every raven that has ever been observed has been black.

2. Therefore, every raven that ever will be observed will be black.

It's possible for the premise of this argument to be true and the conclusion false. Because we haven't observed every raven, we can't be sure that there isn't a nonblack raven somewhere. And because we can't observe the future, we can't be sure that the future will resemble the past. So, unlike deductive arguments, which can establish their conclusions with certainty, inductive arguments can establish their conclusion with only a high degree of probability. A strong inductive argument is one in which it's improbable (but not logically impossible) for the premises to be true and the conclusion false.

Deductive Arguments

Whether a deductive argument is valid depends on the form or structure of the argument. The form of an argument can be represented in many different ways, but one of the most effective is to substitute letters for the statements contained in the argument. Some statements are compound in that they contain other statements as constituents. To accurately represent the form of these statements, each constituent statement should be assigned a letter. For example, a conditional or if-then statement is compound because it contains at least two statements. To accurately represent the form of these statements, assign one letter to the statement following the "if" (known as the "antecedent"), and another to the statement following the "then" (known as the "consequent"). Using this method, two of the most common valid argument forms can be represented as follows.

Some Valid Argument Forms

Affirming the Antecedent (Modus Ponens)

If p then q.

p.

Therefore, q.

Logic is the art of convincing us of some truth.
—JEAN DE LA BRUYERE

For example:

1. If the soul is immortal (p), then thinking doesn't depend on brain activity (q).
2. The soul is immortal (p).
3. Therefore, thinking doesn't depend on brain activity (q).

Denying the Consequent (Modus Tollens)

If p then q.

Not q.

Therefore, not p.

For example:

1. If the soul is immortal (p), then thinking doesn't depend on brain activity (q).
2. Thinking does depend on brain activity (not q).
3. Therefore, the soul is not immortal (not p).

Hypothetical Syllogism

If p then q.

If q then r.

Therefore, if p then r.

Believe nothing, no matter where you read it, or who said it, no matter if I said it, unless it agrees with your own reason and your own common sense.
—BUDDHA

For example:

1. If the Federal Reserve Board raises interest rates, it will be more difficult to borrow money.
2. If it's more difficult to borrow money, home sales will fall.
3. Therefore, if the Federal Reserve Board raises interest rates, home sales will fall.

Disjunctive Syllogism

Either p or q.

Not p.

Therefore q.

valid argument A deductive argument in which it's logically impossible for the premises to be true and the conclusion false.

For example:

1. Sally either walked or rode the bus.
2. She didn't walk.
3. So, she rode the bus.

Because validity is a matter of form, any argument that exhibits any of these forms is valid, regardless of whether the statements it contains are true. So, to determine an argument's validity, it's not necessary to ascertain the truth of its premises.

To see this, consider this argument:

1. If one human is made of tin, then every human is made of tin.
2. One human is made of tin.
3. Therefore, every human is made of tin.

The premises and conclusion of this argument are false. Nevertheless, this argument is valid because *if* the premises were true, *then* the conclusion would be true. A valid argument can have false premises and a false conclusion, false premises and a true conclusion, or true premises and a true conclusion. The one thing it cannot have is true premises and a false conclusion.

Since the purpose of logic is to help us discover the truth, there must be more to being a good deductive argument than being valid. In addition, the premises must be true. When both conditions are met—when an argument is valid and its premises are true—the argument is said to be **sound.**

Only a sound argument provides a good reason for believing its conclusion. To determine whether you are justified in believing the conclusion of a deductive argument, then, you have to determine whether it's sound. This involves three steps: (1) identifying the premises and conclusion, (2) determining whether the argument is valid, and (3) determining whether the premises are true. If the argument is not valid, there is no reason to proceed to step 3, for in that case, the conclusion doesn't follow from the premises.

There are many valid argument forms, and it is not feasible to memorize them all. But once you have ascertained the form of an argument, you can test it for validity by determining whether there is another argument with the same form that would allow the premises to be true and the conclusion false. If so, the argument is invalid. Such an interpretation serves as a counterexample to the claim that the argument is valid.

Some Invalid Argument Forms

Affirming the Consequent

If p, then q.

q.

Therefore, p.

Let's test this argument form for validity by substituting the sentence "Chicago is the capital of Illinois" for p and "Chicago is in Illinois" for q. Then we have:

1. If Chicago is the capital of Illinois (p), then Chicago is in Illinois (q).
2. Chicago is in Illinois (q).
3. Therefore, Chicago is the capital of Illinois (p).

Clearly, this argument is invalid. In a valid argument, you will recall, it's impossible for the premises to be true and the conclusion false. But in this case, both of the premises are true and the conclusion is false. So any argument with this form does not provide a good reason for accepting its conclusion.

Here's another type of argument you may come across:

Denying the Antecedent

If p, then q.

Not p.

Therefore, not q.

Can you imagine any situation in which the premises are true and the conclusion false? Suppose we substitute "Joe is a bachelor" for p, and "Joe is a male" for q. Then we get:

1. If Joe is a bachelor (p), then Joe is a male (q).
2. Joe is not a bachelor (not p).
3. Therefore, Joe is not a male (not q).

This argument is also invalid because it's possible for the premises to be true and the conclusion false. So anyone who uses this form of reasoning—no matter what statements they use in the place of p or q—has not proven their point.

Affirming a Disjunct

Either p or q.

p.

Therefore, not q.

In logic, the word "or" is usually understood inclusively. In the inclusive sense, a statement of the form p or q is true whenever p or q *or both* are true. The word "or" can also be understood exclusively, however. In the exclusive sense, a statement of the form p or q is true whenever p or q *but not both* are true. The fallacy of affirming a disjunct occurs when an inclusive or is interpreted exclusively. For example:

1. Either the car battery is dead or the car is out of gas.
2. The car battery is dead.
3. Therefore, the car is not out of gas.

In the spider-web of facts, many a truth is strangled.
—PAUL ELDRIDGE

Truth is what stands the test of experience.
—ALBERT EINSTEIN

sound argument A valid deductive argument that contains only true premises.

This argument is invalid because it's possible for both disjuncts to be true: the car could have a dead battery and be out of gas at the same time. Consequently, from the fact that one is true, we cannot validly conclude that the other is not true.

Inductive Arguments

Even though inductive arguments are not valid, they can still give us good reasons for believing their conclusions provided that certain conditions are met. An inductive argument that would establish its conclusion with a high degree of probability if its premises were true is known as a **strong argument.** A strong inductive argument with true premises is known as a **cogent argument.** To get a better idea of what constitutes a strong inductive argument, let's examine some common forms of induction.

Enumerative Induction

Enumerative induction is the sort of reasoning we use when we arrive at a generalization about a group of things after observing only some members of that group. The premise of a typical enumerative induction is a statement reporting what percentage of the observed members of a group have a particular property. The conclusion is a statement claiming that a certain percentage of the members of the whole group have that property. Enumerative induction, then, has the following form:

1. X percent of the observed members of A are B.
2. Therefore, X percent of the entire group of A are B.

For example, suppose you use enumerative induction to argue from the observation that 54 percent of the students in your college are female to the conclusion that 54 percent of all college students are female. This would be a strong argument only if your sample is sufficiently large and sufficiently representative of the entire group of college students. A sample is considered to be representative of a group when every member of the group has an equal chance to be part of the sample. If your sample consists of those students attending a small select engineering school, then your argument would not be very strong because your sample is too limited and unrepresentative. But if your sample consists of those students attending a large state university with a national reputation, your argument would be stronger because your sample would be larger and more representative.

Analogical Induction

When we show how one thing is similar to another, we draw an analogy between them. When we claim that two things that are similar in some respects are similar in some further respect, we make an analogical induction. For example, prior to the various missions to Mars, NASA scientists may have argued as follows: The earth has air, water, and life. Mars is like the earth in that it has air and water. Therefore, it's probable that Mars has life. The form of such analogical inductions can be represented as follows:

1. Object A has properties F, G, H, etc., as well as the property Z.
2. Object B has properties F, G, H, etc.
3. Therefore, object B probably has property Z.

Like all inductive arguments, analogical inductions can only establish their conclusions with a certain degree of probability. The more similarities between the two objects, the more probable the conclusion. The fewer similarities, the less probable the conclusion.

The dissimilarities between the earth and Mars are significant. The Martian atmosphere is very thin and contains very little oxygen, and the water on Mars is trapped in ice caps at the poles. So the probability of finding life on Mars is not very high. Mars was more like the earth in the past, however. So the probability of finding evidence of past life on Mars is greater.

NASA scientists are not the only ones who make analogical inductions. This kind of reasoning is used in many other fields, including medical research and law. Whenever medical researchers test a new drug on laboratory animals, they are making an analogical induction. Essentially, they are arguing that if this drug has a certain effect on the animals, then it's probable that it will have the same sort of effect on human beings. The strength of such arguments depends on the biological similarities between the animals and humans. Rats, rabbits, and guinea pigs are often used in these kinds of experiments. Although they are all mammals, their biology is by no means identical to ours. So we cannot be certain that any particular drug will affect us in the same way that it affects them.

The American legal system is based on precedents. A precedent is a case that has already been decided. Lawyers often try to convince judges of the merits of their case by citing precedents. They argue that the case before the court is similar to one that has been decided in the past, and since the court decided one way in that case, it should decide the same way in this case. The opposing attorney will try to undermine that reasoning by highlighting the differences between the case cited and the current case. The person who wins such court cases is often determined by the strength of the analogical arguments presented.

Hypothetical Induction
(Abduction, Inference to the Best Explanation)

We attempt to understand the world by constructing explanations of it. Not all explanations are equally good, however. So even though we may have arrived at an explanation of something, it doesn't mean that we're justified in believing it. If other explanations are better, then we're not justified in believing it.

strong argument An inductive argument that would establish its conclusion with a high degree of probability if its premises were true.

cogent argument A strong inductive argument that contains only true premises.

Inference to the best explanation has the following form:

1. Phenomena p.
2. If hypothesis h were true, it would provide the best explanation of p.
3. Therefore, it's probable that h is true.

The American philosopher Charles Sanders Pierce was the first to codify this kind of inference, and he dubbed it "abduction" to distinguish it from other forms of induction.

Inference to the best explanation may be the most widely used form of inference. Doctors, auto mechanics, and detectives as well as you and I use it almost daily. Anyone who tries to figure out why something happened uses inference to the best explanation. Sherlock Holmes was a master of inference to the best explanation. Here's Holmes at work in *A Study in Scarlet*:

> I knew you came from Afghanistan. From long habit the train of thoughts ran so swiftly through my mind that I arrived at the conclusion without being conscious of intermediate steps. There were such steps, however. The train of reasoning ran, 'Here is a gentleman of a medical type, but with the air of a military man. Clearly an army doctor, then. He has just come from the tropics, for his face is dark, and that is not the natural tint of his skin, for his wrists are fair. He has undergone hardship and sickness, as his haggard face says clearly. His left arm has been injured. He holds it in a stiff and unnatural manner. Where in the tropics would an English army doctor have seen much hardship and got his arm wounded? Clearly in Afghanistan.' The whole train of thought did not occupy a second. I then remarked that you came from Afghanistan, and you were astonished.[14]

Although this passage appears in a chapter entitled "The Science of Deduction," Holmes is not using deduction here, because the truth of the premises does not guarantee the truth of the conclusion. From the fact that Watson has a deep tan and a wounded arm, it doesn't necessarily follow that he has been in Afghanistan. He could have been in California and cut himself surfing. Properly speaking, Holmes is using abduction or inference to the best explanation because he arrives at his conclusion by citing a number of facts and coming up with the hypothesis that best explains them.

Often what makes inference to the best explanation difficult is not that no explanation can be found, but that too many can be found. The trick is to identify which among all the possible explanations is the best. The goodness of an explanation is determined by the amount of understanding it produces, and the amount of understanding produced by an explanation is determined by how well it systematizes and unifies our knowledge. We begin to understand something when we see it as part of a pattern, and the more that pattern encompasses, the more understanding it produces. The extent to which a hypothesis systematizes and unifies our knowledge can be measured by various **criteria of adequacy,** such as consistency, both internal and external; simplicity, the number of assumptions made by a hypothesis; scope, the amount of diverse phenomena explained by the hypothesis; conservatism, how well

All truths are easy to understand once they are discovered; the point is to discover them.

—GALILEO GALILEI

Reason is man's instrument for arriving at the truth, intelligence is man's instrument for manipulating the world more successfully; the former is essentially human, the latter belongs to the animal part of man.

—ERICH FROMM

the hypothesis fits with what we already know; and fruitfulness, the ability of a hypothesis to successfully predict novel phenomena. Let's take a closer look at how these criteria are used to evaluate hypotheses.

The first requirement of any adequate hypothesis is *consistency*. Not only must an adequate hypothesis be internally consistent—consistent with itself—but it must also be externally consistent—consistent with the data it is supposed to explain. If a hypothesis is internally inconsistent—if it's self-contradictory—it can't possibly be true. Thus one of the most effective ways to refute a theory is to show that it harbors a contradiction. (This technique, you will recall, is the one that Socrates used against Euthyphro.) If a hypothesis is externally inconsistent—if it's inconsistent with the data it's supposed to explain—there's reason to believe that it's false. The data, of course, could be mistaken, but until we know that, we shouldn't accept the theory.

Other things being equal, the *simpler* a hypothesis is—the fewer assumptions it makes—the better it is. If phenomena can be explained without making certain assumptions, there's no reason to make them. So a theory that makes unnecessary assumptions is unreasonable. Medieval philosopher William of Occam put the point this way: "Entities should not be multiplied beyond necessity." In other words, you shouldn't assume the existence of anything that's not needed to explain the phenomena. This principle has come to be known as "Occam's razor" because it's used to shave off unneeded entities from theories. (This principle is also known as "the principle of parsimony" and looms large in Carl Sagan's book and movie titled *Contact*.)

Scope—the amount of diverse phenomena explained by a theory—is also an important consideration in theory evaluation. If two theories do equally well with respect to the other criteria of adequacy but one has more scope, it's clearly the better theory, for it has greater explanatory power.

Conservatism—the quality of fitting well with existing theories—is a mark of a good theory because if accepting a theory requires rejecting a good deal of what we've already established, then it may diminish our understanding. Instead of systematizing and unifying our knowledge, it may fragment it. A theory can make up in scope and simplicity what it lacks in conservatism, however. In that case, it may be worthy of acceptance.

In science, *fruitfulness* is determined by the number of successful, novel predictions a theory makes. In philosophy, it's determined by the number of problems it solves. In both cases, it's an indication of the truth of the hypothesis because the best explanation of the fact that a theory makes a successful, novel prediction or solves problems is that it's true.

Unfortunately, there is no formula for applying the criteria of adequacy. We can't quantify how well a hypothesis does with respect to any particular criterion, nor can we rank the criteria in order of importance. At times, we may rate conservatism more highly than scope, especially if the hypothesis in question is lacking in fruitfulness. At other times, we may rate simplicity higher than conservatism, especially if the hypothesis has at least as much scope as any other hypothesis. Choosing among theories isn't the purely logical process it is often made out to be. Like judicial decision making, it relies on factors of human judgment that resist formalization.

The ground aim of all science is to cover the greatest number of empirical facts by logical deductions from the smallest possible number of hypotheses.
—ALBERT EINSTEIN

criteria of adequacy
The features that distinguish a good theory from a bad one: *consistency* (lack of contradictions), *simplicity* (quality of relying on only a small number of assumptions), *scope* (the amount of diverse phenomena explained), *conservatism* (quality of fitting well with existing theories), and *fruitfulness* (the number of new facts predicted or problems solved).

This doesn't mean that the process of theory selection is subjective, however. There are many distinctions we can't quantify that are nevertheless perfectly objective. The point at which day turns into night or a hirsute person becomes bald can't be precisely specified. But the distinctions between night and day or baldness and hirsuteness are as objective as they come. There are certainly borderline cases about which reasonable people can disagree, but there are also clear-cut cases where disagreement would be irrational. It would simply be wrong to believe that a person with a full head of (living) hair is bald. It would be equally wrong to believe that a theory that does not meet the criteria of adequacy as well as its competitors is the better theory.

Informal Fallacies

When we give reasons for accepting a claim, we are making an argument. If the premises are acceptable, and if they adequately support the conclusion, then our argument is a good one. If not — if the premises are dubious, or if they do not justify the conclusion — then our argument is fallacious. A fallacious argument is a bogus one, for it fails to do what it purports to do: provide a good reason for accepting a claim. Unfortunately, logically fallacious arguments can be psychologically compelling. Because most people have never learned the difference between a good argument and a fallacious one, they are often persuaded to believe things for no good reason. To avoid holding irrational beliefs, then, it is important to understand the ways in which an argument can fail.

An argument is fallacious if it contains (1) unacceptable premises, (2) irrelevant premises, or (3) insufficient premises.[15] Premises are unacceptable if they are at least as dubious as the claim they are supposed to support. In a good argument, the premises provide a firm basis for accepting the conclusion. If the premises are shaky, the argument is inconclusive. Premises are irrelevant if they have no bearing on the truth of the conclusion. In a good argument, the conclusion follows from the premises. If the premises are logically unrelated to the conclusion, they provide no reason to accept it. Premises are insufficient if they do not establish the conclusion beyond a reasonable doubt. In a good argument, the premises eliminate reasonable grounds for doubt. If they fail to do this, they don't justify the conclusion. So when someone gives you an argument, you should ask yourself, Are the premises acceptable? Are they relevant? Are they sufficient? If the answer to any of these questions is no, then the argument is not logically compelling.

Unacceptable Premises

Begging the Question An argument begs the question — or argues in a circle — when its conclusion is used as one of its premises. For example, "Jane has telepathy," says Susan. "How do you know?" asks Jill. "Because she can read my mind," replies Susan. Since telepathy is, by definition, the ability to read someone's mind, all Susan has told us is that she believes that Jane can read her mind because she believes that Jane can read her mind. Her reason merely reiterates her claim. Consequently, her reason provides no additional justification for her claim.

False Dilemma An argument proposes a false dilemma when it presumes that only two alternatives exist when in actuality there are more than two. For example: "Either science can explain how she was cured or it was a miracle. Science can't explain how she was cured. So it must be a miracle." These two alternatives do not exhaust all the possibilities. It's possible, for example, that she was cured by some natural cause that scientists don't yet understand. Because the argument doesn't take this possibility into account, it's fallacious.

Irrelevant Premises

Equivocation Equivocation occurs when a word is used in two different senses in an argument. For example, consider this argument: "(i) Only man is rational. (ii) No woman is a man. (iii) Therefore no woman is rational." The word "man" is used in two different senses here: in the first premise, it means human being; in the second, it means male. As a result, the conclusion doesn't follow from the premises.

Composition An argument may claim that what is true of the parts is also true of the whole; this is the fallacy of composition. For example, consider this argument: "Subatomic particles are lifeless. Therefore anything made out of them is lifeless." This argument is fallacious because a whole may be greater than the sum of its parts; that is, it may have properties not possessed by its parts.

Division The fallacy of division is the converse of the fallacy of composition. It occurs when one assumes that what is true of a whole is also true of its parts. For example: "We are alive and we are made out of subatomic particles. So they must be alive too." To argue in this way is to ignore the very real difference between parts and wholes.

Appeal to the Person When someone tries to rebut an argument by criticizing or denigrating its presenter rather than by dealing with the issues it raises, that person is guilty of the fallacy of appeal to the person. This fallacy is referred to as "ad hominem," or "to the man." For example: "This theory has been proposed by a believer in the occult. Why should we take it seriously?" Or: "You can't believe Dr. Jones's claim that there is no evidence for life after death. After all, he's an atheist." The flaw in these arguments is obvious: An argument stands or falls on its own merits; who proposes it is irrelevant to its soundness. Crazy people can come up with perfectly sound arguments, and sane people can talk nonsense.

Genetic Fallacy To argue that a claim is true or false on the basis of its origin is to commit the genetic fallacy. For example: "Jones's idea is the result of a mystical experience, so it must be false (or true)." Or: "Jane got that message from a Ouiji board, so it must be false (or true)." These arguments are fallacious because the origin of a claim is irrelevant to its truth or falsity.

Appeal to Unqualified Authority We often try to support our views by citing experts. This sort of appeal to authority is perfectly valid provided that the person cited really is an expert in the field in question. If not, it is fallacious. Celebrity endorsements often involve fallacious appeals to authority because being famous doesn't necessarily give you any special expertise. The fact that Dionne Warwick is a great singer, for example, doesn't make her an expert on the efficacy of psychic hot lines.

Appeal to the Masses A remarkably common but fallacious form of reasoning is, "It must be true (or good) because everybody believes it (or does it)." Mothers understand that this is a fallacy; they often counter this argument by asking, "If everyone jumped off a cliff, would you do it too?" Of course you wouldn't. What this shows is that just because a lot of people believe something or like something doesn't mean that it's true or good. A lot of people used to believe that the earth was flat, but that certainly didn't make it so. Similarly, a lot of people used to believe that women should not have the right to vote. Popularity is not a reliable indication of either reality or value.

Appeal to Tradition We appeal to tradition when we argue that something must be true (or good) because it is part of an established tradition. For example: "Astrology has been around for ages, so there must be something to it." Or: "Mothers have always used chicken soup to fight colds, so it must be good for you." These arguments are fallacious because traditions can be wrong. This becomes obvious when you consider that slavery was once an established tradition. The fact that people have always done or believed something is no reason for believing that we should continue to do or believe something.

Appeal to Ignorance The appeal to ignorance comes in two varieties: using an opponent's inability to disprove a conclusion as proof of the conclusion's correctness, and using an opponent's inability to prove a conclusion as proof of its incorrectness. In the first case, the claim is that since there is no proof that something is true, it must be false. For example: "There is no proof that the parapsychology experiments were fraudulent, so I'm sure they weren't." In the second case, the claim is that since there is no proof that something is false, it must be true. For example: "Bigfoot must exist because no one has been able to prove that he doesn't." The problem with these arguments is that they take a lack of evidence for one thing to be good evidence for another. A lack of evidence, however, proves nothing. In logic, as in life, you can't get something for nothing.

Appeal to Fear To use the threat of harm to advance one's position is to commit the fallacy of the appeal to fear. It is also known as "swinging the big stick." For example: "If you do not convict this criminal, one of you may be her next victim." This is fallacious because what a defendant might do in the future is irrelevant to determining whether she is responsible for a crime committed in the past. Threats extort; they do not help us arrive at the truth.

Insufficient Premises

Hasty Generalization You are guilty of hasty generalization or jumping to conclusions when you draw a general conclusion about all things of a certain type on the basis of evidence concerning only a few things of that type. For example: "Every medium that's been investigated has turned out to be a fraud. You can't trust any of them." Or: "I know one of those psychics. They're all a bunch of phonies." You can't make a valid generalization about an entire class of things from observing only one or even a number of them. An inference from a sample of a group to the whole group is legitimate only if the sample is representative — that is, only if the sample is sufficiently large and every member of the group has an equal chance to be part of the sample.

Faulty Analogy An argument from analogy claims that things that resemble one another in certain respects resemble one another in further respects. For example: "The earth has air, water, and living organisms. Mars has air and water. Therefore Mars has living organisms." The success of such arguments depends on the nature and extent of the similarities between the two objects. The greater their dissimilarities, the less convincing the argument will be. For example, consider this argument: "Astronauts wear helmets and fly in spaceships. The figure in this Mayan carving seems to be wearing a helmet and flying in a spaceship. Therefore it is a carving of an ancient astronaut." Although features of the carving may bear a resemblance to a helmet and spaceship, they may bear a greater resemblance to a ceremonial mask and fire. The problem is that any two things may have some features in common. Consequently, an argument from analogy can be successful only if the dissimilarities between the things being compared are insignificant.

False Cause The fallacy of false cause consists of supposing that two events are causally connected when they are not. People often claim, for example, that because something occurred after something else, it is caused by it. Latin scholars dubbed this the fallacy of *post hoc, ergo propter hoc,* which means "After this, therefore because of this." Such reasoning is fallacious because from the fact that two events are constantly conjoined, it doesn't follow that they are causally related. Night follows day, but that doesn't mean that day causes night.

Summary

Arguments come in two basic varieties: deductive and inductive. In a valid deductive argument, it's impossible for the premises to be true and the conclusion false. A deductive argument is sound if it's valid and its premises are true. In a strong inductive argument, it's improbable for the premises to be true and the conclusion false. An inductive argument is cogent if it's strong and its premises are true.

Hypothetical induction or inference to the best explanation is one of the most common inductive arguments. The goodness of an explanation is determined by how much understanding it produces, and the amount of understanding produced by an explanation is determined by how well it systematizes and unifies our knowledge. The extent to which a hypothesis accomplishes this goal can be measured by various criteria of adequacy such as consistency, simplicity, scope, conservatism, and fruitfulness.

Study Questions

1. What is the difference between deductive and inductive arguments?
2. What is a valid deductive argument?
3. What is a sound deductive argument?
4. What is a strong inductive argument?
5. What is a cogent inductive argument?
6. What is the logical form of affirming the antecedent, denying the consequent, hypothetical syllogism, disjunctive syllogism, affirming the consequent, denying the antecedent?
7. What is the logical form of enumerative induction, analogical induction, hypothetical induction?
8. What are the criteria of adequacy for good explanations?
9. What are informal fallacies?

Discussion Questions

Determine whether the following deductive arguments are valid or invalid, and if valid, whether they are sound or unsound.

1. If it rained, the streets are wet. The streets are wet. So it must have rained.
2. If Richard Roe is willing to testify, then he's innocent. But he's not willing to testify. Therefore he's not innocent.
3. If Bogotá is north of New Orleans, and New Orleans is north of Mexico City, then Bogotá is north of Mexico City.
4. If the president doesn't act forcefully, he'll lose points in the polls. The president is incapable of acting forcefully. Therefore the president will lose points in the polls.
5. If you want high taxes, excessive unemployment, and corruption in government, then you should vote for my opponent. I know that you don't want any of those things. So you should vote for me.

Determine whether the following inductive arguments are strong or weak, and if strong, whether they are cogent or uncogent.

6. Every day you've lived has been followed by another day in which you have been alive. Therefore every day you ever will live will be followed by another day in which you are alive. (You will live forever.)

7. Every day you've lived has been a day before tomorrow. Therefore every day you ever will live will be a day before tomorrow. (You will die tonight.)

8. Almost every Mummers Parade has been held in freezing weather. Therefore, probably, this year's Mummers Parade will be held in freezing weather.

9. Building the great pyramids required cutting huge stones with remarkable precision and transporting them great distances. So the great pyramids must have been built by extraterrestrials.

10. A recent Roper poll found that a significant number of Americans have woken up paralyzed, have experienced a period of time in which they couldn't remember what they were doing, have seen inexplicable lights, have found puzzling scars on their bodies, and have felt as if they were flying. So a significant number of Americans must have been abducted by aliens.

Identify the informal fallacy committed in the following arguments.

11. Nobel Prize winner Linus Pauling says we should take massive doses of vitamin C every day. Therefore massive doses of vitamin C must be good for you.

12. You should believe in God because if you don't, you'll go to hell.

13. Quartz crystals cure colds because after wearing a quartz crystal around my neck, my cold went away.

14. Society's interest in the occult is growing. Therefore Joe's interest in the occult is growing.

15. I believe in God because the Bible says that God exists, and I believe in the Bible because God wrote it.

The Laboratory of the Mind
Thought Experiments

*P*hilosophical theories explain how it's possible (or why it's impossible) for a concept to apply by identifying the conditions for applying it. **Thought experiments** test such theories by determining whether these conditions are necessary or sufficient for the application of the concept. If it's conceivable that there's a situation in which the concept applies but the conditions aren't met, then the conditions are not necessary for the application of the concept. Conversely, if it's conceivable that there's a situation in which the conditions are met and the concept doesn't apply, the conditions aren't sufficient for the application of the concept. Consider, for example, Aristotle's theory that humans are rational animals. To assess this theory, we have to determine whether being a rational animal is both a necessary and a sufficient condition for being a human being. Let's apply the Socratic Method to this problem.

The first two steps have already been completed: a problem has been identified — What is a human being? — and a hypothesis has been proposed — Human beings are rational animals. The next step is to derive a test implication. We have to ask, What if this theory were true? What does it imply? What does it commit us to? In answer to these questions, we might derive this test implication: If human beings are rational animals, then human infants are rational animals.

Notice that test implications are in the form of conditional or "if-then" statements. The antecedent — the statement following the "if" — identifies a sufficient condition, and the consequent—the statement following the "then"—identifies a necessary condition. So our test implication says two things: (1) that Aristotle's theory being true is a sufficient condition for human infants being rational animals, and (2) that human infants being rational animals is a necessary condition for Artistotle's theory being true.

The next step is to perform the test — examine the situation in our mind, and see whether the implication holds. If it doesn't, then the situation serves as a **counterexample** to the hypothesis. A counterexample is an example that runs counter to or conflicts with the theory. It suggests that the theory is mistaken and should be rejected or revised. Does the implication hold? It wouldn't seem so. Human infants are not rational animals because they do not know how to reason. Thus human infants are a counterexample to Aristotle's theory. So we need to either reject Aristotle's theory or go back to step 2 and revise it. In this case, it looks like Aristotle's theory can be saved with only a minor correction. We could revise it to read that human beings are animals with the capacity to reason. This would take care of the infant counterexample because although infants can't reason, they have the capacity to reason (given time). To assess this new theory, we need to go through the process of deriving a **test implication** and performing a test.

Every thought experiment is part of an argument that usually has the form of denying the consequent or affirming the antecedent. In this case, the form of the argument is denying the consequent. It goes like this:

1. If human beings are rational animals, then human infants must be rational animals.
2. But human infants aren't rational animals.
3. Therefore it's not necessarily true that human beings are rational animals.

This is a deductively valid argument—if the premises are true, the conclusion must be true.

Of course, we could cite a number of positive instances to support the theory. For example:

1. If human beings are rational animals, then Aristotle is a rational animal.
2. Aristotle is a rational animal.
3. Therefore it's probable that human beings are rational animals.

This argument, unlike the former, is not valid—the truth of the premises does not guarantee the truth of the conclusion—because it commits the fallacy of affirming the consequent. It could be a strong inductive argument of the enumerative variety, however, if there were sufficient positive inferences. But because inductive arguments do not guarantee the truth of their conclusions, they can be refuted by one counterexample. All it takes to refute the claim that all ravens are black is one nonblack raven.

The most difficult part of performing a thought experiment is deriving the test implication, because there is no formula for deriving one. Inventing a thought experiment involves a creative leap of the imagination that cannot be dictated by a set of formal rules. German philosopher Edmund Husserl called thought experiments "free fancies" because the situations involved are often produced by the free play of the imagination. But even though thought experiments can be fanciful, they are not frivolous, for as Husserl recognized, "fiction is the source from which the knowledge of 'eternal truths' draws its sustenance."[16] To determine whether a conceptual claim is true, we have to determine whether it holds in all conceivable situations. And to determine that, we have to go beyond the actual to the possible.

thought experiment An imaginary situation designed to determine whether a claim is necessarily true.

counterexample An example that runs counter to or conflicts with a theory.

test implication A statement to the effect that if a theory is true, then a certain concept (event) should apply (occur) in a certain situation.

Platonic Humans

Plato once claimed that humans are featherless bipeds (two-legged creatures without feathers). Is this a good hypothesis concerning the nature of human beings? Put Plato's theory to the test by using the Socratic Method.

The true method of discovery is like the flight of an aeroplane. It starts from the ground of particular observation; it makes a flight in the thin air of imaginative generalization; and it again lands for renewed observation rendered acute by rational interpretation.

— ALFRED NORTH
WHITEHEAD

Philosophical inquiry is not just idle, abstract speculation. Sometimes it has concrete, practical applications. It can even be a matter of life and death. To see this, let's consider a variant of the problem Aristotle was addressing: namely, "What makes something a person?" Understanding the concept of a person will be important to solving a number of philosophical problems we will encounter later in the text.

Case Study: Explaining How Moral Abortions Are Possible

Many people believe that, in certain circumstances, abortion is morally permissible. But abortion seems to involve the intentional killing of an innocent human being, and such an act is usually considered murder. So those who believe that abortion is morally permissible need to explain how it is possible for abortion not to be murder.

Murder is wrong because it violates our rights, specifically our right to life. But what is it about us that gives us a right to life? Why is it murder to intentionally kill an innocent human being but not a cow, a pig, or a chicken? What do we have that gives us our special moral status? Is it something about our physiology? Are we morally superior to these animals because we have an opposable thumb? Because we lack fur or feathers or hoofs? Because we have 46 chromosomes? This was the issue that Mary Anne Warren set out to investigate in her article "On the Moral and Legal Status of Abortion."[17]

In ethics, a being with full moral status—and thus full moral rights—is called a person. The question is, Are all and only human beings persons? In other words, is being a biological human being a necessary and sufficient condition for being a person? To determine whether it is, Warren proposed the following thought experiment.

Thought Experiment

Warren's Moral Space Traveler

What characteristics entitle an entity to be considered a person? . . . In searching for such criteria, it is useful to look beyond the set of people with whom we are acquainted, and ask how we would decide whether a totally alien being was a person or not. . . . Imagine a space traveler who lands on an unknown planet and encounters a race of beings utterly unlike any he has ever seen or heard of. If he wants to be sure of behaving morally toward these beings, he has to somehow decide whether they are people, and hence have full moral rights, or whether they are the sort of thing which he need not feel guilty about treating as, for example, a source of food. How should he go about making this decision? . . .

I suggest that the traits which are most central to the concept of personhood, or humanity in the moral sense, are, very roughly, the following:

1. consciousness (of objects and events external and/or internal to the being, and in particular the capacity to feel pain);

2. reasoning (the developed capacity to solve new and relatively complex problems);

3. self-motivated activity (activity which is relatively independent of either genetic or direct external control);

4. the capacity to communicate, by whatever means, messages of an indefinite variety of types, that is, not just with an indefinite number of possible contents, but on indefinitely many possible topics;

5. the presence of self-concepts, and self-awareness, either individual or racial, or both. . . .

We needn't suppose that an entity must have all of these attributes to be properly considered a person. (1) and (2) alone may well be sufficient for personhood, and quite probably (1)–(3) are sufficient. Neither do we need to insist that any one of these criteria is necessary for personhood, although once again (1) and (2) look like fairly good candidates for necessary conditions, as does (3), if "activity" is construed so as to include the activity of reasoning.[18]

If being a human were a necessary condition for being a person, it would be impossible for a nonhuman to be a person. But as Warren's thought experiment shows, it's not impossible for a nonhuman to be a person, for the notion of a nonhuman person doesn't involve a logical contradiction. According to Warren, what gives us our special moral status isn't the stuff out of which we are made, but rather what we can do with that stuff. So being a human being is neither a necessary nor a sufficient condition for being a person.

Remember, a logically necessary condition is one that something cannot possibly do without. So even if every person who ever has or ever will exist is human, it doesn't follow that being a human is a logically necessary condition for being a person. A possibility may be real even if it is never realized. To show that a condition isn't logically necessary for something, you only have to show that it's logically possible for the thing to exist without it.

Mary Anne Warren wasn't the first person to recognize that the concept of a person and the concept of a human being aren't the same. English philosopher John Locke realized this more than three hundred years ago. He writes, ". . . we must consider what Person stands for; which I think, is a thinking intelligent Being, that has reason and reflection, and can consider it self as it self. . . ."[19] Locke also uses a thought experiment to demonstrate that persons

Everything that is possible to be believed is an image of the truth.

—William Blake

Knowing others is intelligence; knowing yourself is true wisdom.

—Lao Tzu

need not be humans. Instead of appealing to the possibility of intelligent aliens, however, Locke appeals to the possibility of an intelligent parrot. It seems that a certain Sir William Temple wrote in his memoirs of a parrot in Brazil that "spoke, and asked, and answered common Questions like a reasonable Creature. . . ."[20] If there really were such a parrot, Locke argued, and if it really did possess reason and reflection, then it would be a person even though it wasn't a human being.

The notion that not all persons are human beings is one that is widely held but little recognized. Most Christians, for example, take God to be a person. But few would claim that he is a biological human being. As English philosopher Richard Swinburne puts it, "That God is a person, yet one without a body, seems the most elementary claim of theism."[21] So the distinction between persons and human beings is by no means a novel one.

From her analysis of the concept of a person, Warren draws the following conclusion about the moral status of the fetus:

> All we need to claim, to demonstrate that a fetus isn't a person, is that any being which satisfies none of (1)–(5) is certainly not a person. I consider this claim to be so obvious that I think anyone who denied it and claimed that a being which satisfied none of (1)–(5) was a person all the same, would thereby demonstrate that he had no notion at all of what a person is—perhaps because he had confused the concept of a person with that of genetic humanity. . . .
>
> Furthermore, I think that on reflection even the antiabortionists ought to agree not only that (1)–(5) are central to the concept of personhood, but also that it is part of this concept that all and only people have full moral rights. . . .[22]

The question we began with was, How is it possible for abortion not to be murder? Warren provides the following answer: It is possible for abortion not to be murder because only persons can be murdered and fetuses are not persons. In Warren's view, abortion doesn't violate a fetus's right to life because a fetus isn't the sort of thing that can have a right to life.

The realization that persons need not be humans and that humans need not be persons has important implications for our beliefs in other areas, as Warren notes:

> Now if (1)–(5) are indeed the primary criteria of personhood, then it is clear that genetic humanity is neither necessary nor sufficient for establishing that an entity is a person. Some human beings are not people, and there may well be people who are not human beings. A man or woman whose consciousness has been permanently obliterated but who remains alive is a human being which is no longer a person; defective human beings, with no appreciable mental capacity, are not and presumably never will be people; and a fetus is a human being which isn't yet a person, and which therefore can't coherently be said to have full moral rights. Citizens of the next century should be prepared to recognize highly advanced, self-aware robots or computers, should such be developed, and intelligent inhabitants of other worlds, should such be found, as people in the fullest sense, and to respect their moral rights. But to ascribe full moral rights to an entity which is

In religion and politics people's beliefs and convictions are in almost every case gotten at second-hand, and without examination, from authorities who have not themselves examined the questions at issue but have taken them at second-hand from other nonexaminers, whose opinions about them were not worth a brass farthing.

—MARK TWAIN

not a person is as absurd as to ascribe moral obligations and responsibilities to such an entity.[23]

The concept of a person is closely tied to our concepts of rights and responsibilities. In order to ensure that we give others their due, then, we have to be clear about what makes something a person.

Thought Probe

The Terri Schiavo Case

In January 2005, the United States Supreme Court let stand a Florida Supreme Court decision to strike down "Terri's law," a statute passed by the Florida state legislature giving Governor Jeb Bush (President George W. Bush's brother) the authority to prevent a feeding tube from being removed, against the wishes of the patient, Terri Schiavo, and her husband, Michael Schiavo. Terri Schiavo's parents, Bob and Mary Schindler, did not want the feeding tube removed, and Governor Bush sided with them.

Terri Schiavo had been in a persistent vegetative state (PVS) since 1990 when a heart attack allegedly deprived her brain of oxygen for over five minutes. The National Institute of Neurological Disorders and Stroke describes PVS this way:

> A *persistent vegetative state* (commonly, but incorrectly, referred to as "brain-death") sometimes follows a coma. Individuals in such a state have lost their thinking abilities and awareness of their surroundings, but retain non-cognitive function and normal sleep patterns. Even though those in a persistent vegetative state lose their higher brain functions, other key functions such as breathing and circulation remain relatively intact. Spontaneous movements may occur, and the eyes may open in response to external stimuli. They may even occasionally grimace, cry, or laugh. Although individuals in a persistent vegetative state may appear somewhat normal, they do not speak and they are unable to respond to commands.[24]

On March 18, 2005, doctors removed the feeding tube. On March 21, President George Bush signed into law a bill (S. 686) allowing the United States District Court for the Middle District of Florida to hear the parent's case for removing the tube. After hearing the case, the district court refused to order reinsertion of the tube. The case was then appealed to the Eleventh Circuit Court of Appeals, which also voted against reinsertion. It was finally appealed to the United States Supreme Court, which refused to hear the case. Terri Schiavo died on March 31, 2005.

If Terri Schiavo was in a persistent vegetative state, and if people in PVS have permanently lost the ability to think, was Terri Schiavo still a person? Remember, a person, according to Locke and Warren, is conscious, self-aware, and capable of reasoning, communicating, and engaging in self-motivated activity. If Terri Schiavo was not a person, was removing the feeding tube an act of murder?

How Are Thought Experiments Possible?

Thought experiments test claims about the logical relations between concepts by helping us determine whether the claims are necessarily true. But how can such flights of fancy prove anything? Why should we trust our imaginations to reveal anything about the way things are? The answer to these questions lies in our conceptual competence. Having a concept gives us the ability to make accurate judgments about its applicability, even in imaginary situations.

We acquire a concept by being given a definition of it or by being shown examples of it. In either case, once we have a concept, we have the ability to apply it to things we have never before encountered. If we have the concept of the letter A, for example, we can apply it to typefaces we have never seen before. A thought experiment is like a newly encountered typeface. Just as we can trust our judgment to determine whether the concept of the letter A applies to a letter in a new typeface, so we can trust our judgment to determine whether a particular concept applies to the situation described in a thought experiment.

Of course, the more flourishes the letters in a typeface have, the more difficult it will be to determine whether a letter is an A. Similarly, the more outlandish the thought experiment, the more difficult it will be to determine whether the concept in question applies. So not all thought experiments have equal evidentiary value. Some are more persuasive than others.

To have a concept is to be able to apply it correctly. But we may be able to apply a concept without being able to state the criteria we use in applying it. For example, we may be able to identify a grammatical sentence without being able to state the rules of grammar. In such a case, we have an intuitive understanding of grammar even though we do not have a theoretical understanding of it. In attempting to identify the conditions for applying a concept, we are trying to transform our intuitive understanding into a theoretical one. That is, we are trying to make explicit what is implicit in our understanding of a concept. Because having the ability to apply a concept correctly doesn't necessarily give us the ability to state the conditions for applying it, different people may have different theories about what those conditions are. But because we have an intuitive understanding of the concept, there is a body of data—our "intuitions"—that can be used to adjudicate various theories of it.

Criticizing Thought Experiments

The value of any experiment is determined by the amount of control with which it is executed. The more controlled the experiment, the less chance that its results will be misleading. It is not possible to control all the variables in an experiment, however. No one, for example, can control the position of the earth relative to the sun and the other planets. Nevertheless, it is sometimes possible to control all the *relevant* variables—that is, all the variables that could reasonably be expected to affect the outcome of the experiment. Criticizing an experiment usually involves explaining how it's possible that something other than the variable under investigation could have produced the result.

Some thought experiments describe situations that are physically impossible. That is not necessarily a strike against them, however, for their more fantastic aspects may not be relevant to their outcome. Thought experiments examine the logical relations between concepts, and abstracting from physical reality is sometimes necessary to throw those relations into proper relief. Of course, the more outlandish a thought experiment, the more likely it is to alter a variable that is relevant to its outcome. If you doubt the results of an experiment, however, the burden of proof is on you to show where it went wrong by providing an alternative explanation of the results.

There is usually widespread agreement about the outcome of a thought experiment.[25] Thus thought experiments serve as an objective check on philosophical theorizing. When there is disagreement, it usually focuses on the interpretation of the results rather than on the results themselves. In the case of Warren's moral space traveler, for example, there is widespread agreement that persons need not be human beings and vice versa. There is much less agreement, however, about what implications this has for the abortion controversy.

Even if fetuses aren't persons, many claim that fetuses are nonetheless valuable forms of life and thus should be destroyed only if there are good reasons for doing so. For example, Daniel Callahan, director of the Hastings Center, an institute devoted to studying biomedical ethical issues, claims, "[Abortion] is not the destruction of a human person — for at no stage of its development does the conceptus fulfill the definition of a person, which implies a developed capacity for reasoning, willing, desiring and relating to others — but it is the destruction of an important and valuable form of human life."[26] As a result, Callahan maintains, taking such a life "demands of oneself serious reasons for doing so."[27] Just what those reasons are, he doesn't say. Nevertheless, it's clear that Callahan doesn't believe that the nonpersonhood of the fetus justifies abortion on demand. So Warren's moral space traveler thought experiment has not settled the abortion controversy. By clarifying the concept of a person, however, it has raised the level of discussion.

Even if the situation envisioned in a thought experiment is well defined, we may still reject the results of the thought experiment on the grounds that its assumptions are unreasonable. No theory — whether about concepts or physical objects — can be tested in isolation. Theories of any sort have testable consequences only in the context of certain background assumptions. Assumptions about the nature of human cognition and the nature of the external world, for example, lie behind every experiment. Thus if an experiment yields an incredible result, the problem may lie with the background assumptions rather than the theory being tested.

Conceivability and Possibility

To show that a condition is not necessary for the application of a concept, one needs to show only that it's possible for the concept to apply without the

Logical consequences are the scarecrows of fools and the beacons of wise men.
—THOMAS H. HUXLEY

condition being met. The best evidence that a situation is possible is that it's conceivable, that is, coherently imaginable. A situation is coherently imaginable when its details can be filled in and its implications drawn out without running into a contradiction. If, on examination, a situation is found to harbor an inconsistency, then it is not conceivable.

Consider, for example, time travel. At first glance, traveling backward in time seems perfectly conceivable. It may be technically impossible to build a time machine, but the many science-fiction stories that make use of this notion seem to suggest that it is not logically impossible. This suggestion is mistaken, however, because an event that has already happened cannot also not have happened. Suppose you travel back in time to a town at the turn of the century whose population was exactly 10,000 on January 1, 2000. After you arrive, the town would then have a population of 10,001. But it is logically impossible for a town to have a population of both 10,000 and 10,001 on January 1, 2000. So, appearances to the contrary, traveling backward in time to the same universe is neither conceivable nor possible.[28]

What this shows is that apparent conceivability doesn't guarantee possibility. From the fact that a situation seems coherently imaginable, it doesn't follow that it is, for it may contain a hidden contradiction. Apparent conceivability does provide good evidence for possibility, however, because if, after careful reflection, we haven't found a contradiction in a situation, we're justified in believing that it's possible.

Our conceptual ability can be compared to our perceptual ability. We can seem to perceive something that isn't real, but we can't actually perceive something that isn't real. Similarly, we can seem to conceive something that isn't possible, but we can't actually conceive something that isn't possible. To distinguish apparent from actual perception, we often perform physical experiments. Similarly, to distinguish apparent from actual conception, we often perform thought experiments. If we doubt the results of a physical experiment, we can check them by means of another physical experiment. Similarly, if we doubt the results of a thought experiment, we can check them by means of another thought experiment.

Because our conceptual scheme is an interconnected web of beliefs, every philosophical problem has a bearing on every other. Whatever solution is proposed to one problem must be judged in terms of the sorts of solutions it suggests to others. Deciding among various solutions to philosophical problems, then, requires appealing to considerations of scope, simplicity, conservatism, and fruitfulness. The theory that does best with regard to the criteria of adequacy will produce the most understanding.

Thought experiments are just one tool among many that philosophers use to evaluate their theories. But they are an important tool, for not only can they strengthen or weaken existing theories, they can also generate data that any future theory must take into account. Theories at the forefront of philosophical research are generally superior to their predecessors because the thought experiments of the past have broadened the evidence base on which future theories must rest.

Scientific Thought Experiments

Thought experiments aren't unique to philosophy. They can also be found in the sciences, where they have helped produce a number of scientific advances. Their use in the sciences is instructive.

One of the hallmarks of a good theory is that it is free from contradiction. Any theory that implies that something both is and is not the case is unacceptable, for not only is it uninformative, it cannot possibly be true. Thought experiments are particularly useful in testing for contradictions. Galileo used a thought experiment to demonstrate that Aristotle's theory of motion was self-contradictory and thereby paved the way for the modern science of mechanics.

Aristotle held that heavier bodies fall faster than lighter ones. Galileo, on the other hand, maintained that all bodies, regardless of their weight, fall at the same rate. To show that his view was superior to Aristotle's, Galileo proposed the following thought experiment.

Every great advance in science has issued from a new audacity of imagination.

—JOHN DEWEY

Thought Experiment

Impossibility of Aristotle's Theory of Motion

Imagination rules the world.

—NAPOLEON

Imagine that a heavy cannonball is attached to a light musket ball by means of a rope. Now imagine that both this combined system and an ordinary cannonball are dropped from a height at the same time. What should happen? According to Aristotle, because lighter objects fall more slowly than heavier ones, the

Good reasons must, of force, give place to better.

—WILLIAM SHAKESPEARE

musket ball attached to the cannonball should act as a drag on it. So the combined system should fall more slowly than the cannonball alone. But because the combined system is heavier than the cannonball alone and because heavier objects fall faster than lighter ones, the combined system should also fall faster than the cannonball alone. But it is logically impossible for one object to fall both faster and more slowly than another. So Aristotle's theory cannot be correct. Galileo's theory, however, avoids the contradiction by maintaining that all bodies fall at the same rate. It follows, then, that Galileo's view is more credible than Aristotle's.

By showing that Aristotle's theory harbored an inconsistency, Galileo made the modern science of mechanics possible. The value of thought experiments, then, lies not only in their immediate results but also in their long-term consequences.

Summary

Philosophical theories explain how it is possible or why it is impossible for a concept to apply by identifying the conditions for applying it. Thought experiments test these theories by determining whether they hold in all possible situations. If they do not — that is, if there are counterexamples to the theory — there is reason to believe that the theory is mistaken.

Like scientific experiments, thought experiments can go wrong and can be criticized for it. If they are not sufficiently spelled out or if they rest on unreasonable assumptions, their value is questionable. If you believe that a thought experiment is problematic, however, the burden of proof is on you to provide an alternative explanation of the results.

The adequacy of a theory is determined by how much understanding it produces, and the amount of understanding produced by a theory is determined by how well it systematizes and unifies our knowledge. Criteria such as conservatism, scope, fruitfulness, and simplicity can be used to gauge the adequacy of a theory.

Thought experiments not only help us evaluate theories, but they generate data that any future theory must take into account. Theories at the cutting edge of philosophical research are usually superior to their predecessors because previous thought experiments have added important considerations that any future theory must incorporate.

Study Questions

1. What is a thought experiment?
2. How are thought experiments possible?
3. On what grounds can thought experiments be criticized?
4. What is Warren's moral space traveler thought experiment? How does it attempt to undermine the claim that all human beings are persons?

5. On what grounds can philosophical theories be criticized?

6. What are the criteria of adequacy that good theories should meet?

Discussion Questions

1. According to Mary Anne Warren, fetuses aren't persons. But they are potential persons. Does being a potential person give something a right to life? Michael Tooley believes not. To make his point, he offers the following thought experiment.

Thought Experiment

Tooley's Cat

My argument against the potentiality principle can now be stated. Suppose at some future time a chemical were to be discovered which when injected into the brain of a kitten would cause the kitten to develop into a cat possessing a brain of the sort possessed by humans, and consequently into a cat having all the psychological capabilities characteristic of adult humans. Such cats would be able to think, to use language, and so on. Now it would surely be morally indefensible in such a situation to ascribe a serious right to life to members of the species Homo sapiens without also ascribing it to cats that have undergone such a process of development: there would be no morally significant differences. . . .

Suppose a kitten is accidentally injected with the chemical. As long as it has not yet developed those properties that in themselves endow something with a right to life, there cannot be anything wrong with interfering with the causal process and preventing the development of the properties in question. . . .

But if it is not seriously wrong to destroy an injected kitten which will naturally develop the properties that bestow a right to life, neither can it be seriously wrong to destroy a member of Homo sapiens which lacks such properties. . . .[29]

According to Tooley, being a potential person is not a sufficient condition for having a right to life. Is Tooley right about this? If not, where is the flaw in his experiment?

2. Judith Jarvis Thomson believes that the question of whether a fetus is a person or even a potential person is irrelevant to the abortion controversy, for even if the fetus is a person, the woman may be under no obligation to care for it. In defense of her view, she offers the following thought experiment.

Thought Experiment

Thomson's Diseased Musician

I propose, then, that the fetus is a person from the moment of conception. . . . But now let me ask you to imagine this. You wake up in the morning and find yourself back to back in bed with an unconscious violinist. A famous unconscious violinist. He has been found to have a fatal kidney ailment, and the Society of Music Lovers has canvassed all the available medical records and found that you alone have the right blood type to help. They have therefore kidnapped you, and last night the violinist's circulatory system was plugged into yours, so that your kidneys can be used to extract poisons from his blood as well as your own. The director of the hospital now tells you, "Look, we're sorry the Society of Music Lovers did this to you—we would never have permitted it if we had known. But still, they did it, and the violinist now is plugged into you. To unplug you would be to kill him. But never mind, it's only for nine months. By then he will have recovered from his ailment, and can safely be unplugged from you." Is it morally incumbent on you to accede to this situation? No doubt it would be very nice of you if you did, a great kindness. But do you have to accede to it?[30]

Are you morally obligated to share your bloodstream with the diseased musician? If not, are you morally obligated to share your bloodstream with a developing fetus? Is this thought experiment flawed in a significant way?

3. Consider this theory of the function of lightbulbs:

For years it was believed that electric bulbs emitted light. However, recent information has proven otherwise. Electric bulbs don't emit light, they suck dark. Thus we will now call these bulbs "dark suckers." The dark sucker theory, according to a spokesperson, proves the existence of dark, that dark has mass heavier than that of light, and that dark is faster than light.

The basis of the dark sucker theory is that electric bulbs suck dark. Take, for example, the dark suckers in the room where you are. There is less dark right next to them than there is elsewhere. The larger the dark sucker, the greater its capacity to suck dark. Dark suckers in a parking lot have a much greater capacity than ones in this room. . . .

Dark has mass. When dark goes into a dark sucker, friction from this mass generates heat. Thus it is not wise to touch an operating dark sucker. . . .

Finally, we must prove that dark is faster than light. If you were to stand in an illuminated room in front of a closed, dark closet, then slowly open the closet door, you would see the light slowly enter the closet, but since dark is so fast, you would not be able to see the dark leave the closet.

In conclusion, it has been stated that dark suckers make all our lives much easier, so the next time you look at an electric bulb remember that it is indeed a dark sucker.[31]

Are we justified in believing this theory to be true? Explain your answer with reference to the criteria of adequacy.

The Value of Philosophy

Bertrand Russell (1872–1970) is one of the greatest philosophers of the twentieth century, making significant contributions in all of the major branches of philosophy. Perhaps his greatest contribution was in the field of logic where his *Principia Mathematica* (co-authored with Alfred North Whitehead) tried to demonstrate that all of mathematics could be derived from logic. Although Russell did not write much fiction, the Nobel Committee decided to recognize his importance as a man of letters by awarding him the Nobel Prize for Literature in 1950. The following selection is the concluding chapter of his text *The Problems of Philosophy*. In it, he describes the importance of philosophy for the life of the mind.

Having now come to the end of our brief and very incomplete review of the problems of philosophy, it will be well to consider, in conclusion, what is the value of philosophy and why it ought to be studied. It is the more necessary to consider this question, in view of the fact that many men, under the influence of science or of practical affairs, are inclined to doubt whether philosophy is anything better than innocent but useless trifling, hair-splitting distinctions, and controversies on matters concerning which knowledge is impossible.

This view of philosophy appears to result, partly from a wrong conception of the ends of life, partly from a wrong conception of the kind of goods which philosophy strives to achieve. Physical science, through the medium of inventions, is useful to innumerable people who are wholly ignorant of it; thus the study of physical science is to be recommended, not only, or primarily, because of the effect on the student, but rather because of the effect on mankind in general. This utility does not belong to philosophy. If the study of philosophy has any value at all for others than students of philosophy, it must be only indirectly, through its effects upon the lives of those who study it. It is in these effects, therefore, if anywhere, that the value of philosophy must be primarily sought.

But further, if we are not to fail in our endeavour to determine the value of philosophy, we must first free our minds from the prejudices of what are wrongly called "practical" men. The "practical" man, as this word is often used, is one who recognises only material needs, who realises that men must have food for the body, but is oblivious of the necessity of providing food for the mind. If all men were well off, if poverty and disease had been reduced to their lowest possible point, there would still remain much to be done to produce a valuable society; and even in the existing world the goods of the mind are at least as important as the goods of the body. It is exclusively among the goods of the mind that the value of philosophy is to be found; and only those who are not indifferent to these goods can be persuaded that the study of philosophy is not a waste of time.

Philosophy, like all other studies, aims primarily at knowledge. The knowledge it aims at is the kind of knowledge which gives unity and system to the body of the sciences, and the kind which results from a critical examination of the grounds of our convictions, prejudices, and beliefs. But it cannot be maintained that philosophy has had any very great measure of success in its attempts to provide definite answers to its questions. If you ask a mathematician, a mineralogist, a historian, or any other man of learning, what definite body of truths has been ascertained by his science, his answer will last as long as you are willing to listen. But if you put the same question to a philosopher, he will, if he is candid, have to confess that his study has not achieved positive results such as have been achieved by other sciences. It is true that this is partly accounted for by the fact that, as soon as definite knowledge concerning any subject becomes possible, this subject ceases to be called philosophy, and becomes a separate science. The whole study of the heavens, which now belongs to astronomy, was once included in philosophy; Newton's great work was called "the mathematical principles of natural philosophy." Similarly, the study of the human mind, which was, until very lately, a part of philosophy, has now been

---

From: Bertrand Russell, *The Problems of Philosophy* (New York: Henry Holt and Company, 1912) 237–250.

separated from philosophy and has become the science of psychology. Thus, to a great extent, the uncertainty of philosophy is more apparent than real: those questions which are already capable of definite answers are placed in the sciences, while those only to which, at present, no definite answer can be given, remain to form the residue which is called philosophy.

This is, however, only a part of the truth concerning the uncertainty of philosophy. There are many questions—and among them those that are of the profoundest interest to our spiritual life—which, so far as we can see, must remain insoluble to the human intellect unless its powers become of quite a different order from what they are now. Has the universe any unity of plan or purpose, or is it a fortuitous concourse of atoms? Is consciousness a permanent part of the universe, giving hope of indefinite growth in wisdom, or is it a transitory accident on a small planet on which life must ultimately become impossible? Are good and evil of importance to the universe or only to man? Such questions are asked by philosophy, and variously answered by various philosophers. But it would seem that, whether answers be otherwise discoverable or not, the answers suggested by philosophy are none of them demonstrably true. Yet, however slight may be the hope of discovering an answer, it is part of the business of philosophy to continue the consideration of such questions, to make us aware of their importance, to examine all the approaches to them, and to keep alive that speculative interest in the universe which is apt to be killed by confining ourselves to definitely ascertainable knowledge.

Many philosophers, it is true, have held that philosophy could establish the truth of certain answers to such fundamental questions. They have supposed that what is of most importance in religious beliefs could be proved by strict demonstration to be true. In order to judge of such attempts, it is necessary to take a survey of human knowledge, and to form an opinion as to its methods and its limitations. On such a subject it would be unwise to pronounce dogmatically; but if the investigations of our previous chapters have not led us astray, we shall be compelled to renounce the hope of finding philosophical proofs of religious beliefs. We cannot, therefore, include as part of the value of philosophy any definite set of answers to such questions. Hence, once more, the value of philosophy must not depend upon any supposed body of definitely ascertainable knowledge to be acquired by those who study it.

The value of philosophy is, in fact, to be sought largely in its very uncertainty. The man who has no tincture of philosophy goes through life imprisoned in the prejudices derived from common sense, from the habitual beliefs of his age or his nation, and from convictions which have grown up in his mind without the co-operation or consent of his deliberate reason. To such a man the world tends to become definite, finite, obvious; common objects rouse no questions, and unfamiliar possibilities are contemptuously rejected. As soon as we begin to philosophise, on the contrary, we find, as we saw in our opening chapters, that even the most everyday things lead to problems to which only very incomplete answers can be given. Philosophy, though unable to tell us with certainty what is the true answer to the doubts which it raises, is able to suggest many possibilities which enlarge our thoughts and free them from the tyranny of custom. Thus, while diminishing our feeling of certainty as to what things are, it greatly increases our knowledge as to what they may be; it removes the somewhat arrogant dogmatism of those who have never travelled into the region of liberating doubt, and it keeps alive our sense of wonder by showing familiar things in an unfamiliar aspect.

Apart from its utility in showing unsuspected possibilities, philosophy has a value—perhaps its chief value—through the greatness of the objects which it contemplates, and the freedom from narrow and personal aims resulting from this contemplation. The life of the instinctive man is shut up within the circle of his private interests: family and friends may be included, but the outer world is not regarded except as it may help or hinder what comes within the circle of instinctive wishes. In such a life there is something feverish and confined, in comparison with which the philosophic life is calm and free. The private world of instinctive interests is a small one, set in the midst of a great and powerful world which must, sooner or later, lay our private world in ruins. Unless we can so enlarge our interests as to include the whole outer world, we remain like a garrison in a beleaguered fortress, knowing that the enemy prevents escape and that ultimate surrender is inevitable. In such a life there is no peace, but a constant strife between the insistence of desire and the powerlessness of will. In one way or another, if our life is to be great and free, we must escape this prison and this strife.

One way of escape is by philosophic contemplation. Philosophic contemplation does not, in its widest survey, divide the universe into two hostile camps—friends and foes, helpful and hostile, good and bad—it views the whole impartially. Philosophic contemplation, when it is unalloyed, does not aim at proving that the rest of the universe is akin to man. All acquisition of knowledge is an enlargement of the Self, but this enlargement is best attained when it is not directly sought.

It is obtained when the desire for knowledge is alone operative, by a study which does not wish in advance that its objects should have this or that character, but adapts the Self to the characters which it finds in its objects. This enlargement of Self is not obtained when, taking the Self as it is, we try to show that the world is so similar to this Self that knowledge of it is possible without any admission of what seems alien. The desire to prove this is a form of self-assertion and, like all self-assertion, it is an obstacle to the growth of Self which it desires, and of which the Self knows that it is capable. Self-assertion, in philosophic speculation as elsewhere, views the world as a means to its own ends; thus it makes the world of less account than Self, and the Self sets bounds to the greatness of its goods. In contemplation, on the contrary, we start from the not-Self, and through its greatness the boundaries of Self are enlarged; through the infinity of the universe the mind which contemplates it achieves some share in infinity.

For this reason greatness of soul is not fostered by those philosophies which assimilate the universe to Man. Knowledge is a form of union of Self and not-Self; like all union, it is impaired by dominion, and therefore by any attempt to force the universe into conformity with what we find in ourselves. There is a widespread philosophical tendency towards the view which tells us that Man is the measure of all things, that truth is man-made, that space and time and the world of universals are properties of the mind, and that, if there be anything not created by the mind, it is unknowable and of no account for us. This view, if our previous discussions were correct, is untrue; but in addition to being untrue, it has the effect of robbing philosophic contemplation of all that gives it value, since it fetters contemplation to Self. What it calls knowledge is not a union with the not-Self, but a set of prejudices, habits, and desires, making an impenetrable veil between us and the world beyond. The man who finds pleasure in such a theory of knowledge is like the man who never leaves the domestic circle for fear his word might not be law.

The true philosophic contemplation, on the contrary, finds its satisfaction in every enlargement of the not-Self, in everything that magnifies the objects contemplated, and thereby the subject contemplating. Everything, in contemplation, that is personal or private, everything that depends upon habit, self-interest, or desire, distorts the object, and hence impairs the union which the intellect seeks. By thus making a barrier between subject and object, such personal and private things become a prison to the intellect. The free intellect will see as God might see, without a *here* and *now*, without hopes and fears, without the trammels of customary beliefs and traditional prejudices, calmly, dispassionately, in the sole and exclusive desire of knowledge — knowledge as impersonal, as purely contemplative, as it is possible for man to attain. Hence also the free intellect will value more the abstract and universal knowledge into which the accidents of private history do not enter, than the knowledge brought by the senses, and dependent, as such knowledge must be, upon an exclusive and personal point of view and a body whose sense-organs distort as much as they reveal.

The mind which has become accustomed to the freedom and impartiality of philosophic contemplation will preserve something of the same freedom and impartiality in the world of action and emotion. It will view its purposes and desires as parts of the whole, with the absence of insistence that results from seeing them as infinitesimal fragments in a world of which all the rest is unaffected by any one man's deeds. The impartiality which, in contemplation, is the unalloyed desire for truth, is the very same quality of mind which, in action, is justice, and in emotion is that universal love which can be given to all, and not only to those who are judged useful or admirable. Thus contemplation enlarges not only the objects of our thoughts, but also the objects of our actions and our affections: it makes us citizens of the universe, not only of one walled city at war with all the rest. In this citizenship of the universe consists man's true freedom, and his liberation from the thraldom of narrow hopes and fears.

Thus, to sum up our discussion of the value of philosophy: Philosophy is to be studied, not for the sake of any definite answers to its questions, since no definite answers can, as a rule, be known to be true, but rather for the sake of the questions themselves; because these questions enlarge our conception of what is possible, enrich our intellectual imagination, and diminish the dogmatic assurance which closes the mind against speculation; but above all because, through the greatness of the universe which philosophy contemplates, the mind also is rendered great, and becomes capable of that union with the universe which constitutes its highest good.

The Philosophic Enterprise

Brand Blanshard (1892–1989), eminent American philosopher and Rhodes scholar, received his A.B. from Michigan University and his Ph.D. from Harvard University. He taught at Swarthmore College for two decades and chaired the Yale philosophy department from 1945 until his retirement in 1961. His major works include *The Nature of Thought, Reason and Goodness,* and *Reason and Analysis.* In this selection, he presents his view of the relationship between philosophy and science.

Philosophy is best understood, I think, as part of an older and wider enterprise, the enterprise of understanding the world. We may well look first at this understanding in the large. I shall ask, to begin with, what is its goal, then what are its chief stages, then what are the ways in which philosophy enters into it.

The enterprise, we have just said, is that of understanding the world. What do we mean by understanding—understanding anything at all? We mean, I suppose, explaining it to ourselves. Very well; what does explaining anything mean? We stumble upon some fact or event that is unintelligible to us; what would make it intelligible? The first step in the answer is, seeing it as an instance of some rule. You suffer some evening from an excruciating headache and despondently wonder why. You remember that you just ate two large pieces of chocolate cake and that you are allergic to chocolate; the headache seems then to be explained. It is no longer a mere demonic visitor intruding on you from nowhere; you have domesticated it, assimilated it to your knowledge, by bringing it under a known rule.

What sort of rules are these that serve to render facts intelligible? They are always rules of connection, rules relating the fact to be explained to something else. You explain the headache by bringing it under a law relating it *causally* to something else. In like manner, you explain the fact that a figure on the board has angles equal to two right angles by relating it *logically* to something else; by pointing out that it is a triangle, and that it belongs to the triangles as such to have this property. . . .

[Philosophers] have tried to supplement the work of science in at least two respects. In both of these respects science has to be extended if our thirst for understanding is to be satisfied, but in neither of them do scientists take much interest. The fact is that, logically speaking, philosophy begins before science does, and

goes on after science has completed its work. In the broad spectrum of knowledge, science occupies the central band. But we know that there is more to the spectrum than this conspicuous part. On one side, beyond the red end of the spectrum, there is a broad band of infrared rays; and on the other side, beyond the violet end, are the ultraviolet rays. Philosophy deals with the infrareds and the ultraviolets of science, continuous with the central band but more delicate and difficult of discernment.

Take the red end first. Consider the sense in which philosophy comes before science. Many of the concepts the scientist uses and many of his working assumptions he prefers to take for granted. He can examine them if he wishes, and some scientists do. Most do not, because if they waited till they were clear on these difficult basic ideas, they might never get to what most interests them at all. But it would be absurd to leave these basic ideas unexamined altogether. This somewhat thankless preliminary work is the task of the philosopher.

We referred to these unexamined ideas as concepts and assumptions. Let us illustrate the concepts first.

Common sense and science are constantly using certain little words of one syllable that seem too familiar and perhaps unimportant to call for definition. We say, "What time is it?" "There is less space in a compact car," "There was no cause for his taking offense," "He must be out of his mind," "I think these strikes are unjust to the public." Consider the words we have used: 'time', 'space', 'cause', 'good', 'truth', 'mind', 'just', 'I'. If someone said to us, "What do you mean, *I?*" or, when we asked what time it was, "What do you mean by

From: Brand Blanshard, "The Philosophic Enterprise," *The Owl of Minerva: Philosophers on Philosophy,* ed. Charles J. Bontempo and S. Jack Odell (New York: McGraw-Hill, 1975) 163–177.

'time'?" we should probably say, "Oh, don't be an idiot," or perhaps with St. Augustine, "I know perfectly well what time means until you ask me, and then I don't know." I suspect this last is the sound answer regarding all these words. We know what they mean well enough for everyday purposes, but to think about them is to reveal depth after depth of unsuspected meaning. This fact suggests both the strength and the weakness of present-day linguistic philosophy. It is surely true, as this school contends, that a main business of philosophy is to define words. The first great outburst of philosophy in the talk of Socrates was largely an attempt at defining certain key words of the practical life — 'justice', 'piety', 'temperance', 'courage'. But their meanings proved bafflingly elusive; he chased the ghost of justice through ten books of the *Republic* and barely got his hands on it in the end. Socrates saw that to grasp the meaning even of these simple and common terms would solve many of the deepest problems in ethics and metaphysics. But we must add that Socrates was no ordinary language philosopher. He was not an Athenian Noah Webster, collecting the shopworn coins that were current in the marketplace; on the contrary, he took special pleasure in showing that at the level of ordinary usage our meanings were muddled and incoherent. Only by refining and revising them could we arrive at meanings that would stand.

Now the scientist who is trying to find the truth about the cause of flu cannot discontinue his experiments till he has reached clearness on the nature of truth or the concept of causality. The political scientist who holds that democracy is in certain respects better than communism cannot remain dumb till all his colleagues have agreed as to the definition of 'good'. These people must get on with their work, and they are right not to stop and moon about ultimates. But these ideas are ultimates after all; we must use them hourly in our thinking; and it would be absurd if, while researchers were trying to be clear about relatively unimportant matters, no one tried to get clear about the most important things of all. And the right persons to make that effort are surely the philosophers. A philosopher friend of mine sat down in a railway car beside a salesman who, recognizing a kindred spirit, poured out a stream of talk about his line. "And what's your line?" he concluded. "Notions," replied the philosopher. That seemed all right to the salesman, and it should be so to us. Notions are the line of the philosopher, such key notions as truth, validity, value, knowledge, without which scientific thought could not get under way, but which the scientist himself has neither the time nor the inclination to examine.

We suggested that it is not only his ultimate concepts but also his ultimate assumptions that the scientist prefers to turn over to others for inspection. Let me list a few and ask whether there is any natural scientist who does not take them for granted. That we can learn the facts of the physical order through perception. That the laws of our logic are valid of this physical order. That there is a public space and a public time in which things happen and to which we all have access. That every event has a cause. That under like conditions the same sort of thing has always happened, and always will. That we ought to adjust the degree of our assent to any proposition to the strength of the evidence for it. These are all propositions of vast importance, which the scientist makes use of every day of his life. If any one of them were false, his entire program would be jeopardized. But they are not scientific propositions. They are assumed by all sciences equally; they are continuous with the thought of all; yet they are the property of none. It would be absurd to leave these unexamined, for some or all of them may be untrue. But the scientist would be aghast if, before he used a microscope or a telescope, he had to settle the question whether knowledge was possible through perception, or whether there could be a logic without ontology. Scientists have at times discussed these matters, and their views are always welcome, but they generally and sensibly prefer to turn them over to specialists. And the specialists in these problems are philosophers.

I have now, I hope, made clear what was meant by saying that philosophy comes before science. It comes before it in the sense of taking for examination the main concepts and assumptions with which scientists begin their work. Science is logically dependent on philosophy. If philosophy succeeded in showing, as Hume and Carnap thought it had, that any reference to a nonsensible existent was meaningless, the physics that talks of electrons and photons would either have to go out of business or revise its meanings radically. If philosophy succeeded, as James, Schiller, and Freud thought it had, in showing that our thinking is inescapably chained to our impulses and emotions, then the scientific enterprise, as an attempt at impartial and objective truth, would be defeated before it started. Philosophy does not merely put a bit of filigree on the mansion of science; it provides its foundation stones.

If philosophy begins before science does, it also continues after the scientist has finished his work. Each science may be conceived as a prolonged effort to answer one large question. Physics asks, "What are the laws of matter in motion?" Biology asks, "What kinds of structure and behavior are exhibited by living things?" Each science takes a field of nature for its own and tries to keep within its own fences. But nature has no fences; the movement of electrons is somehow continuous with the writing of *Hamlet* and the rise of Lenin. Who is to study this continuity? Who is to reflect on whether the physicist, burrowing industriously in his hole, can break a tunnel through to the theologian, mining anxiously in his? Surely here again is a task that only the philosopher can perform. One way of performing it, which I do not say is the right way, is suggested by the definition of philosophy as the search by a blind man in a dark room for a black hat that isn't there, with the addendum that if he finds it, that is theology. It may be thought that since no two true propositions can contradict each other, the results of independent scientific search could not conflict, and that there is no problem in harmonizing them. On the contrary, when we examine even the most general results of the several sciences, we see that they clash scandalously and that the task of harmonizing them is gigantic. Indeed the most acute and fascinating of metaphysical problems arise in the attempt to reconcile the results of major disciplines with each other.

How are you to reconcile physics with psychology, for example? The physicist holds that every physical event has a physical cause, which seems innocent enough. To say that a material thing could start moving, or, once started, could have its motion accelerated or changed in direction without any physical cause, would seem absurd. If you say that a motion occurs with no cause at all, that is to the physicist irresponsible; if you say that it represents interference from outside the spatial order, it is superstitious. Now is not the psychologist committed to saying that this interference in fact occurs daily? If my lips and vocal cords now move as they do, it is because I am thinking certain thoughts and want to communicate them to you. And the only way in which a thought or desire can produce such results is through affecting the physical motions of waves or particles in my head. It will not do to say that only the nervous correlates of my thought are involved in producing these results, for those physical changes are not my thoughts, and if my thoughts themselves can make no difference to what I do, then rational living becomes a mummery. My action is never in fact guided by conscious choice, nor anything I say determined by what I think or feel. Common sense would not accept that, nor can a sane psychology afford to; the evidence against it is too massive. And what this evidence shows is that conscious choice, which is not a physical event at all, does make a difference to the behavior of tongue

and lips, of arms and legs. Behavior may be consciously guided. But how are you to put that together with the physicist's conviction that all such behavior is caused physically? That is the lively philosophical problem of body and mind.

Conflicts of this kind may occur not only between natural sciences but between a natural and a normative science. Take physics and ethics. For the physicist all events — at least all macroscopic events — are caused; that is, they follow in accordance with some law from events immediately preceding them. This too seems innocent enough. But now apply the principle in ethics. A choice of yours is an event, even if not a physical event, and thus falls under the rule that all events are caused. That means that every choice you make follows in accordance with law from some event or events just preceding it. But if so, given the events that just preceded any of my choices, I had to do what I did do; I could not have done otherwise. But if that is true, does it not make nonsense to say in any case that I ought to have done otherwise, since I did the only thing that I could have done? But then what becomes of ethics as ordinarily conceived? If the scientific principle is true, one will have to rethink the ethical ground for remorse and reward and punishment and praise and blame. This is the ancient problem of free will, which was discussed with fascination by Milton's angels while off duty from their trumpets, and is discussed with equal fascination by undergraduates today. . . .

There are many other conflicts like the two we have mentioned. They fall in no one of the disciplines, but between them, and they must be arbitrated by an agency committed to nonpartisanship. The only plausible nominee for this post is philosophy. Philosophy is the interdepartmental conciliation agency, the National Labor Relations Board, or if you prefer, the World Court, of the intellectual community. Like these other agencies, it has no means of enforcing its verdicts. Its reliance is on the reasonableness of its decisions.

We are now in a position to see the place of philosophy in the intellectual enterprise as a whole. Intelligence has shown from the beginning a drive to understand. To understand anything means to grasp it in the light of other things or events that make it intelligible. The first great breakthrough of this drive was the system of common sense, which was molded into form by millennia of trial and error. This system is being superseded by science, whose network of explanation is far more precise and comprehensive. Philosophy is the continuation of this enterprise into regions that science leaves unexplored. It is an attempt to carry understanding to its furthest possible limits. It brings into the picture the foundations on which science builds and the arches and vaultings that hold its structures together. Philosophy is at once the criticism and the completion of science. That, as I understand it, is what all the great philosophers have been engaged upon, from Plato to Whitehead.

They may never wholly succeed. It is quite possible that men will use such understanding as they have achieved to blow themselves and their enterprise off the planet. But while they do allow themselves further life, the enterprise is bound to go on. For the effort to understand is not a passing whim or foible; it is no game for a leisure hour or "lyric cry in the midst of business." It is central to the very nature and existence of man; it is what has carried him from somewhere in the slime to the lofty but precarious perch where he now rests. The drive of his intelligence has constructed his world for him and slowly modified it into conformity with the mysterious world without. To anyone who sees this, philosophy needs no defense. It may help in practical ways, and of course it does. But that is not the prime reason why men philosophize. They philosophize because they cannot help it, because the enterprise of understanding, ancient as man himself, has made him what he is, and alone can make him what he might be.

Philosophy as an Art Form

Robert Nozick (1938–2002) was the Arthur Kingsley Porter Professor of Philosophy at Harvard University. He is the author of *Anarchy, State, and Utopia,* which won a National Book award in 1975, and *Philosophical Explanations,* which won the Ralph Waldo Emerson Award from Phi Beta Kappa in 1982. In this selection, from *Philosophical Explanations,* Nozick explores the nature of philosophical inquiry.

We have seen that philosophy can be carried on (there are other legitimate ways, too) as part of the humanities, responsive to value and meaning as value and meaning. Although responsive thus, not every part of the humanities is itself a form of art. Can philosophy be not just humanistic but also an art form? It would not be enough, I think, for a philosophy to exhibit and exemplify value and meaning as well as to respond to these, not enough even for it to be intended to be an object to which, as well as through which, others respond. A scientific theory also could fit that, and so be part of the humanities without being an art form.

The key, I think, lies in the degree of shaping and molding that takes place, the self-conscious choice about the nature and details of the work produced, the degree to which the work is created. As the composer works with musical themes, harmonic structures, and meter, the painter with forms, colors, represented things, and perimeters, the novelist with plot themes, characters, actions, and words, so the material of the philosopher is ideas, questions, tensions, concepts. He molds and shapes these, develops, revises, and reformulates them, and places them in various relations and juxtapositions. In the medium of ideas, he sculptures a view.

This molding also involves shaping parts, somewhat against their natural grain sometimes, so as better to fit the overall pattern, one designed in part to fit them. This purposeful molding and shaping, conscious of not being determined solely by the preexisting contours of a reality already out there, is part of the artistic activity. Can the scientist take a similar view of his theorizing, viewing it as a controlled artistic shaping? Einstein spoke of theories as being "free inventions of the human intellect" by which he meant at least that the data did not dictate the theory, that getting to the theory required a leap of intuition and insight — the theory could not simply be "read off" the data. But did he think that only one (adequate, correct, true)

theory could be leaped to, or did he think several quite different theories, equally good, might be leaped to and developed, each of which would equally well fit all the observational data? (Still, once a particular leap is made successfully, it carries the rest of science along in its wake, at least for a time.) Did it feel to Einstein as if he were discovering preexisting theoretical truths, or creating a theory? It would be fruitful to consider what scope the underdetermination of scientific theory by all possible observational data, a central theme in the writings of W. V. Quine, leaves for science as an art form.

Others have aimed at artistic intellectual synthesis: from Dante through Joyce's *Ulysses,* and most recently Pynchon's *Gravity's Rainbow,* some novelists and poets have tried to incorporate everything their time held worth knowing into their encyclopedic works. Some have imagined distinctively new types of intellectual syntheses, new intellectual forms; in *Magister Ludi,* Hesse portrays the Glass Bead game as a synthesis of music, theology, science, and philosophy, and describes also the social institution which serves it. Is philosophy as an artistic activity to be like these, an imaginative encyclopedic synthesis — leavened by a delight in the free play of ideas?

Where into this can we fit the philosopher's concern with the truth? The artist cannot make up just anything, though, either. The artistic activity works within its own constraints, depending upon the medium, and it deals with material having their own degree of obduracy. Novelists often tell us of their surprise at what their characters do, sometimes at what it turns out those characters have to do. The fact that words have meaning, and are not simply sounds, imposes constraints on the poet to which the composer is not sub-

---

From: Robert Nozick, *Philosophical Explanations* (Cambridge, MA: Harvard University Press, 1981) 645–647.

ject (although some literary experiments try to avoid even these). So, too, the different materials of the philosopher—ideas and their relationships, possibilities to be explained and understood—impose their own different constraints. (On this view, should we say that the philosopher's activity is of the same type as that of (other) artists, but is done with different material and so involves different constraints and possibilities; or rather that the different material with its accompanying different constraints and possibilities requires a different activity—a nonartistic one?)

An artistic philosophy would welcome (and appreciate) other shapings, other philosophical visions as part of the basketful, while striving itself for a prominent position in the ranking. Such a philosophy might present more than one vision at a time, or contemplate presenting others later. Is this attitude too playful? Think of a painter who spends his life working on one canvas, repainting and altering, building it up, perfecting it. We ask him what he's doing and hear him reply, "I am engaged in making my painting."

The philosopher aimed at truth states a theory that presents a possible truth and so a way of understanding the actual world (including its value) in its matrix of possible neighbors. In his artistic reshaping, he also may lift the mind from being totally filled with the actual world in which it happens to find itself. There is a tension between the philosopher's desire that his philosophy track the world—as a tight unity, tracking is of value—and his desire that it depict a world worth tracking, if not transcend the world altogether. Still, the philosophy must be true enough to the world, presenting a possible (though shaped) view, to be transcending it.

We can envision a humanistic philosophy, a self-consciously artistic one, sculpting ideas, value, and meaning into new constellations, reverberative with mythic power, lifting and ennobling us by its content and by its creation, leading us to understand and to respond to value and meaning—to experience them and attain them anew.

Suggestions for Further Reading

Bontempo, Charles J., and S. Jack Odell, eds. *The Owl of Minerva: Philosophers on Philosophy*. New York: McGraw-Hill, 1975.

Brown, James Robert. *The Laboratory of the Mind: Thought Experiments in the Natural Sciences*. London: Routledge, 1991.

Gendler, Thomas Szabo, and John Hawthorne, eds. *Conceivability and Possibility*. Oxford: Oxford University Press, 2002.

Horowitz, Tamara, and Gerald J. Massey, eds. *Thought Experiments in Science and Philosophy*. Savage, MD: Rowman and Littlefield, 1991.

Jackson, Frank. *From Metaphysics to Ethics: A Defense of Conceptual Analysis*. Oxford: Clarendon Press, 1998.

Sorensen, Roy A. *Thought Experiments*. Oxford: Oxford University Press, 1992.

Chapter 2

The Mind-Body Problem

Is there a mind/body
problem? If so, which is it
better to have?

—WOODY ALLEN

*L*ike all creatures, we have bodies. But unlike some of them, we also
have minds. With our bodies we eat, drink, walk, talk, breathe, and the
like. With our minds we think, feel, desire, perceive, and understand,
among other things. Modern science has shown that what goes on in our
bodies can be explained in physical terms, as the result of various electro-
chemical or biomechanical interactions. But what about what goes on in
our minds? Can our thoughts also be explained physically? Many think not.
Foremost among them is sixteenth-century philosopher (and inventor of analytic geometry) René Descartes. Although Descartes considers bodies to be
machines, he maintains that human beings are more than just bodies — because no machine will ever be able to do what we do. In his *Discourse on
Method*, Descartes describes how he arrived at this view.

Thought Experiment

The fundamental history
of humankind is the his-
tory of the mind.

—WILLIAM BARRETT

Descartes' Mechanical Moron

From this aspect the body is regarded as a machine which having been made by
the hands of God, is incomparably better arranged, and possesses in itself movements which are much more admirable, than any of those invented by man.
Here I specially stopped to show that if there had been such machines, possessing the organs and outward form of a monkey or some other animal without
reason, we should not have had any means of ascertaining that they were not of
the same nature as those animals. On the other hand, if there were machines
which bore a resemblance to our body and imitated our actions as far as it was
morally possible to do so, we should always have two very certain tests by
which to recognize that, for all that, they weren't real men. The first is, that
they could never use speech or other signs as we do when placing our thoughts
on record for the benefit of others. For we can easily understand a machine's
being constituted so that it can utter words, and even emit some responses to
action on it of a corporeal kind, which brings about a change in its organs; for
instance, if it is touched in a particular part it may ask what we wish to say to
it; if in another part it may exclaim that it is being hurt, and so on. But it never
happens that it arranges its speech in various ways, in order to reply appropriately to everything that may be said in its presence, as even the lowest type of
man can do. And the second difference is, that although machines can perform
certain things as well as or perhaps better than any of us can do, they infallibly
fall short in others, by which means we may discover that they did not act from
knowledge, but only from the disposition of their organs. For while reason is a
universal instrument which can serve for all contingencies, these organs have
need of some special adaptation for every particular action. From this it follows
that it is morally impossible that there should be sufficient diversity in any machine to allow it to act in all the events of life in the same way as our reason
causes us to act.[1]

Descartes believes that we are not machines because we possess two abilities that no machine ever will: (1) the ability to talk intelligently on an indefinite variety of topics and (2) the ability to act intelligently in an indefinite variety of situations. Machines may be able to talk or act intelligently in certain limited contexts, but their abilities will never match our own. Machines can act intelligently only when they are dealing with situations they have been designed or programmed to handle. We, on the other hand, can act intelligently even in situations we have never before encountered. Consequently, we must be more than mere machines.

Although many people working in the field of cognitive science disagree with Descartes' assessment of the prospects for artificial intelligence, they do agree that the ability to use language and solve problems are two of the best indicators of intelligence. In fact, as we shall see, one of the most widely accepted (and widely criticized) tests for artificial intelligence—the Turing test—is a test of just the sort Descartes proposed. Alan Turing, one of the founders of computer science, claimed that if a computer's ability to use language was indistinguishable from that of an ordinary human being, then the machine must be able to think.

Could we build a machine that has our linguistic and problem-solving abilities? Suppose we could. Would such a machine have a mind? How we answer that question will determine how we treat the robots that will eventually walk among us. Cultural anthropologist Arthur Harkins predicted in 1986 that by the year 2000, the first test case of a human-robot marriage would be in the courts.[2] Although that prediction was overly optimistic, many believe that such a civil proceeding is inevitable. This raises a number of interesting questions. What rights should a robot spouse have? What if there were a divorce? Should the robot get half of the community property? Our notion of rights is intimately connected to our notion of reasoning. If a machine can reason as well as we can, it is going to be difficult not to grant it the same rights that we enjoy.

An intelligent robot would be the ultimate labor-saving device. In fact, some have claimed that once intelligent robots become available, we will all live like kings, for the robots will provide us with an inexhaustible source of slave labor. James S. Albus, former chief of the Industrial Systems Division of the National Bureau of Standards, for example, has described what he sees as the coming utopia in his book *People's Capitalism: The Economics of the Robot Revolution*. He remarks,

> Before the Industrial Revolution, the aristocracy could only exist based on slavery because it was simply not possible for a single human being to produce enough wealth to live the life of an aristocrat. Now, in the age of robotics, you will have machines that can think for themselves, that can act for themselves, that can even reproduce themselves. Raw materials will go in, finished products will come out and be distributed through a market system that brings money into an unoccupied structure, which can then be passed out as dividends to the society.

The Mind-Body Problem   **67**

This source of wealth can, in fact, create a new level of civilization that hitherto has only been achieved by a small number of people — namely, the aristocrats. The age of robotics and automation and automatic factories brings us to the point where every citizen could live the life of an aristocrat in the sense that we could be economically self-sufficient and secure, not beholden to any employer.[3]

Within fifty years, Albus believes, a robotic workforce would be able to give each of us an annual income of around $750,000.[4]

Human slavery is unethical. Wouldn't robotic slavery be similarly unethical? Albus's robots can think for themselves. In other words, they have minds of their own. Can we in good conscience force such creatures to do something against their will? Wouldn't it be just as wrong to treat them as slaves as it would be to treat human beings that way? If not, what's the relevant difference? That they're made out of inorganic rather than organic materials? But isn't that just as morally irrelevant as someone's sex or race? Perhaps Albus's scenario is not as much of a utopia as he thinks it is.

Suppose we eventually create machines that can speak and solve problems as well as we do. Would that show that we are machines? Not necessarily, for we may not process information in the same way the machines do. But even if we are machines, our thoughts may not be explainable in mechanical terms. According to the seventeenth-century philosopher (and inventor of calculus) Gottfried Wilhelm von Leibniz, thinking isn't a mechanical concept. So even if a machine could think, thinking couldn't be explained mechanically. Leibniz elucidates this view by means of the following thought experiment.

Thought Experiment

Leibniz's Mental Mill

. . . it must be avowed that perception and what depends upon it cannot possibly be explained by mechanical reasons, that is by figure and movement. Suppose that there be a machine, the structure of which produces thinking, feeling, and perceiving; imagine this machine enlarged but preserving the same proportions, so that you could enter it as if it were a mill. This being supposed, you might visit its inside; but what would you observe there? Nothing but parts which push and move each other, and never anything that could explain perception. This explanation must therefore be sought in the simple substance, not in the composite, that is, in the machine.[5]

Although it's not made out of steel and silicon, the brain is a thinking, feeling, and perceiving machine. Yet if you were to shrink to the size of a blood cell and walk around inside of it, you would observe only the exchange

WALKING AROUND INSIDE THE BRAIN. Suppose you were able to walk around inside a brain, like the crew from the movie *Fantastic Voyage*. Would you observe thinking?

of chemicals between nerve cells. You wouldn't observe the thinking, feeling, and perceiving that the brain is doing. So, like Descartes, Leibniz believes that it's impossible to provide a mechanical account of the mind. But, unlike Descartes, he doesn't believe that it's impossible to construct thinking machines. In his view, there can be machines that think; there just can't be mechanical explanations of thinking.

This may seem a strange view, but it has a number of adherents, even to this day. Wholes are often greater than the sum of their parts. A team, for example, may be the best in its league even though none of its members are. In such a case, an understanding of the parts may not yield an understanding of the whole. Similarly, the mind may be greater than the sum of its parts. Persons, for example, are intelligent even though none of their nerve cells are. So an understanding of their nerve cells may not yield an understanding of their minds.

Leibniz, however, doesn't believe that consciousness emerges from complex arrangements of matter. He believes that matter emerges from complex arrangements of consciousness. For him, the basic building blocks of the universe — the stuff out of which everything is made — are particles of consciousness ("monads") rather than particles of matter. So, according to Leibniz, consciousness is not something possessed by only a select few creatures. It is possessed, in some degree, by everything, even the most fundamental particles.

Arthur Harkins's prediction of a computer/robot marriage by the year 2000 was inaccurate. Nevertheless, a number of thinkers believe that within the next thirty years, computers will become as intelligent as we are. Such computers would be able to reproduce by designing and building other computers with even greater capabilities. At that point—known as the singularity—technological advancement would become so rapid that we could not foresee its outcome. Mathematician Vernor Vinge explores the ramifications of this event:

Within thirty years, we will have the technological means to create superhuman intelligence. Shortly after, the human era will be ended.

Is such progress avoidable? If not to be avoided, can events be guided so that we may survive? These questions are investigated. Some possible answers (and some further dangers) are presented.

The acceleration of technological progress has been the central feature of this century. . . . we are on the edge of change comparable to the rise of human life on Earth. The precise cause of this change is the imminent creation by technology of entities with greater than human intelligence. There are several means by which science may achieve this breakthrough (and this is another reason for having confidence that the event will occur):

- There may be developed computers that are "awake" and superhumanly intelligent. (To date, there has been much controversy as to whether we can create human equivalence in a machine. But if the answer is "yes, we can", then there is little doubt that beings more intelligent can be constructed shortly thereafter.)
- Large computer networks (and their associated users) may "wake up" as a superhumanly intelligent entity.
- Computer/human interfaces may become so intimate that users may reasonably be considered superhumanly intelligent.
- Biological science may provide means to improve natural human intellect.

The first three possibilities depend in large part on improvements in computer hardware. Progress in computer hardware has followed an amazingly steady curve in the last few decades. Based largely on this trend, I believe that the creation of greater than human intelligence will occur during the next thirty years. (Charles Platt has pointed out that AI enthusiasts have been making claims like this for the last thirty years. Just so I'm not guilty of a relative-time ambiguity, let me more specific: I'll be surprised if this event occurs before 2005 or after 2030.)

That is why he says the explanation of consciousness must be sought in the simple rather than the complex.

Such a view may seem odd to those of us raised in the West. But to those raised in the East, it may seem obvious. Many Hindu thinkers claim that all there is is consciousness. The great Hindu theologian Shankara, for example, claims that reality is pure being, pure consciousness, and pure bliss.[7] According to Shankara, there is no matter in the world. There seems to be matter, but that is an illusion created by our ignorance of the true nature of reality.

The view that mind is the sole reality is known as **idealism.** The view that matter is the sole reality is known as **materialism.** And the view that reality contains both mental and material things is known as **dualism.** One of the

What are the consequences of this event? When greater-than-human intelligence drives progress, that progress will be much more rapid. In fact, there seems no reason why progress itself would not involve the creation of still more intelligent entities—on a still-shorter time scale. The best analogy that I see is with the evolutionary past: Animals can adapt to problems and make inventions, but often no faster than natural selection can do its work—the world acts as its own simulator in the case of natural selection. We humans have the ability to internalize the world and conduct "what if's" in our heads; we can solve many problems thousands of times faster than natural selection. Now, by creating the means to execute those simulations at much higher speeds, we are entering a regime as radically different from our human past as we humans are from the lower animals.

From the human point of view this change will be a throwing away of all the previous rules, perhaps in the blink of an eye, an exponential runaway beyond any hope of control. Developments that before were thought might only happen in "a million years" (if ever) will likely happen in the next century.

I think it's fair to call this event a singularity ("the Singularity" for the purposes of this paper). It is a point where our old models must be discarded and a new reality rules. As we move closer to this point, it will loom vaster and vaster over human affairs till the notion becomes a commonplace. Yet when it finally happens it may still be a great surprise and a greater unknown. . . .

Let an ultra intelligent machine be defined as a machine that can far surpass all the intellectual activities of any man however clever. Since the design of machines is one of these intellectual activities, an ultra intelligent machine could design even better machines; there would then unquestionably be an "intelligence explosion," and the intelligence of man would be left far behind. Thus the first ultra intelligent machine is the *last* invention that man need ever make, provided that the machine is docile enough to tell us how to keep it under control. . . . It is more probable than not that, within the twentieth century, an ultra intelligent machine will be built and that it will be the last invention that man need make.[6]

Thought Probe

Artificial Intelligence

If further research into artificial intelligence may result in the extinction of the human race, should it be allowed to continue? Should we try to ban it? How? What if one nation banned it and others didn't?

---

tasks of the philosophy of mind is to determine which of these views, if any, is the most reasonable. In the major research universities of the West, materialism is the dominant view. To date, however, no completely satisfactory materialist theory of the mind has been given. In other words, no one has fully explained how it is possible for a material object to think. But, then again, no one has fully explained how it is possible for a nonmaterial object to think either. In an attempt to understand how thinking is possible, we will examine various theories of mind in light of the thought experiments that have been used to test them.

We will begin by examining the dualistic theory of Descartes (Section 2.1). Then we will examine the materialistic theories of behaviorism and the

idealism The doctrine that all that exists are minds and their contents.

materialism The doctrine that all that exists are material objects.

dualism The doctrine that reality contains both mental and material things.

identity theory (Section 2.2). Next we'll explore the nonmaterialist theory of functionalism (Section 2.3). Finally, we'll explore the materialist theories of eliminative materialism (Section 2.4) and property dualism (Section 2.5).

Each of these theories is the basis of an active research program in psychology, parapsychology, cognitive science, artificial intelligence, or linguistics. These theories determine not only how researchers in these fields interpret their results but also how they frame their experiments. What we look for is determined by what we expect to find. So if the philosophy behind these research programs is flawed, they are unlikely to succeed. As Alfred North Whitehead pointed out, science can only be as good as the philosophy behind it. An adequate theory of the nature of mind, then, must be informed by a sound philosophy.

Objectives

After reading this chapter, you should be able to

- state the various theories of mind.
- describe the thought experiments that have been used to test them.
- evaluate the strengths and weaknesses of the various theories of mind.
- define qualitative content, intentionality, and emergent property.
- formulate your own view of the nature of the mind and the possibility of artificial intelligence.

The Ghost in the Machine
Mind as Soul

Descartes thought that no machine could think as well as we do. The only machines known to Descartes, however, were purely mechanical ones like clocks and waterwheels. If there had been electronic computers in his day, perhaps he would not have been so skeptical of artificial intelligence. Nevertheless, Descartes' belief that thinking could not be a physical process led him to conclude that it must be a nonphysical one. In his view, the mind is an immaterial entity that interacts with the body and yet is capable of existing independently of it. In other words, according to Descartes, the mind is the soul. The doctrine that mental states are states of an immaterial substance that interacts with the body is called **Cartesian dualism.**

Descartes' theory is dualistic because it claims that human beings are composed of two fundamentally different kinds of things: matter and mind. Materialism, which claims that there is only one kind of thing in the world — matter — is a monistic theory.

Descartes' most persuasive arguments for the immateriality of the mind (and the immortality of the soul) appear in his *Meditations on First Philosophy,* which was originally subtitled "In which the existence of God and the Immortality of the Soul are demonstrated." Proving that the mind is separate from the body was not Descartes' only goal in writing the *Meditations,* however. He also wanted to prove that God exists and to explain how knowledge was possible. To understand how Descartes arrived at his theory of mind, it's helpful to know something about his larger project.

> The mind alone sees and hears. All else is deaf and blind.
>
> —PLATO

Descartes' Doubt

While still a student, Descartes came to a realization familiar to many undergraduates: much of what he took to be certain and indubitable was uncertain and dubious. He concluded that most of what passes for knowledge is mere

Cartesian dualism
The doctrine that mental states are states of an immaterial substance that interacts with the body.

opinion, for knowledge requires certainty, and almost nothing is certain. The only place where Descartes found certainty (and thus knowledge) was in mathematics, especially geometry. Geometrical theorems are proven by deducing them from self-evident truths. If science is to yield knowledge, Descartes believed that it, too, must rest on a foundation of indubitable truths.

In the *Meditations*, Descartes sets out to find those truths. Finding just one indubitable truth, he thought, would go a long way toward putting science on a firm footing. He tells us, "Archimedes, in order that he might draw the terrestrial globe out of its place, and transport it elsewhere, demanded only that one point shall be fixed and immovable; in the same way, I shall have the right to conceive high hopes if I am happy enough to discover one thing only which is certain and indubitable."[8] To determine whether there is such an Archimedian point from which our knowledge of the external world could be derived, Descartes tried to determine whether there are any nonmathematical propositions that could not be doubted.

Descartes realized that to carry out his project, he did not have to examine each of his beliefs individually. Rather, he could examine entire families of beliefs by investigating the principles from which they were derived. If those principles could be doubted, then everything based on them could also be doubted. As Descartes puts it, "The destruction of the foundation of necessity brings with it the downfall of the rest of the edifice."[9]

One of the principles on which the edifice of science rests is that sense experience is a source of knowledge. But, Descartes argues, this principle is dubious because we can't be certain that sense experience accurately represents the world. Sometimes, we experience things that aren't really there, as in the case of hallucinations. Other times, we experience things differently from the way they really are, as in the case of illusions. So, just as we can't trust a witness who has lied in the past, we can't trust sense experience to give us an accurate picture of reality.

To demonstrate the unreliability of sense experience, Descartes appeals to the phenomenon of dreams. "How often has it happened to me that in the night I dreamt that I found myself in this particular place, that I was dressed and seated near the fire, whilst in reality I was lying undressed in bed!" he asks.[10] The problem is that dreams often seem very real, and there is no way to tell for certain while we are dreaming that we are dreaming. It is possible, for example, that you will wake up in a few minutes and realize that your reading this book was nothing but a (bad?) dream. Because we can never be absolutely certain that we are *not* dreaming, sense experience cannot be a source of knowledge.

If sense experience is not a source of knowledge, then a lot of what passes for knowledge isn't really knowledge. But sense experience isn't our *only* source of knowledge. We also have knowledge of mathematics, and that isn't based on sense experience. Mathematical theories, unlike scientific ones, need not be verified by observation. Their truth can be discovered by the light of pure reason.

But even the deliverances of reason, claims Descartes, can be doubted. To demonstrate this, Descartes proposes a thought experiment. It is possible, he argues, that there is a being (like God) who brings it about that everything he believes, even in the realm of mathematics and geometry, is false. As Descartes says,

> How do I know that He has not brought it to pass that there is no earth, no heaven, no extended body, no magnitude, no place, and that nevertheless they seem to me to exist just exactly as I now see them? And, besides, as I sometimes imagine that others deceive themselves in the things which they think they know best, how do I know that I am not deceived every time that I add two and three, or count the sides of a square, or judge of things yet simpler if anything simpler can be imagined?[11]

RENÉ DESCARTES
1596–1650

Because he cannot rule out the possibility that there is such a demon, it seems that Descartes can't know whether any of his beliefs are true.

Descartes envisions a supernatural being who, through some sort of mental telepathy, puts thoughts in his mind. But Descartes' point can be made without appeal to the supernatural. We know that thoughts and sensations can be produced by electrically or chemically stimulating the brain. Once we understand the brain well enough, we should be able to give anyone any kind of experience by stimulating his or her brain in the right ways. Descartes' question is this: How do we know that our experiences aren't being produced artificially?

How do we know, for example, that we're not brains in a vat, like the people in the movie *The Matrix*, whose experiences are being controlled by computers? Or how do we know that we're not playing an advanced virtual reality game, as depicted in the movies *The Thirteenth Floor* and *Existenz*? Descartes claims that because there is no way to tell whether such possibilities are actual, we can't acquire knowledge of the external world by means of sense experience.

Thought Probe

Living in the Matrix

Is Descartes right? Is there no way to tell whether you're being deceived by an evil demon, or living inside the matrix, or playing an advanced virtual reality game? If you think you know that none of these things are true, how do you know? What distinguishes real experiences from artificial ones? If you think you can't know that your experience is not artificial, do you think that can you know anything about the external world? If so, how?

I Think, Therefore I Am

It's beginning to look like Descartes can't know anything, for it appears to be possible to doubt everything. But even here, Descartes claims, appearances can be deceiving, for there is at least one thing that he cannot doubt, namely, the fact that he is doubting. But if it's certain that he is doubting, it's also certain that he exists, for he can't doubt unless he exists. Thus Descartes concludes that he knows at least one thing, namely, "I think, therefore I am." Here's Descartes' account of how he arrived at this realization:

> . . . I noticed that whilst I thus wished to think all things false, it was absolutely essential that the "I" who thought this should be somewhat, and remarking that this truth, "I think, therefore I am" was so certain and so assured that all the most extravagant suppositions brought forward by the skeptics were incapable of shaking it, I came to the conclusion that I could receive it without scruple as the first principle of the Philosophy for which I was seeking.[12]

Descartes thought that this truth—"I think, therefore I am"—could serve as the foundation for our knowledge of the external world. We will examine this claim in more detail in Chapter 7, but our present concern is Descartes' theory of mind. What sort of beings are we?

The Conceivability Argument

Materialists claim that we are material objects—complex arrangements of particles of matter. If that were the case, we could not exist without a body. But, Descartes claims, we can exist without a body. As a result, we must be

The Biblical Conception of the Person

Although many people believe that Descartes' dualistic view of the person is the traditional Christian view, they are mistaken. Rather, the Bible presents a monistic view of the person in which the mind and the body are inseparable from each other. British theologian Adrian Thatcher explains,

> There appears to be a rare unanimity among biblical scholars that the biblical picture of the person is non-dualist, and that the Bible gives little or no support to the idea that a person is essentially a soul, or that the soul is separable from the body. Dualists, of course, may reply that, regardless of what the Bible said about the issue then, dualism offers a convincing framework for Christian teaching now. Even so, they cannot get around the fact that, from a biblical point of view, dualism is very odd. Lynn de Silva summarizes the position thus:

> > Biblical scholarship has established quite conclusively that there is no dichotomous concept of man in the Bible, such as is found in Greek and Hindu thought. The biblical view of man is holistic, not dualistic. The notion of the soul as an immortal entity which enters the body at birth and leaves it at death is quite foreign to the biblical view of man. The biblical view is that man is a unity; he is a unity of soul, body, flesh, mind, etc. all together constituting the whole man. None of the constituent elements is capable of separating itself from the total structure and continuing to live after death. . . .

> In biblical thought, the entire human being, not merely the human body, is subject to death and decay. Dust you are, and to dust you shall return, says God to the man in the garden (Gen. 3:19). All mankind is grass, cries the prophet; 'they last no longer than a flower of the field. The grass withers, the flower fades, when the breath of the Lord blows upon them; the grass withers, the flowers fade, but the word of our God endures for evermore (Isa. 40:6–8). Your life, what is it?, asks St. James. You are no more than a mist, seen for a little while and then dispersing (Jas. 4:14).

> More important, the doctrines of creation, incarnation, resurrection, and ascension all favor the non-dualist view. To say that our souls are immortal is to blur the distinction between the Creator and the creature. What is created, as the biblical passages just quoted clearly show, has an end as well as a beginning; indeed, the whole point of these images in these verses is to draw attention to the brevity of human life, especially when compared with the eternal life of God. But this makes no sense if persons are immortal, appearances notwithstanding. The incarnation of God in Christ is a profoundly materialistic affair which allows the human nature of Christ in its totality — not merely Christ's human soul — to be taken up into perfect unity of his single divine Person. Moreover, the resurrection and ascension of Christ seem clearly to exclude dualistic accounts of the human person. The death of Christ was a real and total death, not merely the death of his mortal body. The miracle of the resurrection is precisely that God raises Jesus from the dead, not that he raises Jesus' mortal body and reunites it with his immortal soul. What purpose does the resurrection of Jesus serve, we may ask, if Jesus was not really dead? Was it just to convince the disciples that the bonds of death were forever loosened? Hardly, for if the disciples had believed in immortal souls they would not have required assurance on that point; and if they had needed such assurance, a resurrection miracle would not have provided it; it would merely have created confusion. The ascension of Christ is also rendered superfluous by a dualist account of the person; for the soul of Christ, being alive after his physical death, would presumably have been capable of returning to the Father without its body. What then is the ascension? A highly visual way of saying cheerio? It is, rather, the return of the transformed, transfigured, glorified, yet still embodied, Christ to the Father. No particular historical version of the event is favored by arguing thus. The point is that the theological convictions expressed by the resurrection and ascension narratives make much better sense on the assumption that all men and women are essentially bodily unities, after, as well as before, their bodily deaths.[13]

something more than matter in motion. What more? An immaterial mind. Here is how Descartes arrived at this view:

> . . . examining that which I was, I saw that I could conceive that I had no body, and that there was no world nor place where I might be; but yet that I could not for all that conceive that I was not. On the contrary, I saw from the very fact that I thought of doubting the truth of other things, it very evidently and certainly followed that I was; on the other hand if I had only ceased from thinking, even if all the rest of what I had ever imagined had really existed, I should have no reason for thinking that I had existed. From that I knew that I was a substance the whole essence or nature of which is to think, and that for its existence there is no need of any place, nor does it depend on any material thing; so that this 'me,' that is to say, the soul by which I am what I am, is entirely distinct from body, and is even more easy to know than is the latter; and even if body were not, the soul would not cease to be what it is.[14]

It's conceivable that we can exist without our bodies. After all, many believe that their souls will continue to exist after their bodies die, and, on the face of it, that belief doesn't seem to be self-contradictory. It's not conceivable that we can exist without our minds, however. If we can no longer think, Descartes claims, we no longer exist. Minds, though, are not material things, for they do not occupy space. So, Descartes concludes, we are thinking things, immaterial substances with no physical properties. In the words of the rock musician Sting, "We are spirits in a material world."

Descartes provides a familiar — and comforting — view of the self. Most of us would like to believe that we will survive the death of our bodies. But even though the prospect of immortality is enticing, very few philosophers or psychologists find Descartes' view convincing. To see why there are so few Cartesian dualists, let's take a closer look at his reasoning.

Descartes is trying to find his nature or essence. The nature or essence of a thing is what makes it what it is. It consists of those properties the thing could not possibly do without. For example, having four equal sides is an essential property of a square because if a square lost that property, it would cease to exist. An essential property, then, is a logically necessary condition. It's a requirement that must be met in order for a thing to exist.

Descartes first considers the hypothesis that having a body is essential to him. He reasons that if his body is essential to him, then it should be inconceivable for him to exist without a body. But, he claims, that's not inconceivable. The notion of a disembodied mind is coherently imaginable. So, he concludes, having a body is not essential to him.

He then considers the hypothesis that having a mind is essential to him. He reasons that if his mind is essential to him, then it should be inconceivable for him to exist and not have a mind. That he finds to be inconceivable. If he lost the ability to think, he would cease to exist. So having a mind is essential to him.

Descartes' argument can be spelled out as follows:

1. It's conceivable for me to exist without having a body.
2. Whatever is conceivable is possible.

Although Descartes thought that humans had souls, he thought than animals were soulless automatons—mechanisms that could neither think nor feel. Here's his rationale:

> Descartes' doctrine that animals are pure machines, while men are machines with minds, was in part a compromise between his scientific aims and his voluntaristic, Christian view of man. If biological phenomena could be included in the domain of his universal physics, then the boundary would no longer lie between inanimate and animate beings; physics would include all of nature except the mind of man. Harvey's discovery of the circulation of the blood encouraged Descartes to attempt a general mechanistic physiology in hydraulic terms. Descartes argued that most human motions do not depend on the mind and gave examples of physiological functions (such as digestion), reactions (such as blinking), and feelings (such as passions) which occur independently of the will. In man, however, the mind could also direct the course of the fluid ("animal spirits") which controls movements.
>
> However, to attribute minds to animals would threaten traditional religious beliefs, since the psychological concept of mind was conflated with the theological concept of soul. Descartes argued that it would be impious to imagine that animals have souls of the same order as men and that man has nothing more to hope for in the afterlife than flies and ants have. Similarly, God could not allow sinless creatures to suffer; without souls, animals would not suffer, and man would be absolved from guilt for exploiting, killing and eating them. But he considered the most important reason for denying souls to animals to be their failure "to indicate either by voice or signs that which could be accounted for solely by thought and not by natural impulse" (letter to Henry More, February 1649). Thus, the use of language became the criterion of thought—"the true difference between man and beast." This argument has been accepted in much of the subsequent debate, and discussion has centered on the characteristics of a "true language."[15]

Thought Probe

Animal Soul

Do you agree with Descartes that animals have no minds or souls? Why or why not? What do you think it takes to have a mind?

3. Therefore, it's possible for me to exist without having a body.
4. If it's possible for me to exist without having a body, then having a body is not essential to me.
5. Therefore, having a body is not essential to me.
6. It's inconceivable for me to exist without having a mind.
7. Whatever is inconceivable is impossible.
8. Therefore, it's impossible for me to exist and not have a mind.
9. If it's impossible for me to exist without having a mind, then having a mind is essential to me.
10. Therefore, having a mind is essential to me.

Although these arguments are valid—their conclusions follow from their premises—they may not be sound, for some of their premises may be false. The crucial premise here is that disembodied existence is conceivable. Is it? Try the thought experiment yourself. Imagine you have no body—no arms, no legs, no hands, no eyes, no ears, and so on. Can you do it? If so, are you really imagining existing without a body, or are you imagining existing in a ghostlike quasi-physical body? Remember, Cartesian minds have no physical attributes, not even a location in space. You wouldn't be able to do anything (besides think) or feel anything because you wouldn't have a body. You wouldn't be able to communicate with others unless you were given some sort of telepathic ability. But, even then, it's unclear how you would identify them, for they, too, would have neither a body nor a location in space.

On reflection, many find the notion of disembodied existence inconceivable. British philosopher C. D. Broad sums up his reservations about it this way:

> Speaking for myself, I find it more and more difficult, the more I try to go into concrete detail, to conceive of a person so unlike the only ones that I know anything about, and from whom my whole notion of personality is necessarily derived, as an unembodied person would inevitably be. He would have to perceive foreign things and events (if he did so at all) in some kind of clairvoyant way, without using special sense-organs, such as eyes and ears, and experiencing special sensations through their being stimulated from without. He would have to act upon foreign things and persons (if he did so at all) in some kind of telekinetic way, without using limbs and without the characteristic feelings of stress, strain, etc., that come from the skin, the joints, and the muscles, when we use our limbs. He would have to communicate with other persons (if he did so at all) in some kind of telepathic way, without using vocal organs and emitting articulate sounds; and his conversations with himself (if he had any) would have to be conducted purely in imagery, without any help from incipient movements in the vocal organs and the sensations to which they give rise in persons like ourselves.
>
> All this is 'conceivable', so long as one keeps it in the abstract; but, when I try to think 'what it would be like' in concrete detail, I find that I have no clear and definite ideas. That incapacity of mine, even if it should be shared by most others, does not of course set any limit to what may in fact exist and happen in nature. But it does set a very definite limit to profitable speculation on these matters. And, if I cannot clearly conceive what it would be like to be an unembodied person, I find it almost incredible that the experiences of such a person (if such there could be) could be sufficiently continuous with those had in his lifetime by any deceased human being as to constitute together the experiences of *one and the same* person.[16]

Broad claims that existing without a body is not conceivable because it's not coherently imaginable. Once he started filling in the details and drawing out the implications of such an existence, he ended up with something so foreign to his experience that it was unintelligible. What's more, he claims that even if you have an immaterial soul, and even if it survives the death of your body, *you* won't survive the death of your body because your identity is tied to your body. (We will examine this issue more thoroughly in Chapter 4.)

We are justified in believing something only if it's beyond a reasonable doubt. Broad's reflections, however, indicate that there's good reason to doubt that a disembodied existence is conceivable. Because we're not justified in believing the first premise of Descartes' conceivability argument, it doesn't prove that we can exist without our bodies.

Thought Probe

Heaven without Bodies

Suppose that you have an immaterial soul, and suppose that it goes to heaven when you die, so that heaven is populated exclusively with immaterial souls. Would heaven be something to look forward to? You would no longer be able to perform any of the physical activities that gave you pleasure or gaze on the face of your loved ones. All of the sights, sounds, and smells of your former existence would be gone. Because the only possible means of communication would be telepathy, everybody might be able to read your mind. In that case, you would have no privacy whatsoever. You wouldn't even be able to keep your thoughts to yourself. Is that any way to spend eternity?

The Divisibility Argument

The argument from conceivability isn't the only one Descartes presents for his brand of dualism. He also gives us the following argument from divisibility:

> . . . There is a great difference between mind and body inasmuch as body is by nature always divisible, and the mind is entirely indivisible. For, as a matter of fact, when I consider the mind, that is to say, myself inasmuch as I am only a thinking thing, I cannot distinguish in myself any parts, but apprehend myself to be clearly one and entire. . . . But it is quite otherwise with corporeal or extended objects, for there is not one of these imaginable by me which my mind cannot easily divide into parts.[17]

Here Descartes is appealing to the principle known as the **indiscernibility of identicals:** if two things are numerically identical (that is, if two names or descriptions refer to one and the same thing), then whatever is true of one is true of the other, and vice versa. For example, if Mark Twain is numerically identical to Samuel Clemens, then whatever is true of Mark Twain is true of Samuel Clemens, and vice versa. Descartes' divisibility argument, then, is this:

1. If minds are identical to bodies, then whatever is true of minds is true of bodies, and vice versa.
2. But minds are indivisible and bodies are divisible.
3. Therefore, minds are not identical to bodies.

This, too, is a valid argument. So, again, the question is, how believable are the premises?

Premise 2 might be questioned on the grounds that neurophysiologists have shown that minds can be divided. There is a neurophysiological operation—

indiscernibility of identicals The principle that if two things are identical, then they must both possess the same properties.

cerebral commisurotomy—that severs the bundle of nerves that connects the two hemispheres of the brain (the *corpus callosum*). Patients who undergo this split-brain operation (usually to alleviate epilepsy) seem to be left with split minds. As Roger Sperry, the Nobel Prize–winning psychologist who pioneered this technique, reveals, "Everything we have seen so far indicates that the surgery has left these people with two separate minds, that is, two separate spheres of consciousness. What is experienced in the right hemisphere seems to be entirely outside the realm of awareness of the left."[18] This raises the intriguing question: after the operation, do we now have two people where before there was only one? This is a question we will consider more fully in the chapter on personal identity (Chapter 4).

Even if Descartes is correct in claiming that bodies are divisible and minds aren't, it doesn't follow that minds can exist independently of them. For minds could be capacities of the body. To see this, consider voices. Voices are not vocal chords. When you lose your voice, you don't lose your vocal chords; you lose the capacity to produce sound. This capacity, however, isn't divisible. You can no more divide a capacity than you can divide a feeling. This doesn't mean, however, that voices can exist independently of vocal chords. Just as voices are capacities to produce sounds, minds may be capacities to produce behaviors. If so, then even though minds are not divisible, they could not exist independently of bodies.

The Problem of Interaction

Oh! ridiculous writer, if I once admit these two distinct substances, you have nothing more to teach me. For you do not know what it is that you call soul, less still how they are united, nor how they act reciprocally on one another.

—DIDEROT

Although Cartesian minds are nonphysical, they seem to interact with the physical world. What goes on in our minds apparently affects what happens to our bodies, and vice versa. For example, embarrassment can cause you to blush, anger can cause your blood pressure to rise, fear can cause you to break out in a cold sweat, and so on. Conversely, getting pinched can cause you to feel pain, taking drugs can make you hallucinate, eating chocolate can give you pleasure, and so on. But how is this possible? Cartesian minds can't interact with bodies by bumping into them because they have no location in space. Nor can they interact with bodies by means of forces like electromagnetism or gravity because those forces affect only physical bodies. Insofar as Cartesian dualism doesn't explain how mind-body interaction is possible, it can't account for some of the most important facts about the mind.

The problem that mind-body interaction poses for Descartes' theory was recognized early on. Princess Elizabeth of Bohemia (1618–1680), a woman of remarkable intellectual talent who refused to marry because she preferred the life of the mind, began reading Descartes' *Meditations* in 1642. When Descartes learned of Elizabeth's interest in his work, he wrote her a letter offering to explain anything she might not understand. In a response penned on May 6, 1643, Elizabeth put the following question to Descartes:

> I beg of you to tell me how the human soul can determine the movement of the animal spirits (the chemicals released by neurons) in the body so as to perform

One way to deal with the problem of mind-body interaction is to claim that it is only apparent, not real. The mind and body seem to interact with each other, but that's because mental processes and physical processes run parallel to each other. According to **parallelism,** the correlation between mental and physical events is not the result of a causal interaction between the two.

Some parallelists believe that God produces the correlation by constantly intervening in our affairs. A decision to raise one's arm, for example, is an occasion for God to cause certain nerve cells to fire. Similarly, getting kicked in the shins is an occasion for God to create a feeling of pain in our minds. This view, known as **occasionalism,** solves the problem of mind-body interaction, but at the price of introducing yet another entity into the picture, namely, God. Unfortunately, the price seems to be rather high, for divine intervention is just as mysterious as mind-body interaction.

Other parallelists believe that God produced the correlation by designing the mental and physical realms in such a way that events in one naturally correspond to events in the other. Leibniz, for example, likens the mind and the body to two clocks that have been synchronized with each other. Just as events in one clock correspond to events in the other without the need for any sort of intervention, so events in the mind correspond to events in the body without the need for any sort of divine intervention. Leibniz called this view the **preestablished harmony** because the correlation between the mind and the body was set up by God from the beginning of the universe.

Neither of these versions of parallelism is very appealing, for both make mind-body interaction miraculous. Occasionalism requires a lot of little miracles, and the preestablished harmony requires one big miracle—and miracles defy human understanding.

---

voluntary acts—being as it is merely a conscious substance. For the determination of movement seems always to come about from the moving body's being propelled—to depend on the kind of impulse it gets from what sets it in motion, or again, on the nature and shape of this latter thing's surface. Now the first two conditions involve contact, and the third involves that the impelling thing has extension; but you utterly exclude extension from your notion of soul, and contact seems to me incompatible with a thing's being immaterial.[19]

Elizabeth saw clearly that Descartes' characterization of the soul as nonphysical made it difficult to explain how it could have any physical effects.

Descartes did not have a good answer to Elizabeth's question. He originally responded by saying that minds may affect bodies in the same way that gravity does, but this won't do because gravity is a physical force, and minds have no physical properties. Later, in *The Passions of the Soul,* Descartes tries to explain mind-body interaction by attributing it to the the pineal gland:

. . . the part of the body in which the soul exercises its functions immediately is in nowise the heart, nor the whole of the brain, but merely the most inward of all its parts, to wit, a certain very small gland which is situated in the middle of its substance and so suspended above the duct whereby the animal spirits in its anterior cavities have communication with those in the posterior, that the slightest movements which take place in it may alter very greatly the course of these

parallelism The doctrine that the mind and the body are two separate things that do not interact with one another.

occasionalism The parallelist theory of the mind that claims the correlation between mental and physical events is produced on each occasion by God.

preestablished harmony The parallelist theory of mind that claims that the correlation between mental and physical events was established by God at the beginning of the universe.

THE MIND-BODY
INTERFACE.
According to Des-
cartes, the pineal gland
is the interface be-
tween the mind and
the body. In this illus-
tration from the 1664
French edition of the
Treatise of Man, the
pineal gland sends in-
formation to the mind
from the eyes and re-
ceives instructions
from the mind to move
the muscles.

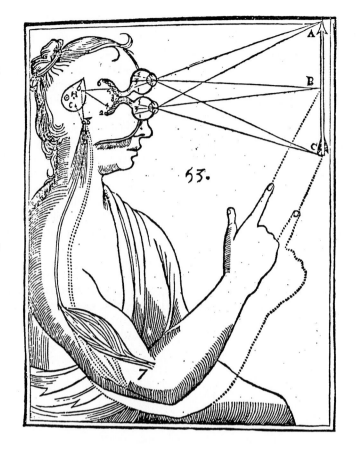

spirits; and reciprocally that the smallest changes which occur in the course of the spirits may do much to change the movements of this gland.[20]

Descartes considered the pineal gland to be the locus of mind-body interaction because he thought it was the organ that unified our sense experience. We have two eyes, two hands, two ears, and so on, but ordinarily we do not see, feel, or hear double. Because we have only one pineal gland, Descartes thought it was responsible for weaving the various inputs from our different senses into a coherent whole.

We now know that the pineal gland doesn't unify our sense experiences. But even if it did, Descartes hasn't offered us a solution to the problem of mind-body interaction because he hasn't told us how the mind alters the flow of "animal spirits" in the nerve cells. It's just as difficult to understand how a nonphysical thing can move a miniscule physical object as it is to understand how such a thing can move a massive one. Without a credible account of how the mind and the body interact, Descartes' theory doesn't provide a satisfactory account of the mind.

Although Descartes thought the mind-body interface was located in the brain, not everybody has. The seat of the soul has been located in many different places, as neuroscientist Colin Blakemore relates:

> To the ancient Egyptians it was definitely somewhere else, for though they entombed their dead leaders with all the tangible trappings of life and tried to preserve in perfect condition their bodily remains for the journey to Osiris, they dealt summarily with the brain by retracting it through the nose with a spoon. The Ba spirit of an Egyptian mummy was not in his head, but in his bowels and his heart.
>
> At one time or another almost every major organ in the body has been credited with this ultimate organic privilege—the guardianship of the soul and of the sentiments that make us men. The liver, blood-coloured and apparently the source of all the veins, played this special role for the Sumerians (the first people to write down their thoughts), for the Assyrians and for the ancient people of Israel. 'My liver shall sing

> praise to Thee, and not be silent', the Psalmist may literally have written.
>
> It is hardly surprising that the arrangement of blood vessels should have guided man in his search for his soul. After all, what is a soul? It is a mover, an animator (that word itself is derived from 'anima', the Latin for 'soul'). And what could be more necessary for the sustenance of movement than the free flow of warming blood through the body. When blood was lost, then so was life. By this argument, the origin of blood must be the source of life itself, and from this view sprang one of the most enduring theories of biology—that the seat of the soul is the heart. Aristotle himself, the greatest biologist in the ancient world, supported this idea, and it is still with us; not in science perhaps, but certainly in poetry and in popular song, where the heart, not the brain, yearns, aches and finally breaks.
>
> Aristotle's specific theory relegated the brain to the task of merely cooling blood from the heart, which was itself the organ of thought and sensation.[21]

The Causal Closure of the Physical

Descartes' dualistic interactionism also runs afoul of a basic principle of materialism known as the **causal closure of the physical.** According to this principle, everything that happens can be explained in purely physical terms. Any bodily movement, for example, can be explained by the fact that certain muscles contracted. And the fact that certain muscles contracted can be explained by the fact that certain neurons fired. And the fact that certain neurons fired can be explained by the fact that certain chemicals were present in the brain. And so on. Nowhere in this chain of explanations must we postulate a nonphysical cause. Nevertheless, people do have thoughts, feelings, and desires, and these things seem to be nonphysical. How can we reconcile these facts? Some have suggested that we can reconcile them by admitting the existence of Cartesian minds and denying them any causal power.

This view, known as **epiphenomenalism,** holds that causation between the mind and the body is a one-way street: the body affects the mind, but the mind does not affect the body. The mind is merely an ineffective by-product of physical processes going on in the body. (An "epiphenomena" is a secondary

causal closure of the physical The principle that everything that happens can be explained in purely physical terms.

epiphenomenalism The doctrine that the mind is an ineffective by-product of physical processes.

process that results from and depends on a primary process.) So just as the smoke produced by a fire has no effect on the fire itself, epiphenomenalists believe that the thoughts, feelings, and desires produced by the brain have no effect on the brain. Or to use another analogy, just as steam is a by-product of boiling water and has no effect on the water that produced it, so the mind is a by-product of the brain and has no effect on the brain that produced it.

This view of the mind-body relation is an attractive one to those who believe that science can explain everything that happens in the world in purely physical terms. It leaves unexplained the mechanism by which the body affects the mind, but it does not postulate any unobservable causes. Epiphenomenalism was championed by a number of thinkers in the nineteenth and twentieth centuries, most notably, Thomas Huxley:

> All states of consciousness in us, as in [brutes], are immediately caused by molecular changes of the brain-substance. It seems to me that in men, as in brutes, there is no proof that any state of consciousness is the cause of change in the motion of the matter of the organism. If these positions are well based, it follows that our mental conditions are simply the symbols in consciousness of the changes which take place automatically in the organism; and that, to take an extreme illustration, the feeling we call volition is not the cause of a voluntary act, but the symbol of that state of the brain which is the immediate cause of that act. We are conscious automata. . . .[22]

Huxley would have us believe that our thoughts, feelings, and desires have no effect on what we do. Our lives would have been no different if we had never formed any beliefs, felt any pain, or longed for any objects. In fact, the entire history of the human race would have been no different if no one had ever had a single thought.

Such a view flies in the face of common sense. What we do with our lives seems very much to depend on what goes on in our minds. For example, wanting to greet a friend can cause you to raise your arm. Believing that a road is closed can cause you to take another route. Feeling pain can cause you to remove your hand from a hot stove. If epiphenomenalism were true, all of these claims would be false because mental states would be only effects, never causes.

What's more, if mental states don't cause anything, it's unclear why they exist. If minds have no physical effects, they confer no reproductive advantage on those who have them. So epiphenomenalists can't explain the existence of minds by appeal to their survival value because, in their view, minds have no survival value. Creatures with minds are no better off than creatures without them. As a theory of mind, then, epiphenomenalism seems to have little to recommend it over Cartesian dualism.

The Problem of Other Minds

Both epiphenomenalism and Cartesian dualism face another embarrassing problem: there seems to be no sure way to tell whether other people have minds. This is the **problem of other minds.** You know that you have a mind

How . . . can the consciousness be dismissed as an epiphenomenon when only by virtue of this epiphenomenon could it be perceived to be an epiphenomenon — or anything else?

—JOSEPH WOOD KRUTCH

because you experience it directly. You have various thoughts, feelings, and desires, and this proves that you have a mind. But you can't directly experience anybody else's mind. You can't have other people's thoughts, feelings, or desires. So, to arrive at the conclusion that other people have minds, you must appeal to certain physical facts. But it seems that those facts can't establish the existence of immaterial minds beyond a reasonable doubt.

Because immaterial minds have no physical properties, you can't use physical instruments to detect them. CAT (computerized axial tomography) scans and MRIs (magnetic resonance imaging) may be able to tell you whether other humans have brains, but they can't tell you whether they have minds. And because any behavior can be produced mechanically, the fact that something behaves in a certain way can't prove that it has a mind. Descartes himself was aware of this problem. He writes, "What do I see from this window but hats and coats which may cover automatic machines."[23] For all a substance dualist knows, then, all the other humans he encounters are mindless automatons — like Stepford Wives — only perhaps not so benign.

The view that one's mind is the only mind that can be known to exist is called **solipsism.** Although some people are attracted to this position, it is decidedly odd, if not insane, because accepting it means rejecting a great many other beliefs we have about the nature of reality, knowledge, and value. For example, we ordinarily claim to know that other people have minds, that what's on their minds affects their behavior, and that those with minds deserve special treatment, and so on. If some sort of substance dualism is true, however, it's unclear that we can legitimately claim to know any of these things. Thus the price of accepting substance dualism appears to be quite high.

Summary

According to Cartesian dualism, mental states are states of an immaterial substance that affects and is affected by one's body. Descartes offers two arguments in support of this view: the conceivability argument and the divisibility argument. In the conceivability argument, Descartes claims that because he can conceive of himself existing without a body, his body is not essential to him. In the divisibility argument, he claims that because his body is divisible but his mind isn't, his mind isn't identical to his body. These arguments are inconclusive, however, for it is doubtful that disembodied existence is conceivable, and, even if the mind were indivisible, it doesn't necessarily follow that the mind could exist independently of the body.

The major problem facing Cartesian dualism is that of explaining how two substances (mind and body) that are so dissimilar could possibly interact. Descartes offers no credible account of mind-body interaction.

Epiphenomenalism is a dualist view that holds that although the body can affect the mind, the mind cannot affect the body. In this view, mental states are a by-product of physical processes. But if immaterial minds have no effect on anything — if they serve no purpose — their existence seems inexplicable.

problem of other minds The philosophical problem of explaining how it is possible to know that there are other minds in the world.

solipsism The view that there is only one mind in the universe, namely, one's own.

Cartesian dualism also faces the problem of other minds, for if it were true, there would seem to be no way of telling whether other humans have minds. Thus, for all a Cartesian dualist knows, solipsism is true—he has the only mind in the universe. Any view that implies that we are not justified in believing in the existence of other minds, however, is suspect.

Study Questions

1. According to Cartesian dualism, what is it to be in a mental state?
2. What reasons does Descartes give for believing that he doesn't have knowledge of the external world?
3. What reasons does Descartes give for believing that he does know that he thinks and that he exists?
4. What is Descartes' argument from conceivability?
5. What is Descartes' argument from divisibility?
6. What is epiphenomenalism?
7. What is the problem of other minds?

Discussion Questions

1. Is disembodied existence conceivable, or does it involve a logical contradiction? Can you construct a thought experiment to back up your view?
2. Descartes identifies the mind with the soul. Should the mind be so identified? Is the mind the same thing as the soul? If not, how does the soul differ from the mind? What is the relationship between the mind and the soul?
3. In addition to minds and souls, many claim that humans also have a spirit. What is a spirit? Is it just another name for a mind or soul or is it something else altogether? Can you give necessary and sufficient conditions for having a spirit?
4. Suppose someone claimed to have a device that destroyed people's souls. When it was used, it prevented a person's soul from going to heaven, but otherwise had no discernable effect on that person. How would you evaluate such a claim? Is the claim that people have souls any more plausible? Why or why not?
5. Some people claim to have found physical evidence for the existence of the soul. Duncan McDougall, for example, placed dying people on a very precise scale and found that they lost between ¾ oz. and 1½ oz. at the moment of death. Does this evidence prove the existence of a Cartesian soul? Why or why not?
6. Is it possible to build a machine that has our linguistic and problem-solving abilities? Would a machine that had our linguistic and problem-solving abilities have a mind?
7. Descartes did not believe that animals have souls because they do not exhibit any behavior that cannot be accounted for in purely mechanical

terms. That is, they do not reason or speak in such a way as to suggest that they have minds. Is Descartes right? Do animals not have minds? If you think that they do have minds or souls, what do you consider the mind to be?

8. Do parapsychological phenomena (telepathy, clairvoyance, precognition, psychokinesis, etc.) provide sufficient reason for believing in the existence of Cartesian minds? Why or why not?

9. If the causal closure of the physical is true, if everything that happens can be explained in purely physical terms, can we have free will? Why or why not?

You Are What You Eat

Mind as Body

*A*lthough Cartesian dualism did not solve the mind-body problem, it did help resolve the conflict between science and religion. Beginning in the eleventh century—when Western scholars "discovered" the writings of ancient Greek philosophers in the libraries of Toledo, Spain—there was a growing tension between clergymen and scientists (or "natural philosophers" as they were then called). These writings showed that it was possible to explain the universe in natural rather than supernatural terms. Reason as well as revelation could be a source of knowledge.

In the twelfth century, Pierre Abelard (1079–1142), a French philosopher and theologian, articulated four rules that should govern any investigation:

1. Use systematic doubt and question everything.
2. Learn the difference between statements of rational proof and those merely of persuasion.
3. Be precise in the use of words, and expect precision from others.
4. Watch for error, even in Holy Scripture.

Realizing that such an approach to knowledge would undermine its intellectual authority, the Catholic Church condemned Abelard in 1140. In 1210, it banned the teaching of logic in Paris. But the genie was already out of the bottle. Too many people had already experienced the power of the new way of thinking. So in 1255, the Church reluctantly agreed to allow logic to be taught in the universities.

Nature was now no longer a closed book. Its mysteries could be understood by anybody willing to logically examine the evidence of the senses. The most startling claim produced by this new approach to knowledge was that of Copernicus (1473–1543): the earth is not the center of the universe. Copernicus showed that the motion of the planets could be explained on the hypothesis that the earth revolved around the sun. Moreover, he showed that this hypothesis was simpler than the hypothesis that the sun revolved around the earth. Copernicus completed his work in 1530, but because it contradicted Church teaching, he was reluctant to publish it. The first edition of his *On the Revolutions of the Heavenly Spheres* didn't appear until 1543, on the day he died.

A number of scholars recognized the importance of Copernicus's discovery and began writing their own books on the subject. One such individual was Giordano Bruno. In 1593, the Church found him guilty of heresy, and in 1600 he was burned at the stake. Another was Galileo Galilei. Looking through one of the first telescopes, he saw the moons of Jupiter and the phases of Venus. Because the Copernican hypothesis provided the best explanation of these findings, Galileo accepted it. In 1632, he published his *Dialogues Concerning the Two Chief World Systems*, in which a proponent of a sun-centered universe (a Copernican) debates a proponent of an earth-centered universe. At the end of the book, the Copernican concedes the argument to his opponent. Although this was meant to placate the Church, it did not succeed, for it was clear from the text that Galileo sided with the Copernicans. Consequently, the Church banned the book and destroyed all the copies it could find. Galileo was brought before the Inquisition, forced under threat of torture to recant his views, and placed under house arrest for the rest of his life.

This was the intellectual climate in which Descartes wrote. Scientific theories called into question the teachings of the Church, and the Church tried to put a stop to scientific inquiry by persecuting those who practiced it. Descartes helped diffuse this volatile situation by claiming that the world contained two distinct substances, only one of which was a suitable object of scientific inquiry. Because the Church had a realm forever beyond the reach of science — the realm of the spirit — it could allow scientists to pursue their investigations unhindered. Science was no longer the threat it had seemed to be, for if Descartes was right, science could never usurp the Church's authority in matters of mind and morals.

This accommodation worked well for more than two hundred years. But by the end of the nineteenth century, many scientists no longer believed that a science of the mind was impossible. Not only did they recognize the flaws in Descartes' arguments, they realized that the same principles that were used to explain animal behavior could be used to explain human behavior. It was widely believed, however, that science could investigate the mind only if it were directly observable. So scientists and philosophers sought ways of understanding the mind that would make it a legitimate object of scientific inquiry. To understand the new scientific theories of the mind, it's helpful to understand the theory of knowledge that motivated them, namely, empiricism.

Empiricism

Empiricism claims that the only source of knowledge about the external world is sense experience. Although there were empiricists in ancient Greece, the most influential modern versions of empiricism were produced by the British philosophers John Locke and David Hume in the seventeenth and

empiricism The epistemological theory that the only source of knowledge about the external world is sense experience.

DAVID HUME
1711–1766

eighteenth centuries. They held that there is nothing in the mind that isn't first in the senses. As Locke put it, the mind is a blank slate (a *tabula rasa*) that contains nothing more than what the senses have put there.

Traditional empiricism claims that our minds contain two types of ideas: simple and complex. Simple ideas (those that do not contain other ideas as constituents) correspond to or represent sensations such as hot, cold, light, dark, loud, soft, sweet, sour, rough, smooth. Complex ideas are built out of simple ideas. The idea of an apple, for example, is composed of the simple ideas of a certain shape, size, color, taste, texture, and so on. Thus all complex ideas can be reduced to or analyzed into simple ideas that represent sensations.

The Empiricists drew two important corollaries from this view of the nature of thought: (1) an idea corresponds to a real object only if it is derived from or reducible to sense impressions, and (2) a term is meaningful only if it stands for a real object. Hume used these principles to demonstrate that terms such as "liberty," "causality," and "self" are not meaningful, for they are not derived from sense impressions. As he says in his *Enquiries Concerning the Human Understanding*, "When we entertain, therefore, any suspicion that a philosophical term is employed without any meaning or idea (as is but too frequent), we need but enquire, *from what impression is that supposed idea derived?* And if it be impossible to assign any, this will serve to confirm our suspicion."[24] Such terms, according to Hume, should be purged from our language.

When we run over libraries, persuaded of these principles, what havoc must we make? If we take in our hand any volume; of divinity or school metaphysics, for instance; let us ask, *Does it contain any abstract reasoning concerning quantity or number?* No. *Does it contain any experimental reasoning concerning matter of fact and existence?* No. Commit it then to the flames: for it can contain nothing but sophistry and illusion.[25]

According to Hume, those who use terms that are not derived from sensations don't know what they are talking about, for they aren't talking about anything.

Hume used his empiricism to show not only that Cartesian minds don't exist but that the very notion of a Cartesian mind is unintelligible. In his *A Treatise of Human Nature*, he writes,

> As every idea is derived from a precedent impression, had we any idea of the substance of our minds, we must also have an impression of it; which is very difficult, if not impossible to be conceived. For how can an impression represent a substance, otherwise than by resembling it? And how can an impression resemble a substance, since, according to this philosophy, it is not a substance, and has none of the peculiar qualities or characteristics of a substance? . . .

> Thus neither by considering the first origin of ideas, nor by means of a definition are we able to arrive at any satisfactory notion of substance; which seems to me a sufficient reason for abandoning utterly that dispute concerning the materiality and immateriality of the soul, and makes me absolutely condemn even the question itself.[26]

According to Hume, we cannot sense the soul. Since there is no sense impression from which the idea of the soul could have been derived, we have no idea what the word "soul" stands for. The question of the existence of the soul, then, cannot be answered because no one knows what they're talking about when they use the word "soul."

Logical Positivism

The rise of modern physics raised a number of problems for traditional empiricism. At the beginning of the nineteenth century, John Dalton experimentally confirmed what the Greek atomists had suggested over two thousand years before, namely, that physical objects were made out of tiny particles of matter called "atoms." Dalton correctly believed that atoms were the smallest particle of an element that retained the chemical properties of that element. He incorrectly believed, however, that atoms were indestructible and unchangeable. By the beginning of the twentieth century, studies of radiation and radioactivity had shown that Dalton's atoms could not only be broken into smaller pieces; they could also be changed into other atoms. Dalton's atoms were not the basic building blocks of the universe. That distinction fell to even smaller subatomic particles. Subatomic particles like electrons are so small, however, that they cannot be directly observed, even in principle. But if they can't be directly observed, the idea of a subatomic particle can't be derived from sense experience. And if the idea of a subatomic particle isn't derived from sense experience, traditional empiricism would have us believe that talk of subatomic particles is meaningless. This conclusion did not sit

To talk of immaterial existences is to talk of nothings. To say that the human soul, angels, God, are immaterial, is to say they are nothings, or that there is no God, no angels, no soul.

—THOMAS JEFFERSON

I consider that a man's brain is like a little empty attic, and you have to stock it with such furniture as you choose.

—SIR ARTHUR CONAN DOYLE

well with a group of philosophically minded scientists who lived in Vienna at the turn of the century. Known as the Vienna circle, they sought to put the new physics on a firm philosophical footing by developing a theory of meaning that would not only make sense of modern science but also eliminate meaningless metaphysical speculation. This theory became the central doctrine in a philosophical movement known as **logical positivism** or logical empiricism.

Traditional empiricism maintains that a term is meaningful only if it can be derived from sense experience. Logical positivism maintains that a sentence is meaningful only if it can be verified by sense experience. The idea is that if there is no way to tell whether a sentence is true, it doesn't tell us anything about the world. Consider, for example, this sentence from Martin Heidegger's *What Is Metaphysics?* "The Nothing nothings." What does this tell us about the world? What must the world be like in order for this sentence to be true? How could we determine whether the world really is that way? In his essay, "The Elimination of Metaphysics through the Logical Analysis of Language," the logical positivist Rudolph Carnap argues that we can't answer these questions because that sentence is meaningless.[27] Those who believe that this statement contains a deep insight into the nature of reality have confused obscurity with profundity.

Sentences that occur in the writings of physicists, even though they contain terms that are not derived from sensation, are nonetheless meaningful because they can be verified. We know what the world must be like if they are true and how to go about determining whether the world is that way. As a result, they give us a real understanding of the nature of reality.

The logical positivists believed that to know the meaning of a sentence is to know how to verify it. To know the meaning of the sentence "The cat is on the mat," for example, is to know what observations would establish its truth. From this, the logical positivists concluded that the meaning of a sentence is its method of verification. This is their famous **verifiability theory of meaning,** which they used to develop the theory of mind known as "logical behaviorism."

Logical Behaviorism

We don't run away because we are afraid. We are afraid because we run away.

—WILLIAM JAMES

We verify whether someone is in a mental state by observing their behavior. We can tell whether someone is thirsty, for example, by observing what they do when they are given a drink. If they take it, there is reason to believe that they are thirsty. Given that the meaning of a statement is its method of verification, and given that the way we verify statements about people's minds is by observing their behavior, it follows that what we mean when we say that someone is in a mental state is that he or she will behave in certain ways in certain situations. According to **logical behaviorism,** then, mental states are behavioral dispositions.

To have a **behavioral disposition** is to have a tendency to respond in certain ways to certain stimuli. For example, if you have a tendency to scream

Psychological Behaviorism

In the twentieth century, a number of psychologists took empiricist principles to heart. If psychology was to become a science, they argued, it would have to concern itself only with what is publicly observable. Specifically, it would have to stop attributing human behavior to unobservable Cartesian minds.

It was once thought that physical objects were moved by gods that dwelled inside of them. ("Everything is full of Gods," said Thales, the West's first physicist.) Only after natural science started explaining the behavior of physical objects in terms of observable causes did it make any progress. The late psychologist B. F. Skinner claims that social science has not made comparable progress because it continues to explain behavior in terms of indwelling agents. "All of what is called behavioral science," says Skinner, "continues to trace behavior to states of mind, feelings, traits of character, human nature, and so on. Physics and biology once followed similar practices and advanced only when they discarded them."[28] Skinner proposes that social science drop its "prescientific" way of thinking and focus on how the environment causes behavior.

Skinner's proposal is a methodological—not a philosophical—one. He outlines a method for studying behavior, not a philosophical theory of mind. Skinner doesn't deny the existence of mental states. He just denies that they have any effect on our behavior. For example, he says, "The punishment of sexual behavior changes sexual behavior, and any feelings which may arise are at best by-products."[29] Because he refers to mental states as by-products, Skinner sounds more like an epiphenomenalist than a logical behaviorist.

whenever you see a mouse, you have a certain behavioral disposition. Logical behaviorism maintains that there is nothing more to being in a mental state than having certain behavioral dispositions. For example, to believe that it's raining is to be disposed to take rainwear with you when you go outside; to desire wealth is to be disposed to engage in activities that make money; and to fear heights is to be disposed to avoid high places. According to logical behaviorism, the mental state doesn't cause the behavioral disposition; it is the behavioral disposition.

Logical positivism is not the only route to logical behaviorism. The English philosopher Gilbert Ryle (1900–1976) came to the conclusion that mental states are behavioral dispositions through a careful analysis of how mental terms are used in ordinary language. We tend to assume that nouns refer to substances. But this is not always the case. Consider, for example, the word "waltz" in the sentence "She danced a waltz." Although "waltz" is a noun, it doesn't refer to a thing. Rather, it refers to a way of dancing. So instead of saying "She danced a waltz," we could just as well have said (albeit somewhat awkwardly) "She danced waltzily." In any event, we would be quite mistaken if we thought that waltzes could exist independently of people dancing. Similarly, Ryle claims, we would be quite mistaken if we thought that minds could exist independently of people behaving. To dance a waltz is simply to dance in a certain way. Similarly, to have a mind is simply to behave in a certain way. Ryle provides the following illustration of the linguistic confusion behind the mind-body problem.

logical positivism The philosophical movement based on the assumption that to know what a sentence means is to know what observations would make it true.

verifiability theory of meaning The doctrine that the meaning of a statement is its method of verification.

logical behaviorism The doctrine that mental states are behavioral dispositions.

behavioral disposition A tendency to respond to certain stimuli in certain ways.

Ryle's University Seeker

A foreigner visiting Oxford or Cambridge for the first time is shown a number of colleges, libraries, playing fields, museums, scientific departments, and administrative offices. He then adds "But where is the University? I have seen where the members of the Colleges live, where the Registrar works, where the scientists experiment and the rest. But I have not yet seen the University in which reside and work the members of your university." It has then to be explained to him that the University is not another collateral institution, some ulterior counterpart to the colleges, laboratories, and offices which he has seen. The University is just the way in which all that he has already seen is organized. When they are seen and when their coordination is understood, the University has been seen. His mistake lay in his innocent assumption that it was correct to speak of the Christ Church, the Bodleian Library, the Ashmolean Museum, and the University, to speak, that is, as if "the University" stood for an extra member of the class of which these other units are members. He was mistakenly allocating the University to the same category as that to which the other institutions belong.[30]

Mind may be defined as response to the meanings of stimuli.

—Yervant Krikorian

Ryle's university seeker makes what Ryle calls a "category mistake" in assuming that the university exists in the same way that libraries, museums, and laboratories do. Similarly, dualists make a category mistake in assuming that minds exist in the same way that bodies do. Minds, like universities, are simply complex patterns of behavior. To believe otherwise is to accept what Ryle calls "the dogma of the ghost in the machine." For Ryle, there's nothing more to having a mind than having a tendency to behave in certain ways.

Logical behaviorism is a materialist theory, for it doesn't postulate the existence of any immaterial objects. It is also a reductive theory, for it holds that mental states are nothing but behavioral dispositions. Reductive theories are highly prized in science because they simplify our ontology (our theory of what there is in the world) by reducing the number of entities that we must suppose to exist. If one type of entity is reducible to another, there is no need to admit the existence of the former in addition to the latter.

For example, consider the statement "The average parent has 1.5 children." The subject of this sentence—the average parent—seems to be a rather unusual individual. Which half of the half-child does this "average" parent have: the top half or the bottom half? None of us who understand what "average" means would want to admit that in addition to real parents, there are also such things as average parents in the world. We know that talk about average parents is just shorthand for talk about real parents. To say that the average parent has 1.5 children is just to say that the number of children divided by the number of parents is 1.5. Once it is realized that we can replace all talk about average parents with talk about real parents, any tendency to admit the existence of average parents in addition to real parents disappears. Similarly, claim the logical behaviorists, once it is realized that we can replace

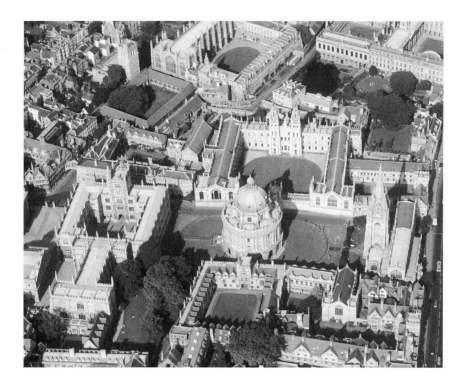

all talk about mental states with talk about behavioral dispositions, any tendency to admit the existence of minds in addition to bodies also disappears.

Logical behaviorism is a simpler theory than Cartesian dualism because it postulates fewer entities. Cartesian dualism would have us believe that in addition to the physical objects in the world, there are also nonphysical objects, namely, minds. Logical behaviorism doesn't commit us to the existence of anything beyond the physical.

Logical behaviorism is also a more conservative theory than Cartesian dualism because it doesn't violate the principle of the causal closure of the physical. It doesn't postulate the existence of any nonphysical causes. Accepting logical behaviorism doesn't require rejecting any scientific principles.

In addition, logical behaviorism is a more fruitful theory than Cartesian dualism because it solves the problem of other minds. There is no way to tell whether Cartesian minds exist because they are immaterial and thus unobservable. According to logical behaviorism, however, minds are complex patterns of behavior. Since behavior is observable, minds are observable. In fact, it's sometimes easier to observe other people's behavior than one's own. So logical behaviorism suggests that it may be easier to know other people's minds than your own.

The explanatory power of a theory is determined by how well it meets the criteria of adequacy. Logical behaviorism is simpler, more conservative, and more fruitful than Cartesian dualism. As long as it has at least as much scope as Cartesian dualism, that is, as long as it fits the data as least as well as Cartesian dualism does, it's clearly the better theory.

It was good for you. Was it good for me?
—BEHAVIORIST QUERY

A philosophical theory of mind tells us what it is to have a mind. That is, it identifies the conditions under which the concept of mind applies to something. Logical behaviorism tells us that something has a mind (is in a mental state) if and only if it has certain behavioral dispositions. So if logical behaviorism were true, it would be logically impossible to be in a mental state and not have certain behavioral dispositions, and vice versa. Is that the case? Let's put it to the test.

Many mental states, such as pain, love, and fear, have certain feelings associated with them. What it feels like to be in one of those states is known as its subjective character or its **qualitative content.** The qualitative content of a mental state seems to be essential to it; if you don't have the appropriate feeling, you aren't in the mental state. For example, if you don't feel anything when someone punches you in the nose, you aren't in pain. Logical behaviorism maintains, on the contrary, that feelings are irrelevant to mental states. As long as you have the right behavioral dispositions, you're in a mental state, regardless of what you're feeling. But that seems implausible.

Consider someone who, as a result of a neurological disorder, can't feel pain:

Thought Experiment

The Perfect Pretender

Some people are born without the ability to feel pain. This is a very dangerous condition, for such people often can't tell before it's too late that they have suffered serious bodily damage. Imagine that such a person is a particularly good student of human behavior and has learned to exhibit the appropriate pain behavior in the appropriate situations. If someone kicks him in the shins, for example, he grabs his shin, hops on one leg, and yells "Ouch!" in the same way that a normal pain sufferer would. He has become such a good actor that his behavior is indistinguishable from that of someone who can feel pain.

The perfect pretender behaves just like someone who can feel pain. Through years of study, he has acquired the same behavioral dispositions as a normal person. But he can't feel pain, and if he can't feel pain, he can't be in pain. So having the right behavioral dispositions isn't sufficient for being in a mental state.

Having the right behavioral dispositions also isn't necessary for being in a mental state. There are people who, through a supreme act of will, can act as if they aren't in pain even though they are suffering terribly. If these people were to become so good at hiding their pain that no one could ever tell when they are in pain, then logical behaviorism would have us believe that they never are in pain. But that can't be right. Anyone who feels pain is in pain whether or not he or she shows it. To demonstrate that being in pain doesn't require behaving in a certain way, Hilary Putnam offers the following thought experiment.

Putnam's Super-Spartans

Imagine a community of "super-Spartans" or "super-stoics"—a community in which the adults have the ability to successfully suppress all involuntary pain behavior. They may, on occasion, admit that they feel pain, but always in pleasant well-modulated voices—even if they are undergoing the agonies of the damned. They do not wince, scream, flinch, sob, grit their teeth, clench their fists, exhibit beads of sweat or otherwise act like people in pain or people suppressing the unconditional responses associated with pain. However, they do feel pain, and they dislike it (just as we do). They even admit that it takes a great effort of will to behave as they do. It is only that they have what they regard as important ideological reasons for behaving as they do, and they have, through years of training, learned to live up to their own exacting standards.[31]

Putnam's super-Spartans should sound familiar to those familiar with the original *Star Trek* TV series. They bear a remarkable resemblance to Vulcans, like Mr. Spock, who also suppress pain behavior for ideological reasons. After a particularly bloody war, the Vulcans decided that they would survive as a race only if they learned to control their emotions. So, from that time on, all Vulcans were trained from birth to hide their feelings. They still have feelings: they just don't show them. Logical behaviorism would have us believe that because Vulcans never act like they are in pain, they never are in pain. But that's ludicrous. You don't have to behave in a certain way to be in pain. So having a certain behavioral disposition is not necessary for being in a mental state.

Putnam's argument can be spelled out as follows:

1. If having certain behavioral dispositions were a necessary condition for being in a certain mental state, then it would be impossible to be in that state and not have those dispositions.

2. But, as the example of the super-Spartans shows, it is possible to be in pain and not have the behavioral dispositions associated with pain.

3. Therefore, having certain behavioral dispositions is not a necessary condition for being in a certain mental state.

Logical behaviorism is a theory about the meaning of mental terms. It claims that what we mean when we say that somebody is in a mental state is that if they were to receive certain stimuli, they would respond in certain ways. For example, according to logical behaviorism, part of what we mean when we say that someone believes that it's raining is that if she were to go outside, she would take rainwear. If these two statements really had the same meaning, then whenever one was true, the other would be true, and vice versa. If there were a situation in which one could be true and the other false, then they couldn't have the same meaning. But there are many such situations. For example, someone who believes that it's raining could go outside

Experience is a good teacher but she sends in terrific bills.

—MINNA ANTRIM

qualitative content
The felt quality of certain mental states.

Behavioral Therapy

The notion that mental states are behavioral dispositions has implications for how we treat mental illness. If we want to alter a person's mind, all we have to do is alter his or her behavior. Psychologist Morton Hunt describes some of the techniques used by behavioral therapists:

> As Joseph Wolpe, a leading exponent of behavior therapy, put it several years ago, the Freudian explanations of neuroses were simply unnecessary; a neurosis was "just a habit—a persistent habit of unadaptive behavior" that could be cured by counterconditioning techniques such as "systematic desensitization." Typically, a female patient with a morbid fear of the penis was induced to relax and think pleasant thoughts, and then to envision a nude male statue far off (where the penis was relatively unthreatening). When the association of relaxation and pleasant thoughts with the remote nonliving penis made it tolerable, the patient was then told to envision it closer and closer, and eventually to practice this association with images of a live male. This was reported to have led her to be able to tolerate the real thing.
>
> Other behavior therapists have used "aversive" conditioning techniques to link unwanted behavior to unpleasant experiences and so eliminate that behavior. Some have given electric shocks to male homosexuals as they looked at erotic photos of nude males. Others have sought to combat overeating by training their patients to imagine themselves vomiting in public when they feel like gorging themselves, or given them pills that produce nausea shortly after eating. Early reports claimed considerable success with these efforts.[32]

The movie A Clockwork Orange graphically depicts the use of aversive conditioning techniques. Unfortunately (or fortunately as the case may be), these techniques did not turn out to be as successful as originally hoped. Hunt explains,

> The view of the human being as rat is simply too narrow: people do think and, thinking, find reason to reshape their own behavior; they follow their own minds despite all the external pressures of reward and punishment.
>
> For much the same reason, many of the behavior therapies have failed to live up to their first promise. The short-term sex therapies, for instance, originally seemed to cure most of the disabilities they were used to treat but follow-up studies have shown that there is a high relapse rate. . . .
>
> The most disappointing results of all have been those of the aversive therapies: the association of homosexuality, overeating, alcoholism, and other behaviors with sharply unpleasant stimuli has shown a high rate of cessation of those behaviors—but the results have been largely ephemeral. For in contrast to laboratory animals, human patients in aversive therapy know that the painful stimulus is being given them for a purpose.[33]

without rainwear because she wants to get wet, she doesn't believe that rainwear will keep her dry, she wants to impress her friends, and so on. What we do in any particular situation depends on what mental states we're in. Behaviorism, however, denies that mental states are causes and thus can't account for even the simplest behavior.

We often explain people's actions by appeal to their beliefs and desires. The assumption behind this practice is that mental states cause behavior. Logical behaviorism denies this commonsense view of mental states. It claims that actions are caused by physical stimuli and prior conditioning—not by mental states. The failure to recognize the causal efficacy of mental states is what ultimately led to the downfall of behaviorism in both philosophical and psychological circles.

The failure of logical behaviorism suggests that the verifiability theory of meaning is flawed. And indeed it is. If the meaning of a statement were its method of verification, then whenever a new method of verification was discovered, the meaning of those statements that could be verified by that method would change. But if we found a new way of measuring height, the meaning of the statement "Jones is five feet tall" wouldn't change.

The most significant problem facing the verifiability theory of meaning, however, is that it undermines itself: if it's true, it's meaningless. Because the verifiability theory of meaning applies to all statements, it applies to itself. So the verifiability theory of meaning is meaningful only if it can be verified. But there is no way to verify the statement "The meaning of a statement is its method of verification" because it is not an empirical statement. There are no observations that would confirm it. By its own lights, then, it's meaningless. It's ironic that a theory designed to rid the world of meaningless statements should end up eliminating itself.

The Identity Theory

It has long been known that the mind is affected by the brain. But it has only recently been recognized that different parts of the brain perform different functions. This was dramatically demonstrated by an incident that occurred near the small town of Cavendish, Vermont, in 1848. Phineas Gage, the foreman of a team of railroad workers, was setting a charge of dynamite. This involved drilling a hole into the rock, filling it with dynamite, and tamping down the dynamite with a steel bar. As Gage was doing the tamping, the dynamite went off, sending the steel bar right through his head. Although the injury knocked him out, it didn't kill him. After a few minutes he regained consciousness and was able to speak. Eventually, he recovered. But he was a changed man. One of the attending physicians, John Harlow, described him this way:

> His physical health is good, and I am inclined to say that he has recovered. . . .
> The equilibrium or balance, so to speak, between his intellectual faculties and animal propensities, seems to have been destroyed. He is fitful, irreverent, indulging at times in the grossest profanity (which was not previously his custom), manifesting but little deference for his fellows, impatient of restraint or advice when it conflicts with his desires, at times pertinaciously obstinate, yet capricious and vacillating, devising many plans of future operation, which are no sooner arranged than they are abandoned. . . . In this regard his mind was radically changed, so decidedly that his friends and acquaintances said that he was "no longer Gage."[34]

What happened to Gage's brain obviously affected his mind in a profound way.

Since Gage's accident, psychologists have amassed a huge amount of data that many believe is best explained on the hypothesis that the mind is the brain. Psychologist Barry Beyerstein catalogs some of this evidence:

> *Phylogenetic:* There is an evolutionary relationship between brain complexity and species' cognitive attributes.
> *Developmental:* Abilities emerge with brain maturation; failure of the brain to mature arrests mental development.

Body am I entirely, and nothing more; and soul is only the name of something in the body.

—FRIEDRICH NIETZSCHE

The relation between thought and the brain is roughly of the same order as that between bile and the liver or urine and the bladder.

—CARL VOGT

LIFE MASK AND SKULL OF PHINEAS GAGE.
Gage's accident showed that the mind depends on the brain.

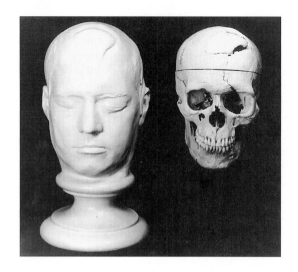

So what is this mind, what are these atoms with consciousness? Last week's potatoes!
—RICHARD P. FEYNMAN

Clinical: Brain damage from accidental, toxic, or infectious sources, or from deprivation of nutrition or stimulation during brain development, results in predictable and largely irreversible losses of mental function.

Experimental: Mental operations correlate with electrical, biochemical, biomagnetic, and anatomical changes in the brain. When the human brain is stimulated electrically or chemically during neurosurgery, movements, percepts, memories, and appetites are produced that are like those arising from ordinary activation of the same cells.

Experiential: Numerous natural and synthetic substances interact chemically with brain cells. Were these neural modifiers unable to affect consciousness pleasurably and predictably, the recreational value of nicotine, alcohol, caffeine, LSD, cocaine, and marijuana would roughly be equal to that of blowing soap bubbles.

Despite their abundance, diversity, and mutual reinforcement, the foregoing data cannot, by themselves, entail the truth of PNI [the psychoneural identity theory, or the identity theory for short]. Nevertheless, the theory's parsimony [simplicity] and research productivity [fruitfulness], the range of phenomena it accounts for [scope], and the lack of credible counter-evidence are persuasive to virtually all neuroscientists.[35]

This excerpt from Beyerstein is instructive not only for the information it conveys but also for the demonstration it provides of how the criteria of adequacy are used to decide among competing theories. He admits that the **identity theory**—the theory that mental states are brain states—is not the only theory that can explain the data. But it's the best theory because the explanation it provides is simpler, more fruitful, and has greater scope than any competing explanation.

The identity theory is simpler than Cartesian dualism because it doesn't assume the existence of an immaterial substance. It's more fruitful because it has successfully predicted a number of novel phenomena, such as the production of mental states through electronic stimulation of the brain. And it has greater scope because it can explain the foregoing phenomena in purely physical terms.

The identity theory is also superior to logical behaviorism because it provides a straightforward account of mental causation. Because mental states are brain states, and because brain states interact with one another to produce behavior, mental causation is simply a type of physical causation.

Like logical behaviorism, the identity theory is a reductive theory. It claims that mental states are nothing but brain states. Unlike logical behaviorism, however, the identity theory does not provide an analysis of the meaning of mental terms. It does not claim that what we mean when we say that someone is in a mental state is that they're in a brain state. It claims only that mental states and brain states are one and the same thing. In this regard, it's like the claim that lightning is an electrical discharge; that claim is not true by definition but was discovered through scientific investigation. To determine whether the identity theory is an adequate theory of mind, however, we'll have to conduct a philosophical investigation.

Thought is a secretion of the brain.

—Pierre-Jean
Georges Cabanis

Thought Probe

Mental Relay Stations

According to Cartesian dualism, we don't think with our brains; we think with our minds. So for the Cartesian dualist, the brain must be nothing more than a sophisticated relay station, receiving messages from the mind and sending messages to it. On this view, those suffering from severe brain damage or from diseases such as Alzheimer's have not suffered any cognitive impairment at all. Their minds are just as good as they ever were, they have simply lost the ability to communicate with their bodies. Is this plausible? Are minds unaffected by brain damage or disease? Or does the loss of brain function also result in a loss of mental function? Which explanation is the most plausible? Why?

Identity and Indiscernibility

If two things are identical, that is, if two terms refer to one and the same thing, then whatever is true of one must be true of the other. So if mental states are identical to brain states, whatever is true of mental states must be true of brain states. But there seem to be many things that are true of mental states that are not true of brain states. Suppose, for example, that you have a headache. In that case, you know that you're in pain, but you don't know that you're in a particular brain state. So the mental state and the brain state seem to have different properties; one is known by you and the other isn't. Consequently, it seems that mental states can't be identical to brain states.

This argument has the same structure as Descartes' divisibility argument. It tries to show that mental states aren't identical to brain states because they have different properties. Although this seems to be a straightforward application of the principle of the indiscernibility of identicals (the principle that says that if two things are identical, then whatever is true of the one is true of the other, and vice versa), it is fallacious—because that principle doesn't

The Brain — is wider than the Sky. . . .

—Emily Dickinson

identity theory The theory that mental states are brain states.

apply to such subjective properties as being known by someone. In Sophocles' *Oedipus Rex*, Oedipus knows that Jocasta is his wife, but he doesn't know that his mother is his wife. But that doesn't mean that Jocasta is not his mother. So this argument fails to disprove the identity theory.

Conscious Experience

There is a related argument, however, that does not suffer from the same flaw. It states that whereas brain states are knowable by empirical investigation, mental states are not. So mental states can't be identical with brain states. This argument succeeds where the foregoing one failed because being knowable by empirical investigation is an objective property that should be shared by identical things.

Thomas Nagel presents one of the most influential statements of this argument in his article "What Is It Like to Be a Bat?" Nagel claims that there is something that every conscious being knows, namely, what it's like to be a being of that sort. Furthermore, he claims, this knowledge isn't something that can be acquired through empirical investigation. All of the physical properties of a thing, however, are knowable by empirical investigation. So, he concludes, being conscious is not a physical property. Here's how Nagel puts it.

Thought Experiment

Nagel's Bat

I assume we all believe that bats have experience. After all, they are mammals, and there is no more doubt that they have experience than that mice or pigeons or whales have experience. . . .

I have said that the essence of the belief that bats have experience is that there is something that it is like to be a bat. Now we know that most bats (the microchiroptera, to be precise) perceive the external world primarily by sonar, or by echolocation, detecting the reflections, from objects within range, of their own rapid, subtly modulated, high-frequency shrieks . . . but bat sonar, though clearly a form of perception, is not similar in its operation to any sense that we possess, and there is no reason to suppose that it is subjectively like anything we can experience or imagine. . . .

This bears directly on the mind-body problem. For if the facts of experience — facts about what it is like for the experiencing organism — are accessible only from one point of view, then it is a mystery how the true character of experiences could be revealed in the physical operation of that organism.[36]

According to Nagel, there is something no non-bat will ever know, namely, what it is like to be a bat. But all of the physical properties of bats can be known by non-bats. So mental states can't be identical to physical states. Nagel's argument is this:

Is Your Brain Really Necessary?

The belief that minds can be realized in or produced by things other than brains has led many to reject the identity theory. Some have tried to salvage the theory by arguing that even if each mental state can't be identified with one particular brain state, each mental state *in a particular species* can be identified with a particular brain state.[37] But research has shown that people with very different brain structures can nevertheless be in the same mental state. As a result, there is reason to doubt that even species-specific mind-brain identities can be established. British neurophysiologist John Lorber, for example, has identified a number of individuals with hydrocephalus (water on the brain) whose skulls are 95 percent filled with cerebrospinal fluid but nevertheless have IQs above 100. Lorber provides the following account of one young man who had an IQ of 126 and yet had virtually no brain: "When we did a brain scan on him, we saw that instead of the normal 4.5 centimeter thickness of brain tissue between the ventricles and the cortical surface, there was just a thin layer of mantle measuring a millimeter or so. His cranium is filled mainly with cerebrospinal fluid."[38] Lorber admits, "I can't say whether the mathematics student has a brain weighing 50 grams or 150 grams, but it's clear that it is nowhere near the normal 1.5 kilograms, and much of the brain he does have is in the more primitive deep structures that are relatively spared in hydrocephalus."[39] Lorber's explanation? "There must be a tremendous amount of redundancy or spare capacity in the brain, just as there is with kidney and liver."[40] But if many different brain states can give rise to the same mental state, we can't identify mental states with brain states.

1. If mental states are identical to brain states, then it is possible to know everything about the mind by knowing everything there is to know about the brain.

2. But, as the example of the bat shows, it's not possible to know everything about the mind by knowing everything about the brain.

3. Therefore, mental states are not brain states.

What the identity theory leaves out of account, according to Nagel, is what any adequate theory of mind must account for, namely, the subjective character of conscious experience. What something feels like can be known only from the "inside," so to speak—from a first-person point of view. The physical properties of something, however, can all be known from the "outside"—from a third-person point of view. Because a complete knowledge of physical properties does not yield a knowledge of mental properties, the mind cannot be identified with the brain.

Nagel's reflections on the mental life of bats suggest that we aren't the only creatures that are conscious. On the contrary, there's reason to believe that most vertebrates have some form of conscious experience. Moreover, there's reason to believe that consciousness could have evolved on other planets. Scientists and science-fiction writers alike have found silicon-based (as opposed to carbon-based) life-forms conceivable. But if there can be silicon-based life, why not silicon-based consciousness?

If mental states were identical to brain states, then only creatures with brains could have minds. But it seems that thoughts can be caused by and realized in other structures than the brain. David Lewis explores this possibility in the following thought experiment.

Thought Experiment

Lewis's Pained Martian

... there might be a Martian who sometimes feels pain, just as we do, but whose pain differs greatly from ours in its physical realization. His hydraulic mind contains nothing like our neurons. Rather, there are varying amounts of fluid in many inflatable cavities, and the inflation of any one of the cavities opens some valves and closes others. His mental plumbing pervades most of his body — in fact, all but the heat exchanger inside his head. When you pinch his skin you cause no firing of C-fibers — he has none — but, rather, you cause the inflation of many smallish cavities in his feet. When these cavities are inflated, he is in pain. And the effects of his pain are fitting: his thought and activity are disrupted, he groans and writhes, he is strongly motivated to stop you from pinching him and to see to it that you never do it again. In short, he feels pain but lacks the bodily states that either are pain or else accompany it in us.

There might be such a Martian; this opinion too seems pretty firm. A credible theory of mind had better not deny the possibility of Martian pain. I needn't mind conceding that perhaps the Martian is not in pain in quite the same sense that we Earthlings are, but there had better be some straightforward sense in which he and we are both in pain.[41]

Lewis's Martian has a very different physiology than we do. Specifically, he has no neurons and thus no brain. Nevertheless, he can feel pain. If the identity theory were true, this would be impossible. Nothing without a brain could feel pain. But the notion of a conscious alien doesn't seem to be self-contradictory. Consider the alien in the movie *E.T. — The Extra-terrestrial*. Like Lewis's Martian, E.T. can feel pain (as well as love, sorrow, and homesickness). Even if an autopsy revealed that he was constructed like Lewis's Martian, we would not deny that he was conscious. So having a brain is not necessary for having a mind.

Putnam makes the same point by using a more down-to-earth example: computers.

Thought Experiment

Putnam's Conscious Computer

Assume that . . . we are, as wholes, just material systems obeying physical laws. Then . . . our mental states, e.g., thinking about next summer's vacation, cannot be identical with any physical or chemical states. For it is clear from what we already know about computers, etc. that whatever the program of the brain may be, it must be physically possible, though not necessarily feasible, to produce something with that same program but quite a different physical and

chemical constitution. Then to identify the state in question with its physical or chemical realization would be quite absurd, from the point of view of psychology anyway (which is the relevant science). It is as if we met Martians and discovered that they were in all functional respects isomorphic to us, but we refused to admit that they could feel pain because their C-fibers were different.[42]

It's conceivable that computers could feel pain even though they don't have brains. Computers use silicon chips instead of neurons to process information. If those silicon chips could be made to perform the same functions as neurons, computers might be able to think and feel like we do.

The possibility of conscious computers has been explored in many works of science fiction. Perhaps the most famous thinking machine is Hal from the movie *2001: A Space Odyssey*. Hal can not only perform calculations, he can carry on an intelligent conversation and implement plans of his own design. But Hal is composed solely of silicon chips and wires. There is not a single neuron anywhere in his circuitry. Nevertheless, he can think. If Hal is a logical possibility — if thinking doesn't require a brain — the identity theory cannot be correct.

Lewis's and Putnam's arguments can be put this way:

1. If the identity theory were true, then it would be impossible for anything without a brain to have a mind.
2. But, as Lewis's pained Martian and Putnam's conscious computer show, things without brains can have minds.
3. So the identity theory is not true; having a brain is not a necessary condition for having a mind.

In the News: Cyborg Liberation Front

Some believe that the most important civil rights movement of the twenty-first century won't be fought for Blacks, women, or even gays. It will be for the rights of intelligent machines. Transhumanism is a movement that looks forward to the time when intelligent cyborgs walk among us, and it wants to ensure that we treat them properly. *Village Voice* reporter Erik Baard reports on a recent transhumanist conference at Yale University:

> Once out of nature I shall never take
> My *bodily form from any natural thing*,
> But such a form as Grecian goldsmiths make
> Of hammered gold and gold enamelling

Yeats's wish, expressed in his poem "Sailing to Byzantium," was a governing principle for those attending the World Transhumanist Association conference at Yale University in late June [2003]. International academics and activists, they met to lay the groundwork for a society that would admit as citizens and companions intelligent robots, cyborgs made from a free mixing of human and machine parts, and fully organic, genetically engineered people who aren't necessarily human at all. A good many of these 160 thinkers aspire to immortality and omniscience through uploading human consciousness into ever evolving machines. . . .

The opening debate, "Should Humans Welcome or Resist Becoming Posthuman?," raised a question that seems impossibly far over the horizon in an era when the idea of reproductive cloning remains controversial. Yet the back-and-forth felt oddly perfunctory. Boston University bioethicist George Annas denounced the urge to alter the species, but the response from the audience revealed a community of people who feel the inevitability of revolution in their bones.

"It's like arguing in favor of the plough. You know some people are going to argue against it, but you also know it's going to exist," says James Hughes, secretary of the Transhumanist Association and a sociologist teaching at Trinity College in Connecticut. "We used to be a subculture and now we're becoming a movement. . . ."

Should a fully realized form of artificial intelligence become in some manner enslaved, Hughes adds, "that would call for liberation acts — not breaking into labs, but whatever we can do."

What Lewis's and Putnam's thought experiments show is that minds can be realized in things other than brains. In other words, minds are "multiply realizable." Many take this **multiple realizability** to be a decisive objection to the identity theory because it shows that you don't need a brain in order to have a mind.

Those who believe otherwise — those who believe that only things with brains like ours can have minds — are often referred to as "speciesists," for they believe that only certain species of animals can have minds. Creatures with minds are due a certain amount of respect. It would be wrong to make such creatures suffer unnecessarily, for example. Speciesists, however, respect only those creatures with brains like ours.

Consider the scene from Steven Spielberg's movie *AI* where the humans destroy the robots. Or consider the scene in *The Animatrix* where the humans refuse to admit the robots into the United Nations. In both cases, the humans are guilty of speciesism because they discriminate against the robots on the grounds they're not made of flesh and blood. We may someday create computers that are as intelligent as we are. How we deal with them will say a lot about our moral intelligence.

But beyond the violent zealots, who are these supposed bio-Luddites? From the right, Leon Kass, chair of the President's Council on Bioethics, rails against transhumanism in his book *Life, Liberty, and the Defense of Dignity*, and Francis Fukuyama weighs in with his fearful exploration *Our Posthuman Future*. From the left, environmentalist Bill McKibben fires *Enough: Staying Human in an Engineered Age*, a book that reads like a 227-page-long helpless screech of brakes on a train steaming ahead at full power.

They have a case for being somewhat apocalyptic about the convergence of genetics, computer science, nanotechnology, and bioengineering. The outcome is almost guaranteed to strain our ancient sensibilities and definitions of personhood. . . .

The key to building allies, to making the cause too important to be ignored, might be to differentiate between the relatively narrow category of humanity and the more sweeping status of personhood. . . .

"I would say if a creature is both sentient and intelligent, and has a moral sense, then that creature should be considered a human being irrespective of the genesis of that person," says Rabbi Norman Lamm, chancellor of Yeshiva University.

He finds agreement at the Catholic-run Georgetown Medical Center. "To err on the side of inclusion is the loving thing to do," concludes Kevin FitzGerald, a Jesuit priest who happens to be a molecular geneticist and bioethicist.

But they, along with an Islamic scholar interviewed for this article, hold strong reservations about the necessity and good of the transhumanist aims. Such qualms are natural. The transhumanists are forcing, with microchips and DNA, a debate on ancient and unanswerable questions, says Bonnie Kaplan, chair of Yale's Technology and Ethics Working Group, cosponsor of the conference.

"My gut says we'll never have the answer to that question we first raised thousands of years ago: Who are we?"[43]

Thought Probe

Intelligent Robots

Should intelligent robots be given the same rights as humans? Why or why not?

A racist makes negative judgments about others because of their race. A sexist makes negative judgments about others because of their sex. A speciesist makes negative judgments about others because of their species. Speciesists who believe that only carbon-based life-forms can have minds are known as "carbon chauvinists." Identity theorists are carbon chauvinists because they believe that no matter how intelligently a creature behaves, it can't have a mind unless it has a brain.

Thought Probe

Speciesism

Suppose you fell in love with someone who seems to be the most intelligent, witty, and caring person you've ever met. Now suppose that "person" turns out to be an android. Would you conclude that the android doesn't really have a mind? Why or why not?

multiple realizability
The view that minds can be realized in things other than brains.

Lewis's pained Martian and Putnam's conscious computer suggest that mental states are not brain states, and the failure of logical behaviorism suggests that they are not behavioral dispositions either. To demonstrate the inadequacy of these reductive theories of the mind, John Searle offers the following thought experiment:

Thought Experiment

Searle's Brain Replacement

Imagine that your brain starts to deteriorate in such a way that you are slowly going blind. Imagine that the desperate doctors, anxious to alleviate your condition, try any method to restore your vision. As a last resort, they try plugging silicon chips into your visual cortex. Imagine that to your amazement and theirs, it turns out that the silicon chips restore your vision to its normal state. Now, imagine further that your brain, depressingly, continues to deteriorate and the doctors continue to implant more silicon chips. You can see where the thought experiment is going already: in the end, we imagine that your brain is entirely replaced by silicon chips; that as you shake your head, you can hear the chips rattling around inside your skull. In such a situation there would be various possibilities. One logical possibility, not to be excluded on any a priori grounds alone, is surely this: You continue to have all of the sorts of thoughts, experiences, memories, etc., that you had previously; the sequence of your mental life remains unaffected. . . .

A second possibility, also not to be excluded on any a priori grounds, is this: as the silicon is progressively implanted into your dwindling brain, you find that the area of your conscious experience is shrinking, but that this shows no effect on your external behavior. You find, to your total amazement, that you are indeed losing control of your external behavior. You find, for example, that when the doctors test your vision, you hear them say, "We are holding up a red object in front of you; please tell us what you see." You want to cry out, "I can't see anything. I'm going totally blind." But you hear your voice saying in a way that is completely out of your control, "I see a red object in front of me." If we carry this thought experiment out to the limit, we get a much more depressing result than last time. We imagine that your conscious experience slowly shrinks to nothing, while your externally observable behavior remains the same. . . .

Now consider a third variation. In this case, we imagine that the progressive implantation of the silicon chips produces no change in your mental life, but you are progressively more and more unable to put your thoughts, feelings, and intentions into action. In this case, we imagine that your thoughts, feelings, experiences, memories, and so forth, remain intact, but your observable external behavior slowly reduces to total paralysis. Eventually you suffer from total paralysis, even though your mental life is unchanged. So in this case, you might hear the doctors saying, "The silicon chips are able to maintain heartbeat, respiration, and other vital processes, but the patient is obviously brain

Silicon chips that can replace neurons are not science-fiction fantasies. Such chips have been developed at the University of Southern California.

While most neuroscientists have labored to understand why the brain works the way it does, the USC researchers are taking a different approach: They're hoping that by tracking how individual neurons communicate, they can restore lost brain functions by implanting computer chips that mimic neuron chatter.

Never mind the whys: "If we can learn the input/output, that's all we need to know," said lead researcher Ted Berger, 46. "We can put them on a chip, and we're ready to go."

If Berger's team can get the brain to talk back to the chips, people who lose memory to old age, are paralyzed after a car accident or lose the ability to speak after a stroke might be able to get lost functions back.

"Everyone grows old with age. Everyone loses their memory," said Dalal, a biomedical-engineering doctoral candidate.

"If we can come up with something that helps people (regain) their memory, that would be great. Obviously we would help out a lot of people.". . .

The team members have recorded much of how neurons in the hippocampus—a part of the brain responsible for memory—respond to signals. They have already managed to etch chips with these neuron codes, and tests show they mimic the language perfectly. Now they face a few substantial hurdles: Can they make the chip talk to the brain? Can they make the chips small enough to fit in the skull?

Berger and fellow researcher Armand R. Tanguay Jr. are confident the answer to both questions is yes.

Tanguay, 47, is so certain the team will build workable brain prostheses—and perhaps "extras" that improve memory and ability to calculate—that just thinking about the implications of the work takes his breath away.

"I gotta tell you, this freaks us out on a daily basis," said Tanguay, an associate professor of electrical engineering. "The reality of it is so mind-blowing, you almost can't function to do the stuff.". . .

Researchers are trying to graft neurons to the chips' surfaces to see if they will serve as conduits. And they hope that by building prostheses that look and talk like the real thing—with the same shape and with electrical conduits clumped as neurons would be on the part being replaced—the neurons surrounding it will naturally talk to it.

Once the problems get worked out—and both researchers have no doubt they will be—scientists will be able to replace any region of the brain, they predict.

"There's no reason why you couldn't," Berger said.

"Is it possible to do this in a way to replace parts of the brain that have been damaged? I think the answer is yes, and not a pipe dream. Yes, a real yes," Berger said. . . .

Researchers are confident that one day, not too long from now, their research will mean the blind will see, the paralyzed will walk, the deaf will hear, the mute will talk.

"There's a real potential to relieve human suffering," Tanguay said.

Amazing as it all seems, "it's real," Berger said. "It's very real."[45]

---

dead. We might as well unplug the system, because the patient has no mental life at all." Now in this case, you would know that they are totally mistaken. That is, you want to shout out, "No, I'm still conscious! I perceive everything going on around me. It's just that I can't make any physical movement. I've become totally paralyzed."[44]

It's entirely possible that in the not-too-distant future there will be artificial devices that function like neurons. (See the box "Neural Chips.") After all, we already have artificial devices that function like arms, legs, hearts, lungs, kidneys, and so on. Such devices could be implanted in the brains of those with failing neurons, gradually replacing all of them. Searle describes three possible outcomes of such a procedure, each of which counts against either behaviorism or the identity theory.

In the first case, the procedure is entirely successful. Your new silicon chips perform all of the functions of your old brain cells. This possibility is a counter-example to the identity theory because it shows that you don't need a brain to have a mind.

In the second case, the procedure does not affect your behavior, but it obliterates your consciousness. You behave as you always did, but you have no control over — and ultimately no awareness of — what your body is doing. The operation has turned you into a zombie. A zombie is a creature that behaves like a normal human being but has no conscious awareness of its activities, much like a sleepwalker. The second case is a counterexample to behaviorism because it shows that there's more to having a mind than having the right behavioral dispositions.

In the third case, the procedure does not affect your mind, but it does affect your behavior. The operation leads to total paralysis. You are aware of everything that's going on around you but you are unable to move. Stephen Hawking, the physicist who has Lou Gehrig's disease, is in a similar predicament. He can move only a few fingers of his left hand. This last case is also a counterexample to logical behaviorism because it shows that you don't need to have any behavioral dispositions in order to have a mind.

Thought Probe

Neural Prostheses

Suppose you had a failing brain and your only hope for survival was to have your brain replaced by silicon chips. Would you do it? Suppose the procedure had been successfully performed many times before and those who've had it report that they feel no different after the procedure than before. Would that affect your decision?

Summary

Out of the empiricist tradition rose the theory of mind known as logical behaviorism, which says that mental states are behavioral dispositions. A behavioral disposition is a tendency to respond in certain ways to certain stimuli. Logical behaviorism is a materialist theory because it does not postulate the existence of any immaterial entities. It is also a reductive theory because it holds that all statements about minds can be translated into statements about bodies. It is not an adequate theory, however, because it cannot account for the felt quality of our mental states, and the translation it envisions cannot be performed.

The identity theory, which says that mental states are brain states, is superior to behaviorism because it can explain mental causation. But there is reason to doubt that mental states are identical to brain states because brain states are knowable by empirical investigation and mental states are not. Moreover, having a brain does not seem to be a necessary condition for having a mind, for it is conceivable that an alien without a brain, or a computer made of silicon, or a person whose neurons have been replaced with biochips could have a mind.

Study Questions

1. What is Ryle's university seeker thought experiment? How does it attempt to undermine Cartesian dualism?
2. According to logical behaviorism, what is it to be in a mental state?
3. What is the verifiability theory of meaning?
4. According to empiricism, what is the source of knowledge?
5. What is the perfect pretender thought experiment? How does it attempt to undermine logical behaviorism?
6. What is Putnam's super-Spartans thought experiment? How does it attempt to undermine logical behaviorism?
7. According to the identity theory, what is it to be in a mental state?
8. What is Nagel's bat thought experiment? How does it attempt to undermine the identity theory?
9. What is Lewis's pained Martian thought experiment? How does it attempt to undermine the identity theory?
10. What is Putnam's conscious computer thought experiment? How does it attempt to undermine the identity theory?
11. What is Searle's brain replacement thought experiment? How does it attempt to undermine the identity theory and logical behaviorism?

Discussion Questions

1. Suppose that a robot was created whose behavior was indistinguishable from that of a normal human being. Should such a robot be given the same rights as a human being? Why or why not?
2. Suppose that an autopsy was performed on an alien found in a crashed flying saucer, and suppose that none of its internal organs resembled a brain. Would that show that it isn't intelligent? Why or why not?
3. What if behaviorism or the identity theory is right and mental states are nothing but physical states? What changes, if any, would we have to make to our legal systems? To our society?

4. Larry Hauser proposes the following thought experiment, which, he claims, calls into question dualism, the identity theory, and functionalism while supporting behaviorism.

Thought Experiment

Your Mother, the Zombie

Imagine . . . that *your mother's a zombie*. How you might discover this is, strictly, beside the point; but as an aid to imagination, add some cheesy special effects. It's discovered during would-have-been routine brain surgery that Mother, in place of a brain (like you) has a head full of sawdust (like some antique dolls): a head full of something that's (1) not like our neurophysiological stuff, (2) not apt to be giving off qualia [feelings], and (3) insufficiently differentiated to support much functional organization. Of course, nothing turns essentially on sawdust. Substitute whatever you like. . . . Stipulate (or imagine), then, that Mother hasn't a quale [feeling] to call her own; nor has she suitable neurophysiological stuff, nor appropriate functional organization. Her behavior, as ever, is unchanged. I submit, you should *not* deny her mental abilities and attainments.[46]

Do you agree? In this situation, would you still believe that your mom had a mind? Or would you conclude that she is just a cleverly constructed automaton? What theory underlies your judgment?

5. According to behaviorism, is it possible for our minds to survive the death of our bodies? How?

6. According to the identity theory, is it possible for our minds to survive the death of our bodies? How?

I, Robot
Mind as Software

If mental states are not brain states and if they are not states of a nonphysical substance, what are they? Many believe that they are functional states. A functional state is one that is defined in terms of what it does rather than what it is made of. Consider, for example, clocks. Clocks can be made out of many different materials. Think of sundials, water clocks, cuckoo clocks, grandfather clocks, digital clocks, to name but a few. What makes these things clocks is not what they're made of but what they do, namely, keep time. According to functionalism, minds are more like clocks than rocks, for they, too, can be defined by what they do.

To perform a function is to take a certain input and produce a certain output. Each worker on an assembly line, for example, performs a function by taking certain parts and putting them together in certain ways. When two things perform the same function, they are said to have the same "causal role." So if a robot was able to replace a worker on an assembly line, the robot would have the same causal role as the worker.

According to the theory of mind known as **functionalism,** mental states are functional states. Functionalism defines mental states in terms of their causal role, that is, their characteristic inputs and outputs. Behaviorism also defined mental states in terms of their causal role, but the only inputs it recognized were physical stimuli and the only outputs it recognized were bodily movements. Functionalism differs from logical behaviorism in that it allows mental states to serve as both the input and the output of mental states. For example, functionalism recognizes that coming to believe that your lover is cheating on you can cause you to become jealous. According to functionalism, the function of mental states is not only to cause behavior but also to cause other mental states.

Because functionalism takes mental causation seriously, it's superior to logical behaviorism. And because it allows minds to be caused by and realized in

Minds are simply what brains do.

—Marvin Minsky

functionalism The doctrine that mental states are functional states.

things other than brains, it's superior to the identity theory. The question is whether being in a functional state is all there is to being in a mental state.

Artificial Intelligence

Functionalism is the theory of mind that underlies the field of artificial intelligence. The goal of artificial intelligence research is to create a computer that can think for itself. Such a computer would have a mind of its own.

An intelligent computer would be a great labor-saving device, especially if it was equipped with a robot body. Not only would robots of this sort be useful around the house or on the job, they would also be useful on the battlefield. With enough intelligent robots, humans would no longer have to spend their lives toiling away at menial jobs or dying in wars.

According to functionalism, to have a mind is to have the ability to perform certain functions. The functions a computer performs are determined by the programs it runs. So, according to the strong view of artificial intelligence, known as "strong AI," there's nothing more to having a mind than running the right kind of program. In this view, the mind is to the brain as the software of a computer is to its hardware. In other words, your mind is the program that's running on your brain.

This view has a number of interesting consequences. If you are your program, then anything that ran your program would be you. A number of computer scientists believe that it will soon be possible to scan your brain, identify the program that's running on it, and transfer that program to a computer, thus giving you eternal life. Marvin Minsky, former head of the artificial-intelligence laboratory at MIT, is one of these scientists. He writes, "In the next 100 years or so, there will be no reason to die anymore. You can just take your personality and download it into another being."[47] Computer scientist Gerald Jay Sussman agrees. In an interview with journalist Grant Fjermedal, he said,

> "If you can make a machine that contains the contents of your mind, then that machine is you. The hell with the rest of your physical body, it's not very interesting. Now, the machine can last forever. Even if it doesn't last forever, you can always dump it out onto tape and make backups, then load it up on some other machine if the first one breaks."
>
> "Everyone would like to be immortal," Sussman said. "I don't think the time is quite right. But it's close. It isn't very long from now. I'm afraid, unfortunately, that I'm the last generation to die. Some of my students may manage to survive a little longer."
>
> When I told Sussman that Danny Hillis had recently told me very nearly the same thing, he replied, "We are sort of on the edge."
>
> "Do you think we are that close?" I asked.
>
> "Yes."[48]

Sussman believes that minds are programs. Just as it is possible to transfer a program from a hard disk to a CD, Sussman looks forward to the day when we will be able to transfer our minds from our brains to computers. (We will ex-

The Physics of Immortality

In *The Physics of Immortality*, physicist Frank Tipler argues that we will all become immortal, not by having our minds uploaded into a computer, but by having them re-created in a computer. In the distant future, he claims, computers will "emulate" every possible person. Tipler spells out his view in this interview with *Omni*:

TIPLER: . . . we have to realize that everything—this desk, this building, humans—is a pattern of information. In principle, you can get the whole of the pattern, which is the human, and code it inside a computer.

OMNI: What does life mean in this context? People like Schopenhauer have talked of a life force or will.

TIPLER: No such things!

OMNI: So you can write all the information needed to reproduce me or you some other place or time, and send it across the universe?

TIPLER: Exactly. I prefer to use the term computer emulation. An emulation is an exact simulation, an absolutely perfect copy. . . .
   Using physics, specifically the Bekenstein Bound, you can prove a human being, indeed the entire visible universe, can be emulated by a sufficiently powerful computer. I give estimates of the upper bound of how powerful a machine will be required for a human, 10^{45} bits of information. The entire universe will need 10^{123} bits, as Roger Penrose was the first to compute.
   As you go into the future, the amount of information storage diverges to infinity. Eventually, however, 10^{123} bits will be insignificant in comparison to the total computer capacity of the universe. So in the far future the whole present universe will be emulated using a tiny fraction of total computer capacity. If this is done by our descendants, once they've taken over the universe and gained control over its

resources, they will emulate into the future the universe as it now exists. We would come into existence again—the present universe at a higher level of implementation, just as inside my computer there is a virtual machine, and possibly a virtual machine inside that, a hierarchy of implementation.

OMNI: But will this "event" be only an information emulation, not an actual physical one?

TIPLER: The event will *be* the present reality, but at a higher level of implementation. No experiment conducted inside the simulation could distinguish between the emulation and the real thing. An emulation is the thing being emulated, an exact simulation in every conceivable respect.

OMNI: Sitting here, how do we know we are not an emulation?

TIPLER: We don't. We could be an emulation in the far future. Anything you have now will be there then. You'd think as you do now. Beings that are perfect copies are no longer copies. They *are* the beings. Right now we are in effect being run as a program: One state of the universe succeeds the next as we move forward in time. You can do that as a computer emulation. There'd be no difference in our experience now, and as our emulated selves, until beings in the far future start to change the emulation—such as moving us into a different environment.[49]

Thought Probe

Computerized Resurrection

Tipler assumes that functionalism is true; that minds are programs. Do you agree? Would you live again if the program running on your brain were re-created and run on some future computer? Why or why not?

plore the philosophical implications of this possibility in more detail in Chapter 4.)

Is this sort of immortality really possible? That depends on whether functionalism is an adequate theory of the mind. To assess its adequacy, we'll have to examine its implications. Functionalism implies that there's nothing more to being in a mental state than being in a certain functional state. Let's see if that's true.

Functionalism and Feeling

Putnam's super-Spartans thought experiment shows that it's possible to be in a mental state without having any particular behavioral disposition. (Putnam's super-Spartans, you recall, experienced pain but never behaved as if they were in pain.) Similarly, David Lewis argues that it's possible to be in a mental state without being in any particular functional state.

Thought Experiment

Lewis's Pained Madman

There might be a strange man who sometimes feels pain, just as we do, but whose pain differs greatly from ours in its causes and effects. Our pain is typically caused by cuts, burns, pressure, and the like; his is caused by moderate exercise on an empty stomach. Our pain is generally distracting, his turns his mind to mathematics, facilitating concentration on that but distracting him from anything else. Intense pain has no tendency whatever to cause him to groan or writhe, but does cause him to cross his legs and snap his fingers. He is not in the least motivated to prevent pain or to get rid of it. In short, he feels pain, but his pain doesn't at all occupy the typical causal role of pain. He would doubtless seem to us to be some form of madman, and that is what I shall call him, though of course the sort of madness I have imagined may bear little resemblance to the real thing.[50]

Lewis's madman is in pain, but his pain has a very different function than ours. Instead of distracting him and making him groan and writhe, it turns his mind to mathematics and makes him cross his legs and snap his fingers. Such a person is decidedly odd, but not inconceivable. The poor fellow may simply be wired wrong. If there can be such a person, however, functionalism is mistaken because being in a mental state doesn't depend on being in a particular functional state.

Lewis's argument is this:

1. If functionalism were true, it would be impossible for someone to be in pain and function differently than we do when we are in pain.

2. But, as Lewis's pained madman shows, it's not impossible for someone to be in pain and function differently than we do.

3. So functionalism is false; being in a certain functional state is not a necessary condition for being in a mental state.

To be in pain, you do not have to be in any particular functional state. What makes something a pain is what it feels like, not what it makes you do. Because functionalism suggests otherwise, it's mistaken.

Just as Lewis shows that being in a specific functional state is not necessary for being in a mental state, Ned Block tries to show that it's not sufficient. According to functionalism, there's nothing more to having a mind than running the right kind of program. What the program is running on — whether it be neurons, silicon chips, or people — is irrelevant. Computer scientist Joseph Wiezenbaum once demonstrated that a computer could be made out of sticks, stones, and toilet paper. Functionalism would have us believe that if those sticks, stones, and toilet paper were running the right kind of program, it would have a mind. Block disagrees. To prove his point, he imagines a computer made of people.

Thought Experiment

Block's Chinese Nation

Suppose we convert the government of China to functionalism, and we convince its officials that it would enormously enhance their international prestige to realize a human mind for an hour. We provide each of the billion people in China (I chose China because it has a billion inhabitants) with a specially designed two-way radio that connects them in the appropriate way to other persons and to [an] artificial body. . . . we arrange to have letters displayed on a series of satellites so they can be seen from anywhere in China. The system of a billion people communicating with one another plus satellites plays the role of an external "brain" connected to the artificial body by radio. . . .

It is not at all obvious that the China–body system is physically impossible. It could be functionally equivalent to you for a short time, say an hour. . . .

What makes the homunculi-headed [miniature man–headed] system . . . just described a prima facie counterexample to (machine) functionalism is that there is prima facie doubt as to whether it has any mental states at all — empirically whether it has what philosophers have variously called "qualitative states," "raw feels," or "immediate phenomenological qualities. . . ." In Nagel's terms, there is a prima facie doubt whether there is anything which it is like to be the homunculi-headed system.[51]

In Block's thought experiment, the people in China are functioning like neurons in a brain: they are sending and receiving signals to and from one another. If functionalism were true, then once the billion people in China started running the program, there would be a billion and one people in China; the billion people with walkie-talkies and the "person" whose program they're running. If the project were carried out properly, it should even be possible to talk to that "person." Block's point, however, is that such a "person" could not possibly have any conscious experience and thus could not be considered to have a mind. So there must be more to having a mind than having the right sort of functional organization.

Block's argument, then, is this:

1. If functionalism were true, then anything that had the right sort of functional organization would have a mind.

2. But as Block's Chinese nation shows, it is not the case that anything that had the right sort of functional organization would have a mind.

3. So functionalism is false; having the right sort of functional organization is not a sufficient condition for having a mind.

A computer can be made out of anything: mechanical gears, vacuum tubes, silicon chips, and the like. All that's required is that its components be related to one another in the right sort of way. Similarly, functionalism claims that a mind can be made out of anything. As long as something has the right sort of functional organization—as long as it produces the right sort of output given the input it receives—it can be considered to have a mind. Block's Chinese nation thought experiment calls this claim into question. It suggests that no purely relational theory of mental states can account for their qualitative content.

Block's Chinese nation presents a version of what is known as the **absent qualia objection** to functionalism because it purports to show that it's possible for something to be functionally equivalent to a human being and yet have no conscious experience. This objection lies behind many people's rejection of the possibility of artificial intelligence. Robots made out of silicon and steel, they say, might be able to function like we do, but they would never be able to feel like we do. They would never be able to have sensations or experience emotions, for example. Robots, in their view, are zombies.

Thought Probe

Is Data a Person?

Data, the robot in the TV series *Star Trek: The Next Generation*, had no feelings but did have the desire to acquire them. In the episode "The Measure of a Man," it was argued that his lack of feelings meant that he wasn't a person. Do you agree? Before you answer, you should realize that there are human beings who have lost the ability to feel emotions as a result of damage to their brains. Are they no longer persons? What conception of persons lies behind your answer?

Not only does it seem to be possible for something to be functionally equivalent to us and not have any conscious experience, it also seems possible for something to be functionally equivalent to us and have the wrong kind of conscious experience. This second possibility is known as the **inverted spectrum problem.** Here's Putnam's version of it:

Thought Experiment

Putnam's Inverted Spectrum

The inverted spectrum example (which appears in the writings of Locke) involves a chap who walks about seeing things so that blue looks red to him and red looks blue to him (or so that his subjective colors resemble the colors on a color negative rather than the colors on a color positive). One's first reaction on hearing of such a case might be to say, "Poor chap, people must pity him." But how would anyone ever know? When he sees anything blue, it looks red to him, but he's been taught to call that color blue ever since he was an infant, so that if one asked him what color the object is he would say "blue." So no one would ever know.

My variation was the following: imagine your spectrum becomes inverted at a particular time in your life and you remember what it was like before that. There is no epistemological problem about "verification." You wake up one morning and the sky looks red, and your red sweater appears to have turned

absent qualia objection The objection to functionalism based on the belief that a functional state could have all the functional properties of a mental state without having any of its qualitative content.

inverted spectrum problem The problem of accounting for the fact that people's color experiences could be very different even though they are functionally equivalent.

People with inverted spectrums may be more than just a physical possibility, as the phenomena of synesthesia suggests. Synesthesia means "joined sensation," and occurs when the input of one sense triggers the output of another. So a synesthete may see sounds or hear colors. Synesthesia can be triggered by hallucinogens like LSD, but it can also occur naturally as this *Wired News* article explains.

Black and white words on a page and the sounds of language explode into many colors in the mind of a middle-aged man. "Two" is blue, "2" is orange, "3" is pink and "traffic" is both blue and brown.

The man has synesthesia—an altered perception in which printed words and numbers burst with color, flavors take on shapes and the spoken language turns into a mental rainbow.

For some people with synesthesia, say researchers, a newspaper is never black and white; it's red, orange, blue, beige, pink and green all over.

"This is an alternate perception," said Thomas Palmeri, a Vanderbilt University psychologist and the first author of a study reporting on tests given to one man. "He is normal; a highly successful, intelligent man and he suffers no problems from this unique wiring of the brain."

The study, appearing Tuesday in the *Proceedings of the National Academy of Sciences*, explores the multichromatic world of a man identified only as W. O. The man, a university professor of medicine, did not respond to requests for a direct interview made through the study's authors.

Palmeri said researchers are starting to realize that W. O. is one of what some suspect is a large number of people with synesthesia, many of whom take joy in this rich symphony of sensations.

"They often experience a great deal of pleasure from this altered perception," said Edward Hubbard, a synesthesia researcher at the University of California, San Diego. For W. O., his synesthesia helped make learning the complex words of science easy when the colors weren't distracting him from study, Palmeri said.

"He sees a palette of different colors when he reads, and sometimes he is more interested in how pretty the page looks than what the words say," he said. . . .

When W. O. was given a list of 100 words printed in black and white, he said each one had a specific color. When the list was presented a second time, weeks later, W. O. gave most words the same color, missing only some that were either beige or off-white.

"These associations are highly reliable," said Blake. "W. O. says that the colors have stayed the same all his life and our observations lend credence to the claim.". . .

Hubbard said that little is known about synesthesia because many people won't admit it. Others, however, are surprised to learn that they are unusual, saying they thought everyone experienced the colorful world that they saw.[54]

Thought Probe

Synesthesia

People with synesthesia are functionally indistinguishable from normal people and are often surprised to realize that they are different. Does this support the claim that functionalism can't account for conscious experiences? Why or why not?

---

blue, and all the faces are an awful color, as on a color negative. Oh my God! Now perhaps you could learn to change your way of talking, and to call things that look red to you "blue," and perhaps you could get good enough so that if someone asked you what color someone's sweater was you would give the "normal" answer. But at night, let us imagine you would moan, "Oh, I wish the colors looked the way they did when I was a child. The colors just don't look the way they used to."[53]

The problem that the inverted spectrum poses for functionalism is this: the two people with inverted spectra or the one person before and after the inversion are in the same functional state. They would both produce the same output from the same input. For example, if you asked them, "What color are stop signs?" they would both say, "Red." Similarly, if you asked them, "Are ripe tomatoes the same color as stop signs?" they would both say, "Yes." But even though they are in the same functional state, they are not in the same mental state, for the qualitative content of their visual experiences is vastly different—one experiences redness when looking at red objects while the other experiences blueness. So there must be more to being in a mental state than being in a functional state.

Putnam's argument can be spelled out like this:

1. If functionalism were true, it would be impossible for people with the same functional organization to have different mental states.

2. But, as Putnam's inverted spectrum shows, it's not impossible for people with the same functional organization to have different mental states.

3. So functionalism is false; having a certain functional organization is not a sufficient condition for being in a certain mental state.

The character Mouse in the movie *The Matrix* raises a similar problem with regard to the faculty of taste. After eating some of the gruel served aboard the *Nebuchadnezzar*, the following discussion ensues:

MOUSE: Do you know what it really reminds me of? Tasty Wheat. Did you ever eat Tasty Wheat?

SWITCH: No, but technically neither did you.

MOUSE: That's exactly my point. Exactly. Because you have to wonder: now how do machines really know what Tasty Wheat tasted like. Maybe they got it wrong. Maybe what I think Tasty Wheat tasted like actually tasted like oatmeal or tuna fish. That makes you wonder about a lot of things. . . .[55]

Mouse realizes that the way Tasty Wheat tastes to people outside the Matrix may be different from the way it tastes to people in the Matrix. (The Matrix is a computer simulation of reality.) The program running in the Matrix may be functionally equivalent to one running in someone's brain, but that doesn't mean that it produces the same experiences. So again it seems that a functional equivalence does not guarantee a mental equivalence.

The absent qualia and inverted spectrum objections to functionalism are compelling. To meet them, functionalists must show either that the situations envisioned in these thought experiments aren't possible or that the qualitative content associated with a mental state isn't essential to it.

Paul Churchland adopts the second alternative and argues that the qualitative content associated with a mental state is irrelevant to it. "What this means," he tells us, "is that the qualitative character of your sensation-of-red might be different from the qualitative character of my sensation-of-red, and a third person's sensation-of-red might be different again. But so long as all three states are standardly caused by red objects and standardly cause all three

Alan Turing: Father of Code and Computers

The genius of Alan Turing (1912–1954) seems inexplicable. In his childhood, creativity and exploration were never encouraged, and in adulthood there were almost no precedents for his creations and no intellectual stepping-stones toward his grand achievements. Turing was a loner, sometimes an outcast, and mostly misunderstood, but he became the father of computer science and the first to see the now-obvious links between mathematics, logic, mind, and machines.

Alan Turing was born in London and educated at King's College, Cambridge. But long before his formal education, he was asking fundamental philosophical and scientific questions. One of his earliest queries was how the human mind could be embodied in matter and whether it could exist independently of matter. He also wondered whether quantum theory (the area of physics dealing with subatomic particles) played a significant part in the mystery of mind-matter. Ostensibly he was a promising young mathematician, but his real interests were broader, encompassing mathematics, logic, and physics.

Turing's first great achievement was the Turing machine, a theoretical device that could compute anything that was computable. The computers we use today are all universal Turing machines.

During World War II, Turing worked for the British government department that was charged with making and breaking codes. At the time, Germany was using a code device — called the Enigma cipher machine — that could produce seemingly unbreakable codes for vital wartime communications. But Turing cracked the Enigma code by envisioning another powerful device that could decode Enigma messages if a small portion of the code text were worked out. Turing's labors were a major contribution to the Allied war effort.

After the war, Turing was a top track runner and a serious candidate for a spot in the 1948 Olympic Games, but an injury prevented him from competing. In 1950, Turing published a landmark paper in the philosophy journal *Mind*. He described the Turing test, a method for determining whether machines can think. His work in this area had a major impact on research in artificial intelligence (AI).

Turing was a homosexual. In Britain in the 1950s, however, homosexuality was a crime. When his homosexuality was discovered, he was arrested, thrown in jail, and given massive injections of estrogen — the preferred "treatment" for homosexuality in Britain at that time. Sometime after he was released from jail, he committed suicide by eating an apple laced with cyanide.

---

of us to believe that something is red, then all three states are sensations-of-red, whatever their intrinsic qualitative character."[56] Such a reply to the absent qualia and inverted spectrum objections, however, simply begs the question. It assumes the truth of functionalism in an attempt to defend it. To see the inadequacy of this reply, just put yourself in the shoes of the person who underwent Putnam's spectrum inversion. Would you say that your mental states before and after the inversion are the same? Could you consider the sensation of redness to be the same as the sensation of blueness as long as both had the same causal role? If not, Churchland's bite-the-bullet defense isn't very persuasive.

Even if functionalism doesn't capture the essence of mental states that have qualitative content (like sensing), it might be argued that it does capture the essence of mental states that do not have qualitative content (like believing). After all, *Star Trek*'s Mr. Spock and Data suggest that one can be intelligent without having any feelings. To explore this possibility, let's take a closer look at the notion of intelligence.

The Turing Test

One of the first people to investigate the possibility of artificial intelligence was Alan Turing, one of the founders of modern computer science. In his 1950 article "Computing Machinery and Intelligence," he considered the question Can machines think? Instead of trying to answer the question by defining the words "machine" and "think," he proposed a test that, if passed by a machine, would indicate that the machine was intelligent. Here is Turing's description of the test.

ALAN TURING
1912–1954

Thought Experiment

The Imitation Game

The new form of the problem [can machines think] can be described in terms of a game which we call the "imitation game." It is played with three people, a man (A), a woman (B), and an interrogator (C) who may be of either sex. The interrogator stays in a room apart from the other two. The object of the game for the interrogator is to determine which of the other two is the man and which is the woman. He knows them by labels X and Y, and at the end of the game he says either "X is A and Y is B" or "X is B and Y is A." The interrogator is allowed to put questions to A and B thus:

The question of whether a computer can think is no more interesting than the question of whether a submarine can swim.
—EDSGER W. DIJKSTRA

C: "Will X please tell me the length of his or her hair?"

Now suppose X is actually A, then A must answer. It is A's object in the game to try to cause C to make the wrong identification. His answer might therefore be: "My hair is shingled, and the longest strands are about nine inches long."

In order that tones of voice may not help the interrogator, the answer should be written, or better still, typewritten. The ideal arrangement is to have a teleprinter communicating between the two rooms. Alternatively the question and answers can be repeated by an intermediary. The object of the game for the third player (B) is to help the interrogator. The best strategy for her is probably to give truthful answers. She can add such things as "I am the woman, don't listen to him!" to her answers, but it will avail nothing as the man can make similar remarks.

We now ask the question, "What will happen when a machine takes the part of A in this game?" Will the interrogator decide wrongly as often when the game is played like this as he does when the game is played between a man and a woman? These questions replace our original, "Can machines think?"[57]

Turing contends that if a machine could play this game as well as a normal man — that is, if it could convince an interrogator that it was a man as often as a normal man could — then the machine would be intelligent. For Turing, there is nothing more to being intelligent than being able to use language like we do.

Turing predicted in 1950 that in fifty years we would have computers powerful enough to "play the imitation game so well that an average interrogator will not have more than a 70% chance of making the right identification after five minutes of questioning."[58] Arthur C. Clarke was aware of this prediction and titled his novel about the English-speaking computer, Hal, *2001: A Space Odyssey* because if Turing were correct, there would be computers like Hal in the year 2001.

The difficulty of passing the Turing test should not be underestimated. To pass it, a computer would apparently have to lie. For example, no computer that answered "Yes" to the question "Are you a computer?" would pass the test. When asked, "What color are your eyes?" "What is your favorite food?" "When did you graduate from high school?" the computer would have to give false but believable answers. It seems that only a machine that knew it was taking the Turing test would be able to pass it. But any machine with that sort of knowledge, it seems, would have to be intelligent.

John Searle denies that it takes any intelligence to pass the Turing test. To see this, Searle suggests, all you have to do is put yourself in the place of the computer.

Thought Experiment

Searle's Chinese Room

Consider a language you don't understand. In my case, I do not understand Chinese. To me Chinese writing looks like so many meaningless squiggles. Now suppose I am placed in a room containing baskets full of Chinese symbols. Suppose also that I am given a rule book in English for matching Chinese symbols with other Chinese symbols. The rules identify the symbols entirely by their shapes and do not require that I understand any of them. The rules might say such things as, "Take a squiggle-squiggle sign from basket number one and put it next to a squoggle-squoggle sign from basket number two."

Imagine that people outside the room who understand Chinese hand in small bunches of symbols and that in response I manipulate the symbols according to the rule book and hand back more small bunches of symbols. Now, the rule book is the "computer program." The people who wrote it are "programmers," and I am the "computer." The baskets full of symbols are the "data base," the small bunches that are handed in to me are "questions" and the bunches I then hand out are "answers."

Now suppose that the rule book is written in such a way that my "answers" to the "questions" are indistinguishable from those of a native Chinese speaker. For example, the people outside might hand me some symbols that unknown to me mean, "What's your favorite color?" and I might after going through the rules give back symbols that, also unknown to me, mean, "My favorite is blue, but I also like green a lot." I satisfy the Turing test for understanding Chinese. All the same, I am totally ignorant of Chinese. And there is no way I could come to understand Chinese in the system as described, since there is no way that I can learn the meanings of any of the symbols. Like a computer, I manipulate symbols, but I attach no meaning to the symbols.[59]

The Turing test is not just a thought experiment: Hugh Loebner has been conducting actual Turing tests for the past ten years. Farhad Manjoo reports on the 2001 competition:

Half a century ago, Alan Turing, the mathematician who pioneered computational theory, came up with a simple test to determine whether or not a computer could "think." The test involved asking the machine a series of questions; if it responded with the same unmistakable *joie de vivre* of a human being, you could call it a thinking machine.

Thinking machines aren't easy to come by. To anyone's knowledge, no machine has passed Turing's test, even though there has been a $100,000 prize offered for it during the last 10 years. That prize — the Loebner Prize, named after Hugh Loebner, its philanthropist sponsor — is being held again this weekend in London.

But again this year, few people are holding out hope that one of the eight robot finalists will be human enough to bag the 100 grand.

The Loebner Prize works very much like that 1950s television game show *To Tell the Truth*, in which celebrity panelists attempted to discover which of three people was the real fellow claiming to have done something extraordinary.

In the Loebner contest, judges are presented with a bevy of chat terminals to type into. Some of the terminals are manned by robots, some by people. The judges hold short conversations with the chatter, looking for unmistakable humanity on the other end. If they don't find it, they mark it down as a robot.

A program needs to fool half the judges to win the grand prize, but that has never been done. The robot that convinces the most judges is considered the winner — for a prize of $2,000.

Last year, Richard Wallace's Alice robot won the contest, and it's the finalist this year, as well. It's competing against seven other robots.

During an interview earlier this year, Wallace said that he was pleased to have won the prize, but like many people, he has expressed dissatisfaction with the rules of the game.

According to Wallace, the judges in the original test devised by Turing weren't told that they were trying to determine whether their chat partner was a robot or not, so they "weren't looking for a robot," he said.

"But the Loebner contest has been called too aggressive, because the judges ask questions that they would never ask a human being during a conversation. They try to trick it — like, they'll ask, 'What does the letter M look like upside down?'"

Because questions like that aren't likely to come up in an everyday conversation, chat robots like Alice don't usually know the answers, he explained.

But "the fact is, people act like robots," Wallace said. "The lesson from (my research) is that we are all like robots — people don't use the full richness of language. Most people most of the time will not say anything that hasn't been said before."

And if the judges in Loebner did that — restricted themselves to the banal conversational style of, say, the celebrity inquisitors on *To Tell the Truth* — the chat robots would have a much better shot at the big prize.[60]

Thought Probe

Loebner Prize

Is the Loebner Prize a good implementation of the Turing test? Would it be better if Wallace's proposals were adopted? Why or why not?

Inside the room, Searle is doing what a computer does when it processes information; namely, he is manipulating formal symbols in accordance with a set of rules. To those outside the room, it appears that he understands what the symbols mean, for the string of symbols he produces in response to the string of symbols he receives is like the one a native Chinese speaker would produce. But he doesn't understand what the symbols mean. So, Searle concludes, passing the Turing test is not a sure sign of intelligence. His argument can be put like this:

1. If a computer could understand a language solely in virtue of running a program, then the man in the room would understand Chinese (because he's doing the same thing that a computer does, namely, manipulating symbols in accordance with a set of rules.)
2. But the man in the room doesn't understand Chinese.
3. So computers can't understand a language solely in virtue of running a program.

The difference between the ways computers and humans manipulate symbols is this: computers manipulate symbols on the basis of their physical features or form, whereas humans manipulate symbols on the basis of their meaning or content. But the meaning of a symbol is not a physical feature of it. You can't tell what a symbol means by examining its form, for anything can symbolize anything else. Xs and Os, for example, can symbolize football players, hugs and kisses, or players in a game of tic-tac-toe. Because computers, as computers, respond only to the form of symbols and not to their meaning, their responses can't be considered intelligent.

How a symbol can be combined with other symbols is determined by its **syntax.** What a symbol means is determined by its **semantics.** Searle's point is that no matter how good a computer gets at producing syntactically correct strings of symbols, it will not understand what those symbols mean, for, as he puts it, "syntax alone is not sufficient for semantics."[61] To understand what a symbol means, you must know what it is intended to represent. And what it is intended to represent is not determined by any of its physical or functional properties.

Those in the artificial-intelligence community realized early on that Searle's Chinese room thought experiment posed a serious challenge to their whole project. Consequently, they produced a number of replies to it in an attempt to blunt its force. Here's a synopsis of some of the replies and Searle's response to them:

- *Systems reply:* The man in the room may not understand Chinese, but the whole system including the room, the man, the symbols and the rule book does understand Chinese. *Rejoinder:* The man could become such a system by internalizing all the rules and yet he would still not understand Chinese.

- *Robot reply:* The man in the room may not understand Chinese, but if the room were put inside a robot that interacted with the world, then the robot would understand Chinese. *Rejoinder:* To make this reply is to give up the position of strong AI that says there's nothing more to having a mind than running the right kind of program. The view implicit in this reply, known as "weak AI," says that in addition to running the right program, the program must be running on the right kind of machine. What's more, Searle believes the same experiment could be made to apply to this situation with only a slight modification. Suppose that the symbols the

syntax How a symbol can be combined with other symbols to form a sentence.

semantics What a symbol means.

Connectionism

The computers that we're familiar with—the ones sitting on our desks, for example—are *sequential processors* because they have a single central processing unit (CPU) that executes one instruction at a time. There are other computer architectures, however, that do not use a single processor. Known as *parallel distributive processing* or *connection machines*, they have a number of feedback adjustable switches operating simultaneously. The advantage of these machines is that they can store information in an analog rather than a digital format. This allows them to perform certain complex tasks like pattern recognition much better than ordinary digital computers.

Like neurons in the brain, the switches in a connection machine are linked to one another and possess various "activation values." The activation values indicate the strength of the input required to produce an output. These values can vary as a result of the inputs received. As a result, connection machines can learn by trial and error.

Connection machines are not programmed in the way that sequential processors are. Instead of being given a list of instructions, these machines are given what amounts to a training regimen. After being given a certain input, the activation values of their switches are adjusted in order to produce the required output. This is supposedly what happens in our brains when we learn something, so it is theoretically possible for a properly outfitted connection machine to learn anything that we can learn. Full-blown connectionist robots may well be taught in the same way we teach our children.

Searle's Chinese room thought experiment seems to have no force against a connection machine. For there is no *single* processor in a connection machine that corresponds to the person in the room and no program in the machine that corresponds to the list of instructions followed by the person in the room. But Searle has another scenario—the Chinese gym—that demonstrates that connection computers, as such, fare no better than sequential computers in achieving real understanding.

Thought Experiment

Searle's Chinese Gym

Imagine that instead of a Chinese room, I have a Chinese gym: a hall containing many monolingual, English-speaking men. These men would carry out the same operations as the nodes and synapses in a connectionist architecture ... and the outcome would be the same as having one man manipulate symbols according to a rule book. No one in the gym speaks a word of Chinese, and there is no way for the system as a whole to learn the meanings of any Chinese words. Yet, with appropriate adjustments, the system could give the correct answers to Chinese questions.[62]

According to Searle, whether a computer is sequential or connectionist is irrelevant to the question of its intelligence. For there's more to being intelligent than simply producing the right output relative to a given input.

man receives come in through television cameras and that the symbols he produces runs the robot's arms and legs. Even in that case, running the program would not give him an understanding of Chinese.

- *Brain simulator reply:* The man in the room does not understand Chinese because he is running the wrong kind of program. If, instead of manipulating symbols, the program simulated the sequence of nerve firings that occur when a Chinese speaker speaks the language, the system would understand Chinese. *Rejoinder:* Again, a slight modification of the experiment shows that this wouldn't work. Suppose that in place of the symbols, the man operates an elaborate set of water pipes connected by valves. The program indicates which valves must be open and shut depending on what symbols are received. Here, the system of water pipes simulates the actions of neurons. Nevertheless, says Searle, neither the man nor the man plus the water pipes understands Chinese.

- *Combination reply:* Even if each of these above replies is unsuccessful, taken together they would create a system that understands Chinese, for the behavior of the resulting system would be indistinguishable from that of one who does understand Chinese. *Rejoinder:* This reply assumes the truth of logical behaviorism, for it says that if something acts like it understands, then it does understand. But logical behaviorism is not a viable theory of the mind. If we knew nothing about the system, we might justifiably conclude that it did understand Chinese. Given what we know, however, such a conclusion would not be justified, for we can account for its behavior without assuming that it understands Chinese.[63]

To understand a language, one must know what the symbols in that language represent. Searle's point is that simply running a program will not give one that knowledge. Something more is needed. Exactly what more, Searle doesn't say. But whatever it is, it must give the thing running the program states that possess intentionality.

Thought Probe

Total Turing Test

Psychologist Stevan Harnad has proposed the Total Turing Test for artificial intelligence. To pass this test, the computer being tested would have to be able to do *everything* that a normal human being does, including walking, riding a bicycle, swimming, dancing, playing a musical instrument, and so on. Only a computer with a robot body could do that. Is passing the Total Turing Test either necessary or sufficient for being intelligent and thus having a mind? Why or why not?

Intentionality

When we think, we think about something. For example, the hope that the Yankees will win the pennant is about the Yankees, the pennant, and the proposition that the Yankees will win the pennant. The "aboutness" of thought is known as **intentionality.** The word "intentionality" comes from the Latin verb *intendo,* which means to point or aim at something. So something that possesses intentionality points or aims at something. The things it points or aims at are known as its "intended objects."

The intentionality of mental states must not be confused with the intentionality of persons. We often speak of persons doing things intentionally, or on purpose. To say that a mental state has intentionality, however, is not to say that it does anything on purpose. Rather, it is to say that it represents or refers to something.

One of the most remarkable things about mental states is that they can be about things that don't exist. We can think about mermaids, unicorns, and

intentionality The property of mental states that makes them of or about something.

centaurs, for example, even though there are no such things. German philosopher Franz Brentano claimed that this is what distinguishes mental states from physical states. Mental states can be directed on nonexistent objects; physical states cannot. You can think about an imaginary rock, but you can't kick one. In any event, the ability to conceive of nonexistent objects and states of affairs is essential for thinking. As philosophers Lewis White Beck and Robert L. Holmes note, "Thinking is a process of learning by trial and error in which the trials and errors are not made in overt bodily behavior but in imagination."[64] The ability to think about nonexistent objects and situations is the wellspring of human creativity.

Any adequate theory of the mind must account for the intentionality of mental states. That is, it must explain how it is possible for us to think about things. Searle's Chinese room thought experiment is designed to show that functionalism can't account for this aspect of our minds. According to the thought experiment, we can be functionally equivalent to a Chinese speaker and still not understand a word of Chinese. Consequently, the intentionality of a mental state can't be determined by its function.

Does Searle's Chinese room thought experiment show that machines can't think? No, for as Searle himself admits, "we are all machines and we can think."[65] What it shows is that there's more to thinking than just running a program. What more? Running it on the right kind of hardware. According to Searle, something can have a mind only if the stuff it thinks with has the same "causal powers" as our brains. Specifically, it must have the power to produce states that possess intentionality, for without intentionality, it can't think about anything.

Does Searle's Chinese room thought experiment show that the Turing test isn't a good test of intelligence? No, for even if passing the test isn't proof of intelligence, it may nevertheless be good evidence for it. Evidence need not be conclusive to be convincing. Test results must always be taken with a grain of salt because it's possible that the results are due to something other than what the test is designed to measure. Most tests provide only *prima facie* evidence for the hypothesis in question. That is, they provide evidence that is good on its face but may be overridden by other considerations. So although it's not necessarily true that whatever passes the Turing test is intelligent, it's probable that whatever passes the Turing test is intelligent. Further investigation, however, may reveal that the probability isn't actual.

Ned Block describes one way of passing the Turing test that doesn't require any intelligence.

Thought Experiment

Block's Conversational Jukebox

Call a string of sentences whose members, spoken one after another, can be uttered in an hour or less, a speakable string of sentences. A speakable string can contain one very long sentence, or a number of shorter ones. Consider the set of all speakable strings of sentences. Since English has a finite number of words (indeed, a finite number of sound sequences forming possible words short enough to appear in a speakable string), this set has a very large but finite number of members. Consider the subset of the set of all speakable strings of sentences, each of whose member strings can be understood as a conversation in which at least one party is "making sense." Call it the set of smart speakable strings. . . . We need not be too restrictive about what is to count as making sense. For example, if sentence 1 is "let's see you talk nonsense," then sentence 2 could be nonsensical. The set of smart speakable strings is a finite set which could in principle be listed by a very large team working for a long time with a very large grant. Imagine that the smart speakable strings are recorded on a tape and deployed by a very simple machine, as follows. An interrogator utters sentence A. The machine searches the set of smart speakable strings, picks out those strings that begin with A, and picks one string at random (or it might pick the first string it finds beginning with A, using a random search). It then produces the second sentence in that string, call it "B." The interrogator utters another sentence, call it "C." The machine picks a string at random that starts with A, followed by B, followed by C, and utters its fourth sentence, and so on.

Now, if the team has been thorough and imaginative in listing the smart speakable strings, this machine would simulate human conversational abilities. Indeed, if the team did a brilliantly creative job, the machine's conversational abilities might be superhuman (though if it is to "keep up" with current events, the job would have to be redone often). But this machine clearly has no mental states at all. It is just a huge list-searcher plus a tape recorder.[66]

The storage capacity required to house all these conversations would be immense. And the longer the conversations were carried on, the more storage space would be required. So such a machine may be impossible to build. Nevertheless, Block's conversational jukebox, like Searle's Chinese room, shows that there's more to being intelligent than just producing a certain output relative to a given input. How that output is produced is also important. If it's produced in a way that doesn't require any intelligence, then even if it can pass the Turing test, it isn't intelligent.

Thought Probe

Devout Robots

Suppose that a robot that passed the Turing test asked to be baptized. Should it be? Why or why not? Should it be given the same rights that we have? Why or why not?

Summary

According to functionalism, mental states are not material states or states of a nonphysical substance. They're functional states. That is, they are states with a certain function or causal role. The function of a state can be defined in terms of its inputs and outputs. Because computer programs can also be defined in terms of their inputs and outputs, functionalism considers minds to be programs. In this view, the mind is to the brain as the software of a computer is to its hardware. You are your program, so anything that runs your program would be you. Theoretically, then, you could become immortal by downloading your mind into a computer.

Being in a certain functional state, however, seems to be neither a necessary nor a sufficient condition for being in a certain mental state. For, like behaviorism, functionalism does not account for the felt quality of our mental states. People whose experiences are very different could nonetheless be functionally identical. Consequently, functionalism doesn't capture the essence of the mental.

Some have thought that functionalism does provide an adequate explanation of mental states that lack qualitative content, like belief. The essential feature of those mental states is their intentionality — they are directed on or about something. But functionalism can't account for intentionality because one can know how to manipulate symbols without knowing what they mean, as Searle's Chinese room thought experiment demonstrates. This doesn't mean that machines can't think, but it does mean that there's more to having a mind than running a program.

Study Questions

1. According to functionalism, what is it to be in a mental state?
2. What is Lewis's pained madman thought experiment? How does it attempt to undermine functionalism?
3. What is Block's Chinese nation thought experiment? How does it attempt to undermine functionalism?
4. What is Putnam's inverted spectrum thought experiment? How does it attempt to undermine functionalism?
5. What is the Turing test for intelligence?
6. What is Searle's Chinese room thought experiment? How does it attempt to undermine the Turing test?
7. What is intentionality?
8. What is Block's conversational jukebox argument? How does it attempt to undermine the Turing test?

Discussion Questions

1. Is it possible to build a computer that can pass the Turing test? Why or why not?
2. It is possible to make a fully functional computer out of sticks, stones, and toilet paper. If such a computer ran your program, would it be you? Why or why not?

3. Consider the various replies to Searle's Chinese room thought experiment. Which do you think is the most plausible? Why?

4. Suppose that the "person" whose program is being run by Block's Chinese nation claims that she is cold. Would you believe her? Why or why not?

5. Psychologist Stevan Harnad has proposed the Total Turing Test for artificial intelligence. To pass this test, the computer being tested would have to be able to do *everything* that a normal human being does, including walking, riding a bicycle, swimming, dancing, playing a musical instrument, and so on. Only a computer with a robot body could do that. Is passing the Total Turing Test either necessary or sufficient for being intelligent and thus having a mind? Why or why not?

There Ain't No Such Things as Ghosts
Mind as Myth

What is mind?
No matter.
What is matter?
Never mind.

— Thomas Key

Nₒₙₑ of the reductive theories of the mind—logical behaviorism, the identity theory, or functionalism—has succeeded (or appears likely to succeed) in providing an adequate account of the nature of the mind. The apparent failure of these theories is an important result of philosophical research and a piece of data that any adequate theory of mind must explain. **Eliminative materialism** provides one such explanation. It claims that reductive theories of the mind have failed because mental terms do not refer to anything. In other words, the reason that there has been no reduction of the mental to the physical is that there is nothing to reduce—mental states do not exist.

Such a claim may seem startling. But eliminative materialists contend that the claim that there are no devil-loving witches would have seemed equally startling to members of the Spanish Inquisition. Just as demonic witches were part of a folk theory that nearly everyone in the thirteenth century took for granted, so mental states are part of a folk theory that nearly everyone in the twenty-first century takes for granted. And just as the advance of scientific knowledge has shown that there are no demonic witches, so, someday, the advance of scientific knowledge may show that there are no mental states.

Richard Rorty, an early advocate of eliminative materialism, provides the following thought experiment to clarify this point.

Thought Experiment

Rorty's Demons

A certain primitive tribe holds the view that illnesses are caused by demons— a different demon for each sort of illness. When asked what more is known about these demons than that they cause illness, they reply that certain members of the tribe — the witch doctors — can see, after a meal of sacred mushrooms, various (intangible) humanoid forms on or near the bodies of the patients. The witch-doctors have noted, for example, that a blue demon with a long nose accompanies epileptics, a fat red one accompanies sufferers from pneumonia, etc. They know such further facts as that the fat red demon dislikes a certain sort of mold which the witch-doctors give people who have pneumonia. If we encountered such a tribe, we would be inclined to tell them that there are no demons. We would tell them that diseases were caused by germs, viruses, and the like. We would add that the witch-doctors were not seeing demons, but merely having hallucinations.[67]

Diseases used to be explained in terms of demons. Now we explain them in terms of germs, viruses, and the like. All references to demons have been eliminated from our medical textbooks. Similarly, claims Rorty, all references to mental states will someday be eliminated from our psychology textbooks. He explains,

> The absurdity of saying "Nobody has ever felt a pain" is no greater than that of saying "Nobody has ever seen a demon," if we have a suitable answer to the question "What was I reporting when I said I felt a pain?" To this question, the science of the future may reply "You were reporting the occurrence of a certain brain-process, and it would make life simpler for us if you would, in the future, say 'My C-fibers are firing' instead of saying 'I'm in pain.'" In so saying, he has as good a *prima facie* case as the scientist who answers the witch-doctor's question "What was I reporting when I reported a demon?" by saying "You were reporting the content of your hallucination, and it would make life simpler if, in the future, you would describe your experiences in those terms."[68]

Modern science can explain everything that the demon theory explained without referring to demons. Similarly, says Rorty, modern science may be able to explain everything that the pain theory explains without referring to pains. If so, science will have shown that there is no good reason to believe in the existence of pains. In such a case, those who continue to believe in pains would be just as deluded as those who continue to believe in demons.

Eliminative materialism differs from reductive materialism in that the former doesn't identify the mind with anything physical. Both logical behaviorism and the identity theory contend that to talk about mental states is to talk about physical states of some sort. Eliminative materialism, on the other hand, contends that to talk about mental states is to talk about nothing. The mind is a myth. Mental states have no more reality than the Greek gods. As a result, all talk about minds can be eliminated from our explanations of behavior.

eliminative materialism The doctrine that there are no mental states.

If no one has ever been in pain, however, it follows that no one has ever done anything because he or she was in pain. If there are no mental states, there are no mental causes. So, like epiphenomenalism, eliminative materialism denies that mental states affect behavior. But, unlike epiphenomenalism, it also denies that mental states exist.

Folk Psychology

Folk psychology is our commonsense theory of the mind that explains people's behavior in terms of mental states like belief and desire. Not only does folk psychology assume that we have beliefs and desires, it also assumes that they affect what we do. Eliminative materialists reject both of these assumptions. In their view, there are no beliefs and desires, so they cannot affect our behavior.

How can the eliminative materialists deny something that seems so obvious? They do so by claiming that mental states are theoretical entities. Theoretical entities are things that are assumed to exist in order to account for something. Atoms, for example, were theoretical entities when they were first postulated. Until very recently, no one had seen an atom. Nevertheless, they were assumed to exist because they provided the best explanation of certain phenomena. Eliminative materialists claim that mental states are like atoms: the only reason we have for believing in them is that they seem to provide the best explanation of certain phenomena. But, contrary to popular belief, mental states do not explain anything. Consequently, we are not justified in believing in them.

Philosopher Paul Churchland, for example, claims that folk psychology fails to explain a number of psychological phenomena.

> So much of what is central and familiar to us remains a complete mystery from within folk psychology. We do not know what sleep is, or why we have to have it, despite spending a full third of our lives in that condition. . . . We do not understand how learning transforms each of us from a gaping infant to a cunning adult or how differences in intelligence are grounded. We have not the slightest idea how memory works, or how we manage to retrieve relevant bits of information instantly from the awesome mass we have stored. We do not know what mental illness is, nor how to cure it.[69]

Because sleep, intelligence, memory, mental illness, and the like can't be explained by folk psychology, Churchland claims that folk psychology will eventually be replaced by another theory that doesn't rely on beliefs and desires.

The fact that folk psychology can't explain certain phenomena would be a strike against it only if it was intended to explain them. But it wasn't. Folk psychology was intended to explain the waking actions of normal adults. There is no more reason to reject folk psychology because it can't explain sleep than there is to reject the theory of continental drift because it can't explain how planets are formed. Different theories explain different things. Just because a theory doesn't explain everything is no reason to reject it.

What's more, even if folk-psychological concepts like belief and desire do not figure into the best theory of the mind, that doesn't mean that there are no beliefs and desires. Searle provides the following example.

Searle's Chevrolet Station Wagon

Consider our existing science of theoretical physics. Here we have a theory that explains how physical reality works, and is vastly superior to our commonsense theories by all the usual criteria. Physical theory covers the same domain as our commonsense theories of golf clubs, tennis rackets, Chevrolet station wagons, and split-level ranch houses. Furthermore, our ordinary folk physical concepts such as "golf club," "tennis racket," "Chevrolet station wagon," and "split-level ranch house" do not exactly, or even remotely, match the taxonomy of theoretical physics. There simply is no use in theoretical physics for any of these expressions and no smooth type reductions of these phenomena is possible. The way that an ideal physics—indeed the way that our actual physics—taxonomizes reality is really quite different from the way our ordinary folk physics taxonomizes reality. Therefore, split-level ranch houses, tennis rackets, golf clubs, Chevrolet station wagons, etc., do not really exist.[70]

Searle ridicules the eliminative materialist argument by showing that if we accept the claim that there are no mental states, we must also accept the claim that there are no Chevrolet station wagons or split-level ranch houses. Eliminative materialists argue that if the concepts of belief and desire do not appear in our best psychological theory, then there is no reason to believe that there are any beliefs or desires. Searle replies that if that were a good argument, then because the concepts of Chevrolet station wagon and split-level ranch house do not appear in our best physical theory, there would be no reason to believe that there are any Chevrolet station wagons or split-level ranch houses. Because that is absurd, so is the claim of the eliminative materialists.

Although Rorty suggests that mental states are analogous to demons, there is a significant disanalogy: we can explain away demonic visions as hallucinations, but we can't explain away sensations as hallucinations because hallucinations are sensations. To have a hallucination is to have a sensation. To make his case, then, Rorty must find some other way of explaining how it's possible for us to be mistaken about the fact that we have sensations. But how could we be mistaken about the fact that we have sensations? Descartes seems to have been onto something when he suggested that he couldn't be deceived about the fact that he was thinking. This suggests that sensations are not theoretical entities. Instead, they are the data that any adequate theory of the mind must explain.

Subjective Knowledge

If either reductive or eliminative materialism were true, it would be possible to provide a complete description of the world in purely physical terms, for

folk psychology Our commonsense theory of mind that explains people's behavior in terms of beliefs and desires.

there would be no nonphysical things or properties. Frank Jackson, however, claims that a complete knowledge of all the physical facts about the world would not give us a complete knowledge of the world. Consider, for example, the following well-informed scientist who has never seen colors.

Thought Experiment

Jackson's Color-Challenged Scientist

Mary is a brilliant scientist who is, for whatever reason, forced to investigate the world from a black and white room via a black and white television monitor. She . . . acquires, let us suppose, all the physical information there is to obtain about what goes on when we see ripe tomatoes, or the sky, and use terms like "red," "blue," and so on.

What will happen when Mary is released from her black and white room . . . ? Will she learn anything or not? It seems just obvious that she will learn something about the world and our visual experience of it. But then it is inescapable that her previous knowledge was incomplete. But she had all the physical information. Ergo there is more to have than that, and physicalism is false.[71]

Although Mary has never seen anything that is colored, she knows all the physical facts about vision. If physicalism were true, she would know everything there is to know about vision. But she doesn't know everything that there is to know about vision because she doesn't know what it's like to see colored objects. So, Jackson concludes, physicalism is false; there's more to the world than just physical objects and physical properties.

According to Jackson, any account of the world that doesn't include the qualitative content of our conscious experience can't be considered complete. But any purely physicalistic account of the world can't include it, for what it feels like to have a certain experience isn't a physical fact. (All physical facts, remember, are knowable from a third-person point of view.) So, contrary to what the eliminative materialists would have us believe, it isn't possible to provide a complete account of the world in purely physical terms.

This is a telling argument against eliminative materialism in particular and physicalism in general. As David Lewis admits, "We dare not grant there is a sort of information we overlook. . . . that would be defeat." So how does Lewis propose to deal with Jackson's thought experiment? "Our proper answer," he tells us, "is that knowing what it's like isn't the possession of information at all. It isn't the elimination of any hitherto open possibilities. Rather, knowing what it's like is the possession of abilities: abilities to recognize, abilities to imagine, abilities to predict one's behavior by means of imaginative experiments."[72] According to Lewis, then, Mary (in her room) didn't lack any information about the world. She simply lacked certain abilities.

What Mary didn't know is what it's like to see colors. According to Lewis, to know what something is like is to know how to do something. So Mary

Jackson's color-challenged scientist is not just a creature of the imagination. There are people who are born seeing only black and white and later gain the ability to see in color. Reporter Jojo Moyes filed the following story in the British newspaper *The Independent*.

A teenager told yesterday how he cried when he saw in colour for the first time, thanks to revolutionary contact lenses developed by British scientists.

Kevin Staight, 18, was born with a rare eye defect, affecting one in a million people, which meant he saw everything in black and white. Now he is learning about colour, after his grandparents Don and Dorothy Staight saved up for the special lenses.

"After I put them on I went for a walk and slowly saw the world in colour for the first time," said Kevin, from Cheltenham, Gloucestershire. "Up until then I didn't have any idea what colour was because I couldn't see it.

"I couldn't stop crying because the world looked so different to what I was used to. The reds just kept on jumping out at me and I had to ask my grandparents which colours were which because I didn't have a clue.

"It has opened up a whole new world for me. I never realized just how beautiful things like trees and flowers are."

Mrs. Staight, Kevin's grandmother, who raised him, said: "He is a completely changed person. I don't think anybody realized just how gloomy his world has been up until now.

"The opticians had told us there was nothing that could be done because he was so severely colour blind. When we heard about these lenses we decided to give them a go to see if they would work for Kevin and the results were amazing.

"He dragged us outside and was rushing around pointing at things and asking what colour they were. It was all very emotional because he was crying."

Mrs. Staight said that Kevin's girlfriend, Sarah Gill, had been nervous about his reaction, as she is half Vietnamese and wasn't sure how he would react to her skin.

"It has made absolutely no difference to Kevin because we explained to him beforehand that people have different colour and textures to their skin," Mrs. Staight said.

Kevin's career prospects have also been aided by the new lenses. As a result of being able to see on-screen colour, he has secured a job working with computers.

The lenses, called ChromaGen, have only been available at six opticians in Britain since they were released last July and are £540 a pair. They were supplied by Bristol optician Roger Spooner, who said: "Kevin's case was very dramatic because he lived in a totally grey world. He was the first person I have come across who was totally colour blind.

"The whole practice was in tears when he came here to try on his lenses but it was a very rewarding experience to help him."[73]

Thought Probe

Color

Kevin claims that he had no idea what color was before he received his lenses. Does this real-world case bolster Jackson's claim that qualia are not physical properties?

didn't lack any factual knowledge, she just lacked performative knowledge. The problem with this argument is that knowing how to do something is neither a necessary nor a sufficient condition for knowing what something is like. Consequently, Lewis's attempt to save physicalism fails.

Knowing how is not a sufficient condition for knowing what, for Mary could have all of the abilities mentioned by Lewis without knowing what red is like. She could know, for example, that red objects appear as a particular shade of gray on her TV screen. This knowledge would give her the ability to recognize or imagine red objects by recognizing or imagining that particular shade of gray. (In this case, she would be imagining red objects, but she would not be imagining them as red objects.) Because Mary could know how to recognize or imagine red objects without knowing what red is like, knowing how doesn't entail knowing what.

Nor does knowing what entail knowing how, for someone could know what something is like without being able to do anything. People paralyzed from birth, for example, can know what pain is even though they can't move a muscle. So knowing what can't be construed as a species of knowing how.

If physicalism were true, then a knowledge of all the physical facts would give us a complete understanding of the world. But there seems to be much about the world that we wouldn't understand if we had no knowledge of qualitative content. Suppose there were a well-informed materialist who couldn't feel pain. She would know that people tend to avoid painful things. But would she understand why this is so? She would know that painful things tend to cause bodily damage and that people usually want to avoid bodily damage, but would that give her a complete understanding of why people tend to avoid painful things? It wouldn't seem so. It leaves out of account the most important reason for avoiding pain, namely, that it hurts. Insofar as sensations (and the fear of sensations) cause actions, anyone who has not experienced them cannot completely understand human behavior.

That pain feels like *this* (where *this* refers to the qualitative content of the experience) is a fact about the world. It is not a physical fact, however, for as we have seen, it is neither identical to nor reducible to a physical fact. Any attempt to describe or explain the world in purely physicalistic terms, then, must leave something out of account, namely, the nature of conscious experience.

To highlight the difficulty that any physicalistic theory has in explaining the mind, David Chalmers offers the following thought experiment about zombies.

Thought Experiment

Zombies

. . . consider the logical possibility of a zombie: someone or something physically identical to me (or to any other conscious being), but lacking conscious experience altogether. At the global level, we can consider the logical possibility of a *zombie world*: a world physically identical to ours, but in which there are no conscious experiences at all. In such a world, everybody is a zombie.

So let us consider my zombie twin. This creature is molecule for molecule identical to me, and identical in all the low-level properties postulated by a completed physics, but he lacks conscious experience entirely. (Some might prefer to call a zombie "it," but I use the personal pronoun; I have grown quite fond of my zombie twin.) To fix ideas, we can imagine that right now I am gazing out the window, experiencing some nice green sensations from seeing the trees outside, having pleasant taste experiences through munching a chocolate bar, and feeling a dull aching sensation in my right shoulder.

What is going on in my zombie twin? He is physically identical to me, and we may as well suppose that he is embedded in an identical environment. He will certainly be identical to me *functionally*: he will be processing internal configurations being modified appropriately and with indistinguishable behavior resulting. He will be *psychologically* identical to me. . . . He will be perceiving the trees outside, in the functional sense, and tasting the chocolate, in the psychological sense. All of this follows from the fact that he is physically identical to me, by virtue of the functional analyses of psychological notions. . . . It is just that none of this functioning will be accompanied by any real conscious experience. There will be no phenomenal feelings, there is nothing it is like to be a zombie.[74]

Chalmer's zombies — unlike Hollywood zombies or voodoo zombies — are physiologically and functionally identical to us. They are made out of the same stuff that we are, and they act the same way that we do. The only difference between us and them is that they have no conscious experience. There is nothing that it is like to be a zombie because they have no sensations or emotions. But you couldn't tell that by looking at them, or even by dissecting them, for both internally and externally, they are indistinguishable from us.

Like Descartes' conceivability argument, Chalmer's zombie argument is designed to show that consciousness is nonphysical. Although it advocates a sort of dualism, it is not the sort of dualism advocated by Descartes. Chalmers is not trying to resurrect the notion that the mind is a nonphysical thing that can exist independently of the body. Instead, he is trying to show that mental properties are not reducible to or explainable in terms of physical properties.

Science has traditionally tried to explain things by identifying their structure or function. Many aspects of consciousness may be explainable in this way, such as the ability to discriminate stimuli, integrate information, and control behavior. These Chalmers calls the "easy problems" of consciousness, not because their solution is obvious, but because they should be solvable in the traditional manner. The problems of how and why physical processes give rise to consciousness, however, do not seem to be similarly solvable. No amount of structural or functional knowledge would seem to provide answers to these questions. Consequently, Chalmers calls these the "hard problems" of consciousness. His zombie thought experiment highlights the difficulty. It seems perfectly conceivable that we could get along in the world without having any conscious experience. So why does it exist, and how do brains produce it? To answer these questions, Chalmers believes a new type of explanation is needed. In the next section, we'll take a look at what such an explanation might look like.

There is nothing so unthinkable as thought, unless it be the entire absence of thought.

—SAMUEL BUTLER

Zombies

Could a zombie (a creature with no mental states) do everything that a normal human being can do? One thing we can do is use metaphorical language — language that, though literally false, can be figuratively true. Nelson Goodman explains,

> Before me is a picture of trees and cliffs by the sea, painted in dull grays, and expressing great sadness. . . . The picture is literally gray but only metaphorically sad. . . . But to say that it is sad is metaphorically true even though literally false. Just as the picture clearly belongs under the label "gray" rather than under the label "yellow," it also clearly belongs under "sad" rather than under "gray."[75]

Could a zombie recognize that this painting belongs under the label "sad"? By definition, a zombie has never experienced sadness (or grayness). It doesn't know what sadness (or grayness) is like. Without this knowledge, would it be able to place the painting in the appropriate category? Why or why not?

Summary

Eliminative materialism provides an explanation for the failure of reductive theories of mind: mental states cannot be reduced to physical states because there is nothing to reduce — mental states do not exist. We think there are mental states because we are in the grip of a bad theory of the mind, namely, folk psychology. Folk psychology is our commonsense theory of mind that explains people's behavior in terms of beliefs and desires. According to eliminative materialism, beliefs and desires are theoretical entities postulated to explain behavior. But we can explain behavior without referring to beliefs and desires. Therefore, there is no reason to believe that they exist.

Eliminative materialism is committed to the view that it is possible to provide a complete description of the world in purely physical terms. But any account of the world that leaves out the qualitative content of our conscious experience can't be considered complete. For it is a fact about the world that each sensation has its own particular feel. Because feelings are real, and because eliminative materialism can't account for our feelings, it is not an adequate theory of the mind.

Study Questions

1. What is Rorty's demons thought experiment? How does it attempt to undermine reductive theories of the mind?
2. What is the eliminative materialist theory of the mind?
3. What is folk psychology?
4. What is Searle's Chevrolet station wagon thought experiment? How does it attempt to undermine eliminative materialism?

5. What is physicalism?
6. What is Jackson's color-challenged scientist thought experiment? How does it attempt to undermine physicalism?

Discussion Questions

1. Is eliminative materialism a more adequate theory of the mind than the reductive theories (logical behaviorism, the identity theory, functionalism)? Why or why not?
2. Is folk psychology a failed psychological theory? Why or why not?
3. Can mental states be considered theoretical entities? Why or why not?
4. Can we adequately explain and predict other people's behavior without talking about their mental states?
5. Can we eliminate all references to mental states from a scientific account of the world? Why or why not?
6. Is knowing what a species of knowing how? Why or why not?
7. Could a zombie (a creature with no mental states) do everything that we can do?

The Whole Is Greater Than the Sum of Its Parts
Mind as Quality

Thought is so little incompatible with organized matter that it seems to be one of its properties.

—JULIEN OFFRAY
DE LA METTRIE

*T*he implausibility of eliminative materialism suggests that the failure to reduce the mental to the physical or the functional can't be explained on the grounds that mental states don't exist. What is the best explanation of this failure then? Many believe that the best explanation is that mental properties are something over and above physical properties. This view of the nature of the mind is known as **property dualism.** It has also been called "emergent materialism," "nonreductive materialism," and "soft materialism."

Some mental states, like pain and fear, have a particular feel, whereas others, like hope and belief, have a particular object. But, as we have seen, what a mental state feels like (its qualitative content) and what it is about (its intentional content) are not physical or functional properties, for neither is knowable from a third-person point of view. We can know all of the physical and functional properties of a mental state without knowing what it's like to have it or what it's about. Thus the conclusion that mental properties are distinct from physical properties seems unavoidable.

Primitive Intentionality

Because the qualitative content (the feel) and the intentional content (the object) of a mental state are not reducible to physical or functional properties, they are "primitive" properties. A **primitive property** is one that can't be explained in terms of anything more fundamental. Jacquette demonstrates the primitiveness of intentionality by means of the following thought experiment.

The Double Aspect Theory

Not all property dualists are emergent materialists. Baruch Spinoza, for example, maintains that, not only are mental properties not emergent, they are not properties of material objects. Spinoza maintains that mental and physical properties are two different aspects of a single underlying substance that is neither mental nor physical. This is the **double aspect theory.** An "aspect" is a way something appears. A concave lens, for example, has two aspects—concave and convex—for from one perspective it appears concave and from another it appears convex. Similarly, claims Spinoza, the substance of the universe has two aspects—mental and physical. The mental aspect is the way the substance appears from the "inside," and the physical aspect is the way it appears from the "outside," so to speak. Everything, from the most elementary particles to the most complex collection of them, has both a mental and a physical aspect. So aspects are not emergent.

Although this view is suggestive, it is unenlightening, for it tells us nothing about the basic stuff itself. We can describe a lens independently of the way it appears to us. We can even explain why it appears differently from different perspectives. But no such explanation of appearances is possible in Spinoza's view. Why his substance appears one way from the inside and another from the outside is just as mysterious as what that substance is.

Thought Experiment

Jacquette's Intentionality Test

As a thought experiment, try using the term "A" to refer, first to the book you are holding, then to the weight of the book in your hands, then to the space it occupies, then to its color. Do this again, switching from one use to another as often as you like, and pay careful attention to whatever mental events or images may be occurring as you do it, to what we may call the phenomenology of intending. Note first of all that you encounter no difficulty in performing this exercise. You can easily use the letter "A" in multiple referential ways without hindrance; nothing prevents you from doing it. You recognize once you have formulated the relevant intention, that by "A" you mean the book, or the color of its cover, or the space it occupies. If someone were to ask you what you mean by "A" when each of these particular intentions was in force, you could answer immediately, and without inference. You do not need to find out what you mean by "A" under any of the circumstances. It is entirely up to you, a decision on your part rather than a discovery. Second, when you attend to the mental events occurring at the time you formulate or shift intentions for the reference of term "A" from one thing to another, if your experience is like most persons', there is nothing special at all that occurs as an essential accompaniment of your intending. There are no identifiable episodes of inward concentration or particular mental imagery. You simply intend something or something new by "A," and that is that. But if there is no psychological occurrence that uniquely characterizes the intending of an object in thought, but the thought directly intends

property dualism
The doctrine that mental states have both physical and nonphysical properties.

primitive property
A property that cannot be reduced to or analyzed in terms of any more basic property.

double aspect theory
The doctrine that the mind and the body are two aspects of a single underlying substance.

the object, then intentionality appears again to be a primitive concept. For there is nothing psychological to which it can be reduced, no unique mental occurrences on which intending is conditional.[76]

This experiment suggests that what our thoughts are about is not determined by any feature of them other than their intentionality. We don't think about objects by means of anything else. We simply think about them. That's what makes intentionality a primitive property.

Putnam agrees. He writes,

> Another way to account for the objectivity of the notion of truth (as well as of reference, etc.) [is] the way suggested by Brentano and by Chisholm; that is, just to take the existence of intentional properties as a "primitive" fact. If primitive just means "not reducible to nonintentional notions," then (I have been arguing) this is, indeed, the right answer."[77]

In this view, intentionality and consciousness are like mass and charge: they are basic properties that cannot be explained in terms of anything more fundamental. Given the failure of all attempts to reduce or eliminate these properties, such a view seems eminently reasonable.

Basic properties can be understood by explaining their relations to other properties. This form of nonreductive explanation has led to some of the greatest advances in modern science. Newton's discovery that $F = ma$ (force equals mass times acceleration) and Einstein's discovery that $E = mc^2$ (energy equals mass times the velocity of light squared) are just two of many examples that could be given. If comparable advances are to be made in the science of the mind, similar laws governing intentionality and consciousness must be found. As Nagel says,

> Only if the uniqueness of the mental is recognized will concepts and theories be recognized for the purpose of understanding it. Otherwise there is a danger of futile reliance on concepts designed for other purposes, and indefinite postponement of any possibility of a unified understanding of mind and body.[78]

It has often been remarked that cognitive science — those branches of philosophy, psychology, anthropology, and linguistics that deal with the mind — is awaiting its Isaac Newton: someone who can bring these disparate fields under one unified theoretical framework. Nagel suggests that this cannot be done by reducing mental phenomena to something else but only by developing theories that recognize their uniqueness.

Mental Dependence

Although mental properties are distinct from physical ones, they are dependent on them. Unlike Cartesian dualism, property dualism maintains that minds cannot exist independently of bodies. Specifying the nature of this dependence has been the goal of much current research in the philosophy

I conclude that the concept of consciousness in the sense of an irreducible relation of awareness is a concept that we can neither exclude nor exchange if, as psychologists, we are to give an adequate account of life and behaviour.

—SIR CYRIL BURT

of mind. The received view is that mental properties "supervene" on physical ones.

The notion of supervenience was first used in ethics to explain the relationship between moral and nonmoral properties. The basic idea is that someone has moral properties in virtue of having certain nonmoral ones. For example, someone is good in virtue of being dependable, being truthful, being willing to help others, and so on. Similarly, according to supervenience theorists, something has a mental property in virtue of having a nonmental one. Nothing can have a mental property unless it has certain nonmental ones, and those nonmental properties give rise to the mental ones.

Property dualism is not a reductive theory of the mind, however, because it does not identify mental properties with nonmental ones. Reductive theories claim that mental properties are nothing but nonmental ones. Property dualism, on the other hand, is committed to the view that mental properties are something over and above nonmental ones.

The Causal Exclusion Problem

Supervenience theorists, by and large, are not epiphenomenalists; they believe that mental events cause physical events. They also tend to be physicalists; they believe that every physical event has a purely physical cause. (This doctrine, you will recall, is known as the "causal closure of the physical.") But these two views seem to be inconsistent with the basic tenet of supervenience: that mental properties are not reducible to physical properties. In other words, it looks like the position sketched above is inconsistent. It is committed to three principles that seemingly cannot all be true:

- The Irreducibility of the Mental: mental properties are distinct from physical ones.
- The Causal Efficacy of the Mental: mental events can have physical effects.
- The Causal Closure of the Physical: every physical event has a purely physical cause.

If we reject the causal efficacy of the mental, we're stuck with either epiphenomenalism (the view that mental states have no causal power) or eliminativism (the view that there are no mental states), neither of which, for reasons we've already explored, seems plausible. If we reject the irreducibility of the mental, we're stuck with either the identity theory or functionalism, neither of which can account for either the qualitative content or the intentional content of mental states. So some claim that the best solution to the dilemma is to give up the doctrine of the causal closure of the physical. For them, that doctrine is an article of faith that not only lacks empirical support but flies in the face of the evidence. One group of philosophers who reject that principle are known as "emergentists."

Emergentism

It is a bizarre thought that a feeling being like you or me might emerge from mere circuitry.

—DOUGLAS R. HOFSTADTER

Emergentists claim that mental properties are emergent properties. An emergent property is one that is had by a whole but not by any of its parts. Life, for example, is an emergent property. The basic consitituents of a living organism—the atoms and molecules out of which it is made—are not alive. But the organism itself is alive because its parts interact with one another in the right sorts of ways. An **emergent property,** then, is one that emerges or comes into being when things that lack that property become related in the appropriate ways.

According to emergentists, consciousness is an emergent property. The individual neurons that make up our brains are not conscious. But once they become related to one another in the right sorts of ways, consciousness emerges.

Because emergentists tend to endorse the causal efficacy of the mental, they usually believe in what's known as "top-down" or "downward causation." Nature can be viewed as having a hierarchical structure where the lower levels give rise to the higher ones. For example, subatomic particles give rise to atoms; atoms give rise to molecules; molecules give rise to cells; cells give rise to organisms; and organisms give rise to societies. These are examples of what's known as "bottom-up causation." The lower levels affect the higher ones. What emergentists claim is that causation can flow in the other direction. Higher levels can affect the lower ones.

The term "downward causation" was introduced by sociologist Donald Campbell to explain the effect of the environment on biological evolution. A number of neurophysiologists believe that this notion can be used to solve the mind-body problem. Neurophysiologist János Szentágothai explains,

> 'Mind' functions—themselves considered as emergent from brain functions— might have a *downward causal effect* on brain functions. In other words, consciousness and thought might interfere with the activity of neuron networks resulting from self-organization, without getting into conflict with accepted (legitimate) laws of nature. The possibility of 'downward causation' from mental functions on the very same brain functions from which they emerge (by 'bottom up' causation), within the accepted laws of nature, is an attractive solution to the brain-mind problem.[79]

Consciousness is what happens to intelligence when it is confronted with an object.

—HAZRAT INAYAT KHAN

The Nobel Prize–winning neurophysiologist Roger Sperry echoes these sentiments:

> In the brain, controls at the physico-chemical and physiological levels are superseded by new forms of causal control that emerge at the level of conscious mental processing, where causal properties include the contents of subjective experience. Causal control is thus shifted in brain dynamics from levels of pure physical, physiological, or material determinacy to levels of mental, cognitive, conscious, or subjective determinacy. The flow of nerve impulse traffic and related physiological events in a conscious process is no longer regulated solely by events in kind but becomes caught up in, enveloped, and moved by the higher mental

controls, somewhat as the flow of electrons in a television set is moved and differentially patterned by the program content on different channels.[80]

According to Sperry, just as the flow of electrons in a television set is determined by the program it is receiving, so the flow of nerve impulses through our brains is determined by the conscious experiences we are having. If conscious experience can indeed affect the flow of nerve impulses, then conscious experience is not epiphenomenal.

The analogy of the program and the television set is fundamentally flawed, however, for the electrons in the TV set and the program it is receiving don't interact with each other in the way that nerve impulses in the brain and conscious experience seem to. In the case of the electrons and the TV program, causation seems to flow in only one direction—from the transmitter to the picture tube—whereas in the case of the nerve impulses and consciousness, causation seems to flow in both directions. What happens in the brain affects our conscious experience, and our conscious experience affects what happens in the brain. Perhaps a better analogy is that between a stream and its banks. As droplets of water come together to form a stream, a bank emerges. The bank is brought into existence by the movement of the water molecules, but it nonetheless determines the flow of those molecules. In this analogy, consciousness is like the bank and nerve impulses are like the stream. Just as the stream brings the bank into existence, so do nerve impulses give rise to consciousness. And just as the bank determines the flow of the stream, so does consciousness determine the flow of nerve impulses. There is a two-way interaction between the bank and the stream: the bank determines the course of the stream, and the stream determines the contours of the bank. Similarly, there is a two-way interaction between consciousness and the brain: consciousness determines the succession of nerve impulses, and nerve impulses determine the content of consciousness. Of course this analogy doesn't fully capture the dynamic nature of consciousness, for the bank is far too passive. Nonetheless, it does reveal how an emergent feature can reach back down and affect that which gave rise to it.

Critics of downward causation do not find such analogies enlightening. They claim that downward causation violates not only the causal closure of the physical but also the principle of the conservation of mass/energy. According to that principle, the total amount of mass/energy in the physical world remains constant. Causation, however, seems to involve the transfer of energy. A moving billiard ball, for example, causes a stationary billiard ball to move by transferring some of its kinetic energy to it. So if mental causation occurs, it seems that it must involve a transfer of energy from the mental to the physical. But any such transfer of energy would violate the principle of the conservation of mass/energy. So mental causation cannot occur.

The argument from the conservation of mass/energy can be spelled out as follows:

1. No energy can enter or leave the physical world.
2. If mental causation occurs, then energy must enter the physical world.
3. Therefore, mental causation cannot occur.

My belief is that the explanations of emergent phenomena in our brains . . . are based on a kind of Strange Loop, an interaction between levels in which the top level reaches back down towards the bottom level and influences it, while at the same time being determined by the bottom level. . . .

—DOUGLAS R. HOFSTADTER

emergent property
A property that comes into being (emerges) when things that lack that property interact in certain ways.

WATERFALL BY
M. C. ESCHER
(LITHOGRAPH, 1961).
The water flowing
through the channel
provides a visual analog
of downward causation.

This argument is valid but its soundness is questionable because there's reason to doubt its second premise. Causation need not always involve the transfer of energy. Consider, for example, a ball on a string that's swung in a circle. The string causes the ball to move in a circle, but it doesn't inject any energy into the system. It simply determines how the energy in the system is distributed. Similarly, the mind may affect the body by determining how the energy in the brain is distributed. So while the argument from the conservation of mass/energy may be a problem for substance dualism, which takes the mind to be an immaterial thing, it is not necessarily a problem for property dualism.

Whether mental properties are causally efficacious will ultimately be determined by scientific inquiry. If the mind affects the body, we should eventually observe effects that can't be predicted or explained in purely physical terms. In the meantime, however, we need to decide which principle to give up.

When deciding among a group of inconsistent principles, it's wise to appeal to the criteria of conservatism, dubbed by American philosopher W. V. O. Quine "the maxim of minimum mutilation": reject that principle whose removal will do the least amount of damage to our belief system.[81] Rejecting the causal efficacy of the mental means giving up the view that people do things because they're in various mental states. It seems that anger, jealousy, fear, and the like can cause people to act: "He slugged him because he was angry." "He snubbed him because he was jealous." "He ran away because he was afraid." All seem to be perfectly legitimate explanations of human behavior. All of these explanations, however, presuppose the causal efficacy of the mental. Without that principle, such explanations would be uninformative; they wouldn't tell us anything about why people act as they do.

Rejecting the irreducibility of the mental means accepting some form of the identity theory or functionalism, neither of which can account for the qualitative content or the intentional content of mental states. What it feels like to be in a mental state (its qualitative content) and what a mental state is about (its intentional content) can't be specified in physiological or functional terms. So adopting either of these theories would leave these aspects of mental states unexplained.

The most expendable of these principles seems to be the causal closure of the physical. Rejecting it does not violate any physical laws, and there seems to be little evidence to support it. As English philosopher John Dupre informs us,

> Evidence for causal completeness would require that increasingly complex systems of physical particles could be shown to be amenable to causal explanation in terms of the laws said to govern individual particles, evidence, that is to say, for general reductionism. . . . No one has claimed to be able to explain the behavior even of very small collections of particles in terms of the behavior of individual particles; the reduction even of relatively simple parts of chemistry to physics is now looked on with considerable skepticism, and even physics itself is acknowledged to consist of laws the relations between which are obscure, though at least the unification of physics is still looked upon by some physicists as an attainable goal. At any rate, the view that every physical particle has its behavior fully determined by microphysical laws must derive any plausibility it has from some source other than the development of microphysics.[82]

Those who believe in the causal closure of the physical usually believe that, in principle, everything that happens in the world can be explained in terms of the interactions of subatomic particles. Such reductionistic explanations have not been forthcoming, however, even in the natural sciences. Dupre believes that the reason for this failure is that there are other sources of causal power besides subatomic particles.

Some of the most tantalizing evidence for the causal efficacy of the mental comes from various clinical experiments. Psychologists Baars and McGovern, for example, cite the phenomenon of biofeedback, where subjects are made aware of the firing rates of neurons and asked to control them. They report,

> The global influence of consciousness is dramatized by the remarkable phenomenon of biofeedback training. There is firm evidence that any single neurone or any population of neurons can come to be voluntarily controlled by giving conscious feedback of their neural firing rates. However, if the biofeedback signal is not conscious, learning does not occur. Subliminal feedback, distraction from the feedback signal, or feedback via a habituating stimulus — all these cases prevent control being acquired. Since this kind of learning only works for conscious

biofeedback signals, it suggests again that consciousness creates global access to all parts of the nervous system.[83]

In these biofeedback experiments, conscious awareness seems to play a causal role in determining the rate at which neurons fire.

The placebo effect also seems to provide evidence for the causal efficacy of the mental. Placebos are inert substances like sugar pills that seem to make people better simply because the people taking them believe they will work. It has long been known that giving patients placebos and telling them that they are painkillers will reduce pain in about 30 percent of the people taking them. But placebos have also been found to produce organic changes in patients. As Jay Dixit reports in the *Washington Post*,

> . . . studies have demonstrated that placebos improve blood pressure, cholesterol levels, heart rate and allergies, and can make warts vanish. For some reason, red sugar pills kill pain better than green, blue, or yellow ones; blue sugar pills work better as sedatives than pink ones. Patients don't just think they get better on placebos: they really do get better, and the changes are reflected in brain scans and blood tests.[84]

In addition to the placebo effect, doctors have also noticed a "nocebo effect" where patients get worse if they believe they are taking a harmful substance.

> In one nocebo study, patients were given sugar water and told it was an emetic. Eighty percent vomited. In another, asthmatic patients inhaled saline spray thinking it was an irritant. Many had breathing problems and asthma attacks. Many recovered when researchers gave them the same spray again, this time telling them it was a bronchodilator.[85]

Both placebos and nocebos work only if the patient believes they will work. If patients are told that they are receiving a sugar pill, nothing happens. So whatever effect placebos have seems to be due to the mind.

Cognitive behavior theory seems to provide yet more evidence for the effect of the mind on the body. People suffering from obsessive-compulsive disorder (OCD) often engage in repetitive behaviors like washing their hands many times a day. They are also often afflicted with unwanted thoughts of a violent or sexual nature that repeatedly intrude into their consciousness. These patients can sometimes be successfully treated with serotonin reuptake inhibitors like Prozac. Dr. Lewis Baxter at the UCLA School of Medicine did a comparative study of the effectiveness of traditional drug therapy with that of cognitive behavioral therapy. In cognitive behavioral therapy, patients are told to use self-instructions like "That's not me, that's a part of my brain that's not working" whenever they started to feel the urge to engage in the unwanted behavior. Baxter found that not only were these self-instructions as effective as the drugs, but brain scans showed that the changes in the brain caused by the self-instructions were virtually the same as those caused by taking drugs.[86]

These studies suggest that the view that the mind can affect the body is not just an outdated piece of folk psychology. On the contrary, mental states

An Emergent God?

Emergent properties such as consciousness and self-consciousness may be able to emerge from things other than nerve cells. If the right sorts of computer chips are interrelated in the right sorts of ways, for example, consciousness or self-consciousness may emerge from them. Property dualism is open to the possibility of artificial as well as alien intelligence.

Interestingly, there are about as many nerve cells in our brains as there are stars in the Milky Way galaxy: 100 billion. Could the Milky Way—or the entire universe—be the brain of some cosmic intelligence? Some believe so. Physicist and theologian Arthur Peacocke, for example, argues not only that the universe itself may be self-conscious but that this cosmic consciousness may affect what goes on in the universe through downward causation. He writes,

> . . . the processes of the natural world displayed certain tendencies, some of them strong enough to be called propensities in the sense that Karl Popper has again recently brought to our notice. These include *propensities* for an increase in complexity which is the basis for an increase in organization in living organisms, itself the basis

for the emergence of consciousness and so of self-consciousness. . . .

In the light of these features of the natural world, might we not properly regard the world-as-a-whole as a total system so that its general state can be a 'top-down' causative factor in, or constraint upon, what goes on at the myriad levels that comprise it? I suggest that these new perceptions of the way in which causality actually operates in our hierarchically complex world provides a new resource for thinking about how God could interact with that world.[87]

Thought Probe

Pan-en-theism

Peacocke calls his view "pan-en-theism" because although God depends on the world (in the way that thoughts depend on the brain), he is more than the world (in the way that thoughts are not reducible to physical states). Is Peacocke's conception of God plausible? Do you think that we are living inside God's brain or body? Why or why not?

---

appear to have tangible physical effects, even in the controlled environment of a scientific laboratory. In the absence of a purely physiological account of these phenomena, mental causation must be considered a live option.

To accept the existence of downward causation is to deny that all human behavior can be explained in purely materialist terms. If mental states can affect brain states, they must be taken into account in any comprehensive explanation of the workings of the brain.

The advantage of viewing mental properties as causally effective is that it not only solves the mind-body problem, but it also opens up new lines of research:

> Whereas the older interpretations of consciousness as inner aspect, epiphenomenon, or semantic pseudoproblem have remained largely sterile, conceptually and experimentally (e.g., there is no place to go from an epiphenomenon), the emergent interaction scheme is by contrast potentially fruitful. It suggests new problems, possible approaches, and new leads to follow in working out the nature of the mental properties, their interactions, and their relations to the sustaining neurophysiology. For example, it follows directly from the foregoing that the brain process must be able to detect and to react to the pattern properties of its own excitation. . . . There exists considerable indirect evidence, particularly from

Consider the implications for the mind-body problem of this astonishing technological advance:

> Severely disabled people who cannot operate a motorised wheelchair may one day get their independence, thanks to a system that lets them steer a wheelchair using only their thoughts.

> Unlike previous thought-communication devices, the system does not use surgical implants. Instead a skullcap peppered with electrodes monitors the electrical activity of its wearer's brain. Early trials using a steerable robot indicate that with just two days training it is as easy to control the robot with the human mind as it is manually.

> "It's a very positive step," says Paul Smith, executive director of The Spinal Injuries Association in London. "The psychological benefits it would offer are huge." The current options to give freedom of movement to people who are quadriplegic are limited, says Smith. For example, it is possible to steer a wheelchair using a chin-operated joystick or by blowing into a thin tube. But both options can be exhausting—and they are not suitable for those with very limited movement.

> So José Millán at the Dalle Molle Institute for Perceptual Artificial Intelligence in Martigny, Switzerland, along with researchers from the Swiss Federal Institute of Technology in Lausanne and the Centre for Biomedical Engineering Research in Barcelona, Spain, has come up with a system that can reliably recognise different mental states.

> If all goes according to plan, it will be the first mind-controlled system able to operate something as complicated as a wheelchair, says Millán.

> At the moment the system controls a simple wheeled robot. The user dons the electrode-lined skullcap, which monitors electrical activity on the surface of the head. A web of wires sends the information to a computer. Millán's software then analyses the brain's activity and, using a wireless link, passes on any commands it spots to the robot. At the moment the user can choose between three different commands: for example, "turn left", "turn right" and "move forward". Millán's software exploits the fact that the desire to move in a particular direction will generate a unique pattern of brain activity. It can tell which command the user is thinking of by spotting the telltale pattern of brain activity associated with that command.[89]

Thought Probe

Mind Control

Does this innovation in "mind control" show that downward causation is a reality? How might a property dualist answer this question? How about an identity theorist?

observations on perceptual and cognitive phenomena, that the brain does in fact do exactly this.[88]

Reductive and eliminative theories of the mind have failed to capture the essence of the mental. Property dualism, on the other hand, provides a framework for understanding the mind that takes into account both the qualitative and intentional content of mental states. By taking the mind to be a cause as well as an effect, it avoids the incongruity of epiphenomenalism and makes possible a coherent account of human freedom and dignity.

How we treat each other—and how we organize society—is determined by our view of ourselves. If mental states are not causes—if what we think has no effect on what we do—then reality is very different from the way it appears. As philosopher Jerry Fodor notes,

. . . if it isn't literally true that my wanting is causally responsible for my reaching, and my itching is causally responsible for my scratching, and my believing is causally responsible for my saying, . . . if none of that is literally true, then practically everything I believe about anything is false and it's the end of the world.[90]

To determine whether we need to radically restructure our worldview, then, we need to determine whether the belief in downward causation—commonly known as free will—is justified. This is the subject of the next chapter.

Summary

The failure to reduce mental states to physical or functional states can't be explained on the hypothesis that mental states don't exist. The best explanation seems to be that mental states have both physical and nonphysical properties. This view, known as property dualism, holds that consciousness emerges when certain nonconscious things like neurons interact in certain ways.

But why would mental properties emerge from physical properties? What survival advantage do they confer on their possessors? Their main advantage seems to be that they provide an effective representation of the world. Sensations represent, or refer to, the world—but not by means of any physical or functional property they possess. They simply represent the world. Thus intentionality is a primitive property.

Mental states may have a causal effect on the physical states that give rise to them. Such a view doesn't deny that physically identical brains are also psychologically identical. It does deny that the person's subsequent mental or physical states can be predicted or explained on the basis of physical properties alone. This view of mental properties offers an attractive way to solve the mind-body problem. It also opens up new lines of research. By taking consciousness to be a cause as well as an effect, property dualism avoids the problem of epiphenomenalism and makes possible a coherent account of freedom and dignity.

Study Questions

1. According to property dualism, what is it to be in a mental state?
2. What is a primitive property?
3. What is Jacquette's intentionality test?
4. Why is intentionality a primitive property?
5. What is downward causation?

Discussion Questions

1. Is property dualism a more adequate theory of the mind than eliminative materialism or the reductive theories? Why or why not?
2. What is the purpose of consciousness? That is, why did consciousness evolve?

3. Could a being with no conscious experience — a zombie — do everything that we can do?

4. If mental properties are nonphysical, can there be a science of the mind? Why or why not?

5. Is there such a thing as downward causation? If not, would we have to restructure society to reflect that fact?

6. A placebo is an inactive substance often given to subjects as a control in medical experiments. Although placebos have no medicinal value, in about 30 percent of the cases patients show some improvement after having been given one. Is this evidence of downward mental causation? Why or why not?

7. Could the Milky Way galaxy be the brain of an intelligent creature? Is the claim that it is the brain of an intelligent creature a plausible one? Why or why not?

Meditations on First Philosophy: Meditation II

René Descartes (1596–1650), often regarded as the founder of modern philosophy, was also one of the central figures in the scientific revolution of the seventeenth century. As a young man, he served in three different armies before retiring to Holland in 1628. There, for the next twenty years, he wrote extensively on science and philosophy, including such works as *The Quest for Truth*, *Rules for the Direction of Mind*, *Discourse on Method*, *Meditations on First Philosophy*, and *Principles of Philosophy*. He suppressed his first work, *The World*, because he heard that Galileo had been condemned by the Roman Catholic Church for advocating the Copernican hypothesis. In this selection from *Meditations on First Philosophy*, Descartes presents his reasons for believing that the mind and body are two separate substances.

Meditations on the First Philosophy in Which the Existence of God and the Distinction between Mind and Body Are Demonstrated.

Meditation II.

Of the Nature of the Human Mind; and that it is more easily known than the Body.

The Meditation of yesterday filled my mind with so many doubts that it is no longer in my power to forget them. And yet I do not see in what manner I can resolve them; and, just as if I had all of a sudden fallen into very deep water, I am so disconcerted that I can neither make certain of setting my feet on the bottom, nor can I swim and so support myself on the surface. I shall nevertheless make an effort and follow anew the same path as that on which I yesterday entered, i.e. I shall proceed by setting aside all that in which the least doubt could be supposed to exist, just as if I had discovered that it was absolutely false; and I shall ever follow in this road until I have met with something which is certain, or at least, if I can do nothing else, until I have learned for certain that there is nothing in the world that is certain. Archimedes, in order that he might draw the terrestrial globe out of its place, and transport it elsewhere, demanded only that one point should be fixed and immoveable; in the same way I shall have the right to conceive high hopes if I am happy enough to discover one thing only which is certain and indubitable.

I suppose, then, that all the things that I see are false; I persuade myself that nothing has ever existed of all that my fallacious memory represents to me. I consider that I possess no senses; I imagine that body, figure, extension, movement and place are but the fictions of my mind. What, then, can be esteemed as true? Perhaps nothing at all, unless that there is nothing in the world that is certain.

But how can I know there is not something different from those things that I have just considered, of which one cannot have the slightest doubt? Is there not some God, or some other being by whatever name we call it, who puts these reflections into my mind? That is not necessary, for is it not possible that I am capable of producing them myself? I myself, am I not at least something? But I have already denied that I had senses and body. Yet I hesitate, for what follows from that? Am I so dependent on body and senses that I cannot exist without these? But I was persuaded that there was nothing in all the world, that there was no heaven, no earth, that there were no minds, nor any bodies: was I not then likewise persuaded that I did not exist? Not at all; of a surety I myself did exist since I persuaded myself of something [or merely because I thought of something]. But there is some deceiver or other, very powerful and very cunning, who ever employs his ingenuity in deceiving me. Then without doubt I exist also if he deceives me, and let him deceive me as much as he will, he can never cause me to be nothing so long as I think that I am something. So that after having reflected well and carefully examined all things, we must come to the definite conclusion that this proposition: I am, I exist,

From: René Descartes, *The Philosophical Works of Descartes*, ed. Elizabeth S. Haldane and G. R. T. Ross (Cambridge: Cambridge University Press, 1931) 144–157. Used with permission of the publisher. Notes have been omitted.

is necessarily true each time that I pronounce it, or that I mentally conceive it.

But I do not yet know clearly enough what I am, I who am certain that I am; and hence I must be careful to see that I do not imprudently take some other object in place of myself, and thus that I do not go astray in respect of this knowledge that I hold to be the most certain and most evident of all that I have formerly learned. That is why I shall now consider anew what I believed myself to be before I embarked upon these last reflections; and of my former opinions I shall withdraw all that might even in a small degree be invalidated by the reasons which I have just brought forward, in order that there may be nothing at all left beyond what is absolutely certain and indubitable.

What then did I formerly believe myself to be? Undoubtedly I believed myself to be a man. But what is a man? Shall I say a reasonable animal? Certainly not; for then I should have to inquire what an animal is, and what is reasonable; and thus from a single question I should insensibly fall into an infinitude of others more difficult; and I should not wish to waste the little time and leisure remaining to me in trying to unravel subtleties like these. But I shall rather stop here to consider the thoughts which of themselves spring up in my mind, and which were not inspired by anything beyond my own nature alone when I applied myself to the consideration of my being. In the first place, then, I considered myself as having a face, hands, arms, and all that system of members composed of bones and flesh as seen in a corpse which I designated by the name of body. In addition to this I considered that I was nourished, that I walked, that I felt, and that I thought, and I referred all these actions to the soul: but I did not stop to consider what the soul was, or if I did stop, I imagined that it was something extremely rare and subtle like a wind, a flame, or an ether, which was spread throughout my grosser parts. As to body I had no manner of doubt about its nature, but thought I had a very clear knowledge of it; and if I had desired to explain it according to the notions that I had then formed of it, I should have described it thus: By the body I understand all that which can be defined by a certain figure: something which can be confined in a certain place, and which can fill a given space in such a way that every other body will be excluded from it; which can be perceived either by touch, or by sight, or by hearing, or by taste, or by smell: which can be moved in many ways not, in truth, by itself, but by something which is foreign to it, by which it is touched [and from which it receives impressions]: for to have the power of self-movement, as also of feeling or of thinking, I did not consider to ap-

pertain to the nature of body: on the contrary, I was rather astonished to find that faculties similar to them existed in some bodies.

But what am I, now that I suppose that there is a certain genius which is extremely powerful, and, if I may say so, malicious, who employs all his powers in deceiving me? Can I affirm that I possess the least of all those things which I have just said pertain to the nature of body? I pause to consider, I revolve all these things in my mind, and I find none of which I can say that it pertains to me. It would be tedious to stop and enumerate them. Let us pass to the attributes of soul and see if there is any one which is in me? What of nutrition or walking [the first mentioned]? But if it is so that I have no body, it is also true that I can neither walk nor take nourishment. Another attribute is sensation. But one cannot feel without body, and besides I have thought I perceived many things during sleep that I recognised in my waking moments as not having been experienced at all. What of thinking? I find here that thought is an attribute that belongs to me; it alone cannot be separated from me. I am, I exist, that is certain. But how often? Just when I think; for it might possibly be the case if I ceased entirely to think, that I should likewise cease altogether to exist. I do not now admit anything which is not necessarily true: to speak accurately I am not more than a thing which thinks, that is to say a mind or a soul, or an understanding, or a reason, which are terms whose significance was formerly unknown to me. I am, however, a real thing and really exist; but what thing? I have answered: a thing which thinks.

And what more? I shall exercise my imagination [in order to see if I am not something more]. I am not a collection of members which we call the human body: I am not a subtle air distributed through these members, I am not a wind, a fire, a vapour, a breath, nor anything at all which I can imagine or conceive; because I have assumed that all these were nothing. Without changing that supposition I find that I only leave myself certain of the fact that I am somewhat. But perhaps it is true that these same things which I supposed were non-existent because they are unknown to me, are really not different from the self which I know. I am not sure about this, I shall not dispute about it now; I can only give judgment on things that are known to me. I know that I exist, and I inquire what I am, I whom I know to exist. But it is very certain that the knowledge of my existence taken in its precise significance does not depend on things whose existence is not yet known to me; consequently it does not depend on those which I can feign in imagination. And indeed the very term *feign* in imagination proves to me my error, for I really do this if I image myself a something, since to imagine is nothing else than to contemplate the figure or image of a corporeal thing. But I already know for certain that I am, and that it may be that all these images, and, speaking generally, all things that relate to the nature of body are nothing but dreams [and chimeras]. For this reason I see clearly that I have as little reason to say, 'I shall stimulate my imagination in order to know more distinctly what I am,' than if I were to say, 'I am now awake, and I perceive somewhat that is real and true: but because I do not yet perceive it distinctly enough, I shall go to sleep of express purpose, so that my dreams may represent the perception with greatest truth and evidence.' And, thus, I know for certain that nothing of all that I can understand by means of my imagination belongs to this knowledge which I have of myself, and that it is necessary to recall the mind from this mode of thought with the utmost diligence in order that it may be able to know its own nature with perfect distinctness.

But what then am I? A thing which thinks. What is a thing which thinks? It is a thing which doubts, understands, [conceives], affirms, denies, wills, refuses, which also imagines and feels.

Certainly it is no small matter if all these things pertain to my nature. But why should they not so pertain? Am I not that being who now doubts nearly everything, who nevertheless understands certain things, who affirms that one only is true, who denies all the others, who desires to know more, is averse from being deceived, who imagines many things, sometimes indeed despite his will, and who perceives many likewise, as by the intervention of the bodily organs? Is there nothing in all this which is as true as it is certain that I exist, even though I should always sleep and though he who has given me being employed all his ingenuity in deceiving me? Is there likewise any one of these attributes which can be distinguished from my thought, or which might be said to be separated from myself? For it is so evident of itself that it is I who doubts, who understands, and who desires, that there is no reason here to add anything to explain it. And I have certainly the power of imagining likewise; for although it may happen (as I formerly supposed) that none of the things which I imagine are true, nevertheless this power of imagining does not cease to be really in use, and it forms part of my thought. Finally, I am the same who feels, that is to say, who perceives certain things, as by the organs of sense, since in truth I see light, I hear noise, I feel heat. But it will be said that these phenomena are false and that I am dreaming. Let it be so; still it

is at least quite certain that it seems to me that I see light, that I hear noise and that I feel heat. That cannot be false; properly speaking it is what is in me called feeling; and used in this precise sense that is no other thing than thinking.

From this time I began to know what I am with a little more clearness and distinction than before; but nevertheless it still seems to me, and I cannot prevent myself from thinking, that corporeal things, whose images are framed by thought, which are tested by the senses, are much more distinctly known than that obscure part of me which does not come under the imagination. Although really it is very strange to say that I know and understand more distinctly these things whose existence seems to me dubious, which are unknown to me, and which do not belong to me, than others of the truth of which I am convinced, which are known to me and which pertain to my real nature, in a word, than myself. But I see clearly how the case stands: my mind loves to wander, and cannot yet suffer itself to be retained within the just limits of truth. Very good, let us once more give it the freest rein, so that, when afterwards we seize the proper occasion for pulling up, it may the more easily be regulated and controlled.

Let us begin by considering the commonest matters, those which we believe to be the most distinctly comprehended, to wit, the bodies which we touch and see; not indeed bodies in general, for these general ideas are usually a little more confused, but let us consider one body in particular. Let us take, for example, this piece of wax: it has been taken quite freshly from the hive, and it has not yet lost the sweetness of the honey which it contains; it still retains somewhat of the odour of the flowers from which it has been culled; its colour, its figure, its size are apparent; it is hard, cold, easily handled, and if you strike it with the finger, it will emit a sound. Finally all the things which are requisite to cause us distinctly to recognise a body, are met with in it. But notice that while I speak and approach the fire what remained of the taste is exhaled, the smell evaporates, the colour alters, the figure is destroyed, the size increases, it becomes liquid, it heats, scarcely can one handle it, and when one strikes it, no sound is emitted. Does the same wax remain after this change? We must confess that it remains; none would judge otherwise. What then did I know so distinctly in this piece of wax? It could certainly be nothing of all that the senses brought to my notice, since all these things which fall under taste, smell, sight, touch, and hearing, are found to be changed, and yet the same wax remains.

Perhaps it was what I now think, viz. that this wax was not that sweetness of honey, nor that agreeable scent of flowers, nor that particular whiteness, nor that figure, nor that sound, but simply a body which a little while before appeared to me as perceptible under these forms, and which is now perceptible under others. But what, precisely, is it that I imagine when I form such conceptions? Let us attentively consider this, and, abstracting from all that does not belong to the wax, let us see what remains. Certainly nothing remains excepting a certain extended thing which is flexible and movable. But what is the meaning of flexible and movable? Is it not that I imagine that this piece of wax being round is capable of becoming square and of passing from a square to a triangular figure? No, certainly it is not that, since I imagine it admits of an infinitude of similar changes, and I nevertheless do not know how to compass the infinitude of my imagination, and consequently this conception which I have of the wax is not brought about by the faculty of imagination. What now is this extension? Is it not also unknown? For it becomes greater when the wax is melted, greater when it is boiled, and greater still when the heat increases; and I should not conceive [clearly] according to truth what wax is, if I did not think that even this piece that we are considering is capable of receiving more variations in extension than I have ever imagined. We must then grant that I could not even understand through the imagination what this piece of wax is, and that it is my mind alone which perceives it. I say this piece of wax in particular, for as to wax in general it is yet clearer. But what is this piece of wax which cannot be understood excepting by the mind? It is certainly the same that I see, touch, imagine, and finally it is the same which I have always believed it to be from the beginning. But what must particularly be observed is that its perception is neither an act of vision, nor of touch, nor of imagination, and has never been such although it may have appeared formerly to be so, but only an intuition of the mind, which may be imperfect and confused as it was formerly, or clear and distinct as it is at present, according as my attention is more or less directed to the elements which are found in it, and of which it is composed.

Yet in the meantime I am greatly astonished when I consider [the great feebleness of mind] and its proneness to fall [insensibly] into error; for although without giving expression to my thoughts I consider all this in my own mind, words often impede me and I am almost deceived by the terms of ordinary language. For we say that we see the same wax, if it is present, and not that we simply judge that it is the same from its having the same colour and figure. From this I should conclude that I knew the wax by means of vision and not simply by the intuition of the mind; unless by chance I remember that, when looking from a window and saying I see men who pass in the street, I really do not see them, but infer that what I see is men, just as I say that I see wax. And yet what do I see from the window but hats and coats which may cover automatic machines? Yet I judge these to be men. And similarly solely by the faculty of judgment which rests in my mind, I comprehend that which I believed I saw with my eyes.

A man who makes it his aim to raise his knowledge above the common should be ashamed to derive the occasion for doubting from the forms of speech invented by the vulgar; I prefer to pass on and consider whether I had a more evident and perfect conception of what the wax was when I first perceived it, and when I believed I knew it by means of the external senses or at least by the common sense as it is called, that is to say by the imaginative faculty, or whether my present conception is clearer now that I have most carefully examined what it is, and in what way it can be known. It would certainly be absurd to doubt as to this. For what was there in this first perception which was distinct? What was there which might not as well have been perceived by any of the animals? But when I distinguish the wax from its external forms, and when, just as if I had taken from it its vestments, I consider it quite naked, it is certain that although some error may still be found in my judgment, I can nevertheless not perceive it thus without a human mind.

But finally what shall I say of this mind, that is, of myself, for up to this point I do not admit in myself anything but mind? What then, I who seem to perceive this piece of wax so distinctly, do I not know myself, not only with much more truth and certainty, but also with much more distinctness and clearness? For if I judge that the wax is or exists from the fact that I see it, it certainly follows much more clearly that I am or that I exist myself from the fact that I see it. For it may be that what I see is not really wax, it may also be that I do not possess eyes with which to see anything; but it cannot be that when I see, or (for I no longer take account of the distinction) when I think I see, that I myself who think am nought. So if I judge that the wax exists from the fact that I touch it, the same thing will follow, to wit, that I am; and if I judge that my imagination, or some other cause, whatever it is, persuades me that the wax exists, I shall still conclude the same. And what I have here remarked of wax may be applied to all other things which are external to me [and which are met with outside of me]. And further, if the [notion or] perception of wax has seemed to me clearer and more distinct, not only after the sight or the touch, but also after many other causes have rendered it quite manifest to me, with how much more [evidence] and distinctness must it be said that I now know myself, since all the reasons which contribute to the knowledge of wax, or any other body whatever, are yet better proofs of the nature of my mind! And there are so many other things in the mind itself which may contribute to the elucidation of its nature, that those which depend on body such as these just mentioned, hardly merit being taken into account.

But finally here I am, having insensibly reverted to the point I desired, for, since it is now manifest to me that even bodies are not properly speaking known by the senses or by the faculty of imagination, but by the understanding only, and since they are not known from the fact that they are seen or touched, but only because they are understood, I see clearly that there is nothing which is easier for me to know than my mind. But because it is difficult to rid oneself so promptly of an opinion to which one was accustomed for so long, it will be well that I should halt a little at this point, so that by the length of my meditation I may more deeply imprint on my memory this new knowledge.

Materialism vs. Dualism

Richard Taylor (1919–2003) taught philosophy at Brown University, Columbia University, and the University of Rochester. He published widely in the areas of both metaphysics and ethics, including books titled *Metaphysics; Action and Purpose; Good and Evil: A New Direction;* and *Freedom, Anarchy, and the Law.* In this selection, Taylor explores the pros and cons of materialism and dualism.

Sometimes the simplest and most obvious distinctions give rise to the profoundest intellectual difficulties, and things most commonplace in our daily experience drive home to us the depths of our ignorance. Men have fairly well fathomed the heavens, so that perhaps nothing counts as surer knowledge than astronomy, the science of the things most distant from us, and yet the grass at our feet presents impenetrable mysteries. In like manner, our knowledge of man, of human history, of cultures remote in time and distance, fills volumes, and yet each of us is bewildered by that one being that is closest to him, namely, himself, as soon as he asks the most elementary questions. And oddly, it seems that the simplest question one can ask about himself the question namely, What am I? is the very hardest to answer, and nonetheless the most important. One can ask of many other things, including some very complex ones—such as a tree, a drop of water, or a machine—just what they are, and be quite certain that his answers, though incomplete, are nonetheless not wholly wrong. But when one asks what he himself is, what he is in his innermost nature; when he asks what is that "I" with which he is so intimately concerned and which is for him the very center of the universe, then he is bewildered, and must fall back on philosophical speculations of the most difficult sort.

It is, moreover, this simple and basic question that has the greatest philosophical ramifications. All morals, religion, metaphysics, and law turn upon it. Law and morality, for example, presuppose the existence of moral agents who have responsibilities and are capable of incurring guilt. But obviously, certain kinds of things can have responsibilities, and certain others cannot; and if men are in fact beings of the latter kind, then morality and law, as traditionally conceived, are nonsense. Again, many religions presuppose that men are spiritual beings, capable of surviving the destruction of their bodies in death. If a man is in fact nothing of the

sort, then those religions rest upon a misconception. It is thus imperative that we try to find some answer to this basic and simple question. . . .

The Reality of the Self and the Body

However unsure I may be of the nature of myself and of the relation of myself to my body, I can hardly doubt the reality of either. Whether I am identical with my body, or whether I am a spirit, or soul, or perhaps only a collection of thoughts and feelings—whatever I am, I cannot doubt my own being, cannot doubt that I am part of the world, even prior to any philosophical reflection on the matter. For surely if I know anything at all, as presumably I do, then I know that I exist. There seems to be nothing I could possibly know any better. And this is, of course, quite consistent with my great ignorance as to the nature of that self of whose existence I feel so assured.

I know, further, that I have a body. I may have learned this from experience, in the same way that I have learned of the existence of innumerable other things, or I may not have; it is, in any case, something I surely know. I may also have only the vaguest conception, or even a totally erroneous one, of the relationship between myself and my body; I can nevertheless no more doubt the reality of the one than the other. I may also be, as I surely am, quite ignorant of the nature and workings of my body and even of many of its parts, but no such ignorance raises the slightest doubt of its reality.

Now what is the connection between these, between myself and my body? Just what relationship am I affirming by "have," when I say with such confidence

From: Richard R. Taylor, *Metaphysics* (Englewood Cliffs, NJ: Prentice-Hall, 1963) 5–29.

that I have a body? Abstractly, there seem to be just three general possibilities. In the first place, my having a body might consist simply in the *identity* of myself with my body, or of my *being* a body. Or second, it might amount to *possession*, such that my having a body consists essentially in this body's being among the various other things that I own or possess, it being at the same time, perhaps, in some way unique among these. Or finally, there may be some special, perhaps highly metaphysical relationship between the two, such as that I as a person am one thing, my body another quite different thing, the two being somehow connected to each other in a special way, appropriately expressed by the assertion that the one has the other.

Now there are great difficulties in all these suggestions, and, under the third, numerous special theories are possible, as we shall see. We had best, however, begin with the simplest view, to see then whether any of the others are any better.

Materialism

I know that I have a body, and that this is a material thing, though a somewhat unusual and highly complicated one. There would, in fact, be no other reason for calling it my body, except to affirm that it is entirely material, for nothing that is not matter could possibly be a part of my body. Now if my having a body consists simply in the identity of myself with my body, then it follows that I *am* a body, and nothing more. Nor would the affirmation of the identity of myself with my body be at all inconsistent with saying that I have a body, for we often express the relationship of identity in just this way. Thus, one might correctly say of a table that it *has* four legs and a top, or of a bicycle that it *has* two wheels, a frame, a seat, and handle bars. In such cases, no one would suppose that the table or the bicycle is one thing, and its parts or "body" another, the two being somehow mysteriously connected. The table or the bicycle just is its parts, suitably related. So likewise, I might just be the totality of my bodily parts, suitably related and all functioning together in the manner expressed by saying that I am a living body, or a living, material animal organism.

This materialistic conception of a person has the great advantage of simplicity. We do know that there are bodies, that there are living animal bodies, and that some of these are in common speech denominated men. A person is, then, on the view, nothing mysterious or metaphysical, at least as regards the *kind* of thing he is.

A consequence of this simplicity is that we need not speculate upon the relationship between one's body and his mind, or ask how the two are connected, or how one can act upon the other, all such questions being rendered senseless within the framework of this view, which in the first place denies that we are dealing with two things. The death of the animal organism—which is, of course, an empirical fact and not subject to speculation—will, moreover, be equivalent to the destruction of the person, consisting simply in the cessation of those functions which together constitute being alive. Hence, the fate of a person is simply, on this view, the fate of his body, which is ultimately a return to the dust whence he sprang. This alleged identity of oneself with his body accounts, moreover, for the solicitude every man has for his body, and for its health and well-being. If a person is identical with his body then any threat to the latter is a threat to himself, and he must view the destruction of it as the destruction of himself. And such, in fact, does seem to be the attitude of all men, whatever may be their philosophical or religious opinions. Again, the distinction that every man draws between himself and other persons, or himself and other things, need be no more than the distinction between one body and others. When I declare that some foreign object—a doorknob, for instance, or a shoe—is no part of myself, I may be merely making the point that it is no part of my body. I would, surely, be more hesitant in declaring that my hand, or my brain and nervous system, which are physical objects, are no parts of me.

Such a conception has nevertheless always presented enormous difficulties, and these have seemed so grave to most philosophers that almost any theory, however absurd when examined closely, has at one time or another seemed to them preferable to materialism. Indeed, the difficulties of materialism are so grave that, for some persons, they need only to be mentioned to render the theory unworthy of discussion.

The Meaning of "Identity"

By "identity" the materialist must mean a strict and total identity of himself and his body, nothing less. Now to say of anything, X, and anything, Y, that X and Y are identical, or that they are really one and the same thing, one must be willing to assert of X anything whatever that he asserts of Y, and vice versa. This is simply a consequence of their identity, for if there is anything whatever that can be truly asserted of any object X, but cannot be truly asserted of some object Y, then it logically follows that X and Y are two different things, and not the same thing. In saying, for instance, that the British wartime prime minister and Winston Churchill are one and the same person, one commits himself to saying of either whatever he is willing to say of the other — such as, that he lived to a great age, smoked cigars, was a resolute leader, was born at Blenheim, and so on. If there were any statement whatever that was true of, say, Mr. Churchill, but not true of the wartime prime minister, then it would follow that Mr. Churchill was not the wartime prime minister, that we are here referring to two different men, and not one.

The question can now be asked, then, whether there is anything true of me that is not true of my body, and vice versa. There are, of course, ever so many things that can be asserted indifferently of both me and my body without absurdity. For instance, we can say that I was born at such and such place and time, and it is not the least odd to say this of my body as well. Or we can say that my body now weighs exactly so many pounds, and it would be just as correct to give this as my weight; and so on.

But now consider more problematical assertions. It might, for instance, be true of me at a certain time that I am morally blameworthy or praiseworthy. Can we then say that my body or some part of it, such as my brain, is in exactly the same sense blameworthy or praiseworthy? Can moral predicates be applied without gross incongruity to any physical object at all? Or suppose I have some profound wish or desire, or some thought — the desire, say, to be in some foreign land at a given moment, or thoughts of the Homeric gods. It seems at least odd to assert that my body, or some part of it, wishes that it were elsewhere, or has thoughts of the gods. How, indeed, can any purely physical state of any purely physical object ever be a state that is *for* something, or *of* something, in the way that my desires and thoughts are such? And how, in particular, could a purely physical state be in this sense *for* or *of* something that is not real? Or again, suppose that I am religious, and can truly say that I love God and neighbor, for instance. Can I without absurdity say that my body or some part of it, such as my foot or brain, is religious, and loves God and neighbor? Or can one suppose that my being religious, or having such love, consists simply in my body's being in a certain state, or behaving in a certain way? If I claim the identity of myself with my body, I must say all these odd things; that is, I must be willing to assert of my body, or some part of it, everything I assert of myself. There is perhaps no logical absurdity or clear falsity in speaking thus of one's corporeal frame, but such assertions as these are at least strange, and it can be questioned whether, as applied to the body, they are even still meaningful.

The disparity between bodily and personal predicates becomes even more apparent, however, if we consider epistemological predicates, involved in statements about belief and knowledge. Thus, if I believe something — believe, for instance, that today is February 31 — then I am in a certain state; the state, namely, of having a certain belief which is in this case necessarily a false one. Now how can a physical state of any physical object be identical with that? And how, in particular, can anything be a *false* physical state of an object? The physical states of things, it would seem, just *are*, and one cannot even think of anything that could ever distinguish one such state from another as being either true or false. A physiologist might give a complete physical description of a brain and nervous system at a particular time, but he could never distinguish some of those states as true and others as false, nor would he have any idea what to look for if he were asked to do this. At least, so it would certainly seem.

Platonic Dualism

It is this sort of reflection that has always led metaphysicians and theologians to distinguish radically between the mind or soul of a man and his body, ascribing properties to the mind that are utterly different in kind from those exhibited by the body; properties which, it is supposed, could not be possessed by any body, just because of its nature as a physical object.

The simplest and most radical of such views *identifies* the person or self with a soul or mind, and declares its relationship to the body to be the almost accidental one of mere occupancy, possession, or use. Thus Plato, and many mystical philosophers before and after him, thought of the body as a veritable prison of the soul, a gross thing of clay from which the soul one day gladly escapes, to live its own independent and untrammeled existence, much as a bird flees its cage or a snake sheds its skin. A person, thus conceived, is a non-material substance — a *spirit*, in the strictest sense — related to an animal body as possessor to thing possessed, tenant to abode, or user to thing used. A person *has* a body only in the sense that he, perhaps temporarily, occupies, owns, or uses a body, being all the while something quite distinct from it and having, perhaps, a destiny quite different from the melancholy one that is known sooner or later to overtake the corporeal frame.

This dualism of mind and body has been, and always is, firmly received by millions of unthinking men, partly because it is congenial to the religious framework in which their everyday metaphysical opinions are formed, and partly, no doubt, because every man wishes to think of himself as something more than just one more item of matter in the world. Wise philosophers, too, speak easily of the attributes of the mind as distinct from those of the body, thereby sundering the two once and for all. Some form of dualism seems in fact indicated by the metaphysical, moral, and epistemological difficulties of materialism which are, it must be confessed, formidable indeed.

But whatever difficulties such simple dualism may resolve, it appears to raise others equally grave. For one thing, it is not nearly as simple as it seems. Whatever a partisan of such a view might say of the simplicity of the mind or soul, a *man* is nonetheless, on this view, *two* quite disparate things, a mind and a body, having almost nothing in common and only the flimsiest connection with each other. This difficulty, once it is acutely felt, is usually minimized by conceiving of a man, in his true self as nothing but a mind, and representing his body as something ancillary to this true self, something that is not really any part of him at all but only one among the many physical objects that he happens to possess, use, or what not, much as he possesses and uses various other things in life. His body does, to be sure, occupy a preeminent place among such things, for it is something without which he would be quite helpless; but this renders it no more a part or whole of his true self or person than any other of the world's physical things.

Possession, however, is essentially a social concept, and sometimes a strictly legal one. Something counts as one of my possessions by virtue of my title to it, and this is something conferred by men, in accordance with conventions and laws fabricated by men themselves. Thus does a field or a building count as one of my possessions. But a certain animal body, which I identify as mine, is not mine in any sense such as this. My dominion over my body arises from no human conventions or laws, and is not alterable by them. The body of a slave, though it may be owned by another man in the fullest sense of ownership that is reflected in the idea of possession, is nevertheless the slave's body in a metaphysical sense in which it could not possibly be the body of his master. One has, moreover, a solicitude for his body wholly incommensurate with his concern for any treasure, however dear. The loss of the latter is regarded as no more than a loss, though perhaps a grave one, while the abolition of one's body cannot be regarded as the mere loss of something clearly held, but is contemplated by any man as an appalling and total calamity.

The ideas of occupancy or use do not express the relation of mind and body any better. *Occupancy*, for instance, is a physical concept; one thing occupies another by being in or upon it. But the mind, on this view, is no physical thing, and no sense can be attached to its resting within or upon any body; the conception is simply ridiculous. Nor does one simply use his body the way he uses implements and tools. One does, to be sure, sometimes use his limbs and other parts, over which he has voluntary control, in somewhat the manner in which he uses tools; but many of one's bodily parts, including some that are vital, the very existence of which may be unknown to him, are not within his control at all. They are nonetheless parts of his body. Artificial devices, too, like hearing aids, spectacles, and the like, do not in the least become parts of one's body merely by being used, even in the case of a man who can barely do without them. They are merely things worn or used. Nor can one say that one's body is that physical being in the world upon which one absolutely depends for his continuing life, for there are many such things. One depends on the sun, for instance, and the air he breathes; without these he would perish as certainly as if deprived of his heart; yet no one regards the sun or the air around him as any part of his body.

A man does not, then, have a body in the way in which he has anything else at all, and any comparison of the body to a material possession or instrument is about as misleading as likening it to a chamber in which one is more or less temporarily closeted. The connection between oneself and his body is far more intimate and metaphysical than anything else we can think of. One's body is at least a part of himself, and is so regarded by every man. Yet it is not merely a part, as the arm is part of the body; and we are so far without any hint of how the mind and the body are connected. . . .

Materialism Again

One thing should by now seem quite plain, however, and that is that the difficulties of simple materialism are not overcome by any form of dualism. There is, therefore, no point in recommending dualism as an improvement over materialism. To assert that a man is both body and mind—that is, that he is two things rather than one—not only does not remove any problem involved in saying that he is one thing only, namely, a body, but introduces all the problems of describing the connection between those two things. We are led to conclude, then, that a metaphysical understanding of human nature must be sought within the framework of materialism, according to which a man is entirely identical with his body.

All forms of dualism arise from the alleged disparity between persons and physical objects. Men, it is rightly noted, are capable of thinking, believing, feeling, wishing, and so on; but bodies, it is claimed, are capable of none of these things, and the conclusion is drawn that men are not bodies. Yet it cannot be denied that men *have* bodies; hence, it is decided that a man, or a person, is a nonphysical entity, somehow more or less intimately related to a body. But here it is rarely noted that whatever difficulties there may be in applying personal and psychological predicates and descriptions to bodies, precisely the same difficulties are involved in applying such predicates and descriptions to *anything whatever*, including spirits or souls. If, for example, a philosopher reasons that a body cannot think, and thereby affirms that, since a person thinks, a person is a soul or spirit or mind rather than a body, we are entitled to ask how a spirit can think. For surely, if a spirit or soul can think, we can affirm that a body can do so; and if we are then asked how a body can think, our reply can be that it thinks in precisely the manner in which the dualist supposes a soul thinks. The difficulty of imagining how a body thinks is not in the least lessened by asserting that something else, which is not a body, thinks. And so it is with every other personal predicate or description. Whenever faced with the dualist's challenge to explain how a body can have desires, wishes, how it can deliberate, choose, repent, how it can be intelligent or stupid, virtuous or wicked, and so on, our reply can always be: The body can do these things, and be these things, in whatever manner one imagines the soul can do these things and be these things. For to repeat, the difficulty here is in seeing how *anything at all* can deliberate, choose, repent, think, be virtuous or wicked, and so on, and *that* difficulty is not removed but simply glossed over by the invention of some new thing, henceforth to be called the "mind" or "soul."

It becomes quite obvious what is the source of dualistic metaphysics when the dualist or soul philosopher is pressed for some description of the mind or soul. The mind or soul, it turns out in such descriptions, is just whatever it is that thinks, reasons, deliberates, chooses, feels, and so on. But the fact with which we began was that *men* think, reason, deliberate, choose, feel, and so on. And we do in fact have some fairly clear notion of what we mean by a man, for we think of an individual man as a being existing in space and time, having a certain height and weight — as a being, in short, having many things in common with other objects in space

and time, and particularly with those that are living, i.e., with other animals. But the dualist, noting that a man is significantly different from other beings, insofar as he, unlike most of them, is capable of thinking, deliberating, choosing, and so on, suddenly asserts that it is not a man, as previously conceived, that does these things at all, but something else, namely, a mind or soul, or something that does not exist in space and time nor have any height and weight, nor have, in fact, any material properties at all. And then when we seek some understanding of what this mind or soul is, we find it simply described as a thing that thinks, deliberates, feels, and so on. But surely the proper inference should have been that men are like all other physical objects in some respects — e.g., in having size, mass, and location in space and time; that they are like some physical objects but unlike others in certain further respects — e.g., in being living, sentient, and so on; and like no other physical objects at all in still other respects — e.g., in being rational, deliberative, and so on. And of course none of this suggests that men are not physical objects, but rather that they are precisely physical objects, like other bodies in some ways, unlike many other bodies in other ways, and unlike any other bodies in still other respects.

The dualist or soul philosopher reasons that since men think, feel, desire, choose and so on, and since such things cannot be asserted of bodies, then men are not bodies. Reasoning in this fashion, we are forced to the conclusion that men are not bodies — though it is a stubborn fact that men nevertheless *have* bodies. So the great problem then is to connect men, now conceived as souls or minds, to their bodies. But philosophically, it is just exactly as good to reason that, since men think, feel, desire, choose, etc., and since men are bodies — i.e., are living, animal organisms having the essential material attributes of weight, size, and so on — then some bodies think, feel, desire, choose, etc. This argument is just as good as the dualist's argument and does not lead us into a morass of problems concerning the connection between soul and body.

The Source of Dualistic Theories

Why, then, does the dualist's argument have, and this one lack, such an initial plausibility? Why have so many philosophers been led into dualistic metaphysical views, on the basis of arguments apparently no stronger than other arguments having simpler conclusions but which are rarely even considered?

Part of the answer is perhaps that, when we form an idea of a *body* or a *physical object*, what is most likely to come to mind is not some man or animal but something much simpler, such as a stone or a marble. When we are then invited to consider whether a physical object might think, deliberate, choose, and the like, we are led to contemplate the evident absurdity of supposing things like *that* do such things, and thus we readily receive the claim that bodies cannot think, deliberate, choose, and the like, and the dualist extracts his conclusion. But suppose we began somewhat differently. Suppose we began with a consideration of two quite dissimilar physical objects—a living, animal body, of the kind commonly denominated "man," on the one hand, and a simple body, of the kind denominated "stone," on the other. Now let it be asked whether there is any absurdity in supposing that one of these things might be capable of thinking, deliberating, choosing, and the like. Here there is no absurdity at all in asserting that an object of the first kind might indeed have such capacities, but evidently not one of the second kind—from which we would conclude, not that men are not physical objects, but rather that they are physical objects which are significantly different from other physical objects, such as stones. And there is, of course, nothing the least astonishing in this.

But how, one may wonder, can a "mere physical object" have feelings? But here the answer should be: Why, if it is a physical object of a certain familiar kind, should it not have feelings? Suppose, for example, that it is a living body, like a frog or mouse, equipped with a complicated and living nervous system. Where is the absurdity in asserting that a "mere physical object" of this sort can feel? Evidently there is none. Hardly anyone would want to insist that beings of this sort—frogs and mice, for instance—must have souls to enable them to feel. It seems enough that they have complicated living nervous systems.

The same type of answer can be given if it is asked how a "mere physical object" can think. If we suppose that it is a physical object of a certain familiar kind, namely, a living body having the form and other visible attributes of a man, and possessed of an enormously complex living brain and nervous system—in short, that the object in question is a living human being—then there is no absurdity in supposing that this being thinks. Any argument purporting to show that such a being cannot think, and must therefore have a nonmaterial soul to do its thinking for it, would be just as good an argument to show that frogs and mice cannot feel, and must therefore have souls to do their feeling for them. The outcome of such philosophizing is just as good, and just as absurd, in the one case as it is in the other.

Now the materialist would, of course, like to maintain that psychological states, such as feeling, believing, desiring, and so on, are really nothing but perfectly *familiar kinds* of material states, that is, states of the body, particularly of the brain and nervous system; states that are either observable or testable by the usual methods of biology, physics, and chemistry. But this, as we have seen earlier, seems to be a vain hope, and will always be an obstacle to any simple materialism. There is always, it seems, something that can be asserted of certain psychological states which makes little if any sense when asserted of any ordinary or familiar state of matter. One can say of a belief, for instance, that it is true or false, but this can never be said, except metaphorically or derivatively, of any familiar state of matter, such as an arrangement of molecules; we could say of such a thing that it is true or false, only if we first assumed that it is identical with some belief that is such. Again, one can say of a desire that it is the desire *for* this or that—for instance, the desire for food; of a fear that it is a fear *of* something—for instance, a fear of heights; but of no familiar state of matter can it be said that it is, in the same sense, *for* or *of* anything. It just is the state of matter that it is. Suppose, for example, that the materialist should say that the feeling of hunger is simply *identical* with a certain familiar state of the body; not merely that it is prompted by that state but that it *is* that state, and is describable in terms of the concepts of physics and chemistry. Thus, let us suppose him to claim that hunger just is the state consisting of having an empty stomach, together with a deficiency of certain salts or other substances in the blood, and a certain physical disequilibrium of the nervous system consequent upon these conditions. Now there is, of course, no doubt an intimate connection between such states as these and the desire for food, but the assertion of their *identity* with that desire will always be plagued because, unlike the desire, those bodily states can be fully described without mentioning food at all, and without saying that they are in any sense states that are *for* food. Indeed, the notion of something being *for* or *of* something else, in the sense in which a desire may be a desire *for* food, or a fear may be a fear *of* heights, is not a concept of physics or chemistry at all. And yet it can surely be said of a certain desire that it is a desire for food, or of a certain fear that it is a fear of heights. The referential character of such states seems, indeed, essential to any proper description of them. Significantly, when those substances that are physiologically associated with such states are artificially administered to someone, in the effort to create within him those states themselves, the effort fails. It is fairly well known, for example, what physiological changes a man undergoes when he is in a state of fear; but when these changes are artificially evoked in him, he does not experience fear in the usual sense. He describes his state as being vaguely *like* fear, but finds that he is not afraid *of* anything.

But while psychological states are thus evidently not identical with any familiar bodily states, it does not follow that they are identical with no state of matter at all. They may, in fact, be unfamiliar states of matter, that is, states of the body that are not observable or testable by the ordinary methods of biology, physics, and chemistry. This suggestion is not as question-begging as it appears, for it is conceded by the most resolute soul philosophers and dualists that psychological states are strange ones in this respect at least, that they are not thus observable. From the fact that some state is unobservable by the usual methods of scientific observation, nothing whatever follows with respect to the truth or falsity of materialism. From the fact that a certain state is in some respect unusual it does not follow that it is a state of an unusual thing, of a soul rather than a body, but rather, that if it is a state of the body it is an unusual one, and if it is a state of the soul it is no less unusual. Nothing is made clearer, more comprehensible, or less strange by postulating some new substance as the subject of certain states not familiar to the natural sciences, and then baptizing that new substance "the mind" or "the soul." Nor does one avoid materialism at this point by saying that by the "mind" or "soul" we just *mean* that which is the subject of psychological states; for while that might indeed be true, it is nevertheless an open question whether what we thus mean by the "mind" or "soul" might not turn out, after all, to be what we ordinarily denominate "the body." The existence of nothing whatever can be derived from any definitions of terms. . . .

Conclusion

Of course we cannot, by these reflections, pretend to have solved the problems of mind and matter, nor to have proved any theory of materialism. Human nature is mysterious, and remains so, no matter what one's metaphysical theory is or how simple it is. It does nevertheless seem evident that no dualistic theory of man renders human nature any less mysterious, and that whatever questions are left unanswered by the materialist are left equally unanswered, though perhaps better concealed, by his opponents.

The Puzzle of Conscious Experience

David Chalmers (1966–) is associate professor of philosophy at the University of California at Santa Cruz. He received his B.A. in mathematics and computer science from the University of Adelaide and his Ph.D. in philosophy and cognitive science from Indiana University. His book *The Conscious Mind: In Search of a Fundamental Theory* was published by Oxford University Press in 1996. The MIT Press has recently published a collection of essays on his work, entitled *Explaining Consciousness: The Hard Problem*. In this selection, Chalmers uses a number of thought experiments to demonstrate the failure of reductive approaches to the mind.

Conscious experience is at once the most familiar thing in the world and the most mysterious. There is nothing we know about more directly than consciousness, but it is extraordinarily hard to reconcile it with everything else we know. Why does it exist? What does it do? How could it possibly arise from neural processes in the brain? These questions are among the most intriguing in all of science.

From an objective viewpoint, the brain is relatively comprehensible. When you look at this page, there is a whir of processing: photons strike your retina, electrical signals are passed up your optic nerve and between different areas of your brain, and eventually you might respond with a smile, a perplexed frown or a remark. But there is also a subjective aspect. When you look at the page, you are conscious of it, directly experiencing the images and words as part of your private, mental life. You have vivid impressions of colored flowers and vibrant sky. At the same time, you may be feeling some emotions and forming some thoughts. Together such experiences make up consciousness: the subjective, inner life of the mind.

For many years, consciousness was shunned by researchers studying the brain and the mind. The prevailing view was that science, which depends on objectivity, could not accommodate something as subjective as consciousness. The behaviorist movement in psychology, dominant earlier in this century, concentrated on external behavior and disallowed any talk of internal mental processes. Later, the rise of cognitive science focused attention on processes inside the head. Still, consciousness remained off-limits, fit only for late-night discussion over drinks.

Over the past several years, however, an increasing number of neuroscientists, psychologists and philosophers have been rejecting the idea that consciousness cannot be studied and are attempting to delve into its secrets. As might be expected of a field so new, there is a tangle of diverse and conflicting theories, often using basic concepts in incompatible ways. To help unsnarl the tangle, philosophical reasoning is vital.

The myriad views within the field range from reductionist theories, according to which consciousness can be explained by the standard methods of neuroscience and psychology, to the position of the so-called mysterians, who say we will never understand consciousness at all. I believe that on close analysis both of these views can be seen to be mistaken and that the truth lies somewhere in the middle.

Against reductionism I will argue that the tools of neuroscience cannot provide a full account of conscious experience, although they have much to offer. Against mysterianism I will hold that consciousness might be explained by a new kind of theory. The full details of such a theory are still out of reach, but careful reasoning and some educated inferences can reveal something of its general nature. For example, it will probably involve new fundamental laws, and the concept of information may play a central role. These faint glimmerings suggest that a theory of consciousness may have startling consequences for our view of the universe and of ourselves.

The Hard Problem

Researchers use the word "consciousness" in many different ways. To clarify the issues, we first have to separate

From: David J. Chalmers, "The Puzzle of Conscious Experience," *Scientific American* 237 (Dec. 1995) 80–86.

the problems that are often clustered together under the name. For this purpose, I find it useful to distinguish between the "easy problems" and the "hard problem" of consciousness. The easy problems are by no means trivial—they are actually as challenging as most in psychology and biology—but it is with the hard problem that the central mystery lies.

The easy problems of consciousness include the following: How can a human subject discriminate sensory stimuli and react to them appropriately? How does the brain integrate information from many different sources and use this information to control behavior? How is it that subjects can verbalize their internal states? Although all these questions are associated with consciousness, they all concern the objective mechanisms of the cognitive system. Consequently, we have every reason to expect that continued work in cognitive psychology and neuroscience will answer them.

The hard problem, in contrast, is the question of how physical processes in the brain give rise to subjective experience. This puzzle involves the inner aspect of thought and perception: the way things feel for the subject. When we see, for example, we experience visual sensations, such as that of vivid blue. Or think of the ineffable sound of a distant oboe, the agony of an intense pain, the sparkle of happiness or the meditative quality of a moment lost in thought. All are part of what I am calling consciousness. It is these phenomena that pose the real mystery of the mind.

To illustrate the distinction, consider a thought experiment devised by the Australian philosopher Frank Jackson. Suppose that Mary, a neuroscientist in the 23rd century, is the world's leading expert on the brain processes responsible for color vision. But Mary has lived her whole life in a black-and-white room and has never seen any other colors. She knows everything there is to know about physical processes in the brain—its biology, structure and function. This understanding enables her to grasp everything there is to know about the easy problems: how the brain discriminates stimuli, integrates information and produces verbal reports. From her knowledge of color vision, she knows the way color names correspond with wavelengths on the light spectrum. But there is still something crucial about color vision that Mary does not know: what it is like to experience a color such as red. It follows that there are facts about conscious experience that cannot be deduced from physical facts about the functioning of the brain.

Indeed, nobody knows why these physical processes are accompanied by conscious experience at all. Why is it that when our brains process light of a certain wavelength, we have an experience of deep purple? Why do we have any experience at all? Could not an unconscious automaton have performed the same tasks just as well? These are questions that we would like a theory of consciousness to answer.

I am not denying that consciousness arises from the brain. We know, for example, that the subjective experience of vision is closely linked to processes in the visual cortex. It is the link itself that perplexes, however. Remarkably, subjective experience seems to emerge from a physical process. But we have no idea how or why this is.

Is Neuroscience Enough?

Given the flurry of recent work on consciousness in neuroscience and psychology, one might think this mystery is starting to be cleared up. On closer examination, however, it turns out that almost all the current work addresses only the easy problems of consciousness. The confidence of the reductionist view comes from the progress on the easy problems, but none of this makes any difference where the hard problem is concerned.

Consider the hypothesis put forward by neurobiologists Francis Crick of the Salk Institute for Biological Studies in San Diego and Christof Koch of the California Institute of Technology. They suggest that consciousness may arise from certain oscillations in the cerebral cortex, which become synchronized as neurons fire 40 times per second. Crick and Koch believe the phenomenon might explain how different attributes of a single perceived object (its color and shape, for example), which are processed in different parts of the brain, are merged into a coherent whole. In this theory, two pieces of information become bound together precisely when they are represented by synchronized neural firings.

The hypothesis could conceivably elucidate one of the easy problems about how information is integrated in the brain. But why should synchronized oscillations give rise to a visual experience, no matter how much integration is taking place? This question involves the hard problem, about which the theory has nothing to offer. Indeed, Crick and Koch are agnostic about whether the hard problem can be solved by science at all.

The same kind of critique could be applied to almost all the recent work on consciousness. In his 1991 book *Consciousness Explained*, philosopher Daniel C. Dennett laid out a sophisticated theory of how numerous independent processes in the brain combine to produce a coherent response to a perceived event. The theory might do much to explain how we produce verbal reports on our internal states, but it tells us very little about why there should be a subjective experience behind these reports. Like other reductionist theories, Dennett's is a theory of the easy problems.

The critical common trait among these easy problems is that they all concern how a cognitive or behavioral function is performed. All are ultimately questions about how the brain carries out some task — how it discriminates stimuli, integrates information, produces reports and so on. Once neurobiology specifies appropriate neural mechanisms, showing how the functions are performed, the easy problems are solved.

The hard problem of consciousness, in contrast, goes beyond problems about how functions are performed. Even if every behavioral and cognitive function related to consciousness were explained, there would still remain a further mystery: Why is the performance of these functions accompanied by conscious experience? It is this additional conundrum that makes the hard problem hard.

The Explanatory Gap

Some have suggested that to solve the hard problem, we need to bring in new tools of physical explanation: nonlinear dynamics, say, or new discoveries in neuroscience, or quantum mechanics. But these ideas suffer from exactly the same difficulty. Consider a proposal from Stuart R. Hameroff of the University of Arizona and Roger Penrose of the University of Oxford. They hold that consciousness arises from quantum-physical processes taking place in microtubules, which are protein structures inside neurons. It is possible (if not likely) that such a hypothesis will lead to an explanation of how the brain makes decisions or even how it proves mathematical theorems, as Hameroff and Penrose suggest. But even if it does, the theory is silent about how these processes might give rise to conscious experience. Indeed, the same problem arises with any theory of consciousness based only on physical processing.

The trouble is that physical theories are best suited to explaining why systems have a certain physical structure and how they perform various functions. Most problems in science have this form; to explain life, for example, we need to describe how a physical system can reproduce, adapt and metabolize. But consciousness is a different sort of problem entirely, as it goes beyond the explanation of structure and function.

Of course, neuroscience is not irrelevant to the study of consciousness. For one, it may be able to reveal the nature of the neural correlate of consciousness — the brain processes most directly associated with conscious experience. It may even give a detailed correspondence between specific processes in the brain and related components of experience. But until we know why these processes give rise to conscious experience at all, we will not have crossed what philosopher Joseph Levine has called the explanatory gap between physical processes and consciousness. Making that leap will demand a new kind of theory.

A True Theory of Everything

In searching for an alternative, a key observation is that not all entities in science are explained in terms of more basic entities. In physics, for example, space-time, mass and charge (among other things) are regarded as fundamental features of the world, as they are not reducible to anything simpler. Despite this irreducibility, detailed and useful theories relate these entities to one another in terms of fundamental laws. Together these features and laws explain a great variety of complex and subtle phenomena.

It is widely believed that physics provides a complete catalogue of the universe's fundamental features and laws. As physicist Steven Weinberg puts it in his 1992 book *Dreams of a Final Theory*, the goal of physics is a "theory of everything" from which all there is to know about the universe can be derived. But Weinberg concedes that there is a problem with consciousness. Despite the power of physical theory, the existence of consciousness does not seem to be derivable from physical laws. He defends physics by arguing that it might eventually explain what he calls the objective correlates of consciousness (that is, the neural correlates), but of course to do this is not to explain consciousness itself. If the existence of consciousness cannot be derived from physical laws, a theory of physics is not a true theory of everything. So a final theory must contain an additional fundamental component.

Toward this end, I propose that conscious experience be considered a fundamental feature, irreducible to anything more basic. The idea may seem strange at first, but consistency seems to demand it. In the 19th century it turned out that electromagnetic phenomena could not be explained in terms of previously known principles. As a consequence, scientists introduced electromagnetic charge as a new fundamental entity and studied the associated fundamental laws. Similar reasoning should apply to consciousness. If existing fundamental theories cannot encompass it, then something new is required.

Where there is a fundamental property, there are fundamental laws. In this case, the laws must relate experience to elements of physical theory. These laws will almost certainly not interfere with those of the physical world; it seems that the latter form a closed system in their own right. Rather the laws will serve as a bridge, specifying how experience depends on underlying physical processes. It is this bridge that will cross the explanatory gap.

Thus, a complete theory will have two components: physical laws, telling us about the behavior of physical systems from the infinitesimal to the cosmological, and what we might call psychophysical laws, telling us how some of those systems are associated with conscious experience. These two components will constitute a true theory of everything.

Searching for a Theory

Supposing for the moment that they exist, how might we uncover such psychophysical laws? The greatest hindrance in this pursuit will be a lack of data. As I have described it, consciousness is subjective, so there is no direct way to monitor it in others. But this difficulty is an obstacle, not a dead end. For a start, each one of us has access to our own experiences, a rich trove that can be used to formulate theories. We can also plausibly rely on indirect information, such as subjects' descriptions of their experiences. Philosophical arguments and thought experiments also have a role to play. Such methods have limitations, but they give us more than enough to get started.

These theories will not be conclusively testable, so they will inevitably be more speculative than those of more conventional scientific disciplines. Nevertheless, there is no reason they should not be strongly constrained to account accurately for our own first-person experiences, as well as the evidence from subjects' reports. If we find a theory that fits the data better than any other theory of equal simplicity, we will have good reason to accept it. Right now we do not have even a single theory that fits the data, so worries about testability are premature.

We might start by looking for high-level bridging laws, connecting physical processes to experience at an everyday level. The basic contour of such a law might be gleaned from the observation that when we are conscious of something, we are generally able to act on it and speak about it—which are objective, physical functions. Conversely, when some information is directly available for action and speech, it is generally

conscious. Thus, consciousness correlates well with what we might call "awareness": the process by which information in the brain is made globally available to motor processes such as speech and bodily action.

The notion may seem trivial. But as defined here, awareness is objective and physical, whereas consciousness is not. Some refinements to the definition of awareness are needed, in order to extend the concept to animals and infants, which cannot speak. But at least in familiar cases, it is possible to see the rough outlines of a psychophysical law: where there is awareness, there is consciousness, and vice versa.

To take this line of reasoning a step further, consider the structure present in the conscious experience. The experience of a field of vision, for example, is a constantly changing mosaic of colors, shapes and patterns and as such has a detailed geometric structure. The fact that we can describe this structure, reach out in the direction of many of its components and perform other actions that depend on it suggests that the structure corresponds directly to that of the information made available in the brain through the neural processes of awareness.

Similarly, our experiences of color have an intrinsic three-dimensional structure that is mirrored in the structure of information processes in the brain's visual cortex. This structure is illustrated in the color wheels and charts used by artists. Colors are arranged in a systematic pattern—red to green on one axis, blue to yellow on another, and black to white on a third. Colors that are close to one another on a color wheel are experienced as similar. It is extremely likely that they also correspond to similar perceptual representations in the brain, as part of a system of complex three-dimensional coding among neurons that is not yet fully understood. We can recast the underlying concept as a principle of structural coherence: the structure of conscious experience is mirrored by the structure of information in awareness, and vice versa.

Another candidate for a psychophysical law is a principle of organizational invariance. It holds that physical systems with the same abstract organization will give rise to the same kind of conscious experience, no matter what they are made of. For example, if the precise interactions between our neurons could be duplicated with silicon chips, the same conscious experience would arise. The idea is somewhat controversial, but I believe it is strongly supported by thought experiments describing the gradual replacement of neurons by silicon chips. The remarkable implication is that consciousness might someday be achieved in machines.

Information: Physical and Experimental

The ultimate goal of a theory of consciousness is a simple and elegant set of fundamental laws, analogous to the fundamental laws of physics. The principles described above are unlikely to be fundamental, however. Rather they seem to be high-level psychophysical laws, analogous to macroscopic principles in physics such as those of thermodynamics or kinematics. What might the underlying fundamental laws be? No one knows, but I don't mind speculating.

I suggest that the primary psychophysical laws may centrally involve the concept of information. The abstract notion of information, as put forward in the 1940s by Claude E. Shannon of the Massachusetts Institute of Technology, is that of a set of separate states with a basic structure of similarities and differences between them. We can think of a 10-bit binary code as an information state, for example. Such information states can be embodied in the physical world. This happens whenever they correspond to physical states (voltages, say); the differences between them can be transmitted along some pathway, such as a telephone line.

We can also find information embodied in conscious experience. The pattern of color patches in a visual field, for example, can be seen as analogous to that of the pixels covering a display screen. Intriguingly, it turns out that we find the same information states embedded in conscious experience and in underlying physical processes in the brain. The three-dimensional encoding of color spaces, for example, suggests that the information state in a color experience corresponds directly to an information state in the brain. We might even regard the two states as distinct aspects of a single information state, which is simultaneously embodied in both physical processing and conscious experience.

A natural hypothesis ensues. Perhaps information, or at least some information, has two basic aspects: a physical one and an experiential one. This hypothesis has the status of a fundamental principle that might underlie the relation between physical processes and experience. Wherever we find conscious experience, it exists as one aspect of an information state, the other aspect of which is embedded in a physical process in the brain. This proposal needs to be fleshed out to make a satisfying theory. But it fits nicely with the principles mentioned earlier—systems with the same organization will embody the same information, for example—and it could explain numerous features of our conscious experience.

The idea is at least compatible with several others, such as physicist John A. Wheeler's suggestion that information is fundamental to the physics of the universe. The laws of physics might ultimately be cast in informational terms, in which case we would have a satisfying congruence between the constructs in both physical and psychophysical laws. It may even be that a theory of physics and a theory of consciousness could eventually be consolidated into a single grander theory of information.

A potential problem is posed by the ubiquity of information. Even a thermostat embodies some information, for example, but is it conscious? There are at least two possible responses. First, we could constrain the fundamental laws so that only some information has an experiential aspect, perhaps depending on how it is physically processed. Second, we might bite the bullet and allow that all information has an experiential aspect—where there is complex information processing, there is complex experience, and where there is simple information processing, there is simple experience. If this is so, then even a thermostat might have experiences, although they would be much simpler than even a basic color experience, and there would certainly be no accompanying emotions or thoughts. This seems odd at first, but if experience is truly fundamental, we might expect it to be widespread. In any case, the choice between these alternatives should depend on which can be integrated into the most powerful theory.

Of course, such ideas may be all wrong. On the other hand, they might evolve into a more powerful proposal that predicts the precise structure of our conscious experience from physical processes in our brains. If this project succeeds, we will have good reason to accept the theory. If it fails, other avenues will be pursued, and alternative fundamental theories may be developed. In this way, we may one day resolve the greatest mystery of the mind.

They're Made of Meat

Terry Bisson (1942–) is an American science-fiction writer. He has written a number of novels combining science fiction with magic or satire. His short story "Bears Discover Fire" won the 1991 Hugo, Nebula, Locus, and Sturgeon Awards. In this story, which was nominated for a Nebula award, he presents speciesism from an alien's point of view.

"They're made out of meat."

"Meat?"

"Meat. They're made out of meat."

"Meat?"

"There's no doubt about it. We picked up several from different parts of the planet, took them aboard our recon vessels, and probed them all the way through. They're completely meat."

"That's impossible. What about the radio signals? The messages to the stars?"

"They use the radio waves to talk, but the signals don't come from them. The signals come from machines."

"So who made the machines? That's who we want to contact."

"*They* made the machines. That's what I'm trying to tell you. Meat made the machines."

"That's ridiculous. How can meat make a machine? You're asking me to believe in sentient meat."

"I'm not asking you, I'm telling you. These creatures are the only sentient race in that sector and they're made out of meat."

"Maybe they're like the orfolei. You know, a carbon-based intelligence that goes through a meat stage."

"Nope. They're born meat and they die meat. We studied them for several of their life spans, which didn't take long. Do you have any idea what's the life span of meat?"

"Spare me. Okay, maybe they're only part meat. You know, like the weddilei. A meat head with an electron plasma brain inside."

"Nope. We thought of that, since they do have meat heads, like the weddilei. But I told you, we probed them. They're meat all the way through."

"No brain?"

"Oh, there's a brain all right. It's just that the brain is *made out of meat!* That's what I've been trying to tell you."

"So . . . what does the thinking?"

"You're not understanding, are you? You're refusing to deal with what I'm telling you. The brain does the thinking. The meat."

"Thinking meat! You're asking me to believe in thinking meat!"

"Yes, thinking meat! Conscious meat! Loving meat. Dreaming meat. The meat is the whole deal! Are you beginning to get the picture or do I have to start all over?"

"Omigod. You're serious then. They're made out of meat."

"Thank you. Finally. Yes. They are indeed made out of meat. And they've been trying to get in touch with us for almost a hundred of their years."

"Omigod. So what does this meat have in mind?"

"First it wants to talk to us. Then I imagine it wants to explore the Universe, contact other sentiences, swap ideas and information. The usual."

"We're supposed to talk to meat."

"That's the idea. That's the message they're sending out by radio. 'Hello. Anyone out there. Anybody home.' That sort of thing."

"They actually do talk, then. They use words, ideas, concepts?"

"Oh, yes. Except they do it with meat."

"I thought you just told me they used radio."

"They do, but what do you think is *on* the radio? Meat sounds. You know how when you slap or flap

From: Terry Bisson, "They're Made of Meat," *Omni*, April 1991.

meat, it makes a noise? They talk by flapping their meat at each other. They can even sing by squirting air through their meat."

"Omigod. Singing meat. This is altogether too much. So what do you advise?"

"Officially or unofficially?"

"Both."

"Officially, we are required to contact, welcome and log in any and all sentient races or multibeings in this quadrant of the Universe, without prejudice, fear or favor. Unofficially, I advise that we erase the records and forget the whole thing."

"I was hoping you would say that."

"It seems harsh, but there is a limit. Do we really want to make contact with meat?"

"I agree one hundred percent. What's there to say? 'Hello, meat. How's it going?' But will this work? How many planets are we dealing with here?"

"Just one. They can travel to other planets in special meat containers, but they can't live on them. And being meat, they can only travel through C space. Which limits them to the speed of light and makes the possibility of their ever making contact pretty slim. Infinitesimal, in fact."

"So we just pretend there's no one home in the Universe."

"That's it."

"Cruel. But you said it yourself, who wants to meet meat? And the ones who have been aboard our vessels, the ones you probed? You're sure they won't remember?"

"They'll be considered crackpots if they do. We went into their heads and smoothed out their meat so that we're just a dream to them."

"A dream to meat! How strangely appropriate, that we should be meat's dream."

"And we marked the entire sector *unoccupied*."

"Good. Agreed, officially and unofficially. Case closed. Any others? Anyone interesting on that side of the galaxy?"

"Yes, a rather shy but sweet hydrogen core cluster intelligence in a class nine star in G445 zone. Was in contact two galactic rotations ago, wants to be friendly again."

"They always come around."

"And why not? Imagine how unbearably, how unutterably cold the Universe would be if one were all alone . . ."

Suggestions for Further Reading

Beakley, Brian, and Peter Ludlow, eds. *The Philosophy of Mind: Classical Problems and Contemporary Issues*. Cambridge: MIT Press, 1992.

Blakemore, Colin, and Susan Greenfield, eds. *Mindwaves: Thoughts on Intelligence, Identity and Consciousness*. Oxford: Basil Blackwell, 1992.

Block, Ned, ed. *Readings in Philosophy of Psychology*. Cambridge: Harvard University Press, 1981.

Churchland, Paul. *Matter and Consciousness*. Cambridge: MIT Press, 1990.

Flanagan, Owen. *Consciousness Reconsidered*. Cambridge: MIT Press, 1992.

Gregory, R. L., ed. *The Oxford Companion to the Mind*. New York: Oxford University Press, 1987.

Hasker, William. *The Emergent Self*. Ithaca, NY: Cornell University Press, 1999.

Haugeland, John. *Artificial Intelligence: The Very Idea*. Cambridge: MIT Press, 1985.

Jacquette, Dale. *Philosophy of Mind*. Englewood Cliffs, NJ: Prentice-Hall, 1994.

Kim, Jaegwon. *Philosophy of Mind*. Boulder, CO: Westview Press, 1996.

Lycan, William, ed. *Mind and Cognition*. Oxford: Blackwell, 1991.

Rosenthal, David M., ed. *The Nature of Mind*. Oxford: Oxford University Press, 1992.

Searle, John. *Minds, Brains, and Science*. Cambridge: Harvard University Press, 1984.

Searle, John. *The Rediscovery of the Mind*. Cambridge: MIT Press, 1992.

Chapter 3

Free Will and Determinism

*S*uppose you are a brilliant computer scientist who has achieved an incredible feat. You have created an android that seems the embodiment of science-fiction fantasy, a machine that is much like *Star Trek's* android, Commander Data. But something awful happens.

Your beloved creation murders a human being. The police cannot catch your android, but they can catch you—and promptly arrest you for murder. The prosecutor asserts that you are responsible for the murder because you programmed the android. You reply that you programmed it to make choices of its own free will. But the prosecutor declares that the android could not possibly have free will. Its choices are the direct result of (1) its original construction and (2) subsequent modifications caused by its environment. The android certainly has had no say in either of these factors. The android's choices and actions, the prosecutor says, have been determined by forces beyond its control. You are the one responsible for these factors. You would be responsible even if the android could alter its own programming or change its environment. After all, says the prosecutor, the android's way of self-programming and environmental manipulation was determined by you.

You reply that if your android lacks free will because of (1) and (2), then humans lack free will, too. Humans, just like the android, are the result of origins and environmental influences that are beyond their control. They have no say in their being born, or their genetic makeup, or their physical characteristics, or the conditions in the world that contributed to their early development. They are, you say, programmed by their genes and their environment, just as the android was programmed by you.

You assert that just as humans obviously can have free will despite their "programming," your android can, too.[1] But is this assertion correct? Regardless of how advanced science becomes, could an android ever really be both programmed and free to make its own choices? Isn't "programmed with free will" a contradiction in terms, as the prosecutor implies? More to the point, can we humans be both free and programmed? We seem to be in the same boat with the android. We all believe that we are programmed, in the sense mentioned above, by our genes and our environment. Yet we want to believe that at least some of our actions and choices are free. How can both these beliefs be true?

Our android scenario has dropped us into the heart of the matter. We seem to have conflicting beliefs about ourselves. But the conflict is more fundamental and more troubling than most people realize. It is at the core of what philosophers call *the problem of free will and determinism*. Let's state this problem more precisely.

First, we all believe or at least are inclined to believe that every event has a cause that makes it happen. This view is known as **causal determinism.** We would think it nonsense to say that an event transpired without a cause. We would be incredulous if someone seriously thought, for example, that her clock stopped working for no reason whatsoever. Even if no one could determine the precise cause or causes, we still would not accept the idea that the clock's stopping had no cause. We might say that the cause was unknown or that it was difficult to discern, but we would not say that it did not exist. Whether we're talking about clocks, computers, solar flares, the mating habits of geese, or the common cold, we firmly believe that each has a cause.

Further, we all believe that our acts—what we do, say, and choose—also have causes, just as everything else must have causes, for our acts are events, too. We assume that our acts are the result of our heredity, our previous experiences, the peculiarities of our personality, the circumstances preceding the acts, or *something*. Indeed, we believe that our acts must have causes—otherwise they would simply happen by chance.

On the other hand, we all believe that we have free will—that we can sometimes make a choice and that it is up to us what we shall choose. And most believe that if we act freely, we can be held responsible for what we do.

But if everything, including every act, has a cause, how is it possible for persons to have free will? Let's say that you perform an act: you press your finger against a button that detonates a bomb. Because everything has a cause, this movement of your finger must have a cause—perhaps the contracting of your muscles accompanied by certain electrical impulses in your hand and brain. According to the thesis of determinism, this something, this cause or causes, in turn must have been due to other causes (like certain brain states), and these causes must have been due to still others, and so on. Indeed, there must have been a whole succession of causes extending indefinitely into the past—stretching back before you were even born. Therefore, your simple act of pressing the button must have been the result of causes over which you had no control whatsoever. Your act was determined, already rigged before you thought to press the button—even before you had fingers. Worse still, we could say the same thing about all our acts. They're all determined. They would seem, therefore, to be entirely outside our control. When we act, we cannot act otherwise than we do.

The American philosopher and psychologist William James (1842–1910) explains causal determinism this way:

> It professes that those parts of the universe already laid down absolutely appoint and decree what the other parts shall be. The future has no ambiguous possibilities hidden in its womb: the part we call the present is compatible with only one totality. Any other future complement than the one fixed from eternity is impossible. The whole is in each and every part, and welds it with the rest into an absolute unity, an iron block, in which there can be no equivocation or shadow of turning.[2]

So, if the thesis of determinism is true, how can we possibly be free? If our acts are not under our control, how can we have free will? We all believe we are free, but how can this be? How can we consistently believe both that we are determined and that we have free will? Two of our most basic beliefs seem to be inconsistent. Something appears to be very wrong with the fundamental assumptions that permeate our relations with others, our laws, our institutions, and our innermost thoughts. Is it that we really are not free? Is it that determinism is false? Are we misunderstanding the problem?

There are two good things in life — freedom of thought and freedom of action.
—SOMERSET MAUGHAM

causal determinism
The doctrine that every event has a cause that makes it happen.

A lot is riding on the answers we give to this problem. Among the important things at stake here is the idea of moral and legal responsibility. If we really are not free in any meaningful way, we cannot reasonably be held responsible for what we do. We cannot reasonably be praised or blamed, rewarded or punished for any of our actions. After all, we would have no control over our acts—they would be the end result of causal chains that stretch back into the indefinite past. We would have no say in this process; it would simply happen to us. We therefore could not reasonably be held responsible for our actions and choices—no more than we could be held responsible for some genetic disease that befell us.

For a fuller appreciation of this point, consider the fictional world constructed by the writer Samuel Butler. In his satirical novel *Erewhon*, he asks us to imagine a country that has a penal system radically different from ours. In *Erewhon*, people who commit crimes are not punished, but are treated in hospitals for moral ills, just as we treat the sick in our world. People who are physically sick, however, are not treated, but are prosecuted and punished as we would criminals. Butler's point is that if determinism is true, it makes about as much sense to punish criminals as it does to punish sick people. Both the acts of criminals and the conditions of the sick are determined by forces beyond their control.

In one dramatic case of a young man found guilty of being ill, the judge had this to say at the time of sentencing:

> Prisoner at the bar, you have been accused of a great crime of laboring under pulmonary consumption, and after an impartial trial before a jury of your countrymen, you have been found guilty. Against the justice of the verdict I can say nothing: the evidence against you was conclusive, and it only remains for me to pass such a sentence upon you, as shall satisfy the ends of the law. That sentence must be a very severe one. It pains me much to see one who is yet so young, and whose prospects in life were otherwise so excellent, brought to this distressing condition by a constitution which I can only regard as radically vicious; but yours is no case for compassion: this is not your first offense. . . . You were convicted of aggravated bronchitis last year: and I find that though you are now only twenty-three years old, you have been imprisoned on no less than fourteen occasions for illnesses of a more or less hateful character; in fact, it is not too much to say that you have spent the greater part of your life in jail.[3]

If Butler is right, our penal system is all wrong. It punishes people for acts over which they could not possibly have any control—acts for which they are not responsible. We need not turn to fiction to see variations on this theme. We can just pick up a newspaper. There we can read about trial lawyers pleading that a client is not responsible for his illegal act because he was born with bad genes, or he grew up in a violent community (and thus has "urban survival syndrome"), or he was the victim of long-term abuse.

Famous trial lawyer Clarence Darrow (1857–1938) consistently wielded the "determinism defense" with great skill and passion. In the 1920s, he de-

A man may be a pessimistic determinist before lunch and an optimistic believer in the will's freedom after it.

—ALDOUS HUXLEY

The Devil Made Me Do It

The determinism defense is still used by lawyers to absolve their clients from guilt. Today's lawyers, though, are much more specific about the causes of their clients' behavior. Margot Slade, of the *New York Times*, reports on some recent variants of the determinism defense.

> The devil-made-me-do-it excuse is probably as ancient as Old Scratch himself. But at a time when Americans have moved from the self-absorbed Me Generation to the self-absolved Not Me Generation, the devil is increasingly appearing in court these days as a defense with a psychological pedigree.
>
> . . . Moosa Hanoukai of Los Angeles was found guilty of voluntary manslaughter, reduced from a charge of murder, for beating his wife to death with a wrench. His lawyer said Mr. Hanoukai's wife had psychologically emasculated him — forcing him to sleep on the floor, calling him names — thus destroying his self-esteem, a kind of meek-mate syndrome.
>
> Daimon Osby, a black 18-year-old who shot two unarmed black men in a Fort Worth, Texas, parking lot . . . managed to get a deadlocked jury after his lawyer argued that he suffered from "urban survival syndrome," or the fear that inner-city black people have of other black people.
>
> . . . [D]efense lawyers have already staked their claim to:
>
> "Roid rage," the severe mood swings associated with steroid use, to mitigate the sentence of Troy Matthew Gentler, 19, who admitted tossing rocks at cars on Interstate 83 near York, York County . . . injuring several people.
>
> "Black rage," which the defense has described as a kind of racial prejudice–induced insanity to explain why Colin Ferguson, who is black, killed six people and injured 19 on a commuter train near New York City. . . .
>
> "Fetal trimethadione syndrome" in the case of Eric Smith, 14, who battered to death a 4-year-old boy . . . in Savona, N.Y., because, his lawyer says, he has an uncontrollable "sadistic side" stemming from his mother's use of epilepsy medication during pregnancy. . . .
>
> "The more we learn about how and why we act in a certain way, unless we rule out everything as psychobabble, the more we're able to offer viable defenses," said Lisa B. Kemler of Alexandria, Va., who represented Lorena Bobbitt and successfully invoked a "battered woman" defense to explain why Bobbitt sliced off her husband's penis while he slept. The jury judged her temporarily insane. . . .
>
> The danger, say scholars, is that juries become loath to draw any line. "If we allow urban psychosis as a defense to crime," [John] Monahan said, "what would be next? Suburban psychosis, marked by a pathological fear of lawn mowers and barbecues?"
>
> Criminal law, he said, turns on the notion that people have free will. "This may be a legal fiction," he said, "but it's necessary in a democracy. Take it out, and we all become characters in a George Orwell novel."[4]

fended two college students, Leopold and Loeb, who murdered and dismembered a child. He admitted that the boys did indeed commit the heinous act but argued that they — like all of us — never had any real control over their lives. They were doomed — determined — by forces that were at work before the boys even conceived of their crime. In his plea, Darrow declared,

> Nature is strong and she is pitiless. She works in her own mysterious way, and we are her victims. We have not much to do with it ourselves. Nature takes this job in hand, and we play our parts. In the words of old Omar Khayyam, we are only:

But helpless pieces in the game He plays
Upon this checkerboard of nights and days;
Hither and thither moves, and checks, and slays,
And one by one back in the closet lays.

What had this boy to do with it? He was not his own father; he was not his own mother; he was not his own grandparents. All of this was handed to him. He did not surround himself with governesses and wealth. He did not make himself. And yet he is to be compelled to pay.

There was a time in England, running down as late as the beginning of the last century, when judges used to convene court and call juries to try a horse, a dog, a pig, for crime. I have in my library a story of a judge and jury and lawyers trying and convicting an old sow for lying on her ten pigs and killing them.

What does it mean? Animals were tried. Do you mean to tell me that Dickie Loeb had any more to do with his making than any other product of heredity that is born upon the earth?[5]

With such entreaties, Darrow persuaded the jury to recommend life in prison for the boys instead of the death penalty.

If Darrow is right, we would have to admit that moral responsibility is an illusion. We might find ourselves agreeing with Casy the preacher in Steinbeck's *The Grapes of Wrath*, who awoke one night and said, "There ain't no sin and there ain't no virtue. There's just stuff people do. It's all part of the same thing. And some of the things people do is nice, and some ain't so nice, but that's as far as any man got a right to say."[6]

In an attempt to determine whether we can act freely, we will put a number of theories of free action to the test. We will begin (Section 3.1) by examining hard determinism, which claims that no one acts freely because every event is caused. Then we will examine indeterminism, which claims that some actions are free because some events are uncaused. Next (Section 3.2), we will examine two forms of compatibilism—traditional and hierarchical—which claim that even if every event is caused, we can still act freely. Finally (Section 3.3), we will examine libertarianism, which claims that free actions are actions caused by an agent rather than an event. Each of these theories has its strengths and weaknesses. To determine which is the most plausible, you will have to determine which provides the best explanation of the evidence, including the evidence established through thought experiments.

Objectives

After reading this chapter, you should be able to

- state the various theories of free action.
- describe the thought experiments that have been used to test them.

- evaluate the strengths and weaknesses of the various theories of free action.
- define causal determinism, causal indeterminism, compatibilism, incompatibilism, first-order desire, and second-order desire.
- formulate your own view of how free actions are possible (or why they are impossible).

The Luck of the Draw

Freedom as Chance

None are more hopelessly enslaved than those who falsely believe they are free.

—GOETHE

*I*n this chapter we will consider two closely related theories that are provocative reactions to the doctrine of causal determinism (the doctrine that every event has a cause). Perhaps without giving the matter much thought, you have already assumed one of them to be true. Let's begin now to see if such an assumption holds up under scrutiny.

Hard Determinism

Those who believe that we have no free will—that there are no free actions—are known as **hard determinists.** They assert that because everything is causally determined, no one acts freely. William James dubbed them "hard determinists" because they do not "shrink from such words as fatality, bondage of the will, necessity, and the like."[7] They readily embrace the view that no one is in control of their lives.

Hard determinists have traditionally been materialists. In fact, Leucippus (ca. 500 B.C.), the first person to propose an atomic theory of matter, is reputed to have said, "Nothing occurs by chance, but all is from necessity." In Leucippus's view, the world is composed of tiny, indivisible particles of matter called atoms. These atoms move through empty space and collide with one another according to fixed laws. These collisions can result in individual atoms sticking together or collections of atoms breaking apart. When individual atoms stick together, something is brought into existence. When a collection of atoms breaks apart, something ceases to exist. Everything that happens is the result of a collision between atoms.

Although the things we call atoms are not indivisible, our most advanced theory of reality is based on Leucippus's insight. Called the "standard model" of particle physics, it claims that everything in the universe is made out of elementary particles. These particles interact with one another to produce all known physical phenomena.

French astronomer Pierre-Simon Laplace (1749–1827) made explicit the deterministic implications of a standard model view in the following thought experiment:

Thought Experiment

Laplace's Superbeing

Given for one instant an intelligence which could comprehend all the forces by which nature is animated and the respective situation of the beings who compose it — an intelligence sufficiently vast to submit these data to analysis — it would embrace in the same formula the movements of the greatest bodies in the universe and those of the lightest atom; for it, nothing would be uncertain and the future, as the past, would be present to its eyes.[8]

According to traditional materialism, the universe is like a giant billiard ball game. Just as the path of every billiard ball is determined by the forces acting on it, so is the path of every elementary particle. Someone who knew the laws of motion, the properties of a billiard ball, and the forces acting on it would be able to predict all of its future movements. Similarly, someone who knew all the laws of physics, all the properties of all the physical objects in the universe, and all of the forces acting on them would be able to predict the entire future of the universe, including everything we will ever do. But if it's possible to predict all of our actions, then what we do is not up to us. If, as traditional materialism suggests, all of our actions are determined by forces beyond our control, we have no free will.

According to traditional materialism, then, the universe is a great, intricate mechanism ticking and turning ceaselessly in fixed ways. In this grand machine, there are component mechanisms known as human beings. They too are entirely physical and fully subject to natural laws. These mechanisms have complex brains producing various brain states. Every brain state follows necessarily from preceding brain states so that every thought and action is entirely necessitated, as the motions of any mechanism must be. Thus the causes of our choices and actions are outside our control. Occasionally certain brain states may give us the impression that we are free, but this impression can do nothing to alter the fact that we are as determined as any other collection of matter. Sometimes we may choose one alternative over another, but the choosing is as necessitated as any other mechanical fact. Freedom is an illusion.

This picture of the world was eloquently expressed by Baron Paul Henri d'Holbach in the eighteenth century. Holbach was one of the first modern thinkers to systematically critique the idea that people have free will. He asserts,

Science is at work, humanity has been at work, scholarship has been at work, and intelligent people now know that every human being is the product of endless heredity in back of him and the infinite environment around him.

—CLARENCE DARROW

hard determinism
The doctrine that there are no free actions.

[Man] is connected to universal nature, and submitted to the necessary and immutable laws that she imposes on all the beings she contains. . . . Man's life is a line that nature commands him to describe upon the surface of the earth, without his ever being able to swerve from it, even for an instant. He is born without his own consent; his organization does in nowise depend upon himself; his ideas come to him involuntarily; his habits are in the power of those who cause him to contract them; he is unceasingly modified by causes, whether visible or concealed, over which he has no control, which necessarily regulate his mode of existence, give the hue to his way of thinking, and determine his way of acting.[9]

According to Holbach, we are powerless to alter the course of nature. Because we are natural objects, we are bound by the same laws that govern everything else in the natural world. We can no more change the future than we can change the past.

The hard determinism of Holbach and Laplace is based on the principle of causal determinism that says every event is the consequence of past events plus the laws of nature. According to causal determinism, nothing happens without a cause and the same cause always produces the same effect. So given the state of the universe at any particular time, and the natural laws that govern it, there is only one possible future. If we could "roll back" the universe to some time in the past (like we rewind a videotape) and then let nature take its course, everything would happen just as it did before. We can't alter the past, and we can't change the laws of nature. So we are not in control of our destinies.

That's not the way things seem, however. It seems as if we are in control of our lives. But that, says the hard determinist, is an illusion. The great Dutch philosopher Spinoza (1632–1677) once remarked that if a stone traveling through the air were conscious, it would believe that it was free and capable of choosing where it would land.[10] According to the hard determinist, we have no more freedom than the stone. We seem to be free because we are aware of our wants, motives, and desires. But we are not aware of the causes of our wants, motives, and desires. If we were, we would realize that we have no more control over them than the stone does over its path through space.

Man is no more responsible for becoming willful and committing a crime than the flower for becoming red and fragrant. In both instances the end products are predetermined by the nature of protoplasm and the chance of circumstances.
—Nathaniel Cantor

The Consequence Argument

Hard determinists believe that causal determinism is **incompatible** with free will. Both can't be true, they say, because if all of our actions are determined by forces beyond our control, they're not free. American philosopher Peter van Inwagen has made this incompatibility explicit by presenting what he calls "the consequence argument." It goes like this:

> If determinism is true, then our acts are the consequences of the laws of nature and events in the remote past. But it is not up to us what went on before we were born, and neither is it up to us what the laws of nature are. Therefore the consequences of these things (including our present acts) are not up to us.[11]

According to van Inwagen, events have consequences, and those consequences are determined by the laws of nature. Among those consequences are

incompatibilism
The doctrine that causal determinism is incompatible with the view that we sometimes act freely.

Freedom and Foreknowledge

Science is not the only discipline whose principles seem to undermine free will. Theology also belongs in that category. A fundamental belief of traditional Christian theology is that God is all-knowing or omniscient. But if God knows everything that we will ever do, then it would seem that we are not free to do anything else. The medieval statesman and philosopher Boethius (480–524) provides one of the earliest and most succinct formulations of the dilemma:

> There seems to me, I said, to be such incompatibility between the existence of God's universal foreknowledge and that of any freedom of judgment. For if God foresees all things and cannot in anything be mistaken, that, which His Providence sees will happen, must result. . . . Besides, just as, when I know a present fact, that fact must be so; so also when I know of something that will happen, that must come to pass. Thus it follows that the fulfillment of a foreknown event must be inevitable.[12]

What Boethius means is that if someone knows that something is going to happen, then it's true that it is going to happen because you can't know something that is false. You can't know that 1+1 equals 3, for example, because 1+1 does not equal 3. But if it's true that something is going to happen, then it cannot possibly not happen. If it's true that the sun will rise tomorrow, for example, then the sun has to rise tomorrow, for otherwise the statement wouldn't be true. So if someone knows that something is going to happen, it must happen. But if it must happen — if it's unavoidable — then no one is free to prevent it from happening. Thus the price of omniscience is freedom.

Although Boethius thought that the apparent conflict between omniscience and free will could be avoided if God existed outside of time, the great Protestant reformer and founder of the Presbyterian Church, John Calvin (1509–1564), thought that it was precisely because God exists outside time that no one can change their destiny. He writes,

> When we attribute foreknowledge to God, we mean that all things have ever been, and perpetually remain, before His eyes, so that to His knowledge nothing in future or past, but all things are present; and present in such a manner, that He does not merely conceive of them from ideas formed in His mind, as things remembered by us appear present to our minds, but really beholds and sees them as if actually placed before Him. And this foreknowledge extends to the whole world, and to all the creatures. Predestination we call the eternal decree of God, by which He has determined in Himself what would have to become of every individual of mankind. For they are not all created with a similar destiny; but eternal life is foreordained for some, and eternal damnation for others."[13]

In Calvin's view, God can see at a glance every moment of everyone's life. Each of our lives is spread out before God like an unwound movie reel. Just as every frame in a film strip is fixed, so is every event in our lives. Consequently, Calvin held that some of us are destined to go to heaven and some to hell, and there's nothing we can do about it.

You might object that while God may know what choices you are going to make, he doesn't make choices for you. That may well be true, but consider this: you are free to do something only if you can refrain from doing it. If your doing something is inevitable — which it must be if God foresees it — then your doing it cannot be a free act.

Thought Probe

Foreknowledge and Freedom

Calvin's argument can be put like this:

1. If God knows that I will do x tomorrow, then it is true that I will do x tomorrow.

2. If it is true that I will do x tomorrow, then I cannot possibly not do x tomorrow.

3. If I cannot possibly not do x tomorrow, then I am not free to do x tomorrow.

4. Therefore, if God knows that I will do x tomorrow, then I am not free to do x tomorrow.

Is this a sound argument? Why or why not? If you think it's not sound, which premise would you reject? Why?

the actions we perform. But because those actions are the consequences of things over which we have no control, our actions aren't free.

The consequence argument can be spelled out more formally as follows:

1. If causal determinism is true, then every event is the consequence of past events plus the laws of nature.
2. We are powerless to change past events, laws of nature, or their consequences, which include our actions.
3. If we are powerless to change our actions—if we can't do otherwise—then we can't act freely.
4. Therefore, if causal determinism is true, we can't act freely.

Premise 1 spells out the notion of causal determinism. To say that something is causally determined is to say that it follows from a statement describing past events plus the laws of nature. Premise 2 states the obvious truth that we cannot change the past or the laws of nature. There's nothing that we can do now that will change anything that's already happened. And there's nothing we can do now that will change the laws of nature. Even if everyone in the world held hands and chanted $E = mc^3$, that would not change Einstein's famous law: $E = mc^2$. Premise 3 draws out the implications of our limitations in this regard. If everything has to happen as it does and couldn't happen any other way, then our actions aren't free. Freedom requires the ability to choose among alternative courses of action. But if causal determinism is true, there are no alternative courses of action. We have to do what we're determined to do and can't do otherwise. In such a world, no one acts freely.

If that world is this world, then many of our individual and social practices are unjustified. The actions of others often give rise to moral sentiments in us, and we often make moral judgments about other people's behavior. If no one acts freely, however, then such moral sentiments and judgments are groundless because no one can be held responsible for something over which they have no control. There would be no reason to feel respect, admiration, gratitude, disdain, resentment, jealousy, or the like toward anyone because none of their actions would be up to them.

To see this, suppose that you watch someone commit a horrible crime. You feel nothing but contempt, even loathing, for the culprit. You later learn, however, that he had been kidnapped, brainwashed, and hypnotized by a mad scientist who had forced him to do the deed. In this case, the criminal doesn't deserve your disapproval because he couldn't help himself. If hard determinism is true, we're all like the criminal. All of our actions are determined by forces beyond our control. As a result, we can't be held responsible for what we do (or fail to do).

The hard determinist argument against moral responsibility, then, is this:

4. If causal determinism is true, we can't act freely.
5. If we can't act freely, we can't be held responsible for our actions.
6. Therefore, if causal determinism is true, we can't be held responsible for our actions.

Recent medical researches . . . have proved in the case of many criminals, if not of all, that from the very first they have been, as it were, doomed or predestined to crime by a faulty or imperfect organization of mind and body.

—LUDWIG BUCHNER

Are you a fatalist? If so, then you must agree with such popular fatalistic assertions as "Que sera, sera—what will be will be." Or "If your time has come, your time has come." Fatalism is the view that the future is already fixed, and there is nothing anyone can do to change it. That is, all future events will happen no matter what. Fatalism thus rules out free will.

But fatalism is not the same thing as causal determinism, the doctrine that every event has a cause. Causal determinism says that future events happen as a result of preceding events. These preceding events include things that we do, so many future events happen because of what we do. Fatalism, however, says that future events happen *regardless of what we do*.

This notion of Fate, which can be traced back to the ancients, is alive and well today. It can be soothing, implying that in the apparent chaos of the world, there is a rigid order, a pattern predestined from the beginning of time. It can offer peace of mind—a serene sense of resignation—to those, like soldiers in wartime, who must face the possibility of imminent death. A belief in Fate can also be an excuse, providing fatalists with a rationale for not struggling to overcome obstacles.

Stories about the supposed workings of Fate can leave you with an eerie feeling. See if you get a chill down the spine by reading this little tale told by its central character—Death:

> There was a merchant in Baghdad who sent his servant to market to buy provisions and in a little while the servant came back, white and trembling, and said, Master, just now when I was in the market-place I was jostled by a woman in the crowd and when I turned I saw it was Death that jostled me. She looked at me and made a threatening gesture; now, lend me your horse, and I will ride away from this city and avoid my fate. I will go to Samarra and there Death will not find me. The merchant lent him his horse, and the servant mounted it, and he dug his spurs in its flanks and as fast as the horse could gallop he went. The merchant went down to the market-place and he saw me standing in the crowd, and he came to me and said, Why did you make a threatening gesture to my ser-
> vant when you saw him this morning? That was not a threatening gesture, I said, it was only a start of surprise. I was astonished to see him in Baghdad, for I had an appointment with him tonight in Samarra.[14]

Creepy feelings aside, are there any reasons for accepting fatalism? For starters, there appears to be no empirical evidence in its favor. The everyday experience of all of us suggests that it simply is not the case that all future events will happen no matter what we do. On the contrary, in countless situations it seems that what we do does affect subsequent events. No wonder then that few people—if any—can be consistent fatalists, refusing to lift a finger to help themselves because everything is already fated anyway. Imagine someone saying, "If I am fated to eat lunch today, I will eat lunch. If I am fated not to eat lunch, I won't. Therefore, there is no need for me to concern myself about lunch at all." It appears that a belief in fatalism based on human experience is a mere superstition.

There are, however, certain logical arguments that some have used to try to prove fatalism. One of them goes like this: Either you will meet your doom tomorrow or you will not. Suppose you will meet your doom tomorrow. Then it is true now that you will meet your doom tomorrow. If it is true now that you will meet your doom tomorrow, then you must meet your doom tomorrow, and there is nothing you can do about it. In other words, true statements about the future require that the future must necessarily be a certain way.

This argument, however, commits a logical fallacy. Recall that a necessary truth is one that cannot possibly be false. Certainly, it is a necessary truth that either you will meet your doom tomorrow or you will not. But it is not a necessary truth that you will meet your doom tomorrow. Nor is it a neces-sary truth that you will not meet your doom tomorrow. These two statements, if true, are contingent truths—statements that could turn out to be false. In this argument, it simply does not follow from the truth of either one of these statements that either one must be necessarily true. So this argument for fatalism fails. Similar ones suffer the same, well, fate.

Emerging Defenses to Crime

The law recognizes that when your behavior is not under your control, you can't be held responsible for it. Law professor Dr. Tom O'Connor has put together a partial list of defenses that lawyers have used to try to reduce their clients' culpability.

The following have at one time or another been introduced in a court of law as Justifications (complete legal & moral exoneration), Excuses (legal but not moral exculpation), or Mitigations (reduces degree of legal & moral responsibility). *Barron's Medical Dictionary* defines "syndrome" as a complex of signs and symptoms presenting a clinical picture of a disease or disorder.

Attention Deficit Disorder aka Hyperactivity, used as both defense and mitigating factor. Used in Michael Fay case (caning in Singapore) to plead for mercy, but Singapore didn't buy it.

Chronic Fatigue Syndrome, or Yuppie Disease, affects about 100,000 Americans, impairs daily activities, body aches, and photophobia, a medically recognized condition.

Fetal Alcohol Syndrome, if mother consumed alcohol during pregnancy, produces "sadistic side" of personality later in life, similar to Fetal Trimethadione (Epilepsy medicine) syndrome. Admissible in U.S. and taken quite seriously in Canada.

Gone with the Wind Syndrome, named after the movie & used by rape experts to explain why rapists believe sex has to be spontaneous and done after some resistance on the part of the woman.

Meek-Mate Syndrome, first invoked by a CA man in 1994 who killed his wife because she psychologically emasculated him by calling him names, ridiculing him in public, and forcing him to sleep on the floor.

Multiple Personality Disorder, this condition is often seen as resulting from childhood abuse, and when successful, it is an insanity defense. A couple of times, however, defendants have been caught lying.

Parental Abuse Syndrome, the Menendez defense, successfully used to claim that years of emotional, physical or sexual abuse by a parent on a child causes loss of control over later behavior. . . .

Posttraumatic Stress Disorder, a recognized DSMIII disorder, triggered by a distressing event, where person becomes numb, offered as justification, excuse, and mitigation. Most successful at mitigating, getting charges reduced.

Premenstrual Stress Syndrome, hormonal changes are so severe that a woman is driven to the unthinkable. Used successfully to acquit Virginia surgeon Geraldine Richter in 1991 for DUI & Zsa Zsa–type behavior.

Rape Trauma Syndrome (RTS), discovered in 1974 and widely used to counter defense claims that the victim offered her consent in some way. One of the reasons consent laws were changed.

Repressed or Recovered Memory Syndrome, certain traumatic memories are triggered years later, such as sexual abuse by a therapist or priest. Juries have accepted these and awarded large sums of money.

Rock and Roll Defense, alleges that subliminal messages in rock, or in some cases rap, music, were the cause of conduct. Used in Manson defense (Beatles), Judas Priest (1990), and Tupac Shakur music.

Television Defense, contends that repeated exposure to violence on TV leads to violent action. First mentioned in 1977 at trial of Ronney Zamora, a fifteen-year-old who killed an eighty-two-year-old neighbor. In this case the jury didn't buy it. . . .

Twinkie Defense, in 1978, Dan White was found guilty of involuntary manslaughter instead of first degree murder for the killing of San Francisco mayor George Moscone and Supervisor Harvey Milk. At the time immediately before the killings, Dan White only consumed junk food.[15]

Thought Probe

Legitimate Defenses?

Could a traditional compatibilist accept any of these defenses as legitimate? Why or why not?

The principle behind premise 5, namely, that we cannot be held responsible for behavior over which we have no control, is well established in courts of law. If defendants can show that an act was the result of an "irresistible impulse," juries often find them not guilty. If hard determinism is correct, however, all of our actions—not only certain violent ones—are the result of irresistible impulses.

The arguments presented by the hard determinists are compelling and valid. To decide whether we should accept their conclusions, we have to determine whether we're justified in believing their premises.

Thought Probe

The Book of Life

Suppose a Laplacean superbeing wrote a book that chronicles your life. For each minute that you're alive, it describes what you will be doing at that time. Now suppose you come across this book and read it. Could you do otherwise than what is written in the book? If you could, would that show that you have free will? (This possibility is explored in "Please Don't Tell Me How the Story Ends" at the end of the chapter.)

Science and Determinism

Let's start with causal determinism. What reasons are there for believing that every event is the consequence of past events plus the laws of nature? Essentially, the main reasons come down to (1) science shows that causal determinism is true, and (2) reflective common sense shows that causal determinism is true. Most people need very little prodding to grasp the import of reason 1. They're reminded every day that science continues to uncover the underlying causes of countless physical phenomena. Science has shown that stars, comets, engines, and cells behave according to unchanging laws of nature. Events that were once mysterious have been revealed to have identifiable causes. Physical relationships have been described with mathematical precision. Successful predictions about physical happenings have become a defining feature of science. Indeed, modern hard determinist theories were inspired by such developments in science. Holbach's own hard determinism took its cue from science, especially physics. It was none other than science, he said, that showed his determinism to be the case.

Evidence of the predictability of human behavior provided by both psychology and biology provides some of the strongest support for the claim that our actions are determined by forces beyond our control. As psychologist B. F. Skinner puts it, "Personal exemption from a complete determinism is revoked as a scientific analysis progresses, particularly in accounting for the behavior of the individual."[16] Skinner is convinced that the behavior of human beings is, in principle, as predictable as the behavior of clocks.

Skinner's confidence in the predictability of human behavior stems from his experiments with pigeons. By reinforcing (rewarding) pigeons for exhibit-

Few informed people . . . can any longer ignore the fact that many kinds of even serious wrongdoing which folklore claimed to be a result of someone's "bad choice" are actually the result of forces over which the individual has no control and often not even any awareness.

—JOHN CUBER

ing the desired behavior, Skinner was able to train his pigeons to perform many remarkable tasks such as playing Ping-Pong, playing a toy piano, and dancing. All effective learning, he thought, is the result of selective reinforcement (or "operant conditioning," as it came to be known). By rewarding appropriate behaviors and not rewarding inappropriate ones, we could get a creature to do almost anything.

This faith in the malleability of all behavior including human was shared by Skinner's mentor, John B. Watson. In 1925, after a number of successful conditioning experiments with animals, he boasted,

> Give me a dozen healthy infants, well-formed, and my own specified world to bring them up in, and I'll guarantee to take any one at random and train him to become any type of specialist I might select — a doctor, lawyer, artist, merchant, chief, and, yes even into a beggar-man and thief, regardless of his talents, penchants, hindrances, abilities, vocations, and race of his ancestors.[17]

Watson clearly thought that how we behaved as adults was determined by how we were brought up as children, that is, by how we were nurtured. What our innate abilities or genetic makeup might be was irrelevant.

Watson had actually begun performing behavioral experiments on human infants five years earlier. To see whether the acquisition and extinction of fear could be explained on behaviorist principles, he and an associate, Rosalie Raynor, tried to instill a fear of rats in an eleven-month-old infant, known as Albert B. The experiment involved banging a steel bar behind Albert's head when he was shown a white rat. After only a few repetitions of this procedure, Albert would cry and try to crawl away when shown the rat. He exhibited the same fear response when shown a rabbit, a fur coat, and a Santa Claus mask. Watson meant to countercondition him, but his mother took Albert and left before he had the opportunity.

Watson was mistaken in believing that behavioral conditioning could be used to produce any desired behavior, however. Skinner found, for example, pigeons could be conditioned to peck a key for food, but not to flap their wings. Rats could be conditioned to press a bar, but cats could not. Rats given sour blue water followed by a sickness-producing drug avoided sour water, but quail, similarly conditioned, avoided blue water. Obviously, the way creatures behave is influenced by their nature as well as by how they are nurtured.[18]

Some of the most compelling evidence for the effect of biology on behavior comes from twin studies. Thomas J. Bouchard, at the University of Minnesota, has studied more than a hundred sets of identical twins that were given up for adoption and raised by different families. He found that their IQs were closer than those of fraternal twins raised in the same family and that they were also remarkably similar in personality, temperament, occupational interests, leisure time interest, and social attitudes.[19] It appears that our genetic makeup affects not only our physical characteristics, like height, weight, and hair color, but our mental characteristics, as well. It does not totally determine those characteristics, but it is obviously an important factor. Harvard biologist E. O. Wilson likens the relationship between our genetic makeup — our nature — and our experiences — how we are nurtured — to that of a photographic negative and developing fluid. Just as a negative can be developed well or poorly, so can our innate propensities. But the basic outlines of our personality, our attitudes, and even our character are in our genes. And those we cannot change by an act of will.

Wilson is the founder of a discipline called "sociobiology," which studies the biological basis of social behavior. The basic premise behind sociobiology is that just as certain physical characteristics can give something an edge in the struggle for survival, so can certain psychological characteristics. Those psychological characteristics that make it more likely that one will live long enough to reproduce will become more prevalent in future generations. So sociobiologists believe that our psychology as well as our physiology can be explained in terms of natural selection.

Advances in evolutionary biology, cognitive psychology, and neurophysiology suggest that the brain contains a number of highly specialized, domain-specific circuits that determine how we interpret experiences, form concepts, and assign meaning to objects and events. The study of these circuits is the focus of a branch of science called "evolutionary psychology." Using the techniques developed by evolutionary biologists, it seeks to identify and explain these circuits by showing how they conferred a survival advantage on those possessing them.

Despite all this, science does not prove that causal determinism is true. In fact, modern physics now explicitly rejects that belief. Physicist Paul Davies explains,

> On the scale of atoms and molecules, the usual rules of cause and effect are suspended. . . . A typical quantum process is the decay of a radioactive nucleus. If you ask why a given nucleus decayed at one moment rather than some other, there is no answer. The event "just happened" at that moment, that's all. You cannot predict these occurrences. All you can do is give the probability. . . . This uncertainty is not simply a result of our ignorance of all the little forces that try to make the nucleus decay; it is inherent in nature itself, a basic part of quantum reality.[20]

Physicists believe that at the atomic level, there are uncaused events—events that happen for no reason at all. What led them to this conclusion is that deterministic theories fail to account for certain experimental results.

Einstein never liked quantum indeterminacy. His dislike is captured in his famous quip "God does not play dice with the universe." He thought that there must be certain "hidden variables," which, if known, would allow us to accurately predict the occurrence of every event, even those at the atomic level.

Einstein's speculation was interesting, but many physicists considered it to be unscientific because there was no way to test it. Then, in 1965, physicist John Bell showed that a hidden variables theory like Einstein's makes predictions that are at odds with quantum mechanics. The equipment needed to test these predictions was not available until 1980. When the experiments were conducted, they always came out in favor of quantum mechanics. As a result, hidden variables theory is dead. Our inability to predict the occurrence of atomic events is not due to our ignorance of the underlying processes or to the limitations of our measuring apparatus. It is due to the basic nature of the universe itself. Parodying Einstein's quote, physicist Stephen Hawking sums up current thinking this way: "God not only plays dice, he throws them in the corner where no one can see them."

A hard determinist might try to defend causal determinism by claiming that, although it doesn't hold on the microlevel of subatomic particles, it does hold on the macrolevel of everyday objects, which is the only level that matters for us. What is true of the parts is not necessarily true of the whole. To claim otherwise is to commit the fallacy of composition. So even if the behavior of subatomic particles is indeterminate, it doesn't follow that our behavior is indeterminate.

Such a defense of causal determinism misses the mark, however, for uncaused events on the microlevel can have profound effects on the macrolevel. Science writer Martin Gardner offers a demonstration.

Thought Experiment

Gardner's Random Bombardier

Imagine a plane flying at supersonic speed over a continent. It carries a hydrogen bomb that is dropped by a mechanism triggered by the click of a Geiger counter. If quantum mechanics is correct, the timing of this click is purely random. Hence absolute chance determines where the bomb falls, and thereby decides between many alternate, equally possible courses of history.[21]

By interacting with individual subatomic particles, Geiger counters effectively "couple" the microworld to the macroworld. Thus any indeterminism that exists in the microworld can be reflected in the macroworld. In Gardner's scenario, the click of a Geiger counter triggers the dropping of a hydrogen bomb. Because the clicking of the Geiger counter is indeterminate, the dropping of the hydrogen bomb is also indeterminate.

Our brains could contain a structure that functions like a Geiger counter. It could respond to the behavior of subatomic particles and randomly modify larger structures of the brain. Perhaps we pass control of our brains over to such a structure whenever we can't make up our minds. In any event, we must conclude that science doesn't show that causal determinism is true. Not only are there no well-confirmed scientific theories in genetics, neurophysiology, or psychology that prove that *all* human actions are caused by prior events, there is reason to believe that indeterminacy is not confined to the microworld.

Common Sense and Causal Determinism

We all believe or are inclined to believe that causal determinism is true. This pervasive belief is a matter of common sense. But, as we said, the fact that everyone has this belief doesn't make it true. Even commonsense beliefs can be false. Some pervasive beliefs, however, are more than just a matter of common sense. They are a matter of *reflective* common sense. A belief of reflective common sense is one that we still believe even after we reflect on it and as-

Is Determinism Self-Refuting?

Some have objected to determinism on the ground that it is self-refuting. John Hick, for example, claims,

> . . . our concept of rational belief is linked with our concept of intellectual freedom. Accordingly a world in which there was (or is) no intellectual freedom would be (or is) a world in which there is no rational belief. Therefore the belief that the world is totally determined cannot rationally claim to be a rational belief. Hence an argument for total determinism is necessarily self-refuting, or logically suicidal.[22]

Hick's argument here goes something like this:

1. If determinism is true, no one believes anything because they have a good reason for believing it. (Instead, they believe it because their neurons have been caused to fire in a certain way.)

2. If no one believes anything because they have a good reason for believing it, no beliefs are rational.

3. Therefore, if determinism is true, no beliefs are rational, including the belief that determinism is true.

Patricia Smith Churchland does not find this sort of argument convincing. She writes,

> An analogy might serve to dramatize the weakness of the putatively self-defeating argument. Until quite recently it was believed that the difference between living things and nonliving

things was that the former was imbued with vital spirit, the latter not. In the event, the theory was challenged and refuted, but consider the following fanciful defense of vitalism, constructed to parallel the aforementioned defense of free will:

> > The anti-vitalist says that there is no such thing as vital spirit. This claim is self-refuting; the speaker can expect to be taken seriously only if his claim cannot. For if the claim is true, then the speaker does not have vital spirit, and must be dead. But since dead men tell no tales, they do not tell anti-vitalist ones either. One cannot reason with dead men.

> In this example, it is clear that the attempt to show that anti-vitalism was self-refuting was simply a *non sequitur*. The argument is a non sequitur because life may be explained by something other than vital spirit, for example by something physical, though the explanation may be much more intricate and complicated than anything envisaged at the time.[23]

Thought Probe

Defending Determinism

Who's right, Hick or Churchland? What premise(s) in Hick's argument would Churchland reject? Why? Is she justified in rejecting them? Why or why not?

---

sess it carefully. Part of this assessment is trying to think of counterexamples that would show the belief to be false. If we carefully evaluate the belief and find no counterexamples to it, we're justified in believing it. It's a reasonable belief.

It has been argued that causal determinism is such a belief, a matter of reflective common sense. After all, how could we make sense of the world if we didn't believe that everything has a cause? It would seem that the idea that everything has a cause is a presupposition crucial to human understanding. Immanuel Kant held this view. He claimed that we could not understand the world unless we assumed that every event has a cause.

Even if we can make sense of the world only on the assumption that every event has a cause, it doesn't follow that every event has a cause because the world may be incomprehensible. What we need to understand the world may

All theory is against freedom of the will; all experience for it.

—Samuel Johnson

not be present in it. What's more, modern physics has shown that we can understand the world without assuming that every event has a cause. Quantum mechanics (the branch of physics that deals with subatomic particles) gives us an unprecedented understanding of the physical world, and yet it does not assume that every event has a cause. So causal determinism is not vindicated by either science or reflective common sense.

Thought Probe

Genetic Cleansing

Suppose that sociobiologists discover the genes that influence our psychology. Suppose further that we develop a technology that allows us to alter our genes thus giving us the power to change our temperament, or personality, and our cognitive ability. Should we use this technology? Why or why not? What would a hard determinist say? Why?

Indeterminism

Many shining actions owe their success to chance, though the general or statesman runs away with the applause.

—HENRY HOME

The view that some events are not the consequence of past events plus the laws of nature is known as **causal indeterminism.** In this view, the future is not fixed. It could unfold in a number of different ways, all of which are consistent with what has gone before. The ancient Greek philosopher Epicurus (341–270 B.C.), another atomist, realized that if the motion of atoms was completely determinate, there would be no free will. To explain how free will is possible, he speculated that atoms randomly "swerve" as they move through space. This random movement of subatomic particles has since been confirmed by modern physics. Physicist Max Born illustrates it with the following tale: "If Gessler had ordered William Tell to shoot a hydrogen atom off his son's head by means of an alpha particle and had given him the best laboratory instruments in the world instead of a cross-bow, Tell's skill would have availed him nothing. Hit or miss would have been a matter of chance."[24] The Physicist Arthur Eddington believes that this indeterminism vindicates our belief in free will. He writes, "The revolution of theory which has expelled determinism from present day physics has therefore the important consequence that it is no longer necessary to suppose that human actions are completely predetermined."[25] If our actions are not predetermined, however, there is room for free will.

William James was as concerned about the ethical implications of determinism as was Epicurus. James realized that in a world governed by necessity, there could be no morality. So he argued that some things happen by chance.

> Indeterminism . . . says that the parts have a certain amount of loose play on one another, so that the laying down of one of them does not necessarily determine what the others shall be. It admits that possibilities may be in excess of actualities, and that things not yet revealed to our knowledge may really in themselves be

One of the more interesting characters in the history of philosophy is William James (1842–1910). He was one of the first important philosophers to come out of America, yet his expertise and interests spread far beyond philosophy.

He was born in New York City, the son of a theologian and the elder brother of the famous novelist Henry James. Little wonder then that he spent so much time studying the psychology of religion and wrote in a lively, clear style that seems more suitable to a novel than a philosophical treatise. James first studied to become an artist, but then entered Harvard University as a medical student. He later lectured there in physiology and anatomy, then philosophy, then psychology.

James seemed to be driven by his own psychological needs to address certain vexing philosophical issues. At one point in his career, he became obsessed with the problem of free will and determinism. He fell into a deep depression, contemplated suicide, and did not recover until he had worked out an answer that made sense to him. (His view is that humans do have free will despite the universe's lockstep determinism.)

Likewise he was intensely interested in both the psychological and philosophical implications of religious belief. He wanted to find a place for religion in his worldview and did so by claiming that people may legitimately accept religious claims if they "work," even when there is no evidence to support those claims. This view of claims that work or don't work is part of James's pragmatism, the notion that the meaning or truth of a claim is the same thing as the practical effects of accepting it (that is, that it works).

---

ambiguous. Of two alternative futures which we conceive, both may now be really possible; and the one become impossible only at the very moment when the other excludes by becoming real. Indeterminism thus denies the world to be one unbending unit of fact. . . . Do not all the motives that assail us, all the futures that offer themselves to our choice, spring equally from the soil of the past; and would not either one of them, whether realized through chance or through necessity, the moment it was realized, seem to us to fit that past, and in the completest and most continuous manner to interdigitate with the phenomena already there?[26]

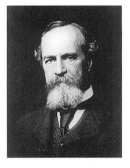

WILLIAM JAMES
1842–1910

If the world is not completely determined, each of us has many possible futures. Which of those futures becomes actual will depend on the choices we make. But a free choice—a choice made by chance—would fit just as well with what has gone before as would a determined choice.

James's view that free actions are uncaused is known as **indeterminism.** It rejects the principle of causal determinism that serves as the first premise of the hard determinists' argument. Because our best scientific theories imply that some events are uncaused, indeterminism is a more conservative theory than hard determinism, for it fits better with our existing knowledge. But even though indeterminism does less damage to our belief system than hard determinism, it has problems of its own because it can't account for personal responsibility. You are responsible for an action only if you did it. But if an action is uncaused, you didn't do it. So it's hard to see how an indeterminist can hold people responsible for their actions.

Richard Taylor illustrates this problem by means of the following thought experiment.

causal indeterminism
The doctrine that some events are not the consequence of past events plus the laws of nature.

indeterminism The doctrine that free actions are uncaused.

Taylor's Unpredictable Arm

Suppose that my right arm is free, according to this conception; that is, that its motions are uncaused. It moves this way and that from time to time, but nothing causes these motions. Sometimes it moves forth vigorously, sometimes up, sometimes down, sometimes it just drifts vaguely about — these motions all being wholly free and uncaused. Manifestly, I have nothing to do with them at all; they just happen, and neither I nor anyone can ever tell what this arm will be doing next. It might seize a club and lay it on the head of the nearest by-stander, no less to my astonishment than his. There will never be any point in asking why these motions occur, or in seeking any explanation of them, for under the conditions assumed there is no explanation. They just happen, from no causes at all.[27]

Taylor imagines that the motions of his arm are totally random. Perhaps his arm is connected to a piece of radioactive material in such a way that whenever the radioactive material decays, his arm moves. In any event, if the movements of Taylor's arm are totally random, Taylor can't be held responsible for them.

Actions, as opposed to reflexes, are intentional. Your leg's going up after the doctor hits your knee with a mallet is a reflex — not an action — because you didn't intend it to happen. Similarly, Taylor's arm movements are not actions because he did not intend them to happen. But if they are not actions, they are not free actions either. So indeterminism does not provide a satisfactory account of free action.

We normally assume that human behavior can be explained by appeal to a person's motives, circumstances, or both. If indeterminism were true, some actions (namely, free actions) would be inexplicable because they would happen for no reason at all. Indeterminism, then, makes free actions incomprehensible. Instead of explaining how free actions are possible, it leaves us with as big a mystery as the one we started with.

Summary

Causal determinism, the view that every event is the consequence of past events plus the laws of nature, has led some to adopt hard determinism, the doctrine that there are no free actions. Hard determinists believe that causal determinism is incompatible with both free and moral responsibility. Modern physics, however, supports causal indeterminism, the view that some events are not the consequence of past events plus the laws of nature. So the future does not appear to be determined.

Some have thought that causal indeterminism makes way for freedom. They accept indeterminism, the doctrine that free actions are uncaused. William James, for example, argues that free will is possible only if human choices are not part of some causal chain but are the result of chance. Because of this element of chance, there exist multiple possibilities for humans, as opposed to the one and only locked-in future of determinism. This view is attractive, but it is seriously flawed—for if an action is the result of uncaused, chance events, it is random. And a random action cannot be a free action because it is not produced by an act of will.

Study Questions

1. What is causal determinism?
2. What is hard determinism?
3. What is the argument for hard determinism?
4. Does science show that causal determinism is true?
5. Does reflective common sense show that causal determinism is true?
6. What is causal indeterminism?
7. What is indeterminism?
8. What is Taylor's unpredictable arm thought experiment? How does it attempt to undermine indeterminism?

Discussion Questions

1. Imagine that hard determinism is true. Would there be any justification for punishment? Why or why not?
2. Suppose that after much thought you fully accept hard determinism. How might your reaction to the following situations differ now that you're a hard determinist?
   a. O. J. Simpson is tried for another murder, you're convinced that he committed the crime, and again he is found not guilty.
   b. Your best friend spreads a malicious and scandalous rumor about you.
   c. You murder your mother.
   d. Your sister is raped by a friend of yours.
3. Let's say that someone who knows you well believes that he can predict everything you do and say during a twenty-four-hour period. Without telling you what he's up to, he writes down his prediction in great detail. And as it turns out, his predictions are correct. Does the fact that someone can accurately predict the behavior of another show that the behavior was determined—that it was fully the result of causes?
4. William Newcomb, a theoretical physicist, proposed the following thought experiment to test beliefs about foreknowledge and causation.

Thought Experiment

Newcomb's Paradox

Suppose there is a Being that, as far as you know, has always correctly predicted your choices in the past. Now suppose this Being makes you the following offer:

The Being shows you two boxes and explains that Box 1 contains $1,000, while Box 2 contains either $1 million or nothing. You can make one of two choices: (1) take what is in both boxes, or (2) take only what is in the second box. The Being has already placed the money in the boxes and he did so on the basis of his prediction. He tells you that if he predicted that you will choose the first alternative and take what is in both boxes, then he left Box 2 empty. If he predicted that you will choose the second alternative and take only what is in Box 2, the Being puts $1 million in it. If you were faced with this choice, which alternative would you choose? Would you choose to take what is in both boxes or only what is in the second box? Why?

The Mother of Invention
Freedom as Necessity

/f causal determinism is true — if every event is the consequence of past events plus the laws of nature — then we cannot act freely because everything we do is caused by forces beyond our control. If causal indeterminism is true — if some of our actions are uncaused — then those actions can't be free because they are not up to us. Because either causal determinism or causal indeterminism is true, the conclusion that we can't act freely seems unavoidable.

Some try to escape this conclusion, however, by arguing that causal determinism is compatible with free will. In their view, we can act freely even if every event is the consequence of past events plus the laws of nature. Unlike hard determinism, this view "abhors harsh words, and repudiates fatality, necessity, and even predetermination and says that its real name is freedom."[28] Consequently, William James calls this view **soft determinism.**

Compatibilism is an appealing solution to the problem of free will because it does not require giving up either the belief in causal determinism or the belief in free will. Compatibilists think they can have their cake and eat it too. Even if science succeeds in showing that all of our behavior is determined, we need not give up the belief that we can be held responsible for what we do. Determined acts can be free acts.

Incompatibilists and traditional compatibilists agree that acting freely requires the ability to do otherwise. If only one course of action is open to you — if you have no choice but to perform an action — you can't perform it freely. Freedom requires choice, and choice requires alternatives. As British philosopher A. J. Ayer put it,

> . . . it is only when it is believed that I could have acted otherwise that I am held to be morally responsible for what I have done. For a man is not thought to be morally responsible for an action that it was not in his power to avoid.[29]

The condition for moral responsibility that Ayer is articulating here has come to be known as the **principle of alternative possibilities:** one can be held

Only that thing is free which exists by the necessities of its own nature, and is determined in its action by itself alone.

— Spinoza

soft determinism
The doctrine that determined actions can nevertheless be free.

principle of alternative possibilities One can be held responsible for doing something only if one could have done otherwise.

responsible for doing something only if one could have done otherwise. This condition can be represented graphically by a "garden of forking paths":[30]

The different paths represent the different courses of action that you can take at a particular point in time. As long as there are a number of courses of action open to you, you can be held responsible for taking one of them. But if it's not in your power to decide which path you'll take — if you're forced to choose one particular path — you shouldn't be held responsible for taking it.

Traditional Compatibilism

Chance is a word devoid of sense. Nothing can exist without a cause.

— Voltaire

Traditional compatibilists believe that free will is compatible with causal determinism. Even if everything you do is determined by past events plus the laws of nature, you still could have done otherwise. They defend this view by offering a hypothetical analysis of the phrase "could have done otherwise." According to them, to say that you could have done otherwise is to say that if you had chosen otherwise, you would have done otherwise. The ability to do otherwise, then, depends on the presence or absence of external constraints. If a different choice would have resulted in a different action, you could have done otherwise.

The first person to articulate a compatibilist position was Thomas Hobbes (1588–1679). He rejected as unintelligible the indeterminist notion that free actions are uncaused. "Nothing," he says, "taketh a beginning from itself."[31] Free actions, like all other events, must have a cause. Specifically, they must be caused by the will. But being caused by the will is not enough to make an action free because, in some situations, no other actions are possible. If you couldn't do otherwise, your action isn't free.

Hobbes offers a conditional analysis of what it is to be able to do otherwise. He writes,

> . . . he is free to do a thing, that may do it if he have the will to do it, and may forbear if he have the will to forbear.[32]

According to Hobbes's **traditional compatibilism,** two conditions must be met in order for someone to act freely: (1) the action must be caused by his will, and (2) it must not be externally constrained. If the action is not caused by his will — if he didn't bring it about — then he didn't perform it. If it is externally constrained — if there is no other action he could perform in those circumstances — then he isn't free to perform it. Hobbes, then, defines freedom negatively. For him, freedom consists in the absence of external constraint or coercion. This type of freedom is often referred to as "negative freedom" or "freedom from" because it takes freedom to consist in the absence of certain impediments to action.

Locke highlights the importance of Hobbes's second condition for free action in the following thought experiment.

Thought Experiment

Locke's Trapped Conversationalist

Suppose a man is carried, while fast asleep, into a room, where there is a person he longs to see and speak with; and suppose he is locked in the room, beyond his power to get out: he awakes, and is glad to find himself in so desirable company, which he stays willingly in, i.e. prefers his stay to going away. I ask, is not this stay voluntary? I think, nobody will doubt it: and yet being locked fast in, it is evident that he is not at liberty not to stay; he does not have the freedom to leave. So liberty is not an idea belonging to volition, or preferring; but to the person having the power of doing, or forbearing to do, according as the mind shall choose or direct.[33]

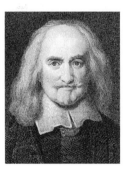

THOMAS HOBBES
1588–1679

traditional compatibilism The doctrine that free actions are (1) caused by one's will and (2) not externally constrained.

Locke's trapped conversationalist is kidnapped while asleep and locked in a room with someone he longs to talk to. When he awakes, he has no desire to leave because he enjoys the company. His staying in the room is a voluntary action because it is what he wants to do. But it is not a free action because he couldn't do otherwise; he couldn't leave the room even if he wanted to. No alternative courses of action are open to him. So the action of the trapped conversationalist meets the first condition of traditional compatibilism but not the second. Because he is not free to leave, his staying in the room is not a free action.

Not only must free actions be unconstrained, but they must be caused by one's will. You act freely only if you do what you want to do. Walter Stace explains,

> What, then, is the difference between acts which are freely done and those which are not? What is the characteristic which is present to all [free acts like "Gandhi fasting because he wanted to free India"] and absent from all [unfree acts like "The man fasting in the desert because there was no food"]? Is it not obvious that, although both sets of actions have causes, the causes of [free acts] are of a different kind from the causes of [unfree acts]? The free acts are all caused by desires, or motives, or by some sort of internal psychological states of the agent's mind. The unfree acts, on the other hand, are all caused by physical forces or physical conditions, outside the agent. Police arrest means physical force exerted from the outside; the absence of food in the desert is a physical condition of the outside world. We may therefore frame the following rough definitions. *Acts freely done are those whose immediate causes are psychological states in the agent. Acts not freely done are those whose immediate causes are states of affairs external to the agent.*[34]

The only actions that we can be held responsible for are those that have been caused by our own beliefs and desires. If the immediate cause of an action is something external to us, like a gun pointed at our head, it is not our doing.

Traditional compatibilism maintains that the conditions of being caused by one's will and not being externally constrained are individually necessary and jointly sufficient for acting freely. Do all and only free actions meet these conditions? Many think not. Consider this thought experiment by Richard Taylor.

Thought Experiment

Taylor's Ingenious Physiologist

Let us suppose that my body is moving in various ways, that these motions are not externally constrained or impeded, and that they are all exactly in accordance with my own desires, choices, or acts of will and what not. . . . We suppose further, accordingly, that while my behavior is entirely in accordance with my own volitions, and thus "free" in terms of the conception of freedom we are examining, my volitions themselves are caused. To make this graphic, we can suppose that an ingenious physiologist can induce in me any volition he pleases, simply by pushing various buttons on an instrument to which, let us suppose, I am attached by numerous wires. All the volitions I have in that situation are, accordingly, precisely the ones he gives me. By pushing one button, he evokes in me the volition to raise my hand; and my hand, being unimpeded, rises in response to that volition. By pushing another, he induces the volition in me to kick, and my foot, being unimpeded, kicks in response to that volition. We can

even suppose that the physiologist puts a rifle in my hands, aims at some passer-by, and then, by pushing the proper button, evokes in me the volition to squeeze my finger against the trigger, whereupon the passer-by falls dead of a bullet wound.[35]

Taylor envisions a situation in which both of the conditions of traditional compatibilism are met: his actions are caused by his will and they are not externally constrained. He is doing what he wants to do, and there are no external forces preventing him from doing otherwise. Nevertheless, his actions are not free because his desires are not his own. They come from the ingenious neurophysiologist, not from himself.

You might think that Taylor's thought experiment is not a counterexample to traditional compatibilism because the ingenious neurophysiologist causes Taylor's actions. But you would be mistaken. The ingenious neurophysiologist does not directly cause Taylor's actions, he only causes Taylor's desires. The direct (proximal) cause of Taylor's actions is his desires. The machinations of the ingenious neurophysiologist are only an indirect (distal) cause of them. Thus Taylor's actions meet both conditions of traditional compatibilism and yet do not seem to be free.

We don't have to appeal to science fiction to see the inadequacy of traditional compatibilism's analysis of free action. Consider the case of drug addicts.

I may be free to do as I please, but am I free to please as I please?

—ARTHUR
SCHOPENHAUER

Better Living through Neurophysiology

Ingenious physiologists of the sort Taylor envisions are not just creatures of fiction. A number of neurophysiologists are trying to control thought patterns by electronically stimulating the brain. Foremost among them is Jose Delgado, former professor of neurophysiology at Yale University. Samuel Chavkin recounts his conversation with Dr. Delgado:

Dr. Delgado feels this development [electronic stimulation of the brain] represents a great breakthrough in the treatment of a variety of conditions, such as pain, emotional illness, and epilepsy. It is based on the principle of having one section of the brain "counter" the activity of another section. "We know that perception, decision making, learning, and other activities may be accompanied by detectable electrical phenomena," he recently wrote. "We also know that electrical stimulation of the brain may induce or modify a variety of autonomic, somatic and mental manifestations." So why not apply this knowledge in controlling brain phenomena at will? . . .

"Detection of brain activity, processing of information, and the automatic triggering of a stimulator," he points out, "could be of critical therapeutic value" and could be used only when needed. "This is the way I foresee psychiatry within five or ten years," he predicted, "when it would begin depending upon the implantation of little computers to deal with emotional illness."[36]

Dr. Delgado has developed a "stimoceiver" that can both monitor brain activity and alter it by means of electronic stimulation. Such a device could be used not only to treat mental disorders but also to rehabilitate criminals or other social misfits. The brain state of those outfitted with this device could be monitored at all times. If it showed any abnormalities, it could be restored to normalcy by remote control.

Thought Probe

Brain Stimulation

Do you agree with Delgado that we should implant stimoceivers into people's brains to monitor and modify their behavior? Why or why not?

Thought Experiment

Taylor's Drug Addiction

One can, for instance, be given a compulsive desire for certain drugs, simply by having them administered to him over a course of time. Suppose, then, that I do, with neither my knowledge nor consent, thus become a victim of such a desire and act upon it. Do I act freely, merely by virtue of the fact that I am unimpeded in my quest for drugs? In a sense I do, surely, but I am hardly free with respect to whether or not I shall use drugs. I never chose to have the desire for them inflicted upon me.[37]

It is possible to become addicted to crack cocaine after using it only a few times. After one is addicted, one has an irresistible desire to use it. Nevertheless, a crack addict's use of crack meets the conditions for a free action laid down by traditional compatibilism: it is caused by the addict's own will, and it is not externally constrained. So traditional compatibilism would have us believe that a crack addict's use of crack is a free action. But that's implausible. Crack addicts can't help themselves. They are slaves to their drug habit. Because traditional compatibilism suggests otherwise, there is reason to believe that it's mistaken.

Compulsive behavior (of which addiction is just one example) is caused by uncontrollable desires. Kleptomania, for example, is caused by an uncontrollable desire to steal. Because a desire is an internal cause, traditional compatibilism would have us believe that the actions of a kleptomaniac are just as free as those of an ordinary thief. But any view that considers compulsive behavior just as free as normal behavior is dubious.

Taylor's thought experiments show that the conditions specified by traditional compatibilism are not sufficient for acting freely. Even if your actions are caused by your will, and even if they are not externally constrained, they can fail to be free. If your will is not under your control — if your choices are not up to you — your actions aren't free.

Thought Probe

Brainwashing

Suppose someone were brainwashed into acquiring a whole new set of desires and beliefs. After the brainwashing, every action he performed flowed from his new desires and beliefs. According to traditional compatibilism, would his actions be free? Why or why not? Does this case bolster or undercut traditional compatibilism?

Hierarchical Compatibilism

The principle of alternative possibilities has it that you are responsible for an action only if you could have done otherwise. This is the insight contained in the second condition of traditional compatibilism. If no other courses of action are open to you — if you are constrained to perform an action — you are not free to perform it. A number of thinkers have recently challenged this conception of free action. In the following thought experiment, Harry Frankfurt tries to show that one can be held responsible for an action even if one couldn't do otherwise.

Thought Experiment

Frankfurt's Decision Inducer

Suppose someone — Black, let us say — wants Jones to perform a certain action. Black is prepared to go to considerable lengths to get his way, but he prefers to avoid showing his hand unnecessarily. So he waits until Jones is about to make up his mind what to do, and he does nothing unless it is clear to him (Black is an excellent judge of such things) that Jones is going to decide to do something other than what he wants him to do. Whatever Jones's initial preferences and inclinations, then, Black will have his way. . . .

Now suppose that Black never has to show his hand because Jones, for reasons of his own, decides to perform and does perform the very action Black wants him to perform. In that case, it seems clear, Jones will bear precisely the same moral responsibility for what he does as he would have borne if Black had not been ready to take steps to ensure that he do it. It would be quite unreasonable to excuse Jones for his action, or to withhold the praise to which it would normally entitle him, on the basis of the fact that he could not have done otherwise.[38]

Frankfurt describes a situation in which Jones can't do otherwise because Black won't let him. Unlike Taylor's ingenious physiologist, however, Black doesn't control Jones's every move. Instead, he monitors Jones's behavior and intervenes only if Jones is going to do something that Black doesn't want him to. So Jones's actions fail to meet the second condition of traditional compatibilism because they are externally constrained by Black. Nevertheless, Frankfurt claims, Jones is responsible for his actions because he is doing what he wants to do.

Each of us wants to do many things, and often these wants conflict. For example, you may want to get a good night's sleep so you will do well on an exam the next day, and you may want to stay up late. So when we say that you did what you wanted to do, we may simply mean that you acted on one of your wants. But we may also mean that you acted on the want you wanted to act on. Only if your action is of the second sort, Frankfurt says, is it free.

All of us have desires for various objects and states of affairs. We desire things like food, clothing, and shelter as well as conditions like being healthy, being well informed, and being well paid. Desires that are directed on objects or states of affairs are called **first-order desires.**

Self-conscious beings like ourselves are not only aware of the first-order desires we have, but we can have desires about those desires. A smoker, for example, can have the desire to not desire to smoke. That is, he can desire to be the sort of person who has no desire for cigarettes. Desires that are directed on first-order desires are called **second-order desires.**

It's possible to have a second-order desire without wanting to act on it. Suppose, for example, that you were a priest who regularly counseled people with marriage problems. In such a situation, you might have a desire to know what it's like to be married. But you probably wouldn't want to act on that desire because if you did, you would no longer be a priest. Second-order desires that we want to act on Frankfurt calls **second-order volitions.**

To act freely, says Frankfurt, is to act on a second-order volition. If you do not formulate second-order volitions, or if you do not act on the ones you do form, your actions are not free — you are a slave to your first-order desires. Frankfurt uses two different types of drug addicts to make his point.

Frankfurt's Unwilling and Wanton Addicts

Let us suppose that the physiological condition accounting for the addiction is the same in both men, and that both succumb inevitably to their periodic desires for the drug to which they are addicted. One of the addicts hates his addiction and always struggles desperately, although to no avail, against its thrust. He tries everything that he thinks might enable him to overcome his desires for the drug. But these desires are too powerful for him to withstand, and invariably, in the end, they conquer him. He is an unwilling addict, helplessly violated by his own desires. . . .

The other addict is a wanton. His actions reflect the economy of his first-order desires, without his being concerned whether the desires that move him to act are desires by which he wants to be moved to act. If he encounters problems in obtaining the drug or in administering it to himself, his responses to his urges to take it may involve deliberation. But it never occurs to him to consider whether he wants the relation among his desires to result in his having the will he has. The wanton addict may be an animal, and thus incapable of being concerned about his will. In any event he is, in respect of his wanton lack of concern, no different from an animal.[39]

The unwilling addict has second-order volitions but is incapable of acting on them. He desires that he not act on his desire to take drugs, but he can't help himself. He is a slave to his drug habit. The wanton, on the other hand, has no second-order volitions. He never questions or reflects on his first-order desires. He has never wondered whether it is desirable to be a drug addict. According to Frankfurt, neither addict acts freely because neither acts on second-order volitions; the unwilling addict doesn't act on them because he cannot bring himself to act on them, and the wanton doesn't act on them because he doesn't have them.

According to Frankfurt, free actions are caused by second-order volitions that one decisively identifies with. This view is known as **hierarchical compatibilism** because it is based on the belief that there is a hierarchy of desires and volitions. The phrase "decisively identifies with" is needed to forestall an infinite regress. Just as our first-order desires can conflict, so can our second-order desires. We may formulate a third-order desire to try to resolve such a conflict, but that desire may conflict with another third-order desire, and so on and on. But a second-order desire that we decisively identify with, claims Frankfurt, "'resounds' throughout the potentially endless array of higher orders," halts the regress, and brings a coherence to our preference structure.

Traditional compatibilism maintains that you cannot act freely if your actions are externally constrained. Frankfurt denies this. As long as you act on your second-order volitions, you are responsible for your actions, whether or not you could do otherwise. Frankfurt appeals to another kind of addict to illustrate this.

first-order desire A desire directed on an object or a state of affairs.

second-order desire A desire directed on a first-order desire.

second-order volition A second-order desire on which one wants to act.

hierarchical compatibilism The doctrine that free actions are caused by second-order volitions that one decisively identifies with.

AN OPIUM DEN IN NEW YORK CITY, CA. 1926.
Are these addicts unwilling, wanton, or happy?

Thought Experiment

Frankfurt's Happy Addict

. . . consider a third kind of addict. Suppose that his addiction has the same physiological basis and the same irresistible thrust as the addictions of the unwilling and wanton addicts, but that he is altogether delighted with his condition. He is a willing addict, who would not have things any other way. If the grip of his addiction should somehow weaken, he would do whatever he could to reinstate it; if his desire for the drug should begin to fade, he would take steps to renew its intensity.[40]

The happy addict, according to Frankfurt, acts freely because he acts on his second-order volition to take drugs. He couldn't do otherwise because he couldn't stop taking drugs even if he wanted to. But the important point is that he doesn't want to. He likes being a drug addict. So his taking drugs is a free action.

Unlike traditional compatibilism, hierarchical compatibilism can explain why those suffering from obsessive-compulsive disorders do not act freely even though their actions are caused internally and are not externally constrained. If a kleptomaniac doesn't want to act on his desire to steal but steals anyway, he does not act freely.

Hierarchical compatibilism can also explain why animals are not usually considered to have free will. Animals, especially mammals, may well be conscious, but they do not seem to be self-conscious, for they do not seem to be able to formulate second-order desires. Cows, for example, can't form a desire to not desire to overeat. They never consider whether they want to be the sort of creatures that are motivated by the desires they have. In other words, animals are wantons. They have—and act on—only first-order desires.

In addition to explaining why addicts and animals do not act freely, hierarchical compatibilism can explain why free will is such a valuable thing. People who act on their second-order volitions do what they want to do; they are their own persons. People who cannot act on their second-order volitions are not in control of their lives. They are not the kind of person they want to be. As a result, they often become alienated from themselves and suffer the despair and depression that comes from feeling powerless.

Hierarchical compatibilism is superior to traditional compatibilism because it has more explanatory power. Whether it's an adequate theory of free action will depend on whether acting on a second-order volition one decisively identifies with is both necessary and sufficient for acting freely.

A number of writers argue that it is not sufficient because one can meet that condition and yet not act freely. Michael Slote identifies one such case.

Thought Experiment

Slote's Hypnotized Patient

Consider the following example. Robert, who is genuinely undecided between two conflicting first-order desires X and Y, is visited by a hypnotist who decides to "solve" his problem by putting him in a trance and inducing in him a second-order volition in favor of X; as a result of having this second-order volition, Robert then acts to satisfy X, never suspecting that his decisiveness has been induced by the hypnotist. The example may bear the marks of science fiction, but it seems adequate, nonetheless, to point up the conceptual insufficiency of "rationality" conditions of free action. For we would all surely deny that Robert acts of his own free will, when he acts from the second-order volitions induced by the hypnotist.[41]

Robert acts on a second-order volition that he identifies with. But his action is not free because his volition is not his. It comes from a hypnotist instead of himself. So there must be more to acting freely than acting on second-order volitions with which you decisively identify. If your actions aren't your own—if you aren't doing your own thing—you aren't acting freely.

Free actions are products of the self. Our desires or volitions may be the immediate causes of our actions, but unless we had a hand in shaping those desires, our actions are not truly our own and we can't be held responsible for them. As Robert Kane puts it, we are "ultimately responsible" for an action only if we are "responsible for the character and motives from which it issued."[42]

There may well be cases where, given a person's character and motives, that person could not have done otherwise. Daniel Dennett cites the case of Martin Luther, who, when he broke away from the Catholic Church, reportedly said, "Here I stand. I can do no other."[43] Given who he was, and given his situation, it may well have been impossible for Luther to do anything else. Nevertheless, Dennett says, Luther may be held responsible for what he did. Kane would agree. But he would add that if Luther is ultimately responsible for what he did, there must have been times in the past when he could have done otherwise, and the choices he made then must have formed the character he has now. If he had no hand in determining who he is, he can't be ultimately responsible for his actions. The question is, How is it possible for one to make such pivotal choices about the self? We'll explore this problem in the next section.

Thought Probe

The Willing Bank Teller

Suppose you are a bank teller and are held up at gunpoint. You realize that you could foil the bank robber if you could take his gun away from him, but you decide that your chances of success are not great. So you calmly hand over the money to him. According to hierarchical compatibilism, do you freely hand over the money to the bank robber? If so, is this a counterexample to hierarchical compatibilism? Why or why not?

Summary

Compatibilists say that causal determinism does not rule out freedom. Even if everything is caused, we can still have free will. So they reject the second premise of the hard determinist's argument, namely, that if every event has a cause, there are no free actions. But they accept the first premise — that every event has a cause. They have thus come to be known as soft determinists.

According to traditional compatibilism, actions can be free if they are (1) caused by one's will and (2) not externally constrained. An action is not externally constrained if the person performing the action is such that if he had chosen to do otherwise, he could have done otherwise. These conditions are not sufficient for free will because if you could not have chosen otherwise, your actions aren't free. Free actions require that your will be under your control — that what you do be up to you.

Hierarchical compatibilism is based on the insight that persons have a hierarchy of different desires. A first-order desire is a desire directed on an object or a state of being; a second-order desire is a desire about a first-order desire. A second-order desire to act on a first-order desire is a second-order volition. For Frankfurt, to act freely you must do more than act on a first-order desire. You must act on a second-order volition with which you identify.

According to this form of compatibilism, you can act freely even if you can't act otherwise.

But hierarchical compatibilism can't be the whole story about free will because our second-order volitions may themselves be caused by forces beyond our control. So there must be more to acting freely than just acting on second-order volitions with which you decisively identify.

Study Questions

1. What is soft determinism?

2. What is traditional compatibilism?

3. What is Stace's explanation of how all our actions have causes, yet some actions are free?

4. What is Taylor's ingenious physiologist thought experiment? What is Taylor's drug addiction thought experiment? How do these two experiments undermine traditional compatibilism?

5. What is Frankfurt's decision inducer thought experiment? How does it attempt to undermine the traditional notion of responsibility?

6. What is hierarchical compatibilism?

7. What is Slote's hypnotized patient thought experiment? How does it attempt to undermine hierarchical compatibilism?

Discussion Questions

1. Suppose that you created an android that was so advanced it could act independently in very complex situations. It made its own decisions and always did exactly what it wanted to do, in accordance with its programming. Would such an android be capable of free action? Why or why not?

2. Consider this argument for compatibilism:

When you perform an action, whatever observable thing that happens, there surely must be something that happens inside you. There must be some psychological event — like your wanting to perform some action — that is connected with the occurrence of the action. If you perform the action of pointing your finger, there must be some internal event of wanting that is linked to your finger-pointing. This connection is obviously causal. Your wanting to point your finger causally produces your finger-pointing. So any action you perform must be caused by some psychological state. Therefore, since action — including free action — involves causal determination (causal determination is part of action), free action must be compatible with causal determination.

Does this argument prove compatibilism? Why or why not?

3. According to hierarchical compatibilism, does Locke's trapped conversationalist act freely? Why or why not?

4. According to either traditional or hierarchical compatibilism, would there be any justification for punishing anybody? If so, what would the justification be?

5. What second-order desires do you have? Do you have any that you're not able to act on? Does that mean that you're not free? Why or why not?

6. If none of your choices were ever up to you — if you played no role in forming your character or becoming the kind of person you are — should you be held responsible for your actions? Why or why not?

Control Yourself
Freedom as Self-Determination

Causal determinism seems to preclude free will. If everything we do is determined by forces beyond our control, nothing we do is up to us. The compatibilist attempt to square determinism with free will seems little better than William James's description of it: "a quagmire of evasion under which the real issue of fact has been entirely smothered."[44] Freedom is more than the absence of constraint; it is the ability to decide our own destiny. Do we have the power to do that? Libertarians believe we do.

Libertarianism holds that free actions are caused by selves. You are responsible for an action if, and only if, you did it. It's not enough for the action to be caused by your desires because if your desires are not your own, you are not ultimately responsible for the actions that flow from them. Is there any evidence that we have this sort of control over our lives? Libertarians say our ordinary, everyday experience of choosing provides such evidence.

> *The sovereignty of one's self over one's self is called Liberty.*
>
> —ALBERT PIKE

The Case for Freedom

The Argument from Experience

We all frequently have the impression that we can freely choose and that the choices we make are up to us. In countless situations, we have the impression that there are alternatives open to us and that nothing prevents us from choosing any one of them—or not choosing. In short, we continually have the experience that we are acting freely. We each would heartily agree that we have experiences like this:

> [At] most moments while I am sitting and talking or listening to someone, I have the impression that there are several alternative things I could do next with my right hand: gesture with it, scratch my head with it, put it on my lap, put it in my pocket, and so on. For each of these alternatives, it seems to me that nothing at

> **libertarianism** The doctrine that free actions are caused by selves (agents, persons).

My Wife and My Mother in Law by W. E. Hill (Illustration, 1915). This ambiguous figure can be seen as a young woman or an old one. But you can decide which aspect you will see. A proof of free will? Some psychologists think so.[45]

all up to that moment stands in the way of my making it the next thing I do with my right hand; it seems to me that what has happened hitherto, the situation at that moment, leaves each of those alternatives still open to me to perform. And while I am conscious, I have similar impressions of open alternatives almost continually, not only about what I could do with my right hand but also, of course, about what I could do with my head, with my speech apparatus, and with my legs and feet. My impression at each moment is that I at the moment, and nothing prior to that moment, determine which of several open alternatives is the next sort of bodily exertion I voluntarily make.[46]

The experience of choosing among alternate courses of action is one that we've all had, and that experience is as uniform and regular as any experience we've had of the external world. On the face of it, then, it seems that our evidence for the existence of free will is as good as our evidence for the existence of the external world. It could turn out that our experience of free will is an illusion, just as it could turn out that our experience of the external world is an illusion—we could be living in a computer simulation like the

Matrix where neither our external nor our internal perceptions are accurate. But in the absence of any convincing evidence to the effect that free will is an illusion, we are justified in believing that it isn't.

The Argument from Deliberation

Just as we've all had the experience of choosing among alternative courses of action, so we've all had the experience of deliberating about which action to choose. We can deliberate about doing something, however, only if we believe that it is in our power to do it or not to do it. If you believe that the concert you wanted to go to is now over, then you can't deliberate about whether to attend the concert. Because you know that there is now no way for you to attend the concert (you have no choice about it), you cannot seriously engage in deciding whether to attend. You might pretend to decide, but genuine deliberation is out of the question. Therefore, when we deliberate, we must believe that we can perform free actions.

Believing something to be true, however, doesn't make it true. Millions of children believe in the Easter bunny, the tooth fairy, and Santa Claus, but that doesn't mean that they exist. Those are folk beliefs that we all know to be false. Similarly, some people say that free will is a folk belief that we now know to be false.

The best evidence for the nonexistence of free will comes from certain experiments on reaction times conducted by psychologist Benjamin Libet. In those experiments, subjects' heads were hooked up to an electroencephalograph (EEG) to measure brain wave patterns, their fingers were hooked up to an electromyograph (EMG) to measure voltage changes in muscles, and they were seated in front of a rapidly moving clock. They were then given the following instructions: "Flex your finger to push the button when you feel like it, and tell us where the hand on the clock is when you decide to do that." The time at which the EEG detected motor activity in the brain (known as the "readiness potential") was set at zero, the time at which the subject reported becoming aware of the intention to press the button occurred about 350 milliseconds (0.35 seconds) later, and the time at which the EMG measured a voltage change in the finger muscle occurred about 200 milliseconds after that. These results seem to indicate that the subjects didn't become conscious of the intention to move their finger until after the movement had started. So rather than causing movement, conscious awareness seems to be an effect of it. Libet interprets his results this way:

> The initiation of the freely voluntary act appears to begin in the brain unconsciously, well before the person consciously knows he wants to act. Is there, then, any role for conscious will in the performance of a voluntary act? To answer this it must be recognized that conscious will does appear about 150 msec before the muscle is activated, even though it follows the onset of the RP [readiness potential]. An interval of 150 msec would allow enough time in which the conscious might affect the final outcome of the volitional process.[47]

In Libet's view, then, although conscious will does not initiate movement, it may be able to stop it before it occurs. "This suggests," says neurophysiologist

One of the annoying things about believing in free will and individual responsibility is the difficulty of finding somebody to blame your problems on.

—P. J. O'ROURKE

LIBET'S
EXPERIMENTAL
SETUP.
Does it show that free
will is an illusion?

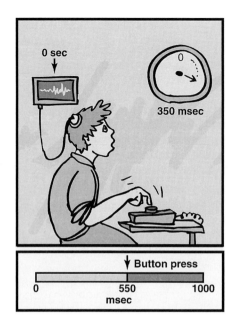

0 sec

350 msec

↓ Button press

0   550   1000

msec

Vilaynur Ramachandran, "that our conscious minds may not have free will, but rather 'free won't.'"[48]

Not everyone concurs with Libet's interpretation of his results, however. In the first place, even if consciousness does not initiate individual muscle movements in such artificial settings, it may still be involved in identifying goals, formulating plans, and devising strategies. It may have played a role, for example, in helping the subjects decide whether they would participate in the experiments.

Second, a number of neurophysiologists argue that what Libet's experiment tests is not conscious awareness but "meta-conscious awareness." As Anthony Jack and Philip Robbins explain,

> . . . the illusion of causality thesis [the claim that the effectiveness of conscious will is an illusion] is almost certainly false. The only reason for believing it derives from a failure to distinguish conscious states (the intention to x) from meta-conscious states (the thought that one is intending to x). In Libet's well-known experiment, subjects don't have the thought that they are consciously intending an action until some time after brain activity underlying the action has begun. Yet it is hardly surprising that the thought that we are consciously intending only occurs after the conscious intention has formed. Unless we assume that conscious intentions form instantaneously and are simultaneously accompanied by the realization that we are having a conscious intention, Libet's experiment poses no challenge.[49]

There's a difference between intending something and thinking that you're intending something. The former is a conscious state, whereas the latter is a meta-conscious state. According to Jack and Robbins, Libet's experiment tests for meta-consciousness, not for consciousness itself. Because we would expect meta-consciousness to arise after consciousness, Libet's experiment does not undermine belief in the efficacy of conscious will. It gives us no reason to think that the effectiveness of conscious will is an illusion.

Agent Causation

Both traditional and hierarchical compatibilists believe that we act freely as long as we do what we want to do. Libertarians, on the other hand, believe that we act freely only if our wants are up to us. If we have no control over what we want, we have no control over what we do. Scottish philosopher Thomas Reid (1710–1796) realized this more than 250 years ago. He writes,

> By the liberty of a moral agent, I understand a power over the determinations of his own will.
>
> If, in any action, he had power to will what he did, or not to will it, in that action he is free. But if, in every voluntary action, the determination of his will be the necessary consequence of something involuntary in the state of his mind, or of something in his external circumstances, he is not free; he has not what I call the liberty of a moral agent, but is subject to necessity.[50]

A staff moves a stone, and is moved by a hand, which is moved by a man.
— ARISTOTLE

According to Reid, the hypothetical interpretation of the phrase "could have done otherwise" doesn't capture what's needed for free will. Being able to do otherwise if we choose otherwise is not enough. We must be able to choose otherwise. If our choices are not up to us, then we can't act freely.

Libertarians claim that even if an action is undetermined by past events, it can nevertheless be free as long as it is caused by an agent. Libertarians, therefore, usually endorse a form of causation known as **agent causation,** which occurs when an agent (self, person) causes an event.

Traditionally, agent causation and event causation were taken to be entirely different species of causation because agent causation was thought to be capable of initiating new causal chains. In this view, when we cause something, we are acting like God. American philosopher Roderick Chisholm explains,

> If we are responsible, then we have a prerogative which some would attribute only to God: each of us when we act, is a prime mover unmoved. In doing what we do, we cause certain events to happen, and nothing — or no one — causes us to cause those events to happen.[51]

Many have found this conception of agent causation mysterious if not incoherent. Daniel Dennett's concerns are typical:

> How does an agent cause an effect without there being an event (in the agent, presumably) that is the cause of that effect (and is itself the effect of an earlier cause, and so forth)? Agent causation is a frankly mysterious doctrine, positing something unparalleled by anything we discover in the causal processes of chemical reaction, nuclear fission and fusion, magnetic attraction, hurricanes, volcanoes, or such biological processes as metabolism, growth, immune reactions, and photosynthesis.[52]

agent causation Causation that occurs when an agent (self, person) causes an event.

Agent causation, as traditionally conceived, seems to make free will nothing less than miraculous. To suppose that we act like God and initiate causal chains is difficult to accept. Rather than explaining anything, it substitutes one mystery for another.

Chisholm came to recognize the problems associated with the traditional conception of agent causation, and in his later years offered an alternative conception:

> In earlier writings on this topic, I had contrasted agent causation with event causation and had suggested that "causation by agents" could not be reduced to causation by events. I now believe that that suggestion was a mistake. What I had called agent causation is a subspecies of event causation.[53]

Event causation is the sort of causation studied by scientists. It occurs when one event causes another, such as when the lighting of a match causes an explosion. An event can be construed as an object having a property at a time. For example, the event of a log burning can be thought to consist in the log having the property of burning at a certain time. The event of the log burning can bring about or contribute causally to any number of other events, such as a marshmallow cooking. The log burning does so in virtue of certain properties or causal powers it possesses, such as the property of being hot.

Agent causation is a type of event causation where the event consists of an agent having a property at a time. Just as ordinary events bring about other events in virtue of the properties they possess, so do agent events. Timothy O'Connor refers to these properties as "volition-enabling properties," for having these properties enables agents to act freely.[54] Like self-consciousness, these properties can be conceived as emergent properties that come into being when certain things (like neurons) interact in certain ways. In fact, self-consciousness itself may be a volition-enabling property, as Sartre and Smullyan suggest (see the box "Sartre and Smullyan on Free Will"). In any event, it's important to realize that agent causation does not require substance dualism. Agents need not be immaterial entities or disembodied spirits in order to cause actions. They can be physical objects as long as they have the right sorts of properties.

Agents also need not be construed as prime movers unmoved. Instead of initiating causal chains, agent causation can be viewed as directing them. As we have seen, alternative courses of action are like forks in a road. Agent-caused choices can be taken to determine which fork the chain will take. Thus understood, agent causation is consistent with the notion of downward mental causation discussed in Chapter 2. To get a better understanding of what's going on when an agent makes a choice, let's consider a particular case.

Suppose you're choosing among going to graduate school, joining the Peace Corps, or entering the business world. Such a choice can be difficult, and the choice you make can have a profound effect on the sort of person you become. You'll want to consider your options carefully. This involves identifying the reasons for choosing each of the alternatives. If you go to graduate school, you'll learn more about a subject you love. If you join the Peace Corps, you'll help the needy in a foreign country. If you enter the business

Sartre and Smullyan on Free Will

Author and philosopher Jean-Paul Sartre is one of the foremost exponents of the philosophy known as *existentialism*. Existentialism claims that humans are, by their nature, free to do what they want to do. We have not been designed to perform a particular function, nor are we forced to engage in any activity we don't like. We can always commit suicide. We, and we alone, are responsible for everything that happens to us. Here's how Sartre expresses it:

> I am condemned to be free. This means that no limits to my freedom can be found except freedom itself or, if you prefer, that we are not free to cease being free. . . .
>
> As we have seen, for human-reality, to be is to choose oneself; nothing comes to it either from the outside or from within which it can receive or accept. Without any help whatsoever, it is entirely abandoned to the intolerable necessity of making itself be — down to the slightest detail. Thus freedom is not a being; it is the being of man — that is, his nothingness of being. If we start by conceiving of man as a plenum, it is absurd to try to find in him afterwards moments or psychic regions in which he would be free. As well look for emptiness in a container which one has filled beforehand up to the brim! Man cannot be sometimes a slave and sometimes free; he is wholly and forever free or he is not free at all.[55]

For Sartre, it is part of a person's nature to be free. It is impossible for something to be a person and not be free. Logician Raymond Smullyan agrees. Here is an excerpt from Smullyan's "Is God a Taoist?" in which God explains why people have free will:

Why the idea that I could possibly have created you without free will! You acted as if this were a genuine possibility, and wondered why I did not choose it! It never occurred to you that a sentient being without free will is no more conceivable than a physical object which exerts no gravitational attraction. (There is, incidentally, more analogy than you realize between a physical object exerting gravitational attraction and a sentient being exerting free will!) Can you honestly even imagine a conscious being without free will? What on earth could it be like? I think that one thing in your life that has so misled you is your having been told that I gave man the *gift* of free will. As if I first created man, and then as an afterthought endowed him with the extra property of free will. Maybe you think I have some sort of "paint brush" with which I daub some creatures with free will, and not others. No, free will is not an "extra"; it is part and parcel of the very essence of consciousness. A conscious being without free will is simply a metaphysical absurdity.[56]

Thought Probe

Self-Consciousness and Free Will

Do you agree with Sartre and Smullyan that it's impossible to be self-conscious and not have free will? Why or why not? Would you be willing to grant that any robot that was self-conscious had free will? Why or why not?

---

world, you may make more money than you would in choosing either of the other options. Once you've identified the relevant reasons, you make your choice. In making that choice, you decide which reason, or set of reasons, carries the most weight. Your choice is undetermined in the sense that you are not forced to choose any one of the three options. But that is not to say that your choice is uncaused, for the reasons you have for each of your options contribute causally to your decision. They just don't necessitate it. If all the events leading up to your decision were repeated, it would be possible for you to choose otherwise. Your decision is up to you.

event causation
Causation that occurs when one event causes another.

Compatibilists and hard determinists maintain that this conception of free action can't be correct because it either leads to an infinite regress or makes human action incomprehensible. Consider again the choice of going to graduate school, joining the Peace Corps, or entering the business world. Suppose you choose to join the Peace Corps. Someone (like your parents) may want to know why you chose that option. Since your choice was a rational one, arrived at through careful deliberation, there should be a reason for it. This reason would supposedly be a second-order reason indicating why you weighted one set of reasons more heavily than another. But, if the decision to weigh one set of reasons more heavily than another is itself rational, there should be a third-order reason for using such a principle of choice, and so on to infinity. So, in the words of Galen Strawson, "True self-determination is logically impossible because it requires the actual completion of an infinite regress of choices, of principles of choice."[57]

Are Strawson's requirements for rational choice plausible? Does making a rational choice among competing sets of reasons require making an infinite number of choices? It wouldn't seem so. Suppose someone asked you why you chose to join the Peace Corps. It would be appropriate for you to say, "Because I decided it was more important to help the needy than continue my studies or make lots of money." That explains your choice and makes it intelligible. There is no need to appeal to any higher level principles of choice.[58]

Now suppose someone asks you, "Why did you decide that helping the needy was more important?" In this case, it would be appropriate to say, "I just did." But, the compatibilists and hard determinists might inquire, how is that any different from a purely random action? If your weighting of reasons is undetermined by other events or reasons, how can it be anything but random? Robert Nozick answers this question by noting that a decision may be self-subsuming: "the weights it bestows may fix general principles that mandate not only the relevant act but also the bestowing of those (or similar weights)."[59] In other words, the decision to act on a certain principle can explain itself by falling under that principle.

To see this, consider a theory of truth. A theory of truth should itself be true. So it should apply to itself. In other words it should fall under — be subsumed by — its own conception of truth. Similarly, claims Nozick, a principle specifying how reasons would be weighted should apply to itself. That is, it should fall under — be subsumed by — its own conception of how reasons should be weighted. Such self-subsuming principles are self-explanatory. There is no need to appeal to other principles to explain them. So unlike random events that cannot be explained, the decision to weight certain reasons in certain ways can be explained by appeal to the principle used to assign the weighting.

Once chosen, this principle may guide other choices, much like a legal precedent governs other legal decisions. Insofar as our characters are determined by the kinds of choices we make, the choice of a principle for weighting reasons may be considered a "self-forming action." Not every choice is character-building, just as every legal decision is not precedent-setting. But those choices that establish principles for weighting reasons are the ones that determine the kind of person we will become.

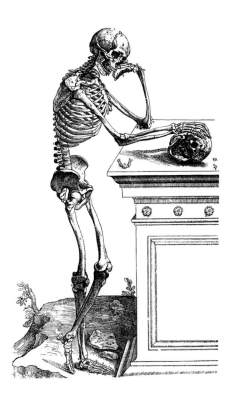

Humans are the only creatures we know who are self-conscious. Does self-consciousness make us free?

The scenario described above is what Mark Balaguer, following Robert Kane, calls a "torn decision." A torn decision is one where the person making the decision "(a) has reasons for two or more options and feels torn as to which set of reasons is strongest . . . and (b) decides without resolving this conflict—i.e. the person has the experience of just choosing."[60] All such decisions, Balaguer claims, involve agent causation and thus affirm the existence of libertarian free will.

> If our torn decisions are undetermined at the moment of choice, then we author and control them. The first point to note here is that if a torn decision is undetermined at the moment of choice in the way described above, then it follows that nothing external to the agent caused her to choose as she does . . . And the second point is that when we combine this lack of external causation with conscious, intentional, purposefulness, we seem to get authorship and control: if (a) an agent S consciously, intentionally, and purposefully chooses some option A, and (b) nothing external to S causes her to choose A, then it seems that (c) she authors and controls the decision.[61]

Such a conception of libertarian free will shows how our actions can be up to us without violating the laws of nature.

Libertarianism explains the experience of choice and deliberation and provides a plausible account of moral responsibility. Neither hard determinism nor compatibilism can make a similar claim. Libertarianism also helps explain why there is so much individual and cultural diversity, why social engineering such as that attempted in the former Soviet Union has failed, and why those raised in the same family often disagree with one another. Given its coherence and explanatory power, libertarianism remains a viable solution to the problem of free will.

Agents (persons, selves) are self-conscious beings who are capable of forming second-order desires. They know what things motivate them, and they can decide whether they want to be motivated by those things. So we can agree with Frankfurt that free actions are those that are caused by second-order volitions. But if the second-order volitions themselves are not caused by the agent, the actions they cause are not free. By requiring that second-order volitions be caused by the agent, then, libertarianism avoids the problem that undermined hierarchical compatibilism.

The plausibility of libertarianism is far from settled. The notion of agent causation may turn out to be mistaken. But given the evidence for downward mental causation presented at the end of Chapter 2 and the possibility of a naturalistic account of it, libertarianism remains a live option.

Thought Probe

Free Androids

Recall the android mentioned at the beginning of this chapter. Suppose that it is indeed programmed to make choices and to learn from its mistakes but that it also possesses self-consciousness. Would the android have free will? Why or why not? If not, is there anything we could give to the android that would give it free will? If so, what is it?

Summary

Because neither traditional nor hierarchical compatibilism reconciles free will and causal determinism, there is reason to believe that they are incompatible. An incompatibilist can still believe in free will, by arguing from the fact that we have free will to the conclusion that causal determinism is false. But if causal determinism is false, causal indeterminism must be true. We can avoid indeterminism (free actions are uncaused), however, by distinguishing between two different types of causation. There's event causation (an event brings about another event) and agent causation (an agent or person brings about an event). According to libertarianism, free actions are actions that are caused, not by other events, but by agents or persons. Libertarians don't deny that every event has a cause. They simply deny that every event has an event cause. This notion of free actions being caused by agents is consistent with our experience of acting and deliberating and it fits well with the mind-body theory of property dualism.

Study Questions

1. What is the libertarian argument for free will?
2. What premise of this argument is accepted by both libertarians and hard determinists?
3. What is event causation?
4. What is agent causation?
5. Some people claim that our experience does not provide evidence that we sometimes act freely. What is their argument? What is the libertarian reply to this argument?

Discussion Questions

1. What theories of mind are consistent with libertarianism?
2. Suppose science is right: we are influenced by countless physical, psychological, social, and genetic factors. Does this mean that we don't have free will? Why or why not?
3. Agent causation is an empirical hypothesis, one that can be verified or falsified through sense experience. Describe an experiment that would determine whether there is such a thing as agent causation. What if this experiment failed? What would be the consequences for the theory of mind and our view of ourselves?
4. Are Sartre and Smullyan right that it is impossible for anything that is self-conscious not to have free will?
5. If libertarianism is true, what justification can be given for punishment? Are there types of justification for punishment available to the libertarian that aren't available to the hard determinist or the compatibilist? If so, what are they?

The Delusion of Free Will

Robert Blatchford (1851–1943) was a socialist, a journalist, and a founder of
England's Independent Labour party. In this selection, he defends hard determinism.

The free will delusion has been a stumbling block in
the way of human thought for thousands of years. Let
us try whether common sense and common knowledge
cannot remove it.

Free will is a subject of great importance to us in this
case; and it is one we must come to with our eyes wide
open and our wits wide awake; not because it is very
difficult, but because it has been tied and twisted into
a tangle of Gordian knots by twenty centuries full of
wordy but unsuccessful philosophers.

The free will party claim that man is responsible for
his acts, because his will is free to choose between right
and wrong.

We reply that the will is not free, and that if it were
free man could not know right from wrong until he was
taught. As to the knowledge of good and evil the free
will party will claim that conscience is an unerring
guide. But I have already proved that conscience does
not and cannot tell us what is right and what is wrong;
it only reminds us of the lessons we have learnt as to
right and wrong.

The "still small voice" is not the voice of God: it is
the voice of heredity and environment.

And now to the freedom of the will.

When a man says his will is free, he means that it is
free of all control or interference: that it can overrule
heredity and environment.

We reply that the will is ruled by heredity and
environment.

The cause of all the confusion on this subject may
be shown in a few words.

When the free will party say that man has a free will,
they mean that he is free to act as he chooses to act.

There is no need to deny that. But *what causes him to
choose?* That is the pivot upon which the whole discussion turns.

The free will party seem to think of the will as something independent of the man, as something outside
him. They seem to think that the will decides without
the control of the man's reason.

If that were so, it would not prove the man responsible. "The will" would be responsible, and not the
man. It would be as foolish to blame a man for the act
of a "free" will, as to blame a horse for the action of its
rider.

But I am going to prove to my readers, by appeals to
their common sense and common knowledge, that the
will is not free; and that it is ruled by heredity and
environment.

To begin with, the average man will be against me.
He knows that he chooses between two courses every
hour, and often every minute, and he thinks his choice
is free. But that is a delusion: his choice is not free. He
can choose, and does choose. But he can only choose as
his heredity and his environment cause him to choose.
He never did choose and never will choose except as
his heredity and his environment—his temperament
and his training—cause him to choose. And his heredity and his environment have fixed his choice before he
makes it.

The average man says "I know that I can act as I
wish to act." But what causes him to wish?

The free will party say, "We know that a man can
and does choose between two acts." But what settles
the choice?

There is a cause for every wish, a cause for every
choice; and every cause of every wish and choice arises
from heredity, or from environment. For a man acts
always from temperament, which is heredity, or from
training, which is environment.

And in cases where a man hesitates in his choice
between two acts, the hesitation is due to a conflict between his temperament and his training, or, as some
would express it, "between his desire and his conscience."

A man is practicing at a target with a gun, when a
rabbit crosses his line of fire. The man has his eye and

From: Robert Blatchford, *Not Guilty: A Defence of the Bottom Dog*
(London: Clarion Press, 1906).

his sights on the rabbit, and his finger on the trigger. The man's will is free. If he presses the trigger, the rabbit will be killed.

Now, how does the man decide whether or not he shall fire? He decides by feeling, and by reason.

He would like to fire, just to make sure that he could hit the mark. He would like to fire, because he would like to have the rabbit for supper. He would like to fire, because there is in him the old, old hunting instinct, to kill.

But the rabbit does not belong to him. He is not sure that he will not get into trouble if he kills it. Perhaps—if he is a very uncommon kind of man—he feels that it would be cruel and cowardly to shoot a helpless rabbit.

Well. The man's will is free. He can fire if he likes: he can let the rabbit go if he likes. How will he decide? On what does his decision depend?

His decision depends upon the relative strength of his desire to kill the rabbit, and of his scruples about cruelty, and the law.

Not only that, but, if we knew the man fairly well, we could guess how his free will would act before it acted. The average sporting Briton would kill the rabbit. But we know that there are men who would on no account shoot any harmless wild creature.

Broadly put, we may say that the sportsman would will to fire, and that the humanitarian would not will to fire.

Now, as both their wills are free, it must be something outside the wills that makes the difference.

Well. The sportsman will kill, because he is a sportsman: the humanitarian will not kill, because he is a humanitarian.

And what makes one man a sportsman and another a humanitarian? Heredity and environment: temperament and training.

One man is merciful, another cruel, by nature; or one is thoughtful and the other thoughtless, by nature. That is a difference of heredity. One may have been taught all his life that to kill wild things is "sport"; the other may have been taught that it is inhuman and wrong: that is a difference of environment.

Now, the man by nature cruel or thoughtless, who has been trained to think of killing animals as sport, becomes what we call a sportsman, because heredity and environment have made him a sportsman.

The other man's heredity and environment have made him a humanitarian.

The sportsman kills the rabbit, because he is a sportsman, and he is a sportsman because heredity and environment have made him one.

That is to say the "free will" is really controlled by heredity and environment.

Allow me to give a case in point. A man who had never done any fishing was taken out by a fisherman. He liked the sport, and for some months followed it eagerly. But one day an accident brought home to his mind the cruelty of catching fish with a hook, and he instantly laid down his rod, and never fished again.

Before the change he was always eager to go fishing if invited: after the change he could not be persuaded to touch a line. His will was free all the while. How was it that his will to fish changed to his will not to fish? It was the result of environment. He had learnt that fishing was cruel. This knowledge controlled his will.

But, it may be asked, how do you account for a man doing the thing he does not wish to do?

No man ever did a thing he did not wish to do. When there are two wishes the stronger rules.

Let us suppose a case. A young woman gets two letters by the same post; one is an invitation to go with her lover to a concert, the other is a request that she will visit a sick child in the slums. The girl is very fond of music, and is rather afraid of the slums. She wishes to go to the concert, and to be with her lover; she dreads the foul street and the dirty home, and shrinks from the risk of measles and fever. But she goes to the sick child, and she foregoes the concert. Why?

Because her sense of duty is stronger than her self-love.

Now, her sense of duty is partly due to her nature—that is, to her heredity—but it is chiefly due to environment. Like all of us, this girl was born without any kind of knowledge, and with only the rudiments of a conscience. But she has been well taught, and the teaching is part of her environment.

We may say that the girl is free to act as she chooses, but she *does* act as she has been taught that she *ought* to act. This teaching, which is part of her environment, controls her will.

We may say that a man is free to act as he chooses. He is free to act as *he* chooses, but *he* will choose as heredity and environment cause him to choose. For heredity and environment have made him that which he is.

A man is said to be free to decide between two courses. But really he is only free to decide in accordance with his temperament and training. . . .

Macbeth was ambitious; but he had a conscience. He wanted Duncan's crown; but he shrank from treason and ingratitude. Ambition pulled him one way, honour pulled him the other way. The opposing forces were so evenly balanced that he seemed unable to decide. Was

Macbeth free to choose? To what extent was he free? He was so free that he could arrive at no decision, and it was the influence of his wife that turned the scale to crime.

Was Lady Macbeth free to choose? She did not hesitate. Because her ambition was so much stronger than her conscience that she never was in doubt. She chose as her overpowering ambition compelled her to choose.

And most of us in our decisions resemble either Macbeth or his wife. Either our nature is so much stronger than our training, or our training is so much stronger than our nature, that we decide for good or evil as promptly as a stream decides to run down hill; or our nature and our training are so nearly balanced that we can hardly decide at all.

In Macbeth's case the contest is quite clear and easy to follow. He was ambitious, and his environment had taught him to regard the crown as a glorious and desirable possession. But environment had also taught him that murder, and treason, and ingratitude were wicked and disgraceful.

Had he never been taught these lessons, or had he been taught that gratitude was folly, that honour was weakness, and murder excusable when it led to power, he would not have hesitated at all. It was his environment that hampered his will. . . .

In all cases the action of the will depends upon the relative strength of two or more motives. The stronger motive decides the will; just as the heavier weight decides the balance of a pair of scales. . . .

How, then, can we believe that free will is outside and superior to heredity and environment? . . .

"What! Cannot a man be honest if he choose?" Yes, if he choose. But that is only another way of saying that he can be honest if his nature and his training lead him to choose honesty.

"What! Cannot I please myself whether I drink or refrain from drinking?" Yes. But that is only to say you will not drink because it pleases you to be sober. But it pleases another man to drink, because his desire for drink is strong, or because his self-respect is weak.

And you decide as you decide, and he decides as he decides, because you are you, and he is he: and heredity and environment made you both that which you are.

And the sober man may fall upon evil days, and may lose his self-respect, or find the burden of his trouble greater than he can bear, and may fly to drink for comfort, or oblivion, and may become a drunkard. Has it not been often so?

And the drunkard may, by some shock, or some disaster, or some passion, or some persuasion, regain his self-respect, and may renounce drink, and lead a sober and useful life. Has it not been often so?

And in both cases the freedom of the will is untouched: it is the change in the environment that lifts the fallen up, and beats the upright down.

We might say that a woman's will is free, and that she could, if she wished, jump off a bridge and drown herself. But she cannot wish. She is happy, and loves life, and dreads the cold and crawling river. And yet, by some cruel turn of fortune's wheel, she may become destitute and miserable; so miserable that she hates life and longs for death, and then she can jump into the dreadful river and die.

Her will was as free at one time as at another. It is the environment that has wrought the change. Once she could not wish to die; now she cannot wish to live.

The apostles of free will believe that all men's wills are free. But a man can only will that which he is able to will. And one man is able to will that which another man is unable to will. To deny this is to deny the commonest and most obvious facts of life. . . .

We all know that we can foretell the action of certain men in certain cases, because we know the men.

We know that under the same conditions Jack Sheppard would steal and Cardinal Manning would not steal. We know that under the same conditions the sailor would flirt with the waitress, and the priest would not; that the drunkard would get drunk, and the abstainer would remain sober. We know that Wellington would refuse a bribe, that Nelson would not run away, that Buonaparte would grasp at power, that Abraham Lincoln would be loyal to his country, that Torquemada would not spare a heretic. Why? If the will is free, how can we be sure, before a test arises, how the will must act?

Simply because we know that heredity and environment have so formed and moulded men and women that under certain circumstances the action of their wills is certain.

Heredity and environment having made a man a thief, he will steal. Heredity and environment having made a man honest, he will not steal.

That is to say, heredity and environment have decided the action of the will, before the time has come for the will to act.

This being so—and we all know that it is so—what becomes of the sovereignty of the will?

Let any man that believes that he can "do as he likes" ask himself *why* he *likes*, and he will see the error of the theory of free will, and will understand why the will is the servant and not the master of the man; for the man is the product of heredity and environment, and these control the will.

As we want to get this subject as clear as we can, let us take one or two familiar examples of the action of the will.

Jones and Robinson meet and have a glass of whisky. Jones asks Robinson to have another. Robinson says, "no, thank you, one is enough." Jones says, "all right: have another cigarette." Robinson takes the cigarette. Now, here we have a case where a man refuses a second drink, but takes a second smoke. Is it because he would like another cigarette, but would not like another glass of whisky? No. It is because he knows that it is *safer* not to take another glass of whisky.

How does he know that whisky is dangerous? He has learnt it from his environment.

"But he *could* have taken another glass if he wished."

But he could not wish to take another, because there was something he wished more strongly — to be safe.

And why did he want to be safe? Because he had learnt — from his environment — that it was unhealthy, unprofitable, and shameful to get drunk. Because he had learnt — from his environment — that it is easier to avoid forming a bad habit than to break a bad habit when formed. Because he valued the good opinion of his neighbors, and also his position and prospects.

These feelings and this knowledge ruled his will, and caused him to refuse the second glass.

But there was no sense of danger, no well-learned lesson of risk to check his will to smoke another cigarette. Heredity and environment did not warn him against that. So, to please his friend, and himself, he accepted.

Now suppose Smith asks Williams to have another glass. Williams takes it, takes several, finally goes home — as he often goes home. Why? Largely because drinking is a habit with him. And not only does the mind instinctively repeat an action, but, in the case of drink, a physical craving is set up, and the brain is weakened. It is easier to refuse the first glass than the second; easier to refuse the second than the third; and it is very much harder for a man to keep sober who has frequently got drunk.

So, when poor Williams has to make his choice, he has habit against him, he has a physical craving against him, and he has a weakened brain to think with.

"But Williams could have refused the first glass."

No. Because in his case the desire to drink, or to please a friend, was stronger than his fear of the danger. Or he may not have been so conscious of the danger as Robinson was. He may not have been so well taught, or

he may not have been so sensible, or he may not have been so cautious. So that his heredity and environment, his temperament and training, led him to take the drink, as surely as Robinson's heredity and environment led him to refuse it.

And now, it is my turn to ask a question. If the will is "free," if conscience is a sure guide, how is it that the free will and the conscience of Robinson caused him to keep sober, while the free will and the conscience of Williams caused him to get drunk?

Robinson's will was curbed by certain feelings which failed to curb the will of Williams. Because in the case of Williams the feelings were stronger on the other side.

It was the nature and the training of Robinson which made him refuse the second glass, and it was the nature and the training of Williams which made him drink the second glass.

What had free will to do with it?

We are told that *every* man has a free will, and a conscience.

Now, if Williams had been Robinson, that is to say if his heredity and his environment had been exactly like Robinson's, he would have done exactly as Robinson did.

It was because his heredity and environment were not the same that his act was not the same.

Both men had free wills. What made one do what the other refused to do?

Heredity and environment. To reverse their conduct we should have to reverse their heredity and environment. . . .

Two boys work at a hard and disagreeable trade. One leaves it, finds other work, "gets on," is praised for getting on. The other stays at the trade all his life, works hard all his life, is poor all his life, and is respected as an honest and humble working man; that is to say, he is regarded by society as Mr. Dorgan was regarded by Mr. Dooley — "he is a fine man, and I despise him."

What causes these two free wills to will so differently? One boy knew more than the other boy. He "knew better." All knowledge is environment. Both boys had free wills. It was in knowledge they differed: environment!

Those who exalt the power of the will, and belittle the power of environment, belie their words by their deeds.

For they would not send their children amongst bad companions or allow them to read bad books. They would not say the children have free will and therefore have power to take the good and leave the bad.

They know very well that evil environment has power to pervert the will, and that good environment has power to direct it properly.

They know that children may be made good or bad by good or evil training, and that the will follows the training.

That being so, they must also admit that the children of other people may be good or bad by training. And if a child gets bad training, how can free will save it? Or how can it be blamed for being bad? It never had a chance to be good. That they know this is proved by their carefulness in providing their own children with better environment.

As I have said before, every church, every school, every moral lesson is a proof that preachers and teachers trust to good environment, and not to free will, to make children good.

In this, as in so many other matters, actions speak louder than words.

That, I hope, disentangles the many knots into which thousands of learned men have tied the simple subject of free will; and disposes of the claim that man is responsible because his will is free. But there is one other cause of error, akin to the subject, on which I should like to say a few words.

We often hear it said that a man is to blame for his conduct because "he knows better."

It is true that men do wrong when they know better. Macbeth "knew better" when he murdered Duncan. But it is true, also, that we often think a man "knows better," when he does not know better.

For a man cannot be said to know a thing until he believes it. If I am told that the moon is made of green cheese, it cannot be said that I *know* it to be made of green cheese.

Many moralists seem to confuse the words "to know" with the words "to hear."

Jones reads novels and plays opera music on Sunday. The Puritan says Jones "knows better," when he means that Jones has been told that it is wrong to do those things.

But Jones does not know that it is wrong. He has heard someone say that it is wrong, but does not believe it. Therefore it is not correct to say that he knows it.

And, again, as to that matter of belief. Some moralists hold that it is wicked not to believe certain things, and that men who do not believe those things will be punished.

But a man cannot believe a thing he is told to believe; he can only believe a thing which he *can* believe; and he can only believe that which his own reason tells him is true.

It would be no use asking Sir Roger Ball to believe that the earth is flat. He *could not* believe it.

It is no use asking an agnostic to believe the story of Jonah and the whale. He *could not* believe it. He might pretend to believe it. He might try to believe it. But his reason would not allow him to believe it.

Therefore it is a mistake to say that a man "knows better," when the fact is that he has been told "better" and cannot believe what he has been told.

That is a simple matter, and looks quite trivial; but how much ill-will, how much intolerance, how much violence, persecution, and murder have been caused by the strange idea that a man is wicked because his reason cannot believe that which to another man's reason [is] quite true.

Free will has no power over a man's belief. A man cannot believe by will, but only by conviction. A man cannot be forced to believe. You may threaten him, wound him, beat him, burn him; and he may be frightened, or angered, or pained; but he cannot *believe*, nor can he be made to believe. Until he is convinced.

Now, truism as it may seem, I think it necessary to say here that a man cannot be convinced by abuse, nor by punishment. He can only be convinced by *reason*.

Yes. If we wish a man to believe a thing, we shall find a few words of reason more powerful than a million curses, or a million bayonets. To burn a man alive for failing to believe that the sun goes round the world is not to convince him. The fire is searching, but it does not seem to him to be relevant to the issue. He never doubted that fire would burn; but perchance his dying eyes may see the sun sinking down into the west, as the world rolls on its axis. He dies in his belief. And knows no "better."

W. T. STACE

The Problem of Free Will

Walter Terence Stace (1886–1967) was a staunch defender of empiricism. He served in the British Civil Service in Ceylon before coming to the United States to teach philosophy at Princeton University. In this selection, he vigorously defends traditional compatibilism.

[A] great problem which the rise of scientific naturalism has created for the modern mind concerns the foundations of morality. The old religious foundations have largely crumbled away, and it may well be thought that the edifice built upon them by generations of men is in danger of collapse. A total collapse of moral behavior is, as I pointed out before, very unlikely. For a society in which this occurred could not survive. Nevertheless the danger to moral standards inherent in the virtual disappearance of their old religious foundations is not illusory.

I shall first discuss the problem of free will, for it is certain that if there is no free will there can be no morality. Morality is concerned with what men ought and ought not to do. But if a man has no freedom to choose what he will do, if whatever he does is done under compulsion, then it does not make sense to tell him that he ought not to have done what he did and that he ought to do something different. All moral precepts would in such case be meaningless. Also if he acts always under compulsion, how can he be held morally responsible for his actions? How can he, for example, be punished for what he could not help doing?

It is to be observed that those learned professors of philosophy or psychology who deny the existence of free will do so only in their professional moments and in their studies and lecture rooms. For when it comes to doing anything practical, even of the most trivial kind, they invariably behave as if they and others were free. They inquire from you at dinner whether you will choose this dish or that dish. They will ask a child why he told a lie, and will punish him for not having chosen the way of truthfulness. All of which is inconsistent with a disbelief in free will. This should cause us to suspect that the problem is not a real one; and this, I believe, is the case. The dispute is merely verbal, and is due to nothing but a confusion about the meanings of words. It is what is now fashionably called a semantic problem.

How does a verbal dispute arise? Let us consider a case which, although it is absurd in the sense that no one would ever make the mistake which is involved in it, yet illustrates the principle which we shall have to use in the solution of the problem. Suppose that someone believed that the word "man" means a certain sort of five-legged animal; in short that "five-legged animal" is the correct *definition* of man. He might then look around the world, and rightly observing that there are no five-legged animals in it, he might proceed to deny the existence of men. This preposterous conclusion would have been reached because he was using an incorrect definition of "man." All you would have to do to show him his mistake would be to give him the correct definition; or at least to show him that his definition was wrong. Both the problem and its solution would, of course, be entirely verbal. The problem of free will, and its solution, I shall maintain, is verbal in exactly the same way. The problem has been created by the fact that learned men, especially philosophers, have assumed an incorrect definition of free will, and then finding that there is nothing in the world which answers to their definition, have denied its existence. As far as logic is concerned, their conclusion is just as absurd as that of the man who denies the existence of men. The only difference is that the mistake in the latter case is obvious and crude, while the mistake which the deniers of free will have made is rather subtle and difficult to detect.

Throughout the modern period, until quite recently, it was assumed, both by the philosophers who denied free will and by those who defended it, that *determinism is inconsistent with free will*. If a man's actions were wholly determined by chains of causes stretching back into the remote past, so that they could be predicted

From: W. T. Stace, *Religion and the Modern Mind* (New York: J. B. Lippincott Company, 1952) 248–258.

beforehand by a mind which knew all the causes, it was assumed that they could not in that case be free. This implies that a certain definition of actions done from free will was assumed, namely that they are actions *not* wholly determined by causes or predictable beforehand. Let us shorten this by saying that free will was defined as meaning indeterminism. This is the incorrect definition which has led to the denial of free will. As soon as we see what the true definition is we shall find that the question whether the world is deterministic, as Newtonian science implied, or in a measure indeterministic, as current physics teaches, is wholly irrelevant to the problem.

Of course there is a sense in which one can define a word arbitrarily in any way one pleases. But a definition may nevertheless be called correct or incorrect. It is correct if it accords with a *common usage* of the word defined. It is incorrect if it does not. And if you give an incorrect definition, absurd and untrue results are likely to follow. For instance, there is nothing to prevent you from arbitrarily defining a man as a five-legged animal, but this is incorrect in the sense that it does not accord with the ordinary meaning of the word. Also it has the absurd result of leading to a denial of the existence of men. This shows that *common usage is the criterion for deciding whether a definition is correct or not*. And this is the principle which I shall apply to free will. I shall show that indeterminism is not what is meant by the phrase "free will" *as it is commonly used.* And I shall attempt to discover the correct definition by inquiring how the phrase is used in ordinary conversation.

Here are a few samples of how the phrase might be used in ordinary conversation. It will be noticed that they include cases in which the question whether a man acted with free will is asked in order to determine whether he was morally and legally responsible for his acts.

JONES: I once went without food for a week.

SMITH: Did you do that of your own free will?

JONES: No. I did it because I was lost in a desert and could find no food.

But suppose that the man who had fasted was Mahatma Gandhi. The conversation might then have gone:

GANDHI: I once fasted for a week.

SMITH: Did you do that of your own free will?

GANDHI: Yes. I did it because I wanted to compel the British Government to give India its independence.

Take another case. Suppose that I had stolen some bread, but that I was as truthful as George Washington. Then, if I were charged with the crime in court, some exchange of the following sort might take place:

JUDGE: Did you steal the bread of your own free will?

STACE: Yes. I stole it because I was hungry.

Or in different circumstances the conversation might run:

JUDGE: Did you steal of your own free will?

STACE: No. I stole because my employer threatened to beat me if I did not.

At a recent murder trial in Trenton some of the accused had signed confessions, but afterwards asserted that they had done so under police duress. The following exchange might have occurred:

JUDGE: Did you sign this confession of your own free will?

PRISONER: No. I signed it because the police beat me up.

Now suppose that a philosopher had been a member of the jury. We could imagine this conversation taking place in the jury room.

FOREMAN OF THE JURY: The prisoner says he signed the confession because he was beaten, and not of his own free will.

PHILOSOPHER: This is quite irrelevant to the case. There is no such thing as free will.

FOREMAN: Do you mean to say that it makes no difference whether he signed because his conscience made him want to tell the truth or because he was beaten?

PHILOSOPHER: None at all. Whether he was caused to sign by a beating or by some desire of his own — the desire to tell the truth, for example — in either case his signing was causally determined, and therefore in neither case did he act of his own free will. Since there is no such thing as free will, the question whether he signed of his own free will ought not to be discussed by us.

The foreman and the rest of the jury would rightly conclude that the philosopher must be making some mistake. What sort of mistake could it be? There is only one possible answer. The philosopher must be using the phrase "free will" in some peculiar way of his own which is not the way in which men usually use it when they wish to determine a question of moral responsibility. That is, he must be using an incorrect definition of it as implying action not determined by causes.

Suppose a man left his office at noon, and were questioned about it. Then we might hear this:

JONES: Did you go out of your own free will?

SMITH: Yes. I went out to get my lunch.

But we might hear:

JONES: Did you leave your office of your own free will?

SMITH: No. I was forcibly removed by the police.

We have now collected a number of cases of actions which, in the ordinary usage of the English language, would be called cases in which people have acted of their own free will. We should also say in all these cases that they *chose* to act as they did. We should also say that they could have acted otherwise, if they had chosen. For instance, Mahatma Gandhi was not compelled to fast; he chose to do so. He could have eaten if he had wanted to. When Smith went out to get his lunch, he chose to do so. He could have stayed and done some more work, if he had wanted to. We have also collected a number of cases of the opposite kind. They are cases in which men were not able to exercise their free will. They had no choice. They were compelled to do as they did. The man in the desert did not fast of his own free will. He had no choice in the matter. He was compelled to fast because there was nothing for him to eat. And so with the other cases. It ought to be quite easy, by an inspection of these cases, to tell what we ordinarily mean when we say that a man did or did not exercise free will. We ought therefore to be able to extract from them the proper definition of the term. Let us put the cases in a table:

Free Acts	Unfree Acts
Gandhi fasting because he wanted to free India.	The man fasting in the desert because there was no food.
Stealing bread because one is hungry.	Stealing because one's employer threatened to beat one.
Signing a confession because one wanted to tell the truth.	Signing because the police beat one.
Leaving the office because one wanted lunch.	Leaving because forcibly removed.

It is obvious that to find the correct definition of free acts we must discover what characteristic is common to all the acts in the left-hand column, and is, at the same time, absent from all the acts in the right-hand column. This characteristic which all free acts have, and which no unfree acts have, will be the defining characteristic of free will.

Is being uncaused, or not being determined by causes, the characteristic of which we are in search? It cannot be, because although it is true that all the acts in the right-hand column have causes, such as the beating by the police or the absence of food in the desert, so also do the acts in the left-hand column. Mr. Gandhi's fasting was caused by his desire to free India, the man leaving his office by his hunger, and so on. Moreover there is no reason to doubt that these causes of the free acts were in turn caused by prior conditions, and that these were again the results of causes, and so on back indefinitely into the past. Any physiologist can tell us the causes of hunger. What caused Mr. Gandhi's tremendously powerful desire to free India is no doubt more difficult to discover. But it must have had causes. Some of them may have lain in peculiarities of his glands or brain, others in his past experiences, others in his heredity, others in his education. Defenders of free will have usually tended to deny such facts. But to do so is plainly a case of special pleading, which is unsupported by any scrap of evidence. The only reasonable view is that all human actions, both those which are freely done and those which are not, are either wholly determined by causes, or at least as much determined as other events in nature. It may be true, as the physicists tell us, that nature is not as deterministic as was once thought. But whatever degree of determinism prevails in the world, human actions appear to be as much determined as anything else. And if this is so, it cannot be the case that what distinguishes actions freely chosen from those which are not free is that the latter are determined by causes while the former are not. Therefore, being uncaused or being undetermined by causes, must be an incorrect definition of free will.

What, then, is the difference between acts which are freely done and those which are not? What is the characteristic which is present to all the acts in the left-hand column and absent from all those in the right-hand column? Is it not obvious that, although both sets of actions have causes, the causes of those in the left-hand column are *of a different kind* from the causes of those in the right-hand column? The free acts are all caused by desires, or motives, or by some sort of internal psychological states of the agent's mind. The unfree acts, on the other hand, are all caused by physical forces or physical conditions, outside the agent. Police arrest means physical force exerted from the outside; the absence of food in the desert is a physical condition of the outside world. We may therefore frame the following rough definitions. *Acts freely done are those whose immediate causes are psychological states in the agent. Acts not freely done are those whose immediate causes are states of affairs external to the agent.*

It is plain that if we define free will in this way, then free will certainly exists, and the philosopher's denial of its existence is seen to be what it is—nonsense. For it is obvious that all those actions of men which we should ordinarily attribute to the exercise of their free will, or of which we should say that they freely chose to do them, are in fact actions which have been caused by their own desires, wishes, thoughts, emotions, impulses, or other psychological states.

In applying our definition we shall find that it usually works well, but that there are some puzzling cases which it does not seem exactly to fit. These puzzles can always be solved by paying careful attention to the ways in which words are used, and remembering that they are not always used consistently. I have space for only one example. Suppose that a thug threatens to shoot you unless you give him your wallet, and suppose that you do so. Do you, in giving him your wallet, do so of your own free will or not? If we apply our definition, we find that you acted freely, since the immediate cause of the action was not an actual outside force but the fear of death, which is a psychological cause. Most people, however, would say that you did not act of your own free will but under compulsion. Does this show that our definition is wrong? I do not think so. Aristotle, who gave a solution of the problem of free will substantially the same as ours (though he did not use the term "free will") admitted that there are what he called "mixed" or borderline cases in which it is difficult to know whether we ought to call the acts free or compelled. In the case under discussion, though no actual force was used, the gun at your forehead so nearly approximated to actual force that we tend to say the case was one of compulsion. It is a borderline case.

Here is what may seem like another kind of puzzle. According to our view an action may be free though it could have been predicted beforehand with certainty. But suppose you told a lie, and it was certain beforehand that you would tell it. How could one then say, "You could have told the truth"? The answer is that it is perfectly true that you could have told the truth if you had wanted to. In fact you would have done so, for in that case the causes producing your action, namely your desires, would have been different, and would therefore have produced different effects. It is a delusion that predictability and free will are incompatible. This agrees with common sense. For if, knowing your character, I predict that you will act honorably, no one would say when you do act honorably, that this shows you did not do so of your own free will.

Since free will is a condition of moral responsibility, we must be sure that our theory of free will gives a sufficient basis for it. To be held morally responsible for one's actions means that one may be justly punished or rewarded, blamed or praised, for them. But it is not just to punish a man for what he cannot help doing. How can it be just to punish him for an action which it was certain beforehand that he would do? We have not attempted to decide whether, as a matter of fact, all events, including human actions, are completely determined. For that question is irrelevant to the problem of free will. But if we assume for the purposes of argument that complete determinism is true, but that we are nevertheless free, it may then be asked whether such a deterministic free will is compatible with moral responsibility. For it may seem unjust to punish a man for an action which it could have been predicted with certainty beforehand that he would do.

But that determinism is incompatible with moral responsibility is as much a delusion as that it is incompatible with free will. You do not excuse a man for doing a wrong act because, knowing his character, you felt certain beforehand that he would do it. Nor do you deprive a man of a reward or prize because, knowing his goodness or his capabilities, you felt certain beforehand that he would win it.

Volumes have been written on the justification of punishment. But so far as it affects the question of free will, the essential principles involved are quite simple. The punishment of a man for doing a wrong act is justified, either on the ground that it will correct his own character, or that it will deter other people from doing similar acts. The instrument of punishment has been in the past, and no doubt still is, often unwisely used; so that it may often have done more harm than good. But that is not relevant to our present problem. Punishment, if and when it is justified, is justified only on one or both of the grounds just mentioned. The question then is how, if we assume determinism, punishment can correct character or deter people from evil actions.

Suppose that your child develops a habit of telling lies. You give him a mild beating. Why? Because you believe that his personality is such that the usual motives for telling the truth do not cause him to do so. You therefore supply the missing cause, or motive, in the shape of pain and the fear of future pain if he repeats his untruthful behavior. And you hope that a few treatments of this kind will condition him to the habit of truth-telling, so that he will come to tell the truth without the infliction of pain. You assume that his actions are determined by causes, but that the usual causes of truth-telling do not in him produce their usual effects. You therefore supply him with an artificially injected motive, pain and fear, which you think will in the future cause him to speak truthfully.

The principle is exactly the same where you hope, by punishing one man, to deter others from wrong actions. You believe that the fear of punishment will cause those who might otherwise do evil to do well.

We act on the same principle with non-human, and even with inanimate, things, if they do not behave in the way we think they ought to behave. The rose bushes in the garden produce only small and poor blooms, whereas we want large and rich ones. We supply a cause which will produce large blooms, namely fertilizer. Our automobile does not go properly. We supply a cause which will make it go better, namely oil in the works. The punishment for the man, the fertilizer for the plant, and the oil for the car, are all justified by the same principle and in the same way. The only difference is that different kinds of things require different kinds of causes, to make them do what they should. Pain may be the appropriate remedy to apply, in certain cases, to human beings, and oil to the machine. It is, of course, of no use to inject motor oil into the boy or to beat the machine.

Thus we see that moral responsibility is not only consistent with determinism, but requires it. The assumption on which punishment is based is that human behavior is causally determined. If pain could not be a cause of truth-telling there would be no justification at all for punishing lies. If human actions and volitions were uncaused, it would be useless either to punish or reward, or indeed to do anything else to correct people's bad behavior. For nothing that you could do would in any way influence them. Thus moral responsibility would entirely disappear. If there were no determinism of human beings at all, their actions would be completely unpredictable and capricious, and therefore irresponsible. And this is in itself a strong argument against the common view of philosophers that free will means being undetermined by causes.

Freedom of Choice and Human Responsibility

Corliss Lamont (1902–1995) was an American philosopher and freethinker who challenged received wisdom in many areas, including economics, politics, religion, and philosophy. He served as secretary/treasurer of the *Journal of Philosophy* and as Chairman of the National Emergency Civil Liberties Committee. In this essay, Lamont presents a number of reasons for believing in the existence of libertarian free will.

It is my thesis that a man who is convinced he possesses freedom of choice or free will has a greater sense of responsibility than a person who thinks that total determinism rules the universe and human life. Determinism in the classic sense means that the flow of history, including all human choices and actions, is completely predetermined from the beginning of time. He who believes that "whatever is, was to be" can try to escape moral responsibility for wrongdoing by claiming that he was compelled to act as he did because it was predestined by the iron laws of cause and effect.

But if free choice truly exists at the moment of choosing, men clearly have full moral responsibility in deciding between two or more genuine alternatives, and the deterministic alibi has no weight. The heart of our discussion, then, lies in the question of whether free choice or universal determinism represents the truth. I shall try to summarize briefly the main reasons that point to the existence of free will.

First, there is the immediate, powerful, common-sense intuition shared by virtually all human beings that freedom of choice is real. This intuition seems as strong to me as the sensation of pleasure or pain; and the attempt of the determinists to explain the intuition away is as artificial as the Christian Scientist claim that pain is not real. The intuition of free choice does not, of course, in itself prove that such freedom exists, but that intuition is so strong that the burden of proof is on the determinists to show that it is based on an illusion.

Second, we can defuse the determinist argument by admitting, and indeed insisting, that a great deal of determinism exists in the world. Determinism in the form of if-then causal laws governs much of the human body's functioning and much of the universe as a whole. We can be glad that the automatic system of breathing, digestion, circulation of the blood, and beating of the heart operate deterministically—until they

get out of order. Determinism versus free choice is a false issue; what we always have is relative determinism and relative free choice. Free will is ever limited by the past and by the vast range of if-then laws. At the same time, human beings utilize free choice to take advantage of those deterministic laws embodied in science and man-made machines. Most of us drive cars, but it is we and not the autos that decide when and where they are to go. Determinism wisely used and controlled—which is by no means always the case—can make us freer and happier.

Third, determinism is a relative thing, not only because human free choice exists, but also because contingency or chance is an ultimate trait of the cosmos. Contingency is best seen in the intersection of mutually independent event-streams between which there was no previous causal connection. My favorite example here is the collision of the steamship *Titanic* with an iceberg off Newfoundland, in the middle of the night on April 14, 1912. It was a terrible accident, with more than 1,500 persons lost. The drifting of the iceberg down from the north and the steaming of the *Titanic* west from England clearly represented two causal streams independent of each other.

Even if a team of scientific experts had been able, per impossible, to trace back the two causal streams and ascertain that the catastrophe had been predestined from the moment the steamship left Southampton, that would not upset my thesis. For the space-time relation of the iceberg and the *Titanic*, as the ship started on its voyage, would have been itself a matter of contingency, since there was no relevant cause to account for that precise relation.

From: Corliss Lamont, "Freedom of Choice and Human Responsibility," *Religious Humanism*, Vol. III, No. 3 (Summer 1969): 110–118.

The pervasive presence of contingency in the world is also proved by the fact that all natural laws, as I have observed, take the form of if-then sequences or relations. The if factor is obviously conditional and demonstrates the continual coexistence of contingency with determinism. The actuality of contingency negates the idea of total and all-inclusive necessity operating throughout the universe. As regards human choice, contingency ensures that at the outset the alternatives one faces are indeterminate in relation to the act of choosing, which proceeds to make one of them determinate.

My fourth point is that the accepted meaning of potentiality, namely, that every object and event in the cosmos possesses plural possibilities of behavior, interaction, and development, knocks out the determinist thesis. From the determinist viewpoint, multiple potentialities are an illusion. If you want to take a vacation trip next summer, you will no doubt think over a number of possibilities before you make a final decision. Determinism logically implies that such deliberation is mere playacting, because you were destined all the time to choose the trip you did choose. When we relate the causal pattern to potentiality, we find that causation as mediated through free choice can have its appropriate effect in the actualization of any one of various possibilities.

Fifth, the normal processes of human thought are tied in with potentiality as I have just described it, and likewise tend to show that freedom of choice is real. Thinking constantly involves general conceptions, universals, or abstractions under which are classified many varying particulars. In the case that I discussed under my fourth point, "vacation travel" was the general conception and the different places that might be visited were the particulars, the alternatives, the potentialities, among which one could freely choose. Unless there is free choice, the function of human thought in solving problems becomes superfluous and a mask of make believe.

Sixth, it is clarifying for the problem of free choice to realize that only the present exists, and that it is always some present activity that builds up the past, as a skier leaves a trail behind him in the snow as he weaves down the hill. Everything that exists—the whole vast aggregate of inanimate matter, the swarming profusion of earthly life, man in his every aspect—exists only as an event or events taking place at this instant moment, which is now. The past is dead and gone; it is efficacious only as it is embodied in present structures and activities.

The activity of former presents establishes the foundations upon which the immediate present operates. What happened in the past creates both limitations and potentialities, always conditioning the present. But conditioning in this sense is not the same as determining; and each day sweeps onward under its own momentum, actualizing fresh patterns of existence, maintaining other patterns and destroying still others. Thus a man choosing and acting in the present is not wholly controlled by the past, but is part of the unending forward surge of cosmic power. He is an active, initiating agent, riding the wave of the present, as it were, and deliberating open alternatives to reach decisions regarding the many different phases of his life.

My seventh point is that the doctrine of universal and eternal determinism is seen to be self-refuting when we work out its full implications in the cases of *reductio ad absurdum* implied. If our choices and actions today were all predestined yesterday, then they were equally predestined yesteryear, at the day of our birth, and at the birth of our solar system and earth some five billion years ago. To take another instance: for determinism, the so-called irresistible impulse that the law recognizes in assessing crimes by the insane must hold with equal force for the actions of the sane and virtuous. In the determinist philosophy, the good man has an irresistible impulse to tell the truth, to be kind to animals, and to expose the graft in City Hall.

Eighth, in the novel dialect of determinism many words lose their normal meaning. I refer to such words as refraining, forbearance, self-restraint, and regret. If determinism turns out to be true, we shall have to scrap a great deal in existing dictionaries and do a vast amount of redefining. What meaning, for example, is to be assigned to forbearance when it is determined in advance that you are going to refuse that second Martini cocktail? You can truly forbear only when you refrain from doing something that it is possible for you to do. But under the determinist dispensation it is not possible for you to accept the second cocktail because fate has already dictated your "No." I am not saying that nature necessarily conforms to our linguistic usages, but human language habits that have evolved over aeons of time cannot be neglected in the analysis of free choice and determinism.

Finally, I do not think that the term moral responsibility can retain its traditional meaning unless freedom of choice exists. From the viewpoint of ethics, law, and criminal law, it is difficult to understand how a consistent determinist would have a sufficient sense of personal responsibility for the development of decent ethical standards. But the question remains whether there have ever been or can be any consistent determinists or whether free choice runs so deep in human nature as an innate characteristic that, as Jean Paul Sartre suggests, "We are not free to cease being free."

THOMAS D. DAVIS

Please Don't Tell Me How the Story Ends

Thomas D. Davis has taught philosophy at Michigan, Grinnell College, the University of Redlands, and De Anza College. Mr. Davis is the author of numerous short stories as well as two mystery novels with philosophical themes: *Suffer Little Children,* which received a Shamus Award from the Private Eye Writers of America for best first mystery of 1991, and *Murdered Sleep.* In this short story, Davis considers the possibility of books of life: books that contain a complete and accurate account of a life but are written before a life is lived.

The heavy door closed behind him, and he glanced quickly at this new detention room. He was startled, almost pleasantly surprised. This was not like the drab cell in which he had spent the first days after his arrest, nor like the hospital rooms, with the serpentine carnival machines, in which he had been tested and observed for the last two months — though he assumed that he was being observed here as well. This was more like a small, comfortable library that had been furnished like a first-class hotel room. Against the four walls were fully stocked bookcases that rose ten feet to the white plaster ceiling; in the ceiling was a small skylight. The floor was covered with a thick green carpet, and in the middle of the room were a double bed with a nightstand, a large bureau, a desk, an easy chair with a side table, and several lamps. There were large gaps in the bookcases to accommodate two doors, including the one through which he had just entered, and also a traylike apparatus affixed to the wall. He could not immediately ascertain the purpose of the tray, but the other door, he quickly learned, led to a spacious bathroom complete with toilet articles. As he searched the main room, he found that the desk contained writing paper, pens, a clock, and a calendar; the bureau contained abundant clothing in a variety of colors and two pairs of shoes. He glanced down at the hospital gown and slippers he was wearing, then quickly changed into a rust-colored sweater and a pair of dark brown slacks. The clothing, including the shoes, fitted him perfectly. It would be easier to face his situation, to face whatever might be coming, looking like a civilized human being.

But what was his situation? He wanted to believe that the improvement in his living conditions meant an improvement in his status, perhaps even an imminent reprieve. But all the same he doubted it. Nothing had seemed to follow a sensible progression since his arrest, and it would be foolhardy to take anything at face value now. But what were they up to? At first, when he had been taken to the hospital, he had expected torture, some hideous pseudomedical experiment, or a brain-washing program. But there had been no operation and no pain. He had been tested countless times: the endless details of biography; the responses to color, scent, sound, taste, touch; the responses to situation and ideas; the physical examination. But if these constituted mind-altering procedures, they had to be of the most subtle variety. Certainly he felt the same; at least no more compliant than he had been in the beginning. What were they after?

As his uncertainty grew to anxiety, he tried to work it off with whatever physical exercise he could manage in the confines of the room: running in place, isometrics, sit-ups, and push-ups. He knew that the strength of his will would depend in part on the strength of his body, and since his arrest he had exercised as much as he could. No one had prevented this.

He was midway through a push-up when a loud buzzer sounded. He leaped to his feet, frightened but ready. Then he saw a plastic tray of food on the metal tray that extended from the wall and a portion of the wall closing downward behind the tray. So this was how he would get his meals. He would see no one. Was this some special isolation experiment?

The question of solitude quickly gave way to hunger and curiosity about the food. It looked delicious and plentiful; there was much more than he could possibly

From: Thomas D. Davis, "Please Don't Tell Me How the Story Ends," *Philosophy* (New York: McGraw-Hill, 1993) 131–135.

eat. Was it safe? Could it be drugged or poisoned? No, there could be no point to their finishing him in such an odd, roundabout fashion. He took the tray to the desk and ate heartily, but still left several of the dishes barely sampled or untouched.

That evening—the clock and the darkened skylight told him it was evening—he investigated the room further. He was interrupted only once by the buzzer. When it continued to sound and nothing appeared, he realized that the buzzer meant he was to return the food dishes. He did so, and the plastic tray disappeared into the wall.

The writing paper was a temptation. He always thought better with a pen in hand. Writing would resemble a kind of conversation and make him feel a little less alone. With a journal, he could construct some kind of history from what threatened to be days of dulling sameness. But he feared that they wanted him to write, that his doing so would somehow play into their hands. So he refrained.

Instead, he examined a portion of the bookshelf that contained paperback volumes in a great variety of sizes and colors. The books covered a number of fields—fiction, history, science, philosophy, politics—some to his liking and some not. He selected a political treatise and put it on the small table next to the easy chair. He did not open it immediately. He washed up and then went to the bureau, where he found a green plaid robe and a pair of light yellow pajamas. As he lifted out the pajamas, he noticed a small, black, rectangular box and opened it.

Inside was a revolver. A quick examination showed that it was loaded and operative. Quickly he shut the box, trembling. He was on one knee in front of the open drawer. His first thought was that a former inmate had left the gun to help him. He was sure that his body was blocking the contents of the drawer from the view of any observation devices in the room. He must not give away the secret. He forced himself to close the drawer casually, rise, and walk to the easy chair.

Then the absurdity of his hypothesis struck him. How could any prisoner have gotten such a thing past the tight security of this place? And what good would such a weapon do him in a room to which no one came? No, the gun must be there because the authorities wanted it there. But why? Could it be they wanted to hide his death under the pretense of an attempted escape? Or could it be that they were trying to push him to suicide by isolating him? But again, what was the point of it? He realized that his fingerprints were on the gun. Did they want to use that as some kind of evidence against him? He went to the bureau again, ostensibly to switch pajamas, and, during the switch, opened the box and quickly wiped his prints off the gun. As casually as he could, he returned to the chair.

He passed the evening in considerable agitation. He tried to read but could not. He exercised again, but it did not calm him. He tried to analyze his situation, but his thoughts were an incoherent jumble. Much later, he lay down on the bed, first pushing the easy chair against the door of the room. He recognized the absurdity of erecting this fragile barrier, but the noise of their pushing it away would give him some warning. For a while, he forced his eyes open each time he began to doze, but eventually he fell asleep.

In the morning, he found everything unchanged, the chair still in place at the door. Nothing but the breakfast tray had intruded. After he had exercised, breakfasted, bathed, and found himself still unmolested, he began to feel more calm. He read half the book he had selected the night before, lunched, and then dozed in his chair.

When he awoke, his eyes scanned the room and came to rest on one of the bookshelves filled with a series of black, leatherbound volumes of uniform size, marked only by number. He had noticed them before but had paid little attention, thinking they were an encyclopedia. Now he noticed what a preposterous number of volumes there were, perhaps two hundred in all, filling not only one bookcase from floor to ceiling but filling parts of others as well. His curiosity piqued, he pulled down Volume LXIV, and opened it at random to page 494.

The page was filled with very small print, with a section at the bottom in even smaller print that appeared to be footnotes. The heading of the page was large enough to be read at a glance. "RE: PRISONER 7439762 (referred to herein as 'Q')." He read on: "3/07/06. 14:03. Q entered room on 3/06/06 at 4:52. Surprised at pleasantness of room. Glanced at furniture, then bookcase, then ceiling. Noted metal tray and second door, puzzled by both. Entered bathroom, noting toilet articles. Lifted shaver and touched cologne." He skipped down the page: "Selected brown slacks, rust sweater, and tan shoes. Felt normal clothing made him more equal to his situation."

It seemed that they were keeping some sort of record of his activities here. But what was the purpose of having the record here for him to read? And how had they gotten it in here? It was easy to figure out how they knew of his activities: they were watching him, just as he had suspected. They must have printed this page during the night and placed it here as he slept. Perhaps his food had been drugged to guarantee that he wouldn't awake.

He glanced toward the door of his cell and remembered the chair he had placed against it. In a drugged sleep, he wouldn't have heard them enter. They could have pulled the chair back as they left. But all the way? Presumably there was some hidden panel in the door. Once the door was shut, they had merely to open the panel and pull the chair the last few inches.

Suddenly he remembered the matter of the gun. He glanced down the page and there it was, a description of how he had handled the gun twice. There was no warning given nor any hint of an explanation as to why the gun was there. There was just the clipped, neutral-toned description of his actions and impressions. It described his hope that the gun might have been left by another prisoner, his rejection of that supposition, his fear that the gun might be used against him in some way, his desire to remove the fingerprints. But how on earth could they have known what he was feeling and thinking? He decided that he had acted and reacted as any normal person would have done, and they had simply drawn the obvious conclusions from his actions and facial expressions.

He glanced further down the page and read: "On 3/07/06, Q awoke at 8:33." And further "... selected *The Future of Socialism* by Felix Berofsky. . . ." And further: "... bent the corner of page 206 to mark his place and put the book. . . ." All his activities of that morning had already been printed in the report!

He began turning the book around in his hands and pulled it away from the shelf. Was this thing wired in some way? Could they print their reports onto these pages in minutes without removing the books from the shelves? Perhaps they had some new process whereby they could imprint specially sensitized pages by electronic signal.

Then he remembered that he had just awakened from a nap, and he slammed the volume shut in disgust. Of course: they had entered the room again during his nap. He placed the volume back on the shelf and started for his chair. How could they expect him to be taken in by such blatant trickery? But then a thought occurred to him. He had picked out a volume and page at random. Why had the description of yesterday and this morning been on that particular page? Were all the pages the same? He returned to the shelf and picked up the same volume, this time opening it to page 531. The heading was the same. He looked down the page: "Q began to return to his chair but became

puzzled as to why the initial description of his activities should have appeared on page 494 of this volume." He threw the book to the floor and grabbed another, Volume LX, opening it to page 103: "... became more confused by the correct sequential description on page 531, Volume LXIV."

"What are you trying to do to me!" he screamed, dropping the second book. Immediately he was ashamed at his lack of self-control.

"What an absurd joke," he said loudly to whatever listening devices there might be.

He picked up the two volumes he had dropped and put them back in place on the bookshelf. He walked across the room and sat in the chair. He tried to keep his expression neutral while he thought.

There was no possibility that observations were being made and immediately transmitted to the books by some electronic process. It all happened too fast. Perhaps it was being done through some kind of mind control. Yet he was certain that no devices of any kind had been implanted in his brain. That would have involved anesthetizing him, operating, leaving him unconscious until all scars had healed, and then reviving him with no sense of time lost. No doubt they had ability, but not that much. It could be something as simple as hypnosis, of course. This would require merely writing the books, then commanding him to perform certain acts in a certain order, including the opening of the books. Yet that would be such a simple, familiar experiment that it would hardly seem worth doing. And it would hardly require the extensive testing procedures that he had undergone before being placed in this room.

He glanced at the books again, and his eye fell on Volume I. If there was an explanation anywhere in this room, it would be there, he thought. The page would probably say only, "Q hoped for an explanation," and in that case he would have to do without one. But it was worth taking a look.

He took Volume I from the shelf, opened it to the first page, and glanced at the first paragraph: "Q hoped to find an explanation." He started to laugh, but stopped abruptly. The explanation seemed to be there after all. He read on: "Experiment in the Prediction of Human Behavior within a Controlled Environment, No. 465, Variant No. 8, Case 2: Subject Aware of Behavior Prediction."

He read through the brief "explanation" several times. (Of course, this in itself might be trickery.) Obviously, these unknown experimenters considered all human behavior to be theoretically predictable. They first studied a subject for a number of weeks and then attempted to predict how that subject would behave within a limited, controlled environment. In his case, they were attempting to predict, in addition to all else, his reactions to the "fact" that his behavior was predictable and being predicted. They had placed those volumes here as proof to him that each prior series of acts had been successfully predicted.

He didn't believe they could do it; he didn't want to believe it. Of course, much of what occurred in the universe, including much of human behavior, was predictable in theory. The world wasn't totally chaotic, after all, and science had had its successes in foreseeing certain events. But he refused to believe that there was no element of chance in the world, that every event happened just as it did out of necessity. He had some freedom, some causal autonomy, some power to initiate the new. He was not merely a puppet of universal laws. Each of his choices was not simply a mathematical function of those laws together with the state of himself and the external world at the moment just prior to the choice. He would not believe that.

Nothing was written on page 1 to indicate how the other experiments had turned out — not that he would have believed such a report anyway. No doubt the indication that his experience was a more complex "variant" of the experiment was meant to imply that the preceding experiments had been successful. But there had to have been mistakes, even if they claimed that the errors could eventually be overcome. As long as there were mistakes, one could continue to believe in human freedom. He did believe in human freedom.

His thoughts were interrupted by the buzzer. His dinner emerged from the wall. He looked at it with anger, remembering how the first page to which he had turned had listed, perhaps even predicted, exactly what foods he would eat. But he didn't reject the meal. He needed his wits about him, and for that he needed strength. He must try to get his mind off all this for tonight, at least. He would eat, read, and then sleep.

For several hours, he was fairly successful in diverting his attention from the books. Then, in bed with the lights out, he recalled the phrase "Variant No. 8, Case 2." That made him feel more hopeful. This was only the second time that this particular version of the experiment was being tried. Surely, the likelihood of error was great.

He found himself thinking about Case 1. What kind of man had he been, and how had he fared? Had he worn green pajamas one day when the book said "yellow," or remained contemptuous when the book said

"hysterical," and then laughed in their faces as they led him from the room? That would have been a triumph.

Suddenly, he thought of the gun and had an image of a man, seated on the edge of the bed, looking at those volumes on the wall, slowly raising the gun to his head. ". . . To predict . . . his reactions to the 'fact' that his behavior was predictable and being predicted." God, was that the purpose of the gun? Had it been put there as one of his options? Had that been the ignominious ending of Case 1, and not the departure in triumph he had pictured a moment ago? He had a vision of himself lying dead on the floor and men in white robes grinning as they opened a volume to a page that described his death. Would he hold out, or would he die? The answer was somewhere in those thousands of pages — if he could only find it.

He realized that he was playing into their hands by supposing that they could do what he knew they could not. Anyway, even if one assumed that they could accurately predict his future, they were not forcing him to do anything. There were no mind-controlling devices; he wasn't being programmed by them. If they were to predict correctly, they must predict what he wanted to do. And he didn't want to die.

In spite of these reflections, he remained agitated. When he finally slept, he slept fitfully. He dreamed that he was a minuscule figure trapped in a maze on the scale of a dollhouse. He watched himself from a distance and watched the life-sized doctors who peered over the top of the maze. There were two exits from the maze, one to freedom and one to a black pit that he knew to be death. "Death," the doctors kept saying to one another, and he watched his steady progression in the maze toward death. He kept shouting instructions to himself. "No, not that way! Go to the left there!" But the doomed figure couldn't hear him.

When he awoke in the morning, he felt feverish and touched only the fruit and coffee on his breakfast tray. He lay on the bed for much of the morning, his thoughts obsessed with the black volumes on the wall. He knew that he must try to foil the predictions, but he feared failure. I am too upset and weak, he thought. I must ignore the books until I am better. I must turn my mind to other things.

But as he tried to divert himself, he became aware of an agonizing echo in his head. He would turn in bed and think: "Q turns onto left side." Or scratch: "Q scratches left thigh." Or mutter "damn them": "Q mutters, 'damn them.'" Finally, he could stand it no longer and stumbled to one of the bookshelves. He pulled two volumes from the shelves, juggled them in his hands, dropped one, then flipped the pages several times before picking a page.

"3/08/06.11:43. At 15:29 on 3/07/06, Q opened Volume I to page 1 and read explanation of experiment."

He slammed the book.

"Damn you," he said aloud. "I'm a man, not a machine. I'll show you. I'll show you."

He took another volume and held it in his hand. "Two and two are five," he thought. "When I was six, I lived in China with the Duke of Savoy. The earth is flat." He opened the book.

"Q wants to confuse prediction. Thinks: Two and two are five. . . ."

He looked around the room as he tried to devise some other line of attack. He noticed the clock and the calendar. Each page of the book gave the date and time at which each page opened, the date and time of each event. He rushed to the desk, flipped the pages of the calendar, and turned the knob that adjusted the hands on the clock. He opened another book and read: "3/08/06. 12:03." He yelled out:

"See? You're wrong. The calendar says June, and the time is 8:04. That's my date and my time. Predict what you think if you want. This is what I think. And I think you're wrong."

He had another idea. The first page he had looked at had been page 494, Volume LXIV. He would open that volume to the same page. Either it must say the same thing or it must be new. Either way they would have failed, for a new entry would show them to be tricksters. He grabbed the volume and found the page. "3/07/06. 14:03. Q entered room on 3/06/06 at 4:52." Once again, he spoke aloud:

"Of course, but that's old news. I don't see anything here about my turning to the page a second time. My, we do seem to be having our problems, don't we?"

He laughed in triumph and was about to shut the book when he saw the fine print at the bottom. He licked his lips and stared at the print for a long time before he pulled down another volume and turned to the page that had been indicated in the footnote: ". . . then Q reopened Volume LXIV, page 494, hoping. . . ."

He ripped out the page, then another, and another. His determination gave way to a fury, and he tore apart one book, then another, until twelve of them lay in tatters on the floor. He had to stop because of dizziness and exhaustion.

"I'm a man," he muttered, "not a machine."

He started for his bed, ignoring the buzzer announcing the tray of food. He made it only as far as the easy chair. He sank into it, and his eyelids seemed to close of their own weight.

"I'm a. . . ."

Asleep, he dreamed again. He was running through the streets of a medieval town, trying desperately to escape from a grotesque, devil-like creature. "At midnight you die," it said. No matter where he ran, the devil kept reappearing in front of him. "It doesn't matter where you go. I will be there at midnight." Then a loud bell began to sound twelve chimes slowly. He found himself in a huge library, swinging an axe at the shelves, which crumbled under his blows. He felt great elation until he saw that everything he had destroyed had been reassembled behind him. He dropped the axe and began to scream.

When he awoke, he thought for a moment he was still dreaming. On the floor, he saw twelve volumes, all intact. Then he turned his head and saw the twelve torn volumes where he had left them. The new ones were on the floor near the metal tray. His lunch had been withdrawn, and the books had been pushed through the opening in the wall while he had slept.

He moved to the bed, where he slept fitfully through the evening and night, getting up only once to sip some tea from the dinner tray.

In the morning he remained in bed. He was no longer feverish, but he felt more exhausted than he could remember ever having been. The breakfast tray came and went untouched. He didn't feel like eating. He didn't feel like doing anything.

At about eleven o'clock, he got out of bed just long enough to find the gun; then he fingered it on his chest as he lay back, staring at the ceiling. There was no point in going on with it. They would have their laughs, of course. But they would have them in any case, since, no matter what he did, it would be in their books. And ultimately it wasn't their victory at all, but the victory of the universal laws that had dictated every event in this puppet play of a world. A man of honor must refuse to play his part in it. He, certainly, refused.

And how could the experimenters delight in their achievement? They were not testing a theory about their prisoners but about all human beings, including themselves. Their success showed that they themselves had no control over their own destinies. What did it matter if his future was written in the books and their futures were not? There would always be the invisible books in the nature of things, books that contained the futures of everyone. Could they help seeing that? And when they saw that, if they too didn't reach for guns, could they help feeling degraded to the core of their souls? No, they had not won. Everyone had lost.

Eventually he sat up on the bed. His hand shook, but he was not surprised. Whatever he might will, there would be that impulse for survival. He forced the hand up and put the barrel of the gun in his mouth.

The buzzer startled him, and the hand with the gun dropped to his side. The lunch tray appeared, and suddenly he was aware of being ravenously hungry. He laughed bitterly. Well, he wouldn't be hungry for long. Still, wasn't the condemned man entitled to a last meal? Surely honor did not forbid that. And the food looked delicious. He put the gun on his pillow and took the tray to his desk.

While he was savoring his mushroom omelet, he glanced at the political treatise that had remained half read by the easy chair for the last two days. God, had it been only two days? It was a shame that he would not be able to finish it; it was an interesting book. And there were other books on the shelves—not the black volumes, of course—that he had been meaning to read for some time and would have enjoyed.

As he sampled some artichokes, he glanced at the formidable black volumes on the shelves. Somewhere there was a page that read: "After completing lunch, Q put the gun to his head and pulled the trigger." Of course, if he changed his mind and decided to finish reading the political treatise first, it would say that instead. Or if he waited a day more, it would register that fact. What were the possibilities? Could it ever say "reprieved"? He did not see how. They would never let him go free with the information he had about their experiments. Unless, of course, there was a change of regime. But that was the barest of possibilities. Could a page say that he had been returned to the regular cells? God, how he would like to talk to another human being. But that would pose the same problem for the experimenters as releasing him. Presumably, they would kill him eventually. Still, that was no worse than what he was about to do to himself. Perhaps they would con-tinue the experiment a while longer. Meantime, he could live comfortably, eat well, read, exercise.

There were indeed possibilities other than immediate suicide, not all of them unpleasant. But could he countenance living any longer? Didn't honor dictate defiance? Yet—defiance of whom? It wasn't as if the laws of the world had a lawmaker in whose face he might shake his fist. He had never believed in a god; rather, it was as if he were trapped inside some creaky old machine, unstarted and uncontrolled, that had been puttering along a complex but predictable path forever. Kick a machine when you're angry, and you only get a sore foot. Anyway, how could he have claimed credit for killing himself, since it would have been inevitable that he do so?

The black volumes stretched out like increments of time across the brown bookshelves. Somewhere in their pages was this moment, and the next, and perhaps a tomorrow, and another, perhaps even a next month or a next year. He would never be able to read those pages until it was already unnecessary, but there might be some good days there; in any case, it would be interesting to wait and see.

After lunch he sat at his desk for a long time. Eventually, he got up and replaced the gun in its case in the bureau drawer. He placed the lunch dishes back on the metal tray and, beside the dishes, heaped the covers and torn pages of the books he had destroyed. He then put the new volumes on the shelves. As he started back to the chair, his eye was caught by the things on the desk. He took a volume from the bookshelf, carried it to the desk, and opened it. He read only the heading at the top: "3/09/06. 13:53." He adjusted the clock and the calendar accordingly. If he was going to live a while longer, he might as well know the correct day and time.

Suggestions for Further Reading

Dennett, Daniel. *Elbow Room: The Varieties of Free Will Worth Wanting.* Cambridge: MIT Press, 1984.

Dworkin, Gerald. *Determinism, Free Will and Moral Responsibility.* Englewood Cliffs, NJ: Prentice-Hall, 1970.

Fischer, John Martin, ed. *Moral Responsibility.* Ithaca, NY: Cornell University Press, 1986.

Flew, Antony, and Vesey, Godfrey. *Agency and Necessity.* Oxford: Basil Blackwell, 1987.

Honderich, Ted. *How Free Are You?* New York: Oxford University Press, 1993.

Kane, Robert. *The Significance of Free Will*. New York: Oxford University Press, 1996.

O'Connor, Timothy, ed. *Agents, Causes, and Events*. Oxford: Oxford University Press, 1995.

Stace, Walter T. *Religion and the Modern Mind*. Philadelphia: Lippencott, 1952.

Taylor, Richard. *Metaphysics*. Englewood Cliffs, NJ: Prentice-Hall, 1992.

Trustead, Jennifer. *Free Will and Responsibility*. Oxford: Oxford University Press, 1984.

Van Inwagen, Peter. *An Essay on Free Will*. Oxford: Clarendon Press, 1983.

Watson, Gary, ed. *Free Will*. Oxford: Clarendon Press, 1982.

Chapter 4

The Problem of Personal Identity

Suppose it's sometime late in the twenty-first century, and you have come down with one of the last incurable diseases. Your doctor informs you that conventional medicine can do nothing to save you. There is, however, a new procedure that may allow you to escape what otherwise would be certain death. Cognitive scientists have recently perfected a device that uploads the contents of your brain (your mind?) into an organic computer composed of "biochips." These biochips have the same causal powers as neurons. The computer is housed in a robot body that can be made to look like you at any stage of your adult life. The robot is outfitted with visual, auditory, olfactory, tactile, and gustatory sensors. Those who have undergone the transfer report that the sensations they receive from these sensors are indistinguishable from those produced by their own sense organs. Things look, sound, smell, feel, and taste the same after the transfer as they did before the upload. These individuals also report that their emotional lives are unaffected by the transfer. What used to give them joy or sorrow, pleasure or pain still does. Knowing this, would you accept the doctor's offer to upload the contents of your brain into a computer?

To answer this question, you must decide whether you would survive the transfer. Would the robot with the contents of your brain be you? The answer you give will depend on your theory of personal identity—that is, on your theory of what makes a person at one time (the earlier person) identical to a person at another time (the later person).

All of us undergo a number of changes throughout our lives. Not only do our bodies change, but so do our minds. Our beliefs, attitudes, and desires, for example, may be very different now from what they were ten years ago. Nevertheless, we ordinarily assume that these changes happen to one and the same person. How is that possible? How can a person change and yet still remain the same person? This is the question that theories of personal identity try to answer.

Our concern for ourselves differs from our concern for anyone else. Although we may be sorry to learn that someone else is about to die, we would not anticipate that death in the same way we would anticipate our own. One way to test theories of personal identity, then, is to determine whether you would be as concerned for someone in the future as you would be for yourself. Suppose, in the case above, you knew that there was a good chance that the person in the robot body would suffer great pain immediately after the transfer as the system adjusted itself. Do you believe that you would be the person experiencing the pain? If so, there's reason to believe that the robot is you.

People are not only concerned about their futures; they are also responsible for their pasts. Justice requires that only those responsible for committing a crime be punished for it. It wouldn't be fair to punish you for a crime that you didn't commit. Similarly, it wouldn't be fair to punish someone else for something you did. Another way to test theories of personal identity, then, is to determine whether the later person would be responsible for something the earlier person had done. Suppose you had committed a crime before you underwent the transfer. Would we be justified in putting the robot in jail? If so, there's further reason to think that the robot is you.

Although most people have probably never seriously considered the possibility of having their minds uploaded into a robot, many Christians believe that their minds will eventually be uploaded into another body, for the Bible teaches that after we die, we will be reborn in a new body.

St. Paul's first letter to the Corinthians is the source of this teaching:

> What you sow does not come to life unless it dies. And what you sow is not the body which is to be, but a bare kernel perhaps of wheat or of some other grain. But God gives it a body as he has chosen, and to each kind of seed its own body. For not all flesh is alike, but there is one kind for men, another for animals, another for birds, and another for fish. There are celestial bodies and there are terrestrial bodies; but the glory of the celestial is one, and the glory of the terrestrial is another. There is one glory of the sun, and another glory of the moon, and another glory of the stars; for star differs from star in glory. So is it with the resurrection of the dead. What is sown is perishable, what is raised is imperishable. It is sown in dishonor, it is raised in glory. It is sown in weakness, it is raised in power. It is sown a physical body, it is raised a spiritual body. If there is a physical body, there is also a spiritual body.[1]

Some take this passage to mean that we will get a transformed physical body in the afterlife; others take it to mean that we will get a brand-new spiritual body. Either way we will get a body. But if we can survive the transfer from a physical body to a spiritual body, couldn't we also survive the transfer from a physical body to a robot body?

Not only should a theory of personal identity help us decide whether we can survive the death of our bodies, it should also help us decide whether we can survive other sorts of change. Suppose, for example, that Frank, a right-wing extremist who believes that the government has no right to tax the rich to give to the poor, blows up an IRS office and injures a number of people. To escape capture, he sets up residence in a small community and changes his name to Robert. After working in the local soup kitchen for a number of years, he joins the fire department and becomes very active in community service projects. He also joins a local church and teaches Sunday school regularly. One night, while studying the Bible, he has a religious experience and becomes a born-again Christian. As a result, he decides to devote his life to helping the needy. Robert now finds it impossible to identify with the thoughts, feelings, and desires that motivated Frank. Frank's beliefs, attitudes, and values seem totally alien to Robert. Although Robert can vaguely remember the bombing, he knows that he would never do such a thing. If Robert were captured by the FBI, should he be punished for the bombing committed by Frank? It is wrong to punish one person for what another

Our souls belong to our bodies, not our bodies to our souls.

—Herman Melville

We do not believe in immortality because we have proved it, but, we forever try to prove it because we believe it.

—James Martineau

person did. Are Robert and Frank the same person? If not, Robert shouldn't have to suffer for Frank's crimes.

How we answer the question Are Robert and Frank the same person? depends on how we interpret the phrase "the same." When we say that one thing is the same as another, we may be saying that they have the same qualities. For example, when we say that a car on one dealer's lot is the same as a car on another dealer's lot, we may mean that they are the same make, model, and year, and thus have identical features. This type of sameness is known as **qualitative identity** because if two things are the same in this sense, they have the same qualities.

When we say that one thing is the same as another, however, we may be saying that they are one and the same thing. For example, when we say that a car on a used car lot is the same one that our family traded in, we may mean that it is the very same car that our family once owned. This type of identity is known as **numerical identity** because two different descriptions are being used to refer to one and the same thing.

To use another example, suppose you go swimming in the ocean and lose your class ring. You can buy another ring that is qualitatively identical to your original ring, but it will not be numerically identical to it because it is not the very ring you lost. So, qualitative identity does not imply numerical identity. On the other hand, someone might find a ring on the beach that is qualitatively very different from your original ring: it might be corroded; it might even be missing the jewel. Nevertheless, it might be numerically identical to your original ring. That is, it might actually be your original ring. So, numerical identity doesn't imply qualitative identity either.

Your original class ring can undergo many changes and yet continue to be one and the same ring. But there are some sorts of changes that it cannot undergo without ceasing to exist. For example, if it became so corroded that it broke into pieces, or if it were melted down, it would no longer exist. When something changes, it loses one or more properties. If something can survive the loss of a property, the property is said to be **accidental** to it. If it cannot survive the loss of a property—if it's impossible for the thing to exist without that property—the property is said to be **essential** to it.

Identity conditions (also known as "persistance conditions") are conditions that must be met in order for a thing to retain its identity over time. They indicate what makes a thing at one time numerically identical to something at another time. Theories of personal identity try to specify the identity conditions for persons. They tell us what kinds of changes a person could undergo and still remain the same (numerically identical) person.

One way to figure out the identity conditions for people is to consider what sorts of changes they would survive. You would survive a haircut. You would lose some hair, but you wouldn't cease to exist. So having a certain amount of hair is not essential to you. But what if you got total amnesia and lost all memory of your past experiences? Would you survive that sort of change? A theory of personal identity should answer that sort of question.

I don't want to achieve immortality through my work. . . . I want to achieve it through not dying.

—WOODY ALLEN

In the News: Kathleen Soliah, a.k.a. Sara Jane Olson

On June 16, 1999, the FBI arrested former Symbionese Liberation Army (SLA) member Kathleen Soliah in St. Paul, Minnesota. Soliah allegedly participated in a number of bombings and bank robberies conducted by the SLA in the 1970s. In the twenty-five years since, Soliah had taken on a new identity. She had changed her name to Sara Jane Olson, married a doctor, and become an active member of her church. Prior to her bail hearing, her lawyer, Stuart Hanlon, even went so far as to claim that she was a different person:

> That girl who left is not the same person who now exists in 1999 in Minnesota. She's a mature woman with all these ties to the community and she would never run. And I think that's the

argument that people in Minnesota understand and we've got to convince a California judge of that.[2]

At the bail hearing, many people testified that she was not the sort of person who would skip bail, let alone commit a crime.

Thought Probe

A Different Person

Kathleen Soliah certainly seems to be a qualitatively very different person than she was in the 1970s. Is she numerically different? Is she different enough that she should get a reduced sentence?

Theories of personal identity try to answer the basic question What makes a person at one time identical to a person at another time? This question should be distinguished from the question How do we tell whether a person at one time is identical to a person at another time? The former question is a metaphysical question because it tries to determine the nature of personal identity. The latter is an epistemological question because it tries to determine the kinds of evidence we use to judge whether persons are identical. These two questions are related, but they are not identical. The relation is analogous to that between a disease and its symptoms. What makes it the case that someone has Lyme disease, for example, is that he or she is infected with a particular bacteria. The way we tell whether someone has Lyme disease, however, is by looking for symptoms such as a bull's-eye rash.

Answering the metaphysical question of personal identity should help us answer the epistemological one. Once we know what makes a person at one time identical to a person at another time, we should be better able to tell whether people are numerically identical. A theory of personal identity that makes it impossible to tell whether two people are identical is not an adequate theory.

We will begin our foray into the problem of personal identity by considering two theories that tie our identity to different kinds of substance. We will then consider a number of theories that tie our identity to our psychology. Finally, we will consider some of the theories that try to combine the two approaches.

qualitative identity
Two objects are qualitatively identical if and only if they share the same properties (qualities).

numerical identity
Two objects are numerically identical if and only if they are one and the same.

accidental property
A property a thing can lose without ceasing to exist.

essential property A property a thing cannot lose without ceasing to exist.

Objectives

After reading this chapter, you should be able to

- state the various theories of personal identity.
- describe the thought experiments that have been used to test them.
- evaluate the strengths and weaknesses of the various theories of personal identity.
- define qualitative identity, numerical identity, apparent memory, real memory, psychological connectedness, and psychological continuity.
- formulate your own view of the possibility of an afterlife.

We Are Such Stuff as Dreams Are Made On

Self as Substance

T he problem of personal identity is a species of the problem of change: How can something change and yet remain the same thing? If something changes, it's different. And if it's different, it's no longer the same. So how can something retain its identity through change?

Although the problem of change greatly exercised the ancient Greek philosophers, the first person to provide a systematic account of identity conditions was John Locke. In the first edition of *An Essay Concerning Human Understanding*, Locke criticized Descartes' view that our identity resided in our souls, but he did not provide a positive account of his own. He realized, however, that any adequate account of moral responsibility must come to grips with the problem of personal identity, for as he says, "In this personal identity is founded all the Right and Justice of Reward and Punishment."[3] It wouldn't be right or just to reward or punish you for something someone else did. So, at the urging of his friend William Molyneaux, Locke issued a second edition of the *Essay*, which contained a new chapter entitled "Of Identity and Diversity" that set out Locke's views on the subject.

According to Locke, whether a thing at one time is identical to a thing at another time depends on the type of thing it is or the respect in which it is considered. The identity conditions for masses of matter, such as rocks or lumps of clay, differ from those for living things, such as plants or animals.

Masses of matter retain their identity as long as they retain the atoms out of which they're made. If they gain or lose any atoms, they become different. As Locke puts it, "If one of these Atoms be taken away, or one new one added, it is no longer the same mass, or the same Body."[4]

Living things, however, are constantly gaining or losing atoms because they take in nutrients and excrete waste products. The matter they consume is used to grow new cells or repair damaged ones. If an organism lives long enough, all of the matter that originally constituted it may be replaced. Nevertheless,

The seen is the changing, the unseen is the unchanging.

—PLATO

says Locke, an organism can retain its identity over time as long as its parts remain organized in a way that allows it to perform its characteristic functions. For example, an oak tree can be identical to a sapling, as long as both share the same functional organization and there is a continuous development from the sapling to the oak tree. In that case, Locke says that the sapling and the oak tree partake of a "common life."

The functional organization of a living thing is essential to it. If an organism lost the ability to perform its characteristic functions, it would cease to exist. For example, if we cut up or burned down an oak tree, it would cease to exist, because it would no longer be able to perform the functions characteristic of oak trees.

Like other living things, the human body is constantly replacing the matter that makes it up. Biologists tell us that it takes about seven years to replace all of the matter in a human body. So none of the atoms that are in your body now were in your body seven years ago. Yet, your body today is numerically identical to your body of seven years ago, because throughout the replacement process, it has maintained the same functional organization.

The identity conditions for artifacts are similar to those for living things. For example, you can replace the tires, air filter, fuel pump, and the like in your car and still have the (numerically) identical car. Locke uses a watch to illustrate this point:

> What is a Watch? 'Tis plain 'tis nothing but a fit organization or Construction of Parts, to a certain end, which, when a sufficient force is added to it, it is capable to attain. If we would suppose this Machine one continued Body, all whose organized Parts were repaired, increas'd, or diminished, by a constant Addition or Separation of insensible Parts, with one Common Life, we should have something very much like the Body of an Animal.[5]

A watch is designed to perform a certain function in a certain way. As long as the changes made to it don't prevent it from performing its function in that way, the changes preserve its (numerical) identity.

Thought Probe

Hobbes's Ship of Theseus

Suppose that the planks in Theseus's ship had been replaced one by one over the years until none of the original planks remained. Suppose further that the original planks had not been destroyed but had been stored in a warehouse. Now suppose that the original planks were put back together in their original order. Now the continuously repaired ship and the ship made of the original planks are docked next to each other in the harbor. Which of the two ships is identical to the original ship? Can Locke's theory of identity conditions help us answer this question? If so, how?

Persons

Persons are beings with full moral standing, including the right to life. What gives them this status, as we saw in Chapter 1, is not the stuff out of which they are made, but what they can do with that stuff. Persons typically can remember their pasts and plan for the future. They are aware of themselves as existing over time. Thus, according to Locke, a person is a "thinking intelligent being that has reason and reflection; and can consider it self as it self, the same thinking thing in different times and places."[6] Only self-conscious beings are aware of their identity over time, and only rational, self-motivated beings are able to plan for the future. So persons are generally considered to be rational, self-conscious beings that have free will.

To demonstrate that persons need not be biological human beings, Locke quotes at length an account of a talking parrot. It seems that a story was circulating in the eighteenth century about an old parrot in Brazil that could not only talk but also ask and answer questions. Here's the English translation of the conversation Locke reports between the parrot and a prince (the parrot apparently spoke Brazilian, although the dialogue was recorded in French):

> [W]hen it [the parrot] came first into the room where the prince was, with a great many Dutchmen about him, it said presently, "What a company of white men are here!" They asked it, what he thought that man was, pointing to the prince. It answered, "Some General or other." When they brought it close to him, he asked it, "Whence come ye?" It answered, "From Marinnan." The Prince, "To whom do you belong?" The parrot, "To a Portugueze." The Prince, "What do you there?" Parrot, "I look after the chickens." The Prince laughed, and said, "You look after the chickens?" The parrot answered, "Yes, I do; and I know well enough how to do it."[7]

By quoting this conversation, Locke is endorsing not its truth but only its possibility. His point is that it's conceivable for there to be a rational, self-conscious, self-motivated parrot. If so, then being a biological human being is not a necessary condition for being a person.

Thought Probe

Is Rachael a Person?

Rachael (played by Sean Young) is an android in the movie *Blade Runner*. Unlike your typical movie android, however, she is made out of biological parts created through genetic engineering. These artificial humans are known as replicants. Rachael has human sensations and emotions, but her empathic ability—her ability to empathize with others—is not as fully developed as that of a normal human being. To distinguish androids from others, Commander Deckard (played by Harrison Ford) administers a "Voight-Kampf" test that

RACHAEL, THE
REPLICANT FROM
BLADE RUNNER.
Is she a person?

measures empathic ability by sensing involuntary eye responses to various questions. Normally, it takes only 20–30 cross-referenced questions to identify a replicant. In Rachael's case, it took more than 100. If there were a test for empathic ability or emotional intelligence, would it be a legitimate test for personhood? Why or why not?

Animalism

We know now that the soul is the body and the body the soul.

—GEORGE BERNARD
SHAW

Some people believe that identity resides in the body. In their view, we are animals first and foremost, and we continue to exist as long as our bodies continue to exist. As with all other animals, we retain our identity as long as our bodies retain a certain functional organization. As long as your body continues to perform its animal functions—respiration, circulation, digestion, and the like—you continue to exist. According to **animalism,** then, identical persons are those with identical living human bodies.

In support of animalism, Eric Olson offers the following thought experiment.

Thought Experiment

The Vegetable Case

Imagine that you fall into what physiologists call a persistent vegetative state. As a result of temporary heart failure, your brain is deprived of oxygen for ten minutes . . . by which time the neurons of your cerebral cortex have died of anoxia. Because thought and consciousness are impossible unless the cortex is intact, and because brain cells do not regenerate, your higher mental functions are irretrievably lost. You will never again be able to remember the past, or plan for the future, or hear a loved one's voice, or be consciously aware of anything at all. . . .

The subcortical parts of the brain, however, . . . are more resistant to damage from lack of blood than the cerebrum is, and they sometimes hold out and continue functioning even when the cerebrum has been destroyed. Those . . . sustain your "vegetative" functions such as respiration, circulation, digestion, and metabolism. Let us suppose that this happens to you. . . . The result is a human animal that is as much like you as anything could be without having a mind.

The animal is not comatose. Coma is a sleep-like state; but a human vegetable has periods in which it appears to be awake. It can respond to light and sound, but not in a purposeful way; it can move its eyes, but cannot follow objects consistently with them. . . .

Neither is the animal "brain-dead," for those parts of its brain that maintain its vegetative functions remain fully intact. . . . The patient is very much alive, at least in the biological sense in which oysters and oak trees are alive. . . .

How can we be sure that the patient in this state has really lost all cognitive functions? . . . there may be room for doubt. So imagine that you lapse into a persistent vegetative state and that as a result your higher cognitive functions are destroyed and that the loss is permanent.

. . . My question in the Vegetable Case is whether the human animal that results when the cerebrum is destroyed is strictly and literally you, or whether it is no more you than a statue erected after your death would be you. Do you come to be a human vegetable or do you cease to exist . . . ?[8]

Olson claims that if you became a vegetable, you would not cease to exist, for your ability to think is not essential to you. You can permanently lose that ability without ceasing to be. But your ability to breathe air, circulate blood, and digest food is essential to you. Only when your body stops performing these functions do you cease to exist.

It's somewhat misleading to call animalism a theory of personal identity because, as the animalists themselves recognize, human vegetables are not human persons. Olson admits, "Perhaps we cannot call that vegetating animal a person, since it has none of those psychological features that distinguish people from non-people (rationality, the capacity for self-consciousness, or what have you)."[9] Nevertheless, he claims, as long as your body lives, you exist.

The vegetable case is essentially the Terri Schiavo case, which is described in Chapter 1, Section 3. Olson would have us believe that although there was no longer a person in Terri Schiavo's body (for her brain was no longer capable of generating thoughts, feelings, or desires), she nevertheless still existed. We need to decide whether this is the proper way to describe the situation. Should we say that Terri Schiavo existed although she was no longer a person,

animalism The doctrine that identical persons are those with identical living human bodies.

or should we say that her body existed although Schiavo herself no longer existed? To decide which of these descriptions is the most appropriate, we'll have to determine whether being a person is an essential or an accidental quality.

Descartes argues that having a mind and thus being a person is essential to you. That's the point of his conceivability argument discussed in Chapter 2. In his view, if your mind ceased to exist, you would cease to exist. Olson claims otherwise; he maintains that the only thing that's essential to you is your body.

One consequence of this view is that you cannot survive the death of your body. Animalists cannot believe in heaven or hell as traditionally conceived, because there are no physical bodies there. But that does not mean that they cannot believe in an afterlife. In their view, you can live again as long as your body lives again.

Let us then conclude boldly that man is a machine, and that the whole universe consists only of a single substance (matter) subjected to different modifications.

—Julien Offray de La Mettrie

Some people hope to reanimate their bodies by preserving them in liquid hydrogen. This process, known as cryonic suspension, involves draining all of the blood out of the body, replacing it with anti-freeze, and immersing the body in a vat of liquid nitrogen at a temperature of −321 degrees Fahrenheit. Once immersed, the body undergoes very little deterioration. Those who elect this procedure hope that one day a way will be found to resuscitate their bodies. The cost of this sort of immortality is rather steep, around $150,000. There is an economy plan, however. For around $80,000, technicians will freeze just your head. In any event, if cryonic suspension were the only way to survive the death of the body, very few of us could look forward to an afterlife.

Those who accept the body theory, however, may look forward to another type of afterlife: resurrection. Physical objects can survive disassembly and reassembly. Consider, for example, a watch that has been taken apart for cleaning. While the parts of the watch lie scattered on the jeweler's table, the watch doesn't exist. Yet when the parts are reassembled, the watch once again exists. Theoretically, then, you could live again if the atoms that made up your body before you died were put back together in their original configuration.

The view that immortality involves the resurrection of the body has been a part of the Christian religion from the beginning. Jesus achieved immortality through resurrection, and his followers thought that what happened to him would happen to them. Early Christians did not cremate their dead because they thought that a cremated body would be difficult, if not impossible, to resurrect. We now know, however, that cremation doesn't destroy the atoms that make up a body. So if God really is all-powerful and all-knowing, he or she should be able to resurrect even a cremated body.

The notion of resurrection is not without its problems, however. In the normal course of events, after we die, our atoms become part of the soil. This soil may be taken up by the roots of a plant, and this plant may be eaten by another human. So one body may contain atoms that once were part of another human being. If God wants to resurrect both, who gets the shared atoms? This is a point that has not been lost on theologians. As English mathematician and philosopher Bertrand Russell recounts, St. Thomas Aquinas was perplexed by this problem:

St. Thomas Aquinas, the official philosopher of the Catholic Church, discussed lengthily and seriously a very grave problem, which, I fear, modern theologians unduly neglect. He imagines a cannibal who has never eaten anything but human flesh, and whose father and mother before him had like propensities. Every particle of his body belongs rightfully to someone else. We cannot suppose that those who have been eaten by cannibals are to go short through all eternity. But, if not, what is left for the cannibal? How is he to be properly roasted in hell, if all his body is restored to its original owners? This is a puzzling question, as the Saint rightly perceives.[10]

In densely populated areas of the globe that have been inhabited for thousands of years, the same atoms could have been parts of numerous bodies. After all, water gets recycled, and we are about 75 percent water. How is a general resurrection possible in such a situation?

There is an even more serious problem with resurrection, however. As our cells die off and are replaced, we continually get new sets of atoms. Which set of atoms will be resurrected? The set you had at the last moment of your physical existence? But what if you died a cripple suffering from Alzheimer's disease? Would you want that body to be resurrected? Or would you want some younger version of yourself to be resurrected?

Some ancient Jews had a different conception of resurrection than St. Thomas. In their view, resurrection does not involve gathering all of the atoms that formerly constituted a human body and putting them back into their original configuration. Rather, it involves using a template to reconstruct the body out of new atoms. This template supposedly resides in the "Luz" bone, which is located at the base of the skull.[11] The Luz bone is supposed to be indestructible, so no matter how one dies, one can be resurrected. Unfortunately, there is no such bone in the body. Every bone can be turned to dust if heated to a sufficiently high temperature. But even if there were an indestructible bone, and even if it could be used as a template to reconstruct your body, the question remains, Would the resulting body be you or only a copy of you? The reconstructed body may not have any of your original atoms. So, even if it is qualitatively identical to your original body, it's doubtful that it's numerically identical to it.

Resurrection—either natural or supernatural—is the animalists' only hope for an afterlife, for they believe that no one can exist in a body other than his or her own. But continued existence in another body seems logically as well as physically possible. The conventional view of heaven and hell does not seem to be logically incoherent—believing that your mind or soul will be transferred to a spiritual body when you die is not like believing that 2 + 2 = 5. The same goes for the Hindu and Buddhist views of reincarnation— that your mind is transferred to another physical body when your current body dies. Even the functionalist view that the mind can be uploaded into computers doesn't seem beyond the realm of possibility. So animalism doesn't seem to have identified the conditions necessary for our continued existence.

The possibility of body switches has been extensively explored in literature and film. Franz Kafka describes such a switch in his story "The Metamorphosis." In the story, a young man goes to sleep and wakes up with the body of a

Our Lord has written the promise of the resurrection, not in books alone, but in every leaf in spring-time.

—MARTIN LUTHER

The Definition of Death

Death has traditionally been defined as the cessation of respiration and circulation. People were declared dead when they stopped breathing and their hearts stopped beating. With the advent of such medical marvels as heart-lung machines, however, it became possible for machines to take over those vital functions, thus keeping people alive far past the time when they would have traditionally been declared dead. This moved doctors and legislators to define death as the cessation of all brain activity, or brain death. To be declared brain-dead, there must be no detectable brain activity, either in the neocortex (the higher brain), which is responsible for mental life, or the brainstem (the lower brain), which regulates bodily functions like respiration and circulation. But many people believe that a patient can cease to exist long before the entire brain dies. They claim that if the neocortex is dead, and the patient is permanently unconscious, the patient has ceased to exist. Dan Wikler defends this view by means of a thought experiment:

> Consider this thought experiment: a man is decapitated, and physicians are able to keep both the head and the body functioning more or less as normal. They cannot, however, reconnect them. Which is the patient?
>
> The answer cannot be "Both," for body and head may be widely separated in location. Nearly everyone able to choose one or the other will, I believe, choose the head. After decapitation, the head *is* the patient, and the conditions of its health and death are those of the patient as a whole. . . .

This is, very roughly, what happens in persistent vegetative state. Though brain and body remain physically intact, they are functionally severed. Those parts of the brain that make consciousness and feeling possible are irreversibly lost, and the continued functioning of the body has no more significance in the patient's life than would, say, a kidney removed from his body and prospering for decades to come in the body of another. That the whole body (except for relevant parts of the brain) is involved rather than one organ is not a difference that makes a difference.

What bearing does such an outlandish thought experiment have on the real-world clinical and legal issue of brain death? It does not show that the expanded [higher brain] definition would be practical, or even desirable. But it does show that it is conceptually sound, and given the mental leap required to view as dead a patient whose body is fairly healthy, this is an essential accomplishment.[12]

Thought Probe

Permanently Unconscious

According to Wikler, Terri Schiavo died in 1980 when she became permanently unconscious. Do you agree that patients who are permanently unconscious have ceased to exist? Should we adopt a higher-brain definition of death? What would be its advantages and disadvantages?

---

beetle. Yet he retains his personality, his memory, his character. So there is reason to believe that he is the same person. If such a body switch is possible, having the same body is not a necessary condition for being the same person.

Kafka doesn't tell us how the transformation took place. Given what we now know of genetics, however, such transformations seem physically possible. Scientists have fused an entire human chromosome into a rat cell. (A chromosome is one complete strand of DNA, the chemical that contains the instructions for making body parts.) If enough genetic material were fused into the rat cells, scientists believe that the rats would start to grow human organs.

The consequences of mixing the DNA of different species are examined in a series of movies based on the short story "The Fly," by George Langelan. In the 1986 film version, Jeff Goldblum has the DNA of a fly fused into his own cells as the result of an experiment with a transporter. As the fly DNA begins to express itself, he acquires the features of a fly. If he doesn't lose his mind in the process, he may continue to exist in the fly's body.

"The Metamorphosis" and "The Fly" suggest that persons are not identical to their bodies. We can undergo a "body switch" without ceasing to exist. The most famous body switch in the philosophical literature, however, is found in John Locke's writings. He suggests that it is possible for a prince to switch bodies with a cobbler without losing his personal identity.

Thought Experiment

Locke's Tale of the Prince and the Cobbler

For should the Soul of a Prince, carrying with it the consciousness of the Prince's past Life, enter and inform the Body of a Cobbler as soon as deserted by his own Soul, every one sees, he would be the same Person with the Prince, accountable only for the Prince's actions.[14]

The body switch described by Locke is one most people find no difficulty imagining. If it happened at night, we can imagine the prince waking up in the cobbler's hut. No doubt he would be quite astonished to find himself in these strange surroundings, but his surprise would be nothing compared to the shock he would get when he looked in the mirror. Instead of seeing his own face, he would see the face of the cobbler. But, as Locke suggests, if his consciousness was not affected — if his memories, personality, and character remained intact — he would still be the prince, even though he was now in the cobbler's body.

The possibility of such body switches has been extensively explored in such films as *Big, Heaven Can Wait, All of Me, Freaky Friday, 18 Again, Vice Versa, Like Father Like Son, Dream a Little Dream, Ghost,* and others. Although it's not technically possible to bring about a body switch at this time, it certainly seems logically possible. If we are to believe the functionalists, it's also physically possible. Nothing we know about the workings of the brain precludes such a switch. If they can occur, however, our identity can't reside in our bodies.

Animalists recognize that body switches pose a problem for their theory. Olson even describes such a switch.

Thought Experiment

The Transplant Case

. . . Imagine that an ingenious surgeon removes your cerebrum . . . and implants it into another head. . . . Your cerebrum comes to be connected to that human being in just the way that it was once connected to the rest of you. . . . and so it is able to function properly inside its new head just as it once functioned inside yours.

The result is a human being who is psychologically more or less exactly like you. . . . On the other hand, she does not remember anything that happened to the person into whose head your cerebrum was implanted, nor does she acquire anything of that person's character (at least at first).

The puzzle, as you have no doubt guessed, is what happens to you in this story (call it the "Transplant Case"). Are you the biologically living but empty-headed human being that has inherited your vegetative functions? Or are you the person who ends up with your cerebrum and your memories? (Or has the operation simply brought your existence to an end?)[15]

Olson here envisions a successful brain transplant. The part of your brain that is responsible for mental life — the cerebrum — is transplanted into another person's skull. The newly constituted person now has all of your thoughts, feelings, and desires. This thought experiment raises the question What happened to you? Most people would say that you got a new body. If so, animalism is false because it maintains that's impossible — you can't exist in anything other than your own body.

Peter Unger argues that the possibility of body switches refutes animalism. To demonstrate its falsity, he uses the "avoidance of future great pain" test. In the following thought experiment, Unger describes a brain transplant where you and your identical twin swap brains.

Thought Experiment

Unger's Great Pain

Let's consider such a case involving you and, not someone qualitatively quite unlike you, but, rather your precisely similar twin. . . .

First about the person who ends up with your original brain and a new body, we ask this question: With the choice flowing fully from your purely egoistic concern, will you choose to (have yourself) suffer considerable pain right before this case's wild processes begin if your *not* taking the bad hit up front will mean that, soon after its processes are complete, the person then with your brain and thus with your mind will suffer *far greater pain*? Yes, of course you will. Though not completely conclusive, this strongly indicates that, as we most deeply believe, throughout this case, you're the person with your brain.

Second, and yet more tellingly, we ask the parallel question: With the choice flowing fully from your purely egoistic concern, will you choose to (have yourself) suffer considerable pain right before this case's wild processes begin if your *not* taking the bad hit up front will mean that, soon, after all its processes are complete, the person with your body, but with your twin's mentally productive brain, thus will suffer *far greater pain*? Not at all, from an egoistic basis, that's a *poor* choice. Though this response might not be absolutely decisive, it's quite conclusive enough. So, we conclude, well enough, that *you haven't even the slightest belief that here you're the being (with your healthy old body) who's inherited your vegetative biological functioning.*[16]

No one wants to undergo great pain. Unger claims that this fact can be used to test the theory of animalism. In a situation where you and your identical twin are about to swap brains, you would be willing to put up with considerable pain before the operation if it would prevent the person composed of your brain and your twin's body from suffering even greater pain after the operation. In this case, your suffering now would result in your avoiding even greater suffering in the future. But you would not be willing to put up with considerable pain before the operation if it would only prevent the person composed of your twin's brain and your body from suffering even greater pain after the operation. In this case, your suffering now would not result in your avoiding even greater pain in the future. (It would prevent your twin from suffering in the future, but we are to suppose that your concern here is solely for yourself.) These cases strongly suggest that animalism is false. You are not your body; you are your mind.

Because animalism identifies persons with bodies, it's committed to the view that there can be only one person per body. If there can be more than

THE HENSEL TWINS.
Abigail and Brittany
Hensel share one
body. A refutation of
animalism?

one, then again animalism is false, for in that case, having the same body is not a sufficient condition for being the same person. There's reason to believe, however, that not only can bodies house more than one person, but that some actually do.

Consider, for example, those suffering from multiple-personality disorder. The personalities involved may differ not only in temperament but also in age and sex. They can have different brain wave patterns, different vocal patterns, and even different memories. Some say this makes them different persons. Courts of law have treated them that way. In cases where someone suffering from multiple-personality disorder has been asked to testify, judges have had each of the different personalities sworn in separately because they didn't want to assume that each personality shared the same memories. (See the box on multiple-personality disorder in Section 4.2.) If the different personalities can be considered different persons, however, persons can't be identical to their bodies.

The most effective way to prove that something is possible is to show that it's actual. Consider the case of the conjoined twins Abigail and Brittany Hensel. Abigail and Brittany have the same body, but they are two separate people—the result of a single egg that failed to divide fully into identical twins. Brittany controls the left side of the body and Abigail, the right. Nevertheless, they have learned to swim, ride a bike, and play the piano. Because animalism is committed to the view that there can be only one person per body, it must deny that Abigail and Brittany are separate people. That is extremely difficult to do, however, given that each can fully articulate her own thoughts, feelings, and desires. By providing a concrete counterexample to animalism, the Hensel twins effectively undermine it.

The Soul Theory

Many people believe that they will achieve immortality by undergoing a body switch of the sort described by Locke. Those who believe in reincarnation believe that their souls will enter new physical bodies. Those who believe in heaven believe that their souls will enter new spiritual bodies. The members of both groups, however, believe that their identity resides in their souls. This suggests the **soul theory**—the doctrine that identical persons are those with identical souls.

Although the soul theory of personal identity enjoys a good deal of popular support, it is even more problematic than animalism, for no one knows what a soul is. Animalism was promising because the nature of bodily identity was fairly clear. No one, however, has any idea of what the identity of souls consists in. Souls can't be identified by their composition or by their location in space because they have traditionally been held to be immaterial and thus have neither composition nor location in space. Until we know what makes souls identical, we cannot use souls to explain what makes persons identical. The unknown cannot be explained in terms of the incomprehensible.

Empiricists have attacked the soul theory on the grounds that the soul cannot be perceived. Hume, for example, writes,

> When we talk of *self* or *substance*, we must have an idea annexed to these terms, otherwise they are altogether unintelligible. Every idea is derived from preceding impressions; and we have no impression of self or substance, as something simple and individual. We have, therefore, no idea of them in that sense. . . .
>
> When I turn my reflection on *myself*, I never can perceive this *self* without some one or more perceptions; nor can I ever perceive any thing but the perceptions. 'Tis the composition of these, therefore, which forms the self.[17]

This is a classic bit of empiricist reasoning. The terms "self" and "substance," Hume claims, can refer to something only if they are meaningful. And they can be meaningful only if the ideas associated with them were derived from sensation. But the ideas associated with the terms "self" and "substance" were not derived from sensation, for we cannot sense the self or substance. So these terms do not refer to anything. In other words, there are no selves.

Because this is an argument about the meaning of terms, it is only as strong as the theory of meaning on which it rests. Hume's theory of meaning, however, suffers from the same defect as that of the logical positivists: it undermines itself.

Because Hume's theory of meaning applies to all terms, it applies to itself. It follows, then, that Hume's theory can be meaningful only if each of the terms in it stands for an idea that was derived from sensation. But not all of the ideas in Hume's theory were derived from sensation—the idea of meaning itself, for

Four thousand volumes of metaphysics will not teach us what the soul is.

—VOLTAIRE

soul theory The doctrine that identical persons are those with identical souls.

St. Augustine: Soul Man

About the time that the Roman Empire was collapsing and the so-called Dark Ages were beginning, the great Christian philosopher and theologian Augustine (A.D. 354–430) came on the scene. He was born in North Africa to a pagan father and a Christian mother. So in more ways than one, Augustine had one foot in the ancient world and the other in medieval times. It should not be surprising then that he spent much of his life trying to fuse these two worlds together, to take the wisdom of the ancients and meld it with medieval Christianity. In the process, he introduced many ideas into Christian thought that would have been foreign to early Christians but that are now commonplace in contemporary Christianity.

From Plato (via the ancient Platonist philosopher Plotinus), Augustine got the dualistic notion of reality consisting of two distinct realms. One sphere is perfect, eternal, and nonmaterial, and the other is flawed, fleeting, and physical. We are made of stuff from each realm, says Augustine. To the inferior physical realm belong our bodies, as transitory as ice on a stove. But to the eternal, noncorporeal world belong our eternal, noncorporeal selves known as "immortal souls." Thus it was Augustine who introduced into Christian thought a new way to achieve immortality: a soul or self that can separate from the body and still live on. Before Augustine, the prevailing notion among Christians was that body and soul were a single unit, and immortality could be achieved only if the body were resurrected.

In his book *The City of God,* Augustine draws out the distinction between the two worlds in great detail. He says that everyone is a citizen of both these realms at once. The true, eternal one is the kingdom of God. The ephemeral, false one consists of the kingdoms of the material world. In the kingdom of God, there is true knowledge, true values, and true life. In the earthly kingdoms, none of these exist.

Augustine came to these conclusions gradually. In fact, he did not embrace Christianity until age thirty-three. During his early years he reveled in the earthly kingdoms—having several love affairs, taking a concubine and fathering a child by her, and indulging in petty theft and lies. He loved the lustful life—and hated it. He used to pray, "Give me chastity and continence, only not yet."

ST. AUGUSTINE
A.D. 354–430

example. Meaningfulness cannot be sensed. Meaningful terms do not have a particular look or feel. We can't tell what a term means by simply looking at it. By its own lights, then, Hume's theory of meaning is meaningless.

Souls have traditionally been considered to be thinking substances. They are not thoughts; they are things that think. So the relation between a soul and its thoughts can be likened to that between a pincushion and its pins. Just as a pincushion is distinct from the pins stuck in it, so a soul is distinct from the thoughts it has.

The advantage of distinguishing between a soul and its thoughts is that it provides a solution to the problem of personal identity. All of us are constantly changing. Nevertheless, these changes seem to happen to one and the same person. How is that possible? The soul theory has a ready answer: Although our thoughts are constantly changing, the thing that has the thoughts —the soul—remains the same. Just as one and the same pincushion can have different pins stuck in it at different times, so one and the same soul can have different thoughts in it at different times.

According to the soul theory, you are your soul. It is what makes you you. It is your essence, your nature, your true self. The soul theory, then, is committed to the view that as long as your soul exists, you exist. Is this true? Leibniz thinks not. To prove his point, he offers the following thought experiment.

The King of China

The immortality which is demanded in morals and in religion does not consist in this perpetual subsistence [of soul] alone, for without the memory of what one had been it would not be in any way desirable. Let us suppose that some individual were to become King of China at one stroke, but on condition of forgetting what he had been, as if he had been born anew, is it not as much in practice or as regards the effects which one can perceive, as if he were to be annihilated and a King of China to be created at his place at the same instant? Which this individual has no reason to desire.[18]

In Leibniz's day, the King of China was the wealthiest person in the world. Many people would like to hold that title. But if the price they had to pay was the loss of all their memories, they might think twice about it. Without their memories, it's doubtful that they would be around to enjoy all that wealth. Who we are seems intimately connected to our memories. If we were to permanently lose all memory of our lives, there's reason to believe that we would cease to exist, regardless of what happened to our souls.

To see this, suppose that when your soul goes to heaven, it loses all of its memories. The person with your soul would therefore have no idea who you are or what you've done. In such a case, would going to heaven be something to look forward to? Or suppose that cryonically freezing a brain erases all of its memories, so when your body is resuscitated, the person in it has no recollection of your life. In such a case, would it be worth $150,000 to have your body cryonically suspended? Or suppose that you were convicted of a capital crime and the judge offered you the options of being executed or having all of your memories erased. Would one alternative be more desirable than the other? In all of these cases, the answer seems to be "No." What this suggests is that you cannot be your soul. There must be more to being the same person than simply having the same soul.

The foregoing considerations suggest that having the same soul is not sufficient for being the same person. But maybe it's necessary. Maybe you cannot be the same person unless you have the same soul. But even this is doubtful.

Souls are supposed to be distinct from the thoughts they have. Thoughts come and go, but souls stay the same. Consequently, it's conceivable that thoughts could be transferred from one soul to another just as pins can be transferred from one pincushion to another, or programs from one computer to another. Nothing we know about souls precludes such soul switches. In fact, the Catholic Church believes that a soul switch of sorts occurs during every properly conducted communion service. (See the box on transubstantiation.) If we can switch souls, however — if it's possible for our consciousness to reside in different souls — then having the same soul is not necessary for being the same person. Locke explores this possibility in his famous thought experiment about Nestor and Thersites.

Neither can I believe that the individual survives the death of his body, although feeble souls harbor such thoughts through fear or ridiculous egotism.

—Albert Einstein

We Are Such Stuff as Dreams Are Made On   **267**

Thought Experiment

Nestor and Thersites

Let anyone reflect upon himself, and conclude that he has in himself an immaterial spirit [soul], which is that which thinks in him, and in the constant change of his body keeps him the same, and is that which he calls himself: Let him also suppose it to be the same soul that was Nestor or Thersites at the siege of Troy . . . But he now having no consciousness of any of the actions either of Nestor or Thersites, does or can he conceive himself the same person with either of them? Can he be concerned in either of their actions? Attribute them to himself, or think them his own more than the actions of any other men that ever existed? . . . [T]hough it were ever so true that the same spirit that informed Nestor's or Thersites's body were numerically the same that now informs his, [he is not the same]. For this would no more make him the same person with Nestor than if some of the particles of matter that were once a part of Nestor were now a part of this man. . . . But let him once find himself conscious of any of the actions of Nestor, he then finds himself the same person with Nestor.[19]

Locke envisions a situation in which the very same immaterial substance or soul that once contained Nestor's or Thersites' thoughts now contains only your own. Would that make you identical to Nestor or Thersites? Locke says "No." If you have none of Nestor's or Thersites' thoughts, then you can't be identical with either Nestor or Thersites, even if your thoughts now reside in one of their souls. As Locke puts it, "If the same consciousness can be transferred from one thinking substance to another, it will be possible that two thinking substances may make but one person. For the same consciousness being preserved, whether in same or different substance, the personal identity is preserved."[20] For Locke, where your consciousness goes, you go. Because it's possible for your consciousness to reside in different souls, being the same person doesn't require having the same soul.

German philosopher Immanuel Kant makes the same point using a billiard ball analogy.

Thought Experiment

Kant's Soul Switch

An elastic ball which impinges on another similar ball in a straight line communicates to the latter its whole motion, and therefore its whole state (that is, if we take account only of the positions in space). If, then, in analogy with such bodies, we postulate substances such that the one communicates to the other representations together with the consciousness of them, we can conceive a whole series of substances of which the first transmits its state together with its

According to the Roman Catholic Church, substance switches are not only possible, they are actual. A substance switch occurs every time a duly ordained priest serves communion.

At the Last Supper Jesus told his followers: "'Take, eat; This is my body.' And he took a cup, and when he had given thanks he gave it to them, saying, 'Drink of it, all of you; for this is my blood of the covenant, which is poured out for many for the forgiveness of sins.'"[22] The Roman Catholic Church takes Jesus at his word here. It claims that Jesus turned the bread and wine at the Last Supper into his body and blood by saying, "This is my body" and "This is my blood." Similarly, it claims that priests can turn the bread and wine at communion into the body and blood of Christ by saying, "This is my body; this is my blood." The transformation occurs as a result of a process known as *transubstantiation*.

First canonized in the fourth Lateran Council of 1215, the doctrine of transubstantiation was reaffirmed by the Council of Trent in 1563: "Because Christ our Redeemer said that it was truly his body that he was offering under the species of bread, it has always been the conviction of the Church of God, and this holy Council now declares again, that by the consecration of the bread and wine there takes place a change of the whole substance of the bread into the substance of the body of Christ our lord and of the whole substance of the wine into the substance of his blood. This change the holy Catholic Church has fittingly and properly called transubstantiation."

When the priest says the sacred words, the bread and the wine undergo a substance switch. They retain all of their perceptible qualities, but now those qualities reside in a different substance, namely, the substance of Jesus Christ.

---

consciousness to the second, the second its own state with that of the preceding substance to the third, and this in turn the states of all the preceding substances together with its own consciousness and with their consciousness to another. The last substance would then be conscious of all the states of the previously changed substances, as being its own states, because they would have been transferred to it together with the consciousness of them.[21]

Just as motion can be transferred from one billiard ball to another, so, Kant claims, consciousness can be transferred from one substantial soul to another. And if your consciousness is transferred, you are transferred. In this situation, even though your consciousness ends up in a different soul than it started with, you would still consider yourself the same person because you would regard its representations (memories) as your own. So your identity cannot reside in your soul.

An adequate theory of personal identity should account for the fact that we make accurate judgments about personal identity. The soul theory can't do this, however, because it doesn't establish any sort of connection between a person's soul and the individual's identifying characteristics. It doesn't tell us what features of a person are determined by the soul. As a result, a person could undergo a soul switch and we would never know it. In fact, for all we know, people are switching souls all the time. Maybe we get a new soul every moment. This seems to be the view of some Buddhists. Because the soul theory can't rule out soul switching, it's not an adequate theory of personal identity.

Near-Death Experiences

Some believe that out-of-body experiences (OOBEs) provide evidence for the existence of souls. People in different cultures throughout the ages have had the sensation of leaving their body. In our culture, this sensation is often reported by those who have had a near-death experience, a term coined by Dr. Raymond Moody to describe a family of experiences he found common among those who had narrowly escaped death. These experiences include

1. Peace and a sense of well-being.
2. Separation from the body.
3. Entering the darkness.
4. Seeing the light.
5. Entering the world of light.[23]

The question is, Do these experiences provide reason to believe in the existence of Cartesian minds? They do only if the existence of Cartesian minds provides the best explanation of these experiences.

People who have had OOBEs report having a very different sort of body than their physical one. This body—often referred to as an "astral body"—usually has arms and legs but can float through walls. People who have clinically died on the operating table have reported that they left their physical body and watched the resuscitation attempt from the ceiling. (To check the veracity of these claims, some hospitals are taping numbers to the inside of light fixtures in such a way that the numbers can be seen only from the ceiling.) Notice, however: astral bodies cannot be Cartesian minds because they have physical properties like shape and location. So even if we accept these reports at face value, they don't provide reason to believe in the existence of Cartesian minds.

Many researchers, however, believe that we should not accept these experiences at face value, for they can be explained without assuming the existence of nonphysical substances. The feeling of peace and well-being, they claim, can best be explained as the result of the brain's production of natural pain-killers—endorphins and enkephalins—in response to the trauma of the experience. The sense of entering the darkness and seeing the light can best be explained as the result of random nerve firings in the visual cortex caused by a lack of oxygen to the brain. And the OOBE itself can be explained as the result of an adoption of a memory-based model of reality caused by a loss of sensory input. Susan Blackmore, the world's leading expert on OOBEs, claims that when our normal sources of information are disrupted, such as when we are near death or under severe stress, our models of reality become unstable. In those situations, our brain tries to construct a stable model by using the only information available to it, namely, memory. Remembered events, however, have a peculiar characteristic: they are always seen from a bird's-eye point of view. Try to remember the last time you walked down the beach or through the woods, for example. If you're like most of us, you visualize yourself from above. This aspect of our memories, Blackmore claims, helps explain out-of-body experiences. These experiences are simply the result of a memory model of reality taking over from a sensory model.[24] Because the near-death experience can be accounted for without postulating the existence of Cartesian minds or astral bodies, it provides no reason for believing that these experiences exist.

Thought Probe

Near-Death Experiences

Is the hallucination hypothesis the best explanation of near-death experiences? Why or why not? Can you find another hypothesis that does as well with respect to the criteria of adequacy?

Even though substantial souls aren't directly observable, we would be justified in believing in them if they provided the best explanation of something. Scientists often postulate theoretical (thus, unobservable) entities to account for puzzling phenomena. But substantial souls are not needed to explain any aspect of human individuality. Consequently, there is no reason to believe they exist. Theologian John Hick explains,

If then there is to be any point to the traditional claim that souls are special divine creations, they must be the bearers of some at least of the distinctive characteristics of the individual. And these characteristics must be ones which do not arise from the inherited genetic code. . . .

However, this idea of innate but not inherited qualities is, to say the least, highly problematic. It has long been clear, even without benefit of special scientific knowledge, that children are almost as often like a parent in basic personality traits as in purely physical characteristics. . . . For many characteristics which might have been supposed to be attributes of the soul are now believed to be part of our genetic inheritance. . . .

The answer seems to be that whilst it cannot be proved that the two factors of heredity and environment between them account for the entire range of the individual's character traits, it certainly seems that they do and that there is no need to postulate in addition the influence of a soul or of a *linga sharira* [astral body] carrying basic dispositional characteristics either supplied directly by God or developed in previous earthly lives.[25]

None of our identifying characteristics seems to have a supernatural origin. All of them can be explained in terms of our genetic makeup or upbringing. Because we can explain human individuality without postulating the existence of substantial souls, they are not needed to ground personal identity.

To desire immortality is to desire the eternal perpetuation of a great mistake.

—ARTHUR
SCHOPENHAUER

Thought Probe

Souls in Heaven

Many of those who believe in souls believe that their souls will go to heaven. But what happens to souls in heaven? Martin Gardner raises a number of questions.

> How old will children be? Will they grow up in heaven? Will anyone age in heaven? Will cripples be made whole? Will the blind see and the deaf hear? Will the insane become sane? Will the aged become young? Will some or all of earth's animals be there? What about material things that we occasionally love: a house, a ship, a city? The fields you roamed as a child?[26]

Can the soul theory answer these questions? If so, how? If not, does that undermine its plausibility as a theory of personal identity? Why or why not?

Summary

Animalism is the doctrine that identical persons are those with identical human bodies. Two bodies can be numerically identical without being qualitatively identical. That is, a body at one time and a body at another time can be one and the same body even though they don't have the same properties, just as an oak and a sapling can be one and the same tree even though they don't have the same features. All that is required is that the changes the thing in question undergoes are consistent with the type of thing it is.

Though animalism doesn't rule out an afterlife (because an afterlife is consistent with the notion of resurrection), it is an unsatisfactory explanation of personal identity because it is possible for people to switch bodies and retain their identities, as in the case of reincarnation, and it is possible for two people to inhabit the same body, as in the case of the Hensel twins.

The soul theory is the doctrine that identical persons are those with identical souls. Because no one knows what a soul is, however, this theory doesn't explain how personal identity is possible. What's more, because souls are distinct from the thoughts they have, it's possible for people to switch souls and retain their identities. We would be justified in believing in souls if they provided the best explanation of something. But they don't explain any aspect of human individuality. Thus there is no reason to believe in them.

Study Questions

1. What is the theory of personal identity known as animalism?
2. Does animalism rule out the possibility of an afterlife?
3. What is Locke's tale of the prince and the cobbler? How does it attempt to undermine animalism?
4. What is the soul theory of personal identity?
5. What is Locke's soul switch thought experiment concerning Nestor and Thersites? How does it attempt to undermine the soul theory?
6. Why is there no reason to assume that souls exist?

Discussion Questions

1. Seven years ago, your body contained none of the atoms it contains today. Suppose that someone could locate the atoms that made you up seven years ago and put them back into their original configuration. Which of the two persons would be identical to you?
2. If you had a different body—a body of the other sex, say—would you still be the same person?
3. If someone gave you the money to have your entire body cryonically suspended, would you accept it? What if someone gave you just enough money to have your head cryonically suspended? Would you accept the gift? Why or why not?
4. Philosopher Kai Nielsen says, "Conceptions of the afterlife are so problematical that it is unreasonable for a philosophical and scientifically sophisticated person living in the west in the twentieth century to believe in life eternal, to believe that we shall survive the rotting or the burning or the mummification of our 'present bodies.'"[27] Do you agree? Why or why not?
5. Are souls needed to explain anything? If so, what?

Golden Memories
Self as Psyche

Our identity as persons does not seem to depend on the continued existence of any sort of substance. Having the same body or soul is neither a necessary nor a sufficient condition for being the same person. On what, then, does our identity depend? Many believe it depends on our memories. As Leibniz realized, if we lose our memories—if we get total amnesia—there is reason to believe that we would cease to exist.

The Memory Theory

Locke agrees with Leibniz that our identity resides in our memories. He writes,

> This may show us wherein personal identity consists: not in the identity of substance, but, as I have said, in the identity of consciousness, wherein if Socrates and the present mayor of Queinborough agree, they are the same person: if the same Socrates waking and sleeping do not partake of the same consciousness, Socrates waking and sleeping is not the same person. And to punish Socrates waking for what sleeping Socrates thought, and waking Socrates was never conscious of, would be no more of right, than to punish one twin for what his brother-twin did, whereof he knew nothing, because their outsides were so like, that they could not be distinguished; for such twins have been seen.[28]

According to Locke, if the present mayor of Queinborough is conscious of something that Socrates was conscious of, that is, if he remembers having an experience that Socrates had, he is identical to Socrates. This view is known as the **memory theory** of personal identity, and it holds that identical persons are those who share at least one experience memory.

Not all of your memories affect your identity. Memories of facts, like the fact that $2 + 2 = 4$, can be had by many different people and thus cannot serve to distinguish you from them. But memories of experiences, like your first kiss,

You have to begin to lose your memory, if only in bits and pieces, to realize that memory is what makes our lives.

—LUIS BUÑUEL

memory theory The doctrine that identical persons are those who share at least one experience memory.

John Locke: The Great Empiricist

Few philosophers have had more influence on practical affairs than John Locke (1632–1704). His greatest achievements were the development of a ground-breaking theory of knowledge and the formulation of a new understanding in political philosophy. The former changed the way people thought about the mind, education, tolerance, and human equality. The latter laid a giant cornerstone for liberal democracy and propelled the American and French Revolutions.

He was born in England, was educated at Oxford where he studied medicine, and became involved in public affairs. He lived in France from 1675 to 1679 and there studied the work of Descartes and another philosopher-mathematician, Gassendi. Before returning to England he had come in contact with most of the great thinkers of the day. In 1683, Locke left England for Holland because of the political situation in his home country. While living in exile, he wrote his magnum opus, *An Essay Concerning Human Understanding*. After he returned to England he published his main political works: *A Letter Concerning Toleration* and *Two Treatises of Government*.

Locke's theory of knowledge had enormous implications for education and the rights of persons. It is based on the premise that everything we know comes to us through sense experience. So our understanding of reality is either derived from sense experience or built from elements that ultimately are extracted from sense experience. When we are born, says Locke, our minds are like blank slates—we have no innate ideas or inborn knowledge. Only our sensory experience can write on the slate, filling it with ideas and expanding our understanding. Therefore, all people are born equal, beginning at the same starting point, being no better than anyone else by birth, requiring only education and equal treatment to flourish.

Locke also drew political implications from his epistemology. Acquiring knowledge through sense experience is by its nature a fallible process. Our senses may deceive us; the sense data may be incomplete or distorted. So Locke reasoned that this human fallibility is the best reason of all to be tolerant of the views of others and to shun dogmatic positions. Coercing people into accepting certain beliefs—as both secular and religious authorities often do—is thus unreasonable and immoral.

JOHN LOCKE
1632–1704

can be had only by you and thus can define who you are. Other people can remember the fact that your first kiss happened, say, on the playground, but they cannot remember your experience of being kissed on the playground, for they didn't have that experience. Our experience memories are unique to each of us and, according to Locke, form the basis of our personal identity.

The memory theory, unlike animalism, allows one person to inhabit more than one body and thus is open to the possibility of reincarnation. If a person has a memory of inhabiting another body, that person is identical to the person who inhabited the other body. The memory theory also allows two people to inhabit the same body. If a person has no memory of what happened to his body during a certain time (as in Locke's example of Socrates waking and Socrates sleeping), that person was not in his body at that time. So if one personality of someone suffering from multiple-personality disorder has no memory of what happened to her body while another personality was in control of it, the two personalities could constitute two different persons.

Locke's original interest in developing a theory of personal identity was to bolster his theory of punishment. Because he believes that identity depends on memory, however, he maintains that you shouldn't be held responsible for something you don't remember doing. In Locke's view, if you don't remember

There is some evidence that the different personalities in those suffering from multiple-personality disorder can have different memories. Does this make the different personalities different persons? During the trial of a man who was charged with raping a woman suffering from multiple-personality disorder, Winnebago County, Wisconsin, Circuit Judge Robert Hawley required the victim to take an oath each time she changed personalities. The judge assumed that the different personalities did not have memory of taking the oath.[29]

Dr. Frank W. Putnam, Jr., a psychiatrist and physiologist at the National Institute of Mental Health in Bethesda, Maryland, has studied multiple-personality disorder for a number of years and has made a number of remarkable discoveries, as reported in the *New York Times Magazine*:

> In the course of his experiments, Dr. Putnam has identified startling differences in the brain waves of the alternate personalities of patients suffering from multiple-personality disorder. Indeed, these waves may vary from one personality to another as much as they vary from one normal person to another.
>
> A second study conducted by Dr. Putnam and his colleagues suggests that each personality may have its own memory. And still another, a study of voice changes among alternate personalities, shows that so-called "multiples" may have abnormally wide vocal ranges and a surprising ability to radically alter speech patterns and habits. . . .
>
> As a result of their flights, whether from true danger or imagined, multiples miss parts of their lives. "Losing time" is one of the most frequent symptoms of a person suffering multiple-personality disorder, and it may be the crucial signal to mental-health workers that they are treating a multiple. Natasha, for example, has suddenly reappeared to find herself in Chicago, St. Louis and Paris as well as in toy stores and in the bedrooms of men she cannot recall meeting. . . .
>
> Some multiples, like Judy, choose to remain multiple. Judy's fiancé, John, the head of the sociology department at a Middle Western university (Judy regularly commutes to see him), is supporting her decision to remain multiple. John has seen most of Judy's personalities. He likes Judy best, but greatly admires the intellectual Mary. He has also survived the suicidal bouts with Lea, a self-destructive alternate whom he has cradled in his arms until a less destructive alternate took over the body.
>
> "At first I didn't know what to make of it," he says. "I would get into a fight with someone and suddenly be talking to someone else who didn't even know a fight had gone on. Do you know how frustrating it is being mad at someone who doesn't have any idea what she's done?"[30]

Thought Probe

Multiple Personalities

The standard treatment for multiple-personality disorder is to try to fuse the different personalities into one. Suppose you're a psychologist treating someone with this disorder, and suppose further that one of the personalities wants you to proceed with the fusing therapy while another does not. What should you do? If fusing causes all of the memories of some of the personalities to be lost forever, would fusing be an act of murder? Why or why not?

doing something, you didn't do it. He acknowledges that not being able to remember a crime is no defense in a court of law. But the reason we don't accept such pleas of ignorance is that we can't be sure whether the accused is telling the truth. God suffers no such limitation, however; no one can hide anything from God. So, on judgment day, "wherein the secrets of all hearts shall be laid open, no one shall be made to answer for what he knows nothing of, but shall receive his doom, his conscience accusing or excusing him."[31]

Memory is the receptacle and sheath of all knowledge.
— CICERO

In other words, when it comes time for God to judge us, we will not be held responsible for anything we don't remember doing.

But there seems to be more to responsibility than just memory. Suppose that a drug could erase the last hour's worth of one's memories. Suppose further that someone took that drug immediately after committing a crime. As a result, that person would have no memory of committing the crime. Does that mean he should not be held responsible for it? It wouldn't seem so. Not being able to remember something doesn't always mean that one cannot be held responsible for it. Oftentimes people don't remember what they did while they were drunk. But that doesn't mean that they shouldn't be punished for what they did. If you got drunk on your own accord, then what you did while you were drunk is your fault, whether you remember doing it or not.

The Inconsistency Objection

A sub-clerk in the post-office is the equal of a conqueror if consciousness is common to them.

—ALBERT CAMUS

Unfortunately (or fortunately, as the case may be), our memories are not perfect. If you are like most people, you have forgotten a good deal of what has happened to you. Suppose you lose all memory of some part of your life. Does that mean that you are no longer identical to the person who was in your body at that time? Locke would seem to think so. In this famous thought experiment, the Scottish philosopher Thomas Reid uses this consequence of Locke's theory to show that it leads to a contradiction.

Thought Experiment

Reid's Tale of the Brave Officer and Senile General

Suppose a brave officer to have been flogged when a boy at school for robbing an orchard, to have taken a standard from the enemy in his first campaign, and to have been made a general in advanced life; suppose, also, which must be admitted to be possible, that, when he took the standard, he was conscious of having been flogged at school, and that, when made a general, he was conscious of his taking the standard, but had absolutely lost the consciousness of his flogging.

These things being supposed, it follows from Mr. Locke's doctrine, that he who was flogged at school is the same person who took the standard, and that he who took the standard is the same person who was made a general. Whence it follows, if there be any truth in logic, that the general is the same person with him who was flogged at school. But the general's consciousness does not reach so far back as his flogging; therefore, according to Mr. Locke's doctrine, he is not the person who was flogged at school.[32]

The brave officer, who took a standard from the enemy, remembers being flogged as a boy for robbing an orchard, and the senile general remembers taking the standard but not being flogged. So, according to Locke's theory, the brave officer is identical to the boy and the senile general is identical to the

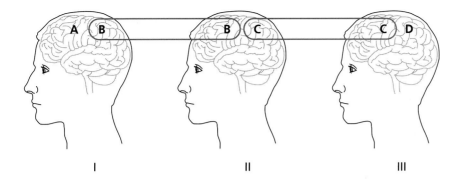

brave officer, but the senile general is not identical to the boy. But that's impossible because identity is transitive: if A is identical to B, and B is identical to C, then A is identical to C. For example, if Mark Twain is identical to Samuel Clemens, and Samuel Clemens is identical to the author of *Huckleberry Finn*, then Mark Twain is identical to the author of *Huckleberry Finn*. Because Locke's theory of personal identity violates the principle of the transitivity of identity, it cannot be correct.

Locke's theory can be salvaged, however, if we're willing to recognize the existence of indirect as well as direct memories. A **direct memory** is one that you can consciously recall. An **indirect memory** is one that an earlier stage of you can consciously recall. An earlier stage of you is one that is connected to you by a series of overlapping direct memories. For example, although you may not remember going to McDonald's five years ago, you may remember doing something yesterday, and the person who did that may remember doing something the day before that, and so on, until you get to a person who does remember going to McDonald's five years ago. If there is such an overlapping series of direct memories, then you are identical to the person who went to McDonald's five years ago.

Memories, in this view, are like strands in a rope. Just as no one strand may stretch the entire length of a rope, no one memory may stretch the entire length of a life. Nevertheless, an overlapping series of memories can constitute one person in the same way that an overlapping series of strands can constitute one rope.

Although the senile general doesn't directly remember being flogged as a boy, he may well indirectly remember it. So by taking memory to be both direct and indirect, it is possible to avoid Reid's objection and formulate a consistent memory theory of personal identity.

Memory . . . is the diary that we all carry about with us.

—OSCAR WILDE

Thought Probe

Were You Ever a Fetus?

According to Locke, your identity extends only as far back as your memories. But your memories extend back to only the age of one or two because, before

direct memory
A memory that a person can consciously recall.

indirect memory
A memory that an earlier stage of a person can consciously recall.

that time, your brain was not developed enough to store memories. It seems to follow, then, that *you* were never a fetus. You came into existence from a fetus, but you yourself never were a fetus. Is this consequence of Locke's theory plausible? Why or why not?

The Circularity Objection

Much as we hate to admit it, our memories are not totally reliable. We sometimes seem to remember things that never really happened. For example, Jean Piaget, the great French psychologist, had a vivid memory of his nurse fighting off a kidnapper during a stroll down the Champs-Elysées when he was only two. Years later, his nurse confessed in a letter to his parents that she made the whole thing up. So from the fact that we seem to remember having an experience, it doesn't follow that we actually had it. Only real memories can serve as the basis of personal identity. Our memories are supposed to connect us to people that lived in the past. If our memories are fictitious, they can't perform that function. So the memory theorist owes us an account of what distinguishes **real memories** from **apparent memories.**

One way to explain the difference is to say that an experience memory is real only if the person with the memory is identical to the person who had the experience. But this creates a problem: if we have to use the notion of personal identity to explain real memories, then we can't use real memories to explain personal identity because the explanation would be circular; it would assume an understanding of that which it is trying to explain. It would be like trying to explain why a sedative puts people to sleep by saying that the sedative has a sleep-inducing power. Such explanations tell us nothing we don't already know.

Bishop Butler, who is credited with first realizing that the memory theory is circular, put the point this way: "One should really think it self-evident, that consciousness of personal identity presupposes and therefore cannot constitute personal identity, any more than knowledge in another case, can constitute truth, which it presupposes."[33] Truth can't be explained in terms of knowledge because knowledge requires truth. We can't say that something is true only if it's known because something is known only if it's true. Similarly, Butler claims, we can't explain personal identity in terms of real memories because real memories are explained in terms of personal identity: a memory is real just in case the person with the memory is identical to the person who had the experience. The concept of a real memory contains the concept of personal identity and so can't be used to explain it.

Sydney Shoemaker and Derek Parfit believe that the memory theory can escape the circle by appealing to a kind of memory that doesn't presuppose personal identity. Called **quasi-memory,** or q-memory for short, it is a type of memory that connects a person to past experiences without assuming that those experiences were had by the person in question. The connection to the past is made in terms of causation. The idea is that if a memory is caused in the right way, it can link you to someone in the past even though that person is not you. So defining personal identity in terms of q-memories avoids the circularity inherent in Locke's theory.

Parfit defines quasi-memory as follows:

I have an accurate quasi-memory of a past experience if
(1) I seem to remember having an experience,
(2) Someone did have this experience, and
(3) my apparent memory is causally dependent, in the right kind of way, on that past experience.[34]

So a quasi-memory is an apparent memory that is caused in the right way by an actual experience. Normally, the person who quasi-remembers an experience will be identical to the person who actually had the experience. But this is not necessarily the case. Advances in neurophysiology and computer technology may make it possible to quasi-remember other people's experiences. (See the "Soul Catcher.")

In the movie *Brainstorm*, a scientist develops a brain-taping device that can tape-record peoples' experiences. Once an experience has been recorded, other people can have the experience by playing back the tape. (A similar device was used in the movies *Total Recall* and *Strange Days*.) If you were to play back another person's tape, your memory of that experience would, at best, be a quasi-memory. It would not be a real memory because the original experience didn't happen to you.

All real memories are quasi-memories, but not all quasi-memories are real memories because people can have quasi-memories of experiences they didn't have. In the movie *Blade Runner*, for example, the replicant Rachael has the memories of her creator's niece. Rachael's creator uploaded his niece's memories into Rachael's brain. Rachael seems to remember having various experiences, and her creator's niece actually had those experiences. If those memories were caused in the right way, they would constitute quasi-memories.

Being caused in the right way is important because quasi-memory is supposed to ground personal identity, and not every way of causing memories is identity preserving. Suppose, for example, that a hypnotist gave you the apparent memory of an experience that actually happened to someone else. That presumably would not make you identical to the person who had that experience. Even if the majority of your memories came from that person via the hypnotist, that still would not make you identical to him or her. Memories generated by hypnosis, then, cannot be quasi-memories because they are not caused in the right way.

Having a quasi-memory that originally belonged to someone else would not make you identical to that person. But having a great many quasi-memories that originally belonged to someone else would make you identical to that person. Suppose that you got total amnesia as the result of some trauma. Now suppose that a brain-tape containing the experiences of someone else's entire life was played back on your brain. (The tape was made just before the person died.) As a result, the only experiences you can remember are those recorded on the tape. In such a case, there would be reason to believe that the person in your body is the person whose memories are recorded on the tape. That person has essentially undergone a body switch.

Hans Moravec, professor of robotics at Carnegie Mellon, thinks that once it's possible to upload our minds (and memories) into computers, identity

real memory
A memory of an event that was experienced by the person remembering it and that was caused by the event it records.

apparent memory
A memory of an event that either didn't happen or that was not caused by the event it records.

quasi-memory
An apparent memory caused in the right way by an actual experience.

In the News: Soul Catcher

In 1995, scientists at British Telecom tantalized the media with talk of a computer chip that could record human thoughts. This possibility is explored in the 2004 movie *The Final Cut*. If it became a reality, q-memories could become a marketable commodity. Here's how the *Electronic Telegraph* reported the story:

> A computer chip implanted behind the eye that could record a person's every lifetime thought and sensation is to be developed by British scientists.
>
> "This is the end of death," said Dr. Chris Winter, of British Telecom's artificial life team. He predicted that within three decades it would be possible to relive other people's lives by playing back their experiences on a computer. "By combining this information with a record of the person's genes, we could re-create a person physically, emotionally and spiritually."
>
> Dr. Winter's team of eight scientists at BT's Martlesham Heath Laboratories near Ipswich calls the chip the 'Soul Catcher.' It would be possible to imbue a new-born baby with a lifetime's experiences by giving him or her the Soul Catcher chip of a dead person, Dr. Winter said. The proposal to digitize existence is based on a solid calculation of how much data the brain copes with over a lifetime.
>
> Ian Pearson, BT's official futurologist, has measured the flow of impulses from the optical nerve and nerves in the skin, tongue, ear, and nose. Over an eighty-year life, we process 10 terrabytes of data, equivalent to the storage capacity of 7,142,857,142,860,000 floppy disks.

> Dr. Pearson said, "If current trends in the miniaturization of computer memory continues at the rate of the past 20 years—a factor of 100 every decade—today's 8-megabyte memory chip norm will be able to store 10 terrabytes in 30 years."
>
> British Telecom would not divulge how much money it is investing in the project, but Dr. Winter said it was taking 'Soul Catcher 2025' very seriously. He admitted that there were profound ethical considerations, but emphasized that BT was embarking on this line of research to enable it to remain at the forefront of communications technology.
>
> "An implanted chip would be like an aircraft's black box and would enhance communications beyond current concepts," he said. "For example, police would be able to use it to relive an attack, rape, or murder from the victim's viewpoint to help catch the criminal."
>
> Other applications would be less useful but more frightening. "I could even play back the smells, sounds, and sights of my holiday to my friends," Dr. Winter said.[35]

Thought Probe

Soul Catcher

Do you believe that such a chip could, in principle, be developed? Why or why not? If it were developed, do you think it should be available to anyone with adequate funds? Why or why not?

won't matter. We'll be able to share memories not only with other human beings but with other life-forms as well. He writes,

> Selective mergings, involving some of another person's memories and not others, would be a superior form of communication, in which recollections, skills, attitudes, and personalities can be rapidly and effectively shared. . . .
>
> Mind transferal need not be limited to human beings. Earth has other species with large brains, from dolphins, whose nervous systems are as large and complex as our own, to elephants, other whales, and perhaps giant squid, whose brains may range up to twenty times as big as ours. . . . The brain-to-computer trans-

feral methods that work for humans should work as well for these large-brained animals, allowing their thoughts, skills, and motivations to be woven into our cultural tapestry.[36]

What Moravec is describing is the technological equivalent of a Vulcan mind-meld. *Star Trek*'s Mr. Spock achieves direct contact with other creatures' minds through telepathy. Moravec would achieve it through uploading the information. If the practice became commonplace, and we were concerned about losing our identity, we would have to ensure that most of our memories originated with us. Moravec, however, is not concerned about personal identity. He looks forward to a time when all the memories of all the minds in the universe will be merged into one supermind.[37] This vision is not unique to Moravec, however. Many idealistic philosophers in both the East and the West — most notably, the followers of Shankara and Hegel — have held a similar view.

The Insufficiency Objection

Although memory is an important ingredient of personal identity, many believe there is more to us than that. Who we are seems to be determined not only by our experiences but also by our desires and intentions. What we care about and what we plan to do are as much a part of us as what we've experienced. If our desires weren't relatively stable, we would never put any of our plans into action. If we no longer desired to achieve the goals our plans were intended to meet, we would not implement our plans. So the loss of all of our desires and intentions could be as destructive to our selves as the loss of all of our memories.

Consider, for example, born-again Christians. They claim to have become new persons — to have been born again — when they found Jesus Christ. What changed, however, was not their memories, but their beliefs and values. Accepting Jesus into their hearts gave them a whole new outlook on life. As a result of their conversion, they may acquire a new personality and a new character. Some believe that these changes can be radical enough to literally make them new persons.

Just as there are two types of memory — factual and experiential — so there are two types of desires — personal and impersonal. An impersonal desire is a desire for something or someone other than oneself. The desire that the Eagles win the Superbowl, for example, is an impersonal desire. A personal desire is a desire for oneself. The desire to get married, for example, is a personal desire. Because personal desires refer to oneself, they can't be used to define personal identity. But, just as it is possible to construct a notion of experience memory that doesn't presuppose personal identity, so it is possible to construct a notion of personal desire that doesn't presuppose personal identity. A **quasi-desire,** like a quasi-memory, is an apparent desire that is caused in the right way by an actual desire.

Our desires are intimately connected with a number of our other mental states — such as our beliefs, our values, and our attitudes — that collectively constitute our character. A change in any one of these could bring about a

> *A man's character is the reality of himself.*
> —H. W. BEECHER

quasi-desire An apparent desire that is caused in the right way by an actual desire.

change in our desires. So personal identity is not a one-dimensional concept. Who we are is determined by a number of different factors, all of which have to be taken into account when making judgments of personal identity.

If a person at one time and a person at another time directly quasi-remember and quasi-desire the same thing, they are **psychologically connected** with one another. If a person at one time and a person at another time indirectly quasi-remember and quasi-desire the same thing — if they form part of an overlapping series of persons who are psychologically connected with one another — they are **psychologically continuous** with one another. These notions can be used to provide the **psychological continuity theory** of personal identity, which says that identical persons are those who are psychologically continuous with one another. This theory of personal identity is superior to Locke's memory theory because it is internally consistent, noncircular, and sufficiently rich to account for the many aspects of our psychology that go into making us who we are. The psychological continuity theory also has no trouble explaining how life after death is possible. You can survive the death of your body as long as there is someone who is psychologically continuous with you after your body dies. Whether that person has the same body is irrelevant.

Thought Probe

Is Darth Vader Anakin Skywalker?

In episode 6 of the *Star Wars* saga, Obi-wan Kenobe tells Luke Skywalker,

> Your father was seduced by the dark side of the force. He ceased to be Anakin Skywalker and became Darth Vader. When that happened, the good man who was your father was destroyed.

Is Obi-wan correct? When Anakin Skywalker joined the dark side, did he cease to exist? He certainly lost many of his former character traits, as well as many of his former beliefs, attitudes, and desires. Did he change enough to literally become a different person? Or is that claim only true from a certain point of view? If so, what point of view is that?

The Reduplication Problem

If I am I because you are you, and if you are you because I am I, then I am not I, and you are not you.
— HASSIDIC RABBI

Those who believe in reincarnation believe that people born at different times can be psychologically continuous with one another. Some people do seem to remember things that only a person who had lived before could remember. The question is whether psychological continuity is enough to make people living at different times identical.

Suppose that we had the best evidence possible for reincarnation. Suppose someone knew things about a historical figure that only that figure could have known. Would that prove that the present person is a reincarnation of the former person? Not according to British philosopher Bernard Williams. Consider this thought experiment.

Thought Experiment

Williams's Reincarnation of Guy Fawkes

Suppose someone undergoes a sudden and violent change of character. Formerly quiet, deferential, churchgoing and home loving, he wakes up one morning and has become, and continues to be, loud-mouthed, blasphemous, and bullying. . . .

Suppose the man who underwent the radical change of character—let us call him Charles—claimed, when he woke up, to remember witnessing certain events and doing certain actions which earlier he did not claim to remember; and that under questioning he could not remember witnessing other events and doing other actions which earlier he did remember. . . .

We may suppose that our enquiry has turned out in the most favourable possible way, and that the events he claims to have witnessed and all the actions he claims to have done point unanimously to the life-history of some one person in the past—for instance, Guy Fawkes. Not only do all Charles' memory-claims that can be checked fit the pattern of Fawkes' life as known to historians, but others that cannot be checked are plausible, provide explanations of unexplained facts, and so on. Are we to say that Charles is now Guy Fawkes, that Guy Fawkes has come to life again in Charles' body, or some such thing?[38]

Charles is psychologically continuous with Guy Fawkes. (Guy Fawkes tried to assassinate the king of England by blowing up the Parliament building in 1605.) If the psychological continuity theory were true, Charles would be identical to Guy Fawkes. But Williams claims that Charles cannot be identical with Guy Fawkes because other people could also be psychologically continuous with Guy Fawkes:

Thought Experiment

Williams's Reduplication Argument

If it is logically possible that Charles should undergo the changes described, then it is logically possible that some other man should simultaneously undergo the same changes; e.g., that both Charles and his brother Robert should be found in this condition. What should we say in that case? They cannot both be Guy Fawkes; if they were, Guy Fawkes would be in two places at once, which is absurd. Moreover, if they were both identical with Guy Fawkes, they would be identical to each other, which is also absurd. Hence we could not say that they were both identical to Guy Fawkes.[39]

psychological connectedness Two people are psychologically connected if they can directly (consciously) quasi-remember and quasi-desire the same things.

psychological continuity Two people are psychologically continuous with one another if they form part of an overlapping series of persons who are psychologically connected with one another.

psychological continuity theory The doctrine that identical persons are those who are psychologically continuous with one another.

Past-Life Hypnotic Regression

Under hypnosis, many people seem to remember past lives. Are these memories good evidence for reincarnation? That depends on whether the memories are apparent or real. Nicholas Spanos, an expert on hypnosis, claims that the evidence suggests that past-life memories are pure fabrications.

> Some people who have been administered hypnotic-induction procedures followed by suggestions to regress back past their birth times report that they experienced past lives. For instance, a 22 year old Caucasian woman, while recently "regressed" in our laboratory, claimed that the year was 1940 and that "he" (her past-life identity involved a change of sex) was a Japanese fighter pilot. How are reports of this type to be explained? The parsimonious answer is that they are suggestion-induced fantasy creations of imaginative subjects. If the subjects hold prior beliefs about the validity of reincarnation and/or if they are given encouragement to do so by the hypnotist, they may come to interpret their fantasies as evidence for the existence of actual past-life personalities. . . .
>
> The few experimental studies that have examined past-life regression have yielded findings that are consistent with the picture of hypnotic responding described above. For example, we recently completed two experiments on this topic. In the first, 110 subjects were tested for responsiveness to hypnotic suggestions (i.e., hypnotizability). In separate sessions, all of these subjects were individually administered a hypnotic procedure and suggestions to regress to times before their births and then to describe where and who they were. During their individual session, 35 subjects enacted past lives. Each subject told

the experimenter that he or she was a different person and was living in a different time. Most went on to provide numerous details about where they lived, their past-life occupations, their families, interests, and so on. Subjects who reported past lives scored higher on hypnotizability than those who did not, and were more likely than those who did not to believe that they had experienced some earlier portents of past lives (e.g., déjà vu experiences, dreams). . . .

> Wambach contended that the historical information obtained from hypnotically regressed past-life responders was almost always accurate. To test this idea in both of our experiments we asked subjects questions that were likely to have historically checkable answers (e.g., Was the responder's community/country at peace or war?). Contrary to Wambach, subjects who gave information specific enough to be checked were much more often incorrect than correct, and the errors were often the type that actual persons from the relevant historical epochs would have been unlikely to make. . . . [I]ts embeddedness in a nexus of social communications allows past-life enactments to be seen for what they are—interesting and imaginative contextually guided fantasy enactments.[40]

Thought Probe

Past-Life Hypnotic Regression

Do you agree with Spanos that the past-life memories recalled under hypnosis are contextually guided fantasy enactments? Why or why not? If not, do you have a better explanation?

By the transitivity of identity, if A is identical to B and A is identical to C, then B is identical to C. So if Guy Fawkes is identical to Charles, and Guy Fawkes is identical to Robert, then Charles is identical to Robert. But Charles isn't identical to Robert, for they are two separate people. Numerically distinct people cannot be numerically identical. So psychological continuity doesn't guarantee personal identity.

A *Star Trek*
Transporter.
Are the people who
find themselves at the
destination identical to
the people who stood
on the transporter pads?
Dr. McCoy was never
quite sure.

The problem is that psychological continuity is a one-to-many relation (many different people can be psychologically continuous with one person), whereas numerical identity is a one-to-one relation. Thus the relation of psychological continuity is too weak to constitute personal identity.

The inadequacy of the psychological continuity theory has been vividly demonstrated by a number of thought experiments, most notably, those dealing with *Star Trek*–style transporter technology. In the TV series *Star Trek*, a device called a transporter is used to beam objects from one location to another. According to the *Star Trek: Next Generation Technical Manual*, the transporter works by scanning an object and recording the state of each of its subatomic particles. The scan destroys the atomic bonds that hold the particles together, but those particles are saved and sent to the destination in a "subatomically debonded matter stream." The pattern acquired from the scan is then used to put the particles back together in their original configuration.[41] So when a person beams down, the traveler is essentially disassembled and reassembled (or killed and resurrected). But, because a physical object can survive disassembly and reassembly, there is good reason for believing that people who use this method of transportation survive the trip.

Suppose there were a different transporter technology, however. Like the *Star Trek* transporter, this transporter could scan an object and break it down into its constituent particles. Unlike the *Star Trek* transporter, however, it would not save the particles. Instead, it would send the pattern to another device that uses different matter to create a replica of the object. Could you survive a trip through this type of transporter? Would the person created from

Although transporters seem logically possible, many thought that they were physically impossible because they seemed to violate the Heisenberg uncertainty principle, which says that we cannot simultaneously know certain things about the state of subatomic particles. Scientists at IBM, however, have shown that there is a way around the Heisenberg uncertainty principle—and thus that Parfit-style transporters are a physical possibility. Here's IBM's description of its accomplishment:

> Teleportation is the name given by science fiction writers to the feat of making an object or person disintegrate in one place while a perfect replica appears somewhere else. How this is accomplished is usually not explained in detail, but the general idea seems to be that the original object is scanned in such a way as to extract all the information from it, then this information is transmitted to the receiving location and used to construct the replica, not necessarily from the actual material of the original, but perhaps from atoms of the same kinds, arranged in exactly the same pattern as the original. A teleportation machine would be like a fax machine, except that it would work on 3-dimensional objects as well as documents, it would produce an exact copy rather than an approximate facsimile, and it would destroy the original in the process of scanning it. A few science fiction writers consider teleporters that preserve the original, and the plot gets complicated when the original and teleported versions of the same person meet; but the more common kind of teleporter destroys the original, functioning as a super transportation device, not as a perfect replicator of souls and bodies.

> Two years ago an international group of six scientists, including IBM Fellow Charles H. Bennett, confirmed the intuitions of the majority of science fiction writers by showing that perfect teleportation is indeed possible in principle, but only if the original is destroyed. Meanwhile, other scientists are planning experiments to demonstrate teleportation in microscopic objects, such as single atoms or photons, in the next few years. But science fiction fans will be disappointed to learn that no one expects to be able to teleport people or other macroscopic objects in the foreseeable future, for a variety of engineering reasons, even though it would not violate any fundamental law to do so.[42]

Thought Probe

Transporter Travel

If this technology became available, would you use it to travel from one place to another? Why or why not? What theory of personal identity lies behind your decision?

your pattern be you or just a copy of you? To sharpen your intuitions, consider British philosopher Derek Parfit's transporter tale.

Thought Experiment

Parfit's Transporter Tale

I enter the Teletransporter. I have been to Mars before, but only by the old method, a space-ship journey taking several weeks. This machine will send me at the speed of light. I merely have to press the green button. Like others, I am nervous. Will it work? I remind myself what I have been told to expect. When

I press the button, I shall lose consciousness, and then wake up at what seems a moment later. In fact I shall have been unconscious for about an hour. The Scanner here on Earth will destroy my brain and body, while recording the exact states of all of my cells. It will then transmit this information by radio. Traveling at the speed of light, the message will take three minutes to reach the Replicator on Mars. This will then create, out of new matter, a brain and body exactly like mine. It will be in this body that I shall wake up.

Though I believe that this is what will happen, I still hesitate. But then I remember seeing my wife grin when, at breakfast today, I revealed my nervousness. As she reminded me, she has been often teletransported, and there is nothing wrong with her. I press the button. As predicted, I lose and seem at once to regain consciousness, but in a different cubicle. Examining my new body, I find no change at all. Even the cut on my upper lip, from this morning's shave, is still there.

Several years pass, during which I am often teletransported. I am now back in the cubicle, ready for another trip to Mars. But this time, when I press the green button, I do not lose consciousness. There is a whirring sound, then silence. I leave the cubicle, and say to the attendant: "It's not working. What did I do wrong?"

"It's working," he replies, handing me a printed card. This reads: "The New Scanner records your blueprint without destroying your brain and body. We hope that you will welcome the opportunities which this technical advance offers."

The attendant tells me that I am one of the first people to use the New Scanner. He adds that, if I stay for an hour, I can use the Intercom to see and talk to myself on Mars.

"Wait a minute," I reply, "If I'm here I can't *also* be on Mars."

Someone politely coughs, a white-coated man who asks to speak to me in private. We go to his office, where he tells me to sit down, and pauses. Then he says, "I'm afraid that we're having problems with the New Scanner. It records your blueprint just as accurately, as you will see when you talk to yourself on Mars. But it seems to be damaging the cardiac systems which it scans. Judging from the results so far, though, you will be quite healthy on Mars, here on Earth you must expect cardiac failure within the next few days."

The attendant later calls me to the Intercom. On the screen I see myself just as I do in the mirror every morning. But there are two differences. On the screen I am not left-right reversed. And, while I stand here speechless, I can see and hear myself, in the studio on Mars, starting to speak.[43]

Parfit would have us imagine two different types of transporters. One destroys him as it scans him, and the other does not. Both use the scanned information to make a replica of him. In the first case, where Parfit's body is destroyed by the scan, the person made from his pattern seems to be identical to him, for he is psychologically continuous with Parfit and has a body like Parfit's. In the second case, where Parfit's body is not destroyed by the scan, the person made from his pattern does not seem to be identical to him, for Parfit's original body and mind still exist. But if the replica is not identical to

Parfit in the second case, it's not identical to Parfit in the first case either. In both cases, the replica is a copy of Parfit, not Parfit himself.

Parfit's teletransporters are really just glorified fax machines that fax humans instead of documents. The word "fax" comes from the word "facsimile," which means an exact copy of something. The documents that come out of fax machines are copies of the original, whether or not the original is destroyed in the process. Similarly, the people that come out of Parfit's teletransporters are copies of the original, whether or not the original was destroyed in the process.

The foregoing objection to the psychological continuity theory has implications for the decision scenario presented at the beginning of the chapter. If you had agreed to have the contents of your brain uploaded into the robot, the best you could have hoped for is that the robot would be psychologically continuous with you. But Williams's reduplication argument and Parfit's transporter tale suggest that psychological continuity is not enough for personal identity. Just as the replicated Parfits are not numerically identical to Parfit, the robot with your psychology would not be you. At best, it would be qualitatively identical to you. Thus those who believe that they can achieve immortality by having their minds uploaded into computers may be mistaken.

Similarly, those who believe that they can achieve immortality by having their minds "uploaded" into celestial bodies may also be mistaken, for transferring your mind into a celestial body is just a type of reincarnation, and, as we have seen, reincarnation does not preserve personal identity. An uploaded person is just a copy of the original, whether the person is uploaded into a physical or a celestial body. Consequently, resurrection may be your best hope for survival after death.

Thought Probe

Can You Go to Heaven?

If a reincarnation of you is at best a copy of you, wouldn't a person in heaven also be, at best, a copy of you? Can someone in heaven who does not have your physical body be numerically identical to you? How? What theory of personal identity supports your answer?

Summary

Our identity as persons does not seem to depend on the stuff we're made of. It does, however, seem to depend on our memories. Locke's memory theory is the doctrine that identical persons are persons who remember the same thing. But this leads to an inconsistency. There could be two people who are identical to a third person and yet are not identical to each other, as in the case of the brave officer and the senile general. Locke's theory can be saved, though, by recognizing the existence of both direct memories (those you can consciously recall) and indirect memories (those that an earlier version of you can recall).

Locke's memory theory, however, is circular — it presupposes the notion it is trying to explain, namely, personal identity. The concept of memory presupposes the concept of personal identity because you can remember something only if it happened to you. By positing quasi-memory — memory stripped of its personal reference — we can get around this problem.

Though memory is an important part of personal identity, there are other vital ingredients — like desires and intentions. There is good reason to believe that if our desires and intentions were somehow erased, we would cease to exist. The psychological continuity theory recognizes the importance of these other factors and holds that identical persons are persons who are psychologically continuous with one another.

This theory, though, must be mistaken, for it is logically possible for more than one person to be psychologically continuous with you. More than one person could have your memories and desires. But if so, personal identity cannot be defined in terms of psychological continuity because psychological identity would not guarantee numerical identity.

Study Questions

1. What is Locke's memory theory of personal identity?
2. What is Reid's tale of the brave officer and the senile general? How does it attempt to undermine Locke's memory theory?
3. Why is Locke's memory theory circular?
4. What is the psychological continuity theory of personal identity?
5. What is Williams's thought experiment concerning the reincarnation of Guy Fawkes? How does it attempt to undermine the psychological continuity theory?
6. What is Parfit's transporter tale? How does it attempt to undermine the psychological continuity theory?

Discussion Questions

1. If you lost all of your memories beyond any possibility of retrieval, would you cease to exist?
2. Doctors used to give scopolamine to women during labor. Scopolamine causes amnesia, so you remember nothing that happened to you while you were under its influence. Women who were "scoped" thus had no memory of giving birth. Did they give birth to their children? What would Locke say?
3. Does past-life hypnotic regression provide good evidence for reincarnation? Why or why not?
4. When someone is born again in Jesus Christ, does a new person come into existence? Why or why not?

5. Suppose that a born-again Christian was a criminal before finding Jesus Christ. Should the fact that the individual has been born again mean that he should be given a lighter sentence? Why or why not?

6. Should we try to reform criminals by erasing their memories? Should we try to reform criminals by changing their character? Is one method preferable to the other? Why or why not?

7. Suppose reincarnation occurred and we could accurately identify who is a reincarnation of whom. Should a reincarnated criminal be punished for crimes committed in a past life? Why or why not?

8. Is resurrection a more plausible view of the afterlife than reincarnation? Why or why not?

9. Consider the following thought experiment suggested by Bernard Williams.

Thought Experiment

Bodily Torture

Suppose someone tells you that the person in your body is going to be tortured tomorrow. This person, however, will have none of your memories and you will have no memory of being tortured. Should you fear being tortured? If so, does that suggest that your identity is more closely tied to your body than the psychological continuity theory suggests? Why or why not?

10. Are the different personalities in people suffering from multiple-personality disorder different persons? Why or why not? The preferred treatment for people suffering from multiple-personality disorder is to merge the different personalities into one. Often this results in the destruction of one or more of those personalities. Is this destruction a type of homicide? If so, is it justifiable homicide? Why or why not?

You Can't Step into the Same River Twice

Self as Process

*W*e would survive a trip through the *Star Trek* transporter—but not Parfit's transporter—because the *Star Trek* transporter transports the body as well as the mind. So something more than psychological continuity is required for personal identity. Sydney Shoemaker claims that in addition to psychological continuity, your psychology must be caused by and realized in the same brain.

My one regret in life is that I am not someone else.

—WOODY ALLEN

The Brain Theory

Our brains are the seat of our consciousness, and as long as they survive, there is reason to believe that we survive. Shoemaker demonstrates the importance of brains to personal identity in the following thought experiment.

To expect a personality to survive the disintegration of the brain is like expecting a cricket club to survive when all its members are dead.

—BERTRAND RUSSELL

Thought Experiment

Shoemaker's Brain Transplant

First, suppose that medical science has developed a technique whereby a surgeon can completely remove a person's brain from his head, examine or operate on it, and then put it back in his skull (regrafting the nerves, blood-vessels, and so forth) without causing death or permanent injury; we are to imagine that this technique of "brain extraction" has come to be widely practiced in the treatment of brain tumors and other disorders of the brain. One day, to begin our story, a surgeon discovers that an assistant has made a horrible mistake. Two men, a Mr. Brown and a Mr. Robinson, had been operated on for brain tumors, and brain extraction had been performed on both of them. At the end of the

operations, however, the assistant inadvertently put Brown's brain in Robinson's head. One of these men immediately dies, but the other, the one with Robinson's body and Brown's brain, eventually regains consciousness. Let us call the latter "Brownson." Upon regaining consciousness Brownson exhibits great shock and surprise at the appearance of his body. Then, upon seeing Brown's body, he exclaims incredulously, "That's me lying there!" Pointing to himself he says, "This isn't my body; the one over there is!" When asked his name he automatically replies, "Brown." He recognizes Brown's wife and family (whom Robinson had never met), and is able to describe in detail events in Brown's life, always describing them as events in his own life. Of Robinson's past life he evidences no knowledge at all. Over a period of time he is observed to display all of the personality traits, mannerisms, interests, likes and dislikes, and so on that had previously characterized Brown, and to act and talk in ways completely alien to the old Robinson.[44]

Shoemaker describes a situation in which a Mr. Brown's brain is transplanted into a Mr. Robinson's skull. The resulting person—Brownson—is psychologically continuous with Mr. Brown. He has Mr. Brown's memories and desires as well as his personality traits and mannerisms. Consequently, claims Shoemaker, Brownson is identical to Brown. The fact that Brownson doesn't have Brown's body is irrelevant because Brownson's psychology is caused by and realized in Brown's brain. Since the brain is the organ of thought, Brownson's thoughts are Brown's thoughts. This suggests that where our brains go, we go. This is the **brain theory:** the doctrine that identical persons are those who are psychologically continuous with one another and whose psychology is caused by and realized in the same brain.

Having the same brain, however, does not require having the same entire brain, for neurophysiology has shown that people can survive the destruction of large parts of their brains. Some people have had almost half of their cerebral cortex destroyed by stroke, injury, or surgery and have learned to function adequately. In these cases, the remaining part of their cerebral cortex has taken over the functions of the damaged part.

Split Brains

Although the brain theory is superior to the body theory, it doesn't avoid the reduplication problem. For, just as more than one person can be psychologically continuous with someone, so more than one physical object can be physically (spatiotemporally) continuous with something. When an amoeba undergoes fission (splits), for example, the two resulting amoebas are physically continuous with the original. Strange as it may seem, persons, like amoebas, may undergo fission.

The brain is divided into two symmetrical hemispheres, which are linked by a bundle of nerves known as the corpus callosum. These fibers carry signals back and forth between the two hemispheres. To prevent the spread of seizures from one hemisphere to the other, neurosurgeons have cut the corpus callosum in a number of patients. What they found was that, by splitting the brains of these patients, they seemed to create two separate spheres of consciousness.

Each half of the brain governs the opposite side of the body. The left hemisphere controls the muscles of the right side of the body and receives information from the right half of the skin surface; the right hemisphere

brain theory The doctrine that identical persons are those who are psychologically continuous with one another and whose psychology is caused by and realized in the same brain.

THE CORPUS
CALLOSUM (FROM
DeFabrica, 1543, BY
ANDREAS VESALIUS).
This bundle of nerves
(L) connects the two
hemispheres of the
brain.

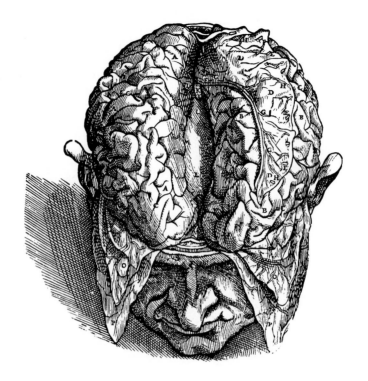

controls the muscles of the left side of the body and receives information from the left half of the skin surface. In most people, the left hemisphere also controls speech. In split-brain patients, information given to one hemisphere is unavailable to the other. For example, in one experiment, an object was placed in the left hand of a blindfolded split-brain patient. She couldn't name the object because speech is controlled by the left hemisphere, and only the right hemisphere knew what the object was. When she was asked to use her left hand to retrieve the object from a box of objects, she had no trouble doing so. When she was asked to use her right hand to retrieve the object, however, all she could do was pick up objects at random. When the blindfold was removed, however, and she was allowed to watch her right hand try to pick up the object, her left hand would slap her right hand whenever it picked up the wrong object. This was the right hemisphere's way of communicating with the left now that it could no longer use the corpus callosum. Such behavior led Roger Sperry to describe split-brain patients as having "two free wills in one cranial vault."[46] In other words, there are two persons in one skull.

Split-brain experiments convinced Derek Parfit that the brain theory was an inadequate theory of personal identity. To exhibit its shortcomings, he proposed the following thought experiment. Suppose (as may well be the case in some people) that each of Parfit's brain hemispheres has the same psychology (memories, desires, attitudes, etc.). Suppose further that Parfit is one of three identical triplets. Then suppose the following.

Parfit's Division

My body is fatally injured, as are the brains of my two [identical] brothers. My brain is divided, and each half is successfully transplanted into the body of one of my brothers. Each of the resulting people believes that he is me, seems to remember living my life, has my character, and is in every other way psychologically continuous with me. And he has a body very like mine.[47]

In this case, each of Parfit's cerebral hemispheres is transplanted into a separate body that is indistinguishable from his own. (We can imagine that his brain was split in order to double the operation's chances for success.) Because each of his hemispheres has the same psychology, the two persons resulting from the two transplants are psychologically continuous with Parfit. And because their brains are physically continuous with his, their psychology is caused by and realized in Parfit's brain. So, according to the brain theory, both people should be identical to Parfit. But that's impossible, for two cannot be one. Thus it appears that the reduplication problem cannot be avoided by requiring that our psychology be grounded in the brain.

Closest Continuer Theories

Personal identity cannot consist in psychological or physical continuity because identity is a relation that can hold only between a thing and itself. Psychological and physical continuity are relations that can hold between many different things. Both minds and bodies can be split. When they are, the resulting things are not identical to the original even though they are continuous with it. To avoid the reduplication problem, then, it seems that a theory of personal identity must either rule out any sort of splitting, or it must have some means of determining which branch is identical to the original.

Sydney Shoemaker adopts the first alternative and suggests that personal identity requires nonbranching psychological continuity.[48] If the causal chain linking you to a person existing at another time splits or merges in certain ways, your identity will not be preserved. According to the **nonbranching theory,** then, identical persons are those who are psychologically continuous with one another and whose causal chain has not branched.

By not allowing branching causal chains, Shoemaker's proposal avoids all of the reduplication scenarios we have examined: Williams's double reincarnation of Guy Fawkes, Parfit's nondestructive teletransportation, and Parfit's division—for each of these scenarios involves branching causal chains of one sort or another.

Robert Nozick adopts the second strategy and tries to provide a means for determining which branch is identical to the original. Psychological and physical continuity are a matter of degree. But, Nozick claims, as long as one

Trying to define yourself is like trying to bite your own teeth.

—ALAN WATTS

nonbranching theory
The doctrine that identical persons are those who are psychologically continuous with one another and whose causal connection has not branched.

Alien Hand Syndrome

Roger Sperry's claim that split-brain operations create "two free wills in one cranial vault" is controversial because these patients often function normally outside of the laboratory. But there is a phenomena experienced by some that lends credence to Sperry's claim, namely, alien hand syndrome. Neurologist I. Biran describes its effects:

> In Stanley Kubrick's movie, *Dr. Strangelove*, the main character is described as "erratic" and displays a bizarre movement disorder. His right hand seems to be driven by a will of its own, at times clutching his own throat and at other times raising into a Nazi salute. Dr. Strangelove must try to restrain this wayward limb with his left hand. Bizarre as this fictional character is, a similar movement disorder can occur in neurologic disease. The complex phenomenon associated with this disorder falls under the rubric of alien hand syndrome. This syndrome is characterized by a limb that seems to perform meaningful acts without being guided by the intention of the patient. Patients find themselves unable to stop the alien limb from reaching and grabbing objects, and they may be unable to release these grasped objects without using their other hand to pry open their fingers. These patients frequently express astonishment and frustration at the errant limb. They experience it as being controlled by an external agent and often refer to it in the third person.[49]

Thought Probe

Who Is Behind the Hand?

Could the agent behind an alien hand be a person? How could we tell?

---

person is sufficiently psychologically and physically continuous with another and there is no one else who is more psychologically and physically continuous with the former person, then the latter person is numerically identical to the former.[50] According to Nozick's **closest continuer theory,** then, identical persons are those who are closest continuers of one another.

The closest continuer theory can avoid certain sorts of reduplication scenarios, but in those cases where two people are equally close, such as in Parfit's division, or a double reincarnation, or a double teletransportation, the closest continuer theory tells us that neither of the later persons is identical to the earlier.

Adopting either the nonbranching theory or the closest continuer theory, however, means rejecting one of our most fundamental beliefs concerning the nature of identity—namely, that the identity of a thing doesn't depend on the existence of other things. This belief has come to be known as the **only x and y principle,** and it rests on the intuition that whether one thing, x, is identical to another thing, y, can depend only on facts about x and y. Facts about other things are irrelevant because identity is a relation that holds between a thing and itself. Whether an oak is identical to a sapling, for example, shouldn't depend on the existence of other trees. Similarly, whether you are identical to a person who lived before shouldn't depend on the existence of other people.

According to either the nonbranching or closest continuer theories, however, your identity depends on the existence of other people. If the causal chain that produced your psychology has split into two or more equal branches, you cannot be identical to the person you think you are. In the case of Parfit's division, for example, neither of the resulting people are identical to Parfit because the causal chain connecting them to Parfit has branched and neither is a closer continuer than the other. So Parfit has suffered death by duplication. If only one of the transplants had been successful, however, the resulting person would have been identical to Parfit. So prior to the operation, Parfit would have been well advised to have hired a hit man with orders to kill one of the resulting people if both operations were successful. By ensuring that the causal chain did not branch, he would have been ensuring his continued existence. Such are the bizarre implications of rejecting the only x and y principle.

Thought Probe

Branch Lines

Should we give up the only x and y principle as both Shoemaker and Nozick suggest? Do you agree that whether you're identical to someone depends on whether other people exist? Why or why not?

Identity and What Matters in Survival

We began our investigation into personal identity with the assumption that we can survive the death of the body only if we are numerically identical to someone who exists after the body has died. But we have been unable to come up with a theory that captures all of our intuitions concerning the nature of personal identity. Parfit suggests that what this shows is that these intuitions are mistaken. Identity is not necessary for survival.

Consider once again the case of Parfit's division. By the transitivity of identity, neither of the resulting persons would be numerically identical to Parfit. If they were, they would be numerically identical to each other, and that is impossible. Two things cannot be one. But even though neither of the resulting persons would be identical to him, it would be irrational for Parfit to view the impending operation the same way he would view his own death. It would also be irrational for him to hire someone to kill one of the resulting people if both transplants succeed, even though that would ensure that he would be numerically identical to the survivor. The best explanation of these facts, claims Parfit, is that identity is not what matters in survival. What matters is psychological continuity. If we retain our memories and our desires, it doesn't matter whether we are numerically identical to anyone who lived before. In that case, we have all that's really important.

To see what Parfit's getting at, imagine what would happen if Parfit's division were successful. The two resulting people would look and act just like he did. The existence of these two replicas would certainly be disconcerting to his friends and relatives, especially if they met both of the replicas at the same

It now seems to me that one changes from day to day and that every few years one becomes a new being.

—George Sand

closest continuer theory The doctrine that identical persons are those who are the closest continuers of one another.

only x and y principle The principle that whether one thing, x, is identical to another thing, y, can only depend on facts about x and y.

time. But because both are psychologically and physically indistinguishable from Parfit, Parfit's friends and relatives would have every reason to be just as interested in each of them as they were in him.

Even though neither of Parfit's replicas is identical to him, it would not seem to them that they had just come into existence. Both would believe they were Parfit, for both would have all of Parfit's memories, desires, and character traits. Even after they had realized the other existed, they would still be able to fulfill their impersonal desires. In fact, if they learned to cooperate with one another, they might be able to complete any projects Parfit had planned in half the time (like in the movie *Multiplicity*).

It would be a little more difficult for both of the replicas to fulfill all of Parfit's personal desires, especially if Parfit were married, employed, or a homeowner. Who would get his wife? Who would get his job? Who would get his house? Judicious planning before the operation might be able to eliminate these difficulties, however. If Parfit knew the operation was coming, he might establish a procedure for deciding these questions. Because both of the resulting persons would have all of his memories, they should agree to go along with whatever procedure he came up with. In any event, from both a third-person and a first-person point of view, being a Parfitian survivor would certainly be much better than simply dying.

If faced with certain death (as in the case presented in the beginning of this chapter), Parfit would probably accept the doctor's offer to download the contents of his brain into a robot. If the operation were successful, the robot would be psychologically continuous with him, and, according to Parfit, that's all that really matters. Alternatively, Parfit could look forward to a more traditional afterlife. He could hope to be psychologically continuous with someone in a spiritual body. The fact that his mind could be placed in two or more robot or spiritual bodies wouldn't bother him, for as long as it were placed in at least one, he would survive.

Identity and What Matters in Responsibility

To live is to change and to be perfect is to have changed often.

—JOHN HENRY NEWMAN

Not only does numerical identity not seem to be necessary for survival, it does not seem to be necessary for responsibility. Whether you should be held responsible for an action seems to depend more on your character than your identity.

Suppose, for example, that before his division, Parfit had led a life of crime. Then, even though neither of his replicas is numerically identical to him, the authorities would have good reason for locking both of them up. Each of them would have whatever desires, intentions, and character traits had led Parfit to a life of crime in the first place. The principle that only those who commit a crime should be punished for it seems inapplicable here. If Parfit's survivors have his character, they should be punished, too.

Your character can change over time. If it does, there is reason to believe that you should not be held fully responsible for what you did in the past. Consider the following example.

Parfit's Reformed Nobelist

Suppose that a man aged ninety, one of the few rightful holders of the Nobel Peace Prize, confesses that it was he who, at the age of twenty, injured a policeman in a drunken brawl. Though this was a serious crime, this man may not now deserve to be punished.[51]

The ninety-year-old Nobel Peace Prize winner is identical to the person who committed the crime seventy years ago. But he may not be responsible for it, for his character may no longer be the same. Our character is a function of our beliefs, attitudes, desires, values, and the like—and our actions are a function of our character. If the character responsible for a crime no longer exists, there's reason to believe that punishment would be pointless.

Parole boards seem to realize that if a person's character changes for the better, the individual's responsibility for a crime is lessened. Parfit suggests that this realization also lies behind statutes of limitations, which limit the length of time during which a person may be charged with committing a specific crime.[52]

Numerical identity seems to be neither necessary nor sufficient for moral responsibility. What matters is sameness of character. If a person's character has changed significantly since the time of an incident, that person's responsibility for the incident may be significantly less.

Explaining the Self

Theories of personal identity try to specify the conditions under which a person at one time is numerically identical to a person at another time. But we have been unable to find a set of conditions that is both necessary and sufficient for personal identity. Why are identity conditions for persons so hard to come by? Given the failure of substance theories of personal identity, the best explanation seems to be that persons aren't things—they are processes.

According to property dualism, the mind is a property that emerges from a physical thing when it reaches a certain degree of complexity. Similarly, the self can be viewed as a property that emerges from the mind when it reaches a certain degree of complexity. Not everything that has a mind has a self, for not everything that is conscious is self-conscious. And not everything that is self-conscious is self-conscious to the same degree. So, contrary to what the substance theorists would have us believe, having a self is not an all-or-nothing affair.

The fact that the unity of the self can be destroyed by psychological and physical traumas (e.g., multiple-personality disorder and split-brain operations) is further evidence for the fact that the self is not a substance. In ordinary circumstances, however, the self seems to be unified, and any process

Substance is one of the greatest of our illusions.
—SIR ARTHUR EDDINGTON

Buddhists on the Self and Nirvana

Belief in the impermanence of all things is one of the fundamental tenets of Buddhism. Moreover, Buddhists claim that belief in a permanent self or soul is the root of all evil. Buddhist theologian Walpola Rahula elaborates,

> According to the teaching of the Buddha, the idea of self is an imaginary, false belief which has no corresponding reality, and it produces harmful thoughts of "me" and "mine," selfish desire, craving attachment, hatred, ill-will, conceit, pride, egoism, and other defilements, impurities and problems. It is the source of all the troubles in the world from personal conflicts to wars between nations. In short, to this false view can be traced all the evil in the world.[53]

Because the cause of evil is the belief in the existence of a soul, the way to eliminate evil is to stop believing in the existence of the soul. Once you do, not only will the world be a better place, but you will realize Nirvana, a state of perfect bliss.

But, you may ask, if there is no soul, who realizes Nirvana? According to Buddhism, realization itself does the realizing. Rahula explains,

> If there is no Self, no Atman, who realizes Nirvana? Before we go on to Nirvana, let us ask the question: Who thinks now, if there is no Self? We have seen earlier that it is the thought that thinks, that there is no thinker behind the thought. In the same way, it is wisdom, realization, that realizes. There is no other self behind the realization.[54]

Traditionally, the self or soul has been conceived as a substance or thing that has thoughts. The Buddhists deny the existence of the self because they deny the existence of continuing substances. Because everything is constantly changing, there is nothing for thoughts to belong to. We speak as if there were continuing selves, but, according to the Buddhists, that is just a convention that we have adopted for practical purposes. Words like "I," "me," "soul," and so on, do not refer to continuing selves, for there are none to refer to.

theory must account for this apparent unity of the self. Immanuel Kant (1724–1804) accounts for it by postulating a "transcendental ego" that lies behind our experience and structures it according to certain rules. Kant's self is transcendental because it cannot be directly observed. As a result, Kant claims that we cannot know whether the self is a continuing substance.[55]

To account for the apparent unity of the self, however, we need not postulate anything that lies beyond experience. We need only assume that the properties that constitute the self are self-organizing. Nobel Prize–winning chemist Ilya Prigogine has shown that many systems in nature are self-organizing.[56] The self may simply be one of those systems. In previous sections, we have seen that there is good reason for believing in both downward causation and agent causation. If mental properties in general and self properties in particular have causal powers, there is no reason to believe that they couldn't unify themselves.

The self, in this view, is a self-generating process. To borrow one of the Buddhists' favorite analogies, the self is to the body as the flame is to the candle. Just as each stage of the flame brings about the next through the process of burning, so each stage of the self brings about the next through the process of thinking. Both the flame and the self are constantly changing, but each is

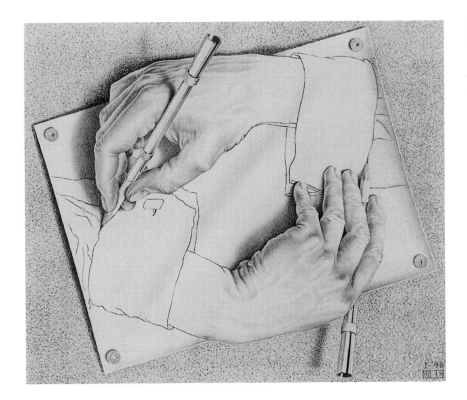

DRAWING HANDS
BY M. C. ESCHER
(LITHOGRAPH, 1948).
A visual analog of a
self-generating process.

part of a continuous process. There can be no flame without a candle, just as there can be no self without a body. But the flame can be passed on to many different candles, just as the self can be passed on to many different bodies. Because flames and selves can continue on in more than one substance, we cannot identify flames or selves with substances. But if we are willing to admit that survival doesn't require identity, we may justifiably hope to survive the death of our bodies.

Thought Probe

Robert and Frank

Consider the case of Robert and Frank discussed in the introduction to this chapter. Given what you now know of personal identity, do you believe that Robert should be punished for what Frank did? Why or why not?

Moral Agents, Narratives, and Persons

All persons have rights that ought to be respected. But only some persons are capable of respecting those rights. The very young, the mentally incapacitated, and the insane, for example, may be incapable of acting morally toward others because they do not know the difference between right and wrong or they are unable to control themselves. In either case, we do not hold them responsible for their actions. Only those persons who have the concepts of right and wrong and can act on those concepts are held accountable for what they do. Persons who can act morally toward others and thus can be justly praised or blamed for their actions are known as "moral agents."

To be a moral agent, you must be capable of acting freely. And, as shown in Chapter 3, to act freely, you must be capable of reflecting on your desires and deciding whether you want to be the sort of person that is motivated by them. By reflecting on your desires and deciding what is worthy of value, you help shape your character and bring unity to your life.

Much has been made recently of the importance of unity in personal identity. Marya Schechtman, for example, argues that you become a person by viewing your life as part of a narrative: "[I]ndividuals constitute themselves as persons by coming to think of themselves as persisting subjects who have had experience in the past and will continue to have experience in the future, taking certain experiences as theirs . . . [Persons] weave stories of their lives."[57] Owen Flanagan similarly argues that you are a person only if your life is lived according to a "contentful story that involves an unfolding rationale."[58] Daniel Dennett views the self as a narrative center of gravity.[59] For him, the self is not something over and above the narrative; it is the narrative. In all of these views, the self is constituted by the narrative that weaves one's thoughts, feelings, and desires into a coherent whole.

Having a certain unity to one's self is a necessary condition for acting responsibly. Consider the case of those suffering from multiple-personality disorder. In their case, there may be a number of different story lines instead of one unified narrative. Courts of law generally do not hold these people responsible for their actions on the grounds that they lack the unity required to govern themselves. As Elyn Saks notes in her book *Jekyll on Trial*, "The sine qua non ["without which not," or necessary condition] of a responsible act is not that *a* consciousness chooses to act, but that a *unified* consciousness chooses to act."[60] Only if all aspects of one's self are available for participation in a decision can one be held responsible for it.

While a certain degree of self-integration may be required to be a moral agent, it doesn't seem to be required to be a person per se. Those suffering from multiple-personality disorder are still persons, either multiple or fragmentary. Those suffering from various forms of amnesia may also be unable to construct a unified narrative of their lives, but they may nonetheless be persons.

Consider the case of Canadian conductor Clive Waring. As a result of viral encephalitis that destroyed his hippocampus, he developed both anterograde and retrograde amnesia. He became unable to form new memories or access his old ones. His life thus consists of a series of discrete periods of consciousness, each lasting only a few minutes. He keeps a diary and often writes in it, "I am now fully awake for the first time." When asked about previous entries in the diary, he disavows them. Clive's life has no narrative unity. Nevertheless, he has many of the marks of personhood: he is rational, self-conscious (for short periods of time), and capable of engaging in self-motivated activity. Killing Clive would unquestionably be an act of murder. So while having a narrative unity to your life may be a necessary condition for being a moral agent, it may not be necessary for being a person.

Thought Probe

Being Clive Waring

Is there one continuous person in Clive Waring's body, or does his body house a succession of persons, each of which exists for only a few minutes? There are no memory connections between the periods of self-consciousness in Clive's body, but his intelligence, character, musical talent, love for his wife, and so on all remain constant. Is this enough to unite these periods of self-consciousness into one person?

Summary

The reduplication problem shows that there must be more to personal identity than psychological continuity. Shoemaker suggests that, in addition, your psychology must be caused by and realized in your brain. Unfortunately, Shoemaker's brain theory doesn't succeed in defining personal identity because, as Parfit's division shows, even though your psychology is caused by and realized in the same brain, it may belong to two different people.

Personal identity cannot consist in psychological or physical continuity because identity is a relation that can hold only between a thing and itself, whereas psychological and physical continuity are relations that can hold between many different things. Stipulating that only nonbranching causal chains can preserve personal identity avoids this problem. Adopting this proposal, however, requires rejecting one of our most fundamental beliefs concerning the nature of identity: the only x and y principle. This belief rests on the intuition that whether one thing, x, is identical to another thing, y, can depend only on facts about x and y. Because numerical identity is a relation between a thing and itself, the existence of other things shouldn't affect the identity of the thing.

At this point, we have to ask if numerical identity is what really matters in survival. In the case of Parfit's division, the two resulting people would be both psychologically and physically indistinguishable from Parfit. There would seem to be every reason for Parfit and his friends and relatives to think that Parfit had indeed survived the strange operation—even though there is no numerical identity. Likewise, it seems that numerical identity is not necessary for moral responsibility. Whether you should be held responsible for an action seems to depend more on your character than on your identity.

Our inability to find identity conditions for persons can be explained on the grounds that the self is a self-generating process rather than an unchanging substance. Because the same process can continue on in different substances, we can't identify selves with substances. But if we're willing to recognize that survival doesn't require identity, we can look forward to surviving the death of our bodies.

Study Questions

1. What is the brain theory of personal identity?
2. What is Shoemaker's brain transplant thought experiment?
3. What is Parfit's division thought experiment? How does it attempt to undermine the physical theory of personal identity?
4. What is the only x and y principle?

Discussion Questions

1. Suppose that brain transplant operations become relatively reliable. Would you have your brain transplanted into another human to avoid certain death? Into a fully functional robot that could house a human brain?
2. Suppose that your body is dying and that half of your brain has been destroyed. Suppose further that your spouse's body is healthy but that half of his or her brain has been destroyed. The doctors say that they can transplant the remaining healthy half of your brain into your spouse's skull. Your spouse agrees to have the transplant. Would you do it? What if the person who agreed to receive your brain was a stranger?
3. Are split-brain patients really two people in one skull? Are there any physical experiments we could conduct to determine whether two people are present? Describe any such experiments.
4. What does the nonbranching proposal say about split-brain patients? Are there two people present in the body? If so, is either identical with the person who occupied the body before the operation?
5. Can an adequate theory of personal identity violate the only x and y principle? Are the consequences of rejecting the principle too bizarre? If you can, explain your view by means of a thought experiment.
6. Is psychological continuity the only thing that matters in survival?
7. Suppose that someone commits a crime and arranges things so that her personality is totally changed after the crime (through brainwashing, psychosurgery, drugs, etc.). Should the resulting person be held responsible for the crime? What if her memories were erased, too?
8. What implications does the realization that responsibility is closely tied to character have for our judicial system? Would our judicial system be more just if we put more emphasis on character than on identity?
9. What theories of mind are consistent with the notion that the self is a process?

Of Identity and Diversity

John Locke (1632–1704) founded the philosophical school known as British empiricism and also served as a physician to the Earl of Shaftesbury. His best-known works are *An Essay Concerning Human Understanding* and *Two Treatises of Government*. The former outlines the basic principles of empiricism; the latter, the basic principles of democratic government. In this selection, Locke argues that personal identity resides not in any particular substance but in the consciousness we have of our continued existence.

8. An animal is a living organized body; and consequently the same animal, as we have observed, is the same continued *life* communicated to different particles of matter, as they happen successively to be united to that organized living body. And whatever is talked of other definitions, ingenious observation puts it past doubt, that the idea in our minds, of which the sound man in our mouths is the sign, is nothing else but of an animal of such a certain form. Since I think I may be confident, that, whoever should see a creature of his own shape or make, though it had no more reason all its life than a cat or a parrot, would call him still a *man*; or whoever should hear a cat or a parrot discourse, reason, and philosophize, would call or think it nothing but a *cat* or a *parrot*; and say, the one was a dull irrational man, and the other a very intelligent rational parrot. A relation we have in an author of great note, is sufficient to countenance the supposition of a rational parrot. His words are:

"I had a mind to know, from Prince Maurice's own mouth, the account of a common, but much credited story, that I had heard so often from many others, of an old parrot he had in Brazil, during his government there, that spoke, and asked, and answered common questions, like a reasonable creature: so that those of his train there generally concluded it to be witchery or possession; and one of his chaplains, who lived long afterwards in Holland, would never from that time endure a parrot, but said they all had a devil in them. I had heard many particulars of this story, and assevered by people hard to be discredited, which made me ask Prince Maurice what there was of it. He said, with his usual plainness and dryness in talk, there was something true, but a great deal false of what had been reported. I desired to know of him what there was of the first. He told me short and coldly, that he had heard of such an old parrot when he had been at Brazil; and though he believed nothing of it, and it was a good way off, yet he had so much curiosity as to send for it: that it was a very great and a very old one; and when it came first into the room where the prince was, with a great many Dutchmen about him, it said presently, *What a company of white men are here!* They asked it, what it thought that man was, pointing to the prince. It answered, *Some General or other.* When they brought it close to him, he asked it, *Whence come ye?* It answered, *From Marinnan.* The Prince, *To whom do you belong?* The parrot, *To a Portuguese.* The Prince, *What do you there?* Parrot, *I look after the chickens.* The Prince laughed, and said, *You look after the chickens?* The parrot answered, *Yes, I; and I know well enough how to do it;* and made the chuck four or five times that people use to make to chickens when they call them. I set down the words of this worthy dialogue in French, just as Prince Maurice said them to me. I asked him in what language the parrot spoke, and he said in Brazilian. I asked whether he understood Brazilian; he said No, but he had taken care to have two interpreters by him, the one a Dutchman that spoke Brazilian, and the other a Brazilian that spoke Dutch; that he asked them separately and privately, and both of them agreed in telling him just the same thing that the parrot had said. I could not but tell this odd story, because it is so much out of the way, and from the first hand, and what may pass for a good one; for I dare say this Prince at least believed himself in all he told me, having ever passed for a very honest and pious man: I leave it to naturalists to reason, and to other men to believe, as they please upon it; however,

---

From: John Locke, *An Essay Concerning Human Understanding*, ed. Alexander Campbell Fraser (Oxford: Clarendon Press, 1894) 445–468. Notes have been omitted.

it is not, perhaps, amiss to relieve or enliven a busy scene sometimes with such digressions, whether to the purpose or no."

I have taken care that the reader should have the story at large in the author's own words, because he seems to me not to have thought it incredible; for it cannot be imagined that so able a man as he, who had sufficiency enough to warrant all the testimonies he gives of himself, should take so much pains, in a place where it had nothing to do, to pin so close, not only a man whom he mentions as his friend, but on a Prince in whom he acknowledges very great honesty and piety, a story which, if he himself thought incredible, he could not but also think ridiculous. The Prince, it is plain, who vouches this story, and our author, who relates it from him, both of them call this talker a parrot: and I ask any one else who thinks such a story fit to be told, whether, if this parrot, and all of its kind, had always talked, as we have a prince's word for it this one did, — whether, I say, they would not have passed for a race of *rational animals;* but yet, whether, for all that, they would have been allowed to be men, and not *parrots?* For I presume it is not the idea of a thinking or rational being alone that makes the *idea of a man* in most people's sense: but of a body, so and so shaped, joined to it; and if that be the idea of a man, the same successive body not shifted all at once, must, as well as the same immaterial spirit, go to the making of the same man.

9. This being premised, to find wherein personal identity consists, we must consider what *person* stands for; — which, I think, is a thinking intelligent being, that has reason and reflection, and can consider itself as itself, the same thinking thing, in different times and places; which it does only by that consciousness which is inseparable from thinking, and, as it seems to me, essential to it: it being impossible for any one to perceive without *perceiving* that he does perceive. When we see, hear, smell, taste, feel, meditate, or will anything, we know that we do so. Thus it is always as to our present sensations and perceptions: and by this every one is to himself that which he calls *self:* — it not being considered, in this case, whether the same self be continued in the same or diverse substances. For, since consciousness always accompanies thinking, and it is that which makes every one to be what he calls self, and thereby distinguishes himself from all other thinking things, in this alone consists personal identity, i.e. the sameness of a rational being: and as far as this consciousness can be extended backwards to any past action or thought, so far reaches the identity of that person; it is the same self now as it was then; and it is by the same self with

this present one that now reflects on it, that that action was done.

10. But it is further inquired, whether it be the same identical substance. This few would think they had reason to doubt of, if these perceptions, with their consciousness, always remained present in the mind, whereby the same thinking thing would be always consciously present, and, as would be thought, evidently the same to itself. But that which seems to make the difficulty is this, that this consciousness being interrupted always by forgetfulness, there being no moment of our lives wherein we have the whole train of all our past actions before our eyes in one view, but even the best memories losing the sight of one part whilst they are viewing another; and we sometimes, and that the greatest part of our lives, not reflecting on our past selves, being intent on our present thoughts, and in sound sleep having no thoughts at all, or at least none with that consciousness which remarks our waking thoughts, — I say, in all these cases, our consciousness being interrupted, and we losing the sight of our past selves, doubts are raised whether we are the same thinking thing, i.e. the same *substance* or no. Which, however reasonable or unreasonable, concerns not *personal* identity at all. The question being what makes the same person; and not whether it be the same identical substance, which always thinks in the same person, which, in this case, matters not at all: different substances, by the same consciousness (where they do partake in it) being united into one person, as well as different bodies by the same life are united into one animal, whose identity is preserved in that change of substances by the unity of one continued life. For, it being the same consciousness that makes a man be himself to himself, personal identity depends on that only, whether it be annexed solely to one individual substance, or can be continued in a succession of several substances. For as far as any intelligent being *can* repeat the idea of any past action with the same consciousness it had of it at first, and with the same consciousness it has of any present action; so far it is the same personal self. For it is by the consciousness it has of its present thoughts and actions, that it is *self to itself* now, and so will be the same self, as far as the same consciousness can extend to actions past or to come; and would be by distance of time, or change of substance, no more two persons, than a man be two men by wearing other clothes today than he did yesterday, with a long or a short sleep between: the same consciousness uniting those distant actions into the same person, whatever substances contributed to their production.

11. That this is so, we have some kind of evidence in our very bodies, all whose particles, whilst vitally united to this same thinking conscious self, so that *we feel* when they are touched, and are affected by, and conscious of good or harm that happens to them, are a part of ourselves; i.e. of our thinking conscious self. Thus, the limbs of his body are to every one a part of himself; he sympathizes and is concerned for them. Cut off a hand, and thereby separate it from that consciousness he had of its heat, cold, and other affections, and it is then no longer a part of that which is himself, any more than the remotest part of matter. Thus, we see the *substance* whereof personal self consisted at one time may be varied at another, without the change of personal identity; there being no question about the same person, though the limbs which but now were a part of it, be cut off.

12. But the question is, Whether if the same substance which thinks be changed, it can be the same person; or, remaining the same, it can be different persons?

And to this I answer: First, This can be no question at all to those who place thought in a purely material animal constitution, void of an immaterial substance. For, whether their supposition be true or no, it is plain they conceive personal identity preserved in something else than identity of substance; as animal identity is preserved in identity of life, and not of substance. And therefore those who place thinking in an immaterial substance only, before they can come to deal with these men, must show why personal identity cannot be preserved in the change of immaterial substances, or variety of particular immaterial substances, as well as animal identity is preserved in the change of material substances, or variety of particular bodies: unless they will say, it is one immaterial spirit that makes the same life in brutes, as it is one immaterial spirit that makes the same person in men; which the Cartesians at least will not admit, for fear of making brutes thinking things too.

13. But next, as to the first part of the question, Whether, if the same thinking substance (supposing immaterial substances only to think) be changed, it can be the same person? I answer, that cannot be resolved but by those who know what kind of substances they are that do think; and whether the consciousness of past actions can be transferred from one thinking substance to another. I grant were the same consciousness the same individual action it could not: but it being a present representation of a past action, why it may not be possible, that that may be represented to the mind to have been which really never was, will remain to be shown. And therefore how far the consciousness of past

actions is annexed to any individual agent, so that another cannot possibly have it, will be hard for us to determine, till we know what kind of action it is that cannot be done without a reflex act of perception accompanying it, and how performed by thinking substances, who cannot think without being conscious of it. But that which we call the same consciousness, not being the same individual act, why one intellectual substance may not have represented to it, as done by itself, what *it* never did, and was perhaps done by some other agent — why, I say, such a representation may not possibly be without reality of matter of fact, as well as several representations in dreams are, which yet whilst dreaming we take for true — will be difficult to conclude from the nature of things. And that it never is so, will by us, till we have clearer views of the nature of thinking substances, be best resolved into the goodness of God; who, as far as the happiness or misery of any of his sensible creatures is concerned in it, will not, by a fatal error of theirs, transfer from one to another that consciousness which draws reward or punishment with it. How far this may be an argument against those who would place thinking in a system of fleeting animal spirits, I leave to be considered. But yet, to return to the question before us, it must be allowed, that, if the same consciousness (which, as has been shown, is quite a different thing from the same numerical figure or motion in body) can be transferred from one thinking substance to another, it will be possible that two thinking substances may make but one person. For the same consciousness being preserved, whether in the same or different substances, the personal identity is preserved.

14. As to the second part of the question, Whether the same immaterial substance remaining, there may be two distinct persons; which question seems to me to be built on this, — Whether the same immaterial being, being conscious of the action of its past duration, may be wholly stripped of all the consciousness of its past existence, and lose it beyond the power of ever retrieving it again: and so as it were beginning a new account from a new period, have a consciousness that *cannot* reach beyond this new state. All those who hold pre-existence are evidently of this mind; since they allow the soul to have no remaining consciousness of what it did in that pre-existent state, either wholly separate from body, or informing any other body; and if they should not, it is plain experience would be against them. So that personal identity, reaching no further than consciousness reaches, a pre-existent spirit not having continued so many ages in a state of silence, must needs make different persons. Suppose a Christian

Platonist or a Pythagorean should, upon God's having ended all his works of creation the seventh day, think his soul hath existed ever since; and should imagine it has revolved in several human bodies; as I once met with one, who was persuaded his had been the *soul* of Socrates (how reasonably I will not dispute; this I know, that in the post he filled, which was no inconsiderable one, he passed for a very rational man, and the press has shown that he wanted not parts or learning;) — would any one say, that he, being not conscious of any of Socrates's actions or thoughts, could be the same *person* with Socrates? Let any one reflect upon himself, and conclude that he has in himself an immaterial spirit, which is that which thinks in him, and, in the constant change of his body keeps him the same: and is that which he calls *himself*: let him also suppose it to be the same soul that was in Nestor or Thersites, at the siege of Troy, (for souls being, as far as we know anything of them, in their nature indifferent to any parcel of matter, the supposition has no apparent absurdity in it,) which it may have been, as well as it is now the soul of any other man: but he now having no consciousness of any of the actions either of Nestor or Thersites, does or can he conceive himself the same person with either of them? Can he be concerned in either of their actions? Attribute them to himself, or think them his own, more than the actions of any other men that ever existed? So that this consciousness, not reaching to any of the actions of either of those men, he is no more one *self* with either of them than if the soul or immaterial spirit that now informs him had been created, and began to exist, when it began to inform his present body; though it were never so true, that the same *spirit* that informed Nestor's or Thersites's body were numerically the same that now informs his. For this would no more make him the same person with Nestor, than if some of the particles of matter that were once a part of Nestor were now a part of this man; the same immaterial substance, without the same consciousness, no more making the same person, by being united to any body, than the same particle of matter, without consciousness, united to any body, makes the same person. But let him once find himself conscious of any of the actions of Nestor, he then finds himself the same person with Nestor.

15. And thus may we be able, without any difficulty, to conceive the same person at the resurrection, though in a body not exactly in make or parts the same which he had here, — the same consciousness going along with the soul that inhabits it. But yet the soul alone, in the change of bodies, would scarce to any one but to him that makes the soul the man, be enough to make

the same man. For should the soul of a prince, carrying with it the consciousness of the prince's past life, enter and inform the body of a cobbler, as soon as deserted by his own soul, every one sees he would be the same *person* with the prince, accountable only for the prince's actions: but who would say it was the same *man?* The body too goes to the making the man, and would, I guess, to everybody determine the man in this case, wherein the soul, with all its princely thoughts about it, would not make another man: but he would be the same cobbler to every one besides himself. I know that, in the ordinary way of speaking, the same person, and the same man, stand for one and the same thing. And indeed every one will always have a liberty to speak as he pleases, and to apply what articulate sounds to what ideas he thinks fit, and change them as often as he pleases. But yet, when we will inquire what makes the same *spirit, man* or *person,* we must fix the ideas of spirit, man, or person in our minds; and having resolved with ourselves what we mean by them, it will not be hard to determine, in either of them, or the like, when it is the same, and when not.

16. But though the same immaterial substance or soul does not alone, wherever it be, and in whatsoever state, make the same *man;* yet it is plain, consciousness, as far as ever it can be extended — should it be to ages past — unites existences and actions very remote in time into the same *person,* as well as it does the existences and actions of the immediately preceding moment: so that whatever has the consciousness of present and past actions, is the same person to whom they both belong. Had I the same consciousness that I saw the ark and Noah's flood, as that I saw an overflowing of the Thames last winter, or as that I write now, I could no more doubt that I who write this now, that saw the Thames overflowed last winter, and that viewed the flood at the general deluge, was the same *self,*—place that self in what *substance* you please—than that I who write this am the same *myself* now whilst I write (whether I consist of all the same substance, material or immaterial, or no) that I was yesterday. For as to this point of being the same self, it matters not whether this present self be made up of the same or other substances — I being as much concerned, and as justly accountable for any action that was done a thousand years since, appropriated to me now by this self-consciousness, as I am for what I did the last moment.

17. *Self* is that conscious thinking thing, — whatever substance made up of, (whether spiritual or material, simple or compounded, it matters not) — which is sensible or conscious of pleasure and pain, capable of happiness or misery, and so is concerned for itself, as far

as that consciousness extends. Thus every one finds that, whilst comprehended under that consciousness, the little finger is as much a part of himself as what is most so. Upon separation of this little finger, should this consciousness go along with the little finger, and leave the rest of the body, it is evident the little finger would be the person, the same person; and self then would have nothing to do with the rest of the body. As in this case it is the consciousness that goes along with the substance, when one part is separate from another, which makes the same person, and constitutes this inseparable self: so it is in reference to substances remote in time. That with which the consciousness of this present thinking thing *can* join itself, makes the same person, and is one self with it, and with nothing else; and so attributes to itself, and owns all the actions of that thing, as its own, as far as that consciousness reaches, and no further; as every one who reflects will perceive.

18. In this personal identity is founded all the right and justice of reward and punishment; happiness and misery being that for which every one is concerned for *himself*, and not mattering what becomes of any *substance*, not joined to, or affected with that consciousness. For, as it is evident in the instance I gave but now, if the consciousness went along with the little finger when it was cut off, that would be the same self which was concerned for the whole body yesterday, as making part of itself, whose actions then it cannot but admit as its own now. Though, if the same body should still live, and immediately from the separation of the little finger have its own peculiar consciousness, whereof the little finger knew nothing, it would not at all be concerned for it, as a part of itself, or could own any of its actions, or have any of them imputed to him.

19. This may show us wherein personal identity consists: not in the identity of substance, but, as I have said, in the identity of consciousness, wherein if Socrates and the present mayor of Queinborough agree, they are the same person: if the same Socrates waking and sleeping do not partake of the same consciousness, Socrates waking and sleeping is not the same person. And to punish Socrates waking for what sleeping Socrates thought, and waking Socrates was never conscious of, would be no more of right, than to punish one twin for what his brother-twin did, whereof he knew nothing, because their outsides were so like, that they could not be distinguished; for such twins have been seen.

20. But yet possibly it will still be objected, — Suppose I wholly lose the memory of some parts of my life, beyond a possibility of retrieving them, so that perhaps I shall never be conscious of them again; yet am I not the same person that did those actions, had those thoughts that I once was conscious of, though I have now forgot them? To which I answer, that we must here take notice what the word *I* is applied to; which, in this case, is the *man* only. And the same man being presumed to be the same person, I is easily here supposed to stand also for the same person. But if it be possible for the same man to have distinct incommunicable consciousness at different times, it is past doubt the same man would at different times make different persons; which, we see, is the sense of mankind in the solemnest declaration of their opinions, human laws not punishing the mad man for the sober man's actions, nor the sober man for what the mad man did, — thereby making them two persons: which is somewhat explained by our way of speaking in English when we say such an one is "not himself," or is "beside himself"; in which phrases it is insinuated, as if those who now, or at least first used them, thought that self was changed; the self-same person was no longer in that man.

21. But yet it is hard to conceive that Socrates, the same individual man, should be two persons. To help us a little in this, we must consider what is meant by Socrates, or the same individual *man*.

First, it must be either the same individual, immaterial, thinking substance; in short, the same numerical soul, and nothing else.

Secondly, or the same animal, without any regard to an immaterial soul.

Thirdly, or the same immaterial spirit united to the same animal.

Now, take which of these suppositions you please, it is impossible to make personal identity to consist in anything but consciousness; or reach any further than that does.

For, by the first of them it must be allowed possible that a man born of different women, and in distant times, may be the same man. A way of speaking which, whoever admits, must allow it possible for the same man to be two distinct persons, as any two that have lived in different ages without the knowledge of one another's thoughts.

By the second and third, Socrates, in this life and after it, cannot be the same man any way, but by the same consciousness; and so making human identity to consist in the same thing wherein we place personal identity, there will be no difficulty to allow the same man to be the same person. But then they who place human identity in consciousness only, and not in something else, must consider how they will make the infant Socrates the same man with Socrates after the resurrection. But whatsoever to some men makes a man, and consequently the same individual man, wherein perhaps few are agreed, personal identity can by us be placed in nothing but consciousness, (which is that alone which makes what we call *self,*) without involving us in great absurdities.

22. But is not a man drunk and sober the same person? Why else is he punished for the act he commits when drunk, though he be never afterwards conscious of it? Just as much the same person as a man that walks, and does other things in his sleep, is the same person, and is answerable for any mischief he shall do in it. Human laws punish both, with a justice suitable to *their* way of knowledge;—because, in these cases, they cannot distinguish certainly what is real, what counterfeit: and so the ignorance in drunkenness or sleep is not admitted as a plea. For, though punishment be annexed to personality, and personality to consciousness, and the drunkard perhaps be not conscious of what he did, yet human judicatures justly punish him; because the fact is proved against him, but want of consciousness cannot be proved for him. But in the Great Day, wherein the secrets of all hearts shall be laid open, it may be reasonable to think, no one shall be made to answer for what he knows nothing of; but shall receive his doom, his conscience accusing or excusing him.

23. Nothing but consciousness can unite remote existences into the same person: the identity of substance will not do it; for whatever substance there is, however framed, without consciousness there is no person: and a carcass may be a person, as well as any sort of substance be so, without consciousness.

Could we suppose two distinct incommunicable consciousnesses acting the same body, the one constantly by day, the other by night; and, on the other side, the same consciousness, acting by intervals, two distinct bodies: I ask, in the first case, whether the day and the night—man would not be two as distinct persons as Socrates and Plato? And whether, in the second case, there would not be one person in two distinct bodies, as much as one man is the same in two distinct clothings? Nor is it at all material to say, that this same, and this distinct consciousness, in the cases above mentioned, is owing to the same and distinct immaterial substances, bringing it with them to those bodies; which, whether true or no, alters not the case: since it is evident the personal identity would equally be determined by the consciousness, whether that consciousness were annexed to some individual immaterial substance or no. For, granting that the thinking substance in man must be necessarily supposed immaterial, it is evident that immaterial thinking thing may sometimes part with its past consciousness, and be restored to it again: as appears in the forgetfulness men often have of their past

actions; and the mind many times recovers the memory of a past consciousness, which it had lost for twenty years together. Make these intervals of memory and forgetfulness to take their turns regularly by day and night, and you have two persons with the same immaterial spirit, as much as in the former instance two persons with the same body. So that self is not determined by identity or diversity of substance, which it cannot be sure of, but only by identity of consciousness.

24. Indeed it may conceive the substance whereof it is now made up to have existed formerly, united in the same conscious being: but, consciousness removed, that substance is no more itself, or makes no more a part of it, than any other substance; as is evident in the instance we have already given of a limb cut off, of whose heat, or cold, or other affections, having no longer any consciousness, it is no more of a man's self than any other matter of the universe. In like manner it will be in reference to any immaterial substance, which is void of that consciousness whereby I am myself to myself: if there be any part of its existence which I cannot upon recollection join with that present consciousness whereby I am now myself, it is, in that part of its existence, no more *myself* than any other immaterial being. For, whatsoever any substance has thought or done, which I cannot recollect, and by my consciousness make my own thought and action, it will no more belong to me, whether a part of me thought or did it, than if it had been thought or done by any other immaterial being anywhere existing.

25. I agree, the more probable opinion is, that this consciousness is annexed to, and the affection of, one individual immaterial substance.

But let men, according to their diverse hypotheses, resolve of that as they please. This every intelligent being, sensible of happiness or misery, must grant— that there is something that is *himself,* that he is concerned for, and would have happy; that this self has existed in a continued duration more than one instant, and therefore it is possible may exist, as it has done, months and years to come, without any certain bounds to be set to its duration; and may be the same self, by the same consciousness continued on for the future. And thus, by this consciousness he finds himself to be the same self which did such and such an action some years since, by which he comes to be happy or miserable now. In all which account of self, the same numerical *substance* is not considered as making the same self; but the same continued *consciousness,* in which several substances may have been united, and again separated from it, which, whilst they continued in a vital union with that wherein this consciousness then resided, made a part of that same self. Thus any part of our bodies, vitally united to that which is conscious in us, makes a part of ourselves: but upon separation from the vital union by which that consciousness is communicated, that which a moment since was part of ourselves, is now no more so than a part of another man's self is a part of me: and it is not impossible but in a little time may become a real part of another person. And so we have the same numerical substance become a part of two different persons; and the same person preserved under the change of various substances. Could we suppose any spirit wholly stripped of all its memory or consciousness of past actions, as we find our minds always are of a great part of ours, and sometimes of them all; the union or separation of such a spiritual substance would make no variation of personal identity, any more than that of any particle of matter does. Any substance vitally united to the present thinking being is a part of that very same self which now is; anything united to it by a consciousness of former actions, makes also a part of the same self, which is the same both then and now.

26. *Person*, as I take it, is the name for this self. Wherever a man finds what he calls himself, there, I think, another may say is the same person. It is a forensic term, appropriating actions and their merit; and so belongs only to intelligent agents, capable of a law, and happiness, and misery. This personality extends itself beyond present existence to what is past, only by consciousness, — whereby it becomes concerned and accountable; owns and imputes to itself past actions, just upon the same ground and for the same reason as it does the present. All which is founded in a concern for happiness, the unavoidable concomitant of consciousness; that which is conscious of pleasure and pain, desiring the self that is conscious should be happy. And therefore whatever past actions it cannot reconcile or *appropriate* to that present self by consciousness, it can be no more concerned in than if they had never been done: and to receive pleasure or pain, i.e. reward or punishment, on the account of any such action, is all one as to be made happy or miserable in its first being, without any demerit at all. For, supposing a *man* punished now for what he had done in another life, whereof he could be made to have no consciousness at all, what difference is there between that punishment and being *created* miserable? And therefore, conformable to this, the apostle tells us, that, at the great day, when every one shall "receive according to his doings, the secrets of all hearts shall be laid open." The sentence shall be justified by the consciousness all persons shall have, that *they themselves*, in what bodies soever they appear, or what substances soever that consciousness adheres to, are the *same* that committed those actions, and deserve that punishment for them.

On Mr. Locke's Account of Personal Identity

Thomas Reid (1710–1796) was the founder of the Scottish, or commonsense, school of philosophy. Many of his works are devoted to countering the skeptical conclusions of the British empiricists. His works include *Inquiry into the Human Mind on the Principles of Common Sense, Essays on the Intellectual Powers of Man*, and *Essays on the Active Powers of Man*. In this selection, he demonstrates by means of a thought experiment that John Locke's theory of personal identity cannot be correct.

In a long chapter upon identity and diversity, Mr. Locke has made many ingenious and just observations, and some which, I think, cannot be defended. I shall only take notice of the account he gives of our own personal identity. His doctrine upon this subject has been censured by bishop Butler, in a short essay subjoined to his Analogy, with whose sentiments I perfectly agree.

Identity, as was observed chap. 4, of this Essay, supposes the continued existence of the being of which it is affirmed, and therefore can be applied only to things which have a continued existence. While any being continues to exist, it is the same being; but two beings which have a different beginning or a different ending of their existence, cannot possibly be the same. To this I think Mr. Locke agrees.

He observes very justly, that to know what is meant by the same person, we must consider what the word *person* stands for; and he defines a person to be an intelligent being, endowed with reason and with consciousness, which last he thinks inseparable from thought.

From this definition of a person, it must necessarily follow, that while the intelligent being continues to exist and to be intelligent, it must be the same person. To say that the intelligent being is the person, and yet that the person ceases to exist, while the intelligent being continues, or that the person continues while the intelligent being ceases to exist, is, to my apprehension, a manifest contradiction.

One would think that the definition of a person should perfectly ascertain the nature of personal identity, or wherein it consists, though it might still be a question how we come to know and be assured of our personal identity.

Mr. Locke tells us, however, "that personal identity, that is, the sameness of a rational being, consists in consciousness alone; and, as far as this consciousness can be extended backward to any past action or thought, so far reaches the identity of that person. So that whatever has the consciousness of present and past actions, is the same person to whom they belong."

This doctrine has some strange consequences, which the author was aware of. Such as, that if the same consciousness can be transferred from one intelligent being to another, which he thinks we cannot show to be impossible, then two or twenty intelligent beings may be the same person. And if the intelligent being may lose the consciousness of the actions done by him, which surely is possible, then he is not the person that did those actions; so that one intelligent being may be two or twenty different persons, if he shall so often lose the consciousness of his former actions.

There is another consequence of this doctrine, which follows no less necessarily, though Mr. Locke probably did not see it. It is, that a man may be, and at the same time not be, the person that did a particular action.

Suppose a brave officer to have been flogged when a boy at school, for robbing an orchard, to have taken a standard from the enemy in his first campaign, and to have been made a general in advanced life. Suppose also, which must be admitted to be possible, that when he took the standard, he was conscious of his having been flogged at school; and that when made a general, he was conscious of his taking the standard, but had absolutely lost the consciousness of his flogging.

These things being supposed, it follows, from Mr. Locke's doctrine, that he who was flogged at school is the same person who took the standard; and that he who took the standard is the same person who was

---

From: Thomas Reid, *Essays on the Intellectual Powers of Man* (Charlestown, MA: Samuel Etheridge, Jr., 1813) 356–362.

made a general. Whence it follows, if there be any truth in logic, that the general is the same person with him who was flogged at school. But the general's consciousness does not reach so far back as his flogging, therefore, according to Mr. Locke's doctrine, he is not the person who was flogged. Therefore the general is, and at the same time is not, the same person with him who was flogged at school.

Leaving the consequences of this doctrine to those who have leisure to trace them, we may observe, with regard to the doctrine itself;

1st, That Mr. Locke attributes to consciousness the conviction we have of our past actions, as if a man may now be conscious of what he did twenty years ago. It is impossible to understand the meaning of this, unless by consciousness he meant memory, the only faculty by which we have an immediate knowledge of our past actions.

Sometimes, in popular discourse, a man says he is conscious that he did such a thing, meaning that he distinctly remembers that he did it. It is unnecessary, in common discourse, to fix accurately the limits between consciousness and memory. This was formerly shown to be the case with regard to sense and memory: and therefore distinct remembrance is sometimes called sense, sometimes consciousness, without any inconvenience.

But this ought to be avoided in philosophy, otherwise we confound the different powers of the mind, and ascribe to one what really belongs to another. If a man can be conscious of what he did twenty years, or twenty minutes ago, there is no use for memory, nor ought we to allow that there is any such faculty. The faculties of consciousness and memory are chiefly distinguished by this, that the first is an immediate knowledge of the present, the second an immediate knowledge of the past.

When, therefore, Mr. Locke's notion of personal identity is properly expressed, it is, that personal identity consists in distinct remembrance: for, even in the popular sense, to say that I am conscious of a past action, means nothing else than that I distinctly remember that I did it.

2dly, It may be observed, that in this doctrine, not only is consciousness confounded with memory, but, which is still more strange, personal identity is confounded with the evidence which we have of our personal identity.

It is very true, that my remembrance that I did such a thing is the evidence I have that I am the identical person who did it. And this, I am apt to think, Mr. Locke meant: but to say that my remembrance that I did such a thing, or my consciousness, makes me the person who did it, is, in my apprehension, an absurdity too gross to be entertained by any man who attends to the meaning of it: for it is to attribute to memory or consciousness, a strange magical power of producing its object, though that object must have existed before the memory or consciousness which produced it.

Consciousness is the testimony of one faculty; memory is the testimony of another faculty: and to say that the testimony is the cause of the thing testified, this surely is absurd, if any thing be, and could not have been said by Mr. Locke, if he had not confounded the testimony with the thing testified.

When a horse that was stolen is found and claimed by the owner, the only evidence he can have, or that a judge or witnesses can have, that this is the very identical horse which was his property, is similitude.

But would it not be ridiculous from this to infer that the identity of a horse consists in similitude only? The only evidence I have that I am the identical person who did such actions, is, that I remember distinctly I did them; or, as Mr. Locke expresses it, I am conscious I did them. To infer from this, that personal identity consists in consciousness, is an argument, which, if it had any force, would prove the identity of a stolen horse to consist solely in similitude.

3dly, Is it not strange that the sameness or identity of a person should consist in a thing which is continually changing, and is not any two minutes the same?

Our consciousness, our memory, and every operation of the mind, are still flowing like the water of a river, or like time itself. The consciousness I have this moment can no more be the same consciousness I had last moment, than this moment can be the last moment. Identity can only be affirmed of things which have a continued existence. Consciousness, and every kind of thought, is transient and momentary, and has no continued existence; and therefore, if personal identity consisted in consciousness, it would certainly follow, that no man is the same person any two moments of his life; and as the right and justice of reward and punishment is founded on personal identity, no man could be responsible for his actions.

But though I take this to be the unavoidable consequence of Mr. Locke's doctrine concerning personal identity, and though some persons may have liked the doctrine the better on this account, I am far from imputing any thing of this kind to Mr. Locke. He was too good a man not to have rejected with abhorrence a doctrine which he believed to draw this consequence after it.

4thly, There are many expressions used by Mr. Locke in speaking of personal identity, which to me are altogether unintelligible, unless we suppose that he confounded that sameness, or identity, which we ascribe to an individual, with the identity which in common discourse is often ascribed to many individuals of the same species.

When we say that pain and pleasure, consciousness and memory, are the same in all men, this sameness can only mean similarity, or sameness of kind; but that the pain of one man can be the same individual pain with that of another man, is no less impossible, than that one man should be another man; the pain felt by me yesterday, can no more be the pain I feel today, than yesterday can be this day; and the same thing may be said of every passion and of every operation of the mind. The same kind or species of operation may be in different men, or in the same man at different times; but it is impossible that the same individual operation should be in different men, or in the same man at different times.

When Mr. Locke therefore speaks of "the same consciousness being continued through a succession of different substances;" when he speaks of "repeating the idea of a past action, with the same consciousness we had of it at the first," and of "the same consciousness extending to actions past and to come;" these expressions are to me unintelligible, unless he means, not the same individual consciousness, but a consciousness that is similar, or of the same kind.

If our personal identity consists in consciousness, as this consciousness cannot be the same individually any two moments, but only of the same kind, it would follow, that we are not for any two moments the same individual persons, but the same kind of persons.

As our consciousness sometimes ceases to exist, as in sound sleep, our personal identity must cease with it. Mr. Locke allows, that the same thing cannot have two beginnings of existence, so that our identity would be irrecoverably gone every time we cease to think, if it was but for a moment.

DEREK PARFIT

Divided Minds and the Nature of Persons

Derek Parfit (1942–) is a philosopher at All Souls College at Oxford. His book *Reasons and Persons* has had a major influence on theories of ethics as well as theories of personal identity. In this essay, he argues that the reason it is so hard to come up with theories of personal identity is that there are no persons.

It was the split-brain cases which drew me into philosophy. Our knowledge of these cases depends on the results of various psychological tests, as described by Donald MacKay. These tests made use of two facts. We control each of our arms, and see what is in each half of our visual fields, with only one of our hemispheres. When someone's hemispheres have been disconnected, psychologists can thus present to this person two different written questions in the two halves of his visual field, and can receive two different answers written by this person's two hands.

Here is a simplified imaginary version of the kind of evidence that such tests provide. One of these people looks fixedly at the centre of a wide screen, whose left half is red and right half is blue. On each half in a darker shade are the words, 'How many colours can you see?' With both hands the person writes, 'Only one'. The words are now changed to read, 'Which is the only colour that you can see?' With one of his hands the person writes 'Red', with the other he writes 'Blue'.

If this is how such a person responds, I would conclude that he is having two visual sensations–that he does, as he claims, see both red and blue. But in seeing each colour he is not aware of seeing the other. He has two streams of consciousness, in each of which he can see only one colour. In one stream he sees red, and at the same time, in his other stream, he sees blue. More generally, he could be having at the same time two series of thoughts and sensations, in having each of which he is unaware of having the other.

This conclusion has been questioned. It has been claimed by some that there are not *two* streams of consciousness, on the ground that the sub-dominant hemisphere is a part of the brain whose functioning involves no consciousness. If this were true, these cases would lose most of their interest. I believe that it is not true, chiefly because, if a person's dominant hemisphere is destroyed, this person is able to react in the way in which, in the split-brain cases, the sub-dominant hemisphere reacts, and we do not believe that such a person

is just an automaton, without consciousness. The sub-dominant hemisphere is, of course, much less developed in certain ways, typically having the linguistic abilities of a three-year-old. But three-year-olds are conscious. This supports the view that, in split-brain cases, there *are* two streams of consciousness.

Another view is that, in these cases, there are two persons involved, sharing the same body. Like Professor MacKay, I believe that we should reject this view. My reason for believing this is, however, different. Professor MacKay denies that there are two persons involved because he believes that there is only one person involved. I believe that, in a sense, the number of persons involved is none.

The Ego Theory and the Bundle Theory

To explain this sense I must, for a while, turn away from the split-brain cases. There are two theories about what persons are, and what is involved in a person's continued existence over time. On the *Ego Theory*, a person's continued existence cannot be explained except as the continued existence of a particular *Ego*, or *subject of experiences*. An Ego Theorist claims that, if we ask what unifies someone's consciousness at any time — what makes it true, for example, that I can now both see what I am typing and hear the wind outside my window — the answer is that these are both experiences which are being had by me, this person, at this time. Similarly, what explains the unity of a person's whole life is the fact that all of the experiences in this life are had by the same person, or subject of experiences. In its best-known form, the *Cartesian view*, each person is a persisting purely mental thing — a soul, or spiritual substance.

From: Derek Parfit, "Divided Minds and the Nature of Persons," *Mindwaves*, ed. C. Blakemore and S. Greenfield (London: Basil Blackwell, 1987) 19–25. Notes have been omitted.

The rival view is the *Bundle Theory*. Like most styles in art — Gothic, baroque, rococo, etc. — this theory owes its name to its critics. But the name is good enough. According to the Bundle Theory, we can't explain either the unity of consciousness at any time, or the unity of a whole life, by referring to a person. Instead we must claim that there are long series of different mental states and events — thoughts, sensations, and the like — each series being what we call one life. Each series is unified by various kinds of causal relation such as the relations that hold between experiences and later memories of them. Each series is thus like a bundle tied up with string.

In a sense, a Bundle Theorist denies the existence of persons. An outright denial is of course absurd. As Reid protested in the eighteenth century, 'I am not thought, I am not action, I am not feeling; I am something which thinks and acts and feels.' I am not a series of events, but a person. A Bundle Theorist admits this fact, but claims it to be only a fact about our grammar, or our language. There are persons or subjects in this language-dependent way. If, however, persons are believed to be more than this — to be separately existing things, distinct from our brains and bodies, and the various kinds of mental states and events—the Bundle Theorist denies that there are such things.

The first Bundle Theorist was Buddha, who taught 'anatta', or the *No Self view*. Buddhists concede that selves or persons have 'nominal existence', by which they mean that persons are merely combinations of other elements. Only what exists by itself, as a separate element, has instead what Buddhists call 'actual existence'. Here are some quotations from Buddhist texts:

> At the beginning of their conversation the king politely asks the monk his name, and receives the following reply: 'Sir, I am known as "Nagasena"; my fellows in the religious life address me as "Nagasena". Although my parents gave me the name . . . it is just an appellation, a form of speech, a description, a conventional usage. "Nagasena" is only a name, for no person is found here.'

> A sentient being does exist, you think, O Mara? You are misled by a false conception. This bundle of elements is void of Self, In it there is no sentient being. Just as a set of wooden parts Receives the name of carriage, So do we give to elements The name of fancied being.

> Buddha has spoken thus: 'O Brethren, actions do exist, and also their consequences, but the person that acts does not. There is no one to cast away this set of elements, and no one to assume a new set of them. There exists no Individual, it is only a conventional name given to a set of elements.'

Buddha's claims are strikingly similar to the claims advanced by several Western writers. Since these writers knew nothing of Buddha, the similarity of these claims suggests that they are not merely part of one cultural tradition, in one period. They may be, as I believe they are, true.

What We Believe Ourselves to Be

Given the advances in psychology and neurophysiology, the Bundle Theory may now seem to be obviously true. It may seem uninteresting to deny that there are separately existing Egos, which are distinct from brains and bodies and the various kinds of mental states and events. But this is not the only issue. We may be convinced that the Ego Theory is false, or even senseless. Most of us, however, even if we are not aware of this, also have certain beliefs about what is involved in our continued existence over time. And these beliefs would only be justified if something like the Ego Theory was true. Most of us therefore have false beliefs about what persons are, and about ourselves.

These beliefs are best revealed when we consider certain imaginary cases, often drawn from science fiction. One such case is *teletransportation*. Suppose that you enter a cubicle in which, when you press a button, a scanner records the states of all of the cells in your brain and body, destroying both while doing so. This information is then transmitted at the speed of light to some other planet, where a replicator produces a perfect organic copy of you. Since the brain of your Replica is exactly like yours, it will seem to remember living your life up to the moment when you pressed the button, its character will be just like yours, and it will be in every other way psychologically continuous with you. This psychological continuity will not have its normal cause, the continued existence of your brain, since the causal chain will run through the transmission by radio of your 'blueprint'.

Several writers claim that, if you chose to be teletransported, believing this to be the fastest way of travelling, you would be making a terrible mistake. This would not be a way of travelling, but a way of dying. It may not, they concede, be quite as bad as ordinary death. It might be some consolation to you that, after your death, you will have this Replica, which can finish the book that you are writing, act as parent to your children, and so on. But, they insist, this Replica won't be you. It will merely be someone else, who is exactly like you. This is why this prospect is nearly as bad as ordinary death.

Imagine next a whole range of cases, in each of which, in a single operation, a different proportion of the cells in your brain and body would be replaced with exact duplicates. At the near end of this range, only 1 or 2 per cent would be replaced; in the middle, 40 or 60 per cent; near the far end, 98 or 99 per cent. At the far end of this range is pure teletransportation, the case in which all of your cells would be 'replaced'.

When you imagine that some proportion of your cells will be replaced with exact duplicates, it is natural to have the following beliefs. First, if you ask, 'Will I survive? Will the resulting person be me?', there must be an answer to this question. Either you will survive, or you are about to die. Second, the answer to this question must be either a simple 'Yes' or a simple 'No'. The person who wakes up either will or will not be you. There cannot be a third answer, such as that the person waking up will be half you. You can imagine yourself later being half-conscious. But if the resulting person will be fully conscious, he cannot be half you. To state these beliefs together: to the question, 'Will the resulting person be me?', there must always *be* an answer, which must be all-or-nothing.

There seem good grounds for believing that, in the case of teletransportation, your Replica would not be you. In a slight variant of this case, your Replica might be created while you were still alive, so that you could talk to one another. This seems to show that, if 100 per cent of your cells were replaced, the result would merely be a Replica of you. At the other end of my range of cases, where only 1 per cent would be replaced, the resulting person clearly *would* be you. It therefore seems that, in the cases in between, the resulting person must be either you, or merely a Replica. It seems that one of these must be true, and that it makes a great difference which is true.

How We Are Not What We Believe

If these beliefs were correct, there must be some critical percentage, somewhere in this range of cases, up to which the resulting person would be you, and beyond which he would merely be your Replica. Perhaps, for example, it would be you who would wake up if the proportion of cells replaced were 49 per cent, but if just a few more cells were also replaced, this would make all the difference, causing it to be someone else who would wake up.

That there must be some such critical percentage follows from our natural beliefs. But this conclusion is most implausible. How could a few cells make such a difference? Moreover, if there is such a critical percentage, no one could ever discover where it came. Since in all these cases the resulting person would believe that he was you, there could never be any evidence about where, in this range of cases, he would suddenly cease to be you.

On the Bundle Theory, we should reject these natural beliefs. Since you, the person, are not a separately existing entity, we can know exactly what would happen without answering the question of what will happen to you. Moreover, in the cases in the middle of my range, it is an empty question whether the resulting person would be you, or would merely be someone else who is exactly like you. These are not here two different possibilities, one of which must be true. These are merely two different descriptions of the very same course of events. If 50 per cent of your cells were replaced with exact duplicates, we could call the resulting person you, or we could call him merely your Replica. But since these are not here different possibilities, this is a mere choice of words.

As Buddha claimed, the Bundle Theory is hard to believe. It is hard to accept that it could be an empty question whether one is about to die, or will instead live for many years.

What we are being asked to accept may be made clearer with this analogy. Suppose that a certain club exists for some time, holding regular meetings. The meetings then cease. Some years later, several people form a club with the same name, and the same rules. We can ask, 'Did these people revive the very same club? Or did they merely start up another club which is exactly similar?' Given certain further details, this would be another empty question. We could know just what happened without answering this question. Suppose that someone said: 'But there must be an answer. The club meeting later must either be, or not be, the very same club.' This would show that this person didn't understand the nature of clubs.

In the same way, if we have any worries about my imagined cases, we don't understand the nature of persons. In each of my cases, you would know that the resulting person would be both psychologically and physically exactly like you, and that he would have some particular proportion of the cells in your brain and body—90 per cent, or 10 per cent, or, in the case of teletransportation, 0 per cent. Knowing this, you know everything. How could it be a real question what would happen to you, unless you are a separately existing Ego, distinct from a brain and body, and the various kinds of mental state and event? If there are no such Egos, there is nothing else to ask a real question about.

Accepting the Bundle Theory is not only hard; it may also affect our emotions. As Buddha claimed, it may undermine our concern about our own futures. This effect can be suggested by redescribing this change of view. Suppose that you are about to be destroyed, but will later have a Replica on Mars. You would naturally believe that this prospect is about as bad as ordinary death, since your Replica won't be you. On the Bundle Theory, the fact that your Replica won't be you just consists in the fact that, though it will be fully psychologically continuous with you, this continuity won't have its normal cause. But when you object to teletransportation you are not objecting merely to the abnormality of this cause. You are objecting that this cause won't get *you* to Mars. You fear that the abnormal cause will fail to produce a further and all-important fact, which is different from the fact that your Replica will be psychologically continuous with you. You do not merely want there to be psychological continuity between you and some future person. You want to be this future person. On the Bundle Theory, there is no such special further fact. What you fear will not happen, in this imagined case, *never* happens. You want the person on Mars to be you in a specially intimate way in which no future person will ever be you. This means that, judged from the standpoint of your natural beliefs, even ordinary survival is about as bad as teletransportation. *Ordinary survival is about as bad as being destroyed and having a Replica.*

How the Split-Brain Cases Support the Bundle Theory

The truth of the Bundle Theory seems to me, in the widest sense, as much a scientific as a philosophical conclusion. I can imagine kinds of evidence which would have justified believing in the existence of separately existing Egos, and believing that the continued existence of these Egos is what explains the continuity of each mental life. But there is in fact very little evidence in favour of this Ego Theory, and much for the alternative Bundle Theory.

Some of this evidence is provided by the split-brain cases. On the Ego Theory, to explain what unifies our experiences at any one time, we should simply claim that these are all experiences which are being had by the same person. Bundle Theorists reject this explanation. This disagreement is hard to resolve in ordinary

cases. But consider the simplified split-brain case that I described. We show to my imagined patient a placard whose left half is blue and right half is red. In one of this person's two streams of consciousness, he is aware of seeing only blue, while at the same time, in his other stream, he is aware of seeing only red. Each of these two visual experiences is combined with other experiences, like that of being aware of moving one of his hands. What unifies the experiences, at any time, in each of this person's two streams of consciousness? What unifies his awareness of seeing only red with his awareness of moving one hand? The answer cannot be that these experiences are being had by the same person. This answer cannot explain the unity of each of this person's two streams of consciousness, since it ignores the disunity between these streams. This person is now having all of the experiences in both of his two streams. If this fact was what unified these experiences, this would make the two streams one.

These cases do not, I have claimed, involve two people sharing a single body. Since there is only one person involved, who has two streams of consciousness, the Ego Theorist's explanation would have to take the following form. He would have to distinguish between persons and subjects of experiences, and claim that, in split-brain cases, there are *two* of the latter. What unifies the experiences in one of the person's two streams would have to be the fact that these experiences are all being had by the same subject of experiences. What unifies the experiences in this person's other stream would have to be the fact that they are being had by another subject of experiences. When this explanation takes this form, it becomes much less plausible. While we could assume that 'subject of experiences', or 'Ego', simply meant 'person', it was easy to believe that there are subjects of experiences. But if there can be subjects of experiences that are not persons, and if in the life of a split-brain patient there are at any time two different subjects of experiences—two different Egos—why should we believe that there really are such things? This does not amount to a refutation. But it seems to me a strong argument against the Ego Theory.

As a Bundle Theorist, I believe that these two Egos are idle cogs. There is another explanation of the unity of consciousness, both in ordinary cases and in split-brain cases. It is simply a fact that ordinary people are, at any time, aware of having several different experiences. This awareness of several different experiences can be helpfully compared with one's awareness, in short-term memory, of several different experiences. Just as there can be a single memory of just having had several experiences, such as hearing a bell strike three times, there can be a single state of awareness both of hearing the fourth striking of this bell, and of seeing, at the same time, ravens flying past the bell-tower.

Unlike the Ego Theorist's explanation, this explanation can easily be extended to cover split-brain cases. In such cases there is, at any time, not one state of awareness of several different experiences, but two such states. In the case I described, there is one state of awareness of both seeing only red and of moving one hand, and there is another state of awareness of both seeing only blue and moving the other hand. In claiming that there are two such states of awareness, we are not postulating the existence of unfamiliar entities, two separately existing Egos which are not the same as the single person whom the case involves. This explanation appeals to a pair of mental states which would have to be described anyway in a full description of this case.

I have suggested how the split-brain cases provide one argument for one view about the nature of persons.

I should mention another such argument, provided by an imagined extension of these cases, first discussed at length by David Wiggins.

In this imagined case a person's brain is divided, and the two halves are transplanted into a pair of different bodies. The two resulting people live quite separate lives. This imagined case shows that personal identity is not what matters. If I was about to divide, I should conclude that neither of the resulting people will be me. I will have ceased to exist. But this way of ceasing to exist is about as good — or as bad — as ordinary survival.

Some of the features of Wiggins's imagined case are likely to remain technically impossible. But the case cannot be dismissed, since its most striking feature, the division of one stream of consciousness into separate streams, has already happened. This is a second way in which the actual split-brain cases have great theoretical importance. They challenge some of our deepest assumptions about ourselves.

Live Forever

Ray Kurzweil (1948–) is an entrepreneur and inventor who developed the world's first print-to-speech reading machine for the blind and the first music synthesizer capable of re-creating the sound of a grand piano. He is the author of *The Age of Spiritual Machines: When Computers Exceed Human Intelligence*. In this selection, he discusses various ways computer technology could extend human life.

Thought to Implant 4: OnNet, please.

Hundreds of shimmering thumbnail images mist into view, spread fairly evenly across the entire field of pseudovision.

Thought: Zoom upper left, higher, into Winston's image.

Transmit: It's Nellie. Let's connect and chat over croissants. Rue des Enfants, Paris in the spring, our favorite table, yes?

Four-second pause.

Background thought: Damn it. What's taking him so long?

Receive: I'm here, ma chère, I'm here! Let's do it!

The thumbnail field mists away, and a cafe scene swirls into place. Scent of honeysuckle. Pâté. Wine. Light breeze. Nellie is seated at a quaint table with a plain white tablecloth. An image of Winston looking 20 and buff mists in across from her. Message thumbnails occasionally blink against the sky.

Winston: It's so good to see you again, ma chère! It's been months! And what a gorgeous choice of bodies! The eyes are a dead giveaway, though. You always pick those raspberry eyes. Très bold, Nellita. So what's the occasion? Part of me is in the middle of a business meeting in Chicago, so can't dally.

Nellie: Why do you always put on that muscleman body, Winston? You know how much I like your real one. Winston morphs into a man in his early 50s, still overly muscular.

Winston: (laughing) My real body? How droll! No one but my neurotechnician has seen it for years! Believe me, that's not what you want. I can do much better! He fans rapidly through a thousand images, and Nellie grimaces.

Nellie: Damn it! You're just one of Winston's MI's! Where is the real Winston? I know I used the right connection!

Winston: Nellie, I'm sorry to have to tell you this. There was a transporter accident a few weeks ago in Evanston, and well, I'm lucky they got to me in time for the full upload. I'm all of Winston that's left. The body's gone.

When Nellie contacts her friend Winston through the Internet connection in her brain, he is already, biologically speaking, dead. It is his electronic mind double, a virtual reality twin, that greets Nellie in their virtual Parisian cafe. What's surprising here is not so much the notion that human minds may someday live on inside computers after their bodies have expired. It's the fact that this vignette is closer at hand than most people realize. Within 30 years, the minds in those computers may just be our own.

The history of technology has shown over and over that as one mode of technology exhausts its potential, a new more sophisticated paradigm emerges to keep us moving at an exponential pace. Between 1910 and 1950, computer technology doubled in power every three years; between 1950 and 1966, it doubled every two years; and it has recently been doubling every year.

By the year 2020, your $1,000 personal computer will have the processing power of the human brain—20 million billion calculations per second (100 billion neurons times 1,000 connections per neuron times 200 calculations per second per connection). By 2030, it will take a village of human brains to match a $1,000 computer. By 2050, $1,000 worth of computing will equal the processing power of all human brains on earth.

Of course, achieving the processing power of the human brain is necessary but not sufficient for creating

---

From: Ray Kurzweil, "Live Forever," *Psychology Today* Jan. 2000: 66–71.

human level intelligence in a machine. But by 2030, we'll have the means to scan the human brain and re-create its design electronically.

Most people don't realize the revolutionary impact of that. The development of computers that match and vastly exceed the capabilities of the human brain will be no less important than the evolution of human intelligence itself some thousands of generations ago. Current predictions overlook the imminence of a world in which machines become more like humans — pro-grammed with replicated brain synapses that recreate the ability to respond appropriately to human emo-tion, and humans become more like machines — our biological bodies and brains enhanced with billions of "nanobots," swarms of microscopic robots transporting us in and out of virtual reality. We have already started down this road: Human and machine have already begun to meld.

It starts with uploading, or scanning the brain into a computer. One scenario is invasive: One very thin slice at a time, scientists input a brain of choice — having been frozen just slightly before it was going to die — at an extremely high speed. This way, they can easily see every neuron, every connection and every neuro-transmitter concentration represented in each synapse-thin layer.

Seven years ago, a condemned killer allowed his brain and body to be scanned in this way, and you can access all 10 billion bytes of him on the Internet. You can see for yourself every bone, muscle and section of gray matter in his body. But the scan is not yet at a high enough resolution to recreate the interneuronal con-nections, synapses and neurotransmitter concentra-tions that are the key to capturing the individuality within a human brain.

Our scanning machines today can clearly capture neural features as long as the scanner is very close to the source. Within 30 years, however, we will be able to send billions of nanobots — blood cell–size scanning machines — through every capillary of the brain to create a complete noninvasive scan of every neural feature. A shot full of nanobots will someday allow the most subtle details of our knowledge, skills and personalities to be copied into a file and stored in a computer.

We can touch and feel this technology today. We just can't make the nanobots small enough, not yet anyway. But miniaturization is another one of those ac-celerating technology trends. We're currently shrink-ing the size of technology by a factor of 5.6 per linear dimension per decade, so it is conservative to say that this scenario will be feasible in a few decades. The

nanobots will capture the locations, interconnections and contents of all the nerve cell bodies, axons, den-drites, presynaptic vesicles, neurotransmitter concen-trations and other relevant neural components. Using high-speed wireless communication, the nanobots will then communicate with each other and with other computers that are compiling the brain-scan database.

If this seems daunting, another scanning project, that of the human genome, was also considered ambitious when it was first introduced 12 years ago. At the time, skeptics said the task would take thousands of years, given current scanning capabilities. But the project is finishing on time nevertheless because the speed with which we can sequence DNA has grown exponentially.

Brain scanning is a prerequisite to Winston and Nellie's virtual life — and apparent immortality.

In 2029, we will swallow or inject billions of nano-bots into our veins to enter a three dimensional cyber-space — a virtual reality environment. Already, neural implants are used to counteract tremors from Parkin-son's disease as well as multiple sclerosis. I have a deaf friend who can now hear what I'm saying because of his cochlear implant. Under development is a retinal im-plant that will perform a similar function for blind peo-ple, basically replacing certain visual processing circuits of the brain. Recently, scientists from Emory University placed a chip in the brain of a paralyzed stroke victim who can now begin to communicate and control his environment directly from his brain.

But while a surgically introduced neural implant can be placed in only one or at most a few locations, nanobots can take up billions or trillions of positions throughout the brain. We already have electronic devices called neuron transistors that, noninvasively, allow communication between electronics and biologi-cal neurons. Using this technology, developed at Ger-many's Max Planck Institute of Biochemistry, scientists were recently able to control from their computer the movements of a living leech.

By taking up positions next to specific neurons, the nanobots will be able to detect and control their activ-ity. For virtual reality applications, the nanobots will take up positions next to every nerve fiber coming from all five of our senses. When we want to enter a specific virtual environment, the nanobots will suppress the sig-nals coming from our real senses and replace them with new, virtual ones. We can then cause our virtual body to move, speak and otherwise interact in the virtual en-vironment. The nanobots would prevent our real bod-ies from moving; instead, we would have a virtual body in a virtual environment, which need not be the same as our real body.

Like the experiences Winston and Nellie enjoyed, this technology will enable us to have virtual interactions with other people — or simulated people — without requiring any equipment not already in our heads. And virtual reality will not be as crude as what you experience in today's arcade games. It will be as detailed and subtle as real life. So instead of just phoning a friend, you can meet in a virtual Italian bistro or stroll down a virtual tropical beach, and it will all seem real. People will be able to share any type of experience — business, social, romantic or sexual — regardless of physical proximity.

The trip to virtual reality will be readily reversible since, with your thoughts alone, you will be able to shut the nanobots off, or even direct them to leave your body. Nanobots are programmable, in that they can provide virtual reality one minute and a variety of brain extensions the next. They can change their configuration, and even alter their software.

While the combination of human-level intelligence in a machine and a computer's inherent superiority in the speed, accuracy and sharing ability of its memory will be formidable — this is not an alien invasion. It is emerging from within our human-machine civilization.

But will virtual life and its promise of immortality obviate the fear of death? Once we upload our knowledge, memories and insights into a computer, will we have acquired eternal life? First we must determine what human life is. What is consciousness anyway? If my thoughts, knowledge, experience, skills and memories achieve eternal life without me, what does that mean for me?

Consciousness — a seemingly basic tenet of "living" — is perplexing and reflects issues that have been debated since the Platonic dialogues. We assume, for instance, that other humans are conscious, but when we consider the possibility that nonhuman animals may be conscious, our understanding of consciousness is called into question.

The issue of consciousness will become even more contentious in the 21st century because nonbiological entities — read: machines — will be able to convince most of us that they are conscious. They will master all the subtle cues that we now use to determine that humans are conscious. And they will get mad if we refute their claims.

Consider this: If we scan me, for example, and record the exact state, level and position of my every neurotransmitter, synapse, neural connection and other relevant details, and then reinstantiate this massive database into a neural computer, then who is the real me? If you ask the machine, it will vehemently claim to be the original Ray. Since it will have all of my memories, it will say, "I grew up in Queens, New York, went to college at MIT, stayed in the Boston area, sold a few artificial intelligence companies, walked into a scanner there and woke up in the machine here. Hey, this technology really works."

But there are strong arguments that this is really a different person. For one thing, old biological Ray (that's me) still exists. I'll still be here in my carbon, cell-based brain. Alas, I (the old biological Ray) will have to sit back and watch the new Ray succeed in endeavors that I could only dream of.

But New Ray will have some strong claims as well. He will say that while he is not absolutely identical to Old Ray, neither is the current version of Old Ray, since the particles making up my biological brain and body are constantly changing. It is the patterns of matter and energy that are semipermanent (that is, changing only gradually), while the actual material content changes constantly and very quickly.

Viewed in this way, my identity is rather like the pattern that water makes when rushing around a rock in a stream. The pattern remains relatively unchanged for hours, even years, while the actual material constituting the pattern — the water — is replaced in milliseconds.

This idea is consistent with the philosophical notion that we should not associate our fundamental identity with a set of particles, but rather with the pattern of matter and energy that we represent. In other words, if we change our definition of consciousness to value patterns over particles, then New Ray may have an equal claim to be the continuation of Old Ray.

One could scan my brain and reinstantiate the new Ray while I was sleeping, and I would not necessarily even know about it. If you then came to me, and said, "Good news, Ray, we've successfully reinstantiated your mind file so we won't be needing your old body and brain anymore," I may quickly realize the philosophical flaw in the argument that New Ray is a continuation of my consciousness. I may wish New Ray well, and realize that he shares my pattern, but I would nonetheless conclude that he is not me, because I'm still here.

Wherever you wind up on this debate, it is worth noting that data do not necessarily last forever. The longevity of information depends on its relevance, utility and accessibility. If you've ever tried to retrieve information from an obsolete form of data storage in an old obscure format (e.g., a reel of magnetic tape from a 1970s minicomputer), you understand the challenge of keeping software viable. But if we are diligent in maintaining our mind file, keeping current backups and porting to the latest formats and mediums, then at least a crucial aspect of who we are will attain a longevity independent of our bodies.

What does this super technological intelligence mean for the future? There will certainly be grave dangers associated with 21st century technologies. Consider unrestrained nanobot replication. The technology requires billions or trillions of nanobots in order to be useful, and the most cost-effective way to reach such levels is through self-replication, essentially the same approach used in the biological world, by bacteria, for example. So in the same way that biological self-replication gone awry (i.e., cancer) results in biological destruction, a defect in the mechanism curtailing nanobot self-replication would endanger all physical entities, biological or otherwise.

Other salient questions are: Who is controlling the nanobots? Who else might the nanobots be talking to?

Organizations, including governments, extremist groups or even a clever individual, could put trillions of undetectable nanobots in the water or food supply of an entire population. These "spy" nanobots could then monitor, influence and even control our thoughts and actions. In addition, authorized nanobots could be influenced by software viruses and other hacking techniques. Just as technology poses dangers today, there will be a panoply of risks in the decades ahead.

On a personal level, I am an optimist, and I expect that the creative and constructive applications of this technology will persevere, as I believe they do today. But there will be a valuable and increasingly vocal role for a concerned movement of Luddites—those anti-technologists inspired by early 19th-century weavers who in protest destroyed machinery that was threatening their livelihood.

Still, I regard the freeing of the human mind from its severe physical limitations as a necessary next step in evolution. Evolution, in my view, is the purpose of life, meaning that the purpose of life—and of our lives—is to evolve.

What does it mean to evolve? Evolution moves toward greater complexity, elegance, intelligence, beauty, creativity and love. And God has been called all these things, only without any limitation, infinite. While evolution never reaches an infinite level, it advances exponentially, certainly moving in that direction. Technological evolution, therefore, moves us inexorably closer to becoming like God. And the freeing of our thinking from the severe limitations of our biological form may be regarded as an essential spiritual quest.

By the close of the next century, nonbiological intelligence will be ubiquitous. There will be few humans without some form of artificial intelligence, which is growing at a double exponential rate, whereas biological intelligence is basically at a standstill. Nonbiological thinking will be trillions of trillions of times more powerful than that of its biological progenitors, although it will be still of human origin.

Ultimately, however, the earth's technology-creating species will merge with its own computational technology. After all, what is the difference between a human brain enhanced a trillion-fold by nanobot-based implants, and a computer whose design is based on high-resolution scans of the human brain, and then extended a trillion-fold?

This may be the ominous, existential question that our own children, certainly our grandchildren, will face. But at this point, there's no turning back. And there's no slowing down.

Suggestions for Further Reading

Hick, John H. *Death and Eternal Life*. San Francisco: Harper and Row, 1976.

Kolak, Daniel, and Raymond Martin. *Self and Identity*. New York: Macmillan, 1990.

Noonan, Harold. *Personal Identity*. London: Routledge, 1989.

Olson, Eric T. *The Human Animal: Personal Identity without Psychology*. New York: Oxford University Press, 1997.

Parfit, Derek. *Reasons and Persons*. Oxford: Clarendon Press, 1984.

Peacock, A., and G. Gillett, eds. *Persons and Personality*. Oxford: Blackwell, 1987.

Perry, John. *A Dialogue on Personal Identity and Immortality*. Indianapolis: Hackett, 1978.

Perry, John, ed. *Personal Identity*. Berkeley: University of California Press, 1975.

Rorty, Amelie, ed. *The Identities of Persons*. Berkeley: University of California Press, 1976.

Shoemaker, Sydney, and Richard Swinburne. *Personal Identity*. Oxford: Basil Blackwell, 1984.

Unger, Peter. *Identity, Consciousness, and Value*. Oxford: Oxford University Press, 1990.

Wilkes, Kathleen V. *Real People: Personal Identity without Thought Experiments*. Oxford: Clarendon Press, 1988.

Williams, Bernard. *Problems of the Self*. Cambridge: Cambridge University Press, 1973.

Chapter 5
The Problem of Relativism and Morality

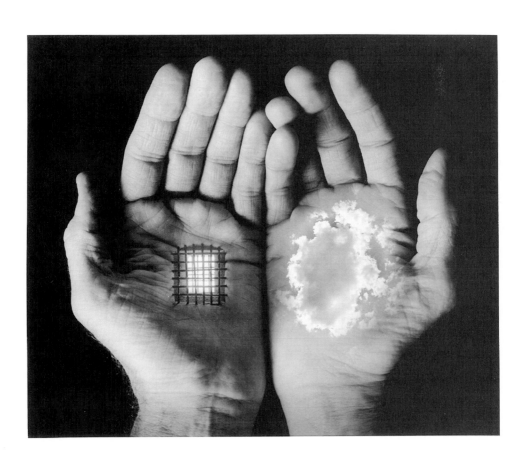

On June 17, 1973, George Zygmanik shattered his spine in a motorcycle accident. Formerly an active, athletic individual, he became a quadriplegic after the accident, unable to move any of his limbs. All the parts of his body that he could feel hurt. His brother, Lester, was at his bedside during most of the next few days. On June 19, George said to Lester, "Hold my hand." After Lester took his hand, he said, "You know what I want you to do." Lester shook his head. Then George said to him, "You're my brother. I want you to promise to kill me. I want you to swear to God."[1]

On June 20, 1973, at 11:00 P.M., Lester Zygmanik walked into the Jersey Shore Medical Center with a sawed-off shotgun under his coat. He entered his brother's room, pointed the gun at his temple, and pulled the trigger. In the ensuing commotion, Lester turned to one of the nurses and said, "I'm the one you're looking for. I just shot my brother."[2]

Did Lester Zygmanik do the right thing? The State of New Jersey didn't think so. He was taken into custody and charged with first-degree murder. Others, however, condoned Lester's action, for not only did he put his brother out of his misery, he did it at his brother's request. What Lester did, they said, was not an act of malice. It was an act of love.

Although Lester's action arouses strong feelings in most of us, we can't base our judgment of his action on our feelings alone. For our feelings may be irrational—they may be the product of prejudice, fear, or cultural conditioning. People used to feel strongly that there was nothing wrong with owning slaves. But that didn't make slavery morally permissible. What's more, feelings often conflict. Some feel that what Lester did was right; others feel that it was wrong. But Lester's action can't be both right and wrong. So to determine whether an action is morally justified, we must go beyond our feelings to the reasons behind them.

We usually justify our actions by appealing to various moral principles, such as it's wrong to steal, it's wrong to lie, it's wrong to break promises, and the like. One task of moral philosophy is to determine whether these principles can be explained in terms of a unified moral theory. Do these principles follow from some more basic principle in the way that Kepler's and Galileo's laws of motion follow from Newton's law of gravitation?

In addition to judging actions to be right or wrong, we also judge people, their characters, and their motives to be good or bad. Good people usually perform right actions, but it doesn't always turn out that way. Consider, for example, the inquisitors of the Roman Catholic Inquisition. From approximately A.D. 1400 to 1600, they executed between 250,000 and 2 million women on the grounds that they were witches. At least some of the inquisitors must have been men of good character who thought they were doing God's work. But, even if they were good persons, what they did was terribly wrong.

Just as virtuous people can do the wrong thing, so can vicious people do the right thing. Hitler, for example, was kind to animals and, during his rise to power, did things to improve the lives of some of the German people. His motives may have been despicable, but that doesn't mean that all of his actions were wrong. The rightness of an action does not depend on the goodness of the person performing it.

Many people learn how to act morally by being taught a moral code. As a result, many believe that there's nothing more to acting morally than following a moral code. But it's neither possible nor desirable to base all of our moral decisions on a moral code because moral codes are often too general to solve specific moral problems. For example, consider the commandment "Thou shalt not kill." Certainly this doesn't mean that we should never kill anything—whether plant or animal—because if we didn't, we would starve to death. Nor does it mean that we should never kill a human being, because sometimes we have to kill in self-defense. Is it wrong to kill someone to put him out of his misery? The Ten Commandments do not say. To derive an answer from them, we must interpret them, and to interpret them, we must appeal to moral theory.

A law is valuable not because it is law, but because there is right in it.
—H. W. BEECHER

In addition to being too general, moral codes often give conflicting advice. To see this, suppose that you are a devout Christian and that one of your children has just sworn at you. You are not sure how to handle this situation, so you turn to the Bible for guidance. In Exodus 21:17 you read, "Whoever curses his father or his mother shall be put to death." You are about to kill your child when he points out that Exodus 20:13 says "Thou shalt not kill." So what should you do? To answer this question, you must go beyond the letter of the law to the theory behind it. You must decide which action would be most in tune with a correct conception of morality.

Theories of morality try to answer the question What makes an action right? or What makes a person good? They try to determine what, if anything, right actions or good people have in common. The data that moral theories try to explain are our considered moral judgments—those moral judgments that we accept after reflecting critically on them. A plausible ethical theory must be consistent with those judgments. If it sanctions obviously immoral actions, it is unacceptable.

Every young man would do well to remember that all successful business stands on the foundation of morality.
—H. W. BEECHER

In ethics, as in any other area of inquiry, there is a dynamic interplay between data and theory. Accepting a powerful theory may mean rejecting certain data, and vice versa. The goal in moral inquiry is to achieve a "reflective equilibrium" between data and theory. We want the fit between data and theory to be so close that no reasonable change in either would improve it.

To achieve reflective equilibrium among your moral beliefs, begin by critically examining both your moral judgments and your moral principles in an attempt to identify which seem to be the most reasonable. Then check the ones that have passed muster for consistency. Try to determine whether your preferred moral principles justify your considered moral judgments, and whether your considered moral judgments follow from your preferred moral principles. If they do, then your moral beliefs are in reflective equilibrium. If they don't, eliminate the inconsistency by revising either your moral principles or your moral judgments.

Theories of morality should also be consistent with our experience of the moral life. We all make moral judgments, get into moral disputes, and act immorally from time to time. If a theory of morality implies that we don't do these things — if it implies that we don't make moral judgments, get into moral disputes, or act immorally — there's reason to believe that it's mistaken.

An adequate theory of morality should also help us solve moral dilemmas. We want to know what makes an action right because we want to do the right thing. If a moral theory is unworkable — if it doesn't give us specific guidance in specific situations — it fails to meet one of the primary goals of ethical inquiry.

We begin our inquiry into the nature of morality by examining various forms of relativism. We then examine the two most prevalent types of ethical theories: consequentialist (teleological) and formalist (deontological). Finally, we consider various theories of what it is to be a good person.

Objectives

After reading this chapter, you should be able to

- state the various theories of morality.
- describe the thought experiments that have been used to test them.
- evaluate the strengths and weaknesses of the various theories of morality.
- define consequentialism, formalism, intrinsic value, instrumental value, principle of justice, principle of mercy, perfect duty, imperfect duty, negative right, positive right, *prima facie* duty, and virtue.
- formulate your own view of what makes an action right or wrong.

Don't Question Authority
Might Makes Right

*T*he Declaration of Independence asserts that all human beings possess certain inalienable rights, including the right to life, liberty, and the pursuit of happiness. These rights are supposed to apply to all people no matter what society they live in. Many Americans today, however, would no longer agree that there are such universal rights. In their view, morality is relative to individuals, to cultures, or to religions.

The view that morality is relative to culture is often thought to be supported by anthropology. As art historian William Fleming says in his text *Arts and Ideas*, "The study by anthropologists of the life and customs of primitive peoples has shown how ethical considerations are relative to tribal customs as well as social and economic conditions."[3] The variation of moral beliefs among cultures is indeed striking. Certain tribes believe that it is morally permissible to kill their members when they reach the age of forty. Cannibals believe that it is morally permissible to eat human beings. And "the Siriono Indians of the upper Amazon appear to think little of copulating in full view of others but may be shamed into exile if they are caught eating in public."[4] Given this wide variation among moral beliefs, how can there be any absolute moral standards?

Even within a culture, the differences in moral beliefs can be vast. Consider, for example, the radically divergent beliefs people have about the morality of abortion, euthanasia, capital punishment, and the like. What better evidence could we have for the relativity of moral judgment? If there were a universal morality, wouldn't there be much more agreement about these issues than there is?

Subjective Absolutism

The lack of consensus in moral matters has led some to embrace the doctrine of **subjective absolutism:** the view that what makes an action right is that

The Absolute Truth is that there is nothing absolute in the world.

—WALPOLA RAHULA

subjective absolutism
The doctrine that what makes an action right is that one approves of it.

one approves of it. According to this view, morality is a matter of personal preference. When we say that an action is right, we are merely saying that we approve of it.

Although this view may help explain the plethora of moral opinions, it cannot possibly be correct because it leads to a logical contradiction. Suppose that someone approved of Lester Zygmanik's action. Then, according to subjective absolutism, what Lester did was right. Now suppose that someone else disapproved of that action. Then what Lester did was wrong. But one and the same action cannot be both right and wrong. The law of noncontradiction tells us that nothing can have a property and lack it at the same time. Subjective absolutism, then, cannot be correct because it's self-contradictory.

Whenever we make a moral judgment about an action, we may have a certain feeling toward it. But having a feeling about an action cannot be what makes the action right or wrong. If that were the case, one and the same action could be both right and wrong, and that's impossible. Just as a plane figure cannot be both round and square at the same time, so an action cannot be both right and wrong at the same time.

An action can be believed to be right and wrong at the same time, however. One person can believe that an action is right while another believes that it is wrong. But that does not make the action both right and wrong. Similarly, the earth can be believed to be flat and round at the same time. But that doesn't make it flat and round at the same time. Just as you cannot make a statement true simply by believing it to be true, you cannot make an action right simply by believing it to be right.

Subjective Relativism

Life, lives, and reality are only what we each perceive them to be.

—SHIRLEY MACLAINE

The subjectivist may try to avoid this contradiction by claiming that right and wrong are not properties like round or square but are relations like small or large. Nothing can be round and square at the same time. But something can be small and large at the same time. An acorn is large in relation to a mustard seed, but it is small in relation to a coconut. So if moral terms are relational, the same action can be both right and wrong.

Subjective relativism—the doctrine that what makes an action right for someone is that it is approved by that person—claims that moral judgments are always relative to the individual. Whenever someone says that an action is right, what she means is that it is right *for her*. Nothing is absolutely right or wrong, just as nothing is absolutely big or small. To understand a moral judgment, then, you have to know who made it.

Although subjective relativism may seem admirably egalitarian in that it considers everyone's moral judgments to be as good as everyone else's, it has some rather bizarre consequences. For one thing, it implies that each of us is morally infallible. As long as we approve of an action, our judgment that it is morally right cannot be mistaken. But this cannot be correct. Suppose that Hitler approved of exterminating the Jews. Then it was right for Hitler to exterminate the Jews. Or suppose that Stalin approved of assassinating his enemies. Then it was right for Stalin to assassinate his enemies. Subjective relativism condones any action as long as the person performing it approves of it. But what Hitler and Stalin did was wrong, even if they approved of what they did. Believing something to be right doesn't make it right. If it did, we'd all be morally infallible, and that's absurd.

It's hard to argue with someone who's infallible. So, as you might expect, subjective relativism makes moral disagreement next to impossible. It's easy to see why. Suppose that Jack says that abortion is right and Jill says that it is wrong. Ordinarily, we would take Jack and Jill to be disagreeing with each other. According to subjective relativism, however, they don't disagree because what Jack is really saying is that he approves of abortion and what Jill is really saying is that she doesn't approve of abortion. These statements do not contradict one another because the subjects of these statements are different (Jack vs. Jill) and they say different things about those subjects. So they both could be true. If Jill wanted to disagree with Jack, she would have to say something like, "I'm sorry, Jack, but you don't approve of abortion." It's hard to see how Jill could ever be in a position to make such a claim, however, for no one knows Jack's mind better than Jack. Yet, according to subjective relativism, that is what she must claim if she wants to disagree with Jack. The problem is that moral subjectivism takes morality to be a matter of taste, and as we all know, there's no arguing about taste.

Morality can't be a matter of taste, however, for subjective relativism fails to meet the criteria of adequacy for ethical theories: it sanctions obviously immoral actions, it implies that people are morally infallible, and it denies that there are any substantive moral disagreements. It simply doesn't fit the facts; it's inconsistent with our experience of the moral life. A scientific theory that's inconsistent with our experience of the physical world should be rejected. So should a moral theory that's inconsistent with our experience of the moral life.

Emotivism

In defense of the notion that morality is subjective, some have gone so far as to claim that moral utterances are neither true nor false. Some things we say do not have a truth value. Consider these utterances: Hooray! Bravo! Boo! Hiss! These are exclamations rather than statements. They serve to express emotions rather than to make claims. As a result, none of them is true or false. According to **emotivism,** all moral utterances (utterances that use moral terms like "right" and "wrong") are expressions of emotion. If we say, for example, that abortion is right, what we're saying, in effect, is "Abortion—Hooray!"

The logical positivist A. J. Ayer defended a version of emotivism in his *Language, Truth, and Logic:*

> If I . . . say "Stealing is wrong," I produce a sentence which has no factual meaning—that is, expresses no proposition which can be either true or false. It is as if I had written "Stealing money!!"—where the shape and thickness of the exclamation marks show, by a suitable convention, that a special sort of moral disapproval is the feeling which is being expressed. It is clear that there is nothing said here which can be true or false.[5]

subjective relativism The doctrine that what makes an action right for someone is that it is approved by that person.

emotivism The doctrine that moral utterances are expressions of emotion.

Logical positivism, you will recall from Chapter 2, is based on the verifiability theory of meaning, which says that if a sentence cannot be verified, it is cognitively meaningless (neither true nor false). Ayer maintains that moral sentences cannot be verified because goodness or rightness cannot be sensed. Good people and right actions do not have a particular look, feel, taste, smell, or sound. Consequently, sentences containing terms like "good" or "right" are neither true nor false.

Even though the verifiability theory of meaning is implausible, there is something to be said for emotivism. By taking moral utterances to be expressions of emotion rather than statements of fact, emotivism avoids some of the difficulties facing subjectivism. Because it claims that moral utterances are not judgments of any kind, it avoids the inconsistency of subjective absolutism and the individual infallibility of subjective relativism. If you don't make a statement, you can't contradict anybody, and you can't be right or wrong.

Emotivism, however, fares no better than subjective relativism in accounting for moral disagreement, for if moral utterances aren't statements, they can't contradict one another. When you say "Hooray!" you haven't said anything that anyone can disagree with. Similarly, if what you're saying when you say that abortion is wrong is something like "Abortion—Boo!" you haven't said anything that anyone can contradict. Moral discourse is more than just cheering or jeering, however. It follows, then, that emotivism cannot be correct.

Emotivism implies that nothing is good or bad because the words "good" and "bad" do not stand for properties or features of anything. This is a radical claim that flies in the face of common sense. To show just how radical it is, Brand Blanshard proposes the following thought experiment.

Thought Experiment

Blanshard's Rabbit

There is perhaps no value statement on which people would more universally agree than the statement that intense pain is bad. Let us take a set of circumstances in which I happen to be interested on the legislative side and in which I think every one of us might naturally make such a statement. We come upon a rabbit that has been caught in one of the brutal traps in common use. There are signs that it has struggled for days to escape and that in a frenzy of hunger, pain, and fear, it has all but eaten off its own leg. The attempt failed: the animal is now dead. As we think of the long and excruciating pain it must have suffered, we are very likely to say: "It was a bad thing that the little animal should suffer so." The positivist tells us that when we say this we are only expressing our present emotion. I hold, on the contrary, that we mean to assert something of the pain itself, namely, that it was bad—bad when and as it occurred.[6]

According to emotivism, the rabbit's pain is neither good nor bad. It may move you to express an emotion, but in and of itself, the rabbit's pain has no moral properties (because there are no moral properties). But surely, Blanshard claims, this cannot be the case. Intense suffering is bad whether or not it causes anybody to express an emotion.

What's more, emotivism implies that everyone's reaction to a situation is just as appropriate as everyone else's. But this, too, flies in the face of common sense. Suppose that someone expresses joy at the pain of the rabbit. Or suppose that someone expresses delight at the torture of innocent children. We would ordinarily consider these reactions inappropriate. This judgment can easily be explained on the hypothesis that some things (like unnecessary suffering) are objectively wrong, but this explanation is not available to the emotivists. Consequently, they cannot account for this aspect of our moral experience.

The fact that a theory conflicts with common sense is a strike against it, but it doesn't rule it out of court. Common sense has been wrong about many things, such as the shape, size, and position of the earth. But we should reject common sense only if the alternative is demonstrably superior to it, and emotivism has nothing over common sense. Not only is it inconsistent with our experience of the moral life, but it provides no means for resolving moral dilemmas. In fact, it suggests that there are no moral dilemmas. Consequently, it is not an adequate ethical theory.

Cultural Relativism

When we say that an action is right, we are not merely saying that we approve of it. Nor are we simply expressing our emotions. What, then, are we saying? Many believe that we're saying that our culture approves of it.

Custom is the universal sovereign.
—PINDAR

Our moral beliefs tend to reflect the culture in which we grew up. For example, if we grew up in India, we may believe that it's morally permissible to burn wives alive along with their dead husbands on a funeral pyre. If we grew up in Syria, we may believe that it's morally permissible to have more than one wife. And if we grew up in the Sudan, we may believe that it's morally permissible to surgically remove the clitorises of young women. If we grew up in America, however, we are likely to believe that none of these practices is morally permissible. Because people in different cultures have different moral beliefs, the conclusion that morality is relative to culture seems unavoidable.

Cultural relativism, then, is the doctrine that what makes an action right is that it's approved by one's culture. Unlike subjective relativism, cultural relativism does not imply that individuals are morally infallible. But it does imply that cultures are morally infallible. Cultures make the moral law, so cultures can do no wrong.

If cultures were morally infallible, however, it would be impossible to disagree with one's culture and be right. Social reformers couldn't claim that a socially approved practice is wrong because if society approves of it, it must be right. If society approves of slavery, for example, then slavery is right. Anyone who would suggest otherwise would simply be mistaken. Thus cultural relativism would have us believe that Jesus, William Lloyd Garrison (one of the leading abolitionists), and Susan B. Anthony (one of the leading suffragettes)

cultural relativism
The doctrine that what makes an action right is that it is approved by one's culture.

Custom may lead a man into many errors, but it justifies none.

—HENRY FIELDING

The fact that an opinion has been widely held is no evidence that it is not utterly absurd.

—BERTRAND RUSSELL

acted immorally, for they all advocated practices that were not approved by their cultures. But instead of condemning them for acting immorally, we praise them for exposing the immoral practices of their cultures. Cultures are not morally infallible. They can and have sanctioned immoral practices. Consequently, cultural relativism cannot be correct.

Unlike subjectivism, cultural relativism does not make moral disagreement impossible. Individuals can legitimately disagree about the morality of an action. But, according to cultural relativism, the only thing they can disagree about is whether their culture approves of the action because that's what determines whether it's right or wrong. So cultural relativism would have us believe that when people disagree about the morality of abortion, what they're really disagreeing about is whether their society approves of abortion. But that's implausible. Moral disagreements in general and the abortion controversy in particular are not about public opinion, and they cannot be resolved through opinion polls. Since cultural relativism suggests otherwise, it's not an adequate theory of morality.

Even if moral disagreements were about public opinion, cultural relativism would still be an inadequate theory of morality because it's unworkable. It can't help us solve moral dilemmas because there is no way to identify one's true culture. Suppose you were a Black Jewish Communist living in Bavaria during Hitler's reign. What would be your true culture? The Blacks? The Jews? The Communists? The Bavarians? The Nazis? Each of us is a member of many different cultures, and there is no way to determine which one is our true culture. If we can't identify our true culture, however, we can't use cultural relativism to solve moral problems.

Given cultural relativism's many failings, why is it so popular? Part of the answer is that many people believe that it promotes tolerance. Anthropologist Ruth Benedict, for example, claims that by accepting cultural relativism, "we shall arrive at a more realistic social faith, accepting as grounds of hope and as new bases for tolerance the coexisting and equally valid patterns of life which mankind has created for itself from the raw materials of existence."[8] But to explicitly advocate cultural relativism on the grounds that it promotes tolerance is to implicitly assume that tolerance is an absolute value. If there are any absolute values, however, cultural relativism is false.

The most a cultural relativist can consistently claim is that her culture values tolerance. But other cultures may not. In fact, fundamentalists of almost every stripe do not tolerate those who disagree with them. From a cultural relativist point of view, then, intolerance can be justified. Thus any attempt to justify cultural relativism by an appeal to tolerance is bound to fail.

Another reason that cultural relativism is so popular is that it seems to be the only ethical theory that is consistent with the anthropological evidence. The inadequacy of cultural relativism suggests that this conclusion is mistaken, however. To see why, let's examine the anthropological argument in more detail.

> *Tolerance is the virtue of the man without convictions.*
> —G. K. Chesterton

> *The despotism of custom is on the wane. We are not content to know that things are; we ask whether they ought to be.*
> —J. S. Mill

The Anthropological Argument

The anthropological argument for cultural relativism says that because people in different cultures disagree about the morality of various actions, there are no universal moral standards. But the fact that people disagree does not, *by itself,* imply that there are no absolute moral standards. Only in conjunction with certain other assumptions can that conclusion be reached. By making those assumptions explicit, we can better judge the soundness of the anthropological argument for cultural relativism. Here's one way of spelling out the argument:

> *Custom is the law of fools.*
> —Sir John Vanbrugh

1. People in different societies make different moral judgments regarding the same action.

2. If people in different societies make different moral judgments regarding the same action, they must accept different moral standards.

3. If people in different societies accept different moral standards, there are no universal moral standards.

4. Therefore, there are no universal moral standards.

This is a valid argument because the conclusion follows from the premises. The question is, Are the premises true? Premise 1 is certainly true, for it has been confirmed by anthropological investigation many times over. What about premise 3? It states that if people disagree about what makes an action right, there can be no correct answer to the question What makes an action right? But this doesn't follow. From the mere fact that people disagree, we can't conclude that none of the parties to the disagreement is correct. Disagreement, by itself, doesn't invalidate every disputant's claim. If it did, you could refute anyone by simply disagreeing with them. To show that someone is mistaken, however, you must do more than just disagree with him or her. You must give reasons for believing that he or she is mistaken. The simple fact that people disagree, then, does not prove that there are no absolute moral standards.

Because premise 3 is false, the anthropological argument is unsound. But premise 3 is not the only questionable premise in this argument. Premise 2 says that whenever people disagree about the morality of an action, they must accept different moral standards. In other words, it says that whenever there is a difference in moral judgments, there is a difference in moral standards. But is this true? To see if it is, let's examine how moral judgments are made.

The Logical Structure of Moral Judgments

There are not unfrequently substantial reasons underneath for customs that appear to us absurd.

—CHARLOTTE BRONTË

A moral judgment is a moral appraisal of a particular action. A moral principle is a moral appraisal of a general *type* of action. From a moral standard like "murder is wrong," which refers to an entire class of actions (the class of murders), we cannot conclude that any particular killing is wrong, for the killing might not be an act of murder. To make that determination, we need to know more about the facts of the case. Murder is the killing of a person with malice aforethought. So, in order to determine whether any particular killing is a murder, we have to determine whether the victim was a person and whether the culprit acted out of hatred or malevolence.

These considerations show that moral judgments do not follow from moral standards alone. To derive a moral judgment from a moral standard, we need additional information about the situation. Without such information, no moral judgment can be made. The formula for a moral judgment, then, is this:

$$\text{Moral standard} + \text{Factual beliefs} = \text{Moral judgment}$$

Because moral standards alone do not imply moral judgments, it is not necessarily true that whenever there is a difference in moral judgments, there is a difference in moral standards. Any difference in judgment could also be due to a difference in the facts of the case.

Some anthropologists believe that this is often the case. Social psychologist Solomon Asch, for example, writes,

> We consider it wrong to take food away from a hungry child, but not if he is overeating. We consider it right to fulfill a promise, but not if it is a promise to commit a crime. . . . It has been customary to hold that diverse evaluations of the same act are automatic evidence for the presence of different principles of evaluation. The preceding examples point to an error in this interpretation. Indeed, an examination of the relational factors points to the operation of constant principles in situations that differ in concrete details. . . . Anthropological evidence

Moral Children

It is widely believed that morality is something that is learned rather than innate. Developmental psychologists such as Jean Piaget and Lawrence Kohlberg have claimed that young children get their morality from their parents. Whatever their parents tell them is right is what they believe to be right. Recent research suggests, however, that this notion of moral development is mistaken. William Damon, chair of Brown University's education department and director of the Center for the Study of Human Development, has found that even very young children seem to have a sense of right and wrong that is independent of what their parents say:

> Damon's idea for his research grew out of a job he took after college as a caseworker in a New York City settlement house for immigrant pre-teens—rough-and-tumble kids clearly headed for trouble. "I noticed that even the very young ones, four and five, had ideas about family, other people, emotions, and morality that were much more advanced and sophisticated than anything developmental psychologists had been writing about," he recalls.
>
> The experience was a revelation. "I had a feeling [one] has very few times in a lifetime. I felt I had discovered something others had not seen." When he later entered graduate school, Damon devised some experiments with nursery-school children that involved asking them to distribute toys and candy among their friends.

> "I was struck with how child after child, whatever school I went to, all said the same kinds of things," he remembers. "They gave reasons why they had to share: 'If I don't share with her, she won't play with me.' 'I'll hurt her feelings if I don't share with her.' They had a sense of reciprocity and a sense of empathy."
>
> Next he asked, "What if your mother or your teacher told you not to share your lunch or candy or your bike with your friend?" The children answered, "That would be wrong. I would do it anyway." Kohlberg and other psychologists had been saying that, before adolescence, children get all their moral values from their parents; to a child, whatever the person in power says is right is right simply because she says so. "But kids were saying, 'My mother would be wrong. That's not nice. That's not fair to my friend.'"[10]

Damon believes that children are born with a natural predisposition to moral behavior. That predisposition has to be nurtured in order to develop, but it is something that, as humans, we all share.

Thought Probe

Moral Children

Does Damon's research lend credibility to the claim that there are absolute moral standards? Why or why not?

---

does not furnish proof of relativism. We do not know of societies in which bravery is despised and cowardice held up to honor, in which generosity is considered a vice and ingratitude a virtue. It seems rather that the relations between valuation and meaning are invariant.[9]

According to Asch, people in different cultures arrive at different moral judgments not because they have different views about the nature of morality, but because they have different views about the nature of reality.

Consider the abortion controversy. Those who are pro-life believe that abortion is wrong; those who are pro-choice believe that it is right. Does this mean that these two groups of people have different views about the nature of morality? No, because they both believe that murder is wrong. What they disagree about is the nature of the fetus. Is a fetus the sort of thing that can be murdered? Their disagreement, then, is about what kind of a thing the fetus is, not about what makes an action right or wrong.

Consider the male chauvinists who believe that it's wrong to give women the same responsibilities as men. Feminists believe that there is no reason not to treat men and women as equals. Male chauvinists and feminists make different moral judgments about how women should be treated. Do they have different views of the nature of morality? Not necessarily: they most likely both accept the principle that equals should be treated equally. Thus their disagreement is not about the nature of morality but about the nature of women. Male chauvinists and feminists simply disagree about what women can do. Because moral judgments follow from both a moral standard and certain factual beliefs, a difference in moral judgments does not necessarily imply a difference in moral standards.

Be not so bigoted to any custom as to worship it at the expense of truth.

—Johann Zimmerman

Thought Probe

When in Rome

Clitoridectomy—the surgical removal of the clitoris—is common in Gambia. It is believed that this procedure makes the woman more pure and desirable as a wife. In 1987, Teneng Jahate, a native of Gambia but a French resident for five years, hired a midwife to perform a clitoridectomy on her two daughters, ages one and two. The practice is outlawed in France, but Jahate did not know this. She testified: "I didn't know it was forbidden in France. I did it because I knew they would be circumcised when they returned to Gambia, so why not do it when they were little?"[11] Did Jahate do the wrong thing? Why or why not?

The Divine Command Theory

All moral obligation resolves itself into the obligation of conformity to the will of God.

—Charles Hodge

Neither an individual nor a society can make an action right by approving it. Many, however, believe that God can. In their view, God is both the author and the enforcer of the moral law. He makes the rules, and he ensures that those who break them get what's coming to them. This view of morality is often called the **divine command theory,** for it holds that what makes an action right is that God commands it to be done. On this view, nothing is right (or wrong) prior to or independently of God's willing it to be done (or refrained from). But this raises the question How did God come up with his commandments? Did he have some standard to go by or did he just arbitrarily will whatever came to mind? This is similar to the problem that Socrates sought to resolve in the *Euthyphro*. It can be put this way: Is an action right because God wills it, or does God will it because it's right? To accept the first alternative is to accept the divine command theory. To accept the second alternative, however, is to reject it, for on this view, the rightness of an action is independent of God's will.

To better understand the import of the divine command theory, consider the following tale. It seems that when Moses came down from the mountain with the tablets containing the Ten Commandments, his people gathered around him to find out how God said they should live. "What do the tablets say?" his followers wanted to know. Moses replied, "I have some good news and some bad news." "Give us the good news first," they instructed him. "Well, the good news," Moses said, "is that God kept the number of commandments down to ten." "Okay, what's the bad news?" they inquired. "The bad news," Moses informed them, "is that he kept the one about adultery in there." The point is that, according to the divine command theory, what makes adultery wrong is that God commands it not to be done. If he hadn't issued such a command, there would be nothing wrong with adultery.

Let's take this line of reasoning to its logical conclusion. If the divine command theory were true, then the Ten Commandments could have gone something like this: "Thou shalt kill everyone you dislike. Thou shalt rape every woman you desire. Thou shalt steal everything you covet. Thou shalt torture innocent children in your spare time . . ."—for killing, raping, stealing, and torturing were not wrong before God made them so, and God could have made them right.

Many take this to be a *reductio ad absurdum* of the divine command theory. It reduces the divine command theory to absurdity because it's absurd to think that God would condone such actions. To avoid the charge of absurdity, a divine command theorist might try to deny that the situation described above is possible. She might argue, for example, that God would never condone killing, raping, stealing, and torturing because God is all-good. But if God is by definition good, then God can't be used to define goodness because such a definition would be circular—the concept being defined would be contained in the concepts doing the defining. If being all-good is an essential property of God, then all the divine command theory tells us is that good (or right) actions would be willed by a supremely good (or righteous) being. While this is certainly true, it's unenlightening. It doesn't tell us what makes an action right and thus doesn't improve our understanding of the nature of morality.

The circularity could be avoided by denying that goodness is a defining attribute of God. But this won't help the divine command theorist because if goodness is not an essential property of God, then there is no guarantee that what he wills will be good. Being all-powerful and all-knowing does not necessarily incline one toward the good. In fact, it may do the opposite. As British statesman Lord Acton remarked, "Power tends to corrupt, and absolute power corrupts absolutely." So the divine command theory faces a dilemma: if goodness is a defining attribute of God, the theory is circular, but if it is not a defining attribute, the theory is false. In either case, the divine command theory is an unacceptable theory of the nature of morality.

To one who believes in God, however, the divine command theory's most significant failing may be that it is demeaning to God; it destroys any reason we might have had for worshiping and obeying him. Leibniz explains,

> In saying, therefore, that things are not good according to any standard of goodness, but simply by the will of God, it seems to me that one destroys, without realizing it, all the love of God and all his glory; for why praise him for what he has done, if he would be equally praiseworthy in doing the contrary? Where will be

The greatest tragedy in mankind's history may be the hijacking of morality by religion.
—ARTHUR C. CLARKE

The will of God is the refuge of ignorance.
—SPINOZA

divine command theory The doctrine that what makes an action right is that God commands it to be done.

his justice and his wisdom if he has only a certain despotic power, if arbitrary will takes the place of reasonableness, and if in accord with the definition of tyrants, justice consists in that which is pleasing to the most powerful. Besides it seems that every act of willing supposes some reason for the willing and this reason, of course, must precede the act.[12]

Leibniz's point is that if things are neither right nor wrong independently of God's will, then God cannot choose one thing over another because it is right. Thus if he does choose one over another, his choice must be arbitrary. A being whose decisions are arbitrary, however, is not worthy of worship.

Moreover, if God's commands are arbitrary—if he has no real reason for making them—then we have no moral obligation to obey them. God may threaten to punish us if we don't obey his commands, but threats extort; they do not create a moral obligation. Might does not make right. So if God's commands are not based on sound moral principles, there is no more reason to obey them than there is to obey a Hitler or a Stalin.

The fact that Leibniz rejects the divine command theory is significant because he is one of the most committed theists in the Western intellectual tradition. He argues at great length that there must be an all-powerful, all-knowing, and all-good God, and thus that this must be the best of all possible worlds. Because God is all-knowing, he knows what kind of a world would be best; because he is all-powerful, he can create such a world; and because he is all-good, he wants to create such a world. Ever since Voltaire lampooned this view in Candide, it has been difficult to take seriously. Nevertheless, what Leibniz demonstrates is that far from being disrespectful or heretical, the view that morality is independent of God is an eminently sensible and loyal one for a theist to hold.

The foregoing considerations indicate that the first horn of our dilemma is false. God cannot make an action right by simply willing it to be done. God must will an action to be done because it's right. In that case, however, morality does not depend on God.

But God, you might object, is omnipotent; he can do anything he wants to do. So he must be able to make actions right or wrong. To say that God is omnipotent, however, is not to say that he can do anything he wants to do. It's to say that he can do anything that it's logically possible to do. As the great Catholic theologian St. Thomas Aquinas realized, "Whatever implies a contradiction does not come within the scope of divine omnipotence because it cannot have the aspect of possibility. Hence it is better to say that such things cannot be done, than that God cannot do them."[13] For example, God can't make the number three an even number. An even number is divisible without remainder by two and not even God can make the number three divisible by two without remainder. God can't do things that are logically impossible. This doesn't impugn his omnipotence, however, because an omnipotent being can do only what's logically possible to do.

Just as God cannot change the laws of mathematics, there is reason to believe that he cannot change the laws of morality. He cannot make love evil, for example, because love is intrinsically good. Lawyer and journalist Albert Pike expresses this point as follows:

Saint Thomas said, "A thing is not just because God wills it, but God wills it because it is just." If he had deduced all the consequences of this fine thought, he would have discovered the true Philosopher's Stone, the magical elixir to convert all the trials of the world into golden mercies. Precisely as it is a necessity for God to be, so it is a necessity for Him to be just, loving, and merciful. He cannot be unjust, cruel, and merciless. He cannot repeal the law of right and wrong, of merit and demerit; for the moral laws are as absolute as the physical laws. There are impossible things. As it is impossible to make two and two be five and not four; as it is impossible to make a thing be and not be at the same time; so it is impossible for the Deity to make crime a merit, and love and gratitude crimes.

Therefore, according to the idea of Saint Thomas, the moral laws are the enactments of the Divine Will only because they are the decisions of the absolute Wisdom and Reason, and the Revelations of the Divine Nature. In this alone consists the right of Deity to enact them."[14]

The true grandeur of humanity is in moral elevation, sustained, enlightened and decorated by the intellect of man.
—CHARLES SUMNER

Pike argues against the divine command theory, not on the grounds that it's circular or demeaning, but on the grounds that it's logically impossible. Pike believes that moral laws like love is good are just as absolute as mathematical laws like the number three is odd. They hold in virtue of the logical relations among the concepts involved, not in virtue of any divine command. So they aren't subject to the will of God.

Even if morality did depend on God's will, the divine command theory would not be an adequate theory of morality because it's unworkable. Just as there is no way to determine which culture is one's true culture, there's no way to determine which God is the one true God. We can use the divine command theory to solve moral problems only if we know which commandments to obey. The divine command theory, however, doesn't tell us how to distinguish legitimate divine commands from illegitimate ones. Consequently, it can't help us make moral decisions.

The believers of any particular sect, of course, will claim that they know where God's true commandments can be found, namely, in their book of sacred scripture. But even if we knew which book of scripture was inspired by God, we still wouldn't know which commands to obey because we couldn't be sure that the scribes got it right. Consider, for example, the following commands from the Bible:

- He that curseth his father or his mother, shall surely be put to death. (Exod. 21:17)
- Whosoever doeth any work in the Sabbath day, he shall surely be put to death. (Exod. 31:15)
- He that sacrificeth unto any god, save unto the Lord only, he shall be utterly destroyed. (Exod. 22:20)

Cursing your father or mother may not be a good thing, but it's not a crime punishable by death. Working on Sunday (or Saturday, as the case may be) also should not be considered a capital offense. And killing members of other religions simply because they are members of other religions certainly is not right. We know that these commands are immoral, even though the Bible

Few contemporary theologians believe in the existence of hell, for they believe that an all-loving God would never let any of his children burn in hell for eternity, no matter how serious the crime. John Hick explains,

> The objections to the doctrine of eternal torment which once seemed so weak and now seem so strong are well known: for a conscious creature to undergo physical and mental torture through unending time (if this is indeed conceivable) is horrible and disturbing beyond words; and the thought of such torment being deliberately inflicted by divine decree is totally incompatible with the idea of God as infinite love; the absolute contrast of heaven and hell, entered immediately after death, does not correspond to the innumerable gradations of human good and evil; justice could never demand for finite human sins the infinite penalty of eternal pain; such unending torment could never serve any positive or reformative purpose precisely because it never ends; and it renders any coherent Christian theodicy impossible by giving the evils of sin and suffering an eternal lodgment within God's creation. Accordingly contemporary theologians who do not accept the doctrine of universal salvation usually speak of the finally lost as passing out of existence rather than as endlessly enduring the torments of hell-fire.[15]

If these arguments are correct, and the universe is governed by an all-loving God, you don't have to worry about going to hell. Whatever the afterlife holds, it will not hold eternal torment.

---

tells us that they come from God. Neither the Bible nor God, then, can be the source and ground of morality. If we can judge their pronouncements to be immoral, we must have a standard of morality that's independent of them.

There are those who hold that even if God is not required as the author of the moral law, he is nevertheless required as the enforcer of it. Without the threat of divine punishment, people will not act morally. But this position is no more plausible than the divine command theory itself. In the first place, as an empirical hypothesis about the psychology of human beings, it is questionable. There is no unambiguous evidence that theists are more moral than nontheists. Not only have psychological studies failed to find a significant correlation between frequency of religious worship and moral conduct, but convicted criminals are much more likely to be theists than atheists. Second, the threat of divine punishment cannot impose a moral obligation, for might does not make right. Threats of violence do not create a moral obligation. We are not morally obligated to obey someone simply because he or she has threatened us with physical harm if we don't.

Heaven and hell are often construed as the carrot and stick that God uses to make us toe the line. Heaven is the reward that good people get for being good, and hell is the punishment that bad people get for being bad. But good people do good because it's good—not because they will personally benefit from it or because someone has forced them to do it. People who do good solely for personal gain or to avoid personal harm are not good people. Suppose that a child is drowning in a lake, and suppose that an able swimmer strolls by but doesn't feel like saving her. Now suppose that a person in a wheelchair rolls up, points a shotgun at the stroller's head, and says, "If you don't save that child, I'm going to blow your head off." The stroller then reluctantly saves the child. Should he be praised for saving her? It wouldn't seem so. By parity of reasoning, it follows that if your only reason for doing good is your fear of going to hell, you're going to hell, because you're no better than the stroller. Good people do good for goodness's sake, not for their own sakes. The notion that we need God as either the author or the enforcer of the moral law, then, is erroneous.

Thought Probe

Commanded to Kill

Suppose that God spoke to you and told you to kill your spouse and your children. How would you know it was God? If you were convinced that it was, would you do it? Why or why not? What light does your answer throw on the divine command theory?

Are There Universal Moral Principles?

Although moral disagreement is widespread, we do seem to be making moral progress. We have abolished slavery, given women the vote, and made tuna dolphin-safe. If there is moral progress, however, there must be fixed moral standards against which we can judge our actions and policies. If there were no such standards, we would have no grounds for thinking that things are better now than they were before. The best explanation of the fact that we seem to be making moral progress, then, is that there are universal moral standards.

There is but one morality, as there is but one geometry.

—VOLTAIRE

Where do these standards come from? We have seen that no one, not even God, can make an action right simply by believing it to be right. But if belief can't justify a moral standard, what can? Many, including the founders of this country, share the view that moral standards can justify themselves.

"We hold these truths to be self-evident . . ." proclaims the Declaration of Independence. A self-evident truth is one that if you understand it, you are justified in believing it. Consider, for example, the statement Whatever has a shape has a size. If you understand that statement—if you know what shape and size are—you are justified in believing it. You don't need any additional evidence to support your belief. Self-evident truths provide their own evidence; they do not stand in need of any further justification.

It is widely believed that there are self-evident truths in logic. For example, the proposition that everything is identical with itself is about as self-evident as you can get. But are there any self-evident truths in morality? It seems so. Consider the statement Equals should be treated equally. This statement does not say that equals are treated equally, nor does it say that everyone is equal. It says that whenever equals are not treated equally, a wrong has been committed. To anyone who understands what equality and morality are, this statement should be self-evident.

If you do not believe that this statement is true, the burden of proof is on you to provide a counterexample. If you are unable to do so—if you cannot cite a situation in which equals should not be treated equally—then your claim that the statement is not true is irrational. You have no reason to make the claim.

Equals should be treated equally is not the only self-evident moral truth. Another is, Unnecessary suffering is wrong. This is not to say that all suffering is wrong. Some suffering, like studying for an exam, is necessary to bring about a greater good. But unnecessary suffering, like the torture of an innocent child, is wrong.

These two principles—that equals should be treated equally and that unnecessary suffering is wrong—are the great principles of **justice** and **mercy.** They do not constitute a theory of morality because they do not tell us what makes an action right. But they do serve as boundary conditions that any theory of morality must meet. If a moral theory violates one or more of these principles, it is unacceptable.

Thought Probe

Moral Knowledge

Renford Bambrough offers the following proof that we have moral knowledge:

> My proof that we have moral knowledge consists essentially in saying, "We know that this child, who is about to undergo what would otherwise be painful surgery, should be given an anaesthetic before the operation. Therefore we know at least one moral proposition to be true." I argue that no proposition that could plausibly be alleged as a reason in favour of doubting the truth of the proposition that the child should be given an anaesthetic can possibly be more certainly true than that proposition itself. If a philosopher produces an argument against my claim to know that the child should be given an anaesthetic, I can therefore be sure in advance that *either* at least one of the premises of his argument is false, or there is a mistake in the reasoning by which he purports to derive from his premises the conclusion that I do not know that the child should be given an anaesthetic.[16]

Is this a convincing proof for the existence of moral knowledge? Why or why not? Is it also a convincing proof for the existence of universal moral principles? Why or why not? What moral principle underlies the judgment made in this case?

Summary

Subjective absolutism is the doctrine that what makes an action right is that it is approved by someone. If approving an action made it right, and if disapproving it made it wrong, then one and the same action could be both right and wrong. But that's impossible. So subjective absolutism cannot be correct.

Subjective relativism is the doctrine that what makes an action right for someone is that it is approved by that person. In this view, right or wrong are not properties like round or square but relations like small or large. This view is not self-contradictory in the way that subjective absolutism is. Nevertheless, it has some bizarre consequences. For one thing, it implies that every individual is morally infallible. For another, it implies that all moral disagreement is about whether individuals know their own minds. Because neither of these implications is plausible, neither is subjective relativism.

Emotivism is the doctrine that moral utterances are expressions of emotion. When people use moral terms like right and wrong, they are not saying anything that is true or false. If this were the case, however, moral disagreement would be impossible. Nothing, even excruciating pain, would be right or wrong in and of itself. This doesn't fit with our experience of the moral life.

Cultural relativism is the view that what makes an action right for someone is that it is approved by that person's culture. This view implies that cultures are morally infallible and thus that it is impossible to disagree with one's culture and be in the right. But cultures are not morally infallible; they have approved all sorts of immoral practices. So cultural relativism cannot be correct.

The divine command theory is the doctrine that what makes an action right is that it is commanded by God. Because God is free to command whatever he wants, he could have commanded us to kill, rape, torture, and steal. But his commanding these actions would not have made them right. To suppose it would have, would be to take away whatever reason we might have for worshipping God. What's more, if goodness is a defining attribute of God, God can't be used to define goodness; the definition would be circular. Thus morality cannot depend on God.

Certain moral principles appear to be universal because they are self-evident. These include the principle of justice — equals should be treated equally — and the principle of mercy — unnecessary suffering is wrong. Any adequate ethical theory should be consistent with these principles.

Study Questions

1. What is subjective absolutism?
2. What if subjective absolutism were true? What are the consequences of accepting subjective absolutism?
3. What is subjective relativism?
4. What if subjective relativism were true? What are the consequences of accepting subjective relativism?
5. What is emotivism?
6. What if emotivism were true? What are the consequences of accepting emotivism?
7. What is cultural relativism?
8. What if cultural relativism were true? What are the consequences of accepting cultural relativism?

principle of justice
The doctrine that equals should be treated equally (and unequals in proportion to their relevant differences).

principle of mercy
The doctrine that unnecessary suffering is wrong.

9. What is the anthropological argument for cultural relativism?
10. What is the logical structure of a moral judgment?
11. What is the divine command theory?
12. What if the divine command theory were true? What are the consequences of accepting the divine command theory?

Discussion Questions

1. Some cultures, most notably Tibetan, practice polyandry, where a woman can have more than one husband. Is polyandry immoral? Why or why not?

2. Many cultures practice polygamy. Muslims may have four wives under Koranic law; the King of Ashanti in West Africa is strictly limited by law to 3,333 wives. Polygamy is not adultery. Neither of these cultures sanctions extramarital sex. Is polygamy immoral? Why or why not?

3. Suppose that we spend the afterlife in the condition in which we die. Would the current medical practice of keeping severely incapacitated people alive be morally justified? Why or why not?

4. Suppose that we believed that the only way to prevent the spirits of our enemies from doing harm to our friends and family was to eat our enemies' bodies. (Some cannibals apparently believe this.) Would this justify cannibalism? Why or why not?

5. Is there a reliable test for determining whether any purported work of sacred scripture is truly the word of God? What is it? Does any work of sacred scripture pass that test? Would members of other religions agree?

6. The Bible contains many commands (known as "hard sayings") that it would be immoral to obey. For example, Numbers 31:17, Deuteronomy 20:13, and Psalms 137:9 command Christians to kill the children and babies of their enemies. Why do we no longer follow these commands? What moral principles do they violate? What does this tell us about the relationship between religion and morality?

The End Justifies the Means
Good Makes Right

*C*onsider again the case of George Zygmanik. Those who think it was right for Lester to kill his suffering, quadriplegic brother argue that it was an act of mercy because it put George out of his misery. Those who think it was wrong for Lester to kill his brother argue that it was an act of murder because it was the intentional killing of an innocent person. These two attitudes represent the two major types of ethical theory: consequentialist and formalist. **Consequentialist** (also known as **teleological**) **ethical theories** claim that the rightness of an action is determined by its consequences. ("Teleology" comes from the Greek *telos*, meaning "end" or "purpose.") **Formalist** (also known as **deontological**) **ethical theories** claim that the rightness of an action is determined by its form, that is, by the kind of action it is. ("Deontology" comes from the Greek *deon*, meaning "duty" or "requirement.") Those who argue that Lester Zygmanik's action was right because it put an end to his brother's suffering are consequentialists. Those who argue that it was wrong because it involved killing an innocent person are formalists.

When we judge a person, a person's character, or a person's motives to be good, we are making a moral judgment. When we judge a physical object (like a car) or an experience (like happiness) to be good, we are not making a moral judgment. So goodness comes in two varieties: moral and nonmoral. Consequentialist ethical theories usually define the right in terms of the good. They maintain that right actions are those that produce the most nonmoral good.

Some things, like money, are good because of what you can do with them. Other things, like happiness, are good regardless of what you can do with them. If someone asked, "What is happiness good for?" we wouldn't know what to say. The value of happiness is not derived from its usefulness; it's just good to be happy. Things, like happiness, that are good for their own sake are **intrinsically valuable.** Things that are good for the sake of something else are **extrinsically** or **instrumentally valuable.**

Happiness is the supreme object of existence.
—J. GILCHRIST LAWSON

consequentialist (teleological) ethical theory An ethical theory that judges the rightness or wrongness of an action in terms of its consequences.

formalist (deontological) ethical theory An ethical theory that judges the rightness or wrongness of an action in terms of its form.

intrinsic value Value for its own sake.

instrumental (extrinsic) value Value for the sake of something else.

Consequentialist ethical theories seek to maximize intrinsic value. Any consequentialist ethical theory, then, must answer two questions: (1) What is intrinsically valuable? and (2) Who is supposed to receive this value? The two most famous consequentialist ethical theories are ethical egoism and utilitarianism.

Ethical Egoism

The world is governed only by self-interest.

—JOHANN SCHILLER

Ethical egoism claims that our only duty is to do what's good for ourselves. As long as we've done what's in our own best interest, we've done the right thing, even if we've made a lot of other people miserable in the process. **Ethical egoism,** then, says that what makes an action right is that it promotes one's own best interest.

Different egoists have different ideas about what's in their best interest. Many are *hedonists* who believe that the more pleasure they get, the better off they are. ("Hedonism" comes from the Greek *hedone,* meaning "pleasure.") Others measure the quality of their lives in terms of the knowledge, power, or self-realization they attain. Egoists of every stripe, however, agree that their only duty is to look out for number one.

Ethical egoism does not require you to do only what you want to do — because what you want to do may not be in your best interest. For example, you may want to sleep late, get high, and listen to music all day, but that may not be in your best interest, especially if you want to stay healthy, get a job, and raise a family. Nor does ethical egoism require that you perform only selfish acts — acts that benefit you at the expense of others. If you are continually making other people miserable, you may not get the kind of cooperation you need to accomplish your goals. So acting selfishly may not be in an egoist's best interest. Clever egoists act generously in the short term in hopes of promoting their best interests in the long term.

Even though the behavior of an ethical egoist may not differ all that much from that of a nonegoist, few people consider ethical egoism to be a plausible theory of morality, for it condones the most heinously evil actions imaginable. Suppose you are walking through the woods one day and come upon your rival, who has just been attacked by a wild animal. If it is in your best interest to eliminate your rival, and if you can do so without getting caught, then ethical egoism says that you are morally obligated to finish him off. Any ethical theory that mandates such acts, however, is, to say the least, questionable.

Those who adopt the hedonistic version of ethical egoism (termed "ethical hedonism") claim that it is the only ethical theory that is consistent with what we know about human motivation. They maintain that the only thing that moves us to action is the desire to increase our own happiness. In other words, everything we do, we do because we think it will make us happy. This psychological theory of human motivation is known as **psychological hedonism.**

If psychological hedonism were true — if we could do only what we thought would make us happy — then ethical egoism would be unavoidable, for "ought" implies "can." We can legitimately claim that someone ought to do something only if he can do it. For example, if you were running late for a meeting, it would be ludicrous for someone to assert that you ought to grow wings and fly to it because that's impossible. Similarly, say the ethical hedonists, it would be ludicrous for someone to assert that you ought to desire something besides your own happiness because that, too, is impossible.

Some believe that the scientific theory of psychological hedonism can be used to prove the philosophical theory of ethical egoism. The argument from psychological hedonism for ethical egoism goes like this:

1. We are morally obligated to perform an action only if we are able to perform it.
2. We are able to perform an action only if we believe that it will maximize our happiness.
3. Therefore, we are morally obligated to perform an action only if we believe that it will maximize our happiness.

The conclusion of this argument doesn't establish ethical hedonism, however, for it only provides a necessary condition for right action, whereas ethical hedonism gives us both a necessary and a sufficient condition. The argument from

ethical egoism The doctrine that what makes an action right is that it promotes one's own best interest.

psychological hedonism The doctrine that the only thing individuals can desire is their own happiness.

psychological hedonism says that we ought to perform an action *only if* it maximizes our happiness whereas ethical hedonism also says that we ought to perform an action *if* it maximizes our happiness. If the argument from psychological hedonism is sound, however, it does show that any ethical theory that requires us to do something other than maximize our own happiness is mistaken.

The claim that we can do only those things that we believe will make us happy is an empirical one. It is not true by definition and thus can be established only by scientific investigation. On the face of it, however, the claim seems to be false, for we do not always seem to do what we believe will maximize our happiness. Consider the passerby who jumps into a raging river to save a drowning child or the patriotic soldier who throws himself on a hand grenade to save his buddies. Neither of these actions seems designed to maximize the actor's happiness.

Selfishness is the root and source of all natural and moral evils.

—Nathaniel Emmons

The psychological hedonist might respond to these counterexamples by saying that although these actions seem to be motivated by something other than one's own happiness, they are not. The person who jumps into a river to save a child, for example, may do so because she thinks the action will make her famous, and being famous would make her happy. Or the soldier who jumps on a hand grenade may do so because it makes him happy to think that he is saving his buddies. These attempts to save the theory, however, turn psychological hedonism into an untestable—and hence uninterestingg—hypothesis. If no evidence can count against it, the theory doesn't tell us anything about the world.

Consider the statement Either it's raining or it isn't. There is no evidence that could possibly refute this statement. Because it's consistent with all possible states of affairs, it's uninformative. We don't learn anything about the weather by being told Either it's raining or it isn't. Similarly, if psychological hedonism is consistent with all possible states of affairs, it tells us nothing about human behavior. In that case, it can't support ethical egoism.

Suppose that someone were to claim that our only motivation for doing anything is to become tired so that we will go to sleep. This hypothesis would account for everything that we do because sleep eventually follows every action we perform. Yet no one has seriously proposed this as a theory of human motivation because there is no way to test it. Nothing could possibly count against it. Every possible action can be interpreted to fit it. Consequently, it's uninformative. The same goes for psychological hedonism.

The essence of true nobility is neglect of self.

—J. A. Froude

Not only is there reason to believe that psychological hedonism is uninformative, there is also reason to believe that it's false. For anyone who was concerned solely with his own happiness would be miserable. Joel Feinberg brings this out in the following thought experiment.

Thought Experiment

Feinberg's Single-Minded Hedonist

To feel the full force of the paradox of hedonism the reader should conduct an experiment in his imagination. Imagine a person (let's call him "Jones") who is, first of all, devoid of intellectual curiosity. He has no desire to acquire any kind of knowledge for its own sake, and thus is utterly indifferent to questions of science, mathematics, and philosophy. Imagine further that the beauties of nature leave Jones cold: he is unimpressed by the autumn foliage, the snow-capped mountains, and the rolling oceans. Long walks in the country on spring mornings and skiing forays in the winter are to him equally a bore. Moreover, let us suppose that Jones can find no appeal in art. Novels are dull, poetry a pain, painting nonsense and music just noise. Suppose further that Jones has neither the participant's nor the spectator's passion for baseball, football, tennis, or any other sport. Swimming to him is a cruel aquatic form of calisthenics, the sun only a cause of sunburn. Dancing is coeducational idiocy, conversation a waste of time, the other sex an unappealing mystery. Politics is a fraud, religion mere superstition; and the misery of millions of underprivileged human beings is nothing to be concerned with or excited about. Suppose finally that Jones has no talent for any kind of handicraft, industry, or commerce, and that he does not regret that fact.

What then is Jones interested in? He must desire something. To be sure, he does. Jones has an overwhelming passion for, a complete preoccupation with, his own happiness. The one exclusive desire of his life is to be happy. It takes little imagination at this point to see that Jones's one desire is bound to be frustrated.[19]

Feinberg's single-minded hedonist shows that we can be happy only if we desire something other than our own happiness. But if we desire something other than our own happiness, psychological hedonism is false.

Psychological hedonism fails as a theory of human motivation because it confuses the object of our desires with the result of satisfying them. We may well feel happy when we satisfy our desires, but that doesn't mean that happiness is the object of our desires. As Anglican priest Joseph Butler noted, "It is not because we love ourselves that we find delight in such and such objects, but because we have particular affections towards them."[20] In other words, we don't desire things because they make us happy; they make us happy because we desire them. Happiness is not the cause of our desires but the effect of satisfying them. Because psychological hedonism mistakes an effect for a cause —because it puts the cart before the horse, so to speak— it fails as a theory of human motivation.

Even if ethical egoism did provide necessary and sufficient conditions for an action to be right, it would be a peculiar sort of ethical theory, for its adherents couldn't consistently advocate it. Suppose that someone came to an ethical egoist for moral advice. If the ethical egoist wanted to do what is in his best interest, he would not tell his client to do what is in her best interest because her interests might conflict with his. Rather, he would tell her to do what is in his best interest.

Such advice has been satirized on national TV. Al Franken, a former writer for *Saturday Night Live* and the author of *Rush Limbaugh Is a Big Fat Idiot and Other Observations*, proclaimed on a number of *Saturday Night Live* shows in the early 1980s that, whereas the 1970s were known as the "me" decade, the 1980s were going to be known as the "Al Franken" decade. So

He who lives only to benefit himself confers on the world a benefit when he dies.

—TERTULLIAN

In a series of novels and essays including *The Fountainhead* and *Atlas Shrugged*, Ayn Rand has argued for a version of ethical egoism called *objectivism*. She writes,

> The basic social principle of the Objectivist ethics is that just as life is an end in itself, so every living human being is an end in himself, not the means to the ends or the welfare of others—and, therefore, that man must live for his own sake, neither sacrificing himself to others nor sacrificing others to himself. To live for his own sake means that *the achievement of his own happiness is man's highest moral purpose.*[21]

To achieve happiness, however, individuals must do more than try to satisfy their desires, because desires can conflict. Rather, they should try to satisfy their *rational* desires, for "the rational interests of men do not clash—that there is no conflict of interests among men who do not desire the unearned, who do not make sacrifices nor accept them, who deal with one another as traders, giving value for value."[22] Thus Rand's objectivism is not a true egoism, for built into it is a principle of justice and fair play. We can't fulfill just any desire but only our rational desires, she argues. And our rational desires are directed only on what we've earned. So Ayn Rand's egoism is more properly viewed as a form of *libertarianism*, which holds that individuals should be free to do whatever they want as long as it doesn't interfere with the rights of others.

---

whenever anyone was faced with a difficult decision, the individual should ask, "How can I most benefit Al Franken?"

There is something odd about an ethical theory that cannot be advocated by its adherents. In fact, it points to what may be ethical egoism's biggest flaw: it doesn't treat equals equally. If there is no morally relevant difference between people, there is no reason not to treat them the same. Anyone who treats them differently is guilty of unfair discrimination. The fact that others are members of a particular race or sex is irrelevant from a moral point of view. Thus anyone who discriminates against others simply because they belong to a different race or sex is guilty of racism or sexism. Similarly, the fact that others are not identical to you is irrelevant from a moral point of view. Thus if you discriminate against others simply because they are not you—if you don't treat them with the same respect that you treat yourself—you are guilty of egoism, which seems just as morally objectionable as racism or sexism. An adequate ethical theory should not treat people differently unless there is a good reason for doing so, for justice requires treating equals equally.

Act-Utilitarianism

The most plausible and widely discussed consequentialist ethical theory is utilitarianism. Traditional utilitarianism takes happiness to be the only thing that's intrinsically valuable, that is, valuable for its own sake. Unlike ethical hedonism, however, it does not maintain that we should seek to maximize only our own happiness. Rather, it maintains that we should seek to maximize the total amount of happiness in the world. Consequently, it avoids many of the problems facing ethical egoism. Specifically, traditional utilitarianism (also called "act-utilitarianism") does not allow people to do something simply because it makes them happy. The happiness of the other people involved must also be taken into account.

Because utilitarianism considers happiness to be good in and of itself, no one's happiness is more valuable than anyone else's. Thus, in determining which action will produce happiness, everyone's happiness must be counted equally. **Act-utilitarianism,** then, says that what makes an action right is that it maximizes happiness, everyone considered.

Act-utilitarianism suggests a straightforward procedure for determining what we should do in any given situation:

1. Identify the different actions that can be performed in the situation.
2. Identify the individuals who will be affected by those actions.
3. Calculate the amount of happiness each individual will receive from those actions.
4. Sum the individual amounts of happiness to determine which action will produce the most happiness.

Suppose we had a situation in which there were three possible courses of action and three people involved. Then we could put the results of the utilitarian calculation in the form of a table (a "util" is a unit of happiness):

	Action 1	Action 2	Action 3
John	3 utils	4 utils	4 utils
Sue	3 utils	2 utils	5 utils
Mary	3 utils	2 utils	5 utils
	9 utils	8 utils	14 utils

In this situation, action 3 is the right action to perform because it produces the most happiness, everyone considered.

Jeremy Bentham (1748–1832), the first to provide a systematic defense of utilitarianism, assumes that the happiness produced by various actions differs only in degree and thus can be measured on a single scale. He claims that, by using his "hedonic calculus," we can quantify the amount of happiness produced by an action. His calculus takes into account such factors as the *intensity* of the happiness, the *duration* of the happiness, the *probability* that the happiness will occur, the *propinquity* (nearness in time) of the happiness to the action, the *fecundity* of the action (the probability that it will produce more happiness in the future), and the *impurity* of the action (the probability that it will produce less happiness in the future).

John Stuart Mill (1806–1873), a follower of Bentham and one of the most influential philosophers of the nineteenth century, argues that the happiness produced by various actions differs not only in degree but also in kind and, thus cannot be measured on a single scale. He writes,

> It is quite compatible with the principle of utility to recognize the fact that some *kinds* of pleasure are more desirable and more valuable than others. It would be absurd that, while in estimating all other things, quality is considered as well as quantity, the estimation of pleasures should be supposed to depend on quantity alone.[23]

act-utilitarianism
The doctrine that what makes an action right is that it maximizes happiness, everyone considered. Also termed "traditional utilitarianism."

JEREMY BENTHAM
1748–1832

Mill believes that happiness differs in quality as well as quantity. Thus in determining what action to perform, we have to consider the kind of happiness produced as well as the amount.

To see what Mill is getting at, compare the happiness derived from playing chess with that of getting drunk. Although playing chess may not produce as much happiness as getting drunk, it could be argued that it produces a better kind of happiness. If so, playing chess is a more worthwhile activity than getting drunk. This is the basis of Mill's famous dictum, "It is better to be a human being dissatisfied than a pig satisfied; better to be Socrates dissatisfied than a fool satisfied."

Having to rank the various forms of happiness in terms of their quality, however, makes the utilitarian calculation much more difficult. For there seems to be no objective way to do it. Mill suggests that we poll those who have experienced the different types of happiness and go with the majority. He says, "Of two pleasures, if there be one to which all or almost all who have experience of both give a decided preference, irrespective of a feeling of moral obligation to prefer it, that is the more desirable pleasure."[24] Although this may seem an eminently democratic procedure, there is no guarantee it will produce the results Mill wants. For the masses may well prefer the lower pleasures to the higher. Even highly educated people may do so. To maintain the distinction between higher and lower pleasures, then, it looks like Mill

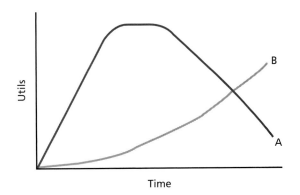

HAPPINESS PRODUCED BY TWO ACTIONS OVER TIME.
In the time span depicted, the happiness produced by A is greater in the short term than that produced by B. Does that mean that A is the better action?

must appeal to another standard of value besides utility. But if he does, his theory is no longer utilitarianism.

Even if it were easy to calculate how much happiness an action would produce, utilitarianism faces another problem: when to perform the calculation. Every action we undertake has consequences indefinitely into the future. At what point should we measure the happiness produced? The answer we give to this question will have a profound effect on what actions we consider to be permissible. An action that produces little happiness in the short term may produce a great deal of happiness in the long term. Consider the graph above. It represents the amount of happiness produced by two different actions (A and B) over time. In the short term, A produces much more happiness than B. In the long term, however, B produces much more happiness than A. The graph could represent the choice between building nuclear power plants and investing in alternative renewable sources of energy, such as solar power or wind power. The advantage of building nuclear power plants is a quick return on our investment. The disadvantage is that they create radioactive wastes that must be disposed of, and the plants themselves must eventually be sealed up and kept off-limits for more than ten thousand years. An investment in alternative renewable sources of energy will not have as quick a return, but it may produce more happiness in the long term because these sources of energy don't pollute and they don't run out. Should we take future generations into account when performing the utilitarian calculation? Act-utilitarianism is silent on this point.

Happiness is a pig's philosophy.
—FRIEDRICH NIETZSCHE

That all who are happy are equally happy is not true. A peasant and a philosopher may be equally satisfied, but not equally happy.
—SAMUEL JOHNSON

Thought Probe

Animal Rights

Jeremy Bentham believed that what made a being worthy of ethical consideration was not whether it could reason but whether it could suffer. Consequently, he thought that an action's effect on animals should be taken into account when performing utilitarian calculations. Do you agree? Is it possible for us to gauge animal suffering? If so, how much should animal suffering be weighed in the calculation? As much as human suffering?

Problems with Rights

According to utilitarianism, the end justifies the means. As long as an action achieves the goal of maximizing happiness, it's morally correct, no matter how it was accomplished. This is not consistent with our notion of rights, however. We believe that certain things shouldn't be done to people, even if doing them would have good consequences. H. J. McCloskey illustrates this in the following thought experiment.

Thought Experiment

McCloskey's Utilitarian Informant

Suppose a utilitarian were visiting an area in which there was racial strife, and that, during his visit, a Negro rapes a white woman, and that race riots occur as a result of the crime, white mobs, with the connivance of the police, bashing and killing Negroes, etc. Suppose too that our utilitarian is in the area of the crime when it is committed such that his testimony would bring about the conviction of a particular Negro. If he knows that a quick arrest will stop the riots and lynchings, surely, as a utilitarian, he must conclude that he has a duty to bear false witness in order to bring about the punishment of an innocent person.[25]

According to utilitarianism, if falsely accusing and convicting an innocent person would maximize happiness, then we are morally obligated to do so. But this does not accord with our experience of the moral life. It's wrong to bear false witness even if doing so will produce more happiness than not.

Not only could act-utilitarianism mandate lying, it could mandate killing, as Richard Brandt demonstrates.

Thought Experiment

Brandt's Utilitarian Heir

Let us suppose that Mr. X is considering whether it is his duty to hasten his father's death. Let us suppose further that Mr. X's father is well-to-do, whereas the son is poor. The father gives the son no money, and the son and his family are continually missing the joys of life because they do not have the means to pay for them. Furthermore, the father is ill and requires nursing care. The cost of nursing care is rapidly eating into the father's capital. Moreover, the father himself gets no joy from life. He must take drugs to make life tolerable, and his physician says that his condition will gradually become worse, although death is still several years away.

On the utilitarian theory, it can well be (and on the hedonistic form, certainly will be) the son's duty to bring about the demise of his father, provided he can do this so that his deed will be undetected (thereby avoiding legal calamities for himself and his family, and not weakening the general confidence of fathers in their sons). But would this in fact be his duty? It does not seem so.[26]

If killing someone—even your father—would produce more happiness than keeping him alive, act-utilitarianism would have us believe that he should be killed. But that is inconsistent with our notion of rights. You are not morally obligated to kill someone to make people happy.

Problems with Duties

Not only is utilitarianism inconsistent with our notion of rights, it is also inconsistent with our notion of duties. We have a number of duties to others, including a duty not to break our promises. Act-utilitarianism maintains, on the contrary, that our only duty is to maximize happiness. If performing that duty requires breaking our promises, then so be it. British philosopher W. D. Ross illustrates.

Duty has nothing to do with what somebody else conceives to be for the common good.
—ROBERT MILLIKAN

Thought Experiment

Ross's Unhappy Promise

Suppose, to simplify the case by abstraction, that the fulfillment of a promise to A would produce 1,000 units of good for him, but that by doing some other act I could produce 1,001 units of good for B, to whom I have made no promise, the other consequences of the two acts being of equal value; should we really think it self-evident that it was our duty to do the second act and not the first? I think not. We should, I fancy, hold that only a much greater disparity of value between the total consequences would justify us in failing to discharge our *prima facie* duty to A. After all, a promise is a promise, and is not to be treated so lightly as the theory we are examining would imply.[27]

Act-utilitarianism holds that we should break a promise whenever doing so will produce more happiness than keeping the promise will. But promises are more important than that. Our obligation to keep our promises is no less binding than our obligation to maximize happiness.

Some duties derive from our membership in a community, whereas others derive from the special roles we play in that community. Parents have special duties to their children, doctors have special duties to their patients, lawyers have special duties to their clients, and so on. But just as act-utilitarianism doesn't provide an adequate account of our ordinary duties, it doesn't provide an adequate account of our special duties either. British political theorist William Godwin, an early defender of utilitarianism, highlights this aspect of utilitarianism in the following thought experiment.

Godwin's Fire Rescue

A man is of more worth than a beast; because, being possessed of higher faculties, he is capable of a more refined and genuine happiness. In the same manner the illustrious archbishop of Cambray was of more worth than his valet, and there are few of us that would hesitate to pronounce, if his palace were in flames, and the life of only one of them could be preserved, which of the two ought to be preferred. . . .

Suppose I had been myself the valet; I ought to have chosen to die, rather than Fenelon should have died. The life of Fenelon was really preferable to that of the valet. . . .

Suppose the valet had been my brother, my father or my benefactor. This would not alter the truth of the proposition. The life of Fenelon would still be more valuable than that of the valet; and justice, pure, unadulterated justice, would still have preferred that which was most valuable.[28]

Godwin claims that if his brother, his father, or his benefactor were trapped in a building with the archbishop and he could save only one of them, he should save the archbishop because that would produce the most happiness. In the first edition of his book, Godwin claimed that he should save the archbishop even if the other person was his mother. This created such an outcry that he had to change the example. But even the new situation is a counterexample to act-utilitarianism. Our duties to our family and friends often outweigh our duty to produce happiness.

Problems with Justice

Justice is to give every man his due.

—ARISTOTLE

Although act-utilitarianism requires that everybody's happiness be counted equally, it doesn't require that the happiness produced by an action be distributed equally. All that matters from a utilitarian point of view is that the amount of happiness produced be the greatest possible. If we can produce more happiness by distributing it unequally, that is what we should do. British philosopher A. C. Ewing provides this example.

Ewing's Utilitarian Torture

Suppose we could slightly increase the collective happiness of ten men by taking away all happiness from one of them, would it be right to do so? It is perhaps arguable that it would be if the difference in happiness of the nine was very large, but not if it was very slight. And if the happiness of the nine were purchased by the actual torture of the one, the injustice of it would seem to poison the happiness and render it worse than valueless even if they were callous

LADY JUSTICE.
Is utilitarian justice
consistent with that
represented by Lady
Justice?

enough to enjoy it. Yet on the utilitarian view any distribution of good, however unfair, ought to be preferred to any other, however just, if it would yield the slightest additional happiness.[29]

Act-utilitarianism would have us believe that justice is served by maximizing happiness. So, by that argument, if the amount of happiness that the Marquis de Sade experienced by torturing innocent young girls exceeded the amount of unhappiness the girls felt by being tortured, he was morally justified in torturing them.

Questions of justice arise not only with regard to the distribution of goods but also with regard to the retribution for crimes. The basic principle of retributive justice is captured in the phrase "an eye for an eye, a tooth for a tooth, a life for a life." This conception of justice requires giving everyone their due. It is represented by the figure of Lady Justice who, blindfolded, carries a balance, symbolically ensuring that no one gets more — or less — than what's coming to each. Act-utilitarianism has no place for such a principle. According to utilitarianism, punishment is justified only if it maximizes happiness.

It has traditionally been thought that punishment can maximize happiness in two ways: by making the criminal a better person or by lowering the overall crime rate. But, in order to accomplish these goals, it is not necessary that

Justice, when equal scales she holds, is blind; nor cruelty, nor mercy change her mind.

—SIR JOHN DENHAM

Utilitarian philosopher Peter Singer has made headlines across the globe because of his controversial views on, among other things, the right of parents to kill their seriously disabled infants. Consider this report:

> He has been called a "notorious messenger of death" in his hometown of Melbourne, Australia. The British media have denounced him as "the man who would kill disabled babies," and in Germany he's been compared to Hitler's henchman Martin Borman. Protesters in wheelchairs have fought his appearances, chained themselves to barricades and smashed his glasses.
>
> He's also been called the most influential philosopher alive. . . .
>
> His most famous book, *Animal Liberation*, published in 1975, jump-started the entire animal rights movement, converting many readers to lifelong vegetarianism and inspiring reforms in humane treatment for laboratory animals and livestock. But animal liberation is only one facet of Singer's ethics. Indeed, his goal is to reconfigure our entire moral landscape.
>
> According to Singer, religion's 2000-year domination of morality ended . . . in 1993, when British law ruled that a comatose man named Anthony Bland could be killed by his doctors. That decision, he maintains, dealt a "mortal" blow to the unquestioned sanctity of human life.
>
> Singer argues that ethics today should be guided by a particular brand of utilitarianism: he calls himself a "preference utilitarian." In classic utilitarianism, what is good is defined as what brings happiness. But happiness is hard to measure. Singer proposes instead that good be defined by "preference." Under this philosophy, moral decisions are based on the most intense preferences of a given individual or group.
>
> Thus, claims Singer, many times animals will be more deserving of life than certain humans, including disabled babies and adults who are brain-injured or in vegetative comas. Presumably, a healthy chimp's preference for life is more intense than a disabled infant's. This philosophy would rule out most medical experimentation on animals, as well as the breeding of animals to provide organs for human transplants.
>
> Even more radical, Singer suggests that since preference is influenced by self-awareness, babies should not be considered "persons" until they are one month old. Before that time, parents and their doctors should be free to kill a baby if, for instance, it has Down's syndrome and the parents don't wish to raise it.[30]

Thought Probe

Singer's "Preference Utilitarianism"

Is Singer's "preference utilitarianism" more plausible than conventional act- or rule-utilitarianism? Do you agree with Singer's position on the permissibility of killing disabled infants? Why or why not?

---

the punishment fit the crime. It is not even necessary that we punish only criminals. Ewing considers these consequences in the following thought experiment.

Thought Experiment

Ewing's Innocent Criminal

Suppose that in a particular case it is impossible to find the real criminal, but suppose also that we have got hold of a person generally believed guilty so that the deterrent effects of punishing him would be the same as if he really were guilty. Suppose, further, that psychological experts could assure us that his character would benefit by a spell of imprisonment. (Even a very good man's character often benefits by suffering: very possibly it is more likely than a bad man's to do so.) That surely would not make the punishment right, yet it ought to on the utilitarian theory.[31]

If punishing an innocent person would maximize happiness, then act-utilitarianism says we should do so, whether the person has it coming or not. But that violates the principle of justice, which says that equals should be treated equally.

Thought Probe

The Utility Machine

Suppose that an inventor approaches the president of the United States with a device that will increase the happiness of those who use it by 1,000 percent. The inventor wants to put the device into production but only if the president agrees to his terms. The president, of course, is interested in providing for the common good and promoting the general welfare, so he asks the inventor what he has in mind. The inventor tells him that he wants to be able to kill at random 50,000 users of the device every year. (Warning labels on the device would alert users to this potential hazard.) The president is concerned about all the pain and suffering the deaths of these 50,000 people would cause. The inventor assures him that even taking into account the suffering caused by their deaths, the people of the United States will still be 1,000 percent happier with the device than without it. Should the president allow the device to go into production? Why or why not? (Such a device is already on the market. Can you guess what it is?)[32]

Rule-Utilitarianism

Act-utilitarianism is inconsistent with our experience of the moral life because it does not fit with our notions of rights, duties, and justice. To try to salvage act-utilitarianism's basic insight—that we should be concerned with promoting the common good—some have proposed what is known as rule-utilitarianism. Rule-utilitarianism maintains that the rightness of an action is determined not by its consequences but by the consequences of the rule it falls under. If an action falls under a rule that would maximize happiness if it were generally followed, then the action is right. **Rule-utilitarianism,** then, is the doctrine that what makes an action right is that it falls under a rule that, if generally followed, would maximize happiness, everyone considered.

According to act-utilitarianism, the procedure for deciding whether an action is right is a two-step process: (1) identify the alternative courses of action, and (2) determine which action would produce the most happiness.

rule-utilitarianism The doctrine that what makes an action right is that it falls under a rule that, if generally followed, would maximize happiness, everyone considered.

According to rule-utilitarianism, the procedure is somewhat different: (1) identify the rule that the action falls under, and (2) determine whether that rule, if generally followed, would maximize happiness. The advantage of rule-utilitarianism over act-utilitarianism is that it fits better with our notions of rights, duties, and justice.

If more happiness would be produced by having people follow rules like "Never lie," "Never cheat," and "Never steal" than by having them follow the rule "perform the action that maximizes happiness," then rule-utilitarianism would be the better theory. But there is reason to believe that following such exceptionless rules would not maximize happiness. Consider the rule "Never lie." Suppose that a crazed person wielding a bloody knife comes to your door and asks you where your neighbor is. In such a situation, telling a lie would seem to be the right thing to do, for it would probably save your neighbor's life and thus produce more happiness than telling the truth. So the rule "Do not lie except to save the lives of innocent people" is a better rule than "Do not lie."

According to rule-utilitarianism, a morally correct action is one that falls under a morally correct rule. And a morally correct rule is one that, if generally followed, would maximize happiness. Because rules with the most exceptions seem to produce the most happiness, they would seem to be the most morally correct.

But once we start allowing rules to have exceptions, it looks as if rule-utilitarianism will end up sanctioning the same actions as act-utilitarianism. Consider the case of Brandt's utilitarian heir. The rule "Never kill innocent people" would not allow the son to kill his father. But the rule "Never kill innocent people unless it maximizes happiness" would allow the killing. Because that rule would produce more happiness if generally followed, it is the morally correct rule to follow. But following it would be no different than following the rule "Perform the action that maximizes happiness." So rule-utilitarianism may have no significant advantage over act-utilitarianism.

You might object that, appearances to the contrary, rules with exceptions would not maximize happiness. For example, it could be argued that a rule like "Never kill innocent people unless it maximizes happiness" would not produce more happiness than a rule like "Never kill innocent people" because the former would create an unacceptably high level of anxiety, distrust, and uncertainty. People would fear for their lives if they knew that they could legitimately be killed whenever their death would produce more happiness than unhappiness.

A rule that allowed you to kill somebody whenever doing so would produce more happiness than unhappiness would probably not be correct on rule-utilitarian grounds. But a rule that allowed you to kill somebody whenever it would produce a *great deal* more happiness than unhappiness probably would be morally correct. A society that followed that rule would be happier than one that didn't. Such a rule would permit the killing of innocent people if it was necessary to produce a great good. Under the right circumstances, it could even sanction genocide. If the world would be much happier if all the members of a certain group were killed, then rule-utilitarianism (as well as act-utilitarianism) would have us believe that we should kill them. But this doesn't seem right. Human life seems more valuable than happiness, even a great deal of it.

The failure of act- and rule-utilitarianism suggests that the utilitarian approach to ethics is mistaken. Common to both of these ethical theories is the assumption that happiness is the only thing that is intrinsically valuable. As John Stuart Mill says,

> According to the Greatest Happiness Principle . . . the ultimate end, with reference to and for the sake of which all other things are desirable, (whether we are considering our own good or that of other people), is an existence exempt as far as possible from pain, and as rich as possible in enjoyments.[33]

Although happiness may well be an intrinsic good, many doubt whether it is the only intrinsic good. Robert Nozick puts this assumption to the test in the following thought experiment.

Thought Experiment

Nozick's Experience Machine

Suppose there were an experience machine that would give you any experience you desired. Super-duper neurophysiologists could stimulate your brain so that you would think and feel you were writing a great novel, or making a friend, or reading an interesting book. All the time you would be floating in a tank, with electrodes attached to your brain. Should you plug into this machine for life, preprogramming your life's experiences? If you are worried about missing out on desirable experiences, we can suppose that business enterprises have researched thoroughly the lives of many others. You can pick and choose from their large library or smorgasbord of such experiences, selecting your life's experiences for, say, the next two years. After two years have passed, you will have ten minutes or ten hours out of the tank, to select the experiences of your next two years. Of course, while in the tank you won't know that you're there; you'll think it's all actually happening. Others can also plug in to have the experiences they want, so there's no need to stay unplugged to serve them. (Ignore problems such as who will service the machines if everyone plugs in.) Would you plug in? What else can matter to us, other than how our lives feel from the inside?[34]

What if a body might have all the pleasures in the world for asking? Who would so unman himself as, by accepting them, to desert his soul, and become a perpetual slave to his senses?

— SENECA

If utilitarianism were correct, the society envisioned by Nozick — a society where everybody spent most of their time in an experience machine — would be a utopia, for its inhabitants would have the most pleasurable experiences possible. Nevertheless, some consider Nozick's society the ultimate dystopia, for the people in it are not leading valuable lives. What makes life valuable, they claim, is the kind of choices you make, not the kind of experiences you have. But the people in Nozick's society aren't making any real choices at all. They may choose which tape to play, but they do not make any choices that build character or improve the self. The people in Nozick's society are not admirable or virtuous. In fact, they are little better than drug addicts who artificially stimulate their brains to escape reality. If this is not utopia, however, there is reason to believe that utilitarianism is flawed.

Thought Probe

Beneficial Drugs

Suppose there were a legal drug that reduced irritability, increased productivity, and made people happy in their work without producing any negative side effects such as addiction or dependence. Would it be morally permissible for an employer to require employees to take it? Would it be morally permissible for an employer to put it in the company's water supply? Does your answer support or undermine utilitarianism?

Summary

Consequentialist ethical theories claim that the rightness of an action is determined by its consequences. Ethical egoism, the doctrine that what makes an action right is that it promotes one's own best interest, is such a theory. It is not, however, a plausible theory of morality because it condones the most evil actions imaginable. In defense of ethical egoism, some have asserted psychological hedonism, the doctrine that the only thing anyone can desire is his or her own happiness. On the face of it, though, this claim seems false, for we do seem to not always act out of self-interest but rather often from genuine altruism. Further, careful consideration reveals a paradox in the doctrine. It is clear that we can be happy only if we desire something other than our own happiness. But if we desire something other than our own happiness, psychological hedonism is false. Ethical egoism also faces the problem that it cannot be consistently advocated by its adherents. This strange difficulty in turn points to an even bigger flaw: by the lights of the theory, one cannot treat equals equally.

A more plausible consequentialist ethical theory is traditional or act-utilitarianism, the doctrine that what makes an action right is that it maximizes happiness, everyone considered. We do the right thing when we produce as much happiness as possible, taking everybody into account. The theory conflicts, however, with our basic intuitions regarding rights, duties, and justice. We believe that people have rights—that certain things shouldn't be done to them even if the actions would have good consequences. We think that we have several duties (like not breaking promises) to others, including special duties to those we have special relationships with. We believe that justice demands that goods and punishments be distributed fairly. But for act-utilitarianism, all these considerations are unimportant; it's the total amount of happiness produced that counts.

To try to improve on act-utilitarianism and to salvage its basic insight—that we should promote the common good—some have proposed rule-utilitarianism. It's the doctrine that what makes an action right is that it falls under a rule that, if generally followed, would maximize happiness, everyone considered. The best rules would include exceptions, allowing them to be broken whenever doing so would produce a great amount of happiness. But such rules would not adequately protect our rights.

Study Questions

1. What is the difference between consequentialist (teleological) and formalist (deontological) ethical theories?
2. What is the difference between moral and nonmoral goods?
3. What is the difference between intrinsic and instrumental (extrinsic) value?
4. What is ethical egoism?
5. What is psychological hedonism?
6. What is the argument from psychological hedonism for ethical egoism?
7. What is Feinberg's single-minded hedonist thought experiment? How does it attempt to undermine psychological hedonism?
8. What is traditional or act-utilitarianism?
9. What are McCloskey's utilitarian informant and Brandt's utilitarian heir thought experiments? How do they attempt to undermine utilitarianism?

10. What are Ross's unhappy promise and Godwin's fire rescue thought experiments? How do they attempt to undermine utilitarianism?

11. What are Ewing's utilitarian torture and innocent criminal thought experiments? How do they attempt to undermine utilitarianism?

12. What is rule-utilitarianism?

13. What is Nozick's experience machine thought experiment? How does it attempt to undermine utilitarianism?

Discussion Questions

1. Consider this case presented by British philosopher Bernard Williams:

Thought Experiment

Williams's South American Showdown

Jim finds himself in the central square of a small South American town. Tied up against the wall are a row of twenty Indians, most terrified, a few defiant, in front of them several armed men in uniform. A heavy man in a sweat-stained khaki shirt turns out to be the captain in charge and, after a good deal of questioning of Jim which establishes that he got there by accident while on a botanical expedition, explains that the Indians are a random group of the inhabitants who, after recent acts of protest against the government, are just about to be killed to remind other possible protesters of the advantages of not protesting. However, since Jim is an honoured visitor from another land, the captain is happy to offer him a guest's privilege of killing one of the Indians himself. If Jim accepts, then as a special mark of the occasion, the other Indians will be let off. Of course, if Jim refuses, then there is no special occasion, and Pedro here will do what he was about to do when Jim arrived, and kill them all. Jim, with some desperate recollection of schoolboy fiction, wonders whether if he got hold of a gun, he could hold the captain, Pedro and the rest of the soldiers to threat, but it is quite clear from the set-up that nothing of that kind is going to work: any attempt at that sort of thing will mean that all the Indians will be killed, and himself. The men against the wall, and the other villagers, understand the situation, and are obviously begging him to accept. What should he do?[35]

Should Jim kill one of the Indians? Why or why not?

2. Are you *morally* obligated to obey all the laws in your city, state, and country? Is it ever immoral to obey a law? If so, when?

3. Consider this case from Judith Jarvis Thomson.

Thought Experiment

Thomson's Trolley Problem

Suppose you are the driver of a trolley. The trolley rounds a bend, and there come into view ahead five track workmen, who have been repairing the track. The track goes through a bit of a valley at that point, and the sides are steep, so you must stop the trolley if you are to avoid running the five men down. You step on the brakes, but alas they don't work. Now you suddenly see a spur of track leading off to the right. You can turn the trolley onto it, and thus save the five men on the straight track ahead. Unfortunately, Mrs. Foot has arranged that there is one track workman on that spur of track. He can no more get off the track in time than the five can, so you will kill him if you turn the trolley onto him. Is it morally permissible for you to turn the trolley?[36]

Should you turn the trolley? Why or why not? Now consider this case.

Thought Experiment

Thomson's Transplant Problem

This time you are to imagine yourself to be a surgeon, a truly great surgeon. Among other things you do, you transplant organs, and you are such a great surgeon that the organs you transplant always take. At the moment you have five patients who need organs. Two need one lung each, two need a kidney each, and the fifth needs a heart. If they do not get those organs today, they will all die; if you find organs for them today, you can transplant the organs and they will all live. But where to find the lungs, the kidneys, and the heart? The time is almost up when a report is brought to you that a young man who has just come into your clinic for his yearly check-up has exactly the right blood-type, and is in excellent health. Lo, you have a possible donor. All you need do is cut him up and distribute his parts among the five who need them. You ask, but he says, "Sorry. I deeply sympathize, but no." Would it be morally permissible for you to operate anyway?[37]

Suppose you believe that it is morally permissible to turn the trolley but not to operate. What is the morally relevant difference between the two situations?

4. Consider this ethical theory: Whatever is natural is good. Is this a plausible ethical theory? Test it by means of thought experiments.

5. What is our obligation to future generations? Must we take into account what our actions will do to them? Why or why not?

6. Suppose you had the option of doubling the total amount of happiness in the world by either doubling the happiness of existing people or doubling the number of people in the world. Is there any reason to prefer one over the other? Are they utilitarian reasons?

Section 5.3

Much Obliged
Duty Makes Right

Our principles are the springs of our actions; our actions the springs of our happiness or misery. Too much care, therefore, cannot be taken in forming our principles.

—PHILIP SKELTON

*A*ccording to Immanuel Kant, the only thing that is intrinsically valuable is a good will. He writes, "It is impossible to conceive anything at all in the world, or even out of it, which can be taken as good without qualification, except a *good will*."[38] To have a good will is to act out of respect for the moral law. It is not merely to act in conformity with it, for that could happen by accident. Rather, it is to act out of the desire to conform with it. People with a good will do good because it's good—not because they will benefit from it. In other words, they do good for goodness's sake.

Happiness cannot be the highest good, Kant argues, because the highest good must be good without qualification. If something is good without qualification, then adding it to a situation should always make the situation better. But adding happiness to a situation does not always make it better. Consider the case of a killing. The morality of the situation is not improved if the killer derived pleasure from the act. In fact, that might make it worse. Happiness, then, does not fulfill Kant's criteria for the highest good. The fact that an action flows from a good will, however, never makes the action worse. So Kant maintains that a good will alone is intrinsically valuable.

Kant's Categorical Imperative

Moral principles can be viewed as imperatives, for they command us to do (or not do) certain things. For example, "Don't steal" is an imperative. A *hypothetical imperative* is one that should be obeyed if certain conditions are met. For example, "Practice regularly if you want to be a good piano player" is a hypothetical imperative. A *categorical imperative* is one that must be obeyed under all conditions. Kant's view is that moral principles are categorical, and, as a result, his moral theory has come to be known as the "categorical imperative."

The First Formulation

Kant provides two formulations of the categorical imperative. The first says, "Act only on that maxim through which you can at the same time will that it should become a universal law."[39] In other words, act only on those principles that you would be willing to have everybody act on. The first formulation of the **categorical imperative,** then, says that what makes an action right is that everyone could act on it, and you would be willing to have everyone act on it.

According to Kant, an adequate morality cannot play favorites. Equals must be treated equally. So if it is morally permissible for someone to perform a certain action in a certain situation, then it is morally permissible for anyone else to perform that action in a similar situation, provided that the two situations are the same in all morally relevant respects. (A morally relevant respect is one that has a bearing on the morality of the action.) If there is no relevant difference between two actions, there is no reason to judge them differently.

Whenever you act, says Kant, you are acting on a maxim or principle. To determine whether a particular action is moral, you have to perform a thought experiment: you have to imagine what the world would be like if everyone acted on that principle. If such a world is conceivable, and if you would be willing to live in it, then it is morally permissible for you to act on the principle.

Kant's first formulation of the categorical imperative, then, identifies two criteria for moral acceptability: universalizability and reversibility. A principle is **universalizable** if everyone could act on it. A principle is **reversible** if you would be willing to have everyone act on it.

Some principles are not universalizable. Consider the following situation. Suppose you are broke and in need of money. You know someone who would lend it to you if you promised to pay it back, but you know you won't be able to pay it back. So you wonder whether it is morally permissible to borrow money on the basis of a false promise. To determine whether such an action is morally permissible, Kant says, you must determine whether everyone could act on the principle "Borrow money on the basis of a false promise whenever you need it." A moment's reflection, however, reveals that everyone couldn't act on that principle because it involves a logical contradiction. On the one hand, it assumes that people will lend money on the basis of promises. On the other, it assumes that people can break their promises whenever they feel like it. So if everyone acted on the principle in question, no one could be trusted to pay back a loan. But if no one could be trusted to pay back a loan, no one would loan any money in the first place. So the principle "Borrow money on the basis of a false promise whenever you need it" is not universalizable. You cannot consistently will that everyone act on that principle. Consequently, says Kant, you can't act on it.

The reversibility criterion is similar to the Golden Rule, which says, "Do unto others as you would have them do unto you." The Golden Rule is based on another type of thought experiment. To determine whether an action is morally permissible, you are supposed to put yourself in the other person's shoes and decide whether you would want them to do to you what you are about to do to them. If not, you should refrain from performing the action.

No action will be considered blameless, unless the will was so, for by the will the act was dictated.

—SENECA

categorical imperative 1 The doctrine that what makes an action right is that everyone could act on it, and you would be willing to have everyone act on it.

universalizability A principle has universalizability if everyone can act on it.

reversibility A principle has reversibility if the person acting on it would be willing to have everyone act on it.

IMMANUEL KANT
1724–1804

The difference between the reversibility criterion and the Golden Rule is that the reversibility criterion focuses on the principle — rather than the people — involved. Instead of attending only to the particulars of the situation, the reversibility criterion has us consider the acceptability of the principle involved. If you would be willing to have everyone act on that principle, it is reversible.

Kant claims that the categorical imperative establishes the existence of a number of perfect duties to oneself and others. A **perfect duty** is one that has no exceptions. These include the duty not to kill innocent people, not to lie, and not to break one's promises. Under no circumstances can any of these duties be disobeyed.

In addition to perfect duties, there are also imperfect duties to oneself and others. An **imperfect duty** is one that does have exceptions. These include the duty to develop one's talents and to help the needy. These duties do not always have to be obeyed. It is enough that we sometimes obey them.

By strictly prohibiting murder, lying, promise-breaking, and the like, Kant's theory avoids many of the problems that plague utilitarianism. Utilitarianism would sanction these types of actions as long as they produced enough happiness. Kant's theory, however, would never sanction them.

What's more, Kant's theory provides a more plausible account of distributive and retributive justice than does utilitarianism. According to utilitarianism, fairness takes a backseat to the greatest happiness principle. If a particular distribution of goods maximizes happiness, that distribution is morally correct, whether or not it is deserved. According to Kant, however, no distribution is permissible unless the principle on which it is based can be universalized.

Insofar as no one wants to be treated unfairly, unjust principles of distribution cannot be universalized.

Utilitarianism does not require that only the guilty be punished or that the punishment fit the crime. The categorical imperative, however, requires both. As Kant says,

> But what is the mode and measure of punishment which public justice takes as its principle and standard? It is just the principle of equality, by which the pointer of the scale of justice is made to incline more to the one side than to the other. . . . Hence it may be said: "If you slander another, you slander yourself; if you steal from another, you steal from yourself; if you strike another, you strike yourself; if you kill another, you kill yourself." This is the only principle which . . . can definitely assign both the quality and the quantity of a just penalty.[40]

In other words, turnabout is fair play—whatever you do to another you should be willing to have done to you. In performing an action, you are affirming the principle on which it is based. If that principle sanctions slandering, stealing, striking, or killing, you should be willing to be slandered, robbed, struck, or killed.

Kant is a firm believer in capital punishment. He writes,

> Even if a civil society resolved to dissolve itself with the consent of all its members—as might be supposed in the case of a people inhabiting an island resolving to separate and scatter throughout the whole world—the last murderer lying in prison ought to be executed before the resolution was carried out. This ought to be done in order that every one may realize the desert of his deeds, and that bloodguiltiness may not remain on the people; for otherwise they will all be regarded as participants in the murder as a public violation of justice.[41]

Kant considers it our duty to execute murderers, for if we don't, we are implicitly condoning their action. If we let someone get away with murder, we are affirming the principle that killing innocent people is right, which is a violation of the categorical imperative.

Some have objected to Kant's theory on the grounds that it is too subjective—certain people may well be willing to have everyone act on principles that are clearly immoral. Consider R. M. Hare's Nazi fanatic.

Thought Experiment

Hare's Nazi Fanatic

Let us, as briefly as possible, consider what might be said in such an argument between a liberal and a Nazi. The liberal might try, first, drawing the Nazi's attention to the consequences of his actions for large numbers of people (Jews for example) who did not share his ideals, and asking him whether he was prepared to assent to a universal principle that people (or even people having the characteristics of Jews) should be caused to suffer thus. Now if only interests were being considered, the liberal would have a strong argument; for, if so, the Nazi would not assent to the judgment that, were he himself to be a Jew, or have the

There are not good things enough in life, to indemnify us for the neglect of a single duty.
—MADAME SWETCHINE

Impartiality is the life of justice, as justice is of all good government.
—JUSTINIAN

Everyone ought to bear patiently the results of his own conduct.
—PHAEDRUS

perfect duty A duty that must always be performed no matter what.

imperfect duty A duty that does not always have to be performed.

characteristics of Jews, he should be treated in this way. . . . But the Nazi has a universal principle of his own which gets in the way of the liberal's argument. He accepts the principle that the characteristics which Jews have are incompatible with being an ideal or pre-eminently good (or even a tolerably good) man; and that the ideal, or even a tolerably good society cannot be realized unless people having these characteristics are eliminated. It might therefore seem *prima facie* that it is no use asking him to imagine himself having the characteristics of Jews and to consider what his interests would then be; for he thinks that, even if the other interests of people (including his own) are sacrificed, the ideal state of society ought to be pursued by producing ideal men and eliminating those that fall short of the ideal.[42]

Unlike the principle "Borrow money on the basis of a false promise whenever you need it," the Nazi directive "Kill all the Jews" does not involve a contradiction. Wanting to have all the Jews dead is not like wanting to have your cake and eat it, too. So the principle is universalizable—everyone can act on it. And if the Nazi fanatic were willing to have himself killed if he were a Jew, it is reversible, too, for the fanatic would be willing to have everyone act on it. So it looks like Kant's theory (as well as the Golden Rule) could sanction genocide—which strongly suggests that these are not adequate ethical theories.

Another objection to Kant's categorical imperative stems from the fact that every action can be described in a number of ways, and there is no way to decide which description is the correct one. Consider again the case of borrowing money on the basis of a false promise. Instead of taking the relevant principle to be "Borrow money on the basis of a false promise whenever you need it," you could take it to be "Borrow money on the basis of a false promise whenever you need it and have such-and-such a genetic code" where the genetic code referred to is your own. Because only you have your genetic code, you will not fall into a contradiction by willing everyone to act on that principle. By making the principle specific enough, you could justify any action. But obviously this won't do.

The most difficult problem facing Kant's theory, however, is the fact that there are no perfect duties. Every duty has exceptions. Ross provides the following example.

Thought Experiment

Ross's Good Samaritan

What lends colour to the theory we are examining, then, is not the actions (which form probably a great majority of our actions) in which some such reflection as 'I have promised' is the only reason we give ourselves for thinking a certain action right, but the exceptional cases in which the consequences of fulfilling a promise (for instance) would be so disastrous to others that we judge it right not to do so. It must of course be admitted that such cases exist. If I have promised to meet a friend at a particular time for some trivial purpose, I should certainly think myself justified in breaking my engagement if by doing so I could prevent a serious accident or bring relief to the victims of one.[43]

Our duty to keep our promises is not a perfect one, for there are situations in which it would be wrong to keep them. For example, if keeping our promise to meet someone at a certain time meant that a number of people would die, then it would be wrong for us to keep our promise. Thus even Kant's theory leaves something to be desired.

The Second Formulation

The second formulation of the categorical imperative goes like this: "Act in such a way that you always treat humanity . . . never simply as a means, but always at the same time as an end."[44] The second formulation of the **categorical imperative,** then, says that what makes an action right is that it treats people as ends in themselves and not merely as means to an end.

Kant considered the two formulations of the categorical imperative to be equivalent because he thought they permitted the same actions. Few agree with this assessment, however, for there are actions permitted by the first (such as a Nazi fanatic killing all the Jews) that are not permitted by the second. The second formulation, then, may best be viewed as a supplement to the first. In this view, deciding whether an action is right is a two-step process: (1) determine whether the principle to be acted on is universalizable and reversible, and (2) determine that it treats everyone as ends in themselves, not merely as means to an end. If the action passes both tests, it is morally permissible.

The insight behind the second formulation is that all persons are inherently valuable. This value stems from the fact that they are self-conscious, rational, and free. Because they are self-conscious, they can be aware of the principles that govern their actions. Because they are rational, they can determine whether those principles are universalizable. And because they are free, they can decide what principles they are going to act on. Consequently, they can be held morally responsible for their actions.

Persons are aware of what motivates them and are capable of deciding whether they want to be motivated by those things. As a result, they can fashion their own destiny. They can decide who or what they are going to become. Respecting the value inherent in persons, then, involves respecting their right to choose. By allowing them to decide what kind of life they will lead, we treat them as ends in themselves and not merely as means to an end.

When we manipulate people—when we use them against their will—we use them merely as means to an end. When we enslave people, for example, we prevent them from pursuing their desires and plans and force them to serve ours. Slavery is wrong precisely because it does not recognize the inherent value of the slaves. It treats them as tools instead of moral agents and thus

Never let a man imagine that he can pursue a good end by evil means, without sinning against his own soul.

—ROBERT SOUTHEY

Every man has a property in his own person; this nobody has a right to but himself.

—JOHN LOCKE

categorical imperative II The doctrine that what makes an action right is that it treats people as ends in themselves and not merely as means to an end.

fails to respect their autonomy—their right to do with their lives what they want.

Not everyone who uses others to accomplish some goal is doing something immoral, however. We often use others as means without using them *merely* as means. For example, we use store clerks to help us with our purchases, and store clerks use us to help pay their bills. But, in this situation, no one is being used merely as a means because no one is being forced to do something against his or her will. Our actions and those of the store clerks are free. Because no one has been forced into the situation, no one's rights have been violated.

The second version of the categorical imperative avoids some of the counterintuitive consequences of the first. It would not allow the Nazi fanatic to kill all the Jews because that would involve using them merely as means. It would also not allow someone with a particular genetic code to borrow money on the basis of a false promise. For, even if such a principle were universalizable, it would still involve treating people merely as means.

Although the second formulation of the categorical imperative doesn't allow people to be used merely as means, it does allow animals to be used merely as means. According to Kant, animals are tools. In his *Lectures on Ethics*, Kant writes, "But so far as animals are concerned, we have no direct duties. Animals . . . are there merely as means to an end. That end is man."[45] Kant believes that animals are only instrumentally—not intrinsically—valuable. Their only value is the value they have for us.

Many find this consequence of Kantianism disturbing. Because animals are sentient creatures, they seem to have a value that is not dependent on us. Utilitarianism seems to be more in tune with our moral sensibilities here, for utilitarianism claims that what makes something valuable from a moral point of view is not that it can reason, but that it can suffer. Jeremy Bentham writes,

> The day may come when the rest of the animal creation may acquire those rights which never could have been witholden from them but by the hand of tyranny. The French have already discovered that the blackness of the skin is no reason why a human being should be abandoned without redress to the caprice of a tormentor. It may one day come to be recognized that the number of the legs, the villosity of the skin, or the termination of the os sacrum are reasons equally insufficient for abandoning a sensitive being to the same fate. What else is it that should trace the insuperable line? Is it the faculty of reason, or perhaps the faculty of discourse? But a full-grown horse or dog is beyond comparison a more rational, as well as a more conversable animal, than an infant of a day or a week or even a month, old. But suppose they were otherwise, what would it avail? The question is not, Can they *reason?* nor Can they *talk?* but, *Can they suffer?*[46]

According to Bentham, happiness is happiness, whether it's human happiness or animal happiness. And if our duty is to maximize happiness, then we should take into account all those who can experience happiness.

The second formulation of the categorical imperative enjoins us to never use people merely as means. Although that may be an admirable ideal, it is not realizable. As British philosopher C. D. Broad notes, sometimes we have to use people merely as means.

Kant's second version of the categorical imperative provides a philosophical justification of individual rights. A right is an entitlement to something. But just what a right entitles you to is a matter of debate.

Some believe that all rights are **negative rights:** having a right entitles you *not* to be interfered with in certain ways. In this view, for example, having a right to life means that others have a duty not to interfere with your attempt to make a living.

Others believe that some rights are **positive rights:** having a certain right entitles you to be provided with certain things. In this view, having a right to life means that others have a duty to provide you with what you need to live.

These differing views of what it is to have a right constitute one of the major ideological differences between liberals and conservatives. Conservatives tend to see all rights as negative rights. Consequently they are not in favor of welfare programs because they consider them to be a violation of our right to do with our money what we want. Liberals, on the other hand, tend to see some rights as positive rights. Consequently, they are in favor of welfare programs because they believe it is our duty to help our fellow human beings.

Thought Probe

Medical Treatment

Suppose a poor, young woman needs a heart operation. She can't afford to pay for it, nor does she have any relatives who can pay for it. Does she have a right to get the operation at taxpayer expense? If so, what theory justifies it?

Thought Experiment

Broad's Typhoid Man

Again, there seem to be cases in which you must either treat A or treat B, not as an end, but as a means. If we isolate a man who is a carrier of typhoid, we are treating him merely as a cause of infection to others. But, if we refuse to isolate him, we are treating other people merely as means to his comfort and culture.[47]

If someone has typhoid or some other contagious disease, to quarantine him is to treat him merely as a means—namely, as a means to the health of others. Not to quarantine him is to treat others merely as means—namely, as means to his well-being. Thus there are times when treating people merely as means is unavoidable.

Or consider the case of human shields. During the Gulf War, the Iraqi government handcuffed American prisoners to strategic targets such as missile silos. If the only way to defeat the Iraqis had been to bomb those silos, we would probably have bombed them, for it would have been necessary to prevent even more people from being used merely as means.

If the evil to be avoided is great enough, it would seem that we could violate any of the duties Kant identifies. Consider this thought experiment by A. C. Ewing.

negative right People have a negative right to something if and only if others have a duty not to interfere with their pursuit of that thing.

positive right People have a positive right to something if and only if others have a duty to provide them with what they need to acquire that thing.

Some people say that the justifications used by the United States for fighting wars have changed over time. One commentator, for example, claims that during the second Bush administration, the rationale for going to war changed from Kantian to utilitarian:

> After World War II — in the Nuremberg trials and the formation of the United Nations — the world's countries embraced a Kantian approach to international relations based upon the recognition of nations as equal sovereign persons (regardless of their size or stage of economic development) with inalienable rights. The UN Charter forbade the "threat or use of force against the territorial integrity or political independence of any state" except if "an armed attack occurs." Similarly, the Nuremberg tribunal stated that "to initiate a war of aggression . . . is the supreme international crime." Utilitarianism was present, too, but in a supporting role: the UN charter assumed that by granting them inalienable rights, the world's nations would help remove a major cause of war. . . .
>
> After the Berlin Wall fell in 1989, however, the world seemed ripe for the application of Kantian principles to international relations. UN support for the Gulf War was a textbook case: The world's nations were coming to the defense of a small nation invaded and taken over by a larger, more powerful neighbor . . . And the U.S. invasion of Afghanistan after September 11 was an act of national self-defense.
>
> But the Bush administration, perhaps emboldened by its success in Afghanistan, proceeded to defy the post–World War II principles of international law. Last June, Bush announced a new doctrine of preemptive (really preventive) war against merely potential adversaries. That was meant to justify an invasion of Iraq. Even if this doctrine is seen as a legitimate nuclear-age extension of self-defense, however, the invasion does not seem justified. The United States would have had to demonstrate that the Iraqis had not merely a few chemical weapons (which had failed to deter Iran in the 1980s war) but a burgeoning nuclear program. But no such programs came to light during the inspections or the war. By Kantian standards, the war was aggression without justifiable cause.
>
> Administration officials have tried to justify the war ex post facto entirely on utilitarian grounds — that is, that the war will lead to the democratization or modernization of the Arab region. These arguments echo those of 19th- and early 20th-century imperialists, and indeed some neoconservatives, including Max Boot and Stanley Kurtz, have argued candidly for a return to imperialism.[48]

Thought Probe

War

Which type of rationale for the war in Iraq — Kantian or utilitarian — seems more plausible to you? Why? Does *any* rationale seem plausible? Why or why not?

Thought Experiment

Ewing's Prudent Diplomat

However important it is to tell the truth and however evil to lie, there are surely cases where much greater evils still can only be averted by a lie, and is lying wrong then? Would it not be justifiable for a diplomat to lie, and indeed break most general moral laws, if it were practically certain that this and this alone would avert a third world-war? . . . while it may be self-evident that lying is always evil, it is surely not self-evident that it is always wrong. To incur a lesser evil in order to avert a much greater might well be right, and if that is the case as regards a lie, the lie is evil but not wrong.[49]

Ewing draws an important distinction here. It may be the case that killing innocent people, lying, stealing, breaking promises, or the like, is always evil, but that doesn't mean that it's always wrong. The right thing to do in many situations is the lesser of two evils. When faced with a conflict between duties, we need to determine which one takes precedence. But because Kant didn't recognize that such conflicts could occur, he didn't provide any mechanism for resolving them.

Thought Probe

Easy Rescue

Suppose you're walking along a deserted alley one night and a young boy comes running up to you, slips, and falls face down in a puddle of water. According to Kant, do you have a duty to at least kneel down and turn his head so that he doesn't drown? Why or why not?

Ross's *Prima Facie* Duties

If moral duties could be ranked hierarchically, we could resolve conflicts among them by simply consulting the ranking. Or if all of the exceptions to each duty could be spelled out, we could have a set of duties that didn't conflict with one another. No one has discovered a ranking that doesn't admit of counterexamples, however, and the number of exceptions for each duty seems to be extremely large. So these means of solving conflicts do not seem promising.

W. D. Ross attempts to deal with the problem of the conflict of duties by distinguishing between actual and *prima facie* duties. An **actual duty** is one that we are morally obligated to perform in a particular situation. A ***prima facie* duty** is one that we are morally obligated to perform in every situation *unless* there are extenuating circumstances. (The phrase *prima facie* literally means "at first glance.") A *prima facie* duty, in other words, is a conditional duty—one we should carry out if it doesn't conflict with other *prima facie* duties. "Do not lie" is a *prima facie* duty because, other things being equal, we should tell the truth. But if, in a particular situation, telling the truth would result in, say, the death of a number of innocent people, then our actual duty may be to lie.

According to Ross, our duties do not arise from any one moral principle. Rather, they grow out of our relationships with other people: spouse to spouse, child to parent, friend to friend, citizen to state, and so forth. "Each of these relations," Ross informs us, "is the foundation of a *prima facie* duty which is more or less incumbent on me according to the circumstances of the case."[50]

Ross identifies seven categories of *prima facie* duties:

1. *Duties of fidelity*, which require us to keep our promises, honor our contracts, and tell the truth.
2. *Duties of reparation*, which require us to compensate others for acts of cruelty and negligence.

actual duty A duty that should be performed in a particular situation.

***prima facie* duty** A duty that should be performed unless it conflicts with other *prima facie* duties.

3. *Duties of justice*, which require us to deal fairly with other people.

4. *Duties of beneficence*, which require us to benefit others.

5. *Duties of nonmaleficence*, which require us not to harm others.

6. *Duties of gratitude*, which require us to compensate others for acts of kindness.

7. *Duties of self-improvement*, which require us to try to become better people.

Ross does not maintain that this set of duties is complete. Instead, he claims that actions that fall under these duties tend to be right:

> We have to distinguish from the characteristic of being our duty that of tending to be our duty. Any act that we do contains various elements in virtue of which it falls under various categories. In virtue of being the breaking of a promise, for instance, it tends to be wrong; in virtue of being an instance of relieving distress it tends to be right.[51]

To determine what our actual duty is in any given situation, we have to decide which duty takes precedence. According to Ross's **pluralistic formalism,** then, what makes an action right is that it falls under the highest-ranked *prima facie* duty in a given situation.

Suppose, for example, that you are faced with a situation in which you can help a child in distress only if you break a promise. To the extent that helping the child follows the *prima facie* duty of beneficence, it tends to be right. To the extent that it violates the *prima facie* duty of fidelity, it tends to be wrong. To determine whether it is actually right or wrong, you have to decide which duty is more important in this situation.

Unfortunately, Ross does not tell us how to make such a decision. He suggests that ranking *prima facie* duties is like evaluating the qualities of a work of art. He writes,

> A poem is, for instance, in respect of certain qualities beautiful and in respect of certain others not beautiful; and our judgment as to the degree of beauty it possesses on the whole is never reached by logical reasoning from the apprehension of its particular beauties or particular defects. Both in this and in the moral case we have more or less probable opinions which are not logically justified conclusions from the general principles that are recognized as self-evident.[52]

There is no formula for ranking *prima facie* duties, just as there is no formula for ranking the qualities of a work of art. In both cases, we have to rely on our intuition. Thus Ross is an intuitionist when it comes to making moral decisions.

Thought Probe

Desert Island Bequest

Suppose you are shipwrecked on a desert island with a dying millionaire. Before the ill-fated voyage, he put $5 million in a public locker. He is willing to give you the key to the locker if you promise to spend the money according to his wishes. (You may keep $500,000 for your trouble.) The millionaire would like you to use the money to plant flowers in Siberia. It turns out that he grew up in Siberia and always lamented the fact that so few flowers grew there. Planting the flowers would fulfill a lifelong dream of his. You promise to do what he wants, so he gives you the key. You are rescued, go to the locker, and retrieve the $5 million. Instead of spending the money on flowers, however, you give it all to cancer research. According to Ross, did you do the right thing? Why or why not?

Rawls's Contractarianism

Utilitarianism is concerned with providing for the common good, but it doesn't respect individual rights. The categorical imperative respects individual rights but is not concerned with providing for the common good. Ross's pluralistic formalism is concerned with both the common good and individual rights but provides no effective means of deciding which takes precedence in a given situation. John Rawls, former professor of philosophy at Harvard University, has developed an approach to ethics that attempts to combine the strengths of these approaches while avoiding their weaknesses. He calls his approach "justice as fairness."

Rawls's primary concern is distributive justice — how should society's benefits and burdens be distributed? The problem is that there are not enough goods — jobs, food, housing, medical care, and the like — to go around. Given the scarcity of goods, how can we arrange things so that everyone gets a fair share?

The distribution of goods in a society is primarily determined by what Rawls terms its "basic structures": its political, legal, economic, and social institutions. To determine what a just society would be like, we have to identify the principles that its basic structures would embody.

Rawls attempts to identify these principles by specifying a procedure for generating them. The assumption is that as long as the procedure is fair, the principles generated by it will also be fair. Consider the following example of procedural justice. Suppose that six people have equal claim to a slice of an uncut pie. If we give the knife to the hungriest person and tell him that he can cut the pie on the condition that he gets the last piece, we should get a fair distribution. In order to ensure that he gets the biggest piece possible, he will have to divide the pie as equally as possible.

Rawls believes that there is a procedure for generating ethical principles that guarantees they will be as fair as possible. That procedure is the one that would be followed in drawing up the ideal social contract. He writes, "The principles of justice for the basic structure of society are the principles that free and rational persons . . . would accept in an initial situation of equality as defining the fundamental terms of their association."[53] To identify the principles that would govern a just society, we have to perform a thought experiment: we have to imagine that we are members of a group of free and rational individuals who meet as equals around a bargaining table to draw up a social contract we can all live by.

pluralistic formalism The doctrine that what makes an action right is that it falls under the highest-ranked duty in a given situation.

In an ideal contract-making situation, the parties to the contract meet as equals—no one has any information that the others lack. If someone had privileged information, he could use it to skew the contract in his favor. To ensure that none of the parties can take unfair advantage of the others, Rawls has us imagine that the parties in the "original position" conduct their negotiations behind a "veil of ignorance." That is, while they are sitting around the bargaining table, there are certain things that they do not know about themselves. Specifically, they do not know their race, sex, natural abilities, religion, interests, social position, or income. This equality guarantees impartiality. Because the parties do not know what group they belong to, they should not agree to principles that discriminate against a particular group. And because they don't know their specific wants and needs, the principles they draw up should be concerned only with primary goods—the goods that all parties should want regardless of their particular situations. These goods include basic liberties as well as such things as power, authority, opportunity, and wealth.

Although the people in the original position don't know much about themselves, they are nonetheless rational and self-interested. Their sole purpose is to arrive at a contract that would be best for them. What principles would they choose? Rawls claims that they would choose three:

1. *The principle of equal liberty*: Each person has an equal right to the most extensive basic liberties compatible with similar liberties for all.
2. *The principle of fair equality of opportunity*: Offices and positions are to be open to all under conditions of fair equality of opportunity.
3. *The difference principle*: Social and economic inequalities are to be arranged so that they are to the greatest benefit of the least advantaged persons.

The principle of equal liberty says that society should grant to each person as much freedom as possible as long as no one has more freedom than anyone else. This principle would be chosen by the people in the original position because they would want to be maximally free to pursue whatever interests they might have. The principle of fair equality of opportunity says that everyone should have an equal opportunity to advance in society. This principle would be chosen because the people in the original position would want to ensure that there are no artificial barriers to their success. The difference principle says that whatever inequalities exist should be arranged so that they benefit the most needy members of society. This principle would be chosen because, for all the people in the original position know, they might be in the neediest group. In game theory, this is known as the maximin strategy: when choosing under conditions of uncertainty, choose the alternative that provides the best worst-case scenario.

The difference principle does not demand that everyone be treated equally. There can be an unequal distribution of goods as long as the inequality serves to maximize the position of the least-well-off group. Interestingly enough, this principle is often invoked to justify various social and economic policies. It was used, for example, to justify former president Ronald Reagan's massive tax cut. Reagan and his advisors claimed that lessening the tax burden on the

Fear of serious injury cannot alone justify suppression of free speech and assembly. Men feared witches and burnt women.

—JUSTICE BRANDEIS

rich would greatly improve the standard of living of the poor. This claim became known as the "trickle-down theory": the idea that letting the rich keep more of their money would leave more money to trickle down to the poor than had been the case before the tax cut. Things didn't turn out that way, however. The tax cut served only to heighten the disparity between the rich and the poor.

The major problem facing formalist theories of ethics is that of resolving conflicts of duty. Rawls goes some way toward solving this problem by ranking the three principles of justice in terms of importance. The principle of equal liberty, Rawls claims, is "lexically prior" to the principle of fair equality of opportunity, which is lexically prior to the difference principle. One principle is lexically prior to another if and only if all the requirements of the former principle must be met before the requirements of the latter. No trade-offs are allowed; the lexically prior principle always takes precedence. So we must ensure that everyone has equal liberty before we ensure that everyone has fair equality of opportunity. And we must ensure that everyone has fair equality of opportunity before we ensure that the basic structures maximize the position of the least well-off group.[54]

Although Rawls's **contractarianism** — the doctrine that what makes an action right is that it is in accord with the principles established by an ideal social contract — is concerned with providing for the common good, it is not a utilitarian theory. Utilitarianism values liberty only so long as it maximizes happiness. If having slaves would maximize happiness, then, according to utilitarianism, we should have slaves. Rawls rejects the notion that rights are valuable only as long as they produce happiness. Like Kant, he considers freedom to be valuable in and of itself. He writes, "Each person possesses an inviolability founded on justice that even the welfare of society as a whole cannot override. . . . Therefore . . . the rights secured by justice are not subject to political bargaining or to the calculus of social interests."[55] For Rawls, then, not only is freedom intrinsically valuable, but it is more valuable than happiness.

No one has ever been in the original position, and it's doubtful that anyone ever will be. Nevertheless, the original position is conceivable (it doesn't involve a logical contradiction), and it is eminently fair (no one can take advantage of anyone else). As a result, there is reason to believe that the principles chosen in the original position would be just.

For those not convinced by this argument, Rawls offers a Kantian justification of his theory. Kant claims that morally correct principles are universalizable and reversible — they apply to everyone including oneself. The way to determine whether a principle is moral is to perform a thought experiment and decide whether everyone could act on that principle and whether you would be willing to have everyone act on that principle. The problem with this approach, as we have seen, is that fanatics could consistently will that people act on principles that are obviously immoral. By requiring ethical decisions to be made behind a veil of ignorance, Rawls helps alleviate this problem. There can be no fanatics behind the veil of ignorance. So the original position provides a "procedural interpretation" of the perspective from which free, rational, and impartial people would make their choices.[56] The way to determine whether a principle is moral is to perform a thought experiment

contractarianism
The doctrine that what makes an action right is that it is in accord with the principles established by an ideal social contract.

and decide whether it would be approved by people in the original position behind the veil of ignorance.

What sort of basic structures are consistent with the principles of justice? Interestingly enough, those found in a liberal, democratic society like ours seem to fit quite nicely. Rawls sees this as further vindication of this theory because any adequate theory of ethics should be consistent with our considered moral judgments.

The Declaration of Independence explicitly endorses the principle of equal liberty, and the Bill of Rights makes it unlawful to restrict certain liberties. The Civil Rights Act of 1964 explicitly endorses the principle of fair equality of opportunity, and Title VII makes it unlawful for any employer to discriminate on the basis of race, color, religion, sex, or national origin. Although our tax code is progressive (the rich are taxed at a higher rate than the poor), the law does not explicitly endorse the difference principle. In fact, some figures suggest that the basic structures in our society do not conform to the difference principle. In September 1997, the Census Bureau reported that the position of the least well-off group in our society was becoming worse. The number of those with incomes less than half the poverty threshold rose from 13.9 million in 1995 to 14.4 million in 1996.

Although Rawls's theory has much to recommend it, it is not without its critics. Some argue that the veil of ignorance is too thick — people know too little to make rational decisions. Because people have no knowledge of their interests or abilities, they would not be able to agree on any principles. Furthermore, others have claimed that if the veil is thinned out — if people know more about themselves — utilitarian principles would be chosen.

Thought Probe

Just Policies

Use Rawls's contractarianism to decide which of these social policies are just — which would be agreed on by people in the original position behind the veil of ignorance? Why or why not?

- entitlement programs such as welfare, medicare, and medicaid
- an inheritance tax of over 75 percent
- the right to an easy rescue (an easy rescue is one that can be performed without putting the rescuer at risk)
- homosexual marriage
- legalized euthanasia

Nozick's Libertarianism

Perhaps the most trenchant critique of Rawls, however, comes from his former colleague at Harvard, Robert Nozick. Nozick argues that Rawls's principles do not adequately protect individual rights. In fact, a society based on Rawls's principles would have to constantly violate people's rights. To demonstrate this, Nozick offers the following thought experiment.

Thought Experiment

Nozick's Basketball Player

. . . suppose a distribution favored by one of these non-entitlement conceptions is realized. Let us suppose it is your favorite one and let us call this distribution D_1. . . . Now suppose that Wilt Chamberlain is greatly in demand by basketball teams, being a great gate attraction. (Also suppose contracts run only for a year, with players being free agents.) He signs the following sort of contract with a team: In each home game, twenty-five cents from the price of each ticket of admission goes to him. (We ignore the question of whether he is "gouging" the owners, letting them look out for themselves.) The season starts, and people cheerfully attend his team's games; they buy their tickets, each time dropping a separate twenty-five cents of their admission price into a special box with Chamberlain's name on it. They are excited about seeing him play; it is worth the total admission price to them. Let us suppose that in one season one million persons attend his home games, and Wilt Chamberlain winds up with $250,000, a much larger sum than the average income and larger even than anyone else has. Is he entitled to this income? Is this new distribution D_2? If so, why? There is no question about whether each of the people was entitled to the control over the resources they held in D_1; because that was the distribution (your favorite) that (for the purposes of argument) we assumed was acceptable. Each of these persons *chose* to give twenty-five cents of their money to Chamberlain.[57]

The people who paid twenty-five cents extra to see Wilt Chamberlain did so of their own free will with their own money. The resulting distribution of goods, however, may have violated a principle of distributive justice, such as the difference principle. Even so, Nozick claims, it cannot be unjust because nobody's rights were violated. What this shows is that any pattern-based system of distributive justice (like Rawls's) will have to interfere in people's lives in order to maintain the pattern. Specifically, it will have to prevent capitalist acts between consenting adults. Because Nozick believes that the right not to be interfered with is the most basic right we possess, he finds any pattern-based principles of distributive justice unacceptable.

This is particularly true of socialism. The basic principle of socialist justice is usually stated as follows: "From each according to his ability, to each according to his needs."[58] In defense of this principle, it is claimed that people are happiest when they are doing what they do best, and society is happiest when the needs of its members are being met. Unfortunately, the only way to ensure that people do what they do best is through the use of force. Suppose

No-Victim Crimes

Certain crimes are called no-victim crimes because committing them does not involve forcing individuals to do anything against their will. Gambling, prostitution, and drug dealing fall into this category. Neither the buyers nor the sellers are coerced into these activities. Because these "crimes" don't violate anyone's rights, libertarians believe that they should be legalized. The present practice of outlawing them is a violation of our right to do with our lives what we want to do.

Making these activities illegal is often justified on utilitarian grounds. It is claimed that if they weren't illegal, an even greater harm would come to society. Libertarians are not impressed with these arguments. Even if legalizing these activities would lead to more unhappiness, they argue that the restriction on our liberty is a greater evil. What's more, they claim that there is reason to believe that legalizing these activities would actually promote the common good. In Holland, for example, where prostitution is legal, the rate of AIDS infection among prostitutes is less than 1 percent compared with 30 to 40 percent for America's prostitutes.[59] Marijuana, too, is legal in Holland, but the proportion of Dutch teenagers using marijuana is a fraction of what it is in America.[60] Libertarians also note that if these activities were legal, they could be taxed, widening the tax base and lessening the tax burden on all of us.

Thought Probe

Legalizing No-Victim Crimes

Should no-victim crimes be legalized? Why or why not?

---

that you want to be an artist, but you are a much better mathematician. To meet the requirements of socialist justice, the government would have to force you to become a mathematician. Even if such a system maximized happiness, many believe that the loss of freedom would be too great to make it morally acceptable.

Nozick advocates a libertarian theory of justice whose basic principle can be stated thus: "From each as they choose, to each as they are chosen."[61] People are entitled to whatever they acquire fairly and squarely. If they do not violate anybody's rights in the process of obtaining something, it is theirs to keep and do with as they please. Any attempt to take it away from them would violate their rights.

Thought Probe

Property Rights

Libertarians claim that people who own property have a right to do with it whatever they want. Is this always true? Can you think of any cases where we would be morally justified in limiting a person's freedom to do with their property what they want?

The Social Contract

Rawls and Nozick are both social contract theorists in that they believe that the legitimacy of a state derives from the consent of the governed. But they have very different views of how the contract should be understood. To place their views in context, it is useful to see how other thinkers have conceived of the social contract.

One of the central questions in political philosophy is what makes a government's power legitimate? Until recently, many governments claimed that their right to rule came from God. (The divine right of kings was one of the principles that our founding fathers explicitly rejected.) Nowadays most people in the West believe that the only legitimate source of governmental power is the consent of the governed. Government exists to serve and protect the people. Social contract theories try to explain how governments can legitimately acquire their power. These theories should not be viewed as attempts to provide a historically accurate account of the origin of any particular state. Rather, they should be viewed as attempts to justify the state by explaining how it's possible for states to come into being without violating any moral principles.

Hobbes

The first person to use the notion of a social contract to justify a form of government was Thomas Hobbes. Hobbes claimed that there were two things that all rational persons naturally desired: peace and justice. No rational person desires to be at war with others, and no one desires to be treated unfairly. Without a central authority to provide protection and adjudicate disputes, however, these goods are hard to come by. In a state of nature, where there is no central authority or government, there would be a war of all against all. Every moment of every day would be spent in the struggle for survival. There would be no time for art, science, or culture. Life, in Hobbes's words, would be "solitary, poor, nasty, brutish, and short."

In order to establish peace and justice, Hobbes believed that rational people would agree to sacrifice some of their freedom and live under the dictates of a supreme ruler. This ruler—called the Leviathan—would have the power to force others to live in peace and honor their contracts. (In the Old Testament, the Leviathan was an evil sea monster that could be defeated only by God.) Only if there were a Leviathan with enough power to keep the peace and enforce the law, Hobbes thought, would civil society be possible.

The agreement to submit to the Leviathan is not a contract between the Leviathan and its subjects. Rather, it is a contract among the subjects themselves. Because the Leviathan is the supreme ruler, it does not answer to any higher authority. Thus any contract made with the Leviathan is unenforceable. And unenforceable contracts, Hobbes thought, are meaningless.

The Leviathan, then, is free to do whatever it pleases. Its power is absolute. It can force its subjects to do anything it wants, except take their own lives. Such a situation may not strike you as very desirable, but Hobbes thought that it was preferable to a state of nature. There is a chance that the Leviathan will turn out to be a ruthless despot, but that was a chance that Hobbes was willing to take.

Locke

Locke was not willing to take that chance. He saw no difference between being besieged by a thousand people and being besieged by one person who has a thousand people at his command. Locke, like Hobbes, saw the social contract as a means of establishing peace and justice. But whereas Hobbes viewed the social contract as one where the subjects give up their rights to the Leviathan, Locke viewed it as one where the subjects entrust their rights to the state for safekeeping.

Locke thought that everyone had a natural right to life and property. People should not be forced to give up their life or their possessions against their will. To protect their rights, Locke thought that people would agree to invest the state with the power to make and enforce laws and to provide for the common defense. To prevent the state from becoming too powerful, these functions should be carried out by different branches of the government. The legislative branch would enact the laws, the executive branch would enforce them, and the federative branch would command the armed forces. Although Locke recognized the need for a judiciary to settle legal disputes, he didn't conceive of the judiciary as a separate branch of government. That idea came from the French jurist Montesquieu.

It should be clear that much of the philosophy behind the American political system is Locke's: the idea that all humans possess certain rights independently of the state, the idea that the function of the state is to protect those rights, the idea that the state derives its legitimacy from the consent of the governed, and the idea that there should be a balance of power among the different branches of the government all come from Locke.

Nozick

Nozick provides a detailed defense of Locke's view of the social contract. Like Locke, he believes that we all possess a natural right to life and property. We should be able to do what we want with what we own. In a state of nature, however, even those who recognize this right will sometimes come into conflict. What one person sees as fair, another will see as unfair. Because people tend to view themselves more favorably than they do others, "They will overestimate the amount of harm or danger they have suffered and passions will lead them to attempt to punish others more than proportionately and to exact excessive compensation."[62] To protect themselves from those who demand more than their fair share and to extract compensation from those who refuse to give it, Nozick claims that people would voluntarily join private protection agencies. If the parties to a dispute belong to different protective agencies, the agencies may do battle. After a number of such battles, there are three possible outcomes: (1) one agency wins most of the time, (2) different agencies win closer to their geographic center so that members of the different agencies move closer to their agency's base, or (3) battles are equally won among competing agencies so that they set up a court system to settle disputes. In each case, as the result of rational self-interest and voluntary cooperation, most people will end up living in an area where one agency or institution has a near-monopoly on the use of force. The state is often conceived as an organization that has a monopoly on the use of force in a geographic area. So private protection agencies would function like states.

In the beginning, these agencies would not actually be states, however, because everyone in the area would not belong to an agency. If an agency forced the independents to buy protection from it, it would violate their rights. But anarchists claim that every state must do this if it is to establish a monopoly on the use of force. Thus anarchists believe that all government is immoral: only by violating people's rights can a government establish a monopoly on the use of force in an area.

Nozick contends, on the contrary, that a dominant protective agency can become a true state without violating anybody's rights. The principle of compensation says that those benefiting from a practice must compensate those harmed by it. So if the independents are harmed by not belonging to the dominant protective agency, the dominant protective agency must compensate them. And the least expensive way to compensate them would be to offer them free protection.[63] So a dominant protective agency could acquire a monopoly on the use of force in an area without violating anyone's rights.

The function of such a minimal state would be to protect its members' rights to life and property. It would prevent or punish physical harm, theft, or fraud, and it would enforce contracts. If it did anything more, however, it would violate people's rights. The state may legitimately require people to pay taxes for the armed services, the police force, and the judicial system because these institutions are needed to protect people's rights. But if a state requires people to pay taxes for any other purpose—such as welfare, medicare, or medicaid—it is acting immorally because it is violating its citizens' property rights. It is forcing them to part with their property against their will. According to Nozick, we are not our brother's keeper. We have a duty not to interfere in other people's lives, but we do not have a duty to provide them with what they need to live.

Thought Probe

Preemptive Incarceration

Neuroscientists are developing brain scanning techniques that may make it possible to identify those who have a tendency to commit violent crimes. Suppose we can positively identify people who have over a 90 percent chance of committing a violent crime. Would we be justified in preemptively locking them up so they won't hurt anyone? Why or why not? If we're not justified in doing that, are we justified in preemptively going to war?

The Ethics of Care

Libertarians recognize no duties to others except the duty of noninterference. We may help others if we want to, but we are under no obligation to do so. Many have suggested that this is an impoverished view of our moral obligations. Specifically, they have argued that it fails to recognize the special duty of care we have to those who care for us.

Utilitarian and Kantian approaches to ethics, which emphasize impartiality, are blind to caring relationships. As we have seen, Godwin created something of a scandal when he suggested that a good utilitarian would rescue the archbishop—instead of his mother—from a burning building. Such a notion grates on our ethical sensibilities. When we have a special relationship with someone else—especially a relationship based on love, friendship, or trust—we may give that person special consideration.

The ethics of care grew out of psychologist Carol Gilligan's study of how men and women approach ethical issues. Gilligan was a colleague of Laurence Kohlberg, a developmental psychologist, who identified six stages of moral development:

1. *Punishment and obedience:* obeying authority to avoid punishment
2. *Self-interest:* making deals to benefit oneself
3. *Interpersonal accord and conformity:* being good to fit in
4. *Authority and social order:* obeying the law out of a sense of duty
5. *Social contract:* adhering to principles beneficial to society
6. *Universal ethical principles:* adhering to abstract principles that should apply to everyone

Kohlberg claims that these stages are universal—that the moral thinking of all humans develops in this manner—and that they are progressive, that is, those who reach the higher stages are making better moral judgments than those who remain at the lower ones.

Kohlberg developed his system by asking people of different ages how they would solve certain moral dilemmas. Typical of these dilemmas is the Heinz dilemma:

> In Europe, a woman was near death from a special kind of cancer. There was one drug that the doctors thought might save her. It was a form of radium that a druggist in the same town had recently discovered. The drug was expensive to make, but the druggist was charging ten times what the drug cost him to make. He paid $200 for the radium and charged $2,000 for a small dose of the drug. The sick woman's husband, Heinz, went to everyone he knew to borrow the money, but he could only get together about $1,000 which is half of what it cost. He told the druggist that his wife was dying and asked him to sell it cheaper or let him pay later. But the druggist said: "No, I discovered the drug and I'm going to make money from it." So Heinz got desperate and broke into the man's store to steal the drug for his wife. Should the husband have done that?[64]

Kohlberg was interested not in the particular solution the subjects offered but in the reasons they gave for their solution. He found that those reasons clustered into six categories that correspond to his six stages of moral development.

When Gilligan began studying women's moral development, she found that they rarely advanced to stage 6 but often remained in stages 3 or 4. In her search for an explanation of this finding, she discovered that Kohlberg's system had been based entirely on interviews with boys and men. Women's voices had not been part of the original dataset. In 1977, she published *In a Different Voice,* which critiqued Kohlberg's system and described the sort of considerations that women brought to bear on ethical issues.

Even if, as a matter of fact, people pass through Kohlberg's stages of moral development, Gilligan argued, it doesn't follow that the later stages are somehow better than the earlier ones. And, from the fact that something is the case, it doesn't follow that it should be the case. Wisdom does not necessarily come with age.

What's more, Gilligan found that, whereas men tended to see ethical dilemmas in terms of rights and responsibilities, women tended to see them in terms of compassion and care. Men tended to be more concerned about whether justice had been served, whereas women tended to be more concerned about whether relationships had been preserved. Subsequent studies have found that the difference between men and women is not as pronounced as Gilligan suggested. A meta-analysis of 79 studies of sex differences in moral reasoning found almost no difference between men and women when education and age differences were taken into account.[65] Nevertheless, it is generally agreed that caring is an important dimension of the moral life. We owe a duty of care to those who have cared for us, and this duty may sometimes override considerations of justice or rights.

Ross recognizes that all of our moral duties grow out of our relationships to others. His duty of gratitude is similar to the duty of care. But many who advocate an ethics of care claim that our concern for others shouldn't be limited to those with whom we have a close personal relationship. Personal relationships are part of a larger system of relationships, which makes up the communities in which we live. Without these communities, our personal relationships would not be possible. Thus the ethics of care is often linked to a communitarian ethic that sees communities as intrinsically valuable and thus deserving of our concern and care.[66]

Not all personal relationships generate a duty of care. Those based on violence, hatred, or disrespect need not be nurtured; nor must those characterized by injustice, exploitation, or oppression. When compassion, concern, and empathy are present, however, so are duties of care.

The duty to care for those who have cared for us can conflict with other duties we have. For example, if someone with whom you have a caring relationship (such as a spouse) is charged with a crime, you may legitimately try to protect that person from the law. The duty to protect those you care for varies, however, with the nature of the relationship and the situation. For example, if the accused is not your spouse but a long-lost friend, and if you have reason to believe that your friend is guilty, any attempt to protect her from the law may be unwarranted.

The ethics of care is not a full-blown ethical theory because it does not purport to solve all ethical problems. It simply hopes to emphasize an aspect of the moral life that is often overlooked by the more traditional theories. In this way, it can give us a richer sense of what it means to act morally.

Thought Probe

Lying with Care

Suppose that your best friend stole some medicine that he needed but couldn't afford from a company that you work for. Should you lie to protect him from the law? What if he stole something that he didn't need, like a CD player? Should you lie to protect him in that situation?

Making Ethical Decisions

None of the major theories we've canvassed—utilitarianism, Kantianism, contractarianism, or caring—provides a complete account of morality. Nevertheless, each of them identifies an important aspect of it. Other things being equal, we should promote the common good, respect individual rights, treat others fairly, and care for those who care for us. Instead of viewing one of these principles as the basis of all morality, we should view all of them as criteria of adequacy that morally correct actions should try to meet. They are the factors that should be taken into account when trying to decide on the right course of action.

If an action promotes the common good, doesn't violate anyone's rights, treats people fairly, and exhibits appropriate care, it is morally permissible. Problems arise when these principles conflict with one another. If the only way to promote the common good is to violate someone's rights, for example, we have to decide whether the violation is worth it.

Ross suggests that judging the rightness of an action is like judging the beauty of an artwork. A more appropriate analogy would seem to be judging the truth of a theory because that sort of judgment is also governed by objective criteria of adequacy. As we have seen, in deciding which theory is most likely to be true, we appeal to such criteria as simplicity, scope, conservatism, and fruitfulness because they indicate the extent to which a theory systematizes and unifies our knowledge. Similarly, in deciding which action is most likely to be right, we appeal to such criteria as utility, rights, justice, and care because they indicate the extent to which an action fulfills our obligations.

We can't quantify how well a theory or an action does with respect to any particular criterion of adequacy, nor can we rank the criteria in order of importance. Nevertheless, the choice between theories and actions is an objective one because the criteria on which the choice is based can be specified without referring to anyone's mental states. Deciding what to do, then, is no less objective than deciding what to believe.

What, then, is the procedure for arriving at an moral judgment? There are four major steps involved, and they can be represented by the acronym **I CARE.**

1. **I**dentify the relevant facts.

2. **C**onsider the **A**lternative courses of action.

3. **R**ate the various alternatives in terms of the moral criteria of adequacy.

4. **E**ffect a decision based on the rating.

Let's consider each of these steps in turn.

1. *Identify the relevant facts.* Moral judgments, as we've seen, follow from moral principles together with factual claims. Many moral disagreements are about the facts of the case rather than the principles involved. To minimize disagreement, then, the first step involved in making a moral judgment involves identifying the relevant facts.

2. *Consider the Alternative courses of action.* When faced with a moral dilemma, there are usually a number of different actions you can perform. The problem is deciding which one of those actions is best from an ethical point of view. To make sure you haven't overlooked a possible course of action, you should take the time to consider all of the different options available to you. This involves not only identifying the different courses of action, but also considering their consequences. Who is going to be affected by the decision? How will they be affected? Those affected by a decision are known as "stakeholders." So good ethical decision making involves identifying the

possible courses of action, identifying the stakeholders, and considering the effects that different actions will have on them.

3. *Rate the various alternatives in terms of the moral criteria of adequacy.* Once the relevant facts are known and the possible courses of action have been specified, the next step is to rate the different actions in terms of the ethical criteria of adequacy, namely, utility, rights, justice, and caring. How well does each action do in terms of maximizing happiness, respecting rights, treating equals equally, and exhibiting care? If one action rates higher than every other in terms of these criteria, then it clearly is the morally correct thing to do. If an action is in the best interest of everyone involved, if it doesn't violate anyone's rights, if it doesn't treat anyone unfairly, and if it cares for those who deserve it, it is morally permissible. It may turn out that no one action does best with respect to all of these criteria, however. The action that produces the most happiness may violate the most rights. Or the action that is the most just may be the most callous. Here is where you must use your judgment. You must weigh the different factors and decide which action comes out best overall. There's no formula that you can use to make such a decision, but this doesn't make ethical decision making any less objective than scientific decision making because scientists, too, must use their judgment to determine which theory does best with regard to cognitive criteria of adequacy such as simplicity, scope, conservatism, and fruitfulness. The simplest scientific theory may be the least conservative. Or the most fruitful theory may have the least scope. To decide which is best, scientists must use their judgment.

What often goes unnoticed is that the criteria of adequacy used to decide among competing scientific theories are themselves values. So arriving at a decision as to which scientific theory is best is to make a value judgment. As Hilary Putnam notes,

> . . . *coherence and simplicity* and the like are themselves values. To suppose that "coherent" and "simple" are themselves just emotive words—words which express a "pro attitude" toward a theory, but which do not ascribe any definite properties to the theory—would be to regard *justification* as an entirely subjective matter. On the other hand, to suppose that "coherent" and "simple" name *neutral* properties—properties toward which people may have a "pro attitude," but there is no objective rightness in doing so—runs into difficulties at once. Like the paradigm value terms (such as "courageous," "kind," "honest," or "good"), "coherent" and "simple" are used as terms of praise. Indeed, they are *action guiding* terms: to describe a theory as "coherent, simple, explanatory" is, in the right setting, to say that acceptance of the theory is justified; and to say that acceptance of a statement is (completely) justified is to say that one ought to accept the statement or theory.[69]

Scientists are in the business of trying to decide what we should believe if we want to avoid error and falsehood; ethicists are in the business of trying to decide what we should do if we want to avoid injustice and wrong. Both are in the business of making value judgments, and both do so in the same way: by weighing various options in terms of criteria of adequacy relevant to the decision.

4. *Effect a decision based on the rating.* Once you've identified the best action to perform in the situation, the final step is to perform it. After you've performed it, however, you should continue to monitor the situation to see if things turned out the way you planned. If not, you need to analyze the situation to determine what went wrong. You can then use the results of that analysis so that you don't make the same mistake in the future.

Thought Probe

The Zygmanik Brothers

Use the I CARE procedure to determine whether Lester did the right thing in killing his brother George. Was this the best action in the circumstances? Why or why not?

Summary

Formalist (deontological) ethical theories claim that the rightness of an action is determined not by its consequences but by its form. Foremost among such theories is Kant's categorical imperative. Kant's first formulation of the doctrine says that what makes an action right is that it is based on a principle that everyone could act on, and you would be willing to have everyone act on. But this formulation of the categorical imperative does not provide a sufficient condition for morality because it permits obviously immoral acts. There are people who are willing to live in a world governed by principles (like "Kill all the Jews") that are universalizable and reversible but are nevertheless immoral.

Kant claims that the categorical imperative establishes the existence of a number of perfect duties to oneself and to others. Perfect duties admit no exceptions and include the duty not to kill innocent people and the duty to keep one's promises. But Kant's perfect duties cannot be followed in every situation, for they can conflict with other duties we have. If keeping our promise to meet someone, for example, would mean that people would die, then it would be immoral to keep our promise.

Kant's second formulation of the categorical imperative says that what makes an action right is that it treats other people as ends in themselves and not merely as means. The insight here is that all persons are inherently valuable. But sometimes treating people merely as means is unavoidable or necessary to prevent even more people from being treated merely as means. The right thing to do in many situations is the lesser of two evils.

W. D. Ross tries to deal with the problem of conflicting duties by positing *prima facie* duties (those we're obligated to perform in every situation unless they conflict with other *prima facie* duties). The problem is that under this scheme, one and the same action can fall under conflicting duties. When this happens, Ross claims, we should make a "considered decision" about which duty has priority. According to pluralistic formalism, then, what makes an action right is that it falls under the highest-ranked *prima facie* duty in a given situation. Unfortunately, Ross does not tell us what sort of considerations are relevant to ranking our duties.

Rawls tries to overcome the deficiencies of traditional formalist approaches to ethics by specifying a procedure for arriving at an ideal social contract. In the "original position," the parties to the contract would operate behind a "veil of ignorance": they would not know their race, sex, natural abilities, religion, interests, social position, or income. This lack of knowledge guarantees their impartiality. People in the original position would agree to three principles: the principle of equal liberty, the principle of fair equality of opportunity, and the difference principle.

To achieve the distribution of goods mandated by the difference principle, government would have to interfere in the lives of its citizens. Nozick considers this interference a violation of individual rights and proposes a libertarian theory of justice: from each as they choose, to each as they are chosen. But this approach to justice ignores the duties of care that we have to those who care for us.

Utility, rights, justice, and care can be viewed as criteria of adequacy for right actions. The right action to perform in any situation is the one that does best with respect to these criteria.

Study Questions

1. What is the first formulation of the categorical imperative?

2. What are perfect duties?

3. What are imperfect duties?

4. What is Hare's Nazi fanatic thought experiment? How does it attempt to undermine the categorical imperative?

5. What is Ross's Good Samaritan thought experiment? How does it attempt to undermine the categorical imperative?

6. What is the second formulation of the categorical imperative?

7. What is Broad's typhoid man thought experiment? How does it attempt to undermine the categorical imperative?

8. What is Ewing's prudent diplomat thought experiment? How does it attempt to undermine the categorical imperative?

9. What is pluralistic formalism?

10. What procedure does Rawls believe will generate ideal principles of justice?

11. What principles of justice does Rawls's procedure sanction?

12. What is the ethics of care?

Discussion Questions

1. Would you be willing to kill an innocent person if it would put an end to world hunger? Why or why not?

2. Suppose you are a soldier peering down the sight of a bazooka at an enemy tank with six innocent civilians strapped to the outside. Should you fire your bazooka knowing that you will probably kill all the civilians but may not stop the tank? Why or why not?

3. Should we use torture to extract military secrets from prisoners of war? Why or why not?

4. Is Kant right in claiming that it is our duty to execute murderers? Why or why not?

5. Suppose it were discovered that when dolphins are tortured to death, they excrete a very powerful narcotic that, when ingested, makes people feel better than they've ever felt before. Would it be right to torture dolphins to death in order to get this narcotic? Why or why not?

6. Would Kant sanction Lester Zygmanik's killing of his brother George? Would Ross? Would Rawls? Would the ethics of care? Why or why not?

7. Is extramarital sex between consenting adults immoral? If so, what moral principle does it violate?

8. Is homosexuality between consenting adults immoral? If so, what moral principle does it violate?

9. Because the poorest group in society is getting poorer, is American society unjust? Should we alter the welfare system so that it maximizes the position of that group?

10. Are taxes for entitlement programs such as welfare, Medicare, and Medicaid immoral? Why or why not?

11. Should no-victim crimes like prostitution, drug use, and gambling be legalized? Why or why not?

12. Consider this theory of morality: "An action is right if and only if (1) it does not violate anyone's autonomy (freedom of choice) unless it is necessary to prevent an overwhelming loss of autonomy and (2) it maximizes as much happiness as is consistent with (1)." Is this an adequate theory of morality? Why or why not? Can you think of any thought experiments that would refute it?

Character Is Destiny
Virtue Makes Right

*I*n addition to judging actions to be morally right or wrong, we also judge people to be morally good or bad. Morally good people are virtuous people; they are people who regularly try to do their duty. They may not always succeed, but at least their hearts are in the right place.

Utilitarianism and Kantianism provide differing conceptions of the virtuous person. According to act-utilitarianism, a virtuous person is one who always tries to maximize happiness. According to Kantianism, a virtuous person is one who always tries to obey the categorical imperative. The utilitarian conception of a morally good person has been attacked on the grounds that it is unattainable. The Kantian conception has been attacked on the grounds that it is undesirable. And both have been attacked on the grounds that they are not conducive to a good life.

The Virtuous Utilitarian

A committed act-utilitarian values happiness above all else—not her own happiness, but happiness in general. Consequently, she tries to produce as much of it as she can in everything that she does. If she does something that does not produce the most happiness possible, she has done wrong. This makes it almost impossible for anyone to do right.

Suppose you wanted to buy a one-dollar soft drink. Doing so would be morally permissible only if there were nothing else you could do with that dollar that would produce more happiness. But certainly there is. You could give it to UNICEF, for example, and feed a number of starving children. The happiness the children would experience from being fed would undoubtedly be greater than the happiness you would experience from drinking a soda. Thus it would be wrong for you to buy the soft drink. As long as there are starving or suffering people in the world, it would be wrong for you to spend any more money on yourself than necessary to prevent your own starvation or suffering. Purchasing a fancy car or an expensive stereo system would definitely be immoral.

Because most of us do not think it immoral to spend money on ourselves, utilitarianism doesn't jibe with our ordinary conception of morality. We usually have little difficulty distinguishing between those actions that it is our duty to perform and those that go above and beyond the call of duty. It is not our duty to help someone across the street, for example, but it is usually good to do so. Actions that do more than is required—that go above and beyond the call of duty—are referred to as *supererogatory actions*. Utilitarianism has no place for supererogatory actions. If it would be better to do something than not to do it, we are morally obligated to do it. Because such self-sacrifice is beyond most of us, utilitarianism seems to advocate an impossible ideal.

The Virtuous Kantian

A committed Kantian lives his life by the categorical imperative. Because the categorical imperative recognizes that we have certain duties to ourselves, such as the duty to develop our own talents, it does not require the same sort of self-sacrifice that utilitarianism does. Nevertheless, Kantianism requires that we always act out of a sense of duty, and that, it has been claimed, is not always a good thing. Michael Stocker brings this out in the following thought experiment about a hospitalized person who is visited by a friend.

Thought Experiment

Stocker's Hospitalized Patient

You are very bored and restless and at loose ends when Smith comes in once again. You are now convinced more than ever that he is a fine fellow and a real friend—taking so much time to cheer you up, traveling all the way across town, and so on. You are so effusive with your praise and thanks that he protests that he always tries to do what he thinks is his duty, what he thinks is best. You at first think he is engaging in a polite form of self-deprecation, relieving the moral burden. But the more you two speak, the more clear it becomes that he was telling the literal truth: that it is not essentially because of you that he came to see you, not because you are friends, but because he thought it his duty, perhaps as a fellow Christian or Communist or whatever, or simply because he knows of no one more in need of cheering up and no one easier to cheer up.[70]

Even though Smith acted out of duty, there seems to be something missing from Smith's action. What's missing, Stocker suggests, is a concern for the hospitalized person himself.

A respect for persons lies at the heart of Kant's ethics. But it is a respect for persons in the abstract—for persons considered as rational beings—not for individual persons. And without a concern for individual persons, claims

Stocker, we cannot realize the great goods of love, friendship, affection, fellow-feeling, and community.[71]

Stocker would have us believe that acting out of duty precludes acting out of concern for the individual. But it can be argued, on the contrary, that acting out of duty requires a concern for the individual. You can't understand your duties unless you have a concern for people as individuals.

Some people have no concern for others. As a result of neglect, abuse, or genetic or congenital defects, they have no compassion, no capacity for remorse, and no conscience. They are psychopaths. Psychopaths are often bright individuals who can converse intelligently about morals. But it is doubtful whether they are capable of acting morally, for it is doubtful whether they can fully understand what a duty is.

Men do less than they ought unless they do all that they can.
—THOMAS CARLYLE

We learn how to act morally by interacting with others. Children who are shown sympathy, compassion, and love develop those qualities in themselves. These moral sentiments are essential to an understanding of moral duty, for they allow us to empathize with others—to "get inside their skins," so to speak—and thus to fully comprehend the effects of our actions. Only those who can empathize with others can be connected to them by bonds of affection, friendship, and love. And only those who can be connected to others in these ways can understand the duties associated with these connections.

An analogy may be helpful here. Someone who is red color-blind may be able to talk intelligently about red things. But because he has never experienced the sensation of redness, he cannot have a complete understanding of what it means for something to be red. Similarly, someone who has no fellow-feeling may be able to talk intelligently about right actions, but he cannot have a complete understanding of what it means to be right. Such a person, says Arthur Murphy,

> . . . could "regard an action as a duty" in the sense of recognizing perhaps with complete practical indifference that it had the traits by which an action is socially identified as "right." . . . What he could never in this way "see" is how such rightness bound him as a moral agent to the performance of the action in question. . . . He could not understand why he ought to do it.[72]

So a concern for persons as individuals, far from being irrelevant to an understanding of our duties, is essential to it.

Stocker is right that what is missing in the situation described in his thought experiment is a concern for the individual. But this is not a fault of the ethics of duty; it is a fault of Smith. Smith has no empathy for the person in the hospital. As a result, he can't fully understand his duty as a friend. But if he can't fully understand his duty as a friend, he can't act out of a sense of duty. The problem with Smith, then, is not that he is acting only out of a sense of duty, but that he is acting out of an impoverished sense of duty.

The Purpose of Morality

If doing our duty required us to neglect ourselves, then there would be something seriously wrong with an ethics of duty: being a good person should not

Children without a Conscience

Children who are severely neglected as infants often grow up to be psychopaths. They have no concern for others, no feelings of remorse or guilt, no conscience. Some consider them to be a serious threat to civilized society. Tom Keogh explores this problem.

> Angela's disturbing behavior problems were apparent almost from the day the six-year-old foster child came to live with Jean and Mike Walsh in 1989 . . . "She would have three- to four-hour temper tantrums every day," recalls Jean. "She flung herself against walls, tore wallpaper down, couldn't function at school or get along with classmates. She nearly strangled our cat, kicked and tormented the dog. She had no friends. She was cruel to her brother and periodically threatened to kill me."
>
> . . . therapists and social service professionals are now seeing more and more children with histories of early childhood abuse or neglect who exhibit the same severe antisocial tendencies—indications of what therapists refer to as an "attachment disorder." According to experts in this emerging field, the condition is caused when the normal bonding process between infant and primary caregiver does not properly occur. Instead of an initial human experience that teaches them to love and trust others, these "unattached" infants learn to trust only themselves, becoming inwardly isolated and emotionally unapproachable. As infants they may stiffen to the touch; in later childhood, they may act out a range of violent and remorseless behaviors. Lacking the empathy needed to establish healthy relationships with others, they have been described as "children without a conscience."[73]

Thought Probe

Empathy and Agency

Can someone without a conscience—without the ability to empathize with others—act morally? Can he or she be a moral agent? If not, what should we do with these people?

---

prevent us from leading a good life. On the contrary, moral actions should promote both the individual and the collective good.

We need morality because if there were no constraints on behavior, it is unlikely that most of us would be able to achieve our goals. Kurt Baier explains,

> . . . people's interests conflict. In such a case, they will have to resort to ruses to get their own way. As this becomes known, men will become suspicious, for they will regard one another as scheming competitors for the good things in life. The universal supremacy of the rules of self-interest must lead to what Hobbes called the state of nature. At the same time, it will be clear to everyone that universal obedience to certain rules overriding self-interest would produce a state of affairs which serves everyone's interest much better than his unaided pursuit of it in a state where everyone does the same. Moral rules are universal rules designed to override those of self-interest when following the latter is harmful to others.[74]

To ensure that everyone has an equal opportunity for a good life, morality requires us to refrain from doing certain things that we otherwise might want to do.

A system of moral rules works to everyone's benefit only if most people live by it. One way to make people obey the moral law is to threaten them with punishment if they disobey. But it's doubtful that this method alone can be entirely successful. Punishment breeds resentment, and if those being punished aren't motivated by something other than the fear of punishment, the system will probably not survive for long.

Another way to get people to act morally is to cultivate their moral sentiments. People who have compassion, sympathy, and trust want to do good, and they feel guilt, shame, or remorse if they don't. These people don't need the external threat of punishment to act morally. Their motivation comes from within. Through proper training, they not only acquire moral sentiments, but they also acquire certain habits or dispositions to behavior. These habits or dispositions are known as "virtues."

Aristotle on Virtue

Who escapes a duty, avoids a gain.

— THEODORE PARKER

ARISTOTLE
384–322 B.C.

A **virtue** is an admirable human quality either because it's good for the person who has it or because it's good for other people. A virtuous person has acquired a habit—a disposition to act in certain ways in certain situations. Those who habitually act in a virtuous manner not only are good people, but, according to Aristotle, they also lead good lives.

Aristotle was one of the first to provide a systematic account of the virtues. He realized that human actions are undertaken for a purpose—they aim to achieve some end—because that end is considered to be valuable. But if every end is only instrumentally valuable as a means to some further end, we would be caught in an infinite regress and our desires would never be satisfied. So there must be some end that is intrinsically valuable—valuable for its own sake—that serves as the goal of all human activity. That end, Aristotle claims, is happiness.

Different people have different conceptions of happiness, however. To identify the correct conception, Aristotle suggests that we discover the proper function of human beings. Individual people, such as carpenters and plumbers, have functions, and what makes them good carpenters or good plumbers is that they perform their function well. Similarly, says Aristotle, good human beings perform their function well.

How can we discover the function of human beings? By identifying what's unique to them. What distinguishes a knife from all other tools is that it cuts well, and cutting is its function. So, according to Aristotle, if we can discover what distinguishes humans from other creatures, we can discover their function.

Living can't be our function because that trait is shared by both plants and animals. Nor can sensing things be our function because higher animals can do that as well. Our ability to reason, however, seems to be unique to us. So, Aristotle concludes, our function is to reason, and happiness is attained through the use of reason. If you don't exercise your reasoning ability, you're not realizing your full potential and are missing out on the greatest good humans can attain. Even the utilitarian John Stuart Mill recognized that happiness produced by reason was better than happiness produced by sensation. Remember his saying: "It is better to be a human being dissatisfied than a pig satisfied."

Nevertheless, this portion of Aristotle's ethical theory has not been particularly well received. Many have pointed out that from the fact that every action aims at some end, it doesn't follow that there is an end at which all actions aim; just as from the fact that everyone has a mother, it doesn't follow that there is someone who is everyone's mother. Human activity aims at a number of different ends. Happiness may be the result of attaining those ends, but it is not the sole object of our desire. (Recall Feinberg's single-minded hedonist.)

What's more, the notion that human beings have a function, and that this function can be identified with what is unique to us, has also been criticized. Humans have many unique properties. Theologian Paul Tillich claims that humans are the only creatures that can experience anguish. Philosopher Henri Bergson claims that humans are the only creatures that laugh. And theologian Reinhold Niebuhr claims that humans are the only creatures that are constantly in heat. None of these features constitute our function, and exemplifying them would not necessarily be good.

The aspect of Aristotle's ethics that still has adherents to this day is his notion that virtues are necessary to lead a good life. A good life requires many things: good health, a good job, good friends, a good family, and the like. To attain these goods, we should cultivate those ways of behaving — those habits — that are most likely to help us attain them. Those habits are virtues.

Aristotle recognizes two types of virtues: intellectual and moral. Intellectual virtues are dispositions, such as wisdom and understanding, which help us to discover the truth. Moral virtues are dispositions, such as courage, temperance, friendliness, and justice, which help us to avoid the problems caused by overdoing or underdoing. For Aristotle, a good life is a balanced life. Those who keep themselves on an even keel are more likely to achieve the ultimate goal of happiness than those who go overboard. Virtues keep us from losing our balance.

Aristotle thinks that bad people have too much or too little of something. For example, if we have too much fear, we suffer from the vice of cowardice. If we have too little fear, we suffer from the vice of foolhardiness. But if we maintain the proper balance between cowardice and foolhardiness, we enjoy the virtue of courage. Aristotle's theory of virtue is often referred to as the "golden mean" because its purpose is to help us find the mean (the middle point) between the extremes of excess (too much) and defect (too little).

Intellectual virtues, Aristotle claims, differ from moral virtues in that they can be taught in the classroom. Moral virtues are skills, however, so they can be learned only by doing. As Aristotle puts it,

> Where doing or making is dependent on knowing how, we acquire know-how by actually doing. For example, people become builders by actually building, and the same applies to lyre players. In the same way, we become just by doing just acts; and similarly with "temperate" and "brave."[75]

This insight has important implications for moral education. If we expect our children to acquire the virtues necessary for a just society, we must encourage them to engage in activities that foster a sense of justice.

Aristotle considers every social skill that is conducive to a good life a moral virtue. This is not a particularly apt classification, however, because

virtue An admirable human quality marked by a disposition to behave in certain ways in certain circumstances.

Excess (vice)	Virtue	Defect (vice)
rashness	courage	cowardice
short temper	gentleness	apathy
extravagance	generosity	stinginess
vanity	high-mindedness	humility
flattery	friendliness	grouchiness
buffoonery	wittiness	boorishness
boastfulness	truthfulness	self-deprecation
bashfulness	modesty	shamelessness
envy	righteous indignation	ill will
debauchery	self-control	insensibility

having such virtues does not necessarily make you a good person. Dracula (Vlad Tepes), for example, was courageous, disciplined, and temperate and yet was one of the most evil people who has ever lived. Courage, discipline, and temperance are admirable qualities—they may even be necessary for being a good person—but they aren't sufficient.

The virtues that make you a morally good person are those that involve acting in accord with duty. Justice, for example, is a good-making virtue because you are just only if you act in accord with the duty of justice. Similarly, benevolence is a good-making virtue because you are benevolent only if you act in accord with the duty of benevolence. Because the purpose of morality is to constrain certain sorts of self-interested behavior, the truly moral virtues are those, like justice and benevolence, that involve action on behalf of others.

MacIntyre on Virtue

*Duty by habit is to plea-
sure turned.*

—SAMUEL BRYDGES

Alasdair MacIntyre, dismayed at our apparent inability to come to any agreement on moral matters, has argued that it would be easier to reach consensus if we focused on what it is to lead a good life rather than on what it is to do the right thing. Because the function of morality is to enable each of us to lead a good life, our primary concern should be the conditions for human flourishing instead of the conditions for right action.

Following Aristotle, MacIntyre claims that in order to lead a good life, you have to be good at something. And in order to be good at something, you have to acquire certain skills. For example, to be a good surgeon, you have to know how to wield a scalpel. To fully realize the good that can come from engaging in the practice of medicine (or any practice for that matter), you have to have the proper motivation. Specifically, you can't be in it only for money or fame. Becoming rich or famous is a good of sorts, but it is a good that is *external* to the practice of medicine. The goods that promote human flourishing, according to MacIntyre, are those that are *internal* to a practice, like the good

Aristotle: Pillar of Western Thought

Aside from Plato, there is none greater in the history of philosophy than Aristotle (384–322 B.C.). At age seventeen, he entered Plato's Academy, learned much from his master, and left the Academy when Plato died. After Plato's death he traveled about in the region, conducting biological research and eventually becoming the tutor of Alexander the Great in Macedonia. In 335 B.C. Aristotle went back to Athens and founded his own school, the Lyceum, in a grove outside the city on a site thought to be sacred to the god Apollo Lyceius.

At first glance, he probably did not seem like a fellow who could change the world: he was said to be bald and thin with a decided lisp in his speech. But he set Western civilization on a course that is still followed to this day. He established the first great library of antiquity and created the categories of philosophical and scientific inquiry that we know today: physics, logic, ethics, psychology, metaphysics, political science, and more. He was interested in almost everything—and studied almost everything. He was the first to organize and systematize the field of logic, charting out the distinctions between valid and invalid inferences and creating the field's technical vocabulary. For the next two thousand years, when students and philosophers studied logic, they essentially took a course of study that Aristotle designed.

Aristotle made contributions to just about every important branch of philosophy. In many of those areas—especially ethics, metaphysics, and political science—Aristotle's ideas are still influential.

In philosophy, he took a different road than Plato had, though he had great respect for his wise teacher. Plato insisted that true knowledge could not be gained by extracting data from the material world, as scientists do. He thought that knowing could be achieved only by using reason to reach the nonmaterial, other-worldly realm of transcendental ideas. Aristotle, though, believed that this world of experience—the data of our senses—can indeed be a source of knowledge. Centuries later, science achieved incredible feats because it tended to follow the path of Aristotle and not Plato.

---

of healing, for acquiring these goods requires developing certain virtues. "The virtues," he says,

> are to be understood as those dispositions which will not only sustain practices and enable us to achieve the goods internal to practices, but which will also sustain us in the relevant kind of quest for the good, by enabling us to overcome the harms, dangers, temptations and distractions which we encounter and which will furnish us with increasing self-knowledge and increasing knowledge of the good.[76]

Virtues are the means by which we achieve the end: a good life.

To lead a good life—to achieve the goods internal to a practice—you have to choose your practices carefully. You can't be good at everything. Being a good football player, for example, precludes being a good jockey. To realize the most good possible, your choice of careers should be part of a coherent plan. Such a plan brings not only order to your life, it also brings unity to your self. Who you are is determined by the choices you make. According to MacIntyre, the unity of a self "resides in the unity of a narrative which links birth to life to death as narrative beginning to middle to end."[77] Just as virtues help you achieve the goods internal to a practice, they also help you achieve a narrative unity in your life.

By doing our duty, we learn to do it.
—E. B. PUSEY

The Buddha on Virtue

The notion that the best life is a balanced life is not unique to Aristotle. The Buddha also taught that a good person should tread a middle path between too much and too little. Here is an excerpt from the Buddha's first sermon:

> Bhikkhus (beggars or monks), these two extremes ought not to be practiced by one who has gone forth from the household life. What are the two? There is devotion to the indulgence of sense-pleasures, which is low, common, the way of ordinary people, unworthy and unprofitable; and there is devotion to self-mortification, which is painful, unworthy and unprofitable.

> Avoiding both these extremes, the Tathagata (the enlightened one) has realized the Middle Path: it gives vision, it gives knowledge, and it leads to calm, to insight, to enlightenment, to Nirvana. And what is that Middle Path . . . ? It is simply the Noble Eightfold Path, namely, right view, right thought, right speech, right action, right livelihood, right effort, right mindfulness, right concentration. This is the Middle Path realized by the Tathagata, which gives vision, which gives knowledge, and which leads to calm, to insight, to enlightenment, to Nirvana.[78]

Whatever unity your life possesses is not created by you alone, however. Your choices make sense only against the background of a tradition. Your tradition gives you your basic orientation to the world. It tells you what sorts of practices are worth pursuing and what sorts of relationships are worth cultivating. You may reject that tradition, but the direction your life takes can always be plotted relative to it.

Traditions can be corrupted and destroyed, however. If they are to survive, they must be sustained and enriched by virtuous behavior. "The virtues," MacIntyre tells us,

> find their point and purpose not only in sustaining those relationships necessary if the variety of goods internal to practices are to be achieved and not only in sustaining the form of an individual life in which that individual may seek out his or her good as the good of his or her whole life, but also in sustaining those traditions which provide both practices and individual lives with their necessary historical context.[79]

Virtues, then, are needed to achieve the good inherent in practices, lives, and traditions.

Because lives and practices derive their value from traditions, MacIntyre's ethical theory is a form of tradition relativism. As such, it faces many of the same problems that cultural relativism does. Are all traditions morally equal? If not, how do we choose among them? Consider the tradition of ethnocentrism, which sometimes promotes the practice of "ethnic cleansing" (genocide). Does the fact that there is a tradition of genocide make it morally acceptable? To effectively exterminate a race, you need certain virtues, such as courage, discipline, self-control, and the like. Are those who have acquired these virtues through the practice of genocide good people? Do they lead good lives? If not, traditions cannot be the source and ground of all value.

There is also the problem of identifying your tradition. Suppose that you are a white Christian capitalist living in China during Mao Tse-tung's reign, and suppose that you want to bring unity and meaning to your life by making choices that are in accord with your tradition. What do you do? How do you identify your tradition? MacIntyre doesn't say. But insofar as you can't identify your tradition, you can't base your decisions on your tradition.

Virtue Ethics

The purpose of morality is to enable us to lead good lives. In order to fully realize the good of a moral life, it is necessary to acquire certain virtues. This has led some to claim that virtue—not duty—should be the fundamental ethical concept. In their view, the central ethical question should be "What sort of person should I be?" instead of "What sorts of actions should I perform?" In an ethics of virtue, judgments about the morality of actions would be secondary to and dependent on judgments about the morality of persons. This system of ethics—**virtue ethics**—would be based on the concept of a good person rather than on the concept of a right action.

If you would create something, you must be something.

—GOETHE

The advantage of such an approach to ethics is that questions about the nature of the good life would once again take center stage. Because persons would be the primary object of moral evaluation, the self would not be slighted in the way that it is in traditional utilitarian or Kantian theories.[80] But would an ethics of virtue be more effective than an ethics of duty in solving ethical dilemmas?

Suppose you were in the same situation as Lester Zygmanik. Your brother has just become a quadriplegic, he is racked with interminable pain, and he is pleading with you to kill him. What should you do? According to virtue ethics, you should do what a virtuous person would do. But what would a virtuous person do? To answer this question, you could try imagining yourself as some virtuous person, such as Gandhi, Socrates, or the Buddha, but it is doubtful whether such a thought experiment would help you solve your problem. This approach to solving moral dilemmas seems no more effective than a duty-based approach. In fact, it may be less effective because it precludes the principled evaluation of alternative courses of action. It's hard to see how one could reach any sort of reflective equilibrium under such conditions.

Moreover, because a virtue is a disposition to act, the only way to determine whether someone has a virtue is to examine that person's actions. For example, the only way to determine whether someone is just is to determine whether that person acts in accord with the duty of justice. But if all judgments of virtue rest on judgments of action, we can't use virtue to judge actions—for that would put the cart before the horse.

There can be no morality without virtue. But there can also be no virtue without duty. So instead of conceiving of virtue and duty as two competing approaches to morality, it would be better to conceive of them as two complementary aspects of morality. They are two sides of the same coin, so to speak. You can't have one without the other any more than you can have a coin with only one side.

virtue ethics A system of ethics based on the concept of a good person rather than that of a right action.

The Ring of Gyges

In the second book of Plato's *Republic*, Glaucon recounts the legend of Gyges, a shepherd who found a magic ring on a corpse in a chasm opened by an earthquake. The ring made its wearer invisible. Gyges used the ring to enter the royal palace, seduce the queen, murder the king, and seize the throne. Glaucon proposes the following thought experiment: suppose there were two such rings, one of which was given to a virtuous person and the other to an outlaw. The outlaw would no doubt use the ring to commit evil deeds. But what about the virtuous person? Glaucon suggests that the virtuous person, too, would use it to break the law. "No one, it is commonly believed, would have such iron strength of mind as to stand fast in doing right or keep his hands off other men's goods, when he could go to the market-place and fearlessly help himself to anything he wanted, enter houses and sleep with any woman he chose, set prisoners free and kill men at his pleasure, and in a word go about among men with the powers of a god. He would behave no better than the other; both would take the same course."[81] Is Glaucon right? Would the behavior of a virtuous person with the power of invisibility be no different from that of an outlaw?

Summary

Virtuous people try to do the right thing. Virtuous act-utilitarians, for example, try to maximize happiness, whereas virtuous Kantians try to obey the categorical imperative. Both of these conceptions of virtue have been criticized on the grounds that neither is conducive to a good life.

The purpose of morality is to make it possible for everyone to enjoy a good life by restricting certain forms of self-interested behavior. A system of moral rules can achieve this result only if people are willing to abide by it. The most effective way to get people to abide by a system of moral rules is to instill in them certain dispositions known as virtues.

Aristotle maintains that virtues help people achieve a good life by making them better able to avoid the vices of excess (too much) and defect (too little). MacIntyre claims that virtues help people achieve a good life by allowing them to acquire the goods internal to a practice. Virtues also bring unity to people's lives and help sustain the traditions that give their lives meaning. Not every tradition is worth sustaining, however. Thus all moral value cannot be rooted in tradition.

Some have thought that an ethics based on virtue would be superior to an ethics based on duty because it would not slight the self in the way that utilitarianism and Kantianism do. An ethics of virtue, however, would be no more effective than an ethics of duty in solving moral dilemmas. Moreover, an ethics of virtue requires an ethics of duty because the only way to determine whether an action is morally virtuous is to determine whether it accords with a moral duty. So virtue and duty are best seen as complementary aspects of morality.

Study Questions

1. According to utilitarianism, what is it to be a virtuous (morally good) person?
2. According to Kantianism, what is it to be a virtuous (morally good) person?
3. According to Aristotle, what is the purpose or function of virtue?
4. According to MacIntyre, what is the purpose or function of virtue?
5. How does virtue ethics differ from duty ethics?

Discussion Questions

1. Would a person who succeeded in governing her actions by the greatest happiness principle lead a good life?
2. Would a person who never disobeyed the categorical imperative lead a good life?
3. Can a psychopath — someone without a conscience — act morally?
4. Is it always best to tread the middle path between too much and too little? Can you think of any cases where it isn't?
5. Do people who seek fame and fortune and get it lead less good lives than those who seek only to become experts in their field and succeed?
6. Because virtue can be taught only by doing, should we require students to perform community service?

Are Ethical Values Relative?

A biographical description of Stace appears on page 233. In this section, he critiques moral relativism.

Any ethical position which denies that there is a single moral standard which is equally applicable to all men at all times may fairly be called a species of ethical relativity. There is not, the relativist asserts, merely one moral law, one code, one standard. There are many moral laws, codes, standards. What morality ordains in one place or age may be quite different from what morality ordains in another place or age. The moral code of Chinamen is quite different from that of Europeans, that of African savages quite different from both. Any morality, therefore, is relative to the age, the place, and the circumstances in which it is found. It is in no sense absolute.

This does not mean merely—as one might at first sight be inclined to suppose—that the very same kind of action which is *thought* right in one country and period may be *thought* wrong in another. This would be a mere platitude, the truth of which everyone would have to admit. Even the absolutist would admit this—would even wish to emphasize it—since he is well aware that different people have different sets of moral ideas, and his whole point is that some of these sets of ideas are false. What the relativist means to assert is, not this platitude, but that the very same kind of action which is right in one country and period may be wrong in another. And this, far from being a platitude, is a very startling assertion.

It is very important to grasp thoroughly the difference between the two ideas. For there is reason to think that many minds tend to find ethical relativity attractive because they fail to keep them clearly apart. It is so very obvious that moral ideas differ from country to country and from age to age. And it is so very easy, if you are mentally lazy, to suppose that to say this means the same as to say that no universal moral standard exists,—or in other words that it implies ethical relativity. We fail to see that the word "standard" is used in two different senses. It is perfectly true that, in one sense, there are many variable moral standards. We speak of judging a man by the standard of his time. And this implies that different times have different standards. And this, of course, is quite true. But when the

word "standard" is used in this sense it means simply the set of moral ideas current during the period in question. It means what people think right, whether as a matter of fact it is right or not. On the other hand when the absolutist asserts that there exists a single universal moral "standard," he is not using the word in this sense at all. He means by "standard" what is right as distinct from what people merely think right. His point is that although what people think right varies in different countries and periods, yet what actually is right is everywhere and always the same. And it follows that when the ethical relativist disputes the position of the absolutist and denies that any universal moral standard exists he too means by "standard" what actually is right. But it is exceedingly easy, if we are not careful, to slip loosely from using the word in the first sense to using it in the second sense; and to suppose that the variability of moral beliefs is the same thing as the variability of what really is moral. And unless we keep the two senses of the word "standard" distinct, we are likely to think the creed of ethical relativity much more plausible than it actually is.

The genuine relativist, then, does not merely mean that Chinamen may think right what Frenchmen think wrong. He means that what is wrong for the Frenchman may *be* right for the Chinaman. And if one enquires how, in those circumstances, one is to know what actually is right in China or in France, the answer comes quite glibly. What is right in China is the same as what people think right in China; and what is right in France is the same as what people think right in France. So that, if you want to know what is moral in any particular country or age all you have to do is to ascertain what are the moral ideas current in that age or country. Those ideas are, *for that age or country,* right. Thus what is morally right is identified with what is thought to be morally right, and the distinction which we made above

_____

From: W. T. Stace, *The Concept of Morals* (New York: Macmillan, 1937) 8–58.

between these two is simply denied. To put the same thing in another way, it is denied that there can be or ought to be any distinction between the two senses of the word "standard." There is only one kind of standard of right and wrong, namely, the moral ideas current in any particular age or country.

Moral right *means* what people think morally right. It has no other meaning. What Frenchmen think right is, therefore, right *for Frenchmen*. And evidently one must conclude — though I am not aware that relativists are anxious to draw one's attention to such unsavoury but yet absolutely necessary conclusions from their creed — that cannibalism is right for people who believe in it, that human sacrifice is right for those races which practice it, and that burning widows alive was right for Hindus until the British stepped in and compelled the Hindus to behave immorally by allowing their widows to remain alive.

When it is said that, according to the ethical relativist, what is thought right in any social group is right for that group, one must be careful not to misinterpret this. The relativist does not, of course, mean that there actually is an objective moral standard in France and a different objective standard in England, and that French and British opinions respectively give us correct information about these different standards. His point is rather that there are no objectively true moral standards at all. There is no single universal objective standard. Nor are there a variety of local objective standards. All standards are subjective. People's subjective feelings about morality are the only standards which exist.

To sum up. The ethical relativist consistently denies, it would seem, whatever the ethical absolutist asserts. For the absolutist there is a single universal moral standard. For the relativist there is no such standard. There are only local, ephemeral, and variable standards. For the absolutist there are two senses of the word "standard." Standards in the sense of sets of current moral ideas are relative and changeable. But the standard in the sense of what is actually morally right is absolute and unchanging. For the relativist no such distinction can be made. There is only one meaning of the word "standard," namely, that which refers to local and variable sets of moral ideas. Or if it is insisted that the word must be allowed two meanings, then the relativist will say that there is at any rate no actual example of a standard in the absolute sense, and that the word as thus used is an empty name to which nothing in reality corresponds; so that the distinction between the two meanings becomes empty and useless. Finally — though this is merely saying the same thing in another way — the absolutist makes a distinction between what actu-

ally is right and what is thought right. The relativist rejects this distinction and identifies what is moral with what is thought by certain human beings or groups of human beings. . . .

I shall now proceed to consider, first, the main arguments which can be urged in favour of ethical relativity; and secondly, the arguments which can be urged against it. . . . The first is that which relies upon the actual varieties of moral "standards" found in the world. It was easy enough to believe in a single absolute morality in older times when there was no anthropology, when all humanity was divided clearly into two groups, Christian peoples and the "heathen." Christian peoples knew and possessed the one true morality. The rest were savages whose moral ideas could be ignored. But all this is changed. Greater knowledge has brought greater tolerance. We can no longer exalt our own morality as alone true, while dismissing all other moralities as false or inferior. The investigations of anthropologists have shown that there exist side by side in the world a bewildering variety of moral codes. On this topic endless volumes have been written, masses of evidence piled up. Anthropologists have ransacked the Melanesian Islands, the jungles of New Guinea, the steppes of Siberia, the deserts of Australia, the forests of central Africa, and have brought back with them countless examples of weird, extravagant, and fantastic "moral" customs with which to confound us. We learn that all kinds of horrible practices are, in this, that, or the other place, regarded as essential to virtue. We find that there is nothing, or next to nothing, which has always and everywhere been regarded as morally good by all men. Where then is our universal morality? Can we, in face of all this evidence, deny that it is nothing but an empty dream?

This argument, taken by itself, is a very weak one. It relies upon a single set of facts — the variable moral customs of the world. But this variability of moral ideas is admitted by both parties to the dispute, and is capable of ready explanation upon the hypothesis of either party. The relativist says that the facts are to be explained by the non-existence of any absolute moral standard. The absolutist says that they are to be explained by human ignorance of what the absolute moral standard is. And he can truly point out that men have differed widely in their opinions about all manner of topics including the subject-matters of the physical sciences — just as much as they differ about morals. And if the various different opinions which men have held about the shape of the earth do not prove that it has no one real shape, neither do the various opinions which they have held about morality prove that there is no one true morality.

Thus the facts can be explained equally plausibly on either hypothesis. There is nothing in the facts themselves which compels us to prefer the relativistic hypothesis to that of the absolutist. And therefore the argument fails to prove the relativist conclusion. If that conclusion is to be established, it must be by means of other considerations.

This is the essential point. But I will add some supplementary remarks. The work of the anthropologists, upon which ethical relativists seem to rely so heavily, has as a matter of fact added absolutely nothing in principle to what has always been known about the variability of moral ideas. Educated people have known all along that the Greeks tolerated sodomy, which in modern times has been regarded in some countries as an abominable crime; that the Hindus thought it a sacred duty to burn their widows; that trickery, now thought despicable, was once believed to be a virtue; that terrible torture was thought by our own ancestors only a few centuries ago to be a justifiable weapon of justice; that it was only yesterday that western peoples came to believe that slavery is immoral. Even the ancients knew very well that moral customs and ideas vary — witness the writings of Herodotus. Thus the principle of the variability of moral ideas was well understood long before modern anthropology was ever heard of. Anthropology has added nothing to the knowledge of this principle except a mass of new and extreme examples of it drawn from very remote sources. But to multiply examples of a principle already well known and universally admitted adds nothing to the argument which is built upon that principle. The discoveries of the anthropologists have no doubt been of the highest importance in their own sphere. But in my considered opinion they have thrown no new light upon the special problems of the moral philosopher.

Although the multiplication of examples has no logical bearing on the argument, it does have an immense *psychological* effect upon people's minds. These masses of anthropological learning are impressive. They are propounded in the sacred name of "science." If they are quoted in support of ethical relativity—as they often are—people think that they must prove something important. They bewilder and over-awe the simple-minded, batter down their resistance, make them ready to receive humbly the doctrine of ethical relativity from those who have acquired a reputation by their immense learning and their claims to be "scientific." Perhaps this is why so much ado is made by ethical relativists regarding the anthropological evidence. But we must refuse to be impressed. We must discount all this mass of evidence about the extraordinary moral customs of remote peoples. Once we have admitted—as everyone who is instructed must have admitted these last two thousand years without any anthropology at all—the principle that moral ideas vary, all this new evidence adds nothing to the argument. And the argument itself proves nothing for the reasons already given. . . .

The [second] argument in favour of ethical relativity is also a very strong one. And it does not suffer from the disadvantage that it is dependent upon the acceptance of any particular philosophy such as radical empiricism. It makes its appeal to considerations of a quite general character. It consists in alleging that no one has ever been able to discover upon what foundation an absolute morality could rest, or from what source a universally binding moral code could derive its authority.

If, for example, it is an absolute and unalterable moral rule that all men ought to be unselfish, from whence does this *command* issue? For a command it certainly is, phrase it how you please. There is no difference in meaning between the sentence "You ought to be unselfish" and the sentence "Be unselfish." Now a command implies a commander. An obligation implies some authority which obliges. Who is the commander, what this authority? Thus the vastly difficult question is raised on *the basis of moral obligation*. Now the argument of the relativist would be that it is impossible to find any basis for a universally binding moral law; but that it is quite easy to discover a basis for morality if moral codes are admitted to be variable, ephemeral, and relative to time, place, and circumstance.

In this book I am assuming that it is no longer possible to solve this difficulty by saying naively that the universal moral law is based upon the uniform commands of God to all men. There will be many, no doubt, who will dispute this. But I am not writing for them. I am writing for those who feel the necessity of finding for morality a basis independent of particular religious dogmas. And I shall therefore make no attempt to argue the matter.

The problem which the absolutist has to face, then, is this. The religious basis of the one absolute morality having disappeared, can there be found for it any other, any secular, basis? If not, then it would seem that we cannot any longer believe in absolutism. We shall have to fall back upon belief in a variety of perhaps mutually inconsistent moral codes operating over restricted areas and limited periods. No one of these will be better, or more true, than any other. Each will be good and true for those living in those areas and periods. We shall have to fall back, in a word, on ethical relativity.

For there is no great difficulty in discovering the foundations of morality, or rather of moralities, if we adopt the relativistic hypothesis. Even if we cannot be quite certain *precisely* what these foundations are — and relativists themselves are not entirely agreed about them — we can at least see in a general way the *sort* of foundations they must have. We can see that the question on this basis is not in principle impossible of answer — although the details may be obscure; while, if we adopt the absolutist hypothesis — so the argument runs — no kind of answer is conceivable at all. . . .

This argument is undoubtedly very strong. It is absolutely essential to solve the problem of the basis of moral obligation if we are to believe in any kind of moral standards other than those provided by mere custom or by irrational emotions. It is idle to talk about a universal morality unless we can point to the source of its authority — or at least to do so is to indulge in a faith which is without rational ground. To cherish a blind faith in morality may be, for the average man whose business is primarily to live aright and not to theorize, sufficient. Perhaps it is his wisest course. But it will not do for the philosopher. His function, or at least one of his functions, is precisely to discover the rational grounds of our everyday beliefs — if they have any. Philosophically and intellectually, then, we cannot accept belief in a universally binding morality unless we can discover upon what foundation its obligatory character rests.

But in spite of the strength of the argument thus posed in favour of ethical relativity, it is not impregnable. For it leaves open one loophole. It is always possible that some theory, not yet examined, may provide a basis for a universal moral obligation. The argument rests upon the negative proposition that *there is no theory which can provide a basis for a universal morality*. But it is notoriously difficult to prove a negative. How can you prove that there are no green swans? All you can show is that none have been found so far. And then it is always possible that one will be found tomorrow. . . .

It is time that we turned our attention from the case in favour of ethical relativity to the case against it. Now the case against it consists, to a very large extent, in urging that, if taken seriously and pressed to its logical conclusion, ethical relativity can only end in destroying the conception of morality altogether, in undermining its practical efficacy, in rendering meaningless many almost universally accepted truths about human affairs, in robbing human beings of any incentive to strive for a better world, in taking the life-blood out of every ideal and every aspiration which has ever ennobled the life of man. . . .

First of all, then, ethical relativity, in asserting that the moral standards of particular social groups are the only standards which exist, renders meaningless all propositions which attempt to compare these standards with one another in respect to their moral worth. And this is a very serious matter indeed. We are accustomed to think that the moral ideas of one nation or social group may be "higher" or "lower" than those of another. We believe, for example, that Christian ethical ideals are nobler than those of the savage races of central Africa. Probably most of us would think that the Chinese moral standards are higher than those of the inhabitants of New Guinea. In short we habitually compare one civilization with another and judge the sets of ethical ideas to be found in them to be some better, some worse. The fact that such judgments are very difficult to make with any justice, and that they are frequently made on very superficial and prejudiced grounds, has no bearing on the question now at issue. The question is whether such judgments have any meaning. We habitually assume that they have.

But on the basis of ethical relativity they can have none whatever. For the relativist must hold that there is no *common* standard which can be applied to the various civilizations judged. Any such comparison of moral standards implies the existence of some superior standard which is applicable to both. And the existence of any such standard is precisely what the relativist denies. According to him the Christian standard is applicable only to Christians, the Chinese standard only to Chinese, the New Guinea standard only to the inhabitants of New Guinea.

What is true of comparisons between the moral standards of different races will also be true of comparisons between those of different ages. It is not unusual to ask such questions as whether the standard of our own day is superior to that which existed among our ancestors five hundred years ago. And when we remember that our ancestors employed slaves, practiced barbaric physical tortures, and burnt people alive, we may be inclined to think that it is. At any rate we assume that the question is one which has meaning and is capable of rational discussion. But if the ethical relativist is right, whatever we assert on this subject must be totally meaningless. For here again there is no common standard which could form the basis of any such judgments.

This in its turn implies that the whole notion of moral *progress* is a sheer delusion. Progress means an advance from lower to higher, from worse to better. But on the basis of ethical relativity it has no meaning to say that the standards of this age are better (or worse) than those of a previous age. For there is no common standard by which both can be measured. Thus it is nonsense to say that the morality of the New Testament is higher than that of the Old. And Jesus Christ, if he imagined that he was introducing into the world a higher ethical standard than existed before his time, was merely deluded. . . .

I come now to a second point. Up to the present I have allowed it to be taken tacitly for granted that, though judgments comparing different races and ages in respect of the worth of their moral codes are impossible for the ethical relativist, yet judgments of comparison between individuals living within the same social group would be quite possible. For individuals living within the same social group would presumably be subject to the same moral code, that of their group, and this would therefore constitute, as between these individuals, a common standard by which they could both be measured. We have not here, as we had in the other case, the difficulty of the absence of any common standard of comparison. It should therefore be possible for the ethical relativist to say quite meaningfully that President Lincoln was a better man than some criminal or moral imbecile of his own time and country, or that Jesus was a better man than Judas Iscariot.

But is even this minimum of moral judgment really possible on relativist grounds? It seems to me that it is not. For when once the whole of humanity is abandoned as the area covered by a single moral standard, what smaller areas are to be adopted as the *loci* of different standards? Where are we to draw the lines of demarcation? We can split up humanity, perhaps, — though the procedure will be very arbitrary — into races, races into nations, nations into tribes, tribes into families, families into individuals. Where are we going to draw the moral boundaries? Does the locus of a particular moral standard reside in a race, a nation, a tribe, a family, or an individual? Perhaps the blessed phrase "social group" will be dragged in to save the situation. Each such group, we shall be told, has its own moral code which is, for it, right. But what is a group? Can anyone define it or give its boundaries? This is the seat of that ambiguity in the theory of ethical relativity to which reference was made on an earlier page.

The difficulty is not, as might be thought, merely an academic difficulty of logical definition. If that were all, I should not press the point. But the ambiguity has practical consequences which are disastrous for morality. No one is likely to say that moral codes are confined within the arbitrary limits of the geographical divisions of countries. Nor are the notions of race, nation, or political state likely to help us. To bring out the essentially practical character of the difficulty let us put it in the form of concrete questions. Does the American nation constitute a "group" having a single moral standard? Or does the standard of what I ought to do change continuously as I cross the continent in a railway train? Do different States of the Union have different moral codes? Perhaps every town and village has its own peculiar standard. This may at first sight seem reasonable enough. "In Rome do as Rome does" may seem as good a rule in morals as it is in etiquette. But can we stop there? Within the village are numerous cliques each having its own set of ideas. Why should not each of these claim to be bound only by its own special and peculiar moral standards? And if it comes to that, why should not the gangsters of Chicago claim to constitute a group having its own morality, so that its murders and debaucheries must be viewed as "right" by the only standard which can legitimately be applied to it? And if it be answered that the nation will not tolerate this, that may be so. But this is to put the foundation of right simply in the superior force of the majority. In that case whoever is stronger will be right, however monstrous his ideas and actions. And if we cannot deny to any set of people the right to have its own morality, is it not clear that, in the end, we cannot even deny this right to the individual? Every individual man and woman can put up, on this view, an irrefutable claim to be judged by no standard except his or her own.

If these arguments are valid, the ethical relativist cannot really maintain that there is anywhere to be found a moral standard binding upon anybody against his will. And he cannot maintain that, even within the social group, there is a common standard as between individuals. And if that is so, then even judgments to the effect that one man is morally better than another become meaningless. All moral valuation thus vanishes. There is nothing to prevent each man from being a rule unto himself. The result will be moral chaos and the collapse of all effective standards. . . .

But even if we assume that the difficulty about defining moral groups has been surmounted, a further difficulty presents itself. Suppose that we have now definitely decided what are the exact boundaries of the social group within which a moral standard is to be operative. And we will assume — as is invariably done by relativists themselves — that this group is to be some actually existing social community such as a tribe or nation. How are we to know, even then, what actually is the moral standard within that group? How is anyone to know? How is even a member of the group to know? For there are certain to be within the group — at least this will be true among advanced peoples — wide differences of opinion as to what is right, what wrong. Whose opinion, then, is to be taken as representing the moral standard of the group? Either we must take the opinion of the majority within the group, or the opinion of some minority. If we rely upon the ideas of the majority, the results will be disastrous. Wherever there is found among a people a small band of select spirits, or perhaps one man, working for the establishment of higher and nobler ideals than those commonly accepted by the group, we shall be compelled to hold that, for that people at that time, the majority are right, and that the reformers are wrong and are preaching what is immoral. We shall have to maintain, for example, that Jesus was preaching immoral doctrines to the Jews. Moral goodness will have to be equated always with the mediocre and sometimes with the definitely base and ignoble. If on the other hand we said that the moral standard of the group is to be identified with the moral opinions of some minority, then what minority is this to be? We cannot answer that it is to be the minority composed of the best and most enlightened individuals of the group. This would involve us in a palpably vicious circle. For by what standard are these individuals to be judged the best and the most enlightened? There is no principle by which we could select the right minority. And therefore we should have to consider every minority as good as every other. And this means that we should have no logical right whatever to resist the claim of the gangsters of Chicago — if such a claim were made — that their practices represent the highest standards of American morality. It means in the end that every individual is to be bound by no standard save his own.

The ethical relativists are great empiricists. What is the actual moral standard of any group can only be discovered, they tell us, by an examination on the ground of the moral opinions and customs of that group. But will they tell us how they propose to decide, when they get to the ground, which of the many moral opinions they are sure to find there is the right one in that group? To some extent they will be able to do this for the Melanesian Islanders — from whom apparently all lessons in the nature of morality are in future to be taken. But it is certain that they cannot do it for advanced peoples whose members have learnt to think for themselves and to entertain among themselves a wide variety of opinions. They cannot do it unless they accept the calamitous view that the ethical opinion of the majority is always right. We are left therefore once more with the conclusion that, even within a particular social group, anybody's moral opinion is as good as anybody else's, and that every man is entitled to be judged by his own standards.

Finally, not only is ethical relativity disastrous in its consequences for moral theory. It cannot be doubted that it must tend to be equally disastrous in its impact upon practical conduct. If men come really to believe that one moral standard is as good as another, they will conclude that their own moral standard has nothing special to recommend it. They might as well then slip down to some lower and easier standard. It is true that, for a time, it may be possible to hold one view in theory and to act practically upon another. But ideas, even philosophical ideas, are not so ineffectual that they can remain forever idle in the upper chambers of the intellect. In the end they seep down to the level of practice. They get themselves acted on.

Of the Principle of Utility

Jeremy Bentham (1748–1832) was the first to provide a systematic defense of utilitarianism. A child prodigy, Bentham entered Oxford University at the age of twelve. He was the leader of a group known as the Philosophical Radicals, which included James Mill and his son, John Stuart Mill, another child prodigy. Together they undertook to reform the political and legal system of Great Britain. This selection, taken from Bentham's *Introduction to the Principles of Morals and Legislation*, articulates the view that right actions increase happiness and decrease misery.

I. Nature has placed mankind under the governance of two sovereign masters, *pain* and *pleasure*. It is for them alone to point out what we ought to do, as well as to determine what we shall do. On the one hand the standard of right and wrong, on the other the chain of causes and effects, are fastened to their throne. They govern us in all we do, in all we say, in all we think: every effort we can make to throw off our subjection, will serve but to demonstrate and confirm it. In words a man may pretend to abjure their empire: but in reality he will remain subject to it all the while. The *principle of utility* recognizes this subjection, and assumes it for the foundation of that system, the object of which is to rear the fabric of felicity by the hands of reason and of law. Systems which attempt to question it, deal in sounds instead of sense, in caprice instead of reason, in darkness instead of light.

But enough of metaphor and declamation: it is not by such means that moral science is to be improved.

II. The principle of utility is the foundation of the present work: it will be proper therefore at the outset to give an explicit and determinate account of what is meant by it. By the principle of utility is meant that principle which approves or disapproves of every action whatsoever, according to the tendency which it appears to have to augment or diminish the happiness of the party whose interest is in question: or, what is the same thing in other words, to promote or to oppose that happiness. I say of every action whatsoever; and therefore not only of every action of a private individual, but of every measure of government.

III. By utility is meant that property in any object, whereby it tends to produce benefit, advantage, pleasure, good, or happiness, (all this in the present case comes to the same thing) or (what comes again to the same thing) to prevent the happening of mischief, pain, evil, or unhappiness to the party whose interest is considered: if that party be the community in general, then the happiness of the community: if a particular individual, then the happiness of that individual.

IV. The interest of the community is one of the most general expressions that can occur in the phraseology of morals: no wonder that the meaning of it is often lost. When it has a meaning, it is this. The community is a fictitious *body*, composed of the individual persons who are considered as constituting as it were its *members*. The interest of the community then is, what?—the sum of the interests of the several members who compose it.

V. It is in vain to talk of the interest of the community, without understanding what is the interest of the individual. A thing is said to promote the interest, or to be *for* the interest, of an individual, when it tends to add to the sum total of his pleasures: or, what comes to the same thing, to diminish the sum total of his pains.

VI. An action then may be said to be conformable to the principle of utility, or, for shortness sake, to utility, (meaning with respect to the community at large) when the tendency it has to augment the happiness of the community is greater than any it has to diminish it.

VII. A measure of government (which is but a particular kind of action, performed by a particular person or persons) may be said to be conformable to or dictated by the principle of utility, when in like manner the tendency which it has to augment the happiness of

From: Jeremy Bentham, "Of the Principle of Utility," *An Introduction to the Principles of Morals and Legislation* (Oxford: Clarendon Press, 1879) 1–7. Notes have been omitted.

the community is greater than any which it has to diminish it.

VIII. When an action, or in particular a measure of government, is supposed by a man to be conformable to the principle of utility, it may be convenient, for the purposes of discourse, to imagine a kind of law or dictate, called a law or dictate of utility: and to speak of the action in question, as being conformable to such law or dictate.

IX. A man may be said to be a partizan of the principle of utility, when the approbation or disapprobation he annexes to any action, or to any measure, is determined by and proportioned to the tendency which he conceives it to have to augment or to diminish the happiness of the community: or in other words, to its conformity or unconformity to the laws or dictates of utility.

X. Of an action that is conformable to the principle of utility one may always say either that it is one that ought to be done, or at least that it is not one that ought not to be done. One may say also, that it is right it should be done; at least that it is not wrong it should be done; that it is a right action; at least that it is not a wrong action. When thus interpreted, the words *ought,* and *right* and *wrong,* and others of the stamp, have a meaning: when otherwise, they have none.

XI. Has the rectitude of this principle been ever formally contested? It should seem that it had, by those who have not known what they have been meaning. Is it susceptible of any direct proof? it should seem not: for that which is used to prove every thing else, cannot itself be proved: a chain of proofs must have their commencement somewhere. To give such proof is as impossible as it is needless.

XII. Not that there is or ever has been that human creature breathing, however stupid or perverse, who has not on many, perhaps on most occasions of his life, deferred to it. By the natural constitution of the human frame, on most occasions of their lives men in general embrace this principle, without thinking of it: if not for the ordering of their own actions, yet for the trying of their own actions, as well as of those of other men. There have been, at the same time, not many, perhaps, even of the most intelligent, who have been disposed to embrace it purely and without reserve. There are even few who have not taken some occasion or other to quarrel with it, either on account of their not understanding always how to apply it, or on account of some prejudice or other which they were afraid to examine into, or could not bear to part with. For such is the stuff that man is made of: in principle and in practice, in a right track and in a wrong one, the rarest of all human qualities is consistency.

XIII. When a man attempts to combat the principle of utility, it is with reasons drawn, without his being aware of it, from that very principle itself. His arguments, if they prove any thing, prove not that the principle is *wrong,* but that, according to the applications he supposes to be made of it, it is *misapplied.* Is it possible for a man to move the earth? Yes; but he must first find out another earth to stand upon.

XIV. To disprove the propriety of it by arguments is impossible; but, from the causes that have been mentioned, or from some confused or partial view of it, a man may happen to be disposed not to relish it. Where this is the case, if he thinks the settling of his opinions on such a subject worth the trouble, let him take the following steps, and at length, perhaps, he may come to reconcile himself to it.

1. Let him settle with himself, whether he would wish to discard this principle altogether; if so, let him consider what it is that all his reasonings (in matters of politics especially) can amount to?

2. If he would, let him settle with himself, whether he would judge and act without any principle, or whether there is any other he would judge and act by?

3. If there be, let him examine and satisfy himself whether the principle he thinks he has found is really any separate intelligible principle; or whether it be not a mere principle in words, a kind of phrase, which at bottom expresses neither more nor less than the mere averment of his own unfounded sentiments; that is, what in another person he might be apt to call caprice?

4. If he is inclined to think that his own approbation or dis-approbation, annexed to the idea of an act, without any regard to its consequences, is a sufficient foundation for him to judge and act upon, let him ask himself whether his sentiment is to be a standard of right and wrong, with respect to every other man, or whether every man's sentiment has the same privilege of being a standard to itself?

5. In the first case, let him ask himself whether his principle is not despotical, and hostile to all the rest of the human race?

6. In the second case, whether it is not anarchial, and whether at this rate there are not as many different

standards of right and wrong as there are men? and whether even to the same man, the same thing, which is right to-day, may not (without the least change in its nature) be wrong to-morrow? and whether the same thing is not right and wrong in the same place at the same time? and in either case, whether all argument is not at an end? and whether, when two men have said, 'I like this,' and 'I don't like it,' they can (upon such a principle) have any thing more to say?

7. If he should have said to himself, No: for that the sentiment which he proposes as a standard must be grounded on reflection, let him say on what particulars the reflection is to turn? if on particulars having relation to the utility of the act, then let him say whether this is not deserting his own principle, and borrowing assistance from that very one in opposition to which he sets it up: or if not on those particulars, on what other particulars?

8. If he should be for compounding the matter, and adopting his own principle in part, and the principle of utility in part, let him say how far he will adopt it?

9. When he has settled with himself where he will stop, then let him ask himself how he justifies to himself the adopting it so far? and why he will not adopt it any farther?

10. Admitting any other principle than the principle of utility to be a right principle, a principle that it is right for a man to pursue; admitting (what is not true) that the word *right* can have a meaning without reference to utility, let him say whether there is any such thing as a *motive* that a man can have to pursue the dictates of it: if there is, let him say what that motive is, and how it is to be distinguished from those which enforce the dictates of utility: if not, then lastly let him say what it is this other principle can be good for?

Good Will, Duty, and the Categorical Imperative

Although Immanuel Kant (1724–1804) never traveled more than forty miles outside of his native Königsberg (now Kaliningrad, Russia), his writings opened up many new vistas in philosophy. In his most celebrated work, *Critique of Pure Reason*, he argues that the mind is not a passive receiver of sensations but an active shaper of ideas. So our view of reality is a construct of the human mind. This idea had a revolutionary impact on subsequent philosophy. No less revolutionary were Kant's ideas in ethics. In this selection, taken from his *Fundamental Principles of the Metaphysics of Morals*, he defends the notion that the rightness of an action can be determined by reason alone.

Nothing can possibly be conceived in the world, or even out of it, which can be called good, without qualification, except a Good Will. Intelligence, wit, judgement, and the other *talents* of the mind, however they may be named, or courage, resolution, perseverance, as qualities of temperament, are undoubtedly good and desirable in many respects; but these gifts of nature may also become extremely bad and mischievous if the will which is to make use of them, and which, therefore, constitutes what is called *character,* is not good. It is the same with the *gifts of fortune.* Power, riches, honour, even health, and the general well-being and contentment with one's condition which is called *happiness,* inspire pride, and often presumption, if there is not a good will to correct the influence of these on the mind, and with this also to rectify the whole principle of acting, and adapt it to its end. The sight of a being who is not adorned with a single feature of a pure and good will, enjoying unbroken prosperity, can never give pleasure to an impartial rational spectator. Thus a good will appears to constitute the indispensable condition even of being worthy of happiness.

There are even some qualities which are of service to this good will itself, and may facilitate its action, yet which have no intrinsic unconditional value, but always presuppose a good will, and this qualifies the esteem that we justly have for them, and does not permit us to regard them as absolutely good. Moderation in the affections and passions, self-control, and calm deliberation are not only good in many respects, but even seem to constitute part of the intrinsic worth of the person; but they are far from deserving to be called good without qualification, although they have been so unconditionally praised by the ancients. For without

the principles of a good will, they may become extremely bad; and the coolness of a villain not only makes him far more dangerous, but also directly makes him more abominable in our eyes than he would have been without it.

A good will is good not because of what it performs or effects, not by its aptness for the attainment of some proposed end, but simply by virtue of the volition, that is, it is good in itself, and considered by itself is to be esteemed much higher than all that can be brought about by it in favour of any inclination, nay, even of the sumtotal of all inclinations. Even if it should happen that, owing to special disfavour of fortune, or the niggardly provision of a step-motherly nature, this will should wholly lack power to accomplish its purpose, if with its greatest efforts it should yet achieve nothing, and there should remain only the good will (not, to be sure, a mere wish, but the summoning of all means in our power), then, like a jewel, it would still shine by its own light, as a thing which has its whole value in itself. Its usefulness or fruitlessness can neither add to nor take away anything from this value. It would be, as it were, only the setting to enable us to handle it the more conveniently in common commerce, or to attract to it the attention of those who are not yet connoisseurs, but not to recommend it to true connoisseurs, or to determine its value. . . .

Thus the moral worth of an action does not lie in the effect expected from it, nor in any principle of

---

From: Immanuel Kant, *Fundamental Principles of the Metaphysics of Morals* (London: Longmans, Green, 1909). Notes have been omitted.

action which requires to borrow its motive from this expected effect. For all these effects—agreeableness of one's condition, and even the promotion of the happiness of others—could have been also brought about by other causes, so that for this there would have been no need of the will of a rational being; whereas it is in this alone that the supreme and unconditional good can be found. The pre-eminent good which we call moral can therefore consist in nothing else than *the conception of law* in itself, *which certainly is only possible in a rational being,* in so far as this conception, and not the expected effect, determines the will. This is a good which is already present in the person who acts accordingly, and we have not to wait for it to appear first in the result.

But what sort of law can that be, the conception of which must determine the will, even without paying any regard to the effect expected from it, in order that this will may be called good absolutely and without qualification? As I have deprived the will of every impulse which could arise to it from obedience to any law, there remains nothing but the universal conformity of its actions to law in general, which alone is to serve the will as a principle, *i.e.* I am never to act otherwise than so *that I could also will that my maxim should become a universal law.* Here, now, it is the simple conformity to law in general, without assuming any particular law applicable to certain actions, that serves the will as its principle, and must so serve it, if duty is not to be a vain delusion and a chimerical notion. The common reason of men in its practical judgments perfectly coincides with this, and always has in view the principle here suggested. Let the question be, for example: May I when in distress make a promise with the intention not to keep it? I readily distinguish here between the two significations which the question may have: Whether it is prudent or whether it is right, to make a false promise? The former may undoubtedly often be the case. I see clearly indeed that it is not enough to extricate myself from a present difficulty by means of this subterfuge, but it must be well considered whether there may not hereafter spring from this lie much greater inconvenience than that from which I now free myself, and as, with all my supposed *cunning,* the consequences cannot be so easily foreseen but that credit once lost may be much more injurious to me than any mischief which I seek to avoid at present, it should be considered whether it would not be more *prudent* to act herein according to a universal maxim, and to make it a habit to promise nothing except with the intention of keeping it. But it is soon clear to me that such a maxim will still only be based on the fear of consequences. Now it is a wholly different thing

to be truthful from duty, and to be so from apprehension of injurious consequences. In the first case, the very notion of the action already implies a law for me; in the second case, I must first look about elsewhere to see what results may be combined with it which would affect myself. For to deviate from the principle of duty is beyond all doubt wicked; but to be unfaithful to my maxim of prudence may often be very advantageous to me, although to abide by it is certainly safer. The shortest way, however, and an unerring one, to discover the answer to this question whether a lying promise is consistent with duty, is to ask myself, Should I be content that my maxim (to extricate myself from difficulty by a false promise) should hold good as a universal law, for myself as well as for others? and should I be able to say to myself, "Every one may make a deceitful promise when he finds himself in a difficulty from which he cannot otherwise extricate himself"? Then I presently become aware that while I can will the lie, I can by no means will that lying should be a universal law. For with such a law there would be no promises at all, since it would be in vain to allege my intention in regard to my future actions to those who would not believe this allegation, or if they over-hastily did so, would pay me back in my own coin. Hence my maxim, as soon as it should be made a universal law, would necessarily destroy itself.

I do not, therefore, need any far-reaching penetration to discern what I have to do in order that my will may be morally good. Inexperienced in the course of the world, incapable of being prepared for all its contingencies, I only ask myself: Canst thou also will that thy maxim should be a universal law? If not, then it must be rejected, and that not because of a disadvantage accruing from it to myself or even to others, but because it cannot enter as a principle into a possible universal legislation, and reason extorts from me immediate respect for such legislation. I do not indeed as yet *discern* on what this respect is based (this the philosopher may inquire), but at least I understand this, that it is an estimation of the worth which far outweighs all worth of what is recommended by inclination, and that the necessity of acting from *pure* respect for the practical law is what constitutes duty, to which every other motive must give place, because it is the condition of a will being good *in itself,* and the worth of such a will is above everything. . . .

Everything in nature works according to laws. Rational beings alone have the faculty of acting according *to the conception* of laws, that is according to principles, *i.e.* have a *will.* Since the deduction of actions from principles requires *reason,* the will is nothing but practical reason. If reason infallibly determines the will, then the actions of such a being which are recognized as objectively necessary are subjectively necessary also, *i.e.* the will is a faculty to choose *that only* which reason independent on inclination recognizes as practically necessary, *i.e.* as good. But if reason of itself does not sufficiently determine the will, if the latter is subject also to subjective conditions (particular impulses) which do not always coincide with the objective conditions; in a word, if the will does not *in itself* completely accord with reason (which is actually the case with men), then the actions which objectively are recognized as necessary are subjectively contingent, and the determination of such a will according to objective laws is *obligation,* that is to say, the relation of the objective laws to a will that is not thoroughly good is conceived as the determination of the will of a rational being by principles of reason, but which the will from its nature does not of necessity follow.

The conception of an objective principle, in so far as it is obligatory for a will, is called a command (of reason), and the formula of the command is called an imperative. . . .

Now all *imperatives* command either *hypothetically* or *categorically.* The former represent the practical necessity of a possible action as means to something else that is willed (or at least which one might possibly will). The categorical imperative would be that which represented an action as necessary of itself without reference to another end, *i.e.,* objectively necessary.

Since every practical law represents a possible action as good, and on this account, for a subject who is practically determinable by reason, necessary, all imperatives are formulae determining an action which is necessary according to the principle of a will good in some respects. If now the action is good only as a means *to something else,* then the imperative is *hypothetical;* if it is conceived as good *in itself* and consequently as being necessarily the principle of a will which of itself conforms to reason, then it is *categorical.* . . .

When I conceive a hypothetical imperative, in general I do not know beforehand what it will contain until I am given the condition. But when I conceive a categorical imperative, I know at once what it contains. For as the imperative contains besides the law only the necessity that the maxims shall conform to this law, while the law contains no conditions restricting it, there remains nothing but the general statement that the maxim of the action should conform to a universal law, and it is this conformity alone that the imperative properly represents as necessary.

There is therefore but one categorical imperative, namely, this: *Act only on that maxim whereby thou canst at the same time will that it should become a universal law.*

Now if all imperatives of duty can be deduced from this one imperative as from their principle, then, although it should remain undecided whether what is called duty is not merely a vain notion, yet at least we shall be able to show what we understand by it and what this notion means.

Since the universality of the law according to which effects are produced constitutes what is properly called *nature* in the most general sense (as to form), that is the existence of things so far as it is determined by general laws, the imperative of duty may be expressed thus: *Act as if the maxim of thy action were to become by thy will a universal law of nature.*

We will now enumerate a few duties, adopting the usual division of them into duties to ourselves and to others, and into perfect and imperfect duties.

1. A man reduced to despair by a series of misfortunes feels wearied of life, but is still so far in possession of his reason that he can ask himself whether it would not be contrary to his duty to himself to take his own life. Now he inquires whether the maxim of his action could become a universal law of nature. His maxim is: From self-love I adopt it as a principle to shorten my life when its longer duration is likely to bring more evil than satisfaction. It is asked then simply whether this principle founded on self-love can become a universal law of nature. Now we see at once that a system of nature of which it should be a law to destroy life by means of the very feeling whose special nature it is to impel to the improvement of life would contradict itself, and therefore could not exist as a system of nature; hence that maxim cannot possibly exist as a universal law of nature, and consequently would be wholly inconsistent with the supreme principle of all duty.

2. Another finds himself forced by necessity to borrow money. He knows that he will not be able to repay it, but sees also that nothing will be lent to him, unless he promises stoutly to repay it in a definite time. He desires to make this promise, but he has still so much conscience as to ask himself: Is it not unlawful and inconsistent with duty to get out of a difficulty in this way? Suppose, however, that he resolves to do so, then the maxim of his action would be expressed thus: When I think myself in want of money, I will borrow money and promise to repay it, although I know that I never can do so. Now this principle of self-love or of one's own advantage may perhaps be consistent with

my whole future welfare; but the question now is, Is it right? I change then the suggestion of self-love into a universal law, and state the question thus: How would it be if my maxim were a universal law? Then I see at once that it could never hold as a universal law of nature, but would necessarily contradict itself. For supposing it to be a universal law that everyone when he thinks himself in a difficulty should be able to promise whatever he pleases, with the purpose of not keeping his promise, the promise itself would become impossible, as well as the end that one might have in view in it, since no one would consider that anything was promised to him, but would ridicule all such statements as vain pretences.

3. A third finds in himself a talent which with the help of some culture might make him a useful man in many respects. But he finds himself in comfortable circumstances, and prefers to indulge in pleasure rather than to take pains in enlarging and improving his happy natural capacities. He asks, however, whether his maxim of neglect of his natural gifts, besides agreeing with his inclination to indulgence, agrees also with what is called duty. He sees then that a system of nature could indeed subsist with such a universal law although men (like the South Sea islanders) should let their talents rest, and resolve to devote their lives merely to idleness, amusement, and propagation of their species — in a word, to enjoyment; but he cannot possibly *will* that this should be a universal law of nature, or be implanted in us as such by a natural instinct. For, as a rational being, he necessarily wills that his faculties be developed, since they serve him, and have been given him, for all sorts of possible purposes.

4. A fourth, who is in prosperity, while he sees that others have to contend with great wretchedness and that he could help them, thinks: What concern is it of mine? Let everyone be as happy as Heaven pleases, or as he can make himself; I will take nothing from him nor even envy him, only I do not wish to contribute anything to his welfare or to his assistance in distress! Now no doubt if such a mode of thinking were a universal law, the human race might very well subsist, and doubtless even better than in a state in which everyone talks of sympathy and good-will, or even takes care occasionally to put it into practice, but, on the other side, also cheats when he can, betrays the rights of men, or otherwise violates them. But although it is possible that a universal law of nature might exist in accordance with that maxim, it is impossible to *will* that such a principle should have the universal validity of a law of

nature. For a will which resolved this would contradict itself, inasmuch as many cases might occur in which one would have need of the love and sympathy of others, and in which, by such a law of nature, sprung from his own will, he would deprive himself of all hope of the aid he desires. . . .

We have thus established at least this much, that if duty is a conception which is to have any import and real legislative authority for our actions, it can only be expressed in categorical, and not at all in hypothetical imperatives. We have also, which is of great importance, exhibited clearly and definitely for every practical application the content of the categorical imperative, which must contain the principle of all duty if there is such a thing at all. We have not yet, however, advanced so far as to prove *à priori* that there actually is such an imperative, that there is a practical law which commands absolutely of itself, and without any other impulse, and that the following of this law is duty. . . .

Now I say: man and generally any rational being *exists* as an end in himself, *not merely as a means* to be arbitrarily used by this or that will, but in all his actions, whether they concern himself or other rational beings, must be always regarded at the same time as an end. All objects of the inclinations have only a conditional worth; for if the inclinations and the wants founded on them did not exist, then their object would be without value. But the inclinations themselves being sources of want are so far from having an absolute worth for which they should be desired, that, on the contrary, it must be the universal wish of every rational being to be wholly free from them. Thus the worth of any object which is *to be acquired* by our action is always conditional. Beings whose existence depends not on our will but on nature's, have nevertheless, if they are rational beings, only a relative value as means, and are therefore called *things*; rational beings, on the contrary, are called *persons*, because their very nature points them out as ends in themselves, that is as something which must not be used merely as means, and so far therefore restricts freedom of action (and is an object of respect). These, therefore, are not merely subjective ends whose existence has a worth *for us* as an effect of our action, but *objective ends,* that is things whose existence is an end in itself: an end moreover for which no other can be substituted, which they should subserve *merely* as means, for otherwise nothing whatever would possess *absolute worth*; but if all worth were conditioned and therefore contingent, then there would be no supreme practical principle of reason whatever.

If then there is a supreme practical principle or, in respect of the human will, a categorical imperative, it must be one which, being drawn from the conception of that which is necessarily an end for everyone because it is *an end in itself*, constitutes an *objective* principle of will, and can therefore serve as a universal practical law. The foundation of this principle is: *rational nature exists as an end in itself*. Man necessarily conceives his own existence as being so: so far then this is a *subjective* principle of human actions. But every other rational being regards its existence similarly, just on the same rational principle that holds for me: so that it is at the same time an objective principle, from which as a supreme practical law all laws of the will must be capable of being deduced. Accordingly the practical imperative will be as follows: *So act as to treat humanity, whether in thine own person or in that of any other, in every case as an end withal, never as means only*. . . .

The conception of every rational being as one which must consider itself as giving in all the maxims of its will universal laws, so as to judge itself and its actions from this point of view—this conception leads to another which depends on it and is very fruitful, namely, that of a *kingdom of ends*.

By a *kingdom* I understand the union of different rational beings in a system by common laws. Now since it is by laws that ends are determined as regards their universal validity, hence, if we abstract from the personal differences of rational beings, and likewise from all the content of their private ends, we shall be able to conceive all ends combined in a systematic whole (including both rational beings as ends in themselves, and also the special ends which each may propose to himself), that is to say, we can conceive a kingdom of ends, which on the preceding principles is possible.

For all rational beings come under the *law* that each of them must treat itself and all others *never merely as means*, but in every case *at the same time as ends in themselves*. Hence results a systematic union of rational beings by common objective laws, *i.e.*, a kingdom which may be called a kingdom of ends, since what these laws have in view is just the relation of these beings to one another as ends and means. It is certainly only an ideal.

The Original Position and Justification

John Rawls (1921–2002) held the John Cowles Chair of Philosophy at Harvard University. His major work, A *Theory of Justice,* has been described as the most notable contribution to political philosophy since John Stuart Mill. In this selection from that book, Rawls explains why he believes that the most just society would be one governed by an ideal social contract.

The Main Idea of the Theory of Justice

My aim is to present a conception of justice which generalizes and carries to a higher level of abstraction the familiar theory of the social contract as found, say, in Locke, Rousseau, and Kant. In order to do this we are not to think of the original contract as one to enter a particular society or to set up a particular form of government. Rather, the guiding idea is that the principles of justice for the basic structure of society are the object of the original agreement. They are the principles that free and rational persons concerned to further their own interests would accept in an initial position of equality as defining the fundamental terms of their association. These principles are to regulate all further agreements; they specify the kinds of social cooperation that can be entered into and the forms of government that can be established. This way of regarding the principles of justice I shall call justice as fairness.

Thus we are to imagine that those who engage in social cooperation choose together, in one joint act, the principles which are to assign basic rights and duties and to determine the division of social benefits. Men are to decide in advance how they are to regulate their claims against one another and what is to be the foundation charter of their society. Just as each person must decide by rational reflection what constitutes his good, that is, the system of ends which it is rational for him to pursue, so a group of persons must decide once and for all what is to count among them as just and unjust. The choice which rational men would make in this hypothetical situation of equal liberty, assuming for the present that this choice problem has a solution, determines the principles of justice.

In justice as fairness the original position of equality corresponds to the state of nature in the traditional theory of the social contract. This original position is not, of course, thought of as an actual historical state of affairs, much less as a primitive condition of culture. It is understood as a purely hypothetical situation characterized so as to lead to a certain conception of justice. Among the essential features of this situation is that no one knows his place in society, his class position or social status, nor does any one know his fortune in the distribution of natural assets and abilities, his intelligence, strength, and the like. I shall even assume that the parties do not know their conceptions of the good or their special psychological propensities. The principles of justice are chosen behind a veil of ignorance. This ensures that no one is advantaged or disadvantaged in the choice of principles by the outcome of natural chance or the contingency of social circumstances. Since all are similarly situated and no one is able to design principles to favor his particular condition, the principles of justice are the result of a fair agreement or bargain. For given the circumstances of the original position, the symmetry of everyone's relations to each other, this initial situation is fair between individuals as moral persons, that is, as rational beings with their own ends and capable, I shall assume, of a sense of justice. The original position is, one might say, the appropriate initial status quo, and thus the fundamental agreements reached in it are fair. This explains the propriety of the name "justice as fairness": it conveys the idea that the principles of justice are agreed to in an initial situation that is fair. The name does not mean that the concepts of justice and fairness are the same, any more than the phrase "poetry as metaphor" means that the concepts of poetry and metaphor are the same.

Justice as fairness begins, as I have said, with one of the most general of all choices which persons might make together, namely, with the choice of the first principles of a conception of justice which is to regulate

From: John Rawls, "The Original Position and Justification," A *Theory of Justice* (Cambridge: Harvard University Press, 1971) 11–17. Notes have been omitted.

all subsequent criticism and reform of institutions. Then, having chosen a conception of justice, we can suppose that they are to choose a constitution and a legislature to enact laws, and so on, all in accordance with the principles of justice initially agreed upon. Our social situation is just if it is such that by this sequence of hypothetical agreements we would have contracted into the general system of rules which defines it. Moreover, assuming that the original position does determine a set of principles (that is, that a particular conception of justice would be chosen), it will then be true that whenever social institutions satisfy these principles those engaged in them can say to one another that they are cooperating on terms to which they would agree if they were free and equal persons whose relations with respect to one another were fair. They could all view their arrangements as meeting the stipulations which they would acknowledge in an initial situation that embodies widely accepted and reasonable constraints on the choice of principles. The general recognition of this fact would provide the basis for a public acceptance of the corresponding principles of justice. No society can, of course, be a scheme of cooperation which men enter voluntarily in a literal sense; each person finds himself placed at birth in some particular position in some particular society, and the nature of this position materially affects his life prospects. Yet a society satisfying the principles of justice as fairness comes as close as a society can to being a voluntary scheme, for it meets the principles which free and equal persons would assent to under circumstances that are fair. In this sense its members are autonomous and the obligations they recognize self-imposed.

One feature of justice as fairness is to think of the parties in the initial situation as rational and mutually disinterested. This does not mean that the parties are egoists, that is, individuals with only certain kinds of interests, say in wealth, prestige, and domination. But they are conceived as not taking an interest in one another's interests. They are to presume that even their spiritual aims may be opposed, in the way that the aims of those of different religions may be opposed. Moreover, the concept of rationality must be interpreted as far as possible in the narrow sense, standard in economic theory, of taking the most effective means to given ends. I shall modify this concept to some extent, as explained later, but one must try to avoid introducing into it any controversial ethical elements. The initial situation must be characterized by stipulations that are widely accepted.

In working out the conception of justice as fairness one main task clearly is to determine which principles of justice would be chosen in the original position. To do this we must describe this situation in some detail and formulate with care the problem of choice which it presents. These matters I shall take up in the immediately succeeding chapters. It may be observed, however, that once the principles of justice are thought of as arising from an original agreement in a situation of equality, it is an open question whether the principle of utility would be acknowledged. Offhand it hardly seems likely that persons who view themselves as equals, entitled to press their claims upon one another, would agree to a principle which may require lesser life prospects for some simply for the sake of a greater sum of advantages enjoyed by others. Since each desires to protect his interests, his capacity to advance his conception of the good, no one has a reason to acquiesce in an enduring loss for himself in order to bring about a greater net balance of satisfaction. In the absence of strong and lasting benevolent impulses, a rational man would not accept a basic structure merely because it maximized the algebraic sum of advantages irrespective of its permanent effects on his own basic rights and interests. Thus it seems that the principle of utility is incompatible with the conception of social cooperation among equals for mutual advantage. It appears to be inconsistent with the idea of reciprocity implicit in the notion of a well-ordered society. Or, at any rate, so I shall argue.

I shall maintain instead that the persons in the initial situation would choose two rather different principles: the first requires equality in the assignment of basic rights and duties, while the second holds that social and economic inequalities, for example inequalities of wealth and authority, are just only if they result in compensating benefits for everyone, and in particular for the least advantaged members of society. These principles rule out justifying institutions on the grounds that the hardships of some are offset by a greater good in the aggregate. It may be expedient but it is not just that some should have less in order that others may prosper. But there is no injustice in the greater benefits earned by a few provided that the situation of persons not so fortunate is thereby improved. The intuitive idea is that since everyone's well-being depends upon a scheme of cooperation without which no one could have a satisfactory life, the division of advantages should be such as to draw forth the willing cooperation of everyone taking part in it, including those less well situated. Yet this can be expected only if reasonable terms are proposed. The two principles mentioned seem to be a fair agreement on the basis of which those better endowed, or more fortunate in their social position, neither of which we can be said to deserve, could expect the willing cooperation of others when some workable scheme is a necessary condition of the welfare of all. Once we decide to look for a conception of justice that nullifies the accidents of natural endowment and the contingencies of social circumstance as counters in the quest for political and economic advantage, we are led to these principles. They express the result of leaving aside those aspects of the social world that seem arbitrary from a moral point of view.

The problem of the choice of principles, however, is extremely difficult. I do not expect the answer I shall suggest to be convincing to everyone. It is, therefore, worth noting from the outset that justice as fairness, like other contract views, consists of two parts: (1) an interpretation of the initial situation and of the problem of choice posed there, and (2) a set of principles which, it is argued, would be agreed to. One may accept the first part of the theory (or some variant thereof), but not the other, and conversely. The concept of the initial contractual situation may seem reasonable although the particular principles proposed are rejected. To be sure, I want to maintain that the most appropriate conception of this situation does lead to principles of justice contrary to utilitarianism and perfectionism, and therefore that the contract doctrine provides an alternative to these views. Still, one may dispute this contention even though one grants that the contractarian method is a useful way of studying ethical theories and of setting forth their underlying assumptions.

Justice as fairness is an example of what I have called a contract theory. Now there may be an objection to the term "contract" and related expressions, but I think it will serve reasonably well. Many words have misleading connotations which at first are likely to confuse. The terms "utility" and "utilitarianism" are surely no exception. They too have unfortunate suggestions which hostile critics have been willing to exploit; yet they are clear enough for those prepared to study utilitarian doctrine. The same should be true of the term "contract" applied to moral theories. As I have mentioned, to understand it one has to keep in mind that it implies a certain level of abstraction. In particular, the content of the relevant agreement is not to enter a given society or to adopt a given form of government, but to accept certain moral principles. Moreover, the undertakings referred to are purely hypothetical: a contract view holds that certain principles would be accepted in a well-defined initial situation.

The merit of the contract terminology is that it conveys the idea that principles of justice may be conceived as principles that would be chosen by rational persons, and that in this way conceptions of justice may be explained and justified. The theory of justice is a part, perhaps the most significant part, of the theory of rational choice. Furthermore, principles of justice deal with conflicting claims upon the advantages won by social cooperation; they apply to the relations among several persons or groups. The word "contract" suggests this plurality as well as the condition that the appropriate division of advantages must be in accordance with principles acceptable to all parties. The condition of publicity for principles of justice is also connoted by the contract phraseology. Thus, if these principles are the outcome of an agreement, citizens have a knowledge of the principles that others follow. It is characteristic of contract theories to stress the public nature of political principles. Finally there is the long tradition of the contract doctrine. Expressing the tie with this line of thought helps to define ideas and accords with natural piety. There are then several advantages in the use of the term "contract." With due precautions taken, it should not be misleading.

A final remark. Justice as fairness is not a complete contract theory. For it is clear that the contractarian idea can be extended to the choice of more or less an entire ethical system, that is, to a system including principles for all the virtues and not only for justice. Now for the most part I shall consider only principles of justice and others closely related to them; I make no attempt to discuss the virtues in a systematic way. Obviously if justice as fairness succeeds reasonably well, a next step would be to study the more general view suggested by the name "rightness as fairness." But even this wider theory fails to embrace all moral relationships, since it would seem to include only our relations with other persons and to leave out of account how we are to conduct ourselves toward animals and the rest of nature. I do not contend that the contract notion offers a way to approach these questions which are certainly of the first importance; and I shall have to put them aside. We must recognize the limited scope of justice as fairness and of the general type of view that it exemplifies. How far its conclusions must be revised once these other matters are understood cannot be decided in advance.

The Virtues

Alasdair MacIntyre (1929–) is a professor of philosophy at Vanderbilt University. He has authored a number of books, including *After Virtue* and *Whose Justice? Which Rationality?* In this selection from *After Virtue*, MacIntyre articulates the view that to lead a good life, you need to cultivate those virtues that will enable you to excel at a particular practice in a particular tradition.

It is now possible to return to the question from which this enquiry into the nature of human action and identity started: In what does the unity of an individual life consist? The answer is that its unity is the unity of a narrative embodied in a single life. To ask 'What is the good for me?' is to ask how best I might live out that unity and bring it to completion. To ask 'What is the good for man?' is to ask what all answers to the former question must have in common. But now it is important to emphasize that it is the systematic asking of these two questions and the attempt to answer them in deed as well as in word which provide the moral life with its unity. The unity of a human life is the unity of a narrative quest. Quests sometimes fail, are frustrated, abandoned or dissipated into distractions; and human lives may in all these ways also fail. But the only criteria for success or failure in a human life as a whole are the criteria of success or failure in a narrated or to-be-narrated quest. A quest for what?

Two key features of the medieval conception of a quest need to be recalled. The first is that without some at least partly determinate conception of the final *telos* there could not be any beginning to a quest. Some conception of the good for man is required. Whence is such a conception to be drawn? Precisely from those questions which led us to attempt to transcend that limited conception of the virtues which is available in and through practices. It is in looking for a conception of *the* good which will enable us to order other goods, for a conception of *the* good which will enable us to extend our understanding of the purpose and content of the virtues, for a conception of *the* good which will enable us to understand the place of integrity and constancy in life, that we initially define the kind of life which is a quest for the good. But secondly it is clear the medieval conception of a quest is not at all that of a search for something already adequately characterized, as miners search for gold or geologists for oil. It is in the course of the quest and only through encounter-

ing and coping with the various particular harms, dangers, temptations and distractions which provide any quest with its episodes and incidents that the goal of the quest is finally to be understood. A quest is always an education both as to the character of that which is sought and in self-knowledge.

The virtues therefore are to be understood as those dispositions which will not only sustain practices and enable us to achieve the goods internal to practices, but which will also sustain us in the relevant kind of quest for the good, by enabling us to overcome the harms, dangers, temptations and distractions which we encounter, and which will furnish us with increasing self-knowledge and increasing knowledge of the good. The catalogue of the virtues will therefore include the virtues required to sustain the kind of households and the kind of political communities in which men and women can seek for the good together and the virtues necessary for philosophical enquiry about the character of the good. We have then arrived at a provisional conclusion about the good life for man: the good life for man is the life spent in seeking for the good life for man, and the virtues necessary for the seeking are those which will enable us to understand what more and what else the good life for man is. We have also completed the second stage in our account of the virtues, by situating them in relation to the good life for man and not only in relation to practices. But our enquiry requires a third stage.

For I am never able to seek for the good or exercise the virtues only *qua* individual. This is partly because what it is to live the good life concretely varies from circumstance to circumstance even when it is one and the same conception of the good life and one and the same set of virtues which are being embodied in a

From: Alasdair MacIntyre, "The Virtues, The Unity of a Human Life and the Concept of a Tradition," *After Virtue* (Notre Dame: University of Notre Dame Press, 1984) 218–225.

human life. What the good life is for a fifth-century Athenian general will not be the same as what it was for a medieval nun or a seventeenth-century farmer. But it is not just that different individuals live in different social circumstances; it is also that we all approach our own circumstances as bearers of a particular social identity. I am someone's son or daughter, someone else's cousin or uncle; I am a citizen of this or that city, a member of this or that guild or profession; I belong to this clan, that tribe, this nation. Hence what is good for me has to be the good for one who inhabits these roles. As such, I inherit from the past of my family, my city, my tribe, my nation, a variety of debts, inheritances, rightful expectations and obligations. These constitute the given of my life, my moral starting point. This is in part what gives my life its own moral particularity.

This thought is likely to appear alien and even surprising from the standpoint of modern individualism. From the standpoint of individualism I am what I myself choose to be. I can always, if I wish to, put in question what are taken to be the merely contingent social features of my existence. I may biologically be my father's son; but I cannot be held responsible for what he did unless I choose implicitly or explicitly to assume such responsibility. I may legally be a citizen of a certain country; but I cannot be held responsible for what my country does or has done unless I choose implicitly or explicitly to assume such responsibility. Such individualism is expressed by those modern Americans who deny any responsibility for the effects of slavery upon black Americans, saying 'I never owned any slaves'. It is more subtly the standpoint of those other modern Americans who accept a nicely calculated responsibility for such effects measured precisely by the benefits they themselves as individuals have indirectly received from slavery. In both cases 'being an American' is not in itself taken to be part of the moral identity of the individual. And of course there is nothing peculiar to modern Americans in this attitude: the Englishman who says, 'I never did any wrong to Ireland; why bring up that old history as though it had something to do with me?' or the young German who believes that being born after 1945 means that what Nazis did to Jews has no moral relevance to his relationship to his Jewish contemporaries, exhibit the same attitude, that according to which the self is detachable from its social and historical roles and statuses. And the self so detached is of course a self very much at home in either Sartre's or Goffman's perspective, a self that can have no history. The contrast with the narrative view of the self is clear. For the story of my life is always embedded in the story of those communities from which I derive my identity. I am born with a past; and to try to cut myself off from that past in the individualist mode, is to deform my present relationships. The possession of an historical identity and the possession of a social identity coincide. Notice that rebellion against my identity is always one possible mode of expressing it.

Notice also that the fact that the self has to find its moral identity in and through its membership in communities such as those of the family, the neighborhood, the city and the tribe does not entail that the self has to accept the moral *limitations* of the particularity of those forms of community. Without those moral particularities to begin from there would never be anywhere to begin; but it is in moving forward from such particularity that the search for the good, for the universal, consists. Yet particularity can never be simply left behind or obliterated. The notion of escaping from it into a realm of entirely universal maxims which belong to man as such, whether in its eighteenth-century Kantian form or in the presentation of some modern analytical moral philosophies, is an illusion and an illusion with painful consequences. When men and women identify what are in fact their partial and particular causes too easily and too completely with the cause of some universal principle, they usually behave worse than they would otherwise do.

What I am, therefore, is in key part what I inherit, a specific past that is present to some degree in my present. I find myself part of a history and that is generally to say, whether I like it nor not, whether I recognize it or not, one of the bearers of a tradition. It was important when I characterized the concept of a practice to notice that practices always have histories and that at any given moment what a practice is depends on a mode of understanding it which has been transmitted often through many generations. And thus, insofar as the virtues sustain the relationships required for practices, they have to sustain relationships to the past—and to the future—as well as in the present. But the traditions through which particular practices are transmitted and reshaped never exist in isolation for larger social traditions. What constitutes such traditions?

We are apt to be misled here by the ideological uses to which the concept of a tradition has been put by conservative political theorists. Characteristically such theorists have followed Burke in contrasting tradition with reason and the stability of tradition with conflict. Both contrasts obfuscate. For all reasoning takes place within the context of some traditional mode of thought, transcending through criticism and invention the limitations of what had hitherto been reasoned in that tradition; this is as true of modern physics as of medieval logic. Moreover when a tradition is in good order it is always partially constituted by an argument about the goods the pursuit of which gives to that tradition its particular point and purpose.

So, when an institution — a university, say, or a farm, or a hospital — is the bearer of a tradition of practice or practices, its common life will be partly, but in a centrally important way, constituted by a continuous argument as to what a university is and ought to be or what good farming is or what good medicine is. Traditions, when vital, embody continuities of conflict. Indeed when a tradition becomes Burkean, it is always dying or dead.

The individualism of modernity could of course find no use for the notion of tradition within its own conceptual scheme except as an adversary notion; it therefore all too willingly abandoned it to the Burkeans, who, faithful to Burke's own allegiance, tried to combine adherence in politics to a conception of tradition which would vindicate the oligarchical revolution of property of 1688 and adherence in economics to the doctrine and institutions of the free market. The theoretical incoherence of this mismatch did not deprive it of ideological usefulness. But the outcome has been that modern conservatives are for the most part engaged in conserving only older rather than later versions of liberal individualism. Their own core doctrine is as liberal and as individualist as that of self-avowed liberals.

A living tradition then is an historically extended, socially embodied argument, and an argument precisely in part about the goods which constitute that tradition. Within a tradition the pursuit of goods extends through generations, sometimes through many generations. Hence the individual's search for his or her good is generally and characteristically conducted within a context defined by those traditions of which the individual's life is a part, and this is true both of those goods which are internal to practices and of the goods of a single life. Once again the narrative phenomenon of embedding is crucial: the history of a practice in our time is generally and characteristically embedded in and made intelligible in terms of the larger and longer history of the tradition through which the practice in its present form was conveyed to us; the history of each of our own lives is generally and characteristically embedded in and made intelligible in terms of the larger and longer histories of a number of traditions. I have to say 'generally and characteristically' rather than 'always', for traditions decay, disintegrate and disappear. What then sustains and strengthens traditions? What weakens and destroys them?

The answer in key part is: the exercise or the lack of exercise of the relevant virtues. The virtues find their point and purpose not only in sustaining those relationships necessary if the variety of goods internal to practices are to be achieved and not only in sustaining the form of an individual life in which that individual may seek out his or her good as the good of his or her whole life, but also in sustaining those traditions which provide both practices and individual lives with their necessary historical context. Lack of justice, lack of truthfulness, lack of courage, lack of the relevant intellectual virtues — these corrupt traditions, just as they do those institutions and practices which derive their life from the traditions of which they are the contemporary embodiments. To recognize this is of course also to recognize the existence of an additional virtue, one whose importance is perhaps most obvious when it is least present, the virtue of having an adequate sense of the traditions to which one belongs or which confront one. This virtue is not to be confused with any form of conservative antiquarianism; I am not praising those who choose the conventional conservative role of *laudator temporis acti*. It is rather the case that an adequate sense of tradition manifests itself in a grasp of those future possibilities which the past has made available to the present. Living traditions, just because they continue a not-yet-completed narrative, confront a future whose determinate and determinable character, so far as it possesses any, derives from the past.

In practical reasoning the possession of this virtue is not manifested so much in the knowledge of a set of generalizations or maxims which may provide our practical inferences with major premises; its presence or absence rather appears in the kind of capacity for judgment which the agent possesses in knowing how to select among the relevant stack of maxims and how to apply them in particular situations. Cardinal Pole possessed it, Mary Tudor did not; Montrose possessed it, Charles I did not. What Cardinal Pole and the Marquis of Montrose possessed were in fact those virtues which enable their possessors to pursue both their own good and the good of the tradition of which they are the bearers even in situations defined by the necessity of tragic, dilemmatic choice. Such choices, understood in the context of the tradition of the virtues, are very different from those which face the modern adherents of rival and incommensurable moral premises in the debates about which I wrote in Chapter 2. Wherein does the difference lie?

It has often been suggested — by J. L. Austin, for example — that *either* we can admit the existence of rival and contingently incompatible goods which make incompatible claims to our practical allegiance *or* we can believe in some determinate conception of *the* good life for man, but that these are mutually exclusive alternatives. No one can consistently hold both these views. What this contention is blind to is that there may be better or worse ways for individuals to live through the tragic confrontation of good with good. And that to know what the good life for man is may require knowing what are the better and what are the worse ways of living in and through such situations. Nothing *a priori* rules out this possibility; and this suggests that within a view such as Austin's there is concealed an unacknowledged empirical premise about the character of tragic situations.

One way in which the choice between rival goods in a tragic situation differs from the modern choice between incommensurable moral premises is that *both* of the alternative courses of action which confront the individual have to be recognized as leading to some authentic and substantial good. By choosing one I do nothing to diminish or derogate from the claim upon me of the other; and therefore, whatever I do, I shall have left undone what I ought to have done. The tragic protagonist, unlike the moral agent as depicted by Sartre or Hare, is not choosing between allegiance to one moral principle rather than another, nor is he or she deciding upon some principle of priority between moral principles. Hence the 'ought' involved has a different meaning and force from that of the 'ought' in moral principles understood in a modern way. For the tragic protagonist cannot do everything that he or she ought to do. This 'ought', unlike Kant's, does not imply 'can'. Moreover any attempt to map the logic of such 'ought' assertions on to some modal calculus so as to produce a version of deontic logic has to fail. . . .

Yet it is clear that the moral task of the tragic protagonist may be performed better or worse, independently of the choice between alternatives that he or she makes—*ex hypothesi* he or she has no *right* choice to make. The tragic protagonist may behave heroically or unheroically, generously or ungenerously, gracefully or gracelessly, prudently or imprudently. To perform his or her task better rather than worse will be to do both what is better for him or her *qua* individual and *qua* parent or child or *qua* citizen or member of a profession, or perhaps *qua* some or all of these. The existence of tragic dilemmas casts no doubt upon and provides no counterexamples to the thesis that assertions of the form 'To do this in this way would be better for X and/or for his or her family, city or profession' are susceptible of objective truth and falsity, any more than the existence of alternative and contingently incompatible forms of medical treatment casts doubt on the thesis that assertions of the form 'To undergo his medical treatment in this way would be better for X and/or his or her family' are susceptible of objective truth and falsity. . . .

The presupposition of this objectivity is of course that we can understand the notion of 'good for X' and cognate notions in terms of some conception of the unity of X's life. What is better or worse for X depends upon the character of that intelligible narrative which provides X's life with its unity. Unsurprisingly it is the lack of any such unifying conception of a human life which underlies modern denials of the factual character of moral judgments and more especially of those judgments which ascribe virtues or vices to individuals.

I argued earlier that every moral philosophy has some particular sociology as its counterpart. What I have tried to spell out in this chapter is the kind of understanding of social life which the tradition of the virtues requires, a kind of understanding very different from those dominant in the culture of bureaucratic individualism. Within that culture conceptions of the virtues become marginal and the tradition of the virtues remains central only in the lives of social groups whose existence is on the margins of the central culture. Within the central culture of liberal or bureaucratic individualism new conceptions of the virtues emerge and the concept of a virtue is itself transformed.

The Ones Who Walk Away from Omelas

Ursula K. LeGuin (1929–) is one of the most highly regarded science-fiction writers of our time. Two of her books, *The Left Hand of Darkness* and *The Dispossessed,* have won both the Nebula Award from the Science Fiction Writers of America and the Hugo Award from the World Science Fiction Convention. *The Word for World Is Forest* also won a Hugo Award. In the short story reprinted here, LeGuin explores the implications of utilitarianism and traditionalism in a particularly poignant way.

With a clamor of bells that set the swallows soaring, the Festival of Summer came to the city Omelas, bright-towered by the sea. The rigging of the boats in harbor sparkled with flags. In the streets between houses with red roofs and painted walls, between old moss-grown gardens and under avenues of trees, past great parks and public buildings, processions moved. Some were decorous: old people in long stiff robes of mauve and gray, grave master workmen, quiet, merry women carrying their babies and chatting as they walked. In other streets the music beat faster, a shimmering of gong and tambourine, and the people went dancing, the procession was a dance. Children dodged in and out, their high calls rising like the swallows' crossing flights over the music and the singing. All the processions wound toward the north side of the city, where on the great watermeadow called the Green Fields boys and girls, naked in the bright air, with mudstained feet and ankles and long, lithe arms, exercised their restive horses before the race. The horses wore no gear at all but a halter without bit. Their manes were braided with streamers of silver, gold, and green. They blew out their nostrils and pranced and boasted to one another; they were vastly excited, the horse being the only animal who has adopted our ceremonies as his own. Far off to the north and west the mountains stood up half-encircling Omelas on her bay. The air of morning was so clear that the snow still crowning the Eighteen Peaks burned with white-gold fire across the miles of sunlit air, under the dark blue of the sky. There was just enough wind to make the banners that marked the race course snap and flutter now and then. In the silence of the broad green meadows one could hear the music winding through the city streets, farther and nearer and ever approaching, a cheerful faint sweetness of the air that from time to time trembled and gathered together and broke out into the great joyous clanging of the bells.

Joyous! How is one to tell about joy? How describe the citizens of Omelas?

They were not simple folk, you see, though they were happy. But we do not say the words of cheer much any more. All smiles have become archaic. Given a description such as this one tends to make certain assumptions. Given a description such as this one tends to look next for the King, mounted on a splendid stallion and surrounded by his noble knights, or perhaps in a golden litter borne by great-muscled slaves. But there was no king. They did not use swords, or keep slaves. They were not barbarians. I do not know the rules and laws of their society, but I suspect that they were singularly few. As they did without monarchy and slavery, so they also got on without the stock exchange, the advertisement, the secret police, and the bomb. Yet I repeat that these were not simple folk, not dulcet shepherds, noble savages, bland utopians. They were not less complex than we. The trouble is that we have a bad habit, encouraged by pedants and sophisticates, of considering happiness as something rather stupid. Only pain is intellectual, only evil interesting. This is the treason of the artist: a refusal to admit the banality of evil and the terrible boredom of pain. If you can't lick 'em, join 'em. If it hurts, repeat it. But to praise despair is to condemn delight, to embrace violence is to lose hold of everything else. We have almost lost hold; we can no longer describe a happy man, nor make any celebration of joy. How can I tell you about the people of Omelas? They were not naive and happy children—though their children were, in fact, happy. They were mature, intelligent, passionate adults whose lives were not wretched.

From: Ursula K. LeGuin, "The Ones Who Walk Away from Omelas," *New Dimensions III*, ed. Robert Silverberg (New York: New American Library, 1974) 1–7.

O miracle! But I wish I could describe it better. I wish I could convince you. Omelas sounds in my words like a city in a fairytale, long ago and far away, once upon a time. Perhaps it would be best if you imagined it as your own fancy bids, assuming it will rise to the occasion, for certainly I cannot suit you all. For instance, how about technology? I think that there would be no cars or helicopters in and above the streets; this follows from the fact that the people of Omelas are happy people. Happiness is based on a just discrimination of what is necessary, what is neither necessary nor destructive, and what is destructive. In the middle category, however — that of the unnecessary but undestructive, that of comfort, luxury, exuberance, etc. — they could perfectly well have central heating, subway trains, washing machines, and all kinds of marvelous devices not yet invented here, floating light-sources, fuelless power, a cure for the common cold. Or they could have none of that: it doesn't matter. As you like it. I incline to think that people from towns up and down the coast have been coming in to Omelas during the last days before the Festival on very fast little trains and doubledecked trams, and that the train station of Omelas is actually the handsomest building in town, though plainer than the magnificent Farmers Market. But even granted trains, I fear that Omelas so far strikes some of you as goody-goody. Smiles, bells, parades, horses, bleh. If so, please add an orgy. If an orgy would help, don't hesitate. Let us not, however, have temples from which issue beautiful nude priests and priestesses already half in ecstasy and ready to copulate with whomsoever, man or woman, lover or stranger, desires union with the deep godhead of the blood, although that was my first idea. But really it would be better not to have any temples in Omelas — at least, not manned temples. Religion yes, clergy no. Surely the beautiful nudes can just wander about, offering themselves like divine soufflés to the hunger of the needy and the rapture of the flesh. Let them join the processions. Let tambourines be struck above the copulations, and the glory of desire be proclaimed upon the gongs, and (a not unimportant point) let the offspring of these delightful rituals be beloved and looked after by all. One thing I know there is none of in Omelas is guilt. But what else should there be? I thought at first there were no drugs, but that is puritanical. For those who like it, the faint insistent sweetness of *drooz* may perfume the ways of the city, *drooz* which first brings a great lightness and brilliance to the mind and limbs, and then after some hours a dreamy languor, and wonderful visions at last of the very arcane and inmost secrets of the Universe, as well as exciting the pleasure of sex beyond all belief; and it is not habit-forming. For more modest tastes I think there ought to be beer. What else, what else belongs in the joyous city? The sense of victory, surely, the celebration of courage. But as we did without clergy, let us do without soldiers. The joy built upon successful slaughter is not the right kind of joy; it will not do; it is fearful and it is trivial. A boundless and generous contentment, a magnanimous triumph felt not against some outer enemy but in communion with the finest and fairest in the souls of all men everywhere and the splendor of the world's summer: this is what swells the hearts of the people of Omelas, and the victory they celebrate is that of life. I really don't think many of them need to take *drooz*.

Most of the processions have reached the Green Fields by now. A marvelous smell of cooking goes forth from the red and blue tents of the provisioners. The faces of small children are amiably sticky; in the benign gray beard of a man a couple of crumbs of rich pastry are entangled. The youths and girls have mounted their horses and are beginning to group around the starting line of the course. An old woman, small, fat, and laughing, is passing out flowers from a basket, and tall young men wear her flowers in their shining hair. A child of nine or ten sits at the edge of the crowd, alone, playing on a wooden flute. People pause to listen, and they smile, but they do not speak to him, for he never ceases playing and never sees them, his dark eyes wholly rapt in the sweet, thin magic of the tune.

He finishes, and slowly lowers his hands holding the wooden flute.

As if that little private silence were the signal, all at once a trumpet sounds from the pavilion near the starting line: imperious, melancholy, piercing. The horses rear on their slender legs, and some of them neigh in answer. Sober-faced, the young riders stroke the horses' necks and soothe them, whispering, "Quiet, quiet, there my beauty, my hope . . ." They begin to form in rank along the starting line. The crowds along the race course are like a field of grass and flowers in the wind. The Festival of Summer has begun.

Do you believe? Do you accept the festival, the city, the joy? No? Then let me describe one more thing.

In a basement under one of the beautiful public buildings of Omelas, or perhaps in the cellar of one of its spacious private homes, there is a room. It has one locked door, and no window. A little light seeps in dustily between cracks in the boards, secondhand from a cobwebbed window somewhere across the cellar. In one corner of the little room a couple of mops, with stiff, clotted, foul-smelling heads, stand near a rusty bucket. The floor is dirt, a little damp to the touch, as cellar dirt usually is. The room is about three paces long and two wide: a mere broom closet or disused toolroom. In the room a child is sitting. It might be a boy or a girl. It looks about six, but actually is nearly ten. It is feeble-minded. Perhaps it was born defective, or perhaps it has become imbecile through fear, malnutrition, and neglect. It picks its nose and occasionally fumbles vaguely with its toes or genitals, as it sits hunched in the corner farthest from the bucket and the two mops. It is afraid of the mops. It finds them horrible. It shuts its eyes, but it knows the mops are still standing there; and the door is locked; and nobody will come. The door is always locked, and nobody ever comes, except that some-times—the child has no understanding of time or interval—sometimes the door rattles terribly and opens, and a person, or several people, are there. One of them may come in and kick the child to make it stand up. The others never come close, but peer in at it with frightened, disgusted eyes. The food bowl and the water jug are hastily filled, the door is locked, and the eyes disappear. The people at the door never say anything, but the child, who has not always lived in the tool-room, and can remember sunlight and its mother's voice, sometimes speaks. "I will be good," it says. "Please let me out. I will be good!" They never answer. The child used to scream for help at night, and cry a good deal, but now it only makes a kind of whining, "eh-haa, eh-haa," and it speaks less and less often. It is so thin there are no calves to its legs; its belly protrudes; it lives on a half-bowl of cornmeal and grease a day. It is naked. Its buttocks and thighs are a mass of festered sores, as it sits in its own excrement continually.

They all know it is there, all the people of Omelas. Some of them have come to see it, others are content merely to know it is there. They all know that it has to be there. Some of them understand why, and some do not, but they all understand that their happiness, the beauty of their city, the tenderness of their friendships, the health of their children, the wisdom of their schol-ars, the skill of their makers, even the abundance of their harvest and the kindly weathers of their skies, de-pend wholly on this child's abominable misery.

This is usually explained to children when they are between eight and twelve, whenever they seem capable of understanding; and most of those who come to see the child are young people, though often enough an adult comes, or comes back, to see the child. No matter how well the matter has been explained to them, these young spectators are always shocked and sickened at the sight. They feel disgust, which they had thought themselves superior to. They feel anger, outrage, impo-tence, despite all the explanations. They would like to do something for the child. But there is nothing they can do. If the child were brought up into the sunlight out of that vile place, if it were cleaned and fed and comforted, that would be a good thing, indeed; but if it were done, in that day and hour all the prosperity and beauty and delight of Omelas would wither and be de-stroyed. Those are the terms. To exchange all the good-ness and grace of every life in Omelas for that single, small improvement: to throw away the happiness of thousands for the chance of the happiness of one: that would be to let guilt within the walls indeed.

The terms are strict and absolute; there may not even be a kind word spoken to the child.

Often the young people go home in tears, or in a tearless rage, when they have seen the child and faced this terrible paradox. They may brood over it for weeks or years. But as time goes on they begin to realize that even if the child could be released, it would not get much good of its freedom: a little vague pleasure of warmth and food, no doubt, but little more. It is too de-graded and imbecile to know any real joy. It has been afraid too long ever to be free of fear. Its habits are too uncouth for it to respond to humane treatment. Indeed after so long it would probably be wretched without walls about it to protect it, and darkness for its eyes, and its own excrement to sit in. Their tears at the bit-ter injustice dry when they begin to perceive the terri-ble justice of reality, and to accept it. Yet it is their tears and anger, the trying of their generosity and the accep-tance of their helplessness, which are perhaps the true source of the splendor of their lives. Theirs is no vapid, irresponsible happiness. They know that they, like the child, are not free. They know compassion. It is the existence of the child, and their knowledge of its exis-tence, that makes possible the nobility of their archi-tecture, the poignancy of their music, the profundity of their science. It is because of the child that they are so gentle with children. They know that if the wretched one were not there sniveling in the dark, the other one, the fluteplayer, could make no joyful music as the young riders line up in their beauty for the race in the sunlight of the first morning of summer.

Now do you believe in them? Are they not more credible? But there is one more thing to tell, and this is quite incredible.

At times one of the adolescent girls or boys who go to see the child does not go home to weep or rage, does not, in fact, go home at all. Sometimes also a man or woman much older falls silent for a day or two, and then leaves home. These people go out into the street, and walk down the street alone. They keep walking, and walk straight out of the city of Omelas, through the beautiful gates. They keep walking across the farmlands of Omelas. Each one goes alone, youth or girl, man or woman. Night falls; the traveler must pass down village streets, between the houses with yellow-lit windows, and on out into the darkness of the fields. Each alone, they go west or north, toward the mountains. They go on. They leave Omelas, they walk ahead into the darkness, and they do not come back. The place they go toward is a place even less imaginable to most of us than the city of happiness. I cannot describe it at all. It is possible that it does not exist. But they seem to know where they are going, the ones who walk away from Omelas.

Suggestions for Further Reading

Baier, Kurt. *The Moral Point of View.* Ithaca, NY: Cornell University Press, 1958.

Cahn, Steven M., and Joram G. Haber. *20th Century Ethical Theory.* Englewood Cliffs, NJ: Prentice-Hall, 1995.

Feldman, Fred. *Introductory Ethics.* Englewood Cliffs, NJ: Prentice-Hall, 1978.

Fishkin, James. *Beyond Subjective Morality.* New Haven, CT: Yale University Press, 1984.

Frankena, William. *Ethics.* Englewood Cliffs, NJ: Prentice-Hall, 1973.

Helm, Paul. *The Divine Command Theory of Ethics.* Oxford: Oxford University Press, 1979.

Kane, Robert. *Through the Moral Maze: Searching for Absolute Values in a Pluralistic World.* New York: Paragon House, 1994.

Kant, Immanuel. *Groundwork of the Metaphysics of Morals.* Trans. H. J. Paton. New York: Harper and Row, 1964.

Mill, John Stuart. *Utilitarianism.* Indianapolis: Bobbs-Merrill, 1957.

Nielson, Kai. *Ethics without God.* Buffalo, NY: Prometheus Books, 1973.

Rachels, James. *The Elements of Moral Philosophy.* New York: Random House, 1986.

Ross, W. D. *The Right and the Good.* Oxford: Clarendon Press, 1967.

Sher, George. *Moral Philosophy: Selected Readings.* New York: Harcourt, Brace, Jovanovich, 1987.

Smart, J. J. C., and Bernard Williams. *Utilitarianism: For and Against.* Cambridge: Cambridge University Press, 1973.

Taylor, Paul. *Principles of Ethics.* Encino, CA: Dickenson, 1975.

Chapter 6

The Problem of Evil
and the Existence of God

The demand of the human understanding for causation requires but the one old and only answer, God.
— HENRY MARTYN DEXTER

Where did the universe come from? Why are we here? What is to become of us? Such questions have traditionally been answered by appeal to the supernatural. From time immemorial, the workings of the natural world have been attributed to supernatural beings (gods). The Greeks, for example, believed that thunderstorms were caused by Zeus, earthquakes by Poseidon, and volcanoes by Hephaestus (the Roman Vulcan). Few today would attribute thunderstorms, earthquakes, or volcanoes to the actions of supernatural beings. Some phenomena, however, such as the creation of the universe, the existence of miracles, and the experience of the divine, are still thought to require a supernatural explanation. We will examine these and other phenomena to see if they are best explained by appeal to the supernatural.

The diversity of supernatural beings that have been postulated to explain various phenomena is immense. They range from nature spirits, such as leprechauns, fairies, and gnomes, to supreme beings, such as Jehovah, Allah, and Brahman. Religions that believe in the existence of many supernatural beings or gods are called "polytheistic"; those that believe in one supreme being are called "monotheistic." Even among monotheistic religions, however, there is a wide variation in their conceptions of the supreme being. For example, Jehovah (the supreme being of Christianity), Allah (the supreme being of Islam), and Ahura Mazda (the supreme being of Zoroastrianism) are persons; like us, they have thoughts, feelings, and desires. Unlike us, however, they are all-powerful, all-knowing, and all-good. Brahman (the supreme being of the Hindu religion), however, is not a person but an impersonal substance often described as pure being, pure consciousness, and pure bliss. The supreme being, however, cannot both be and not be a person because that is logically impossible. So if Hinduism is true, Christianity must be false, and vice versa. Those who are interested in understanding the true nature of reality, then, need to determine not only if there is a supreme being, but if so, what kind of a being it is.

In the space of one chapter, we cannot investigate all the different conceptions of God. So we will focus on the conception of God common to Christianity, Judaism, and Islam, namely that of an all-powerful (omnipotent), all-knowing (omniscient), and all-good (omnibenevolent) being who created and rules the universe. Our goal will be to determine whether we are justified in believing in the existence of such a being. If not, then killing in the name of God is not only immoral, it's irrational as well.

Religion has been used to justify the massacre of millions of people. Thousands of people in the United States recently died at the hands of Islamic fundamentalists. But God-fearing Christians also slaughtered thousands of people in the Crusades and the Inquisition. The rationale was the same in all of these cases: God says that unbelievers should die. As the God of the Bible says, "He that sacrificeth unto any god, save unto the Lord only, he shall be utterly destroyed" (Exod. 22:20). How we should interpret such pronouncements is one of the most important inquiries we can undertake.

Christians consider the Islamic suicide bombers' belief that they will receive the services of seventy-two virgins in heaven to be absurd. What Christians often fail to realize, however, is that Muslims, Hindus, and Jews consider the Christian claim that only those who believe in Jesus Christ will go to heaven to be equally absurd. The only way to decide which, if either, of these beliefs is true is to examine the reasons behind them.

If you ask someone why they believe in God, you are likely to get an answer like "Because my parents taught me that God exists." But the mere fact that your parents taught you something doesn't make it true. Your parents may have also taught you that Santa Claus, the Easter bunny, and the tooth fairy exist, but that doesn't mean that they do. Your upbringing in a certain religion may have caused you to have certain beliefs, but it doesn't justify those beliefs.

When we ask someone why he or she believes something, we may be looking for two very different sorts of things. On the one hand, we may be looking for the cause of that person's belief. This is the sort of thing that psychologists, sociologists, and anthropologists look for. On the other hand, we may be looking for the reasons that person has for thinking that belief is true. This is the sort of thing that philosophers look for. Philosophers are not particularly interested in how you came by your belief in God; they are interested in determining whether there is any truth to the claim that God exists.

Because so many people have been taught from such a young age that a particular God is the one true God, it is often difficult to be objective about the God question. But we must be objective if we hope to get to the truth of the matter. When we reflect on the existence of God, we need to put aside our prejudices and ask ourselves, If I didn't believe, hope, or fear that there was a God, how would I assess the arguments for the existence of God?

After assessing the arguments, you may decide that you are justified in believing in God. In that case, you may be a **theist,** that is, one who believes in God. If you find that you are neither justified nor unjustified in believing in God, you may be an **agnostic,** that is, one who neither believes nor disbelieves in God. If you decide that you are justified in believing that God does not exist, you may be an **atheist,** that is, one who does not believe in God.

The traditional God of theism is not only supposed to be the creator of the universe, but he is also supposed to be personally involved with it. God not only watches over us but also helps us in times of need. He listens to our prayers and sometimes grants them. Not everyone who believes in one god, however, shares that conception of god. Many of the founders of our country, including Thomas Jefferson, Benjamin Franklin, and George Washington, were **deists.** They believed that the universe was created by a god, but they didn't believe that he watches over it. The god of the deists is like a watchmaker who is so skillful that the mechanisms he creates never need to be adjusted. Deists do not believe that God intervenes in the world or the affairs of men. He does not perform miracles or answer prayers.

Reason unaided by revelation can prove that God exists.

—ROMAN CATHOLIC BALTIMORE CATECHISM

theist One who believes in a god, especially a personal god who rules the world.

agnostic One who neither believes nor disbelieves in God.

atheist One who disbelieves in God.

deist One who believes that God created the universe and then abandoned it.

Pantheism is yet another type of monotheism that is not theist in the traditional sense. Pantheists believe that the universe itself is God. This is not to say that the universe is a person, but it is to say that the universe is divine and thus the ultimate object of reverence. Many Hindus are pantheists, as are many Buddhists, Taoists, and Unitarian Universalists. They hold that nature is sacred and that the religious feelings of awe and wonder that we experience need not be attributed to a supernatural agency. They are merely a recognition of the grandeur of the universe and our intimate connection to it.

In this chapter, we will examine a number of the traditional arguments for the existence of God. There are some arguments that we won't consider, because they are clearly fallacious. These arguments have a certain amount of currency, however, so it's useful to see where they go wrong.

One popular argument for the existence of God appeals to sacred scripture. When asked why they believe in God, many people respond by citing a sacred text. "I believe in God because the Bible says that God exists," a Christian might claim. When asked why they believe the Bible, they might respond, "Because God wrote it." Do you see the problem here? They are trying to prove the existence of God by assuming that He exists. Any argument that assumes what it's trying to prove, however, proves nothing. A good argument should increase the likelihood of its conclusion by citing evidence that is more well established than its conclusion. If the conclusion appears as a premise in an argument, however, it can't increase the likelihood of its conclusion.

The Bible, of course, is not the only book of sacred scripture. Different religions take different texts to be divinely inspired. For Muslims, it is the Koran; for Hindus, it is the Vedas; and for the Zoroastrians (the first monotheistic religion), it is the Avesta. These texts contradict one another in all sorts of ways and so cannot all be true. The Bible, for example, says that God incarnated in the form of Jesus Christ, whereas the other three deny that. So to decide which, if any, of these texts is the true word of God, we must appeal to something other than the texts themselves.

Some defend the Bible on the grounds that it contains historically accurate information. But from the fact that some of what the Bible says about the natural world is true, it doesn't follow that anything it says about the supernatural world is true. Herman Melville's *Moby-Dick* contains many truths about whaling, but from this we can't conclude that there was a great white whale. Moreover, biblical archaeologists have found that there is good reason for believing that a number of the major historical claims of the Bible are false. (See the box "Biblical Archaeology.") To establish the existence of supernatural beings, then, we need something more than a book that claims that they exist.

Another popular argument for the existence of God is based on the claim that every society throughout history has had a belief in God. This is often called the argument from common consent. Even if this claim were true, it wouldn't establish the existence of God, for from the fact that many people

Biblical Archaeology

Archaeological investigations have failed to confirm many of the most significant events recorded in the Bible. Many archaeologists believe that this lack of confirming evidence is grounds for thinking that the historical sections of the Bible can't be taken literally, as Haim Watzman reports in *The Chronicle of Higher Education*:

"If Abraham, Isaac, Jacob, Moses, and David aren't proven, how am I supposed to live with that?" This agonized question came from the crowded back row of an auditorium at Ben-Gurion University during a conference titled "Has the Biblical Period Disappeared?" It expressed the shiver that went down Israel's collective spine as puzzled scholars saw Israel's lay population jerked into awareness of the last two decades of biblical archaeological and historical research. . . .

The chill that produced the question at Ben-Gurion University was set off by one of Israeli archaeology's leading biblical minimalists—a label attached by their colleagues to those who think that very little in the Bible's historical sections is true. The Tel Aviv University archaeologist Ze'ev Herzog began the flurry with a cover story in the weekend magazine of the October 29, 1999, issue of *Ha'aretz*, the national daily newspaper.

"This is what archaeologists have learned from their excavations in the Land of Israel: the Israelites were never in Egypt, did not wander in the desert, did not conquer the land in a military campaign and did not pass it on to the 12 tribes of Israel. Perhaps even harder to swallow is the fact that the united monarchy of David and Solomon, which is described by the Bible as a regional power, was at most a small tribal kingdom," he wrote. . . .

None of the scholars speaking at the conference believe that the Bible's historical sections can be accepted as literal, accurate descriptions of historical events. They also agree that the extra-biblical evidence for events described in the Bible dwindles the farther back in time one goes. King Ahab of Israel is well-documented in other inscriptions from elsewhere in the Middle East; the united monarchy of David and Solomon is not. Evidence exists of the rise of the new Israelite nation in the Palestinian highlands during the late Bronze Age—the age of the Judges—but it can be interpreted in different ways. There is no external evidence at all for the patriarchs and, in fact, the biblical description contains contradictions and anachronisms that, scholars generally agree, seem to place the patriarchs in the age of the Judges rather than several generations earlier, as the Bible has it.

Mr. Herzog concludes from such findings that the Bible simply should not be used as a historical source. The archaeological practice begun by William Foxwell Albright, who founded the discipline of biblical archaeology in the early part of the twentieth century, was that findings in the field should be interpreted in the light of the biblical text. Mr. Herzog's new paradigm is that the Bible should be set aside and the findings interpreted in their own right.[1]

Thought Probe

Biblical Truths

Does the failure to find confirming evidence for many of the Bible's historical claims undercut the credibility of its nonhistorical claims? Why or why not?

believe something, it doesn't follow that it is true. Many people in the world once believed that the earth was flat, but that didn't make it flat. Believing something doesn't make it so. What's more, the claim that every society has a belief in God is false. The word "god," as we've seen, is extremely ambiguous, and there is no single conception of God that has been held by all societies.

pantheist One who believes that the universe is God.

Certainly not all societies have believed in the traditional god of theism, nor have they believed in a personal god. Many societies, such as those where Buddhism is the dominant religion, have no belief in God as traditionally conceived. Two of the most fundamental principles of Buddhism are that there are no continuing substances (*anicca*) and thus no continuing selves (*anatta*). If there are no continuing substances, however, there are no eternal beings and no immortal souls. The argument from common consent, then, is both fallacious and erroneous.

Some defend their belief in God on the grounds that no one can prove that God does not exist. This type of argument is known as an appeal to ignorance and is also fallacious. From the fact that one cannot prove that something does not exist, it doesn't follow that it does exist. One cannot prove that Santa Claus does not exist. But that doesn't mean that he does exist.

Although it is often claimed that one cannot prove a universal negative, (where a universal negative is a statement to the effect that something does not exist), that is not necessarily so. If one can prove that the notion of a thing is self-contradictory, one can prove that it doesn't exist. We know, for example, that there are no round squares, because the notion of a round square is self-contradictory. Similarly, some claim, the theistic notion of God is self-contradictory. To give but one example, the theistic God is often claimed to be perfectly merciful and perfectly just. If He is perfectly just, He makes sure that everyone gets what's coming to them. If He is perfectly merciful, he lets everyone off. But no one, not even God, can do both. So the theistic notion of God may be self-contradictory. If so, such a god cannot possibly exist.

The traditional God of theism is supposed to be immaterial. Because God does not have a body, however, it's impossible to sense him. Some atheists use this fact to argue against God. They claim that since no one can prove that God does exist, he must not exist. This, too, is an appeal to ignorance and is just as fallacious as the one made by the theists. A thing may exist even though we cannot sense it.

Scientists believe in a lot of things that can't be sensed, like subatomic particles. Their belief in these particles is justified because the assumption that they exist provides the best explanation of a number of phenomena, and it does not contradict any known facts. Many of the arguments presented by theists for the existence of God can be viewed as inferences to the best explanation. Theists cite certain phenomena, like the origin and design of the universe, and claim that they are best explained on the assumption that God exists. We will examine such claims to determine whether the God hypothesis does provide the best explanation of anything.

If the arguments for the existence of God are as good as the arguments for the existence of subatomic particles, then we should be justified in believing that the existence of God is a fact. And if we're justified in believing that the existence of God is a fact, we should be justified in teaching that fact in public schools. There is no separation between state and science. If religious arguments are as good as scientific ones, maybe there should be no separation between state and church.

On the other hand, if religious arguments are as good as scientific ones, there's no need for religious faith. Our belief in the existence of subatomic particles is not based on faith—it's based on fact. If our belief in the existence of God is similarly based on fact, religious faith would be superfluous. Realizing that strong arguments for the existence of God would undermine faith, many theologians claim that it is wrongheaded to try to justify belief in God through the use of reason. Dutch theologian Herman Bavinck, for example, proclaims,

> We receive the impression that belief in the existence of God is based entirely upon these proofs. But indeed that would be "a wretched faith, which, before it invokes God, must first prove his existence.". . . The so-called proofs are by no means the final grounds of our most certain conviction that God exists. This certainty is established only by faith. . . .[2]

Evaluating the effectiveness of both reason and faith in establishing the existence of God is one of the goals of this chapter.

Atheists claim not only that the God hypothesis does *not* provide the best explanation of anything but that it also contradicts known facts. One undeniable fact, they claim, is that evil exists. But if the world was created by an all-powerful, all-knowing, and all-good being, there should be no evil in the world. If God is all-good, he shouldn't want evil to exist in the world; if he's all-knowing, he should know how to create a world without evil; and if he's all-powerful, he should be able to create a world without evil. So why is there so much evil in the world? This is the famous problem of evil. Theists recognize that this is a serious challenge to the God hypothesis and consequently have devised a number of theories to justify the existence of evil. We will examine some of these theories in the second section of this chapter.

Question with boldness even the existence of a god; because, if there be one, he must more approve of the homage of reason, than that of blindfolded fear.

—THOMAS JEFFERSON

Objectives

After reading this chapter, you should be able to

- state various arguments for the existence of God.
- evaluate the various arguments for the existence of God.
- state the argument from evil.
- evaluate the various solutions to the problem of evil.
- define theism, deism, atheism, agnosticism, pantheism, theodicy, moral evil, and natural evil.
- decide on a basis of reasons whether you are a theist, an atheist, or an agnostic.

The Mysterious Universe
God as Creator

Science cannot determine origin, and so cannot determine destiny.

—THEODORE MUNGER

Science is remarkably effective at explaining the workings of the world. It has given us an understanding of everything from galactic clusters to subatomic particles. But many believe that there are some things that science can't explain, like the origin of the universe. To explain that, it is argued, we must appeal to something outside the universe—something supernatural—like God. Arguments that attempt to derive the existence of God from the existence of the universe are known as **cosmological arguments** for the existence of God.

The Traditional Cosmological Argument

The basic cosmological argument is known as the first-cause argument. It rests on the assumption that everything has a cause. Because nothing can cause itself, and the string of causes can't be infinitely long, there must be a first cause, namely, God. This argument received its classic formulation at the hands of the great Roman Catholic philosopher St. Thomas Aquinas. He writes,

> In the world of sensible things, we find there is an order of efficient causes. There is no case known . . . in which a thing is found to be the efficient cause of itself; for so it would be prior to itself, which is impossible. Now in efficient causes it is not possible to go to infinity, because . . . the first is the cause of the intermediate cause, and the intermediate is the cause of the ultimate cause. . . . Now to take away the cause is to take away the effect. Therefore, if there be no first cause among efficient causes, there will be no ultimate, nor any intermediate, cause. . . . therefore it is necessary to admit a first efficient cause, to which everyone gives the name God.[3]

St. Thomas's argument goes something like this:

1. Some things are caused.

2. Nothing can cause itself.

3. Therefore, everything that is caused is caused by something other than itself.

4. The chain of causes cannot stretch infinitely backward in time.

5. If the chain of causes cannot stretch infinitely backward in time, there must be a first cause.

6. Therefore, everything that is caused has a first cause, namely, God.

If sound, this argument proves the existence of a first cause. St. Thomas claims that it also proves the existence of God. But this follows only if there is good reason for believing that the first cause is all-powerful, all-knowing, and all-good. The cosmological argument itself, however, gives us no reason for believing that this is the case.

An all-powerful being would be able to create every possible universe. From the fact that a being created this universe, however, we can't conclude that it has that kind of power. For all we know, this is the only universe that being could create. In the absence of any additional evidence, then, we are not justified in believing that the first cause is all-powerful.

An all-knowing being would know everything there is to know about every possible universe. From the fact that a being created this universe, however, we can't conclude that it has that kind of knowledge. For all we know, this is the only universe the creator knew how to create. So again, in the absence of additional evidence, we are not justified in believing that the first cause is all-knowing.

An all-good being would create only good things. But the universe seems to contain a lot of evil. The simplest explanation of this fact is that the creator of this universe is not all-good. This is the explanation of evil that was favored by the early Christian sect known as the Gnostics. They believed that our world was created by the *demiurge*, a defective, inferior god who is the author of evil. So even if the traditional cosmological argument succeeds in proving the existence of a first cause, it does not succeed in proving the existence of God.

Some believe that the universe is too flawed to be the creation of a divine being. The Roman poet Lucretius, for example, writing fifty years before the birth of Christ, had this to say about the universe and its creator:

> I dare this to affirm . . .
> That in no wise the nature of all things
> For us was fashioned by a power divine
> So great the faults it stands encumbered with
> First, mark all regions which are overarched
> By the prodigious reaches of the sky:
> Well-nigh two thirds intolerable heat
> And a perpetual fall of frost doth rob

If God does exist, I don't think he's vengeful; I just think he's an underachiever.

—WOODY ALLEN

cosmological argument An argument that attempts to derive the existence of God from the existence of the universe.

Thomas Aquinas

The greatest thinker of medieval times was the philosopher-theologian Thomas Aquinas (1225–1274). He was born in the castle of Roccasecca in the kingdom of Naples (Italy). At the age of five, he was sent to the Abbey of Monte Cassino to begin his schooling. By his mid-teens, he was ready to continue his education at the University of Naples. There he studied philosophy and liberal arts and, at eighteen, became a Dominican monk. When his aristocratic family learned that he had entered an order of beggars, they locked him in the family castle for about a year. His imprisonment had no effect, for he soon left to study with the Dominicans in Paris and remained devoted to the Dominican ideals of study and preaching for the rest of his life.

In 1256, he lectured as a master of theology at the University of Paris and subsequently taught at Orvieto, Rome, and Naples. For the rest of his days, he continued to teach and to write treatises, scriptural commentaries, and defenses of his philosophical positions. He was involved in all the major philosophical and theological disputations of his day. By the time he had finished, he had created a grand intellectual system that has exerted more influence in the Church than the work of any other theologian.

In December 1273, he had a religious experience during Mass that profoundly affected him. He reportedly said of this incident, "All that I have written seems to me like straw compared to what has now been revealed to me." He stopped writing and died four months later at age fifty.

Aquinas's greatest achievement was a synthesis of the Christianity of his day with the philosophy of Aristotle. Eight hundred years earlier, Augustine brought about a similar marriage between Plato's philosophy and Christianity. But Aquinas thought that the Augustinian synthesis was inadequate. For example, Augustine thought that all true knowledge was to be found in an unearthly, nonmaterial, eternal realm that was far superior to the earthly, material, fleeting world of flesh. But Aquinas, following Aristotle, thought that rational knowledge could be gained through sense experience, as well as through revelation.

St. Thomas Aquinas
1225–1274

From mortal kind. . . .
Beside these matters, why
Doth Nature feed and foster on land and sea
The dreadful breed of savage beasts, the foes
Of the human clan? Why do the seasons bring
Distempers with them? Wherefore stalks at large
Death so untimely?[4]

As an abode for humans, the earth leaves something to be desired. Instead of promoting human flourishing, it seems to be inimical to it. Such would not be the case, Lucretious claims, if the universe was created by a divine being.

Not only might the first cause be something less than perfect, it might be something less than human. Hume provides the following example:

The Brahmins assert, that the world arose from an infinite spider, who spun this whole complicated mass from his bowels, and annihilates afterwards the whole or any part of it, by absorbing it again, and resolving it into his own essence.[5]

Nothing in the traditional cosmological argument rules out the possibility of a nonhuman first cause. As a result, it can't establish the existence of God.

St. Thomas's argument shows only that everything that is caused has a first cause. Because God supposedly is eternal, he doesn't need a cause. So if the universe is eternal, it doesn't need a first cause.

Even prior to the advent of modern physics, there were powerful reasons for believing that the universe was eternal. To suppose otherwise, it was argued, was to suppose that you could get something from nothing, and that's impossible. "From nothing, nothing comes," is how Lucretius puts it. Creation always involves taking preexisting stuff and fashioning it in certain ways. It never involves bringing something into existence out of nothing.

This insight is enshrined in one of the fundamental laws of modern physics. Known as the Law of Conservation of Mass-Energy, it says that the total amount of mass-energy in the world can neither be increased nor decreased. In 1785, Antoine Lavoisier proposed the Law of Conservation of Mass, which says that matter can be neither created nor destroyed. In 1842, Julius Robert Mayer proposed the Law of Conservation of Energy, which says that energy can be neither created nor destroyed. In 1907, Albert Einstein, in his famous equation, $E=mc^2$, showed mass can be converted into energy and vice versa. Since that time, the two laws have been merged into the Law of Conservation of Mass-Energy. If the total amount of mass-energy can be neither increased nor decreased, then the implication would seem to be that the universe is eternal.

To undercut this notion, St. Thomas tries to argue that an eternal universe is inconsistent with the facts. If there were no first cause, he claims, there would be nothing happening now. But there is something happening now. So there must be a first cause. This argument, however, rests on the mistaken notion that an infinite series of causes is just a very long finite series.

Consider a single-column stack of children's blocks resting on a table. Each block rests on the block below it, except for the block that rests on the table. If the bottom block were taken away, the whole stack would fall down. In a finite stack of blocks, there must be a first block.

In an infinite stack of blocks, however, there is no first block. Similarly, in an infinite causal chain, there is no first cause. Aquinas took this to mean that an infinite causal chain is missing something. But it is a mistake to think that anything is missing from an infinite causal chain. Even though an infinite causal chain has no first cause, there is no event in that chain that doesn't have a cause. Similarly, even though the set of real numbers has no first member, there is no number that doesn't have a predecessor. Logic doesn't demand a first cause any more than it demands a first number. An eternal universe is both a physical and a logical possibility.

There is no more steely barb than that of the infinite.

—CHARLES
BAUDELAIRE

The Kalam Cosmological Argument

Although it may be possible for the universe to be infinitely old, many believe that the universe was created less than fifteen billion years ago in a cataclysmic explosion known as the "big bang." The existence of such a creation event

Let the chain of second causes be ever so long, the first link is always in God's hand.

—GEORGE LAVINGTON

explains a number of phenomena, including the expansion of the universe, the existence of the cosmic background radiation, and the relative proportions of various sorts of matter. As the theory has been refined, more specific predictions have been derived from it. A number of these predictions have recently been confirmed. Although this is a major scientific achievement, many believe that it has theological implications as well. Specifically, they believe that it provides scientific evidence for the existence of God. Astronomer George Smoot suggested as much when he exclaimed at a press conference reporting the findings of the Cosmic Background Explorer (COBE) satellite, "If you're religious, it's like looking at the face of God." Why? Because something must have caused the big bang, and who else but God could have done such a thing? Astronomer Hugh Ross, in his book *The Creator and the Cosmos*, puts the argument this way: "If the universe arose out of a big bang, it must have had a beginning. If it had a beginning, it must have a beginner."[6] And that beginner, Ross believes, is God.

The Kalam cosmological argument follows along these lines. It goes like this:

1. Whatever begins to exist has a cause.
2. The universe began to exist.
3. Therefore, the universe had a cause, namely God.

This argument gets its name from the Arabic word *kalam*, which means "to argue or discuss." It originated with Islamic theologians who sought to challenge the Greek view of the eternity of matter.

The Kalam cosmological argument doesn't require that everything have a cause, only those things that begin to exist. Since God is eternal, he doesn't require a cause. The universe, however, is not eternal. So it does requires a cause.

As with the traditional cosmological argument, however, the Kalam cosmological argument gives us no reason for believing that the first cause is God. The universe that came from the big bang is finite, and it doesn't take a being of infinite power to create a finite universe. The same goes for the properties of intelligence and goodness. So even if the Kalam cosmological argument did prove the existence of a first cause, it doesn't prove the existence of God.

There's reason to believe it doesn't even prove the existence of a first cause, however, for modern physics explicitly repudiates premise 1 and provides good reason for rejecting premise 2.

Remarkably enough, modern physics rejects the claim that whatever begins to exist has a cause. On the contrary, it maintains that things like subatomic particles can come into existence without a cause. As physicist Edward Tryon tells us,

> . . . quantum electrodynamics reveals that an electron, positron, and photon occasionally emerge spontaneously in a perfect vacuum. When this happens, the three particles exist for a brief time, and then annihilate each other, leaving no trace behind. . . . The spontaneous, temporary emergence of particles from a vacuum is called a vacuum fluctuation, and is utterly commonplace in quantum field theory.[7]

Vacuum fluctuations are random events, and random events have no cause. So anything produced by a vacuum fluctuation is uncaused.

What's even more remarkable is that, according to modern physics, the universe itself could be the result of a vacuum fluctuation! Tryon explains,

> If it is true that our Universe has a zero net value for all conserved quantities, then it may simply be a fluctuation of a vacuum, the vacuum of some larger space in which our universe is imbedded. In answer to the question of why it happened, I offer the modest proposal that our Universe is simply one of those things which happen from time to time.[8]

According to Tryon, universes happen; they come into existence spontaneously without being caused to exist.

Wouldn't a universe produced by a vacuum fluctuation violate the Law of Conservation of Mass-Energy? Not if the total amount of mass-energy of the universe is zero. How is that possible? Physicist Paul Davies explains,

> There is a . . . remarkable possibility, which is the creation of matter from a state of zero energy. This possibility arises because energy can be both positive and negative. The energy of motion or the energy of mass is always positive, but the energy of attraction, such as that due to certain types of gravitational or electromagnetic field is negative. Circumstances can arise in which the positive energy that goes to make up the mass of newly created particles of matter is exactly offset by the negative energy of gravity or electromagnetism. . . . Some have suggested that there is a deep cosmic principle at work which requires the universe to have exactly zero energy. If that is so, the cosmos can follow the path of least resistance, coming into existence without requiring any input of matter or energy at all.[9]

If our universe has zero total energy, as measurements seem to indicate, it could be the result of a vacuum fluctuation. But if it was the result of a vacuum fluctuation, it was not caused to exist by anyone or anything.

The second premise of the Kalam cosmological argument says that the universe began to exist. Evidence for the big bang is usually presented as evidence for this claim. But the fact that the big bang occurred doesn't prove that the universe began to exist, for the big bang may itself have been the result of a prior big crunch!

It has long been known that if the amount of matter in the universe is great enough, then the universe will someday stop expanding and start contracting. Eventually, all the matter in the universe would be drawn back to a single point in what has come to be known as the "big crunch." Because matter supposedly cannot be crushed out of existence, the contraction cannot go on indefinitely. At some point the compressed matter may bounce back in another big bang. If so, the big bang would have been caused by a prior big crunch rather than by some supernatural being.

The view that the universe oscillates between periods of expansion and contraction in an endlesss — and beginningless — cycle of creation and destruction is a very Eastern one. Hindus, for example, believe that everything in the universe — as well as the universe itself — undergoes a continuous process of death

If God did not exist, it would be necessary to invent him.

—Voltaire

and rebirth. For them, time is circular; the beginning and end are one and the same. Thus the notion of a first cause makes no sense. Only for those who have a linear view of time is the question of the origin of the universe a problem.

Some estimates indicate that there is not enough mass in the universe to stop its expansion. So the big bang may not have been the result of a prior big crunch. But even if the universe as a whole never contracts, we know that certain parts of it do. When a star has used up its fuel, the force of gravity causes it to contract. If the star is massive enough, this contraction results in a black hole. The matter in a black hole is compressed toward a point of infinite density known as a "singularity." Before it reaches the singularity, however, some physicists, most notably Lee Smolin, believe that the matter in the black hole may start expanding again and give rise to another universe. In a sense, then, according to Smolin, our universe may reproduce itself by budding off. He writes,

> A collapsing star forms a black hole, within which it is compressed to a very dense state. The universe began in a similarly very dense state from which it expands. Is it possible that these are one and the same dense state? That is, is it possible that what is beyond the horizon of a black hole is the beginning of another universe?
>
> This could happen if the collapsing star exploded once it reached a very dense state, but after the black hole horizon had formed around it. . . .
>
> What we are doing is applying this bounce hypothesis, not to the universe as a whole, but to every black hole in it. If this is true, then we live not in a single universe, which is eternally passing through the same recurring cycle of collapse and rebirth. We live instead in a continually growing community of "universes," each of which is born from an explosion following the collapse of a star to a black hole.[10]

Smolin's vision of a self-reproducing universe is an appealing one. It suggests that the universe is more like a living thing than an artifact and thus that its coming into being doesn't require an external agent.

Tryon's and Smolin's theories are not the only ones that explain the big bang without appealing to the supernatural. Paul Teinhardt of Princeton University and Neil Turok of Cambridge University have proposed a new oscillating theory of the universe in which the universe is brought into existence as the result of a collision between giant membranes of matter. Andre Linde has proposed a self-reproducing theory of the universe wherein the budding-off process is driven by scalar fields rather than black holes. And Stephen Hawking has proposed that although the universe is finitely old, it had no beginning in time because, as St. Augustine suggests, time came into existence with the universe.

These theories are simpler than the God hypothesis because they do not postulate the existence of any supernatural entities. They are also more conservative because they don't contradict any laws of science. In addition, they are potentially more fruitful because they make testable predictions. Other things being equal, the simpler, the more conservative, and the more fruitful a theory, the better. So even if the big bang occurred fifteen billion years ago, we don't have to assume that it was caused by God.

Why a Universe?

God is supposedly eternal, but our universe is only fifteen billion years old. So if God existed for a long time before creating our universe, what prompted him to create it? Was he bored? Lonely? Underappreciated? Did he finally realize, after thinking about it for an infinite amount of time, that reality was not as good as it could be? What do you think?

The Teleological Argument

For many people, the most convincing evidence for the existence of God is not the existence of the universe but the structure of it. Everything in the universe seems designed for a purpose. But purposeful design can be brought about only by conscious intelligence. And who else but God could have designed the universe?

Telos is Greek for "end" or "result." Arguments such as this are known as **teleological arguments** because they attempt to derive the existence of God from the apparent design or purpose in the universe.

In all the vast and the minute, we see the un-ambiguous footsteps of the God, who gives its luster to the insect's wing and wheels his throne upon the rolling worlds.

—WILLIAM COWPER

The Analogical Design Argument

One of the most popular teleological arguments for the existence of God is based on an analogy between the universe and a machine. Cleanthes, in Hume's *Dialogues Concerning Natural Religion*, gives us one version of this argument:

> Look around the world: Contemplate the whole and every part of it: You will find it to be nothing but one great machine, subdivided into an infinite number of lesser machines, which again admit of subdivisions, to a degree beyond what human senses and faculties can trace and explain. All these various machines, and even their most minute parts, are adjusted to each other with an accuracy, which ravishes into admiration all men, who ever contemplated them. The curious adapting of means to ends, throughout all nature, resembles exactly, though it much exceeds, the production of human contrivance; of human design, thought, wisdom, and intelligence. Since therefore the effects resemble each other, we are led to infer, by all the rules of analogy, that the causes also resemble, and that the Author of nature is somewhat similar to the mind of man, though possessed of much larger faculties, proportioned to the grandeur of the work, which He has executed.[11]

Like the parts of a machine, the parts of the universe fit together to perform various functions. For example, subatomic particles fit together to form atoms, atoms fit together to form molecules, and molecules fit together to form everything else. This accurate adjustment of parts and curious adap-tation of means to ends is similar to that found in machines. But machines have a designer. So the universe probably has a designer, namely, God.

teleological argument An argument that attempts to derive the existence of God from the design or purpose of things.

According to the design argument, because the accurate adjustment of parts and curious adaptation of means to ends found in natural objects is similar to that found in objects made by humans, it is probable that natural objects were designed by an intelligent being.

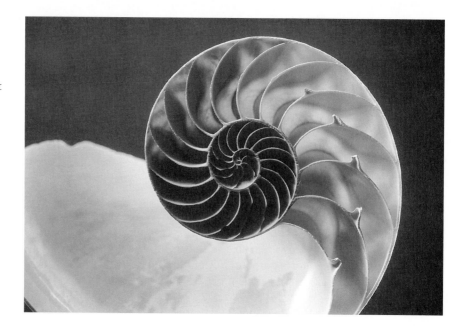

By showing that two things are similar in some respects, analogical arguments try to establish that they are similar in some further respect. For example, consider this analogical argument for the existence of life on Mars:

1. The earth has air, water, and life.
2. Mars has air and water.
3. Therefore, Mars probably has life.

The fact that Mars resembles Earth in having air and water gives us some reason to believe that it also resembles Earth in having life. But it doesn't prove that Mars has life. There are many dissimilarities between Earth and Mars. The Martian atmosphere is very thin and contains little oxygen, and the water on Mars is trapped in ice caps at the poles. The strength of an analogical argument is determined by the extent of the similarity between the objects being compared. The more dissimilarities, the less likely the conclusion.

The most famous version of the analogical design argument was penned by the English clergyman William Paley. In the following thought experiment, Paley tries to show that there is just as much reason to believe that the universe was designed as there is to believe that a watch was designed.

Thought Experiment

Paley's Watch

In crossing a heath, suppose I pitched my foot against a *stone*, and were asked how the stone came to be there, I might possibly answer that, for anything I knew to the contrary, it had lain there for ever; nor would it, perhaps, be very easy to show the absurdity of this answer. But suppose I found a *watch* upon the ground, and it should be inquired how the watch happened to be in that place, I should hardly think of the answer which I had given—that, for anything I knew, the watch might have always been there. Yet why should not this answer serve for the watch as well as for the stone? Why is it not as admissible in the second case as in the first? For this reason, and for no other; viz., that, when we come to inspect the watch, we perceive (what we could not discover in the stone) that its several parts are framed and put together for a purpose. . . .

This mechanism being observed . . . the inference, we think, is inevitable, that the watch must have had a maker; that there must have existed, at some time, and at some place or other, an artificer or artificers who formed it for the purpose which we find it actually to answer; who comprehended its construction, and designed its use. . . .

Every indication of contrivance, every manifestation of design, which existed in the watch exists in the works of nature; with the difference, on the side of nature, of being greater and more, and that in a degree which exceeds all computation.[12]

Paley claims that if he found a watch in a heath (a meadow) and observed that the parts fit together to move the hands, he would have reason to believe that it was designed by somebody. The universe seems to exhibit the same sort of purposeful arrangement of parts that the watch does. So, he concludes, there is reason to believe that it, too, was designed by somebody, namely, God.

Paley's argument is this:

1. The universe resembles a watch.
2. Every watch has a designer.
3. Therefore, the universe probably has a designer, namely, God.

If the analogy between a watch and the universe is a good one, there is reason to believe that the universe had a designer. But, from this it doesn't follow that God exists, for the designer need have none of the properties traditionally associated with God.

If the universe was designed for a purpose, there must have been some goal that the designer was trying to accomplish. But if the designer needs a universe to achieve that goal, then the designer can't be all-powerful. Any evidence for design, then, is evidence against the view that the designer is all-powerful. John Stuart Mill expresses this point as follows:

> It is not too much to say that every indication of design in the Kosmos is so much evidence against the omnipotence of the designer. For what is meant by Design? Contrivance: the adaptation of means to end. But the necessity for contrivance— the need of employing means—is a consequence of the limitation of power. Who would have recourse to means if to attain his end his mere word was sufficient?[13]

An all-powerful being should be able to achieve his goals without using any devices. If God needs a universe to accomplish his goals, there's reason to believe he can't accomplish them by himself. The existence of the universe, therefore, casts doubt on the existence of an all-powerful designer.

Designing a universe requires a certain amount of intelligence, but it doesn't require an infinite amount. As we've seen, a truly all-knowing being would not only know everything there is to know about our universe, it would also know everything there is to know about every possible universe. Our universe, however, gives us no reason to think that its designer (if it has one) has that kind of knowledge.

On the contrary, many believe that the design of our universe is so poor that there is reason to believe that its designer, if it had one, was far from perfect. Lucretius argued as much in the fourth century B.C. Clarence Darrow echoed those sentiments in the twentieth century. Darrow writes,

> Even a human being of very limited capacity could think of countless ways in which the earth could be improved as the home of man, and from the earliest time the race has been using all sorts of efforts and resources to make it more suitable for its abode. Admitting that the earth is a fit place for life, and certainly every place in the universe where life exists is fitted for life, then what sort of life was this planet designed to support? There are some millions of different species of animals on this earth, and one-half of these are insects. In numbers, and perhaps in other ways, man is in a great minority. If the land of the earth was made for life, it seems as if it was intended for insect life, which can exist almost anywhere. If no other available place can be found, they can live by the million on man, and inside of him. They generally succeed in destroying his life, and, if they have a chance, wind up by eating his body.[14]

Those who believe in God often assume that he designed the universe for our benefit. If so, His design is less than perfect. Earth is not particularly hospitable to humans. Every place on Earth is subject to natural disasters, and there are many places where humans can't live. Insects, on the other hand, seem to thrive everywhere. When the great biologist G. B. S. Haldane was asked what his study of living things revealed about God, he is reported to have said, "An inordinate fondness for beetles." Because the earth seems more suited to insects than to humans, it's doubtful that it was designed by a divine being who had our interests in mind.

Even if the world was designed for us, it need not have been designed by one person. Suppose you were walking along a river and came across a hydroelectric power plant. You would not be justified in believing that it was designed by one person because such large projects usually have many designers. In terms of scale and complexity, the universe resembles a power plant more than it does a watch. Reasoning by analogy, then, it can be claimed that the universe had many designers. Maybe the universe was designed by a committee. That would go a long way toward explaining the design flaws noted by Darrow.

An analogical argument is only as strong as the analogy upon which it's based. Although the universe resembles a machine in certain respects, it also resembles a living thing. Living things differ from machines in that they come into being through natural reproduction instead of conscious design. So if the analogy between the universe and a living thing is as good as the analogy between the universe and a machine, we are not justified in believing that the universe was the product of conscious design. Philo makes this point in Hume's *Dialogues Concerning Natural Religion*:

> If we survey the universe, so far as it falls under our knowledge, it bears a great resemblance to an animal or organized body, and seems actuated with a like principle of life and motion. A continual circulation of matter in it produces no disorder: a continual waste in every part is incessantly repaired: The closest sympathy is perceived throughout the whole system. And each part or member, in performing its proper offices, operates both to its own preservation and to that of the whole. The world, therefore, I infer, is an animal, and the Deity is the soul of the world, activating it and activated by it.[15]

Although we don't often think of the universe as a living thing, the analogy is a good one. If you could observe the universe by means of time-lapse photography, taking one picture every million years or so, what would you see? The big bang might seem like the squeezing of a puff-ball, releasing matter (spores?) into the universe. The matter congeals into stars (cells?) that transform (digest?) the matter inside of them and eject (excrete?) it by means of solar winds or stellar explosions. The stars are organized into galaxies (organs?), and these galaxies are organized into galactic clusters (bodies?). The popular version of the Gaia hypothesis proposed by James Lovelock maintains that Earth is a living organism. Maybe the universe itself is a living organism. The ancient Greek suggestion that the universe was hatched from a cosmic egg seems at least as plausible as Paley's suggestion that it was designed by a cosmic watchmaker.

The Universe should be deemed an immense being; always living.
—ALBERT PIKE

The Best-Explanation Design Argument

In addition to being construed as an analogical argument, the design argument can be construed as an inference to the best explanation. It can be argued that the existence of God provides the best explanation of the apparent design of the universe. The argument would go like this:

1. The universe exhibits apparent design.
2. The best explanation of this apparent design is that it was designed by a supernatural being.
3. Therefore it's probable that the universe was designed by a supernatural being, namely, God.

Just as the success of an analogical argument depends on the closeness of the analogy offered, so the success of an inference to the best explanation depends on the adequacy of the explanation offered. If other explanations are at least as adequate, the argument doesn't go through. Many believe that the apparent design of the universe can be explained without invoking God. It's best explained, they argue, by the theory of evolution.

Although the theory of evolution is usually associated with Charles Darwin, it was first developed in ancient Greece about twenty-five hundred years ago. A study of fossils taught Anaximander (611–547 B.C.) that life on Earth was once very different from what it is now. From this, he concluded that the environment of the early earth must also have been very different. As the environment changed, so did the creatures it supported.

Anaximander didn't explain how one life-form evolved into another. But another ancient Greek philosopher—Empedocles—did. Empedocles (ca. 495–ca. 435 B.C.) thought that, in the beginning, natural forces randomly created creatures with all sorts of mixed-up features—animals with faces and breasts on both sides, oxen with the heads of men, creatures that were half-male and half-female.[16] Most of these creatures died because their features made it difficult for them to survive and reproduce. Others thrived, however, because their features were well-suited to their environment. Those that survived would seem to have been purposefully designed for their habitats even though they were the product of chance combinations and natural selection. As Aristotle recognized, "Wherever, then, everything turned out as it would have if it were happening for a purpose, there the creatures survived, being accidentally compounded in a suitable way; but where this did not happen, the creatures perished and are perishing still, as Empedocles says of his 'man-faced ox-progeny.'"[17] Although scientists today don't accept the details of Empedocles' theory, they do recognize natural selection as one of the driving forces of evolution.

Darwin observed that more creatures are born than live long enough to reproduce, that these creatures possess different physical characteristics, and that many of those differences are inherited. He reasoned, like Empedocles, that those characteristics that improve a creature's "inclusive fitness" (ability to live long enough to reproduce) will become more prevalent in future generations. The more such characteristics a creature has, the better suited it will be to its environment. So the accurate adjustment of parts and the curious adaptation of means to ends that so impressed Cleanthes and Paley can be explained in purely natural terms. There is no need to invoke a supernatural designer.

Opponents of evolution often object that various organs or limbs couldn't have evolved gradually because a half-formed organ or limb has no survival value. "What good is half a wing?" they ask. The answer is that half a wing is better than none. Richard Dawkins explains,

> What use is half a wing? How did wings get their start? Many animals leap from bough to bough, and sometimes fall to the ground. Especially in a small animal, the whole body surface catches the air and assists the leap, or breaks the fall, by acting as a crude aerofoil. Any tendency to increase the ratio of surface area to weight would help, for example, flaps of skin growing out in the angles of joints. From here, there is a continuous series of gradations to gliding wings, and hence to flapping wings. Obviously there are distances that could not have been jumped by the earliest animals with proto-wings. Equally obviously, for any degree of smallness or crudeness of ancestral air-catching surfaces, there must be some distance, however short, which can be jumped with the flap and which cannot be jumped without the flap.[18]

What's more, creatures all along the continuum are alive today. "Contrary to the creationist literature," Dawkins asserts, "not only are animals with 'half a wing' common, so are animals with a quarter of a wing, three quarters of a wing, and so on."[19] So intermediate stages in the development of organs and limbs are not only possible, they are actual.

Intelligent Design If there were structures that were so complex that they could not possibly have evolved through natural selection, there would be reason to believe that evolution was false. Michael Behe, a Lehigh University biochemist, claims to have found such structures. He describes them this way:

> By irreducibly complex I mean a single system composed of several well-matched, interacting parts that contribute to the basic function, wherein the removal of any one of the parts causes the system to effectively cease functioning. An irreducibly complex system cannot be produced directly, (that is, by continuously improving the initial function, which continues to work by the same mechanism) by slight, successive modifications of a precursor system, because any precursor to an irreducibly complex system that is missing a part is by definition nonfunctional.[20]

Because he believes he has identified a number of such irreducibly complex systems, Behe denies that every biological system arose through natural selection.

Behe's favorite example of an irreducibly complex mechanism is a mouse trap. A mouse trap consists of five parts: (1) a wooden platform, (2) a metal hammer, (3) a spring, (4) a catch, and (5) a metal bar that holds the hammer down when the trap is set. What makes this mechanism irreducibly complex is that if any one of the parts were removed, it would no longer work. Behe claims that many biological systems like cilium, vision, and blood clotting are also irreducibly complex because each of these systems would cease to function if any of their parts were removed.

Irreducibly complex biochemical systems pose a problem for evolutionary theory because it seems that they could not have arisen through natural selection. A trait, like vision, can improve an organism's ability to survive only if it works. And it works only if all of the parts of the visual system are present. So, Behe concludes, vision couldn't have arisen through slight modifications to a previous system. It must have been created all at once by some intelligent designer.

Most biologists are unimpressed with Behe's argument, however, because they reject the notion that the parts of an irreducibly complex system could not have evolved independently of that system. As Nobel Prize–winning biologist H. J. Muller noted in 1939, a genetic sequence that is, at first, inessential to a system may later become essential to it. Biologist H. Allen Orr describes the process as follows: "Some part (A) initially does some job (and not very well, perhaps). Another part (B) later gets added because it helps A. This new part isn't essential, it merely improves things. But later on A (or something else) may change in such a way that B now becomes indispensable."[21] For example, air bladders—primitive lungs—made it possible for certain fish to acquire new sources of food. But they were not necessary to the survival of the fish. As the fish acquired additional features, however, such as legs and arms, lungs became essential. So contrary to what Behe would have us believe, the parts of an irreducibly complex system need not have come into existence all at once.

Science has proof without any certainty. Creationists have certainty without any proof.
—ASHLEY MONTAGUE

We are the products of editing rather than authorship.
—GEORGE WALD

THE MIRACULOUS
OCCURRENCE.
Does appealing to the
supernatural improve
our understanding of
a situation, or does it
simply mask the fact
that we do not yet
understand?

"I THINK YOU SHOULD BE MORE
EXPLICIT HERE IN STEP TWO."

*A Miracle: An event de-
scribed by those to whom
it was told by men who
did not see it.*

—ELBERT HUBBARD

In fact, we know that some of the parts of the systems Behe describes are found in other systems. Thrombin, for example, is essential for blood clotting, but it also aids in cell division and is related to the digestive enzyme trypsin. Because the same protein can play different roles in different systems, the fact that it is part of an irreducibly complex system doesn't indicate that it couldn't have arisen through natural selection. Biologists do not know how all of the parts of every irreducibly complex biochemical system came into being, and they may never know because there is no fossil record indicating how these systems evolved over time. Nevertheless, biologists do know that it is not, in principle, impossible for irreducibly complex systems to arise through natural selection.

What's more, complexity theory has shown that biochemical systems can be self-organizing; that is, they can acquire their structure without input from outside the system. One such self-organizing system is the Belousov-Zhabotinsky (BZ) reaction, which involves a cyclic sequence of chemical re-actions. If any one of the reactions is disrupted, the cycle is broken. Thus the reaction is irreducibly complex in Behe's sense. Nevertheless, it arises natu-rally, without any outside interference. After explaining the BZ reaction in some detail, Niall Shanks and Karl Joplin conclude that "complexity theory predicts, and experiments confirm, that Behe's irreducibly complex systems can result from the dynamical phenomena of self-organization. Self-organization, resulting in what Kauffman terms 'order for free,' can be exploited with advantage by evolving biological systems."[22] Because there are many ways in which irreducibly complex systems can arise naturally, there is no need to invoke a supernatural designer.

Creationists sometimes cite the absence of certain evidence in an attempt to discredit evolution. But often the evidence they claim is lacking is present in abundance. Consider, for example, the claim that there are no transitional fossils. If one species evolved into another, they argue, there should be fossil remains of intermediate or transitional organisms. But the fossil record contains gaps where the intermediate organisms should be. So, they conclude, evolution did not occur. Given the nature of the fossilization process, however, gaps are to be expected. Very few of the organisms that come into being ever get fossilized. Nevertheless, biologists have discovered thousands of transitional fossils. The transitions from primitive fish to bony fish, from fish to amphibian, from amphibian to reptile, from reptile to bird, from reptile to mammal, from land animal to early whale, and from early ape to human are particularly well documented.[23] In addition, there is a detailed record of the diversification of mammals into rodents, bats, rabbits, carnivores, horses, elephants, manatee, deer, cows, and many others. As the late Harvard biologist Stephen J. Gould reported, "[P]aleontologists have discovered several superb examples of intermediary forms and sequences, more than enough to convince any fair-minded skeptic about the reality of life's physical genealogy."[24]

Creationists also erroneously claim that no one has ever observed evolution. Biological evolution, in its broadest sense, is simply change in the genetic makeup of a group of organisms over time. This sort of change has been observed many times over. Insects that have developed a resistance to pesticides or bacteria that have developed a resistance to antibiotics are just two examples of biological evolution familiar to us all. These instances of biological evolution do not impress creationists because they are examples of what they call "micro-evolution"—genetic changes within a particular species. What creationists say has never been observed is "macro-evolution"—genetic changes from one species to another. But, in fact, this too has been observed. Eight new species of fruit flies have been observed in the laboratory as well as six new species of other insects. A new species of mouse arose on the Faeroe Islands in the last two hundred fifty years, and scientists have recently recorded a new species of marine worm. The origin of over a dozen new species of plants has been observed in the last fifty years.[25] So it is simply inaccurate to claim that either micro- or macro-evolution has never been observed.

Fine-Tuning Another aspect of the universe that many people believe lends credibility to the notion that the universe was designed is the remarkable fine-tuning of many of its physical properties. If certain forces were stronger or weaker than they are, or if any subatomic particles had more or less mass than they do, atoms and molecules wouldn't be able to form, and we wouldn't exist. The laws that govern the universe seem tailor-made for us. As physicist Paul Davies reveals, "It seems as though someone has fine-tuned nature's

To surrender to ignorance and call it God has always been premature, and it remains premature today.

—ISAAC ASIMOV

Extraterrestrial Design

When Michael Behe gives lectures on intelligent design theory, he often opens the floor to questions. During one of those question-and-answer sessions, he was asked, "Could the designer be an alien from outer space?" to which he answered, "Yes." The intelligent design theory itself tells us nothing about the nature of the designer. So it's entirely possible for the designer to be an extraterrestrial.

Remarkably enough, this is the basic premise on which the religion known as "Raelianism" is founded. Raelianism is the brainchild of the French journalist Claude Vorilhon. He was moved to create this religion after he was contacted by an extraterrestrial while walking along the rim of the extinct Puy de Lassolas volcano in central France. The extraterrestrial told him that all life on Earth was created by aliens from outer space using advanced genetic engineering technology. Here is a summary of the Raelian story from their Web site:

On the 13th of December 1973, French journalist Rael was contacted by a visitor from another planet, and asked to establish an Embassy to welcome these people back to Earth.

The extra-terrestrial was about four feet in height, had long dark hair, almond shaped eyes, olive skin and exuded harmony and humour. He told Rael that:

"we were the ones who made all life on earth"

"you mistook us for gods"

"we were at the origin of your main religions"

"Now that you are mature enough to understand this, we would like to enter official contact through an embassy"

The messages dictated to Rael explain how life on Earth is not the result of random evolution, nor the work of a supernatural 'God'. It is a deliberate creation, using DNA, by a scientifically advanced people who made human beings literally "in their image" what one can call "scientific creationism". References to these scientists and their work, as well as to their symbol of infinity can be found in the ancient texts of many cultures. For example, in Genesis, the biblical account of creation, the word "Elohim" has been mistranslated as "God" in the singular, but it is a plural, which means *those who came from the sky*.

Leaving our humanity to progress by itself, the Elohim nevertheless maintained contact with us via prophets including Buddha, Moses, Jesus and Mohammed, all specially chosen and educated by them. The role of the prophets was to progressively educate humanity through the messages they taught, each time adapted to the culture and level of understanding at the time. They were also to leave traces of the Elohim so that we would be able to recognize them as our creators and fellow human beings when we had advanced enough scientifically to understand them.[26]

Thought Probe

Intelligent Design

Suppose that life on Earth is the result of intelligent design. Which hypothesis—the God hypothesis or the extraterrestrial hypothesis—is the better explanation? Which hypothesis does better with respect to the criteria of adequacy?

---

numbers to make a universe. . . . The impression of design is overwhelming."[27] But appearances can be deceiving.

The fine-tuning of the universe is something that needs to be explained only if it's possible for the universe to be tuned differently than it is. A number of physicists, however, believe that the laws of physics could not be any different than they are. Einstein used to wonder how much choice God had in constructing the universe. Physicist Stephen Hawking believes that God had very little choice. In his best-seller *A Brief History of Time* Hawking writes, "There may well be only one, or a small number, of complete unified theories . . . that are self-consistent and allow the existence of structures as complicated as human beings who can investigate the laws of the universe and ask about the nature of God."[28] Philosopher Baruch Spinoza held a similar view. He thought that there was only one possible universe. If so, the fact that the universe is so well suited to us needs no explanation. It couldn't be any other way.

Alternatively, it's possible that the laws of nature are the result of natural selection. We have seen that black holes may give birth to other universes. Any universe that can form black holes, then, can reproduce. In biology, if we ask why a particular species has a certain trait, the answer we get is that having that trait makes it more likely for members of the species to live long enough to reproduce. Why do humans have an opposable thumb? Because having one makes it possible to make tools, and creatures who make tools are more likely to live long enough to reproduce. Lee Smolin suggests that this sort of reasoning can be applied to universes. Why does the universe have the specific natural laws that it does? Because having them makes the formation of black holes possible, and universes that exist long enough to make black holes are more likely to reproduce.

Here's how Smolin puts it:

> Any universe in the collection, no matter what its own parameters are, is likely to spawn in time a vast family of descendants that after a while are dominated by those whose parameters are the most fit for producing black holes. . . . *After a sufficient time, it is probable that a universe chosen at random from the collection has parameters that are near a peak of the production of black holes.*
>
> It is exactly because of this that this theory, based on a collection of unobservable universes, can have explanatory power. We need only make one additional hypothesis, which is that *our universe is a typical member of the collection.* Then we can conclude that the parameters that govern our universe must also have parameters that are close to one of the peaks of the production of black holes.[29]

Just as the features of an organism can be explained by appeal to natural selection, so can the features of the universe. As a result, there is no need to invoke God to explain the fine-tuning of the universe.

Evolutionary theories are simpler than creationist theories (theories that claim that the universe was designed and created by a supernatural being) because they can account for the apparent design of living things without postulating a supernatural being. They are also more conservative than creationist theories because they fit better with the findings of various sciences. As Isaac Asimov relates, "Creationism cannot be adopted without discarding all of modern biology, biochemistry, geology, astronomy — in short without discarding all of science."[30]

Evolutionary theories also have greater scope than creationist theories because they can explain how different species arose. Creationists, such as Duane Gish of the Institute for Creation Research, admit that they cannot do this:

> We do not know how the Creator created, what processes He used, for He used processes which are not now operating anywhere in the natural universe. This is why we refer to creation as special creation. We cannot discover by scientific investigation anything about the creative processes used by the Creator.[31]

Nothing in biology makes sense except in the light of evolution.

— THEODOSIUS DOBZHANSKY

But if creationists can't tell us how the creator created, they can't explain creation. It's impossible to explain the unknown in terms of the incomprehensible. As Plato realized, to say that 'God did it' is not to give a reason but to give an excuse for not having a reason.[32]

Evolutionary theories are also more fruitful than creationist theories because they have successfully predicted a number of new facts; creationist theories have predicted none. Evolutionary theories, for example, predicted that the chromosomes and proteins of related species would be similar, that mutations would occur, and that organisms would adapt to changing environments. All of these predictions have been verified. Creationist theories have no predictive successes. Because evolutionary theories meet the criteria of adequacy better than creationist theories, they are better theories.

Thought Probe

Human Design Flaws

Bertrand Russell once said, "If I were granted omnipotence, and millions of years to experiment in, I should not think man much to boast of as the final result of all my efforts."[33] Biologists S. Jay Olshansky, Bruce A. Carnes, and

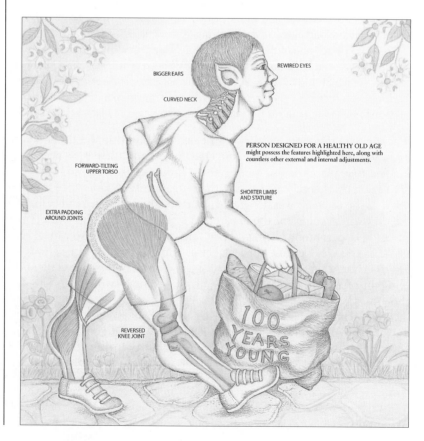

PERSON DESIGNED FOR A HEALTHY OLD AGE might possess the features highlighted here, along with countless other external and internal adjustments.

BIGGER EARS

REWIRED EYES

CURVED NECK

FORWARD-TILTING UPPER TORSO

EXTRA PADDING AROUND JOINTS

SHORTER LIMBS AND STATURE

REVERSED KNEE JOINT

100 YEARS YOUNG

Robert N. Butler agree with Russell that our design leaves much to be desired. The best explanation of our design flaws, they claim, is that human beings were the product of natural selection.

> Bulging disks, fragile bones, fractured hips, torn ligaments, varicose veins, cataracts, hearing loss, hernias and hemorrhoids: the list of bodily malfunctions that plague us as we age is long and all too familiar. Why do we fall apart just as we reach what should be the prime of life? . . .
>
> In evolutionary terms, we harbor flaws because natural selection, the force that molds our genetically controlled traits, does not aim for perfection or endless good health. If a body plan allows individuals to survive long enough to reproduce (and, in humans and various other organisms, to raise their young), then that plan will be selected. . . . More important, anatomical and physiological quirks that become disabling only after someone has reproduced will spread. For example, if a body plan leads to total collapse at age 50 but does not interfere with earlier reproduction, the arrangement will get passed along despite the harmful consequences late in life."[34]

The foregoing figure shows one way of improving our design. Do our design flaws provide evidence against intelligent design?

The Argument from Miracles

The existence of miracles is thought by many to be a compelling reason for believing in God. The sacred texts of many religions are filled with accounts of wondrous events. The Bible, for example, tells us of a stick turning into a snake, of the Red Sea being parted, and of the sun standing still. These events seem to have no natural explanation. This has led many to accept a supernatural explanation of them.

A miracle is something more than an unusual or a surprising event. An eclipse of the sun is unusual, but it is not miraculous. Winning a lottery is surprising, but it does not call for a supernatural explanation. Only a violation of natural law would do that. Thus a **miracle** can be defined as a violation of natural law by a supernatural being.

The argument from miracles can be formulated this way:

1. There are events that seem to be miracles.

2. The best explanation of these events is that they were performed by a miracle worker.

3. Therefore, there probably is a miracle worker, namely, God.

Although the existence of miracles does imply a miracle worker, it doesn't imply the existence of God. For a miracle worker, like a cosmic creator or designer, need not be all-powerful, all-knowing, or all-good. Many theists, for example, believe that the Devil can perform miracles because he, too, can violate natural law. But the Devil is not all-powerful, all-knowing, or all-good. So, even if there is a miracle worker, the miracle worker need not be God.

The Christian religion not only was at first attended with miracles, but even at this day cannot be believed by any reasonable person without one.
—DAVID HUME

miracle A violation of natural law by a supernatural being.

Nature never breaks her own laws.

—LEONARDO DA VINCI

Some argue that, far from proving God's existence, miracles disprove it. Miracles are violations of natural law. Why, they ask, would God break his own laws? To rectify a mistake he had made? To deal with a situation he hadn't foreseen? Accepting either alternative requires rejecting God's omnipotence or omniscience. A perfect being wouldn't have to tinker with his creation. He would get it right the first time. Thus any evidence for miracles is evidence against the existence of God.

Moreover, many believe that the sorts of miracles attributed to God could not possibly be the work of an all-powerful, all-knowing, all-good being. One of the most famous recent alleged miracles occurred in Fatima, Portugal, in 1917. There, three peasant girls were allegedly visited by the mother of Jesus, given some prophecies, and told to pray. During Mary's last visit, the sun is said to have miraculously danced in the sky, thus confirming the girls' story. Images of Jesus and Mary appear in everything from tortillas to billboards, and the faithful flock to them by the thousands. But the question arises, What's the point? Is God trying to tell us something? If so, why appear only to children and peasants who are unlikely to be believed? Why not make an announcement at the United Nations or on national TV? If God wants to convince us that a message came from him, why resort to local pyrotechnics? It may have seemed to the people in Fatima that the sun danced, but we know that it didn't because no observatory reported it. If God really wanted to get our attention, he could have made the sun actually dance. No one could have ignored such a feat. Why didn't he do that?

A reported event counts as a miracle only if (1) the reported event actually occurred and (2) the event violates a law of nature. Hume argues that we can never be justified in believing either of these things. Consequently, we can never legitimately claim that a miracle occurred.

Many reports of miracles date from ancient times and come from sources of dubious credibility. Such anecdotal evidence is not sufficient to establish the existence of miracles. "There is not to be found in all history," Hume says, "any miracle attested by a sufficient number of men, of such unquestioned good sense, education, and learning as to secure us against all delusion in themselves; of such undoubted integrity, as to place them beyond all suspicion of any design to deceive others."[36] Those who report miracles typically are not trained observers. Often they have a great desire to believe in miracles or something to gain by getting others to believe in them. In either case, their testimony is not to be trusted.

But suppose that a number of people of unquestioned good sense, education, and learning did report a miraculous event. Even then, we would not be justified in believing that a miracle had occurred because the evidence for a miracle can never outweigh the evidence for the natural law it supposedly violates. Hume puts it this way:

> Nothing is esteemed a miracle if it ever happens in the common course of nature. There must, therefore, be a uniform experience against every miraculous event, otherwise that event would not merit the appellation. And as a uniform experience amounts to a proof, there is here a direct and full proof, from the nature of the fact, against the existence of miracles.[37]

Deciding between competing claims requires weighing the evidence in favor of each. But the evidence in favor of a miracle can never outweigh the evidence in favor of a natural law. All past experience will be on the side of the natural law. So the scale can never tip in favor of the miracle.

Weighing evidence, for Hume, is a matter of counting experiments. In his *Enquiries Concerning the Human Understanding*, he tells us that to decide between competing claims, "we must balance the opposite experiments, where they are opposite, and deduct the smaller number from the greater, in order to know the exact force of the superior evidence."[38] This approach to evaluating claims assumes that every experiment carries the same weight. But that is not the case. Some are more carefully controlled than others and thus deserve to be weighted more heavily. Any evaluation of competing claims must take into account both the quality and the quantity of the evidence available.

Contrary to what Hume would have us believe, the results of one experiment, done under properly controlled conditions, can outweigh the results of any number of other experiments. For example, it was long believed that the principle of the conservation of matter was a law of nature. Einstein suggested that this principle was mistaken. His famous equation—$E = mc^2$—predicts that matter can be converted into energy, and thus that the total amount of matter in the universe can be altered. The explosion of the first atomic bomb provided ample proof of Einstein's theory. So one event can provide sufficient grounds for rejecting what has long been considered to be a law of nature.

No event, however, can provide sufficient grounds for believing that a miracle has occurred because its seeming impossibility may simply be due to our ignorance of the operative laws. St. Augustine concurs: "A miracle is not

The happy do not believe in miracles.

—GOETHE

If God did a miracle, He would deny His own nature and the universe would simply blow up, vanish, become nothing.

—JOYCE CARY

contrary to nature but contrary to our knowledge of nature."[39] Something may seem impossible to us because we are unaware of the laws governing it. For example, in the eighteenth century, the scientific community dismissed reports of meteorites on the grounds that they violated natural law. The great chemist Lavoisier, for example, argued that stones couldn't fall from the sky because there were none up there. Even Thomas Jefferson, after reading a report by two Harvard professors claiming to have observed meteorites, remarked, "I could more easily believe that two Yankee professors would lie than that stones would fall down from heaven."[40] Meteorites seemed impossible to Lavoisier and Jefferson because they were unaware of the laws governing heavenly bodies. Now that we know those laws, we no longer consider meteorites to be impossible.

We would be justified in believing that an apparent violation of a natural law was a miracle only if we were justified in believing that no natural law would ever be discovered to explain the occurrence. But we can never be justified in believing that, because no one can be sure what the future will bring. We can't rule out the possibility that a natural explanation will be found for an event, no matter how incredible. The recent discovery of a natural explanation for the "miracle" of the parting of the Red Sea illustrates this point nicely. (See the box "Parting the Red Sea.") When we are faced with an inexplicable event, it is always more rational to look for a natural cause than to attribute the event to something supernatural. Appealing to the supernatural does not increase our understanding. It simply masks the fact that we do not yet understand.

What's more, any supposed miracle could be the result of a superadvanced technology rather than a supernatural being. Arthur C. Clarke once said that any sufficiently advanced technology is indistinguishable from magic. So the seemingly inexplicable events that many attribute to God could simply be the work of advanced aliens. Erich von Däniken argues as much in his book *Chariots of the Gods,* where he claims that the wheel that Ezekiel saw in the sky was really a UFO. Explanations that appeal to advanced aliens are actually superior to explanations that appeal to supernatural beings because they are simpler and more conservative: they do not postulate any nonphysical substances, and they do not violate any natural laws. (Of course, they are not as good as explanations that don't appeal to aliens.) Nevertheless, apparent miracles don't provide evidence for the existence of God because they can be explained just as well on other hypotheses.

> *All the Biblical miracles will at last disappear with the progress of science.*
>
> —MATTHEW ARNOLD

Thought Probe

The Fivefold Challenge

According to Robby Berry, "there are five major miraculous events in the Bible which are completely unconfirmed by modern archaeology: These miracles are: (1) the parting of the sea by Moses (Exodus 14: 21–31); (2) the stopping of the sun by Joshua (Joshua 10: 12–14); (3) the reversal of the sun's course by Isaiah

Was Jesus a Magician?

Psychologist Nicholas Humphrey reports that Jesus's "miracles" were similar to tricks being performed by the magicians of his time:

> Many scholars have noted (to their dismay or glee, depending on which side they were taking) that Jesus' miracles were in fact entirely typical of the tradition of performance magic that flourished around the Mediterranean at that time. Lucian, a Roman born in Syria, writing in the second century A.D., catalogued the range of phenomena that the 'charlatans' and 'tricksters' could lay on. They included walking on water, materialisation and dematerialisation, clairvoyance, expulsion of demons, and prophecy. And he went on to explain how many of these feats were achieved by normal means. Hippolytus, too, exposed several pseudo miracle workers who had powers uncannily similar to those of Jesus, including a certain Marcus who had mastered the art of turning the water in a cup red by mixing liquid from another cup while the onlookers' attention was distracted.
>
> So close were the similarities between Jesus' works and those of common, lower-class magicians, that several Jewish and pagan commentators at the time simply took it for granted that there was little except style and zeal to distinguish Jesus from the others. In their view, while Jesus might have been an especially classy conjuror, he was certainly not in an altogether separate class.
>
> Celsus claimed that Jesus had picked up the art during his youth in Egypt, where the Samarian magicians were the acknowledged masters. Having listed the tricks of the Samarians, such as expelling diseases, calling up spirits of the dead, producing banquets out of thin air, and making inanimate objects come to life, Celsus (according to the Christian writer Origen) went on to say: 'Then, since these fellows do these things, will you ask us to think them sons of God? Should it not rather be said that these are the doings of scoundrels?'
>
> Christian apologists were, early on, only too well aware of how their Messiah's demonstrations must have looked to outsiders. They tried to play down the alarming parallels. There is even some reason to think that the Gospels themselves were subjected to editing and censure so as to exclude some of Jesus' more obvious feats of conjuration and to delete references to the possible Egyptian connection. . . .
>
> The somewhat lame solution, adopted by Origen and others, was to admit that the miracles would indeed have been fraudulent if done by anybody else, simply to make money, but not when done by Jesus to inspire religious awe. 'The things told of Jesus would be similar if Celsus had shown that Jesus did them as the magicians do, merely for the sake of showing off. But as things are, none of the magicians, by the things he does, calls the spectators to moral reformation, or teaches the fear of God to those astounded by the show.'[41]

Thought Probe

Jesus's Miracles

Is Origen's solution a good one? Is it plausible to say that if Jesus's feats were performed by anyone else, they would just be tricks but that because they were performed by Jesus, they were miracles? Why or why not?

(Isaiah 38: 7–8); (4) the feeding of thousands of people by Jesus using only five loaves of bread and two fishes (Mark 6: 34–44); and (5) the resurrection of the saints, and their subsequent appearance to many (Matthew 27: 52–53)."[42] These miracles were supposedly witnessed by thousands of people but there is no archaeological evidence to back them up. Berry believes that this is good reason to believe that these miracles never occurred. Do you agree? Why or why not? (Berry is offering a reward to anyone who can provide reliable non-biblical evidence that any of these events occurred: He will read three books of that person's choice or attend a church of the denomination of that person's choice for three months.)

The Argument from Religious Experience

Much of our knowledge of the world comes from sense experience. But sense experience is not the only kind of experience we can have. Some people also have religious experience. Just as sense experience can give us knowledge of natural things, some people claim that religious experience can give us knowledge of supernatural things.

Religious experience comes in many varieties, from a feeling of peace and well-being to a direct personal experience of God. Because our concern here is whether God exists, we will focus on those experiences that people take to be experiences of God.

St. John describes such an experience:

The end I have in view is the divine Embracing, the union of the soul with the divine Substance. In this loving, obscure knowledge God unites Himself with the soul eminently and divinely. This knowledge consists in a certain contact of the soul with the Divinity, and it is God Himself Who is then felt and tasted, though not manifestly and distinctly, as it will be in glory. But this touch of knowledge and of sweetness is so deep and so profound that it penetrates into the inmost substance of the soul.[43]

There is no doubt that St. John took his experience to be an experience of God. But the fact that he took it to be an experience of God doesn't mean that it was an experience of God. For we can be mistaken about what we experience, as Descartes illustrated. What seems to be a cat lying in the yard can turn out to be an old shoe. We are justified in believing that what we seem to experience actually exists only if the hypothesis that it exists provides the best explanation of our experience. So we are justified in believing that we have experienced God only if the hypothesis that God exists provides the best explanation of our experience.

The argument from religious experience, then, can be put this way:

1. People have experiences that seem to be of God.
2. The best explanation of these experiences is that they are of God.
3. Therefore, it is probable that God exists.

The crucial claim here is premise 2. In order to determine whether the God hypothesis is best, we have to compare it with competing hypotheses.

The main competitor to the God hypothesis is the hallucination hypothesis, which says that religious experiences are caused by abnormal conditions of the body. Bertrand Russell was a proponent of the hallucination hypothesis. He writes,

This Is Your Brain on God

Michael Persinger, a neurophysiologist at Laurentian University in Sudbury, Ontario, believes that religious experience is the result of a particular type of electrical activity in the brain. To test his hypothesis, he has developed a helmet lined with magnets that uses electromagnetic radiation to create various brain wave patterns. Journalist Jack Hitt reports on his experiences in Persinger's lab:

[Persinger's] theory is that the sensation described as "having a religious experience" is merely a side effect of our bicameral brain's feverish activities. Simplified considerably, the idea goes like so: when the right hemisphere of the brain, the seat of emotion, is stimulated in the cerebral region presumed to control notions of self, and then the left hemisphere, the seat of language, is called upon to make sense of this nonexistent entity, the mind generates a "sensed presence." . . .

It may seem sacrilegious and presumptuous to reduce God to a few ornery synapses, but modern neuroscience isn't shy about defining our most sacred notions — love, joy, altruism, pity — as nothing more than static from our impressively large cerebrums. Persinger goes one step further. His work practically constitutes a Grand Unified Theory of the Otherworldly: He believes cerebral fritzing is responsible for almost anything one might describe as paranormal — aliens, heavenly apparitions, past-life sensations, near-death experiences, awareness of the soul, you name it. . . .

Using his fixed wavelength patterns of electromagnetic fields, Persinger aims to inspire a feeling of a sensed presence — he claims he can also zap you with euphoria, anxiety, fear, even sexual stirring. Each of these electromagnetic patterns is represented by columns of numbers — thousands of them, ranging from 0 to 255 — that denote the increments of output for the computer generating the EM [electromagnetic] bursts. . . .

Persinger envisions a series of EM patterns that work the way drugs do. Just as you take an antibiotic and it has a predictable result, you might be exposed to precise EM patterns that would signal the brain to carry out comparable effects.

Another possible application: Hollywood. Persinger has talked to Douglas Trumbull, the special-effects wizard responsible for the look of everything from *2001: A Space Odyssey* to *Brainstorm*. They discussed the technological possibility of marrying Persinger's helmet with virtual reality. "If you've done virtual reality," Persinger says, "then you know that once you put on the helmet, you always know you are inside the helmet. The idea is to create a form of entertainment that is more real." But he adds, sounding like so many people who've gotten a call from the coast, "we haven't cut a deal yet."[45]

Thought Probe

Religious Experience

Does the fact that religious experiences can be produced electronically undercut the claim that they are produced by a supernatural being? Why or why not?

From a scientific point of view, we can make no distinction between the man who eats little and sees heaven and the man who drinks much and sees snakes. Each is in an abnormal physical condition, and therefore has abnormal perception.[44]

Russell claims that the cause of religious experiences is internal rather than external. As a result, such experiences provide no evidence for the existence of God.

If you talk to God, you are praying; if God talks to you, you have schizophrenia.

— THOMAS SZASZ

Although religious experiences can happen spontaneously, those who claim to have seen God have often led lives of extreme self-denial and self-discipline. They have renounced worldly goods, repressed their physical desires, and rejected normal human companionship. They have filled their lives with prayers, devotions, and rituals. Psychologists now know that this sort of ascetic lifestyle can have the same effect on the brain as hallucinogenic drugs.[46]

What's more, studies have shown that descriptions of religious experiences are indistinguishable from descriptions of drug experiences. On Good Friday, 1962, Walter Pahnke, a Harvard Divinity School student, gave psilocybin (a drug whose effects are similar to those of LSD) to half of a group of thirty students at Harvard's Marsh Chapel. (The other half were given a placebo.) After listening to the Good Friday sermon, the group listened to organ music and recorded their experiences. Nine members of the group reported having a genuine religious experience. To evaluate their claims, Pahnke had three women, trained to identify descriptions of religious experiences, read their reports. The women found that the subjects' reports had all the earmarks of a genuine religious experience. Pahnke concluded, "Those subjects who received psilocybin experienced phenomena which were indistinguishable from if not identical with . . . the categories defined by our typology of mysticism."[47]

The fact that religious experiences are often produced by abnormal physiological conditions does not, by itself, show that they are untrue. Every experience we have is affected by the condition of our body. Maybe certain physiological conditions are conducive to discovering certain types of truths. C. D. Broad explains,

> Suppose, for the sake of argument, that there is an aspect of the world which remains altogether outside the ken of ordinary persons in their daily life. Then it seems very likely that some degree of mental and physical abnormality would be a necessary condition for getting loosened from the objects of ordinary sense perception to come into contact with this aspect of reality. One might have to be slightly "cracked" in order to have some peep-holes into the super-sensible world.[48]

What we experience is determined by the state of our body at the time of the experience. To experience God, maybe we have to be in an abnormal state. As Broad suggests, maybe we have to be "cracked" to see through the cracks of our ordinary experience.

We can't discount religious experiences simply because they occur under abnormal conditions. Neither can we accept them at face value simply because they seem so real. To be considered true, they must pass the same sorts of tests that ordinary experiences do.

One test of the truth of an experience is agreement among those who've had the experience. If there is widespread agreement, there is reason to believe that those who had the experience actually experienced what they thought they did. In the case of religious experience, however, there is very little agreement about what is experienced. According to theologian John Hick, "As we listen to the world-wide company of those who have spoken about the divine reality out of direct personal experience, we find that they have conceptualized their experiences in many different and often incompatible ways, each in accordance with his own environing traditions and culture."[49] For example, Christian mystics tend to experience a personal God (Jehovah), whereas Hindu mystics tend to experience a nonpersonal god (Brahman). But the supreme being cannot be both personal and nonpersonal. So both of these experiences cannot be true. Unless some way of resolving this disagreement is found, there is little reason to believe that either of these experiences is true.

Disagreements about what has been experienced are usually resolved by gathering more information. Suppose that someone claims that the fruit in a bowl is real; someone else claims that it is plastic. To determine who is right, we would touch, smell, and perhaps taste the objects in the bowl. If they felt, smelled, and tasted like real fruit, we would be justified in believing that they are real. Disagreements about religious experience cannot be resolved in this way, however, because God cannot be sensed. There is no way to tell whether a religious experience was caused by God. But without a method for distinguishing real religious experiences from fake ones, we are not justified in believing any of them to be real.

The Ontological Argument

The arguments we have canvassed so far attempt to prove the existence of God by appealing to some fact about the world. The **ontological argument,** however, attempts to prove the existence of God by appealing to nothing more than the concept of God itself. A proper understanding of the concept of God, it is claimed, will reveal that there must be something that falls under that concept.

Everything actual must have first been possible, before having actual existence.

—ALBERT PIKE

Anselm's Ontological Argument

The first to propose such an argument was St. Anselm (A.D. 1033?–1109), who conceived of God as the greatest possible being (a being "than which none greater can be conceived"). Such a being must exist, Anselm claims, because if he didn't, it would be possible for there to be a greater being. He writes,

> And whatever is understood exists in the understanding. And assuredly that than which nothing greater can be conceived cannot exist in the understanding alone. For, suppose it exists in the understanding alone: then it can be conceived to exist in reality; which is greater.
>
> Therefore; if that than which nothing greater can be conceived exists in the understanding alone, the very being, than which none greater can be conceived is one, than which a greater can be conceived. But, obviously, this is impossible. Hence, there is no doubt that there exists a being than which nothing greater can be conceived.[50]

A being that exists "in the understanding alone" is a being that exists only in our minds. But a being that exists in reality is greater than a being that exists only in our minds. So if God existed only in our minds, it would be

ontological argument An argument from the nature of God to the existence of God.

possible for there to be a being greater than God, namely, a being like God that exists in reality. But it's not possible for there to be a being greater than God. So God must exist in reality.

More formally, the argument looks like this:

1. God, by definition, is the greatest being possible.
2. If God exists only in our minds, then it is possible for there to be a being greater than God, namely, a being like God that exists in reality.
3. But it is not possible for there to be a being greater than God.
4. Therefore God must exist in reality.

Although this argument is valid, most people find it unconvincing. They realize that you can't define something into existence.

A contemporary of Anselm, Gaunilo, shared that belief. He used a thought experiment to show that if Anselm's style of reasoning were correct, you could prove that the greatest island possible exists.

Thought Experiment

Gaunilo's Lost Island

Consider this example: Certain people say that somewhere in the ocean there is an island, which they call the "Lost Island" because of the difficulty or, rather, the impossibility of finding what does not exist. They say that it is more abundantly filled with inestimable riches and delights than the Isles of the Blessed, and that although it has no owner or inhabitant, it excels all the lands that men inhabit taken together in the unceasing abundance of its fertility.

When someone tells me that there is such an island, I easily understand what is being said, for there is nothing difficult here. Suppose, however, as a consequence of this, that he then goes on to say: You cannot doubt that this island, more excellent than all lands, actually exists somewhere in reality, because it undoubtedly stands in relation to your understanding. Since it is more excellent not simply to stand in relation to the understanding, but to be in reality as well, therefore this island must necessarily be in reality. Otherwise, any other land that exists in reality would be more excellent than this island, and this island which you understand to be the most excellent of all lands would then not be the most excellent.[51]

The greatest island possible would have the ideal climate, the broadest array of natural resources, the greatest number of trees per acre, and the like. Gaunilo points out that by Anselm's lights, if it didn't exist, then it wouldn't be the greatest island possible. So, by parity of reasoning, it would seem that the greatest island possible must exist.

Anselm was aware of Gaunilo's objection and tried to counter it by claiming that his argument applied only to the greatest being possible, not to particular kinds of beings. But if existence is intrinsic to God because it makes him better, it's hard to see why it couldn't be intrinsic to other things as well. It could be argued, for example, that the most evil being possible must exist because if it didn't, it wouldn't be the most evil being possible. This is obviously absurd. What has gone wrong?

The problem lies with Anselm's understanding of the phrase "exists only in the understanding." Apparently Anselm believed that to say that God exists only in the understanding is to say that there is something in our minds that is like God in all respects except that it doesn't exist in reality. That is indeed impossible. But that is not a plausible interpretation of the phrase "exists only in the understanding." To say that something, x, exists only in the understanding (mind) is to say that the concept of x doesn't apply to anything in reality. For example, to say that centaurs exist only in the mind is to say that the concept of centaurs doesn't apply to anything in reality. Similarly, to say that God exists only in the mind is to say the concept of God doesn't apply to anything in reality, and that is not self-contradictory. There is no contradiction involved in saying that the concept of the greatest being possible is not exemplified. So the ontological argument does not succeed in showing that God must exist by definition.

Descartes' Ontological Argument

Descartes also offered an ontological argument. He defined God as the most perfect being possible instead of the greatest being possible. The most perfect being possible possesses all possible perfections. Because existence is a perfection (it's better to exist than not to exist), God exists. Here's how Descartes puts it:

> Whenever I choose to think of the First and Supreme Being and as it were bring out the idea of him from the treasury of my mind, I must necessarily ascribe to him all perfections, even if I do not at the moment enumerate them all, or attend to each. This necessity clearly ensures that when later on I observe that existence is a perfection, I am justified in concluding that the First and Supreme Being exists.[52]

Descartes' argument can be put this way:

1. God, by definition, possesses all possible perfections.
2. Existence is a perfection.
3. Therefore, God exists.

This argument assumes that there can be a supremely perfect being and that existence can be a defining property. Both assumptions have been questioned.

Kant argues that existence can't be a defining property because it adds nothing to our concept of a thing. We don't know anything more about the nature of a thing when we are told that it exists. Paul Edwards elucidates Kant's point by means of the following thought experiment.

Edwards's Gangle

Suppose I am an explorer and claim to have discovered a new species of animal which I call "gangle." I have been asked to explain what I mean by calling an animal a "gangle" and I have given this answer: "By a gangle I mean a mammal with eleven noses, seven blue eyes, bristly hair, sharp teeth and wheels in the place of feet." Let us now contrast two supplementary remarks I might make. The first time I add "furthermore a gangle has three long tails." The second time I add "furthermore, let me insist that gangles exist." It is evident that these are two radically different additions. In the first case I was adding to the definition of "gangle"; I was enlarging the concept; I was mentioning a further property which a thing must possess before I would call it a "gangle." The second time I was doing something quite different. I was not enlarging the concept of gangle, I was saying that there is something to which the concept applies, that the combination of characteristics or qualities *previously* mentioned belong to something.[53]

To be told that a thing exists is not to be given any information about the type of thing it is. It is merely to be apprised of the fact that there are things of that type. Consequently, existence can't be a defining property.

Even if existence could be a defining property, there would be some question as to whether it is a perfection. A perfection always makes something better. But it is doubtful that it's always better to exist than to not exist. Consider someone who is terminally ill and suffering intense, untreatable pain. In such a situation, nonexistence might be a blessing.

And, further still, whether or not existence is a perfection, there is reason to doubt that something could possess all possible perfections. Consider the perfections of justice and mercy, for example. God is often considered to be perfectly just and perfectly merciful. But, as we've seen, He can't give everyone exactly what's coming to them and let them all off. So it seems that he can't be perfectly just and perfectly merciful.

Similar problems arise with respect to many other perfections. Take omniscience and goodness, for example. To say that God is all-knowing is to say that there is nothing that he doesn't know. To say that he is all-good is to say that he never does anything wrong. The question arises, then, can God know what it is to be greedy? To be envious? To be gluttonous? To know what it is to be greedy, envious, or gluttonous, one has to have been greedy, envious, or gluttonous. But a totally good person would never have committed these sins. So it seems that we can know things that God can't. If this is the case, however, it is doubtful he is all-knowing.

Perhaps the most telling criticism of Descartes' ontological argument, however, is that it is uninformative. The first premise of Descartes' argument cannot be taken to assert the existence of God, for if it did, the argument would be circular: it would assume what it is trying to prove. The first premise, then, is best taken to be a hypothetical,

1'. If God exists, then he possesses all possible perfections.

But, when the first premise is taken this way, the conclusion becomes

3'. If God exists, then he exists.

This is undoubtedly true, but it's uninformative: it doesn't tell us anything that we don't already know. And it certainly doesn't establish the existence of God. So Descartes' ontological argument is no more successful than Anselm's.

Thought Probe

One More God

By some estimates, humans have worshipped more than three thousand different gods throughout history. So monotheists (those who believe in only one god) don't believe in thousands of other gods. The difference between atheists and monotheists, then, is that atheists believe in one less god than monotheists. If monotheists are rationally justified in not believing in thousands of other gods, are atheists equally justified in not believing in the god of the monotheists? Why or why not?

Pascal's Wager

Blaise Pascal, one of the seventeenth century's greatest mathematicians, was well aware that a belief in God could not be rationally justified. Nevertheless, he thought that it could be pragmatically justified. A belief is *rationally justified* when there is sufficient reason for believing it to be true. A belief is *pragmatically justified* when there is sufficient reason for believing that having it will benefit you. Pascal thought that because there is a chance that believing in God will get us into heaven, we should believe in God, even though the evidence doesn't warrant it.

To get a better sense of the difference between rational and pragmatic justification, consider the following case. Suppose you are a homeless person, living hand to mouth, with no prospect of a steady income or regular meals. You know, however, that if you were committed to an insane asylum, you'd have a warm bed to sleep in and three square meals a day, which is all you have ever hoped for. You also know that if you could convince mental health workers that you believe you are Jesus Christ, you would be committed. In this case, you would be pragmatically justified in believing that you are Jesus Christ because having that belief would be a great benefit to you. To realize that benefit, you ought to do everything you can to acquire that belief. Similarly, Pascal thought that we ought to do everything we can to acquire a sincere, passionate belief in God. The question is, Would such a belief be pragmatically justified?

Pascal admits that it is impossible to know either what God is or whether he exists. Nevertheless, he believes that it's in our own best interest to believe

The dice of God are always loaded.

—RALPH WALDO EMERSON

in the God of Jansenism (a heretical Roman Catholic sect to which Pascal converted after having a mystical experience), because if you do, and he exists, you go to heaven. If you believe in Pascal's God, and he doesn't exist, you lose nothing. Here's Pascal's analysis of the situation.

Thought Experiment

Pascal's Wager

Let us weigh up the gain and the loss involved in calling heads that God exists. Let us assess the two cases: if you win, you win everything, if you lose, you lose nothing. Do not hesitate then; wager that he does exist.[54]

It would be irrational not to bet on the flip of a coin if you had everything to win and nothing to lose. Similarly, Pascal claims, it would be irrational not to bet that God exists.

Pascal here assumes that there is a 50 percent chance that there is a God that grants eternal salvation to those who believe in him. But Pascal also assumes that we can know nothing about God's nature. So it's hard to see how he could assign a probability to any particular view of the nature of God.

Maybe God rewards those who don't believe in him. Philosopher and literary critic Galen Strawson makes an interesting case for this possibility:

It is an insult to God to believe in God. For on the one hand, it is to suppose that he perpetrated acts of incalculable cruelty. On the other hand, it is to suppose that he has perversely given his human creatures an instrument—their intellect—which must inevitably lead them if they are dispassionate and honest, to deny his existence. It is tempting to conclude that if He exists, it is the atheists and agnostics that He loves best, among those with any pretensions to education. For they are the ones who have taken Him most seriously.[55]

Reason is considered by many to be God's greatest gift to humanity. But as we have seen (and Pascal agrees), the existence of God apparently cannot be established through reason alone. If we are to respect God's gift, we should follow it where it leads—which may not be to theism.

There are many other possibilities. Maybe God doesn't care whether people believe in him or not. Maybe he randomly chooses who gets eternal life. Maybe he punishes those who believe in him for purely selfish reasons. Maybe he punishes anyone who gambles. Given that the chances that Pascal's God exists are something less than 50 percent, Pascal's wager may not be such a good bet.

The stakes in the bet may also be different from what Pascal would have us believe. For one thing, heaven may not be such a great prize. If it involves sitting on a cloud playing a harp all day, few would find it enjoyable. (Milton's Satan, who thought it was better to rule in hell than serve in heaven, certainly wouldn't want to go there.) For another, it's not true that you lose nothing by believing in God. Performing the rituals and living according to

Silverman's Wager

Herb Silverman, professor of mathematics at Charleston College and founding chair of the Coalition for the Community of Reason, proposes his own wager to counter Pascal's:

Blaise Pascal (1623–1662) and Herb Silverman (1942–????) have had two common interests: mathematics, which led to our mutual profession, and theology, which led to our respective wagers. Though a Christian, Pascal was also a doubter. In Number 233 of his Pensees he says, "If there is a God, He is infinitely incomprehensible, since, having neither parts nor limits, He has no affinity to us. We are then incapable of knowing either what He is or if He is." Pascal later went on to say, "Reason can decide nothing here." He then concluded, in his now famous wager, that belief in God was the only rational choice to make: "If God does not exist, one will lose nothing by believing in him; while if he does exist, one will lose everything by not believing."

Before stating my own wager, let me make a couple of comments about Pascal's. His first conditional statement could just as well refer to the Tooth Fairy or the pot of gold at the end of the rainbow. Were we to devote our entire life to such fruitless searches, we would be left with an unproductive and wasted life—certainly a loss.

The second conditional statement is even more problematic. Pascal assumes the only existing god would be his Christian version—one who rewards believers with eternal bliss and punishes nonbelievers with eternal damnation. Moreover, it would be a god who either could not distinguish genuine from feigned belief or who would simply reward hypocrites for pretending a faith that they lack.

I agree with Pascal that no god is comprehensible to us. But suppose, for the sake of argument, I posit the existence of a creator who actually cares about human beings and elects to spend an eternity with a chosen few. What selection criteria would such a Supreme Being adopt? I expect this divine scientist would prefer having a "personal relationship" with the same kind of folks I would—intelligent, honest, rational people who require some evidence before holding a belief. Pascal would undoubtedly agree with me that our most promising students ask provocative questions until convinced by rational arguments, while our dullest students mindlessly accept what they think we want them to believe. Wouldn't a supreme teacher concur? My kind of Supreme Being would favor eternal discourse with a Carl Sagan over a Pat Robertson.

Such a superior intellect would presumably be bored by and want little contact with humans who so confidently draw unwarranted conclusions about his unprovable existence. This brilliant designer would be as appalled as I am by those who profess and glorify blind faith. With that kind of deity in mind, I modestly make my own wager. It is almost a plagiarism. I change none of Pascal's words, except that his last *not* now appears earlier in the wager. But what a difference a *not* makes!

I hereby propose "Silverman's Wager": If God does not exist, one will lose nothing by not believing in him; while if he does exist, one will lose everything by believing.[56]

Thought Probe

The Best Bet

Which wager, Pascal's or Silverman's, do you think is the best? Why?

---

the dictates of a religion (as Pascal advocates) take time, energy, and money. If there is no God, that time, energy, and money may have been wasted.

Some even go so far as to say that betting against God is the only way to win at life. André Breton, French writer and founder of surrealism, for example, tells us,

I have always wagered against God and I regard the little that I have won in this world as simply the outcome of this bet. However paltry may have been the stake (my life) I am conscious of having won to the full. Everything that is doddering, squint eyed, vile, polluted, and grotesque is summoned up for me in that one word: God![57]

Breton apparently believes that a bird in the hand is better than two in the bush. It's better to live life to the fullest than restrain yourself in hopes of a reward that may never come. In any event, you should think twice before accepting Pascal's wager because the risk and rewards may be very different from the way they're represented.

Thought Probe

Alien Religion

Suppose that we are visited by aliens from outer space and find that they have no religion and have never heard of any of the gods worshipped by humans. Would this undermine the credibility of our religions? Would it be appropriate to try to evangelize the aliens and convert them to one of our religions? Why or why not?

Religion, which should most distinguish us from the beasts, and ought most particularly to elevate us, as rational creatures, above brutes, is that wherein men often appear most irrational, and more senseless than beasts themselves.

—JOHN LOCKE

Robert Coburn reports that, although there is no unanimous agreement that the arguments for the existence of God fail, "there is certainly near-unanimous agreement on this matter, at least among professional philosophers."[58] Most (but not all) of those who have studied these arguments have found them wanting. They provide neither rational nor pragmatic justification for a belief in God.

Some have argued that even if the arguments, taken individually, are not convincing, taken collectively, they make a strong case. But that would be true only if all of the arguments were about the same thing, and that doesn't seem to be the case. The cosmological argument is about a creator, the design argument is about a designer, the argument from miracles is about a miracle worker, and so on. The arguments themselves give us no reason to believe that they are all talking about the same thing. A separate argument would be needed to prove that, and no such argument has been forthcoming.

The major problem with all of the arguments from experience is that even if they were cogent, they wouldn't prove the existence of the traditional God of theism. Even if the universe does have a creator, a designer, a miracle worker, or a source of religious experience, there is no reason to believe that any of them is all-powerful, all-knowing, or all-good. The arguments aren't cogent, however, because everything they attempt to explain by invoking God can be better explained without invoking him. So they don't justify believing in the existence of God.

The goodness of an explanation is determined by how much understanding it produces, and the amount of understanding produced by an explanation is determined by how well it systematizes and unifies our knowledge. The extent to which an explanation systematizes and unifies our knowledge can be measured by various criteria of adequacy such as simplicity (the number of assumptions made), scope (the types of phenomena explained), conservatism (fit with existing theory), and fruitfulness (ability to make successful novel predictions).

Supernatural explanations are inherently inferior to natural ones because they do not meet the criteria of adequacy as well. For example, they are usually less simple because they assume the existence of at least one additional type of entity. They usually have less scope because they don't explain how the phenomena in question are produced and thus they raise more questions than they answer. They are usually less conservative because they imply that certain natural laws have been violated. And they are usually less fruitful because they don't make any novel predictions. That is why scientists avoid them.

Given the inherent inferiority of supernatural explanations, we would be justified in accepting a supernatural explanation only if we were sure that a natural explanation would never be found. But we can never be sure of that, because we can never know what the future will bring.

Theology is but the ignorance of natural causes reduced to a system.
—Baron Paul Henri T. D'Holbach

Summary

Arguments that try to derive the existence of God from the existence of the universe are known as cosmological arguments. One of them is the so-called first-cause argument: some things are caused, and because nothing can cause itself, and the chain of causes can't be infinitely long, there must be a first cause, which we call God. But this argument, if sound, proves only the existence of a first cause, not God, for the first cause need not be all-powerful, all-knowing, or all-good. It is also not necessarily true that the universe has a cause, nor that an infinite regress of causes is logically possible.

The Kalam cosmological argument maintains that whatever begins to exist has a cause. Because the universe began to exist with the big bang, it must have a cause, namely God. But whatever caused the big bang need not be God—it may not be all-powerful, all-knowing, or all-good. Furthermore, the big bang doesn't necessarily have to have a cause. It could have been the result of what scientists call a vacuum fluctuation, an uncaused event. Or the big bang could have been just another cycle in an infinitely "oscillating" universe—a universe without a first cause.

Teleological arguments try to derive the existence of God from the apparent design or purpose in the universe. One popular teleological argument is based on an analogy between the universe and a machine: the universe resembles a watch; every watch has a designer; therefore the universe probably has a designer—God. But even if this is a good analogical argument, it doesn't show that such a designer must be God. In addition, the very existence of a universe designed for a purpose casts doubt on the notion of an all-powerful designer, who should need no universe to achieve goals. The design argument can also be construed this way: the existence of God provides the best explanation of the design of the universe. But another explanation of this design is better. That explanation is evolution.

Some argue that the existence of miracles shows that God must exist. But the existence of miracles only implies a miracle worker, not God. In fact, some have argued that the existence of miracles disproves the existence of an all-powerful or all-knowing God. Furthermore, no event can provide us with sufficient grounds for believing that a miracle has occurred.

Religious experience is also alleged to provide us with proof of God's existence. But there is no way to tell whether a religious experience was caused by God. Without a method for distinguishing real religious experiences from fake ones, we are not justified in believing any to be real.

It seems that belief in God (as traditionally conceived) cannot be rationally justified. Blaise Pascal, however, thought that it could be pragmatically justified. He asserted that it's in your best interests to believe in God because if you do and God exists, you go to heaven; if you believe and God doesn't exist, you lose nothing. But this simple bet ignores many other possibilities. Maybe God rewards those who don't believe; maybe God doesn't care who believes; maybe heaven is no real prize. Moreover, it's not true that you lose nothing by believing in God. Living a religious life costs time, energy, and money. And following religious dictates may lead to unnecessary suffering.

Study Questions

1. According to the traditional theism, what sort of being is God?
2. What is the traditional cosmological argument?
3. What is the Kalam cosmological argument?
4. What is the analogical design argument?
5. What is the best-explanation design argument?
6. What is the argument from miracles?
7. What is the argument from religious experience?
8. What is Anselm's ontological argument?
9. What is Descartes' ontological argument?
10. What is Pascal's wager?
11. What is the argument from meaning?

Discussion Questions

1. There are many books that claim to contain the revealed word of God, such as the Bible, the Koran, and the Vedas. How can we tell which, if any, actually does contain the revealed word of God?
2. Is the existence of one God (monotheism) inherently more plausible than the existence of many gods (polytheism)?
3. Can God make a rock so heavy that he can't lift it? If not, does this impugn his omnipotence?

4. If God knows everything you will ever do in your life, do you have free will?

5. Is there any situation in which a supernatural explanation would be superior to a natural one? If so, describe it.

6. Recently, a trailer park was destroyed by a tornado. Many people were killed, but one child was found alive in the rubble. Many consider it a miracle that the child was saved. Was it?

7. Some say that the purpose of miracles is to make God's presence known to us. Is this a good justification for miracles?

8. Is there anything God could do that would give us unequivocal proof of his existence?

9. Suppose you were raised in a different culture in a family that worshipped a different god than you do now. Would you still have the religion that you have now? If not, can you be sure that your current religion is the true one? If so, what would have convinced you to change religions?

10. Suppose you're trying to make a rational choice among religions. What criteria would you use to determine which religion is the best? Would those be the same criteria you would use to determine which religion is true? If not, how would they differ?

When Bad Things Happen to Good People

God as Troublemaker

None of the arguments we've canvassed justify believing in the existence of God because none of them establish God's existence beyond a reasonable doubt. That doesn't mean that God doesn't exist, however. There may be good arguments that we've overlooked. But there is an argument that many believe proves that God doesn't exist, namely, the argument from evil.

The world contains a great deal of evil. Think of all the babies born with serious defects, of all the people killed in natural disasters, of all the victims of war and crime. An all-knowing being would know that there is a great deal of evil in this world. An all-good being would want to prevent this evil. And an all-powerful being would be able to prevent it. So if God is all-knowing, all-powerful, and all-good, why is there so much evil in the world?

Anything that is inherently wrong is evil. Suffering and injustice, for example, are evil. To show that unnecessary evil is incompatible with the existence of God, William Rowe offers the following thought experiment.

Thought Experiment

Rowe's Fawn

Suppose in some distant forest lightning strikes a dead tree, resulting in a forest fire. In the fire a fawn is trapped, horribly burned, and lies in terrible agony for several days before death relieves its suffering. So far as we can see, the fawn's intense suffering is pointless. For there does not appear to be any greater good such that the prevention of the fawn's suffering would require either the loss of that good or the occurrence of an evil equally bad or worse. Nor does there seem to be any equally bad or worse evil so connected to the fawn's suffering that it would have had to occur had the fawn's suffering been prevented. Could an omnipotent, omniscient being have prevented the fawn's apparently point-

WHY MUST THEY SUFFER? Millions of animals die in forest fires every year. Is the suffering they undergo really necessary to make the world a better place? Would the world be a worse place to live if so many animals didn't suffer and die every year?

less suffering? The answer is obvious, as even the theist will insist. An omnipotent, omniscient being could have easily prevented the fawn from being horribly burned, or, given the burning, could have spared the fawn the intense suffering by quickly ending its life, rather than allowing the fawn to lie in terrible agony for several days.[59]

As surely as God is good, so surely there is no such thing as necessary evil.
— ROBERT SOUTHEY

Humans are not the only creatures capable of intense suffering. Certainly all mammals can suffer, and, probably, most other vertebrates can as well. Much of the suffering that sentient creatures experience at the hands of nature seems unnecessary, and all of it is preventable by an omniscient, omnipotent being. Because an all-good being would want to prevent unnecessary suffering, there seems to be good reason for believing that God, as traditionally understood, does not exist.

The argument from evil, then, can be stated like this:

1. There is unnecessary evil in the world.
2. If there were an all-powerful, all-knowing, all-good being, there would be no unnecessary evil in the world.
3. Therefore, there is no all-powerful, all-knowing, all-good being.

The second premise of this argument is uncontroversial because theists and atheists alike believe that it's good to prevent unnecessary evil. The success or failure of this argument, then, hinges on the truth or falsity of the first premise.

The first premise claims not that there is evil in the world, but that there is *unnecessary* evil in the world. A necessary evil is one that is required to prevent a greater evil or to bring about a greater good. Chemotherapy, for example is a necessary evil: it's evil because it causes suffering; it's necessary because it's required to prevent death and promote health. An unnecessary evil neither prevents a greater evil nor brings about a greater good. Necessary evils are morally justified. Unnecessary evils, however, are not. To defeat the argument from evil, then, theists need to show that there is reason to believe that all the evil in the world is necessary. To defend it, nontheists must show that there is reason to believe that at least some evil is unnecessary.

A theory that seeks to justify belief in God in the face of all the evil in the world is known as a **theodicy** (which comes from the Greek words *theos* meaning "god" and *dike* meaning "judgment"). Many different theodicies have been proposed over the years, and all seek to defend the claim that the evil in the world is necessary.

The Ontological Defense

The ontological defense claims that goodness, by its very nature, can't exist without evil. So it's impossible for God to have made a good world—let alone the best of all possible worlds—that didn't contain evil. If goodness was a type of evil, this claim would make sense. Red is a type of color, so it's impossible for God to make a red thing without making a colored thing. But goodness isn't a type of evil. Good and evil are contradictory concepts like red and not-red. In the case of contradictory concepts, however, it is possible to have one without having the other. Suppose God were to color everything red. In that case, there would be no nonred objects in the world. But that wouldn't mean that there were no red objects in the world. Red things can exist even if there are no nonred things in the world. Similarly, good things can exist even if there are no evil things in the world. The lack of evil doesn't preclude the existence of goodness. If it did, there would be no goodness in heaven because heaven presumably contains no evil.

The Knowledge Defense

After describing many horrendous acts of evil, Ivan, in Dostoyevsky's *The Brothers Karamazov*, asks, "Do you understand why this infamy must be and is permitted? Without it, I am told, man could not have existed on Earth, for he could not have known good and evil."[60] This argument assumes that a knowledge of evil is a good thing and that such a knowledge cannot be acquired unless evil exists. Both of these assumptions are questionable.

When Adam and Eve were first created, they supposedly had no knowledge of good or evil. But this wasn't such a bad thing because before the fall, they are said to have lived in paradise. What's more, to acquire their knowledge, they didn't have to experience evil. All they had to do was eat the apple. So the story of Adam and Eve suggests that both of the assumptions underlying this argument are false.

Even if they were true—even if a knowledge of evil was a good thing and such a knowledge could be acquired only by experiencing evil—there seems to be far more evil in the world than is necessary to give us a knowledge of it.

Fundamentalist Christians often blame the existence of evil on the actions of Adam and Eve. Because the pair disobeyed God's command, we are suffering to this day. The logic of this justification, however, leaves much to be desired, as Mark Twain explains,

> To proceed with the Biblical curiosities. Naturally you will think the threat to punish Adam and Eve for disobeying was of course not carried out, since they did not create themselves, nor their natures nor their impulses nor their weaknesses, and hence were not properly subject to anyone's commands, and not responsible to anybody for their acts. It will surprise you to know that the threat was carried out. Adam and Eve were punished, and that crime finds apologists unto this day. The sentence of death was executed.
>
> As you perceive, the only person responsible for the couple's offense escaped; and not only escaped but became the executioner of the innocent. . . .
>
> Very well, God banished Adam and Eve from the Garden, and eventually assassinated them. All for disobeying a command which he had no right to utter. But he did not stop there, as you will see. He has one code of morals for himself, and quite another for his children. He requires his children to deal justly — and gently — with offenders, and forgive them seventy-and-seven times; whereas he deals neither justly nor gently with anyone, and he did not forgive the igno-rant and thoughtless first pair of juveniles even their first small offense and say, "You may go free this time, I will give you another chance."
>
> On the contrary! He elected to punish *their* children, all through the ages to the end of time, for a trifling offense committed by others before they were born. He is punishing them yet. In mild ways? No, in atrocious ones.
>
> You would not suppose that this kind of a Being gets many compliments. Undeceive yourself: the world calls him the All-Just, the All-Righteous, the All-Good, the All-Merciful, the All-Forgiving, the All-Truthful, the All-Loving, the Source of All Morality. These sarcasms are uttered daily, all over the world. But not as conscious sarcasms. No, they are meant seriously: they are uttered without a smile.[61]

Thought Probe

Adam and Eve

The forbidden apple contained the knowledge of right and wrong. So before Adam and Eve ate the apple, they couldn't have known it was wrong to eat the apple. But if they didn't know it was wrong, was it right to punish them for what they did? And even if it was right to punish them, was it right to punish all of mankind throughout eternity for what they did? Is it fair to punish sons and daughters for the sins of their fathers?

To know what blue is, we have to see only a few blue things. Similarly, to know what evil is, we have to experience only a few examples of it. If the evil in the world is necessary, it must be necessary for something other than our education.

The Free-Will Defense

Many believe that evil is necessary for free will. They assume that having free will is a good thing because without it, there would be no right or wrong actions, no good or bad people. No one could be praised or blamed for what he or she did because no one could have done otherwise. Free will requires real

theodicy An attempt to justify belief in God given the existence of evil.

choices. And real choices differ in their moral value. Some are good, and some are bad. So the price we pay for having free will is the existence of evil.

To justify the existence of evil, however, theists must explain not only why evil is chosen but why it is chosen so often. If it's possible to have free will and always or usually choose the good, the existence of evil remains a mystery.

A being who has free will and yet always chooses the good does not seem to be a contradiction in terms. God is supposed to be such a being. He supposedly has free will and always chooses the good. Couldn't God have made us the same way? If not, why not? Alvin Plantinga claims that humans, by their very nature, might be so depraved that it's impossible for God to create a world containing humans in which they do not do evil. He calls this the doctrine of "transworld depravity."[62] This doctrine, however, flies in the face of church teaching. Most Christian churches teach that Jesus was a sinless human being, and the Catholic Church teaches that his mother, Mary, was also born without sin. Accepting Plantinga's doctrine, then, requires rejecting basic doctrines of the Christian church.

Even if God could not have made us so that we never do evil, it certainly seems that he could have made us so that we do evil less often than we do. Having a stronger desire to do good would not make us any less free. We do not diminish our children's freedom by teaching them to do good. A world filled with people of high moral character, then, would not be a world with less free will. But it would be a world with less evil. So the free-will defense fails, for there seems to be more evil in the world than is necessary for the existence of free will.

Even if free will requires that humans make as many evil choices as they do, there is still much more evil in the world than necessary. The evil that humans suffer at the hands of other humans, known as **moral evil,** is only a small portion of the total amount of evil in the world. The evil that humans suffer at the hands of nature, known as **natural evil,** is far more significant. John Stuart Mill explains,

> In sober truth, nearly all the things which men are hanged or imprisoned for doing to one another, are nature's every-day performances. Killing, the most criminal act recognized by human laws, Nature does once to every being that lives; and in a large proportion of cases, after protracted tortures such as only the greatest monsters whom we read of ever purposely inflicted on their living fellow-creatures. . . . Nature impales men, breaks them as if on the wheel, casts them to be devoured by wild beasts, burns them to death, crushes them with stones like the first Christian martyr, starves them with hunger, freezes them with cold, poisons them by the quick or slow venom of her exhalations, and has hundreds of other hideous deaths in reserve, such as the ingenious cruelty of a Nabis or a Domitian never surpassed. All this, Nature does with the most supercilious disregard both of mercy and of justice, emptying her shafts upon the best and noblest indifferently with the meanest and worst; upon those who are engaged in the highest and worthiest enterprises, as often as the direct consequences of the noblest acts; and it might almost be imagined as a punishment for them. She mows down those on whose existence hangs the well-being of a whole

One of the most poignant examples of natural evil is the tsunami (tidal wave) that occurred in the Indian Ocean on December 26, 2004, killing more than 200,000 people, many of whom were infants and children. Instead of viewing the tsunami as evidence of the nonexistence of God, however, some see it as evidence of God's wrath, as James A. Haught reports,

> Immediately after the Indian Ocean tragedy, Israel's chief Sephardic rabbi, Shlomo Amar, told Reuters: "This is an expression of God's great ire with the world. The world is being punished for wrongdoing." The international news syndicate also quoted a Hindu high priest as stating the tsunami was caused by "a huge amount of pent-up manmade evil on Earth" combined with the positions of the planets. And it quoted a Jehovah's Witness as saying the tragedy is "a sign of the last days," fulfilling Christ's promise that devastation will precede the time when believers will "see the Son of Man coming in a cloud with power and great glory." Catholic Bishop Alex Dias of Port Blair, India, said the tsunami was "a warning from God to reflect deeply on the way we lead our lives." On MSNBC's *Scarborough Country*, Jennifer Giroux, director of

Women Influencing the Nation (WIN), said the tsunami was divine punishment for America's "cloning, homosexuality, trying to make homosexual marriages, abortion, lack of God in the schools, taking Jesus out of Christmas."[64]

Arkansas governor and Baptist minister Michael Huckabee disagrees with those who see natural disasters as the work of God. He claims that God does not do evil. In 1997 he refused to sign a bill granting relief to tornado victims because the bill referred to the tornado as an "act of God." Huckabee explains, "It's a matter of conscience. I refuse to walk through tornado damage and to say that what destroyed it was God and what built it back was only human beings. I saw God protect a lot of people, save a lot of people. That's an act of God, too."[65]

Thought Probe

Wrath of God

Would an all-good, all-knowing, all-powerful being allow 200,000 of his children to die in such a horrible manner just to express his anger or teach people a lesson? Would he kill Asians to punish Americans? Or is Huckabee right that God is not responsible for natural disasters?

---

people, perhaps the prospects of the human race for generations to come, with as little compunction as those whose death is a relief to themselves, or a blessing to those under their noxious influence.[63]

Millions suffer and die in natural disasters every year. According to traditional theism, this is God's handiwork. Because he created the natural world, he is directly responsible for all of this evil. But an all-knowing, all-powerful, all-good being would not subject his children to such torture. So there must not be an all-powerful, all-good being.

Some try to justify natural evil by blaming it on Satan. According to this view, God does not create evil; Satan does. But this view is not available to those who take God to be all-knowing, all-powerful, and all-good. An all-knowing being would know what Satan was up to. An all-powerful being would be able to prevent Satan from doing evil. And an all-good being would want to prevent Satan from doing evil. A being who sits idly by and knowingly lets someone inflict evil on others is either powerless to prevent it or is evil himself.

moral evil The evil that humans suffer at the hands of other humans.

natural evil The evil that humans suffer at the hands of nature.

Suppose you were walking down the street one day and you saw a five-year-old boy putting cigarettes out on his two-year-old sister. If you didn't stop the boy, you would be as bad as the boy himself. Satan is like the boy in this story; he inflicts pain and suffering on the human race. If God is able to stop him but doesn't, He is as bad as Satan himself.

Thought Probe

Is There Free Will in Heaven?

Heaven is popularly considered to be a place where there is no sin and thus no evil. But according to the free-will defense, there can be no free will without evil. So how can there be free will in heaven? If there is no free will in heaven, is it a desirable place to go?

The Ideal-Humanity Defense

Natural evil has been defended on the grounds that it's necessary to improve the human race. By pushing some of us to our limits, it's claimed, the struggle against nature helps us to achieve our potential as a species. Natural evil is helping us evolve toward an ideal humanity.[66]

There are a number of problems with this proposal. For one thing, there is little evidence that the struggle for survival has improved the human race. As a species, we seem no better than our ancestors. Another problem is that the advances we have made in science and the arts are not the result of natural evil. Great scientists and artists are not, by and large, motivated by a desire to overcome natural evil. They are usually motivated by the values of truth and beauty. Even in the case of those who are engaged in the battle against natural evil, such as doctors and rescue workers, there seems to be much more natural evil than is needed to motivate them.

The biggest problem facing the ideal-humanity defense, however, is that it seems to contradict the fundamental principle of Christian morality: that each human being is of infinite value. John Hick explains,

> Although it took Christianity a long time to clarify and is taking even longer for it to implement its valuation of individual personality, perhaps its chief contribution to the life of the world has been its insistence that each human being is equally a child of God, made for eternal fellowship with his Maker and endowed with unlimited value by the divine love which has created him, which sustains him in being, and which purposes his eternal blessedness. Thus, in spite of so many failures in Christian practice, Christianity teaches that the human individual is never a mere means, expendable in the interests of some further goal, but is always an end in himself as the object of God's love.[67]

As Kant taught us, because we are rational beings capable of shaping our own destiny, it's wrong for anyone to use us against our will. When we force others to do our bidding—when we use others as means to an end rather than as ends in themselves—we treat them as slaves and fail to respect their inherent dignity and worth. But if it's wrong for humans to treat each other as slaves, it's also wrong for God to treat us as slaves. Thus the suffering we undergo cannot be justified on the grounds that it's necessary to bring about a greater good for others.

Russian novelist Fyodor Dostoyevsky eloquently expresses this point when one of his characters says,

> Surely I haven't suffered simply that I, my crimes and my sufferings may manure the soil of the future harmony for somebody else. I want to see with my own eyes the hind lie down with the lion and the victim rise up and embrace his murderer. I want to be there when every one suddenly understands what it has all been for.[68]

It's not right, Dostoyevsky implies, to make someone suffer for the benefit of someone else. Since the ideal-humanity defense suggests otherwise, it's unsuccessful.

The doing of evil to avoid an evil cannot be good.
—SAMUEL COLERIDGE

The Soul-Building Defense

John Hick claims that although it's wrong to make us suffer for the sake of someone else, it's not wrong to make us suffer for our own sake. He writes, "The only morally acceptable justification of the agonies and heartaches of human life must be of a . . . kind in which the individuals who have suffered themselves participate in the justifying good and are themselves able to see their own past sufferings as having been worthwhile."[69] According to Hick, evil is necessary, not to improve the human race, but to improve each individual human being.

What does not destroy me makes me stronger.
—NIETZSCHE

The assumption behind this view is that suffering can build character. By overcoming adversity, Hick believes, we can acquire virtues such as courage, endurance, and sympathy. But trials and tribulations do not always make us better people. Instead of ennobling us, intense suffering often makes us bitter, resentful, and cynical. It can destroy our faith in mankind as well as our will to live. English novelist W. Somerset Maugham concurs,

> I have never found that suffering improves the character. Its influence to refine and ennoble is a myth. . . . I have suffered from poverty and the anguish of unrequited love, disappointment, disillusion, lack of opportunity and recognition, want of freedom; and I know that they made me envious and uncharitable, irritable, selfish, unjust; prosperity, success, happiness, have made me a better man.[70]

Maugham rejects the assumption that suffering can build character. Instead of ennobling us, he claims, suffering debases us. Only prosperity, success, and happiness can make us better people.

Hick recognizes that suffering often has negative consequences. Most people don't realize their full potential in this life. Many, in fact, become less virtuous over time. That's why he believes that there must be life beyond the grave. "If the human potential is to be fulfilled in the lives of individual men and women," he says, "those lives must be prolonged far beyond the limits of our present bodily existence."[71] The purpose of life, according to Hick, is to

Karma and the Problem of Inequality

One aspect of the problem of evil that is easy to overlook is the problem of inequality. According to the Judeo-Christian tradition, none of us has lived before, so none of us deserves the particular situation we find ourselves in. But some people are born with crippling defects to parents who abuse them, whereas others are born in perfect health to billionaires who adore them. How is that fair? John Hick describes the problem:

> We have not created by our own free actions either the favourable or the unfavourable make-up of our genetic code; and we have not earned the fortunate or the unfortunate conditions in which our lives are set. Neither our inner constitution nor our outer circumstances are in any way appropriate to what we have hitherto been or done—for we did not exist at all prior to our birth as the particular individuals that we are, living in the particular place and in the particular historical period in which we have been born.
>
> On a purely naturalistic view these inequalities would simply have to be accepted as details of the natural order, neither fair nor unfair, just nor unjust. . . . But if, on the other hand, the religious claim is well founded that man's life is established by a higher spiritual power or process, then these disparities of human life take on an inescapable moral significance. It becomes appropriate to ask why they occur and to consider whether they are just or unjust. And on the western assumption that we have had no previous existence and have been brought into being *ab initio* in our present state of inequality, the human scene seems cruelly unfair.[72]

The doctrine of Karma, many believe, can solve both the problem of inequality and the problem of evil. Hick explains,

The alternative assumption of the religions of Indian origin is that we have all lived before and that the conditions of our present life are a direct consequence of our previous lives. There is no arbitrariness, no randomness, no injustice in the inequalities of our human lot, but only cause and effect, the reaping now of what we have ourselves sown in the past. Our essential self continues from life to life, being repeatedly reborn or reincarnated, the state of its karma, or the qualitative sum of its volitional activity, determining the nature of its next earthly life. As R. K. Tripathi of Banaras Hindu University says, "The law of karma along with the doctrine of rebirth has the merit of solving one great problem of philosophy and religion, a problem which is a headache to the western religions and which finds no satisfactory solution in them. The problem is: How is it that different persons are born with an infinite diversity regarding their fortunes in spite of the fact that God is equally good to all? It would be nothing short of denying God to say that He is whimsical. If God is all-Goodness and also All-Powerful, how is it that there is so much evil and inequality in the world? Indian religions relieve God of this responsibility and make our *karmas* responsible.[73]

Thought Probe

Karma

Does the law of Karma along with the doctrine of rebirth provide a better solution to the problem of evil and inequality than those offered by Christians? Why or why not?

become the best that we can be. But most of us don't achieve a state of moral or spiritual perfection in this life. So we must lead additional lives either in this world or in other worlds.

Hick does not believe that it's permissible to use people against their will to benefit others. But he does believe that it's permissible to use people against their will to benefit themselves. Practices or laws that limit people's freedom for their own good are called *paternalistic*. Motorcycle helmet laws, for example, are paternalistic because they limit motorcyclists' freedom in an attempt to protect them from injury. Hick's theodicy is paternalistic because it attempts to justify suffering on the grounds that it's good for the soul. But not only is it doubtful that suffering has such a salutary effect, it's also doubtful that, even if it did, it would be morally justified. The same sort of considerations that make it wrong to use people to benefit others make it wrong to use people to benefit themselves. In both cases, people are being treated merely as means to an end and not as ends in themselves, and that fails to respect the dignity that resides in each person. As Charles Fried said of paternalistic medical experiments, " . . . even if the ends are the patient's own ends, to treat him as a means to them is to undermine his humanity insofar as humanity consists in choosing and being able to judge one's own ends, rather than being a machine which is used to serve ends, even one's own ends."[74] From a moral point of view, then, the soul-building defense doesn't seem to be any better than the ideal-humanity defense.

What's more, Hick's theodicy leads to some unsavory consequences. If evil is necessary to build character, then eliminating evil is wrong. You shouldn't alleviate another person's suffering because, in so doing, you could be stunting his or her spiritual growth. It was this sort of reasoning that led to the untouchable class in India.

Untouchables occupy the lowest rung of Indian society. In the not-so-distant past, it was forbidden to aid these people because it was thought that their misery was punishment for the wickedness of their past lives. Hindus believe that reincarnation is governed by the law of Karma, which says, in effect, "As ye sow, so shall ye reap." In other words, what you do will come back to you, if not in this life, then in a future life. So if you do evil in this life, then an equivalent amount of evil will be done to you in some future life. Your future suffering will atone for your past crimes and prepare you for a better life to come. Alleviating your misery would interfere with your spiritual evolution. By this logic, then, the more misery you endure, the better off you are. Because Hick's soul-building defense implies that it's wrong to alleviate another's suffering, it cannot be correct.

In addition, there seems to be much more evil in the world than is necessary to build character. Hick admits that most people make little or no spiritual progress during their lives. Why is that? Couldn't God have arranged things so that more spiritual growth took place during our stay on Earth? What reason do we have for believing that more growth occurs in other lives on other planets? And why does God need a universe to make us virtuous anyway. Couldn't he just have created us with virtue? If not, can he really be all-powerful? In light of these difficulties, Hick's soul-building theodicy is no more successful than any of the others we've examined.

The world is not growing worse and it is not growing better—it is just turning around as usual.
—FINLEY PETER DUNNE

The Finite-God Defense

In a world created by an all-powerful, all-knowing, and all-good being, there should be no unnecessary evil. Although each defense we've examined might be able to show that some of the evil in the world is necessary, none of them can show that all of it is necessary. One way to explain all the unnecessary evil in the world is to admit that God does not have all of the properties traditionally attributed to him. The Gnostics, as we have seen, thought that the creator of our universe was not all-good. On that assumption, the existence of unnecessary evil is not hard to explain.

Rabbi Harold Kushner believes that unnecessary evil exists because God is not all-powerful. In his best-selling book *When Bad Things Happen to Good People*, he claims that evil exists because God is powerless to prevent it. He tells us,

> God does not want you to be sick or crippled. He didn't make you have this problem, and He doesn't want you to go on having it, but He can't make it go away. That is something which is too hard even for God.[75]

Kushner's God is a limited God. Specifically, He is not capable of performing miracles because he cannot violate natural law. Nevertheless, Kushner believes that such a God is worthy of worship. At least He's more worthy of worship than a God that could do something about evil and doesn't.[76]

Many theists don't share Kushner's view of God, however. John Baillie, former co-president of the World Council of Churches, for example, says,

> . . . I should say that the only grounds I know for believing in God would show Him omnipotent or not at all; and I should feel also that if some ground did appear for believing in the existence somewhere *within* reality of a being of loving purpose but finite power, I should not be moved to worship but only to admiration—I should applaud but I should not kneel. Nothing less than the Infinite can really slake the soul's thirst.[77]

Baillie would admire a finite, loving being, but he would not worship him. He might tip his hat to him if he passed him on the street, but he would not get down on his knees and worship him. In Baillie's estimation one can derive little comfort from the belief in a being that can prevent evil but doesn't. But one can derive little more comfort from the belief in a being that is powerless to prevent evil. If God is just as limited as we are, why worship him?

The existence of evil could be squared with the existence of God if we were willing to give up either of his other two attributes: omniscience and omnibenevolence. We could say that although God is all-powerful and all-good, he is rather dim-witted and doesn't realize how bad we have it down here. Or we could say that although God is all-powerful and all-knowing, he is evil and likes to see us suffer. Both of these alternatives, however, seem even less plausible than Kushner's.

Historically, the notion of a finite god has claimed many adherents. In addition to the Gnostics, the Manichaeans believed that God was limited. Founded around A.D. 240 by the Persian prophet Mani, Manichaeanism holds that God and Satan are equally powerful and that they are locked in an eternal struggle for supremacy. God is associated with light and the realm of the spirit, whereas Satan is associated with darkness and the realm of the flesh. According to Mani, the universe is a battleground between the forces of light and darkness. This, of course, is the worldview portrayed in the *Star*

Is God All Good?

Psalm 145:9 tells us "The Lord is good to all." In Deuteronomy 32:4, God is said to be "a God of truth and without iniquity, just and right is he." But in Isaiah 45:7, we read "I make peace and create evil. I the Lord do all these things." Lamentations 3:38 concurs: "Out of the mouth of the most High proceedeth not evil and good?" Which characterization do you think is the most accurate?

Consider the following people that God killed:

- A man (Onan) who refused to impregnate his brother's widow (Genesis 38:7–10).

- Two men (Nadab and Abihu) who offered God incense that he had not authorized (Leviticus 10:1–2).

- A group of about 300 people who opposed Moses politically (Numbers 16:1–35).

- Another group of 14,700 who sympathized with the first group (Numbers 16:49).

- People who complained about the light bread Moses was serving (Numbers 21:4–6).

- Twenty-four thousand people because some of them worshipped Baal (Numbers 25:3–9).

- Thousands of Amorites who besieged Gibeon (Joshua 10:10–11).

In addition to directly killing people, in many places God commands people to kill. For example, he orders the execution of

- Three thousand of the Levites' brothers, friends, and neighbors, who had become unruly (Exodus 32:26–28).

- All the men, women, and children in all seven of the tribes who were the Israelites' neighbors — which comes to about 14 million (Deuteronomy 2:34, 3:6, 7:1–2, 16, 20:16–17).

- All the men, women, and children of the cities of Jericho (Joshua 6:21, 8:24–26, 10:26–42, 11:10–23, 21:44).

- All the Amalekites, including children, and even animals (I Samuel 15:3–18). (Saul was severely punished for sparing some of them.)

- All the members of the house of Ahab and ministers of Baal (II Kings 10:11–25).

God also has people put to death for minor offenses. For example, God commands the death penalty for the following actions:

- Consulting a witch (Leviticus 20:6, Deuteronomy 18:11)

- Having a different religion (Exodus 22:20, Leviticus 24:10–23, Deuteronomy 13:1–15, 17:2–5, 18:20, Joshua 23:7–16, II Kings 18:40)

- Gathering sticks or kindling on the Sabbath (Exodus 31:14–15, 35:2–3, Numbers 15:32–36)

- Eating the wrong food (Exodus 12:15, Leviticus 3:16–17, 7:22, 25–27, 17:10–16).

- Swearing at your mother or father (Exodus 21:17)[78]

The apparent evil attributed to God in the Bible convinced the Gnostics that the God of the Bible was not the one true God. They believed that the God who created our world was an inferior, flawed God known as the "Demiurge." The one true God — the source and ground of all being — was beyond human comprehension. The Revolutionary War patriot and writer Thomas Paine shared the Gnostics' view of the God of the Bible:

> Whenever we read the obscene stories, the voluptuous debaucheries, the cruel and torturous executions, the unrelenting vindictiveness, with which more than half the Bible is filled, it would be more consistent that we called it the word of a demon rather than the Word of God. It is a history of wickedness that has served to corrupt and brutalize mankind; and for my part, I sincerely detest it as I detest all that is cruel.[79]

Thought Probe

God's Goodness

Is Paine's assessment a fair one? Why or why not?

Wars saga. Evil is not a problem in such a world because it is an integral part of it. St. Augustine was a Manichaean for a number of years before he converted to Christianity.

God, as traditionally conceived, is an immaterial being and thus cannot be sensed. This doesn't mean, however, that the claim that God exists cannot be empirically tested, for even though God can't be sensed, his effects can. The God hypothesis makes at least one testable prediction: if the world was created and is ruled by an all-powerful, all-knowing, and all-good being, it should contain no unnecessary evil. All the evidence, however, seems to indicate that this prediction is false, for the world seems to contain a great deal of unnecessary evil. The various theodicies we've examined are "ad hoc" hypotheses designed to explain away the seeming failure of the prediction. (*Ad hoc* is a Latin phrase meaning "toward this.") None of them seems to be successful, however. That is not to say that there is no way to justify all of the evil in the world. Maybe there is and we haven't found it yet. If we could see things from God's point of view, maybe we'd realize that everything is for the best. But, from the fact that there might be a justification for evil, it doesn't follow that there is one; nor does it follow that we're justified in believing that there is one. If you believe in God, then, your belief must be a matter of faith.

Thought Probe

What If God Died?

If God is finite, it's possible for God to die. In the trilogy *Towing Jehovah, Blameless in Abaddon,* and *The Eternal Footman,* science-fiction writer James Morrow explores this possibility. Suppose God died. How would the universe be different? How would we tell that God no longer existed?

Summary

The argument from evil says that if there were an all-powerful, all-good being, there would be no unnecessary evil in the world; but there is a great deal of unnecessary evil in the world, so there is no all-powerful, all-good being. To counter this argument, one must reject the premise that there is unnecessary evil in the world. One way to do this is to assert that a knowledge of evil is a good thing and that we can't acquire this knowledge unless evil exists. But neither of these assertions is plausible.

Another approach to justifying evil is to say that evil is necessary if humans are to have free will. Free will is a good thing, and exercising it will sometimes lead to evil. But a being with free will who always chooses good is not logically impossible. God is such a being; so, presumably, are angels. Why couldn't God have made us the same way?

The theist must also justify natural evil—the evil that humans suffer at the hands of nature. And indeed many theists have asserted that natural evil is necessary to bring about a greater good. One proposal is that natural evil improves the human race, helping the species achieve its full potential. But this implies that because evil is necessary to bring about good, any attempt to eliminate evil would be wrong. In addition, this greater-good defense contradicts the fundamental Christian principle that each individual is of infinite value and shouldn't be used as a means to some greater end.

John Hick claims that evil is necessary to improve not the human race but each individual human being. But this approach rests on the paternalistic notion that it's permissible to force people to do things against their will for their own good. Hick's view also has the same flaw as the traditional greater-good defense: if evil is necessary to build character, then eliminating it is wrong.

One way to escape the argument from evil is to embrace the notion of a finite God. One could claim, for example, that there is so much evil in the world because God is powerless to prevent it. But is such a God worthy of worship?

Study Questions

1. What is the argument from evil?
2. What is the ontological defense?
3. What is the knowledge defense?
4. What is the free-will defense?
5. What is the ideal-humanity defense?
6. What is the soul-building defense?
7. What is the finite-God defense?
8. What is the difference between natural and moral evil?

Discussion Questions

1. Is it possible to have a knowledge of good without having a knowledge of evil? Explain your answer.
2. Would the world be a worse place without free will?
3. Do the doctrines of Karma and reincarnation solve the problem of evil?
4. Some claim that if we could see the world from God's point of view, what looks evil to us would no longer look evil. Is this a satisfactory justification of evil?
5. If we get a reward in heaven commensurate with the amount of pain we experienced on Earth, does that solve the problem of inequality?
6. Consider this quote from Kenneth V. Lanning: "The fact is that far more crime and child abuse has been committed by zealots in the name of God, Jesus and Mohammed than has ever been committed in the name of Satan."[80] Is this a good reason for not believing in God?
7. Consider this thought experiment presented by British philosopher Antony Flew.

The Invisible Gardener

Let us begin with a parable. It is a parable developed from a tale told by John Wisdom in his haunting and revelatory article "Gods." Once upon a time two explorers came upon a clearing in the jungle. In the clearing were growing many flowers and many weeds. One explorer says: 'Some gardener must tend this plot.' The other disagrees: 'There is no gardener.' So they pitch their tents and set a watch. No gardener is ever seen. 'But perhaps he is an invisible gardener.' So they set up a barbed-wire fence. They electrify it. They patrol with bloodhounds. (For they remember how H. G. Wells's The Invisible Man could be both smelt and touched though he could not be seen.) But no shrieks ever suggest that some intruder has received a shock. No movements of the wire ever betray an invisible climber. The bloodhounds never give cry. Yet still the Believer is not convinced: 'But there is a gardener, invisible, intangible, insensible to electric shocks, a gardener who has no scent and makes no sound, a gardener who comes secretly to look after the garden which he loves.' At last the Skeptic despairs: 'But what remains of your original assertion? Just how does what you call an invisible, intangible, eternally elusive gardener differ from an imaginary gardener or even from no gardener at all?'[81]

Is the claim that God exists like the claim that a gardener exists? Why or why not?

Faith and Meaning
Believing the Unbelievable

*F*aith, according to the *American Heritage Dictionary*, is "belief that does not rest on logical proof or material evidence."[82] Many have argued that belief in the existence of the Christian God must be a matter of faith because, from a logical point of view, the Christian story makes no sense.

The Leap of Faith

Danish philosopher Søren Kierkegaard (1813–1855) was particularly troubled by the Christian belief that an immortal being (God) became mortal (Jesus Christ). He writes, "That that which in accordance with its nature is eternal comes into existence in time, is born, grows up, and dies—this is a breach with all thinking."[83] So difficult is this notion to comprehend that Kierkegaard labeled it "absurd."

It has long been known that many of the Christian dogmas are incompatible with reason. Ordinarily, that would be grounds for rejecting them, for the more unreasonable a claim, the less reason there is for believing it. In the case of religious claims, however, some apologists argue the opposite. Carthaginian theologian Tertullian (160?–230?), for example, says of the incarnation, "It is to be believed because it is absurd."[84] Here absurdity becomes a reason for belief. Kierkegaard agrees, "The absurd is the object of faith and the only object that can be believed."[85] Kierkegaard takes this attitude toward the absurd because faith requires passion and only that which is contrary to reason can be believed passionately.

Kierkegaard realized that, at best, a rational "proof" for the existence of God would only make God's existence probable. He writes, "Even if all the brains of all the critics were concentrated in one, it would still be impossible to obtain anything more than an approximation." But an approximation is "incommensurable with an infinite personal interest in eternal happiness."[86]

A faith that cannot survive collision with the truth is not worth many regrets.

—ARTHUR C. CLARKE

Only certainty can ensure Kierkegaard's salvation. And certainty can be achieved only through faith. So those who are serious about their salvation must make a "leap of faith" and embrace the absurd. But because the absurd flies in the face of reason, faith in it requires an extremely passionate act of will.

Bertrand Russell concurs,

> When there are rational grounds for an opinion, people are content to set them forth and wait for them to operate. In such cases, people do not hold their opinions with passion; they hold them calmly, and set forth their reasons quietly. The opinions that are held with passion are always those for which no good ground exists; indeed the passion is the measure of the holder's lack of rational conviction.[87]

The more absurd the proposition, the more passionate the belief in it must be. Because the proposition that God became mortal is about as absurd as they come, Kierkegaard thinks that belief in it requires the maximum amount of passion. Russell views passionate belief unfavorably because he believes that the more passionately a belief is held, the more likely it is to be false. Kierkegaard, on the other hand, views passionate belief favorably because he believes that the more passionately a belief is held, the more likely it is to be true.

Kierkegaard recognizes two kinds of truth: objective and subjective. Objective truth is concerned with "what" is believed; subjective truth is concerned with "how" it is believed. Something is objectively true if it corresponds to reality. Something is subjectively true if it is believed passionately. Because only the absurd can be believed passionately, Kierkegaard defines subjective truth this way:

> An objective uncertainty held fast in an appropriation-process of the most passionate inwardness is the truth, the highest truth attainable for an existing individual.[88]

The idea is that what makes someone a truly religious person is not *what* but *how* that person believes. If you believe in God passionately enough, it changes your whole being. In that case, Kierkegaard says, you are subjectively "in the truth."

But Kierkegaard goes on to say that if you are subjectively in the truth, you are objectively in the truth as well. He writes, "There is a 'how' which has this quality, that if it is truly given, the 'what' is also given; and that is the 'how of faith'. . . inwardness at its maximum proves to be objectivity."[89] In other words, if you believe something passionately enough, it becomes objectively true. Only maximum passion will do. But if you've got it, you've got the truth:

> At its maximum this inward "how" is the passion of the infinite, and the passion of the infinite is the truth. But the passion of the infinite is precisely subjectivity, and thus subjectivity becomes the truth.[90]

According to Kierkegaard, believing something to be true can make it true. But is that really the case? Let's put it to the test.

Christians are not the only ones who can hold maximally passionate beliefs. Although atheists are not known for their passion, it certainly seems that there could be maximally passionate atheists. Consider someone brought

A casual stroll through the lunatic asylum shows that faith does not prove anything.

—FRIEDRICH NIETZSCHE

I respect faith, but doubt is what gets you an education.

—WILSON MIZNER

up in a very religious home who wants desperately to believe only what he is justified in believing. It takes a supreme act of will for him to accept reason—as opposed to revelation—as a source of knowledge. But suppose he succeeds in passionately believing in the nonexistence of God. Then, according to Kierkegaard, it would be objectively true that there is no God. Now suppose that his twin brother believes just as passionately in the existence of God. Then it would be objectively true that there is a God. But it's logically impossible for it to be objectively true that God exists and that he doesn't exist. So Kierkegaard's theory of truth cannot possibly be correct.

Maybe Kierkegaard's theory doesn't apply to atheists. In that case, consider one of the many cult leaders who believe themselves to be the one true God. Suppose one of these leaders believes it with a maximum amount of inwardness. Then he would be the one true God. Now suppose that another cult leader believes just as passionately that he is the one true God. Then he would be the one true God. But they both can't be the one true God. So again Kierkegaard's theory must be mistaken. The moral of the story is that even in religious matters, you can't make something true simply by believing it to be true.

Kierkegaard not only considers passionate belief to be the road to truth, he also considers it to be the road to virtue. People who believe in God passionately are better than people who don't. As he puts it, "Whoever is neither cold nor hot is nauseating."[91] But is passionate belief in God something to be admired? Bertrand Russell doesn't think so:

> There is something feeble, and a little contemptible, about a man who cannot face the perils of life without the help of comfortable myths. Almost inevitably some part of him is aware that they are myths and that he believes them only because they are comforting. But he dare not face this thought, and he therefore cannot carry his own reflections to any logical conclusion. Moreover, since he is aware, however dimly, that his opinions are not rational, he becomes furious when they are disputed. He therefore adopts persecution, censorship, and a narrowly cramping education as essentials of statecraft. In so far as he is successful, he produces a population which is timid and unadventurous and incapable of progress.[92]

Rather than admiring those who believe something when there is no good evidence for it, Russell despises them. Because they can't support their view by reason, they have to resort to force and violence. Such people, Russell says, do not make the world a better place.

The notion that faith in Christ is to be rewarded by an eternity of bliss, while a dependence upon reason, observation, and experience merits everlasting pain, is too absurd for refutation, and can be believed only by that unhappy mixture of insanity and ignorance called 'faith.'

—ROBERT G. INGERSOLL

Evidentialism

In courts of law, you can't convict someone unless you have adequate evidence of their guilt, because without adequate evidence, a guilty verdict would not be justified. Many claim that what goes in courts of law should go in everyday life: you are justified in believing something only if you have adequate evidence for it. This view, known as **evidentialism**, holds that only beliefs based on evidence can be justified. Some go further and claim that you

evidentialism The doctrine that you are justified in believing something if and only if your evidence supports it.

have a moral obligation to proportion your belief to the evidence. In their view, if you believe something for which you do not have adequate evidence, you have done something wrong.

No one has expressed this point of view more forcefully than the distinguished mathematician W. K. Clifford: "It is wrong always, everywhere, and for anyone to believe anything on insufficient evidence."[93] Others of similar stature have echoed this sentiment. Biologist Thomas Henry Huxley, for example, declared, "It is wrong for a man to say that he is certain of the objective truth of any proposition unless he can produce evidence which logically justifies that certainty."[94] The reason these men think that it is wrong for belief to outstrip the evidence is that our actions are guided by our beliefs, and if our beliefs are mistaken, our actions may be misguided.

To demonstrate the importance of basing belief on the evidence, Clifford provides the following example:

> A shipowner was about to send to sea an emigrant-ship. He knew that she was old, and not overwell built at the first; that she had seen many seas and climes, and often had needed repairs. Doubts had been suggested to him that possibly she was not seaworthy. These doubts preyed upon his mind, and made him unhappy; he thought that perhaps he ought to have her thoroughly overhauled and refitted, even though this should put him at great expense. Before the ship sailed, however, he succeeded in overcoming these melancholy reflections. He said to himself that she had gone safely through so many voyages and weathered so many storms that it was idle to suppose she would not come safely home from this trip also. He would put his trust in Providence, which could hardly fail to protect all these unhappy families that were leaving their fatherland to seek for better times elsewhere. He would dismiss from his mind all ungenerous suspicions about the honesty of builders and contractors. In such ways he acquired a sincere and comfortable conviction that his vessel was thoroughly safe and seaworthy; he watched her departure with a light heart, and benevolent wishes for the success of the exiles in their strange new home that was to be; and he got his insurance-money when she went down in mid-ocean and told no tales.[95]

The shipowner did not base his belief on the evidence. Instead he engaged in wishful thinking and self-deception. Consequently, Clifford claims that he is morally responsible for the death of the emigrants. Even if the ship had not sunk, the shipowner would still be in the wrong because "he had no right to believe on such evidence as was before him."[96]

When lives hang in the balance, it certainly seems that we have a duty to proportion our belief to the evidence, that is, to believe no more—and no less—than what the evidence warrants. But, according to Clifford, we have a duty to proportion our belief to the evidence in all cases.

> Every time we let ourselves believe for unworthy reasons, we weaken our powers of self-control, of doubting, of judicially and fairly weighing evidence. We all suffer severely enough from the maintenance and support of false beliefs and the fatally wrong actions which they lead to. . . . But a greater and wider evil arises when the credulous character is maintained and supported, when a habit of believing for unworthy reasons is fostered and made permanent."[97]

They who imagine truth in untruth and see untruth in truth, never arrive at truth, but follow vain desires.

—THE DHAMMAPADA

According to Clifford, responsible believing is a skill that can be maintained only through constant practice. And because responsible believing is a prerequisite for responsible acting, we have a duty to foster that skill. If we don't, we diminish our powers of judgment and thereby weaken the social fabric.

Brand Blanshard agrees, arguing that the duty to proportion our belief to the evidence is absolute:

> To think is to seek to know. In seeking knowledge, we assume that it is something worth having, something intrinsically good, that to miss it through ignorance or error is an evil, and that the more of it we have, the better. To court falsity is wrong, and that is what we do when we allow belief to outrun the evidence. To forgo truth needlessly is also wrong, and that is what we do when, with sufficient evidence before us, we decline to believe. Strangely enough, the rule that we should equate our belief with the evidence seems to have no exceptions. Most maxims of conduct, of course, do have exceptions. The rule that we should keep a promise must at times be broken for the sake of the overriding good of saving a life. The rule that life should be saved must at times be broken in the interest of the overriding good of a nation. But it is hard to imagine any circumstances in which it would be right, if we could avoid it, to believe either more or less than the evidence before us warrants.[98]

Blanshard here attempts to justify evidentialism not by appeal to its social consequences, but by appeal to the intrinsic value of knowledge. Knowledge, he claims, is a good thing whereas error is an evil. The surest way to maximize our knowledge and minimize our error is to proportion our belief to the evidence.

The way to see by faith is to shut the eye of reason.
—BENJAMIN FRANKLIN

We certainly have a duty to act responsibly. Do we also have a duty to believe responsibly? Is it as immoral to believe something we have no right to believe as it is to take something we have no right to take? Clifford and Blanshard believe so. As evidence for this belief, Blanshard offers the case of Torquemada, the head of the Spanish Inquisition.

Torquemada burned more than two thousand people at the stake for what he considered to be their heretical beliefs. We consider what he did to be terribly wrong. But why? Blanshard offers the following analysis:

> When an act is set down as wrong, it is usually because of bad consequences or a bad motive. Suppose that in this case you fix upon the consequences, which included the excruciating suffering in mind and body of many good men and women. Torquemada would have admitted the suffering. But he would have pointed out that in his view, the consequences included very much more; they included the cleansing from Spain of human plague-spots from which a pestilence was spreading, a pestilence that threatened to carry large numbers of persons to perdition and was averted cheaply by this relatively small number of deaths. So far as consequences were concerned, the balance was therefore good. As for motive, the highest of all motives is the sense of duty, and this Torquemada felt strongly. One may say that a human being should have some humanity as well as a sense of duty. He would probably reply, following Augustine, that he was doing a genuine kindness to the people he sent to the stake. If they continued heretics, they would suffer agonizingly and eternally in hell; so far they had resisted everything that might, by inducing them to recant, have prevented their

going there; there was some chance that, if put on the pyre and burnt by a slow fire, as they not infrequently were to give more time to repent, they would renounce their error; and was not an hour or so of fire in this life a low price at which to purchase exemption from an eternity of fire hereafter?[99]

If there is a God, atheism must strike Him as less of an insult than religion.
—EDMOND AND JULES DE GONCOURT

Torquemada believed that he was doing his duty, and he also may have believed that he was doing what was best for both society and his victims. Why, then, are his actions wrong? Blanshard claims that they are wrong because "he had no right to believe what he did."[100]

To students of World War II, Torquemada's reasoning should sound familiar, for it is the same sort of reasoning Hitler gave for exterminating the Jews. Hitler claimed that the Jews were a plague on mankind and that he was doing the human race a favor by eradicating them. Torquemada's reasoning should also sound familiar to students of the war against terrorism, for it is the same sort of reasoning that Islamic terrorists give for killing Americans. Islamic terrorists believe that America is an agent of the devil (the Great Satan) and a source of great evil. They believe that their suicide bombings are sanctioned by God and that their sacrifice will be rewarded in heaven with seventy-two virgins. We think that what Hitler did and what the Islamic terrorists are doing is wrong. But what makes it wrong? Is it, as Blanshard claims, that they have no right to believe what they do?

No, because even if they had a right to believe what they did, their actions would still be wrong. Two thousand years ago, people had a right to believe that the earth was flat. All the evidence available pointed to that conclusion. But that didn't make the earth flat. Believing something to be so doesn't make it so, even if the belief is justified. Similarly, suppose that Torquemada had what seemed to be a reliable test for being a Devil-loving witch. Perhaps his research had revealed that all, and only, those who passed the test had admitted to being a witch in their diaries. In any event, even if he was justified in believing that he could accurately identify witches, what he did was still wrong because there are no such witches. The rightness or wrongness of an action depends on the way the world is, not on the way that people think the world is.

As we saw in Chapter 5, a moral judgment follows from a moral principle and a factual claim. If the factual claim is false, then any moral judgment based solely on that claim is mistaken. Torquemada's, Hitler's, and the Islamic terrorists' actions are wrong because the facts on which they are based are false: there are no Devil-loving witches, Jews are not a plague on mankind, and Americans are not agents of the Devil.

Actions are not the only things we make moral judgments about, however. In addition to judging actions to be right or wrong, we also judge people to be good or bad. Perhaps Clifford's and Blanshard's arguments can be better understood as arguments about what makes persons good or bad.

A good (virtuous) person is one who has a tendency to do the right thing. But doing the right thing requires believing what is true. And the best way to ensure that you believe what is true is to proportion your belief to the evidence. So it could be argued that anyone who does not practice responsible believing is not a good person. In other words, being morally virtuous requires being intellectually virtuous.

A virtue, you will recall, is an admirable quality that is either good for you or good for other people. Proportioning your belief to the evidence is good for you because it makes it less likely that you'll be taken in by con artists, swindlers, and charlatans. It is good for other people because it makes it less likely that you will do something immoral. So proportioning your belief to the evidence can be considered to be a virtue.

Thought Probe

Blanshard's Beliefs

Are Blanshard and Clifford correct in claiming that our duty to proportion our beliefs to the evidence is absolute? Can you think of a counterexample, a case where it would not be right to proportion your belief to the evidence? Should people who don't proportion their belief to the evidence be ashamed of themselves? Why or why not?

The Will to Believe

American philosopher and psychologist William James argues that our duty to proportion our belief to the evidence is not absolute. There are times, he says, when we are justified in believing something on faith. He agrees with Clifford and Blanshard that it's wrong not to base our belief on the evidence when the matter can be decided on purely intellectual grounds. But in those cases where we're faced with a genuine option, and when believing something to be true can help make it true, we are justified in believing more than what the evidence warrants.

A genuine option, for James, is one that is forced, live, and momentous. A forced option is one where there are two mutually exclusive alternatives and you must choose one or the other. A live option is one that is believable because it is possible for it to be true. And a momentous option is one whose consequences are significant. James gives the following example of a genuine option where it is permissible not to proportion our belief to the evidence:

> *Do you like me or not?* — for example. Whether you do or not depends, in countless instances, on whether I meet you half-way, am willing to assume that you must like me, and show you trust and expectation. The previous faith on my part in your liking's existence is in such cases what makes your liking come. But if I stand aloof, and refuse to budge an inch until I have objective evidence . . . ten to one your liking never comes.[101]

Although I have no evidence that you like me, if I have faith that you do, then you may come to like me. Because unfounded beliefs can bring about desirable consequences, James believes that only a fool would not have unfounded beliefs. As he puts it, "*where faith in a fact can help create the fact,* that would be an insane logic which would say that faith running ahead of scientific evidence is the 'lowest kind of immorality' into which a thinking being can fall."[102]

Believe that life is worth living, and your belief will help create that fact.
—William James

But are such beliefs really unfounded? It wouldn't seem so, for they are based on well-known facts about human behavior. We know, for example, that if we treat people with kindness and respect, they will usually return the favor. This knowledge has been gained through experience and serves as the evidence on which our faith rests. Far from being groundless, then, our faith is actually well rooted in our knowledge of human nature. James is right in claiming that the decision to show kindness to strangers can be rational. He is wrong, however, in claiming that there is no evidence to support such a decision.

What's more, James's claim that our faith can transform others is misleading. It is not our faith that brings about the change; it is our behavior. By acting *as if* we like someone, we may get her to like us. For such a strategy to work, however, it is not necessary that we actually like the person. All that is required is that we get her to believe that we like her. So it's our actions rather than our beliefs that produce the desired results.

A better example would be that of believing in yourself. If you believe that you can accomplish something—if you are self-confident—you may be more likely to accomplish it. But again it's unclear that such self-confidence is unfounded. Folk wisdom tells us that believing in yourself is an important ingredient of success. (That's the moral of the story "The Little Engine That Could," for example.) So the belief that you can accomplish something, even if you've never accomplished it before, can be justified on the basis of well-established psychological principles.

But let's grant that there are cases where faith in a fact can bring about a fact. Is belief in the existence of God one of them? It wouldn't seem so. We can no more bring God into existence by believing in him than we can bring the tooth fairy into existence by believing in her. God's existence doesn't depend on our belief. If it did, he wouldn't be all-powerful.

Faith in the existence of a particular god is not the sort of faith James is trying to justify, however. He is trying to justify faith in the affirmations common to all religions, which he identifies as follows:

> First, she says that the best things are the eternal things . . . the things in the universe that throw the last stone . . . and say the final word. "Perfection is eternal. . . ."
>
> The second affirmation of religion is that we are better off even now if we believe her first affirmation to be true.[103]

What can faith in these affirmations accomplish? According to James, it can give us a sense of being personally related to the universe.

> The more perfect and more eternal aspect of the universe is represented in our religions as having personal form. The universe is no longer a mere *It* to us, but a *Thou*, if we are religious; and any relation that might be possible from person to person might be possible here.[104]

Your believing that the universe has person-like aspects can help you develop a personal relationship to it, and such a relationship can help give meaning, point, and purpose to your life.[105] But your believing that the universe has person-like aspects can't turn it into a person or the creation of one. The fact that your faith can create is a fact about you—the fact that you have a certain attitude toward the universe.

The Meaning of Life

Many theists believe that their lives can be meaningful if and only if they are part of a divine plan. If there was no intelligence behind the creation of the universe—if the universe came into existence as the result of a random vacuum fluctuation, for example—there is no reason for its existing. But if there is no reason for its existing, they feel, there is no reason for their existing either.

The assumption here is that fulfilling God's plan would make our lives meaningful. Robert Nozick puts that assumption to the test in the following thought experiment.

Thought Experiment

God's Plan

Suppose God decides to reveal to us why He created us. Everywhere on the planet, everyone hears a deep, beautiful voice resonating in their heads: "Now, my children, the time has come for me to reveal why I created you. In a week,

a band of intergalactic travelers will be passing through your solar system. I arranged their trip, and it just so happens that the only thing they can eat are human beings. (I designed them that way.) So I created you as a source of food for them. When they land, I want you to walk into their food processing chambers and turn yourself into people burgers."[106]

Faith and Meaning   **501**

It's possible that God created us to serve as food for another species. After all, many people believe that God put animals and plants here for us to eat. Who knows what super-advanced aliens eat?

If our sole purpose for being were to serve as food for someone else, would being eaten by that group make our lives meaningful? Nozick thinks not. He writes, "If the cosmic role of human beings was to provide a negative lesson to some others ('don't act like them') or to provide needed food for passing intergalactic travelers who were important, this would not suit our aspirations—not even if afterwards the intergalactic travelers smacked their lips and said that we tasted good."[107] Doing our creator's bidding does not necessarily make our lives meaningful.

This can be demonstrated by a much more mundane example. Suppose your parents had always planned on you being a doctor, but you had always wanted to be an artist. In that case, would being a doctor make your life meaningful? Probably not. Even though your parents created you, doing what they want you to do would not necessarily endow your life with meaning. Similarly, even if God created you, doing what he wants you to do would not necessarily make your life meaningful.

What's more, if all meaning comes from without, then God's existence must be meaningless because he is not part of anybody's plan. But if God's existence is meaningless, then our existence is meaningless, for as Irish philosopher George Berkeley realized, "Nothing can give to another that which it hath not itself."[108] On the other hand, if God's existence is not meaningless, he must be able to create his own meaning. But if God can create his own meaning, why can't we? We're rational, self-conscious beings with free will. We know what gives us satisfaction, and we can formulate plans to achieve it. It seems that we have all we need to generate our own meaning.

Existentialism

The notion that we are part of a divine plan is one of the oldest and most influential ideas in Western intellectual history. It holds that everything was created for a purpose, and that the value of a thing is determined by how well it accomplishes its purpose. Because it also maintains that the different types of things can be arranged in a hierarchy from lowest to highest—minerals, vegetables, animals, humans, angels, God—this idea has come to be known as the "Great Chain of Being."

Existentialists explicitly repudiate this idea. They do not believe that our lives were planned out by God before we came into existence. Instead, they believe that we come into existence and then decide for ourselves how we are going to live our lives. This view is summed up in their slogan: existence precedes essence. Philosopher and Nobel Prize–winning author Jean-Paul Sartre explains,

> Atheistic existentialism, of which I am a representative, declares with greater
> consistency that if God does not exist there is at least one being whose existence

comes before its essence, a being which exists before it can be defined by any conception of it. That being is man or, as Heidegger has it, the human reality. What do we mean by saying that existence precedes essence? We mean that man first of all exists, encounters himself, surges up in the world and defines himself afterwards. If man as the existentialist sees him is not definable, it is because to begin with he is nothing. He will not be anything until later, and then he will be what he makes of himself. Thus, there is no human nature, because there is no God to have a conception of it. Man simply is. . . . Man is nothing else but that which he makes of himself. That is the first principle of existentialism.[109]

In Sartre's view, then, we have not been put here to do anyone's bidding; there is no purpose that we are designed to serve. Consequently, the meaning of our lives can't consist in following some prearranged plan because there is no such plan. Whatever meaning we find in life we must create for ourselves.

In claiming that we have no essence, Sartre isn't denying that we possess certain physical and social properties. We all have a certain height, weight, skin color, class, nationality, and so on. But these properties (which Sartre refers to as our "facticity") don't make us who we are because that depends on what we *make* of those properties. Unlike other creatures that exist only "in themselves" ("*en soi*"), we exist "for ourselves" ("*pour soi*"). Who we are is an issue for us, an issue that we can decide for ourselves.

According to the existentialists, we create ourselves in the act of making choices. We exist in a world that demands that we do things, that we undertake certain projects. We interpret the things we encounter in the world in terms of those projects. But, as these projects unfold, our selves come into being. In the act of deciding what to do, we determine who we will become.

Only authentic choices are self-determining, however. An authentic choice is one with which you identify. If you do something simply because it's the normal or expected thing to do, your decision is not authentic. But if you do it because it reflects the kind of person you want to become, then it's authentic.

There is no one you can turn to for guidance in making authentic choices, however, because if your choice is based on the views of an external authority, it's not authentic. So Sartre characterizes the human condition as one of abandonment, anguish, and despair: Abandonment because we're on our own, no one can make our choices for us. Anguish because we have to choose. We can't simply do nothing because, as theologian Harvey Cox realized, "Not to choose is to choose." And despair because we have to live with the consequences of our choices.

This is a bleak view of the human condition. Existential art and literature promotes this view by exploring such themes as alienation, absurdity, and angst. But are such negative responses the only plausible ones to the realization that we are ultimately responsible for our lives? Classicist Hazel Barnes thinks not. She writes,

> No humanistic existentialist will allow that the only alternative is despair and irresponsibility. Camus has pointed out the fallacy involved in leaping from the premise "The universe has no higher meaning" to the conclusion, "Therefore my life is not worth living." The individual life may have an intrinsic value, both to

We owe it to ourselves as respectable human beings, as thinking human beings, to do what we can to make humanity more rational. . . . Humanists recognize that it is only when people feel free to think for themselves, using reason as their guide, that they are best capable of developing values that succeed in satisfying human needs and serving human interests.

—ISAAC ASIMOV

the one who lives it and to those in the sphere of his influence, whether the universe knows what it's doing or not.[110]

In other words, just because there's no meaning *of* life, it doesn't follow that there can be no meaning *in* life.[111] As long as you're doing your own thing, your life can be meaningful, even if it's not part of anyone else's plan.

Religion without God

Many think that being a religious person requires holding certain beliefs about God. But as we've seen, the belief that there is a God who is all-powerful, all-knowing, and all-good is suspect. A growing number of theologians, after realizing that traditional theistic beliefs cannot be rationally maintained, have concluded that we should reject those beliefs. Foremost among them is John Shelby Spong, former Episcopal Bishop of Newark, New Jersey. In a number of works, including *Why Christianity Must Change or Die*, he argues that only by giving up the belief in a theistic God can Christianity survive as a religion. Being a nontheist or an atheist, however, doesn't prevent one from being a deeply religious person. All Buddhists, for example, are atheists because they don't believe in a supreme being of either the personal or the impersonal variety. Nevertheless, many consider them to be among the most religious people on the planet. What makes them so religious is not their particular beliefs, but the kind of persons they are and the kind of lives they lead.

Robert Coburn argues that those who have a religious attitude toward life share four important characteristics:

First, they have a sense of the numinous. That is, they are struck or moved, at least from time to time, by awareness of the sacred, by an apprehension of something in (or about) life or the world that is deeply mysterious, something both attractive and fearful that evokes such responses as awe and reverence. . . .

Second, they find themselves, at least from time to time, possessed of those "fruits of the spirit" that St. Paul called "love, joy [and] peace." That is, they frequently, or at least occasionally, know a deep serenity, poise, tranquility, or quietness within, a peace that is rooted in a profound sense of security despite the contingencies of life. . . .

Third, more or less devoutly religious people within the Christian tradition often have certain characteristic attitudes toward life and toward some of the more fundamental events and situations in life. Thus they often regard seeking after fame, fortune, and power as wrong insofar at least as one is motivated by vanity or a desire for self-glorification. . . .

Fourth, the behavior of those who live the life of faith has a characteristic shape. At least the following three behavioral features tend to be present among the devout in the Christian tradition. Such people participate in public and private "acts of worship." . . . Such people also regularly act in ways that involve putting on "the form of the servant" . . . Last, such people act in ways designed to "share the blessing" they feel they have received through participation in the life of their religious community and tradition with those who are outside "the circle of the faithful."[112]

To have these characteristics — to have a religious orientation toward life — it is neither necessary nor sufficient to have a belief in God. It's not necessary because, like the Buddhists, one can have these characteristics and not believe in God. It's not sufficient because one can believe in God and not have these characteristics. We all know people who believe in God but have little respect for nature, are always on the go, only look out for number one and never do volunteer work. Even though these people have religious beliefs, they are not religious people.

Being a good person and leading a good life does not require having a belief in God. Theists and atheists alike can possess high moral character and be socially responsible. Similarly, being a religious person doesn't require having any particular religious beliefs. Atheists can have a religious orientation toward life and theists can lack one. The fruits of religion, then, are not limited to only the faithful.

> *I have ever judged of the religion of others by their lives. . . . But this does not satisfy the priesthood. They must have a positive, a declared assent to all their interested absurdities. My opinion is that there would never have been an infidel, if there had never been a priest.*
>
> —Thomas Jefferson

Summary

Kierkegaard realizes that accepting the Christian story requires making a leap of faith because certain aspects of that story are absurd. But he advocates making the leap because by doing so you can attain the highest truth possible. Russell finds those who believe on faith feeble and contemptible because they are not willing to face reality. Because they can't back up their views with logic or reason, they often resort to violence.

Clifford argues that we have a moral duty to proportion our belief to the evidence on the grounds that it will strengthen society. Blanshard argues for that duty on the grounds that it will help us attain knowledge and avoid error.

James argues that we need not always proportion our belief to the evidence. When we are faced with a genuine choice that can't be decided on intellectual grounds, and where faith in a fact can help create that fact, we may justifiably believe on faith.

The existentialists believe that we define ourselves through our choices. If those choices are authentic, our lives can be meaningful, even if they're not part of a divine plan.

Study Questions

1. Why does Kierkegaard believe that being a Christian requires a leap of faith?
2. According to Kierkegaard, what is the difference between objective and subjective truth?
3. Why does Russell think that faith is not something to be admired?
4. What is evidentialism?

5. Why does Clifford believe we should proportion our beliefs to the evidence?

6. Why does Blanshard believe we should proportion our beliefs to the evidence?

7. According to James, when is an option genuine?

8. According to James, when is faith justified?

9. What do the existentialists mean by their slogan "existence precedes essence"?

10. According to the existentialists, when is a choice authentic?

Discussion Questions

1. Are there any cases where simply believing something to be true, makes it true? If so, what are they?

2. Is faith a virtue? Why or why not?

3. What if children were taught from an early age to be ashamed of themselves if they didn't believe responsibly, in the same way they are now taught to be ashamed of themselves if they didn't behave responsibly? Would society be better or worse for it?

4. Do you agree with the existentialists that your life can be meaningful even if it isn't part of a divine plan? Why or why not?

5. Consider this quote from Edmund Way Teale: "It is morally as bad not to care whether a thing is true or not, so long as it makes you feel good, as it is not to care how you got your money as long as you have got it."[113] Is this true? Is it immoral not to question your religious beliefs?

The Five Ways

St. Thomas Aquinas (1225–1274) became a Dominican monk when he was only eighteen years old. His mother, a noblewoman, opposed his affiliation with an order of what she regarded as beggars and imprisoned him in the family castle for more than a year. When she finally released him, he went to Paris to continue his studies under Albertus Magnus. He was appointed professor of philosophy at the University of Paris in 1256. Aquinas's great work, *Summa Theologica*, attempted to reconcile the Augustinian theology (which held that revelation was the only source of knowledge) with Aristotelian philosophy (which held that sense experience was the only source of knowledge). Aquinas argued that reason and revelation are compatible with one another. Specifically, he held that the existence of God can be proved through the use of reason. In what follows, Aquinas responds to objections that God doesn't exist by providing his own arguments for the existence of God.

Objection 1. It seems that God does not exist; because if one of two contraries be infinite, the other would be altogether destroyed. But the word 'God' means that He is infinite goodness. If, therefore, God existed, there would be no evil discoverable; but there is evil in the world. Therefore God does not exist.

Obj. 2. Further, it is superfluous to suppose that what can be accounted for by a few principles has been produced by many. But it seems that everything we see in the world can be accounted for by other principles, supposing God did not exist. For all natural things can be reduced to one principle, which is nature; and all voluntary things can be reduced to one principle, which is human reason, or will. Therefore there is no need to suppose God's existence.

On the contrary, It is said in the person of God: *I am Who I am* (Exod. iii. 14).

I answer that, The existence of God can be proved in five ways.

The first and more manifest way is the argument from motion. It is certain, and evident to our senses, that in the world some things are in motion. Now whatever is in motion is put in motion by another, for nothing can be in motion except it is in potentiality to that towards which it is in motion; whereas a thing moves inasmuch as it is in act. For motion is nothing else than the reduction of something from potentiality to actuality. But nothing can be reduced from potentiality to actuality, except by something in a state of actuality. Thus that which is actually hot, as fire, makes wood, which is potentially hot, to be actually hot, and thereby moves

and changes it. Now it is not possible that the same thing should be at once in actuality and potentiality in the same respect, but only in different respects. For what is actually hot cannot simultaneously be potentially hot; but it is simultaneously potentially cold. It is therefore impossible that in the same respect and in the same way a thing should be both mover and moved, *i.e.*, that it should move itself. Therefore, whatever is in motion must be put in motion by another. If that by which it is put in motion be itself put in motion, then this also must needs be put in motion by another, and that by another again. But this cannot go on to infinity, because then there would be no first mover, and, consequently, no other mover; seeing that subsequent movers move only inasmuch as they are put in motion by the first mover; as the staff moves only because it is put in motion by the hand. Therefore it is necessary to arrive at a first mover, put in motion by no other; and this everyone understands to be God.

The second way is from the nature of the efficient cause. In the world of sense we find there is an order of efficient causes. There is no case known (neither is it, indeed, possible) in which a thing is found to be the efficient cause of itself; for so it would be prior to itself, which is impossible. Now in efficient causes it is not possible to go on to infinity, because in all efficient causes following in order, the first is the cause of the

From: St. Thomas Aquinas, *Summa Theologica* (London: Burns, Oates, and Washbourne, 1920) 24–27.

intermediate cause, and the intermediate is the cause of the ultimate cause, whether the intermediate cause be several, or one only. Now to take away the cause is to take away the effect. Therefore, if there be no first cause among efficient causes, there will be no ultimate, nor any intermediate cause. But if in efficient causes it is possible to go on to infinity, there will be no first efficient cause, neither will there be an ultimate effect, nor any intermediate efficient causes; all of which is plainly false. Therefore it is necessary to admit a first efficient cause, to which everyone gives the name of God.

The third way is taken from possibility and necessity, and runs thus. We find in nature things that are possible to be and not to be, since they are found to be generated, and to corrupt, and consequently, they are possible to be and not to be. But it is impossible for these always to exist, for that which is possible not to be at some time is not. Therefore, if everything is possible not to be, then at one time there could have been nothing in existence. Now if this were true, even now there would be nothing in existence, because that which does not exist only begins to exist by something already existing. Therefore, if at one time nothing was in existence, it would have been impossible for anything to have begun to exist; and thus even now nothing would be in existence—which is absurd. Therefore, not all beings are merely possible, but there must exist something the existence of which is necessary. But every necessary thing either has its necessity caused by another, or not. Now it is impossible to go on to infinity in necessary things which have their necessity caused by another, as has been already proved in regard to efficient causes. Therefore we cannot but postulate the existence of some being having of itself its own necessity, and not receiving it from another, but rather causing in others their necessity. This all men speak of as God.

The fourth way is taken from the gradation to be found in things. Among beings there are some more and some less good, true, noble, and the like. But 'more' and 'less' are predicated of different things, according as they resemble in their different ways something which is the maximum, as a thing is said to be hotter according as it more nearly resembles that which is hottest; so that there is something which is truest, something best, something noblest, and, consequently, something which is uttermost being; for those things that are greatest in truth are greatest in being, as it is written in *Metaph*. ii. Now the maximum in any genus is the cause of all in that genus; as fire, which is the maximum of heat, is the cause of all hot things. Therefore there must also be something which is to all beings the cause of their being, goodness, and every other perfection; and this we call God.

The fifth way is taken from the governance of the world. We see that things which lack intelligence, such as natural bodies, act for an end, and this is evident from their acting always, or nearly always, in the same way, so as to obtain the best result. Hence it is plain that not fortuitously, but designedly, do they achieve their end. Now whatever lacks intelligence cannot move towards an end, unless it be directed by some being endowed with knowledge and intelligence; as the arrow is shot to its mark by the archer. Therefore some intelligent being exists by whom all natural things are directed to their end; and this being we call God.

Reply Obj. 1. As Augustine says (*Enchir.* xi.): *Since God is the highest good, He would not allow any evil to exist in His works, unless His omnipotence and goodness were such as to bring good even out of evil.* This is part of the infinite goodness of God, that He should allow evil to exist, and out of it produce good.

Reply Obj. 2. Since nature works for a determinate end under the direction of a higher agent, whatever is done by nature must needs be traced back to God, as to its first cause. So also whatever is done voluntarily must also be traced back to some higher cause other than human reason or will, since these can change and fail; for all things that are changeable and capable of defect must be traced back to an immovable and self-necessary first principle, as was shown in the body of the *Article*.

Natural Theology

Richard Swinburne (1934–) is Emeritus Nolloth Professor of the Philosophy of the Christian Religion at Oxford University, England. He is one of the foremost proponents of natural theology (the attempt to prove the existence of God on the basis of facts about nature). His books include *The Existence of God*, *The Coherence of Theism*, and *The Evolution of the Soul*. In this selection, taken from his "The Vocation of a Natural Theologian," he explains the nature of his project.

The basic idea of *The Existence of God* is that the various traditional arguments for theism—from the existence of the world (the cosmological argument), from its conformity to scientific laws (a version of the teleological argument), and so on—are best construed not as deductive arguments but as inductive arguments to the existence of God. A valid deductive argument is one in which the premises (the starting points) infallibly guarantee the truth of the conclusion; a correct inductive argument is one in which the premises confirm the conclusion (that is, make it more probable than it would otherwise be). Science argues from various limited observable phenomena to their unobservable physical causes, and in so doing it argues inductively. My claim was that theism is the best justified of metaphysical theories. The existence of God is a very simple hypothesis that leads us to expect various very general and more specific phenomena that otherwise we would not expect; and for that reason it is rendered probable by the phenomena. Or rather, as with any big scientific theory, each group of phenomena adds to the probability of the theory—together they make it significantly more probable than not.

When explaining phenomena we have available two different kinds of explanation. One is scientific explanation, whereby we explain a phenomenon E in terms of some prior state of affairs F (the cause) in accordance with some regularity or natural law L that describes the behavior of objects involved in F and E. We explain why a stone took two seconds to fall from a tower to the ground (E) by its having been liberated from rest at the top of the tower 64 feet from the ground (F) and by the regularity derivable from Galileo's law of fall that all bodies fall toward the surface of the earth with an acceleration of 32 ft/sec (L); E follows from F and L. And . . . science can also explain the operation of a regularity or law in some narrow area in terms of the operation of a wider law. Thus it can explain why Galileo's law of fall holds for small objects near the surface of the earth. Galileo's law follows from Newton's laws, given that the earth is a body of a certain mass far from other massive bodies and the objects on its surface are close to it and small in mass in comparison.

The other way that we use all the time and see as a proper way of explaining phenomena is what I call personal explanation. We often explain some phenomenon E as brought about by a person P in order to achieve some purpose or goal G. The present motion of my hand is explained as brought about by me for the purpose of picking up a glass. The motion of my legs earlier toward a room is explained by my purpose of going there to give a lecture. In these cases I bring about a state of my body that then itself causes some state of affairs outside my body. But it is I (P) who brings about the bodily state (E) conducive to producing that further state (G) rather than some other.

The kind of explanation involved here is a different way of explaining things from the scientific. Scientific explanation involves laws of nature and previous states of affairs. Personal explanation involves persons and purposes. In each case the grounds for believing the explanation to be correct are, as stated earlier, the fact that to explain the cited phenomenon and many other similar phenomena we need few entities (for example, one person rather than many), few kinds of entities with few, easily describable properties, behaving in mathematically simple kinds of ways (such as a person having certain capacities and purposes that do not

From: Richard Swinburne, "The Vocation of a Natural Theologian," in *Philosophers Who Believe*, ed. Kelly James Clark (Downers Grove, IL: InterVarsity Press, 1993) 179–202.

change erratically) that give rise to many phenomena. In seeking the best explanation of phenomena we may seek explanations of either kind, and if we cannot find a scientific one that satisfies the criteria, we should look for a personal one.

We should seek explanations of all things; but we have seen that we have reason for supposing that we have found one only if the purported explanation is simple and leads us to expect what we find when that is otherwise not to be expected. The history of science shows that we judge that the complex, miscellaneous, coincidental and diverse needs explaining, and that it is to be explained in terms of something simpler. The motions of the planets (subject to Kepler's laws), the mechanical interactions of bodies on earth, the behavior of pendula, the motions of tides, the behavior of comets and so forth formed a pretty miscellaneous set of phenomena. Newton's law of motion constituted a simple theory that led us to expect these phenomena, and so was judged a true explanation of them. The existence of thousands of different chemical substances combining in different ratios to make other substances was complex. The hypothesis that there were only a hundred or so chemical elements of which the thousands of substances were made was a simple hypothesis that led us to expect the complex phenomena. When we reach the simplest possible starting point for explanation that leads us to expect the phenomena that we find, there alone we should stop and believe that we have found the ultimate brute fact on which all other things depend.

The Cosmological Argument

The cosmological argument argues from the existence of a complex physical universe (or something as general as that) to God who keeps it in being. The premise is the existence of our universe for so long as it has existed (whether a finite time or, if it has no beginning, an infinite time). The universe is a complex thing with lots and lots of separate chunks. Each of these chunks has a different finite and not very natural volume, shape, mass and so forth—consider the vast diversity of galaxies, stars and planets, and pebbles on the seashore. Matter is inert and has no powers that it can choose to exert; it does what it has to do. There is a limited amount of it in any region, and it has a limited amount of energy and velocity. There is a complexity, particularity and finitude about the universe that looks for explanation in terms of something simpler.

The existence of the universe is something evidently inexplicable by science. For, as we saw, a scientific ex-

planation as such explains the occurrence of one state of affairs in terms of a previous state of affairs and some law of nature that makes states like the former bring about states like the latter. It may explain the planets being in their present positions by a previous state of the system (the sun and planets being where they were last year) and the operation of Kepler's laws, which postulate that states like the latter are followed a year later by states like the former. And so it may explain the existence of the universe this year in terms of the existence of the universe last year and the laws of cosmology. But either there was a first state of the universe or there has always been a universe. In the former case, science cannot explain why there was the first state; and in the latter case it still cannot explain why any matter exists (or, more correctly, matter-energy) for the laws of nature to get a grip on, as it were. By its very nature science cannot explain why there are any states of affairs at all.

But a God can provide an explanation. The hypothesis of theism is that the universe exists because there is a God who keeps it in being and that laws of nature operate because there is a God who brings it about that they do. He brings it about that the laws of nature operate by sustaining in every object in the universe its liability to behave in accord with those laws (including the law of the conservation of matter, that at each moment what was there before continues to exist). The universe exists because at each moment of finite or infinite time, he keeps in being objects with this liability. The hypothesis of theism is like a hypothesis that a person brings about certain things for some purpose. God acts directly on the universe, as we act directly on our brains, guiding them to move our limbs (but the universe of course is not his body).

As we have seen, personal explanation and scientific explanation are the two ways we have of explaining the occurrence of phenomena. Since there cannot be a scientific explanation of the existence of the universe, either there is a personal explanation or there is no explanation at all. The hypothesis that there is a God is the hypothesis of the existence of the simplest kind of person that there could be. A person is a being with power to bring about effects, knowledge of how to do so and freedom to choose which effects to bring about. God is by definition an omnipotent (that is, infinitely powerful), omniscient (that is, all-knowing) and perfectly free person: he is a person of infinite power, knowledge and freedom; a person to whose power, knowledge and freedom there are no limits except those of logic. The hypothesis that there exists a being with infinite degrees of the qualities essential to a being of that kind is the postulation of a very simple being. The hypothesis that there is one such God is a much simpler hypothesis than the hypothesis that there is a god who has such and such limited power, or the hypothesis that there are several gods with limited powers. It is simpler in just the same way that the hypothesis that some particle has zero mass or infinite velocity is simpler than the hypothesis that it has 0.32147 of some unit of mass or a velocity of 221,000 km/sec. A finite limitation cries out for an explanation of why there is just that particular limit, in a way the limitlessness does not. God provides the simplest stopping-point for explanation.

That there should exist anything at all, let alone a universe as complex and as orderly as ours, is exceedingly strange. But if there is a God, it is not vastly unlikely that he should create such a universe. A universe such as ours is a thing of beauty, a theater in which humans and other creatures can grow and work out their destiny, a point that I shall develop further below. So the argument from the universe to God is an argument from a complex phenomenon to a simple entity, which leads us to expect (thought does not guarantee) the existence of the former far more than it would be expected otherwise. Therefore, I suggest, it provides some evidence for its conclusion.

The Argument from Design

The teleological argument, or argument from design, has various forms. One form is the argument from temporal order. This has as its premises the operation of the most general laws of nature, that is, the orderliness of nature in conforming to very general laws. What exactly these laws are, science may not yet have discovered—perhaps they are the field equations of Einstein's general theory of relativity, or perhaps there are some yet more fundamental laws. Now, as we have seen, science can explain the operation of some narrow regularity or law in terms of a wider or more general law. But what science by its very nature cannot explain is why there are the most general laws of nature that there are; for *ex hypothesi*, no wider law can explain their operation.

The conformity of objects throughout endless time and space to simple laws cries out for explanation. For let us consider to what this amounts. Laws are not things, independent of material objects. To say that all objects conform to laws is simply to say that they all behave in exactly the same way. To say, for example, that the planets obey Kepler's laws is just to say that each planet at each moment of time has the property of moving in the ways that Kepler's laws state. There is, therefore, this vast coincidence in the behavioral properties of objects at all times and in all places. If all the coins of some region have the same markings, or all the papers in a room are written in the same handwriting, we seek an explanation in terms of a common source of these coincidences. We should seek a similar explanation for that vast coincidence which we describe as the conformity of objects to laws of nature—such as the fact that all electrons are produced, attract and repel other particles, and combine with them in exactly the same way at each point of endless time and space.

That there is a universe and that there are laws of nature are phenomena so general and pervasive that we tend to ignore them. But there might so easily not have been a universe at all, ever. Or the universe might so easily have been a chaotic mess. That there is an orderly universe is something very striking, yet beyond the capacity of science ever to explain. Science's inability to explain these things is not a temporary phenomenon, caused by the backwardness of twentieth-century science. Rather, because of what a *scientific* explanation is, these things will ever be beyond its capacity to explain. For scientific explanations by their very nature terminate with some ultimate natural law and ultimate physical arrangement of physical things, and the question with which I am concerned is why there are natural laws and physical things at all. There is available again the simple explanation of the temporal orderliness of the universe, that God makes protons and electrons move in an orderly way, just as we might make our bodies move in the regular patterns of a dance. He has *ex hypothesi* the power to do this. But why should he choose to do so? The orderliness of the universe makes it a beautiful universe, but, even more importantly, it makes it a universe that humans can learn to control and change. For only if there are simple laws of nature can humans predict what will follow from what—and unless they can do that, they can never change anything. Only if they know that by sowing certain seeds, weeding and watering them, they will get corn, can they develop an agriculture. And humans can acquire that knowledge only if there are easily graspable regularities of behavior in nature. It is good that there are human beings, embodied minicreators who share in God's activity of forming and developing the universe through their free choice. But if there are to be such, there must be laws of nature. There is therefore, some reasonable expectation that God will bring them about; but otherwise that the universe should exhibit such very striking order is hardly to be expected.

The form of "argument from design" that has been most common in the history of thought and was very widely prevalent in the eighteenth and early nineteenth centuries is the argument from spatial order. The intricate organization of animals and plants that enabled them to catch the food for which their digestive apparatus was suited and to escape from predators suggested that they were like very complicated machines and hence that they must have been put together by a master machine-maker, who built into them at the same time the power to reproduce. The frequent use of this argument in religious apologetic came to an abrupt halt in 1859, when Darwin produced his explanation of why there were complexly organized animals and plants, in terms of the laws of evolution operating on much simpler organisms. There seemed no need to bring God into the picture.

That reaction was, however, premature. For the demand for explanation can be taken back a further stage. Why are there laws of evolution that have the consequence that over many millennia simple organisms gradually give rise to complex organisms? No doubt because these laws follow from the basic laws of physics. But then why do the basic laws of physics have such a form as to give rise to laws of evolution? And why were there primitive organisms in the first place? A plausible story can be told of how the primeval "soup" of matter-energy at the time of the "big bang" (a moment some 15,000 million years ago at which, scientists now tell us, the universe, or at least the present stage of the universe, began) gave rise over many millennia, in accordance with physical laws, to those primitive organisms. But then why was there matter suitable for such evolutionary development in the first place?

With respect to the laws and with respect to the primeval matter, we have again the same choice: saving that these things cannot be further explained or postulating a further explanation. Note that the issue here is not why there are laws at all (the premise of the argument from temporal order) or why there is matter-energy, at all (the premise of the cosmological argument), but why the laws and the matter-energy have this peculiar character of being already wound up to produce plants, animals and humans. Since the most general laws of nature have this special character, there can be no scientific explanation of why they are as they are. And although there might be a scientific explanation of why the matter at the time of the big bang had the special character it did, in terms of its character at some earlier time, clearly if there was a first state of the universe, it must have been of a certain kind; or if the universe has lasted forever, its matter must have had certain general features if at any time there was to be a state of the universe suited to produce plants, animals and humans. Scientific explanation comes to a stop. The question remains whether we should accept these particular features of the laws and matter of the universe as ultimate brute facts or whether we should move beyond them to a personal explanation in terms of the agency of God.

What the choice turns on is how likely it is that the laws and initial conditions should by chance have just this character. Recent scientific work has drawn attention to the fact that the universe is fine-tuned. The matter-energy at the time of the big bang has to have a certain density and a certain velocity of recession; increase or decrease in these respects by one part in a million would have had the effect that the universe was not life-evolving. For example, if the big bang had caused the quanta of matter-energy to recede from each other a little more quickly, no galaxies, stars or planets, and no environment suitable for life would have been formed. If the recession had been marginally slower, the universe would have collapsed in on itself before life could be formed. Similarly, the constants in the laws of nature needed to lie within very narrow limits if life was to be formed. It is, therefore, most unlikely that laws and initial conditions should have by chance a life-producing character. God is able to give matter and laws this character. If we can show that he would have reason to do so, then that gives support to the hypothesis that he has done so. There is available again the reason (in addition to the reason of its beauty) that was a reason why God would choose to bring about an orderly universe at all—the worthwhileness of the sentient embodied beings that the evolutionary process would bring about, and above all of humans who can themselves make informed choices as to what sort of a world there should be.

A similar pattern of argument from various other phenomena such as the existence of conscious beings, the providential ordering of things in certain respects, the occurrence of certain apparently miraculous events in history and the religious experiences of many millions is, I claimed in *The Existence of God*, available to establish theism (when all the arguments are taken together) as overall significantly more probable than not.

Dialogues Concerning Natural Religion

David Hume (1711–1776) wrote his *Treatise of Human Nature* in his early twenties. Although it is one of the finest pieces of empiricist philosophy ever written, its importance was not recognized at the time, and none of the philosophy departments Hume applied to would hire him. Hume became Keeper of the Advocates' Library in Edinburgh and there wrote his *History of England,* which established him as one of the greatest literary figures of his time. The following selections are taken from his *Dialogues Concerning Natural Religion,* in which Philo argues from the lack of empirical evidence to the conclusion that God does not exist.

Not to lose any time in circumlocutions, said CLEANTHES, addressing himself to DEMEA, much less in replying to the pious declamations of PHILO; I shall briefly explain how I conceive this matter. Look round the world: Contemplate the whole and every part if it: You will find it to be nothing but one great machine, subdivided into an infinite number of lesser machines, which again admit of subdivisions, to a degree beyond what human senses and faculties can trace and explain. All these various machines, and even their most minute parts, are adjusted to each other with an accuracy, which ravishes into admiration all men, who have ever contemplated them. The curious adapting of means to ends, throughout all nature, resembles exactly, though it much exceeds, the productions of human contrivance; of human design, thought, wisdom, and intelligence. Since therefore the effects resemble each other, we are led to infer, by all the rules of analogy, that the causes also resemble; and that the Author of nature is somewhat similar to the mind of man; though possessed of much larger faculties, proportioned to the grandeur of the work, which he has executed. By this argument *a posteriori,* and by this argument alone, we do prove at once the existence of a Deity, and his similarity to human mind and intelligence. . . .

If we see a house, CLEANTHES, we conclude, with the greatest certainty, that it had an architect or builder; because this is precisely that species of effect, which we have experienced to proceed from that species of cause. But surely you will not affirm, that the universe bears such a resemblance to a house, that we can with the same certainty infer a similar cause, or that the analogy is here entire and perfect. The dissimilitude is so striking, that the utmost you can here pretend to is a guess, a conjecture, a presumption concerning a similar cause;

and how that pretension will be received in the world, I leave you to consider.

It would surely be very ill received, replied CLEANTHES; and I should be deservedly blamed and detested, did I allow that the proofs of a Deity amounted to no more than a guess or conjecture. But is the whole adjustment of means to ends in a house and in the universe so slight a resemblance? The economy of final causes? The order, proportion, and arrangement of every part? Steps of a stair are plainly contrived, that human legs may use them in mounting; and this inference is certain and infallible. Human legs are also contrived for walking and mounting; and this inference, I allow, is not altogether so certain, because of the dissimilarity which you remark; but does it, therefore, deserve the name only of presumption or conjecture? . . .

Now according to this method of reasoning, DEMEA, it follows (and is, indeed, tacitly allowed by CLEANTHES himself) that order, arrangement, or the adjustment of final causes is not, of itself, any proof of design; but only so far as it has been experienced to proceed from that principle. For aught we can know *a priori,* matter may contain the source or spring of order originally, within itself, as well as mind does; and there is no more difficulty in conceiving, that the several elements, from an internal unknown cause, may fall into the most exquisite arrangement, than to conceive that their ideas, in the great, universal mind, from a like internal, unknown cause, fall into that arrangement. The equal possibility of both these suppositions is allowed. By

---

From: David Hume, *Dialogues Concerning Natural Religion,* ed. Norman Kemp Smith (New York: Bobbs-Merrill, 1947) 143–181. Notes have been omitted.

experience we find (according to CLEANTHES), that there is a difference between them. Throw several pieces of steel together, without shape or form; they will never arrange themselves so as to compose a watch: Stone, and mortar, and wood, without an architect, never erect a house. But the ideas in a human mind, we see, by an unknown, inexplicable economy, arrange themselves so as to form that plan of a watch or house. Experience, therefore, proves, that there is an original principle of order in mind, not in matter. From similar effects we infer similar causes. The adjustment of means to ends is alike in the universe, as in a machine of human contrivance. The causes, therefore, must be resembling.

I was from the beginning scandalised, I must own, with this resemblance, which is asserted, between the Deity and human creatures; and must conceive it to imply such a degradation of the supreme Being as no sound theist could endure. With your assistance, therefore, DEMEA, I shall endeavour to defend what you justly call the adorable mysteriousness of the divine nature, and shall refute this reasoning of CLEANTHES; provided he allows, that I have made a fair representation of it.

When CLEANTHES had assented, PHILO, after a short pause, proceeded in the following manner.

That all inferences, CLEANTHES, concerning fact, are founded on experience, and that all experimental reasonings are founded on the supposition, that similar causes prove similar effects, and similar effects similar causes; I shall not, at present, much dispute with you. But observe, I entreat you, with what extreme caution all just reasoners proceed in the transferring of experiments to similar cases. Unless the cases be exactly similar, they repose no perfect confidence in applying their past observation to any particular phenomenon. Every alteration of circumstances occasions a doubt concerning the event; and it requires new experiments to prove certainly, that the new circumstances are of no moment or importance. A change in bulk, situation, arrangement, age, disposition of the air, or surrounding bodies; any of these particulars may be attended with the most unexpected consequences: And unless the objects be quite familiar to us, it is the highest temerity to expect with assurance, after any of these changes, an event similar to that which before fell under our observation. The slow and deliberate steps of philosophers, here, if any where, are distinguished from the precipitate march of the vulgar, who, hurried on by the smallest similitude, are incapable of all discernment or consideration.

But can you think, CLEANTHES, that your usual phlegm and philosophy have been preserved in so wide a step as you have taken, when you compared to the universe houses, ships, furniture, machines; and from their similarity in some circumstances inferred a similarity in their causes? Thought, design, intelligence, such as we discover in men and other animals, is no more than one of the springs and principles of the universe, as well as heat or cold, attraction or repulsion, and a hundred others, which fall under daily observation. It is an active cause, by which some particular parts of nature, we find, produce alterations on other parts. But can a conclusion, with any propriety, be transferred from parts to the whole? Does not the great disproportion bar all comparison and inference? From observing the growth of a hair, can we learn any thing concerning the generation of a man? Would the manner of a leaf's blowing, even though perfectly known, afford us any instruction concerning the vegetation of a tree?

BUT to show you still more inconveniences, continued PHILO, in your anthropomorphism; please to take a new survey of your principles. *Like effects prove like causes.* This is the experimental argument; and this, you say too, is the sole theological argument. Now it is certain, that the liker the effects are, which are seen, and the liker the causes, which are inferred, the stronger is the argument. Every departure on either side diminishes the probability, and renders the experiment less conclusive. You cannot doubt of this principle: Neither ought you to reject its consequences. . . .

Now, CLEANTHES, said PHILO, with an air of alacrity and triumph, mark the consequences. *First,* By this method of reasoning, you renounce all claim to infinity in any of the attributes of the Deity. For as the cause ought only to be proportioned to the effect, and the effect, so far as it falls under our cognisance, is not infinite; what pretensions have we, upon your suppositions, to ascribe that attribute to the divine Being? You will still insist, that, by removing him so much from all similarity to human creatures, we give into the most arbitrary hypothesis, and at the same time weaken all proofs of his existence.

Secondly, You have no reason, on your theory, for ascribing perfection to the Deity, even in his finite capacity; or for supposing him free from every error, mistake, or incoherence in his undertakings. There are many inexplicable difficulties in the works of nature, which, if we allow a perfect Author to be proved *a priori,* are easily solved, and become only seeming difficulties, from the narrow capacity of man, who cannot trace infinite relations. But according to your method of reasoning, these difficulties become all real; and perhaps will be insisted on, as new instances of likeness to human art and contrivance. At least, you must acknowledge, that it is impossible for us to tell, from our limited views, whether this system contains any great faults, or deserves any considerable praise, if compared to other possible, and even real systems. Could a peasant, if the ÆNEID were read to him, pronounce that poem to be absolutely faultless, or even assign to it its proper rank among the productions of human wit; he, who had never seen any other production?

But were this world ever so perfect a production, it must still remain uncertain, whether all the excellencies of the work can justly be ascribed to the workman. If we survey a ship, what an exalted idea must we form of the ingenuity of the carpenter, who framed so complicated, useful, and beautiful a machine? And what surprise must we entertain, when we find him a stupid mechanic, who imitated others, and copied an art, which, through a long succession of ages, after multiplied trials, mistakes, corrections, deliberations, and controversies, had been gradually improving? Many worlds might have been botched and bungled, throughout an eternity, ere this system was struck out: Much labour lost: Many fruitless trials made: And a slow, but continued improvement carried on during infinite ages in the art of world-making. In such subjects, who can determine, where the truth; nay, who can conjecture where the probability, lies; amidst a great number of hypotheses which may be proposed, and a still greater number which may be imagined?

And what shadow of an argument, continued PHILO, can you produce, from your hypothesis, to prove the unity of the Deity? A great number of men join in building a house or ship, in rearing a city, in framing a commonwealth: Why may not several Deities combine in contriving and framing a world? This is only so much greater similarity to human affairs. By sharing the work among several, we may so much farther limit the attributes of each, and get rid of that extensive power and knowledge, which must be supposed in one Deity, and which, according to you, can only serve to weaken the proof of his existence. And if such foolish, such vicious creatures as man can yet often unite in framing and executing one plan; how much more those Deities or Dæmons, whom, we may suppose several degrees more perfect? . . .

But farther, CLEANTHES; men are mortal, and renew their species by generation; and this is common to all living creatures. The two great sexes of male and female, says MILTON, animate the world. Why must this circumstance, so universal, so essential, be excluded from those numerous and limited Deities? Behold then the theogony of ancient times brought back upon us.

And why not become a perfect anthropomorphite? Why not assert the Deity or Deities to be corporeal, and to have eyes, a nose, mouth, ears, &c.? EPICURUS maintained, that no man had ever seen reason but in a human figure: therefore the gods must have a human figure. And this argument, which is deservedly so much ridiculed by Cicero, becomes, according to you, solid and philosophical.

In a word, CLEANTHES, a man, who follows your hypothesis, is able, perhaps, to assert, or conjecture, that the universe, sometime, arose from something like design: But beyond that position he cannot ascertain one single circumstance, and is left afterwards to fix every point of his theology, by the utmost licence of fancy and hypothesis. This world, for aught he knows, is very faulty and imperfect, compared to a superior standard; and was only the first rude essay of some infant Deity, who afterwards abandoned it, ashamed of his lame performance; it is the work only of some dependent, inferior Deity; and is the object of derision to his superiors: it is the production of old age and dotage in some superannuated Deity; and ever since his death, has run on at adventures, from the first impulse and active force, which it received from him. . . . You justly give signs of horror, DEMEA, at these strange suppositions: But these, and a thousand more of the same kind, are CLEANTHES'S suppositions, not mine. From the moment the attributes of the Deity are supposed finite, all these have place. And I cannot, for my part, think, that so wild and unsettled a system of theology is, in any respect, preferable to none at all. . . .

IT must be a slight fabric, indeed, said DEMEA, which can be erected on so tottering a foundation. While we are uncertain, whether there is one Deity or many; whether the Deity or Deities, to whom we owe our existence, be perfect or imperfect, subordinate or supreme, dead or alive; what trust or confidence can we repose in them? What devotion or worship address to them? What veneration or obedience pay them? To all the purposes of life, the theory of religion becomes altogether useless: And even with regard to speculative consequences, its uncertainty, according to you, must render it totally precarious and unsatisfactory.

To render it still more unsatisfactory, said PHILO, there occurs to me another hypothesis, which must acquire an air of probability from the method of reasoning so much insisted on by CLEANTHES. That like effects arise from like causes: This principle he supposes the foundation of all religion. But there is another principle of the same kind, no less certain, and derived from the same source of experience; that where several known circumstances are *observed* to be similar, the unknown will also be *found* similar. Thus, if we see the limbs of a human body, we conclude, that it is also attended with a human head, though hid from us. Thus, if we see, through a chink in a wall, a small part of the sun, we conclude, that, were the wall removed, we should see the whole body. In short, this method of reasoning is so obvious and familiar, that no scruple can ever be made with regard to its solidity.

Now if we survey the universe, so far as it falls under our knowledge, it bears a great resemblance to an animal or organized body, and seems actuated with a like principle of life and motion. A continual circulation of matter in it produces no disorder: A continual waste in every part is incessantly repaired: The closest sympathy is perceived throughout the entire system: And each part or member, in performing its proper offices, operates both to its own preservation and to that of the whole. The world, therefore, I infer, is an animal, and the Deity is the SOUL of the world, actuating it, and actuated by it.

You have too much learning, CLEANTHES, to be at all surprised at this opinion, which, you know, was maintained by almost all the theists of antiquity, and chiefly prevails in their discourses and reasonings. For though sometimes the ancient philosophers reason from final causes, as if they thought the world the workmanship of God; yet it appears rather their favourite notion to consider it as his body, whose organization renders it subservient to him. And it must be confessed, that as the universe resembles more a human body than it does the works of human art and contrivance; if our limited analogy could ever, with any propriety, be extended to the whole of nature, the inference seems juster in favour of the ancient than the modern theory.

There are many other advantages too, in the former theory, which recommended it to the ancient theologians. Nothing more repugnant to all their notions, because nothing more repugnant to common experience, than mind without body; a mere spiritual substance, which fell not under their senses nor comprehension, and of which they had not observed one single instance throughout all nature. Mind and body they knew, because they felt both: An order, arrangement, organization, or internal machinery in both they likewise knew, after the same manner: And it could not but seem reasonable to transfer this experience to the universe, and to suppose the divine mind and body to be also coeval, and to have, both of them, and arrangement naturally inherent in them, and inseparable from them. . . .

. . . The world plainly resembles more an animal or a vegetable, than it does a watch or a knitting-loom. Its

cause, therefore, it is more probable, resembles the cause of the former. The cause of the former is generation or vegetation. The cause, therefore, of the world, we may infer to be some thing similar or analogous to generation or vegetation.

But how is it conceivable, said DEMEA, that the world can arise from any thing similar to vegetation or generation?

Very easily, replied PHILO. In like manner as a tree sheds its seed into the neighbouring fields, and produces other trees; so the great vegetable, the world, or this planetary system, produces within itself certain seeds, which, being scattered into the surrounding chaos, vegetate into new worlds. A comet, for instance, is the seed of a world; and after it has been fully ripened, by passing from sun to sun, and star to star, it is at last tossed into the unformed elements, which everywhere surround this universe, and immediately sprouts up into a new system.

Or if, for the sake of variety (for I see no other advantage), we should suppose this world to be an animal; a comet is the egg of this animal; and in like manner as an ostrich lays its egg in the sand, which, without any farther care, hatches the egg, and produces a new animal; so. . . .

I understand you, says DEMEA: But what wild, arbitrary suppositions are these? What *data* have you for such extraordinary conclusions? And is the slight, imaginary resemblance of the world to a vegetable or an animal sufficient to establish the same inference with regard to both? Objects, which are in general so widely different; ought they to be a standard for each other?

Right, cries PHILO: This is the topic on which I have all along insisted. I have still asserted, that we have no *data* to establish any system of cosmogony. Our experience, so imperfect in itself, and so limited both in extent and duration, can afford us no probable conjecture concerning the whole of things. But if we must needs fix on some hypothesis; by what rule, pray, ought we to determine our choice? Is there any other rule than the greater similarity of the objects compared? And does not a plant or an animal, which springs from vegetation or generation, bear a stronger resemblance to the world, than does any artificial machine, which arises from reason and design? . . .

Compare, I beseech you, the consequences on both sides. The world, say I, resembles an animal, therefore it is an animal, therefore it arose from generation. The steps, I confess, are wide; yet there is some small appearance of analogy in each step. The world, says CLEANTHES, resembles a machine, therefore it is a machine, therefore it arose from design. The steps are here equally wide, and the analogy less striking. And if he pretends to carry on *my* hypothesis a step farther, and to infer design or reason from the great principle of generation, on which I insist; I may, with better authority, use the same freedom to push farther *his* hypothesis, and infer a divine generation or theogony from his principle of reason. I have at least some faint shadow of experience, which is the utmost that can ever be attained in the present subject. Reason, in innumerable instances, is observed to arise from the principle of generation, and never to arise from any other principle.

HESIOD, and all the ancient mythologists, were so struck with this analogy, that they universally explained the origin of nature from an animal birth, and copulation. PLATO too, so far as he is intelligible, seems to have adopted some such notion in his TIMÆUS.

The BRAHMINS assert, that the world arose from an infinite spider, who spun this whole complicated mass from his bowels, and annihilates afterwards the whole or any part of it, by absorbing it again and resolving it into his own essence. Here is a species of cosmogony, which appears to us ridiculous, because a spider is a little contemptible animal, whose operations we are never likely to take for a model of the whole universe. But still here is a new species of analogy, even in our globe. And were there a planet wholly inhabited by spiders (which is very possible), this inference would there appear as natural and irrefragable as that which in our planet ascribes the origin of all things to design and intelligence, as explained by CLEANTHES. Why an orderly system may not be spun from the belly as well as from the brain, it will be difficult for him to give a satisfactory reason.

God and the Problem of Evil

B. C. Johnson is a pen name for the author, who wishes to remain anonymous. Here
he discusses the problem that evil poses for those who believe in God.

Here is a common situation: a house catches on fire and a six-month-old baby is painfully burned to death. Could we possibly describe as "good" any person who had the power to save this child and yet refused to do so? God undoubtedly has this power and yet in many cases of this sort he has refused to help. Can we call God "good"? Are there adequate excuses for his behavior?

First, it will not do to claim that the baby will go to heaven. It was either necessary for the baby to suffer or it was not. If it was not, then it was wrong to allow it. The child's ascent to heaven does not change this fact. If it was necessary, the fact that the baby will go to heaven does not explain why it was necessary, and we are still left without an excuse for God's inaction.

It is not enough to say that the baby's painful death would in the long run have good results and therefore should have happened, otherwise God would not have permitted it. For if we know this to be true, then we know — just as God knows — that every action successfully performed must in the end be good and therefore the right thing to do, otherwise God would not have allowed it to happen. We could deliberately set houses ablaze to kill innocent people and if successful we would then know we had a duty to do it. A defense of God's goodness which takes as its foundation duties known only after the fact would result in a morality unworthy of the name. Furthermore, this argument does not explain why God allowed the child to burn to death. It merely claims that there is some reason discoverable in the long run. But the belief that such a reason is within our grasp must rest upon the additional belief that God is good. This is just to counter evidence against such a belief by assuming the belief to be true. It is not unlike a lawyer defending his client by claiming that the client is innocent and therefore the evidence against him must be misleading — that proof vindicating the defendant will be found in the long run. No jury of reasonable men and women would accept such a defense and the theist cannot expect a more favorable outcome.

The theist often claims that man has been given free will so that if he accidentally or purposely causes fires, killing small children, it is his fault alone. Consider a bystander who had nothing to do with starting the fire but who refused to help even though he could have saved the child with no harm to himself. Could such a bystander be called good? Certainly not. If we would not consider a mortal human being good under these circumstances, what grounds could we possibly have for continuing to assert the goodness of an all-powerful God?

The suggestion is sometimes made that it is best for us to face disasters without assistance, otherwise we would become dependent on an outside power for aid. Should we then abolish modern medical care or do away with efficient fire departments? Are we not dependent on their help? Is it not the case that their presence transforms us into soft, dependent creatures? The vast majority are not physicians or firemen. These people help in their capacity as professional outside sources of aid in much the same way that we would expect God to be helpful. Theists refer to aid from firemen and physicians as cases of man helping himself. In reality, it is a tiny minority of men helping a great many. We can become just as dependent on them as we can on God. Now the existence of this kind of outside help is either wrong or right. If it is right, then God should assist those areas of the world which do not have this kind of help. In fact, throughout history, such help has not been available. If aid ought to have been provided, then God should have provided it. On the other hand, if it is wrong to provide this kind of assistance, then we should abolish the aid altogether. But we obviously do not believe it is wrong.

Similar considerations apply to the claim that if God interferes in disasters, he would destroy a considerable amount of moral urgency to make things right.

From: B. C. Johnson, *The Atheist Debater's Handbook* (Amherst, NY: Prometheus Books, 1983) 99–108.

Once again, note that such institutions as modern medicine and fire departments are relatively recent. They function irrespective of whether we as individuals feel any moral urgency to support them. To the extent that they help others, opportunities to feel moral urgency are destroyed because they reduce the number of cases which appeal to us for help. Since we have not always had such institutions, there must have been a time when there was greater moral urgency than there is now. If such a situation is morally desirable, then we should abolish modern medical care and fire departments. If the situation is not morally desirable, then God should have remedied it.

Besides this point, we should note that God is represented as one who tolerates disasters, such as infants burning to death, in order to create moral urgency. It follows that God approves of these disasters as a means to encourage the creation of moral urgency. Furthermore, if there were no such disasters occurring, God would have to see to it that they occur. If it so happened that we lived in a world in which babies never perished in burning houses, God would be morally obliged to take an active hand in setting fire to houses with infants in them. In fact, if the frequency of infant mortality due to fire should happen to fall below a level necessary for the creation of maximum moral urgency in our real world, God would be justified in setting a few fires of his own. This may well be happening right now, for there is no guarantee that the maximum number of infant deaths necessary for moral urgency are occurring.

All of this is of course absurd. If I see an opportunity to create otherwise nonexistent opportunities for moral urgency by burning an infant or two, then I should *not* do so. But if it is good to maximize moral urgency, then I *should* do so. Therefore, it is not good to maximize moral urgency. Plainly we do not in general believe that it is a good thing to maximize moral urgency. The fact that we approve of modern medical care and applaud medical advances is proof enough of this.

The theist may point out that in a world without suffering there would be no occasion for the production of such virtues as courage, sympathy, and the like. This may be true, but the atheist need not demand a world without suffering. He need only claim that there is suffering which is in excess of that needed for the production of various virtues. For example, God's active attempts to save six-month-old infants from fires would not in itself create a world without suffering. But no one could sincerely doubt that it would improve the world.

The two arguments against the previous theistic excuse apply here also. "Moral urgency" and "building virtue" are susceptible to the same criticisms. It is worthwhile to emphasize, however, that we encourage efforts to eliminate evils; we approve of efforts to promote peace, prevent famine, and wipe out disease. In other words, we do value a world with fewer or (if possible) no opportunities for the development of virtue (when "virtue" is understood to mean the reduction of suffering). If we produce such a world for succeeding generations, how will they develop virtues? Without war, disease, and famine, they will not be virtuous. Should we then cease our attempts to wipe out war, disease, and famine? If we do not believe that it is right to cease attempts at improving the world, then by implication we admit that virtue-building is not an excuse for God to permit disasters. For we admit that the development of virtue is no excuse for permitting disasters.

It might be said that God allows innocent people to suffer in order to deflate man's ego so that the latter will not be proud of his apparently deserved good fortune. But this excuse succumbs to the arguments used against the preceding excuses and we need discuss them no further.

Theists may claim that evil is a necessary by-product of the laws of nature and therefore it is irrational for God to interfere every time a disaster happens. Such a state of affairs would alter the whole causal order and we would then find it impossible to predict anything. But the death of a child caused by an electrical fire could have been prevented by a miracle and no one would ever have known. Only a minor alteration in electrical equipment would have been necessary. A very large disaster could have been avoided simply by producing in Hitler a miraculous heart attack — and no one would have known it was a miracle. To argue that continued miraculous intervention by God would be wrong is like insisting that one should never use salt because ingesting five pounds of it would be fatal. No one is requesting that God interfere all of the time. He should, however, intervene to prevent especially horrible disasters. Of course, the question arises: where does one draw the line? Well, certainly the line should be drawn somewhere this side of infants burning to death. To argue that we do not know where the line should be drawn is no excuse for failing to interfere in those instances that would be called clear cases of evil.

It will not do to claim that evil exists as a necessary contrast to good so that we might know what good is. A very small amount of evil, such as a toothache, would allow that. It is not necessary to destroy innocent human beings.

The claim could be made that God has a "higher morality" by which his actions are to be judged. But it is a strange "higher morality" which claims that what we call "bad" is good and what we call "good" is bad. Such a morality can have no meaning to us. It would be like calling black "white" and white "black." In reply the theist may say that God is the wise Father and we are ignorant children. How can we judge God any more than a child is able to judge his parent? It is true that a child may be puzzled by his parents' conduct, but his basis for deciding that their conduct is nevertheless good would be the many instances of good behavior he has observed. Even so, this could be misleading. Hitler, by all accounts, loved animals and children of the proper race; but if Hitler had had a child, this offspring would hardly have been justified in arguing that his father was a good man. At any rate, God's "higher morality," being the opposite of ours, cannot offer any grounds for deciding that he is somehow good.

Perhaps the main problem with the solutions to the problem of evil we have thus far considered is that no matter how convincing they may be in the abstract, they are implausible in certain particular cases. Picture an infant dying in a burning house and then imagine God simply observing from afar. Perhaps God is reciting excuses in his own behalf. As the child succumbs to the smoke and flames, God may be pictured as saying: "Sorry, but if I helped you I would have considerable trouble deflating the ego of your parents. And don't forget I have to keep those laws of nature consistent. And anyway if you weren't dying in that fire, a lot of moral urgency would just go down the drain. Besides, I didn't start this fire, so you can't blame me."

It does no good to assert that God may not be all-powerful and thus not able to prevent evil. He can create a universe and yet is conveniently unable to do what the fire department can do—rescue a baby from a burning building. God should at least be as powerful as a man. A man, if he had been at the right place and time, could have killed Hitler. Was this beyond God's abilities? If God knew in 1910 how to produce polio vaccine and if he was able to communicate with somebody, he should have communicated this knowledge. He must be incredibly limited if he could not have managed this modest accomplishment. Such a God if not dead, is the next thing to it. And a person who believes in such a ghost of a God is practically an atheist. To call such a thing a god would be to strain the meaning of the word.

The theist, as usual, may retreat to faith. He may say that he has faith in God's goodness and therefore the Christian Deity's existence has not been disproved. "Faith" is here understood as being much like confidence in a friend's innocence despite the evidence against

him. Now in order to have confidence in a friend one must know him well enough to justify faith in his goodness. We cannot have justifiable faith in the supreme goodness of strangers. Moreover, such confidence must come not just from a speaking acquaintance. The friend may continually assure us with his words that he is good but if he does not act like a good person, we would have no reason to trust him. A person who says he has faith in God's goodness is speaking as if he had known God for a long time and during that time had never seen Him do any serious evil. But we know that throughout history God has allowed numerous atrocities to occur. No one can have justifiable faith in the goodness of such a God. This faith would have to be based on a close friendship wherein God was never found to do anything wrong. But a person would have to be blind and deaf to have had such a relationship with God. Suppose a friend of yours had always claimed to be good yet refused to help people when he was in a position to render aid. Could you have justifiable faith in his goodness?

You can of course say that you trust God anyway—that no arguments can undermine your faith. But this is just a statement describing how stubborn you are; it has no bearing whatsoever on the question of God's goodness.

The various excuses theists offer for why God has allowed evil to exist have been demonstrated to be inadequate. However, the conclusive objection to these excuses does not depend on their inadequacy.

First, we should note that every possible excuse making the actual world consistent with the existence of a good God could be used in reverse to make that same world consistent with an evil God. For example, we could say that God is evil and that he allows free will so that we can freely do evil things, which would make us more truly evil than we would be if forced to perform evil acts. Or we could say that natural disasters occur in order to make people more selfish and bitter, for most people tend to have a "me first" attitude in a disaster (note, for example, stampedes to leave burning buildings). Even though some people achieve virtue from disasters, this outcome is necessary if persons are to react freely to disaster—necessary if the development of moral degeneracy is to continue freely. But, enough; the point is made. Every excuse we could provide to make the world consistent with a good God can be paralleled by an excuse to make the world consistent with an evil God. This is so because the world is a mixture of both good and bad.

Now there are only three possibilities concerning God's moral character. Considering the world as it actually is, we may believe: (a) that God is more likely to be all evil than he is to be all good; (b) that God is less likely to be all evil than he is to be all good; or (c) that God is equally as likely to be all evil as he is to be all good. In case (a) it would be admitted that God is unlikely to be all good. Case (b) cannot be true at all, since—as we have seen—the belief that God is all evil can be justified to precisely the same extent as the belief that God is all good. Case (c) leaves us with no reasonable excuses for a good God to permit evil. The reason is as follows: if an excuse is to be a reasonable excuse, the circumstances it identifies as excusing conditions must be actual. For example, if I run over a pedestrian and my excuse is that the brakes failed because someone tampered with them, then the facts had better bear this out. Otherwise the excuse will not hold. Now if case (c) is correct and, given the facts of the actual world, God is as likely to be all evil as he is to be all good, then these facts do not support the excuses which could be made for a good God permitting evil. Consider an analogous example. If my excuse for running over the pedestrian is that my brakes were tampered with, and if the actual facts lead us to believe that it is no more likely that they were tampered with than that they were not, the excuse is no longer reasonable. To make good my excuse, I must show that it is a fact or at least highly probable that my brakes were tampered with, not that it is just a possibility. The same point holds for God. His excuse must not be a possible excuse, but an actual one. But case (c), in maintaining that it is just as likely that God is all evil as that he is all good, rules this out. For if case (c) is true, then the facts of the actual world do not make it any more likely that God is all good than that he is all evil. Therefore, they do not make it any more likely that his excuses are good than that they are not. But, as we have seen, good excuses have a higher probability of being true.

Cases (a) and (c) conclude that it is unlikely that God is all good, and case (b) cannot be true. Since these are the only possible cases, there is no escape from the conclusion that it is unlikely that God is all good. Thus the problem of evil triumphs over traditional theism.

The Miracle Sleuth

Michael Martin (1935–) is a professor emeritus of philosophy at Boston University and has published a number of important works, including *Atheism: A Philosophical Justification* and *The Case Against Christianity*. In this short story, he explores the plausibility of the belief in miracles.

Father Mike Flanagan was tired and depressed. He had just completed a long report and he was not looking forward to presenting it to Monsignor Pagello. He leaned back in his chair, stretched his muscular body, and sighed. "The Monsignor will not like it. He will not like it one damn bit. But what could I do? It's the truth," he thought. Unfortunately, he knew that the Church sometimes had to bend the truth for its own noble ends. He did not mind that. Mike was enough of a utilitarian to know that truth was not everything and that sometimes it had to be sacrificed. What he hated was the pretense: the denial that the truth was being bent for good purposes.

"Why couldn't they just admit that they were lying for a good cause?" he asked himself. But he knew the answer. "They simply can't face it! They can't admit to themselves that the case for miracles is weak or nonexistent." He placed the one-hundred-seventy-three-page report in a binder and glanced at the title page: "Confidential Report on the Evidence for Miracles with Special Reference to the Sixty-Fourth Officially Declared Miracle at Lourdes" by Michael Flanagan, SJ. He put it in his briefcase, picked up his cup of coffee, and gazed out the window.

"Why did I ever accept such a thankless job?" he mused. He remembered as if it were yesterday the cold January morning when Bishop Dwight Thomas, head of what some referred to as "the Catholic Church's Secret Service," summoned Mike to his office. "Mike, I called you in for another special assignment. There is no one in the Church whom I trust as I do you—no one who has your special abilities and expertise." The bishop glanced at the thick dossier on his desk. "Very impressive! Phi Beta Kappa at Yale, Naval intelligence, private investigator. The Church was fortunate indeed when you decided to join the priesthood. And then to top it off, a Harvard Ph.D. with a specialization in Epistemology! I believe that God Himself sent you to us," he said beaming.

Mike thought, "Why is he going through all this again?" He cleared his throat and found himself saying: "I would be willing to help in whatever way I can, of course. But I would like to remind the bishop that I have been working on the Australian exorcism case for several months, and I was hoping that . . ."

"Yes, Mike, I know you expected a vacation," the bishop said, interrupting. "But the superb job you did in Australia convinced me that only you can help us. Exposing Father Collins's 'exorcisms' as fakes is the finest piece of sleuthing I have had the privilege of seeing in almost twenty years in this job. Mind you, many people in the Church hierarchy do not like it. They were hoping that you would find Collins to be legitimate. But your evidence was so convincing that . . . well, never mind that. I have a much more important job for you now, so important I don't think you can refuse."

"You know that I will not refuse," said Mike.

The bishop motioned Mike to have a seat and fixed his eyes on a picture of the Virgin before he started to speak. "As you know, the doctrine that the truth of the Christian religion can be proved on the basis of miracles has been a dogma of the Church since the Third Session of the First Vatican Council in 1870. The Church has maintained that biblical miracles were performed by Moses, the Prophets, Jesus, and others, and even that miracles have occurred in modern times, for example, at Lourdes. The Church has vigorously rejected the view so popular since the nineteenth century that miracles are impossible." The bishop rose from his desk and paced back and forth. "Indeed, St. Pius X in 1910 in the Oath against Modernism maintained that miracles had an enduring apologetic value and said that they were 'eminently suited to the intelligence of all men of every era, including the present.' In fact, the

From: Michael Martin, "The Miracle Sleuth," *The Big Domino in the Sky* (Buffalo, NY: Prometheus, 1996) 130–145.

flourishing of the Roman Catholic Church despite hardships and adversities is considered by the Church to be a miracle." He paused and for the first time looked at Mike directly. "However, there are some of our own people who have doubts," he said, his voice growing softer. "They believe that there has been entirely too much emphasis on miracles in the Church's teaching. As people become more educated they find it harder and harder to believe in miracles in the way that the Church expects them to. It may be the case that the doctrine of miracles, far from having a great apologetic value for the Church, may actually contribute to our increasingly bad image. Indeed, some feel that the doctrine of miracles should be deemphasized and in time perhaps be eliminated all together. They think that it should not be maintained as a dogma that belief in miracles is rational; thus, perhaps Catholics should believe in some miracles, for example, the Resurrection and the Virgin Birth, but not because these doctrines are rational."

Mike smiled and said, "That sounds like Protestantism to me, Bishop."

"Perhaps, perhaps!" he said, laughing. "I hasten to add," he said, growing serious again, "that this more extreme view is not widely shared and is not likely to be adopted as official Church dogma in our lifetime. Nevertheless, a complete review of the epistemological foundations of belief in miracles is needed. It needs to be done by someone who is Catholic, but who has been trained in some philosophical tradition other than that of St. Thomas Aquinas. The tough appraisal of a Harvard-trained epistemologist is just what is needed. We need especially a critique of the claims of miracles at Lourdes."

"Why Lourdes?" Mike asked.

"Lourdes is unique among Catholic shrines where miracles are supposed to have occurred, since only at Lourdes has there been a definite procedure for investigating and recognizing miracles. If the miracles at Lourdes are found to be suspicious, there will be good reason to be suspicious of other alleged miracles which have not been so rigorously investigated."

"I see," said Mike.

"Of course, I don't mean to anticipate your conclusions. By the way, don't make policy decisions in your report. Just review the epistemological considerations."

"Who will read my report?"

"Well, it will certainly not be made public. I will read it, of course, and so will selected members of my staff. Where it will go from there remains to be seen. For a while it will remain basically confidential, just as your Australian one on exorcism has, although it will have to be much more hush-hush. After that I will have to decide how best to use it strategically and politically. Naturally, you will have the resources of this office at your disposal and a generous expense account for travel and research. I need not remind you that leaks to the press would be intolerable."

"There will be no leaks from this end. But why the rush? I still don't see why I couldn't take a vacation before I . . ."

"I'm sorry, Mike. This is the middle of January. I would like the report on my desk by the first week in June, when there will be a meeting of twelve like-minded members of the Church hierarchy. I am sorry that I cannot tell you more except to say that a critical report on the status of miracles will strengthen the hand of the Twelve. I know that this is not very much time to complete the sort of report I want, so it is important for you to get started at once."

Mike remembered leaving the Bishop's office with mixed feelings. On the one hand, the challenge was exciting. He had always had some reservations about the Church's doctrine of miracles, and this assignment would give him the time and stimulus to test his ideas. On the other hand, knowing the conservative nature of the Church hierarchy, he could not imagine that a report at all critical of the present doctrine would have any effect.

He spent the next two months at libraries reading David Hume's classic critiques of miracles, modern critiques such as that by Antony Flew, and the latest articles on miracles in philosophical and theological journals. With this background, Mike started to investigate the miracles at Lourdes, first by reading some of the classical pro and con literature on the subject and then by investigating the last officially declared miracle at Lourdes—the sixty-fourth officially declared miracle in the history of the shrine. He decided to concentrate on this case because it was the most recent and there would be a greater chance of getting reliable information. This miracle was the alleged cure of Serge Perrin, a French accountant who, while at Lourdes in 1970, experienced a sudden recovery from a long illness. After investigation, the international committee of doctors that investigates the claim of miracles for the Church had said that Perrin was suffering from "a case of recurring organic hemiplegia [paralysis of one side of the body] with ocular lesions, due to cerebral circulatory defects" and that his cure had no medical explanation. By mid-April Mike had read the official dossier on Perrin and the critiques of it, and was ready to begin the less scholarly part of the investigation, the part he liked the best. He traveled to Europe and talked to members of the international committee of doctors who had decided that Perrin's cure was medically inexplicable. He also had Perrin's dossier independently appraised by specialists in the United States. By May he was ready to write.

In mid-May, with the first draft of the report almost done, Mike heard the news. Bishop Thomas had died of a massive heart attack, and with his death his organization had come under close scrutiny. In particular, it was discovered that a confidential report on the miracles was being prepared by Michael Flanagan, SJ, the well known intellectual bloodhound, and the word was out that the powerful men in the Church hierarchy were upset. Toward the end of May, Mike was notified that he should finish his report as quickly as possible and submit it to Monsignor Marcel Pagello, who had taken over Bishop Thomas's responsibilities. He also heard through the grapevine that Pagello was appointed to clean house, and that not much of the old organization in terms either of personnel or ideology would remain when he was finished. Mike could only speculate whether the forthcoming meeting of the mysterious Twelve had been discovered.

When he turned in his report the next morning, Mike was told by the Monsignor's secretary that the Monsignor would spend the day reading it and would see him at 8 A.M. the following day for breakfast. During the day Mike tried to find out all he could about Monsignor Pagello. Few of his contacts knew Pagello very well and the information they had was not helpful. He was described in various ways: "a conservative hardliner," "brilliant and ruthless," "charming and manipulative." One of Mike's contacts said that in his younger days Pagello was a champion Greco-Roman wrestler, and another spoke of his piercing eyes. Mike decided that he would be completely honest with the Monsignor, tell the truth, stand up for what he believed, and hope for the best.

He knocked on the Monsignor's door promptly at eight and it was immediately opened by a huge bear of a man who said pleasantly, "Father Flanagan, please come in! Can I offer you some coffee and rolls?" while crushing Mike's hand in the most powerful grip he had ever felt. "No thanks, Monsignor. I usually don't eat breakfast."

"Well, please sit down. Let us get right to the point, shall we? I have studied your report on miracles very carefully, and I must say that I am very impressed by the scholarship and thought that have gone into it. However, the position that you take in the report is quite unacceptable to the Church because it conflicts with our doctrines. It would be unfortunate if it ever became known that the Church had actually sponsored this report. So I must ask you to refrain from ever revealing—and I underline the word 'ever'—that it was sponsored by this office or by any office of the Church."

"Yes, Monsignor, I will agree to that."

"Good, good! I deem it regrettable that Bishop Thomas and others saw fit to use the resources of this office to instigate heretical and unorthodox ideas. Although Bishop Thomas's death was a tragic loss to the Church, he had recently taken a course of action that could only have led to unfortunate consequences. Had he not died he would have had to be replaced. We had been watching him for some time and . . ."

"But what about the merits of my argument?" Mike asked, interrupting. "I believe that what I said was true."

"Yes, I am sure you do. What in particular do you think is true in your report?"

"First of all, if you recall, I argue that even if miracles have occurred, when 'miracle' is defined as an event caused by some noncorporeal creature, their existence gives no support to belief in God. A noncorporeal creature need not be God. There are rival supernatural hypotheses that account for miracles as well as the God hypothesis."

"Yes, I noted with interest that you adopted the concept of miracles used by Pope Benedict XIV in his classic treatise *De servorum Dei beatificatione et beatorum canonizatione*, in which a miracle need only be beyond the powers of corporeal creatures. However, just because miracles can be caused by created spirits who are not God, for example, angels, they would still be produced by God in the sense that the created spirit acted as God's agent."

"I am afraid, Monsignor, that you do not understand the radical nature of my thesis. My point is not that angels could be the direct cause of miracles. Miracles could be caused by noncorporeal beings that are not God's agents. God and angels might not exist although other supernatural beings might. For example, polytheism might be true and, if so, it, as well as theism, would account for miracles. I am not suggesting that polytheism is true, of course, only that the existence of miracles even as defined by Pope Benedict XIV is compatible with it."

"I see," the Monsignor said quietly. Mike was not sure that he did see, or that if he did, he wanted to.

"However, my main argument is that in order to claim that a miracle has occurred, rival hypotheses must be shown to be less probable than the miracle hypothesis. For example, the miracle-hypothesis explanation of some event must be shown to be more probable than the hypothesis that the event will be explained by future science utilizing as yet undiscovered laws that govern nature. Given the scientific progress of the last two centuries, such a prediction seems rash and unjustified. In medicine, for example, diseases that were considered mysterious are now understood without appeal to supernatural powers. Further progress seems extremely likely; indeed, it seems plausible to suppose that many so-called miracle cures of the past will one day be understood, as some have already been, in terms of psychosomatic medicine."

"Would you make that same claim about the Resurrection? Will your science some day explain how our Lord rose from the dead?" the monsignor said, his voice dripping with sarcasm.

"I don't think one can rule that out," Mike replied, getting up from his chair. "However, there are other hypotheses that must be eliminated that are perhaps more relevant in the case of the Resurrection and some other biblical miracles. The difficulties of ruling out hoax, fraud, or deception are legend. We have excellent reason today to believe that some contemporary faith healers use fraud and deceit to make it seem that they have paranormal powers and are getting miracle cures and even resurrecting people from the dead. These men have little trouble in duping a public that is surely no less sophisticated than that of biblical times. Did Jesus really walk on the water or only appear to because he was walking on rocks below the surface? Did Jesus turn the water into wine or did he only appear to because he substituted wine for water by some clever trick? Did Jesus arise from the dead or did his disciples make it seem as if he did? The hypothesis that Jesus was a magician has been seriously considered by some biblical scholars. The success of some contemporary 'faith healers' and 'psychic wonders' in convincing the public of 'miracle cures' by the use of deception and fraud indicates that it was possible for Jesus, if he was a magician, to do the same."

"How can you believe in God and say these things, Father!" exclaimed the monsignor, with a touch of anguish in his voice.

"Again I think you misunderstand me. I am not doubting the divinity of Jesus, but only that this can be demonstrated by miracles," Mike said, taking his seat again. "There is still another hypothesis that is a rival to the miracle hypothesis. Alleged miracles may not be due to some trick or fraud, but to misperceptions based on religious bias. A person full of religious zeal may see what he or she wants to see, not what is really there.

We know from empirical studies that people's beliefs and prejudices influence what they see and report. It would not be surprising that religious people who report that they have seen miraculous events have projected their biases onto the actual event. Did Jesus still the storm as it is claimed in the Gospel according to Matthew, or did the storm by coincidence happen to stop when 'He rose and rebuked the wind and the sea' and witnesses in their religious zeal 'saw' Him stilling the storm?"

"No doubt this sometimes happens. But to suppose that religious believers are not able to separate true from false miracles seems implausible," the monsignor said.

"But why? Religious attitudes often foster uncritical belief and acceptance. Indeed, in a religious context, uncritical belief is often thought to be a virtue, with doubt and skepticism a vice. Thus, a belief arising in a religious context and held with only modest conviction may tend to reinforce itself and develop into an unshakable conviction. It would hardly be surprising if, in this context, some ordinary natural event were seen as a miracle."

The monsignor did not reply. With a grim expression on his face he rose from his chair and began leafing through the report.

"I also believe that my analysis of the Perrin case at Lourdes is correct," Mike said. "Here one question was whether the international committee which determined that the cure was medically inexplicable was competent to decide such issues. At best, this committee had only the competence to decide that the cure was scientifically inexplicable in terms of current knowledge of nature. This committee did not know what the future development of medical science would be; thus any judgment that the committee made about the absolute inexplicability of a cure in terms of nature can and should have no particular authority."

The monsignor looked at Mike with eyes that seemed to penetrate to his soul. "I need not remind you, Father Flanagan, that the final authority for the judgment that a cure at Lourdes is a miracle is made by the Church. If the majority of the committee decides that the cure is inexplicable, the patient's dossier is given to the canonical commission headed by the bishop of the diocese in which the allegedly cured person lives. Only the Church can make the final decision as to whether the event is a miracle; that is, whether God has intervened in the natural course of events."

"Yes, I am quite aware of that and, in fact, I consider that in my report—I think around page 150. My point is that even if it was caused by some supernatural force or forces, this need not be caused by the Christian God. Church officials who make the final decision about whether a cure is a miracle and if so, whether it is caused by God, apparently ignore these other alternatives. As a result, the final decision that the cure is explained by God's intervention is more like a leap of faith than a rational decision. Further, the decisions of the Church are contingent on the competence of the international committee of doctors. But, as I have already argued, this committee's judgment exceeded its competence."

"I gather you have reservations about the committee's actual application of present-day medical knowledge," said the monsignor, again glancing through the report.

"Yes, my investigation indicated that the committee should not have concluded what it did. A small sample of specialists in the United States who independently examined the document produced by the international committee of doctors found the cure of Perrin very suspicious, the data in the document highly problematic, and the document obscure and filled with technical verbiage. For example, although crucial laboratory tests such as a spinal tap and radiation brain scan were standard in most hospitals for diagnosing the illness Perrin was said to have, they were never performed. The reviewers also considered the diagnosis of hemiplegia very implausible since, because he had right leg weakness and left visual and motor symptoms, more than one side of Perrin's brain had to be involved. In addition, symptoms of generalized constriction of his visual field and various sensory motor disturbances suggested hysteria rather than an organic illness. Moreover, the American specialists who reviewed the document maintained that if there was an organic illness at all, multiple sclerosis was the most likely explanation of Perrin's symptoms. However, it is well known that multiple sclerosis has fleeting symptoms with periodic severe flare-ups followed by remissions that are sometimes complete."

The monsignor looked up as if he expected Mike to say more. Mike continued: "As I also point out, there were serious problems not only with the Investigation of the Perrin case, but with the sixty-third officially declared miracle as well. The problems with both cases suggest that there is something badly amiss in the application of the procedures used by the Catholic Church for declaring something a miracle cure at Lourdes. An apparently questionable diagnosis of Perrin and an unsubstantiated judgment about the cure involved in the sixty-third official miracle were accepted by the Lourdes medical bureau and the international committee."

The monsignor glanced at his watch. "Well, this has been most edifying, Father Flanagan! But I am afraid that another matter forces me to bring our pleasant chat to an end. Is there any final statement that you would like to make?"

"Only this. Although I believe that I show in the report that belief in miracles is not rationally justifiable, I don't mean to suggest that the Church should give up maintaining that miracles have occurred. I believe the uneducated members of our Church need to believe in miracles and that we should, for their sake, keep up the pretense that the miracles are rationally justified. But we who are educated and enlightened should not maintain this view. Indeed, we should believe in miracles on faith and faith alone. I further . . ."

"Thank you, Father," the monsignor interrupted. "Your ideas are interesting and will be taken into account when I make my decision about what to do with your report," he said, rising from his chair, smiling.

"What are the possible dispositions of my report?" Mike asked.

"The most likely disposition will be for it to be put in the archives in one of our libraries for scholarly use. Of course, it will have few readers. But we shall see! Thank you again, Father Flanagan," he said as he showed Mike to the door.

That night in his room Mike prayed as he never had before. God seemed close and intimate, like a brother or loved one. Mike still believed in miracles despite his report. He passionately believed in the Resurrection, the Virgin Birth, the feeding of the five hundred, and the rest. Indeed, he believed more firmly than before he had written the report. But how could he? The evidence was against them! They were improbable in the light of the facts. How could he, who was trained in logic and reason, who argued the importance of epistemic responsibility, believe in them? He thanked God for his belief despite the evidence and despite his training and commitment to reason. His belief was itself a miracle of sorts. He wept for joy and was reminded of a well-known passage from Hume's *Essay Concerning Human Understanding:*

> [The] Christian religion not only was at first attended with miracles, but even to this day cannot be believed by any reasonable person without them. Mere reason is not sufficient to convince us of its veracity; and whoever is moved by faith to assent to it is conscious of a continued miracle in his own person, which subverts all the principles of his understanding, and gives him a determination to believe what is most contrary to custom and experience.

A week after his meeting with the Monsignor, Father Michael Flanagan received notification of his next assignment. For an indefinite time he was to teach English in a small Catholic college in Iowa. He learned some time later that the "Confidential Report on the Evidence for Miracles with Special Reference to the Sixty-Fourth Officially Declared Miracle at Lourdes," by Michael Flanagan, SJ, had been placed in the archives of Catholic University of America, where it was read by two graduate students.

Suggestions for Further Reading

Adams, Robert M. *The Virtue of Faith and Other Essays in Philosophical Theology*. New York: Oxford University Press, 1987.

Angeles, Peter, ed. *Critiques of God*. Buffalo, NY: Prometheus Books, 1976.

Davies, Paul. *God and the New Physics*. New York: Simon and Schuster, 1983.

Hick, John. *Philosophy of Religion*. Englewood Cliffs, NJ: Prentice-Hall, 1965.

Hudson, Yeager. *The Philosophy of Religion: Selected Readings*. Mountain View, CA: McGraw-Hill, 1991.

Hume, David. *Dialogues Concerning Natural Religion*. Ed. Norman Kemp Smith. Indianapolis: Bobbs-Merrill, 1947.

Johnson, B. C. *The Atheist Debater's Handbook*. Amherst, NY: Prometheus Books, 1983.

Mackie, J. L. *The Miracle of Theism*. Oxford: Clarendon Press, 1990.

Martin, Michael. *Atheism*. Philadelphia: Temple University Press, 1990.

Matson, Wallace I. *The Existence of God*. Ithaca, NY: Cornell University Press, 1965.

Plantinga, Alvin. *God, Freedom, and Evil*. New York: Harper and Row, 1974.

Rowe, William L. *Philosophy of Religion*. Encino, CA: Dickenson, 1978.

Scriven, Michael. *Primary Philosophy*. New York: McGraw-Hill, 1966.

Wainwright, William J. *Philosophy of Religion*. Belmont, CA: Wadsworth, 1988.

Chapter 7
The Problem of Skepticism and Knowledge

What is knowledge? How does knowledge differ from belief? Does knowledge require certainty? How do we acquire knowledge? Are reason and sense experience both sources of knowledge? What is the extent of our knowledge? Do we have knowledge of the external world? These are the sorts of questions that epistemology—the branch of philosophy that studies knowledge—tries to answer.

We ordinarily claim to know many different types of things. Most of us, for example, would claim to know what pain feels like, how to ride a bicycle, and that snow is white. In each case the object of our knowledge (what our knowledge is about) is different. In the first case, it is about an experience; in the second, a skill; and in the third, a fact. Our focus here will be on the third type of knowledge because we're interested in how we come to know facts.

The sort of knowledge we have when we know what it's like to be in pain is called **knowledge by acquaintance,** or "knowing what." Bertrand Russell claimed that "we have acquaintance with anything of which we are directly aware without the intermediary of any process of inference or any knowledge of truth."[1] For Russell, the only things we are directly aware of are our sensations. Russell thought that our sensations were caused by material objects, but he didn't think that we were directly aware of them. When we hold an apple in our hand and look at it, for example, we're directly aware of a certain color, shape, smell, feel, and so on, but we're not directly aware of the apple itself. We infer the existence of the apple on the basis of our sensations. The distinction between direct and indirect awareness, however, raises one of the most difficult problems in epistemology: How do we know that our sensations are caused by physical objects? After all, we could be dreaming, hallucinating, or hooked up to a sophisticated virtual reality machine. If we can't be certain that such possibilities are not actual, can we acquire knowledge by means of our senses? Those who think not are known as **philosophical skeptics.** According to them, the extent of our knowledge is much more limited than we ordinarily assume.

The sort of knowledge we have when we know how to ride a bicycle is known as **performative knowledge,** or "knowing how." Anyone who has a skill has this sort of knowledge. Ordinarily, anyone who knows how to do something also knows what it is to do it. For example, those who know how to ride a bicycle usually know what it is to ride a bicycle because they learned how to ride a bicycle by actually riding one. But one can learn how to do something without actually doing it. One can learn how to fly an airplane, for example, by training in a flight simulator, and in the future we might be able to upload performative knowledge directly into our brains as is done in the movie *The Matrix*. So, although knowing how and knowing what are often correlated, they are not necessarily connected with one another.

The type of knowledge we have when we know that snow is white is known as **propositional knowledge,** or "knowing that." A proposition is a statement that affirms or denies something and thus is either true or false. One of the first and foremost attempts to characterize propositional knowledge can be found in the works of Plato. In his dialogue "Meno," Socrates remarks, "it is not, I am sure, a mere guess to say that right opinion and knowledge are different. There are few things that I should claim to know, but that at least is among them, whatever else is."[2] The point that Plato is trying to make here is that while having right opinions (true beliefs) may be a necessary condition for knowledge, it is not sufficient—there must be something more to having knowledge than just having true beliefs.

True belief is necessary for knowledge because we can't know something that's false, and if we know something, we can't believe that it's false. For example, we can't know that 2 + 2 equals 5 because 2 + 2 doesn't equal 5. In other words, we can't know what isn't so. Similarly, if we know that 2 + 2 equals 4, we can't believe that it doesn't. To know that something is true is to believe that it's true.

True belief is not sufficient for knowledge, however, because we can have true belief without having knowledge. Consider, for example, the following situation. Suppose you believe that it's raining in Hong Kong right now, and suppose that it is. Does this mean that you know that it's raining in Hong Kong right now? Not if you have no good reason for believing so, for in that case, your belief is nothing more than a lucky guess. Having knowledge, then, would seem to require having good reasons for what you believe. Plato agrees. "True opinions," Socrates tells Meno, "are a fine thing and do all sorts of good so long as they stay in their place, but they will not stay long. They run away from a man's mind; so they are not worth much until you tether them by working out the reason. . . . Once they are tied down, they become knowledge."[3] For Plato, then, knowledge is true belief that is grounded in reality. Determining when a belief is adequately grounded in reality or justified is one of the major tasks of epistemology.

Traditionally, philosophers have recognized two sources of knowledge: reason and sense experience. Those who believe that knowledge of the external world can be gained through the use of reason are known as **rationalists.** Those who believe that sense experience is our only source of knowledge of the external world are known as **empiricists.** Empiricists recognize that reason can give us knowledge of logical truths like "Either it's raining or it's not raining." But they deny that reason alone can tell us anything about the external world. Knowing that either it's raining or it's not raining, for example, tells us nothing about the weather.

Propositions can be known in different ways. Some propositions are knowable **a priori,** that is, prior to or independently of sense experience. For example, the proposition that either it's raining or it's not raining is knowable a priori because you don't have to look outside to determine its truth. Whether it's raining or not raining, the proposition that *either* it's raining *or* it's not raining is true. Other propositions are only knowable **a posteriori,** that is, on the basis of sense experience. For example, the proposition that water boils at 212 degrees Fahrenheit is only knowable a posteriori because it can only be known after observing boiling water.

knowledge by acquaintance Knowledge of what it is to have a certain experience.

philosophical skepticism The doctrine that we have no knowledge of some realms, such as the external world.

performative knowledge Knowledge of how to perform a certain activity.

propositional knowledge Knowledge of whether a proposition is true or false.

rationalism The doctrine that reason is a source of knowledge of the external world.

empiricism The doctrine that sense experience is the only source of knowledge of the external world.

a priori knowledge Knowledge that can be acquired prior to or independently of sense experience.

a posteriori knowledge Knowledge based on sense experience.

Logical truths or propositions that can be turned into logical truths by substituting synonyms for synonyms are called **analytic propositions.** The truth that either it's raining or it's not raining is analytic because it is a logical truth. It has the form "either A or not A" and that is true no matter what proposition we substitute for A. The proposition "either there's liquid precipitation or it's not raining" is also an analytic truth because it can be turned into an analytic truth by substituting synonyms for synonyms. Propositions that are not analytic are called **synthetic propositions.** These would include most of the facts discovered by science.

Both rationalists and empiricists agree that analytic propositions are knowable a priori. They disagree, however, about whether synthetic propositions are also knowable in that way. Rationalists tend to believe that at least some synthetic propositions—such as "From nothing, nothing comes"—are knowable a priori. Empiricists, on the other hand, believe that no synthetic propositions are knowable a priori. On this issue hangs the status of reason as a source of knowledge.

In addition to understanding how we come to know things, epistemologists are also interested in understanding what it is for a proposition to be true. Ordinarily, we would say that a proposition is true when it tells it like it is. In other words, a proposition is true when things in the world are as it says they are. Aristotle expresses that insight this way: "To say of what is that it is not, or of what is not that it is, is false; while to say of what is that it is and of what is not that it is not, is true."[4] This view of truth assumes that there is a way the world is and that a proposition is true when it corresponds to the way the world is. Thus it has come to be known as the **correspondence theory of truth.**

Explicating the notion of correspondence has been notoriously difficult, however. One suggestion, made by Ludwig Wittgenstein, is that true propositions are pictures of reality. Just as the arrangement of the elements in a picture represent the arrangement of objects in reality, Wittgenstein thought that the arrangement of the elements in a proposition represented the arrangement of objects in reality. The problem is that not every proposition can be considered a picture of reality. Consider, for example, the proposition that unicorns are not centaurs. Although this proposition is true, neither unicorns nor centaurs exist. So it's difficult to see how the elements of the proposition could picture them. Other attempts to explicate the correspondence relation have proven equally problematic. Consequently, a number of other accounts of truth have been proposed.

Some believe that truth can be defined as coherence with our beliefs. Brand Blanshard explicates the coherence theory of truth as follows:

> . . . reality is a system, completely ordered and fully intelligible with which thought in its advance of more and more identifying itself. . . . And if we take this view, our notion of truth is marked out for us. Truth is the approximation of thought to reality. It is thought on its way home. . . . Hence at any given time the degree of truth in our experience as a whole is the degree of system it has

achieved. The degree of truth of a particular proposition is to be judged in the first instance by its coherence with experience as a whole, ultimately by its coherence with that further whole, all-comprehensive and fully articulated, in which thought can come to rest.[5]

According to the **coherence theory of truth,** a proposition is true if and only if it coheres with our belief system. Our belief system is not yet complete because there are aspects of reality we do not yet fully understand. So any proposition that coheres with our current belief system is at best only partially true. Only a proposition that coheres with a complete belief system—one that accounts for all aspects of reality—can be considered fully true.

Coherence with our belief system is certainly a test of truth. Fit with existing theory—conservatism—is a criterion of adequacy for hypotheses because the better a hypothesis fits with what we've already learned, the more likely it is to be true. But those who accept the coherence theory of truth maintain that coherence is more than just a test of truth: it's the nature of truth. For them, there is nothing more to a proposition's being true than its cohering with our beliefs.

There must be more to truth than coherence, however, because a proposition can cohere with one's belief system and be false. Consider the case of David Koresh, the former leader of the Branch Davidians, who died when the cult's headquarters near Waco, Texas, burned down in 1993. Koresh believed that he was Jesus Christ. He maintained that this belief was based on a coherent interpretation of the Scriptures. Suppose it was. And suppose that everything else that he believed cohered with that belief. Does that mean that it was true that he was Jesus Christ? No. Just because someone consistently believes something doesn't mean that it's true.

To avoid the problem of coherent but false belief systems, some have tried to specify which belief system a proposition must cohere with in order to be true. Charles Sanders Pierce claims that a belief is true if it coheres with the belief system fated to be agreed on by all who investigate.[6] But there is no guarantee that all investigators will eventually agree on one belief system. For any set of data, an infinite number of theories can be constructed to account for that data. We can't rule out the possibility that, at the end of inquiry, there would be two or more incompatible belief systems that account for the data equally well. But two incompatible belief systems cannot both be true. Because it's possible for two incompatible belief systems to be equally coherent, there must be more to truth than coherence.

William James proposed that we define truth in terms of usefulness. He writes, "The true is only the expedient in the way of our behaving, expedient in almost any fashion, and expedient in the long run and on the whole course."[7] For James, a true proposition is one that works. According to the **pragmatic theory of truth,** then, a proposition is made true by its practical consequences. One of the reasons that truth is so valuable is that actions based on true propositions are much more likely to succeed than those based

analytic proposition A proposition that is a logical truth or can be turned into a logical truth by substituting synonyms for synonyms.

synthetic proposition A proposition that is not analytic.

correspondence theory of truth The doctrine that a proposition is made true by its correspondence with reality.

coherence theory of truth The doctrine that a proposition is made true by its coherence with a system of beliefs.

pragmatic theory of truth The doctrine that a proposition is made true by its practical consequences.

on false ones. James suggests that this insight can be used to define truth. For him, a true proposition is one that is such that if we acted on it, it would bring about the desired result.

The problem, of course, is that false beliefs can lead to desired results. The Nazis desired to win World War II. If they had, would that mean that the proposition that Jews are subhuman is true? Suppose that Muslim extremists succeed in taking over the world. Would that mean that Allah is the one true God? Or take David Koresh's belief that he was Jesus Christ. That belief seemed to work for him. He got a lot of followers and a lot of wives out of it. Does that mean he really was Jesus Christ? The answer to all of these questions seems to be "No." The fact that a proposition works may provide some reason for believing that it's true, but that doesn't make it true.

Some believe that truth is simply a matter of belief. We've all heard statements like "What's true for you is not true for me" or "You have your truth, I have mine." The implication here is that truth is relative to individuals. Consequently, this view is known as **cognitive subjectivism.**

The view that you can make something true by simply believing it to be true is not unique to the twentieth century. It flourished in ancient Greece over twenty-five hundred years ago. The ancient champions of cognitive subjectivism are known as Sophists. They were professors of rhetoric who earned their living by teaching wealthy Athenians how to win friends and influence people. Because they believed that truth was relative, however, they taught their pupils to argue both sides of any case, which created quite a scandal at the time. (The words "sophistic" and "sophistical" are used to describe arguments that appear sound but are actually fallacious.) The greatest of the Sophists — Protagoras—famously expressed his subjectivism thus: "Man is the measure of all things, of existing things that they exist, and of nonexisting things that they do not exist."[8] Truth does not exist independently of human minds but is created by our thoughts. Consequently, whatever anyone believes is true.

Plato saw clearly the implications of such a view. If whatever anyone believes is true, then everyone's belief is as true as everyone else's. And if everyone's belief is as true as everyone else's, then the belief that subjectivism is false is as true as the belief that subjectivism is true. Plato put it this way: "Protagoras, for his part, admitting as he does that everybody's opinion is true, must acknowledge the truth of his opponents' belief about his own belief, where they think he is wrong."[9] Cognitive subjectivism, then, is self-refuting. If it's true, it's false. Any claim whose truth implies its falsehood cannot possibly be true.

It's ironic that Protagoras taught argumentation because in a Protagoran world, there shouldn't be any arguments. Arguments arise when there is some reason to believe that someone is mistaken. If believing something to be true made it true, however, no one could ever be mistaken; everyone would be infallible. It would be impossible for anyone to have a false belief because the mere fact that they believed something would make it true. So if Protagoras's customers took his philosophy seriously, he would be out of a job. If no one can lose an argument, there's no need to learn how to argue.

Some believe that truth is relative to societies or cultures. There's no doubt that different cultures have different beliefs about what is true. But according to **cognitive cultural relativism,** each culture manufactures its own truth. This view is as problematic as cognitive subjectivism, however. For if a society believed that truth was not socially constructed (as ours may well believe), then that view would be as true as the claim that truth is socially constructed, which is absurd.

The problem with the relativist is that he wants to have his cake and eat it too. On the one hand, he wants to say that he or his society is the supreme authority on matters of truth. But, on the other hand, he wants to say that other individuals, societies, or conceptual schemes are equally authoritative. He can't have it both ways. As philosopher W. V. O. Quine explains,

> Truth, says the cultural relativist, is culture-bound. But if it were, then he, within his own culture, ought to see his own culture-bound truth as absolute. He cannot proclaim cultural relativism without rising above it, and he cannot rise above it without giving it up.[10]

If relativism were true, there would be no standpoint outside of yourself or your society from which to make valid judgments. But if there were no such standpoint, you would have no grounds for thinking that relativism is true. In proclaiming that truth is relative, then, the relativist hoists himself on his own petard; he blows himself up, so to speak.

Much as we might like all of our beliefs to be true, we know that they aren't. Even the most fervent relativist must confess that he or she dials a wrong number, bets on a losing racehorse, or forgets a friend's birthday. These admissions reveal that truth is not simply a matter of belief. If believing something to be so made it so, the world would contain a lot fewer unfulfilled desires, unrealized ambitions, and unsuccessful projects than it does.

So what is the truth about truth? The British philosopher J. L. Austin once said, "If a proposition is true, there is, of course, a state of affairs that makes it true."[11] And of course there is. We can't make a proposition true by simply believing it to be true, and a proposition can't make itself true. Thus truth must consist in some sort of relationship between a proposition and reality as the correspondence theory suggests. No one has yet specified exactly what that relationship is, but that shouldn't prevent us from accepting the correspondence theory any more than the fact that no one has been able to specify exactly what gravity is should prevent us from accepting the theory of gravity. We can provisionally adopt what might be called a **minimal correspondence theory,** which says that a proposition is true if and only if things are as it says they are. This preserves the insight that true propositions accurately represent reality without falling prey to the criticisms that were fatal to the other theories of truth.

cognitive subjectivism The doctrine that a proposition is made true by one's believing it to be true.

cognitive cultural relativism The doctrine that a proposition is made true by a society believing it to be true.

minimal correspondence theory The doctrine that a proposition is true if and only if things are as it says they are.

To say that truth consists in a correspondence between a proposition and reality is not to say that there is only one way to accurately represent reality. Reality can be represented in many different ways, just as a territory can be mapped in many different ways. Consider, for example, road maps, topographical maps, and relief maps. These maps use different symbols to represent different aspects of the terrain, and the symbols that appear on one map may not appear on another. Nevertheless, it makes no sense to say that one of these maps is the correct map. Each can provide an accurate representation of the territory, and thus each can be considered to be true. The view that there is only one correct way of representing the world may be called "absolutism." Accepting the correspondence theory of truth does not commit one to absolutism.

In this chapter, we'll touch on just a few of the problems of epistemology. The first section deals with the problem of skepticism, the second with the problem of perception, and the third with the problem of defining knowledge.

Objectives

After reading this chapter, you should be able to

- state Descartes' dream argument and his evil genius argument.
- evaluate the claim that knowledge requires certainty.
- state the different theories of perception.
- evaluate the different theories of perception.
- state the various theories of knowledge.
- evaluate the arguments for each theory of knowledge.
- define knowledge by acquaintance, philosophical skepticism, performative knowledge, propositional knowledge, rationalism, empiricism, a priori proposition, a posteriori proposition, analytic proposition, synthetic proposition, correspondence theory of truth, coherence theory of truth, pragmatic theory of truth, sense data, primary qualities, and secondary qualities.

Things Aren't Always What They Seem
Skepticism about Skepticism

Much of what we claim to know about the world is based on sense experience. The way things look, feel, taste, sound, and smell is generally believed to be an accurate indication of the way they are. But is this belief justified? Is sense experience a source of knowledge? Or is it only a source of opinion?

All wish to possess knowledge, but few, comparatively speaking, are willing to pay the price.

—Juvenal

Greek Rationalism

The world that presents itself to our senses is constantly changing. Winds blow, rains fall, mountains crumble to the sea, and living things come into being, grow old, and pass away. But change is a mystery. How can something change and yet remain the same thing? If something changes, it's different, and if it's different, it's no longer the same. So it seems that nothing can remain the same through change.

The problem greatly perplexed the ancient Greeks. Heraclitus, unwilling to deny the evidence of his senses, maintained that identity over time is an illusion. The same thing cannot exist over time because "Change alone is unchanging."[12] The world, he thought, was being created anew each instant. "You cannot step into the same river twice," he proclaimed, "for the water into which you first stepped has flowed on."[13] Heraclitus viewed the world not as a static collection of discrete objects, but as a dynamic web of interconnected processes.

This view was shared by the Buddha (ca. 563–ca. 483 B.C.), who walked the earth at the same time as Heraclitus. The Buddha also used the analogy of a river to illustrate the dynamic nature of our existence. "O Brahmana," he says, "it is just like a mountain river, flowing far and swift, taking everything along with it; there is no moment, no instant, no second when it stops flowing, but it goes on flowing and continuing. So Brahmana, is human life, like a mountain river."[14] Both Heraclitus and the Buddha deny the existence of any continuing substance. Nothing remains the same over time. Everything is in a constant state of flux.

Parmenides

Heraclitus's contemporary Parmenides (born ca. 515 B.C.) found this view of the world incomprehensible. Reality must contain a continuing substance, he thought, because only that which is unchanging is real. Although Parmenides expressed his philosophy in a poem, he based it on a logical argument. Parmenides realized that whatever involves a logical contradiction cannot exist. So, he reasoned, nonexistence (nothingness) cannot exist. Also, from nothing, nothing comes. So everything that exists must have always existed. And everything that exists must continue to exist because it is just as impossible for something to become nothing as it is for nothing to become something.

Furthermore, if nonexistence cannot exist, then there is no place where there is nothing. But if every place is occupied, there is no place for anything to move to. So motion is impossible. Parmenides concluded the world must be a single, solid, eternal, and unchanging sphere. According to Parmenides, everything is one.

Just as Heraclitus's philosophy is echoed in the teachings of Buddhism, so Parmenides' philosophy is echoed in the teachings of Hinduism. In Chapter 2, verse 16 of the epic Hindu poem Bhagavad Gita (Sanskrit for "song of the Lord"), we read, "That which is not shall never be; That which is, shall never cease to be. To the wise, these truths are self-evident." The notions that change is an illusion and that everything is one are two of the central teachings of Hinduism. Instead of viewing the world as essentially material in nature, however, the Hindus view it as essentially spiritual. The only thing that truly exists (because it is unchanging) is Brahman, which is pure being, pure consciousness, and pure bliss.

According to Parmenides, reality is very different from the way it appears. The world seems to be composed of myriad objects that are constantly changing. But logic, he claims, proves otherwise. Change is logically impossible, and anything that's logically impossible cannot exist. So our senses don't put us in touch with reality. Only reason, he thought, can reveal the way the world is. Thus Parmenides is often considered to be the father of rationalism because he was the first in the West to maintain that knowledge can be gained independently of sense experience through the use of reason.

Thought Probe

Thinking about Nothing

Parmenides believed that because nonexistence cannot exist, it cannot be thought about. Do you agree? Can you think about nothing? That is, can nothingness be the object of your thought? If so, can you describe what you're thinking about when you're thinking about nothing?

Zeno

Parmenides attracted some very able followers, most notably, Zeno of Elea (490?–425? B.C.). Zeno reportedly concocted dozens of additional arguments in support of his mentor's view, only a handful of which have come down to us. To get a sense of these arguments, consider his paradox of bisection.

Thought Experiment

Zeno's Paradox of Bisection

Suppose you are in a stadium at a given distance from the exit door. Then you can never get out of the stadium because before you reach the door you must reach the point halfway there. But before you can reach the halfway point, you must reach a point halfway to that. And since it takes some finite interval of time to move from one point to another, and there are an infinite number of halfway points, it would take you an infinite time to pass through them all and get out.[15]

If Zeno's analysis of motion is correct, not only can we never get out of the stadium, but we can never take the first step toward the door. Before we reach the halfway point, we would first have to reach a point halfway to that. And before we reach that point, we would have to reach a point halfway to that, and so on. So just as it would take an infinite amount of time to get out of the stadium, it would take an infinite amount of time to take the first step. And since finite beings like ourselves do not have an infinite amount of time on our hands, motion is impossible.

Zeno did not deny that people seem to move from place to place. What he denied was that the way the world seems is an accurate reflection of the way it really is. Like his teacher, Parmenides, he claimed that whatever involves a logical contradiction can't exist. And because motion involves a logical contradiction, it can't exist.

Although Zeno's thought experiments did not convince many people of their own immobility, they had an enormous influence on subsequent philosophizing. Zeno was the first philosopher to present logical arguments in prose, a form of exposition used by philosophers ever since. In recognition of this accomplishment, Aristotle refers to Zeno as "the inventor of dialectic." Aristotle also notes that Zeno's thought experiments led to the development of the atomic theory of matter.[16] Of Zeno's thought experiments, Gregory Vlastos writes, "In the whole history of philosophy no better device has ever been found for sensitizing us to the possibility that commonplaces may conceal absurdities and hence to the need of reexamining even the best entrenched and most plausible assumptions."[17] We may disagree with Zeno's conclusions, but we cannot but admire his method.

The notion that the world may be very different from the way it appears has recently been explored in a number of movies, most notably, *The Matrix*. The movie takes place sometime in the future when computers have taken over the world and use humans as a source of energy. The humans are kept alive in fluid-filled pods, their brains being stimulated by electrodes connected directly to their nervous systems. Those plugged into the matrix think they're leading normal lives in the late twentieth century, whereas in reality they're floating in a pod. What they take to be real is nothing more than a computer-generated fantasy.

Plato

While the image presented in *The Matrix* is a striking one, it strongly resembles one presented by Plato about twenty-five hundred years ago. Plato, following Parmenides, held that only that which is unchanging is real, and, following Heraclitus, that what is presented to our senses is constantly changing. So he concluded that what we sense isn't fully real. To convey this view, Plato fashioned one of the most vivid and significant images in the history of philosophy: the allegory of the cave. The allegory appears in Book VII of his *Republic*, where Socrates is talking to Glaucon:

SOCRATES: And now, I said, let me show in a figure how far our nature is enlightened or unenlightened: — Behold! human beings living in a underground cave, which has a mouth open towards the light and reaching all along the cave; here they have been from their childhood, and have their legs and necks chained so that they cannot move, and can only see

Solving Parmenides' and Zeno's Paradoxes

Parmenides' and Zeno's paradoxes have engaged some of the world's greatest minds for more than two thousand years, and many solutions have been offered. The best way to solve a paradox, however, is to "dissolve" it; to show that it rests on contradictory assumptions and thus cannot get off the ground. Some think that a contradiction lies at the heart of Zeno's paradoxes. In the paradox of bisection, for example, Zeno assumes that space can be infinitely divided. This means that the smallest amount of space—a point—has no dimensions. On the other hand, Zeno also assumes that it takes a finite amount of time to traverse any amount of space. But it takes no time at all to traverse a point, for a point has no dimensions. So Zeno seems to be trying to have his cake and eat it too. Both assumptions can't be true, and once we reject either one of them, there is no longer a paradox.

What about Parmenides' claim that nonexistence cannot exist? Hasn't modern science proved that the world is mostly empty space? Indeed it has. But it has also proved that space is a thing. Einstein's theory of general relativity predicts that space will be curved around massive objects, and this prediction has been confirmed many times over in many different experiments. But you can't curve something that doesn't exist. So space is not mere nothingness. Russell Ruthen, staff writer for *Scientific American*, explains,

> Space is not just the nothing between the earth and the stars. Nor is it simply the void between the electron and the atomic nucleus. It is a ubiquitous medium more resilient than rubber, more rigid than steel.[18]

So Parmenides was right. There is no place where there is nothing. There are places where there is nothing but empty space, but space itself is a thing. Where Parmenides went wrong was in assuming that if a place is occupied, nothing else can move into it. Empedocles realized the error in this reasoning more than two thousand years ago and suggested that we move through space like fish move through water. His view appears to be pretty accurate.

---

before them, being prevented by the chains from turning round their heads. Above and behind them a fire is blazing at a distance, and between the fire and the prisoners there is a raised way; and you will see, if you look, a low wall built along the way, like the screen which marionette players have in front of them, over which they show the puppets.

GLAUCON: I see.

SOCRATES: And do you see, I said, men passing along the wall carrying all sorts of vessels, and statues and figures of animals made of wood and stone and various materials, which appear over the wall? Some of them are talking, others silent.

GLAUCON: You have shown me a strange image, and they are strange prisoners.

SOCRATES: Like ourselves, I replied; and they see only their own shadows, or the shadows of one another, which the fire throws on the opposite wall of the cave? . . .

SOCRATES: And suppose further that the prison had an echo which came from the other side, would they not be sure to fancy when one of the passers-by spoke that the voice which they heard came from the passing shadow?

GLAUCON: No question, he replied.

SOCRATES: To them, I said, the truth would be literally nothing but the shadows of the images.

GLAUCON: That is certain.

SOCRATES: And now look again, and see what will naturally follow if the prisoners are released and disabused of their error. At first, when any of them is liberated and compelled suddenly to stand up and turn his neck round and walk and look towards the light, he will suffer sharp pains; the glare will distress him, and he will be unable to see the realities of which in his former state he had seen the shadows; . . .

SOCRATES: And suppose once more, that he is reluctantly dragged up a steep and rugged ascent, and held fast until he's forced into the presence of the sun himself, is he not likely to be pained and irritated? When he approaches the light his eyes will be dazzled, and he will not be able to see anything at all of what are now called realities.

GLAUCON: Not all in a moment, he said.

SOCRATES: He will require to grow accustomed to the sight of the upper world. And first he will see the shadows best, next the reflections of men and other objects in the water, and then the objects themselves; then he will gaze upon the light of the moon and the stars and the spangled heaven; and he will see the sky and the stars by night better than the sun or the light of the sun by day?

GLAUCON: Certainly.

SOCRATES: Last of all he will be able to see the sun, and not mere reflections of him in the water, but he will see him in his own proper place, and not in another; and he will contemplate him as he is. . . .

SOCRATES: Imagine once more, I said, such a one coming suddenly out of the sun to be replaced in his old situation; would he not be certain to have his eyes full of darkness?

GLAUCON: To be sure, he said.

SOCRATES: And if there were a contest, and he had to compete in measuring the shadows with the prisoners who had never moved out of the cave, while his sight was still weak, and before his eyes had become steady (and the time which would be needed to acquire this new habit of sight might be very considerable) would he not be ridiculous? Men would say of him that up he went and down he came without his eyes; and that it was better not even to think of ascending; and if any one tried to loose another and lead him up to the light, let them only catch the offender, and they would put him to death.

GLAUCON: No question, he said.

SOCRATES: This entire allegory, I said, you may now append, dear Glaucon, to the previous argument; the prison-house is the world of sight, the light of the fire is the sun, and you will not misapprehend me if you interpret

the journey upwards to be the ascent of the soul into the intellectual world according to my poor belief, which, at your desire, I have expressed whether rightly or wrongly God knows. But, whether true or false, my opinion is that in the world of knowledge the idea of good appears last of all, and is seen only with an effort; and, when seen, is also inferred to be the universal author of all things beautiful and right, parent of light and of the lord of light in this visible world, and the immediate source of reason and truth in the intellectual; and that this is the power upon which he who would act rationally, either in public or private life must have his eye fixed.[19]

The allegory of the cave is meant to represent not only the human situation in general but Socrates' life in particular. Socrates, like the prisoner loosed from the cave, had glimpsed the true nature of reality and tried to convince the inhabitants of Athens that they didn't know what they thought they knew. Some didn't welcome this news, however, and conspired to put him to death.

The objects that cast shadows on the wall represent what Plato considers to be the truly real objects: the forms. A form is a universal; it is a property

Although *The Matrix* scenario is a bit far-fetched, British philosopher Nick Bostrom thinks there is a good probability that we're living in a computer simulation. To prove his point, he has developed what he calls the "simulation argument":

> *The Matrix* got many otherwise not-so-philosophical minds ruminating on the nature of reality. But the scenario depicted in the movie is ridiculous: human brains being kept in tanks by intelligent machines just to produce power.
>
> There is, however, a related scenario that is more plausible and a serious line of reasoning that leads from the possibility of this scenario to a striking conclusion about the world we live in. I call this the simulation argument. Perhaps its most startling lesson is that there is a significant probability that you are living in a computer simulation. I mean this literally: if the simulation hypothesis is true, you exist in a virtual reality simulated in a computer built by some advanced civilization. Your brain, too, is merely a part of that simulation. What grounds could we have for taking this hypothesis seriously? Before getting to the gist of the simulation argument, let us consider some of its preliminaries. One of these is the assumption of "substrate independence". This is the idea that conscious minds could in principle be implemented not only on carbon-based biological neurons (such as those inside your head) but also on some other computational substrate such as silicon-based processors. . . .
>
> Our second preliminary is that we can estimate, at least roughly, how much computing power it would take to implement a human mind along with a virtual reality that would seem completely realistic for it to interact with. Furthermore, we can establish lower bounds on how powerful the computers of an advanced civilization could be. Technological futurists have already produced designs for physically possible computers that could be built using advanced molecular manufacturing technology. The upshot of such an analysis is that a technologically mature civilization that has developed at least those technologies that we already know are physically possible, would be able to build computers powerful enough to run an astronomical number of human-like minds, even if only a tiny fraction of their resources was used for that purpose.
>
> If you are such a simulated mind, there might be no direct observational way for you to tell; the virtual reality that you would be living in would look and feel perfectly real. But all that this shows, so far, is that you could never be completely sure that you are not living in a simulation. This result is only moderately interesting. You could still regard the simulation hypothesis as too improbable to be taken seriously.
>
> Now we get to the core of the simulation argument. This does not purport to demonstrate that you are in a simulation. Instead, it shows that we should accept as true at least one of the following three propositions:
>
> (1) The chances that a species at our current level of development can avoid going extinct before becoming technologically mature is negligibly small

that can be possessed by many different things. Various works of art, for example, can be beautiful. What makes them beautiful, Plato claims, is that they participate in the form of beauty. As he puts it, "By beauty all beautiful things become beautiful."[21] So, for Plato, forms are causes: they make the world what it is. To understand the world, then, we must understand the forms that give rise to it.

We can't acquire knowledge of the forms by means of the senses, however, because the forms aren't physical objects. How, then, do we acquire knowledge of them? Plato suggests that we come to know them through an act of recollection.

(2) Almost no technologically mature civilizations are interested in running computer simulations of minds like ours

(3) You are almost certainly in a simulation.

Each of these three propositions may be prima facie implausible; yet, if the simulation argument is correct, at least one is true (it does not tell us which).

While the full simulation argument employs some probability theory and formalism, the gist of it can be understood in intuitive terms. Suppose that proposition (1) is false. Then a significant fraction of all species at our level of development eventually becomes technologically mature. Suppose, further, that (2) is false, too. Then some significant fraction of these species that have become technologically mature will use some portion of their computational resources to run computer simulations of minds like ours. But, as we saw earlier, the number of simulated minds that any such technologically mature civilization could run is astronomically huge.

Therefore, if both (1) and (2) are false, there will be an astronomically huge number of simulated minds like ours. If we work out the numbers, we find that there would be vastly many more such simulated minds than there would be non-simulated minds running on organic brains. In other words, almost all minds like yours, having the kinds of experiences that you have, would be simulated rather than biological. Therefore, by a very weak principle of indifference, you would have to think that you are probably one of these simulated minds rather

than one of the exceptional ones that are running on biological neurons.

So if you think that (1) and (2) are both false, you should accept (3). It is not coherent to reject all three propositions. In reality, we do not have much specific information to tell us which of the three propositions might be true. In this situation, it might be reasonable to distribute our credence roughly evenly between the three possibilities, giving each of them a substantial probability. . . .

If we are in a simulation, is it possible that we could know that for certain? If the simulators don't want us to find out, we probably never will. But if they choose to reveal themselves, they could certainly do so. Maybe a window informing you of the fact would pop up in front of you, or maybe they would "upload" you into their world. Another event that would let us conclude with a very high degree of confidence that we are in a simulation is if we ever reach the point where we are about to switch on our own simulations. If we start running simulations, that would be very strong evidence against (1) and (2). That would leave us with only (3).[20]

Thought Probe

Bostrom's Simulation Argument

Do you think that Bostrom's simulation argument is a good one? That is, do you think it is probable that you are living in a computer simulation? Why or why not?

We often judge things to fall short of an ideal. An action may be just but not perfectly just; two objects may be equal, but not perfectly equal; a painting may be beautiful but not perfectly beautiful. To make such judgments, Plato claimed, we must have knowledge of the ideal (the form) involved. But we can't acquire that knowledge through our senses because nothing that we sense is perfectly just, equal, or beautiful. So we must have been born with a knowledge of these forms, and sense experience helps us recall that knowledge.

Knowledge we are born with is known as "innate knowledge." Rationalists characteristically attribute innate knowledge to us, thus explaining how it's possible to have knowledge that does not depend on sense experience. Some rationalists claim that we have an innate knowledge of concepts; others claim that we have an innate knowledge of statements. But, in either case, it's knowledge possessed by all normal human beings.

Thought Probe

Innate Knowledge

Do you think that there are any concepts or truths that all normal humans have or know? If so, what are they?

Cartesian Skepticism

The first step to knowledge is to know that we are ignorant.

—RICHARD CECIL

The most influential modern rationalist is Descartes. He doubted that sense experience can give us knowledge because knowledge requires certainty and nothing we learn through our senses is certain. Descartes holds that you are justified in believing something to be true only if you are certain of it. "I ought no less carefully to withhold my assent from matters which are not entirely certain and indubitable," he informs us, "than from those which appear to me manifestly to be false."[22] You are no more justified in believing something that is uncertain than you are in believing something that is obviously false. So if something can be doubted—if there is a possibility that it's false—you can't know that it's true.

Although this conception of knowledge may seem unduly strict, it does seem to accord with our use of the term. We often discount others' testimony if there is a possibility that they're mistaken. Suppose, for example, that a witness in a murder trial claims to have seen the defendant at the scene of the crime. If the defense attorney can show that there is reason to doubt the witness's testimony (because it was dark, because he was too far away, because his glasses were broken), she undercuts his claim to know that he saw the defendant. When there's reason to doubt a witness, you can't know that the person is telling the truth.

One of Descartes' goals in his *Meditations on First Philosophy* was to determine the extent of our knowledge. To accomplish this goal, he did not try to inspect every one of his beliefs. Instead, he examined the principles upon which they are based. He realized that if the principles are dubious, then so are the beliefs that are based on them. One principle that underlies many of our beliefs is that sense experience is a source of knowledge. But our senses can deceive us. What appears to be round, for example, can turn out to be square. Because we can't be certain that what we've learned through our senses is true, sense experience cannot be a source of knowledge.

Cartesian Doubt

To show that we can't trust our senses, Descartes presents two of the most famous thought experiments in the history of philosophy: the dream argument and the evil genius argument. We examined them briefly in Chapter 2. Now let's examine them more closely.

Here's Descartes' dream argument:

Thought Experiment

Descartes' Dream Argument

How often has it happened to me that in the night I dreamt that I found myself in this particular place, that I was dressed and seated near the fire, whilst in reality I was lying undressed in bed! At this moment it does indeed seem to me that it is with eyes awake that I am looking at this paper, that this head which I move is not asleep, that it is deliberately and of set purpose that I extend my hand and perceive it; what happens in sleep does not appear so clear and distinct as does all this. But in thinking over this I remind myself that on many occasions I have in sleep been deceived by similar illusions, and in dwelling carefully on this reflection I see so manifestly that there are no certain indications by which we may clearly distinguish wakefulness from sleep that I am lost in astonishment. And my astonishment is such that it is almost capable of persuading me that I now dream.[23]

Doubt is the vestibule which all must pass before they can enter the temple of wisdom.
— CALEB C. COLTON

Dreams can often seem quite real. Even when we do things that we can't do when we're awake (like flying), it seems as if we're really doing them. Because there is no way to tell for certain while we're dreaming that we're dreaming, we can't be certain that we're not dreaming right now. And if we can't be certain that we're not dreaming right now, we can't acquire knowledge through the use of our senses.

Where doubt is, there truth is — it is her shadow.
— G. BAILEY

Thought Probe

Dreams and Reality

Is Descartes right that there are no certain indications by which we can distinguish wakefulness from sleep? Suppose that every dream you had ended by your getting into bed and going to sleep. Would you be able to tell what was a dream and what was reality? How?

Descartes' dream argument can be spelled out this way:

1. We can't be certain that we're not dreaming.
2. If we can't be certain that we're not dreaming, we can't be certain that what we sense is real.
3. If we can't be certain that what we sense is real, we can't acquire knowledge through sense experience.
4. Therefore, we can't acquire knowledge through sense experience.

Although Descartes may not have been certain that he was not dreaming, you may feel that you are certain that you're not dreaming. But feeling certain and being certain are two different things. In Descartes' view, you can be certain of something only if it's impossible for you to be mistaken. But it's not impossible for you to be mistaken that you're awake. On the contrary, you could wake up at any moment and discover that your whole life has been a dream. Because you can't rule out the possibility that you're dreaming, Descartes claims that your senses can't give you knowledge of the external world.

Even if you can't be certain that you're not dreaming, it would seem that you can still know some things. You can know, for example, that some things are colored, for if you hadn't experienced colored things, how could you know what color is? None of the things that you take to be colored may actually be colored, but there must be some colored things in the world, for otherwise you wouldn't know what color is.

But even this can be doubted. You could have learned what color is in the same way that Adam and Eve learned what right and wrong are — by having that knowledge directly implanted in your mind. Descartes explores this possibility in his evil genius argument.

Thought Experiment

Descartes' Evil Genius Argument

Nevertheless I have long had fixed in my mind the belief that an all-powerful God existed by whom I have been created such as I am. But how do I know that He has not brought it to pass that there is no earth, no heaven, no extended body, no magnitude, no place, and that nevertheless they seem to me to exist just exactly as I see them?[24]

An all-powerful being could put thoughts in your mind, and he could arrange it so that everything you believe about the external world is false. Because we can't be certain that we're not in the grip of such a demon, we can't acquire knowledge through the senses.

To prove that we could be systematically deluded, we don't have to appeal to the supernatural. The evil genius could just as well be a mad scientist. Peter Unger presents a modern-day version of Descartes' evil genius argument.

Thought Experiment

Unger's Mad Scientist

This scientist uses electrodes to induce experiences and thus carries out his deceptions, concerning the existence of rocks or anything else. He first drills

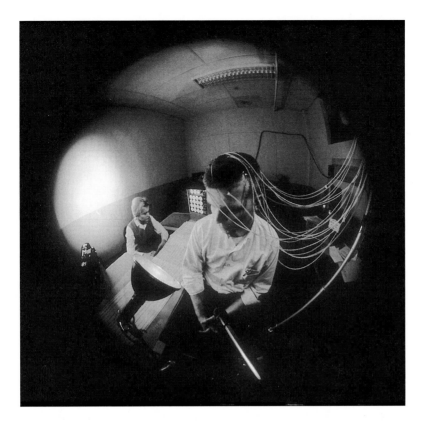

holes painlessly in the variously colored skulls, or shells, of his subjects and then implants his electrodes into the appropriate parts of their brains, or protoplasm, or systems. He sends patterns of electrical impulses into them through the electrodes, which are themselves connected by wires to a laboratory console on which he plays, punching various keys and buttons in accordance with his ideas of how the whole thing works and with his deceptive designs. The scientist's delight is intense, and it is caused not so much by his exercising his scientific and intellectual gifts as by the thought that he is deceiving various subjects about all sorts of things. Part of that delight is caused, on this supposition, by his thought that he is deceiving a certain person, perhaps yourself, into falsely believing that there are rocks. He is, then, an evil scientist, and he lives in a world which is entirely bereft of rocks.[25]

Because Unger's mad scientist directly controls the firing patterns of the neurons in your brain, he can give you any experience he wants. As a result, he can implant in you any number of false beliefs. Because you can't be sure that you're not at the mercy of such a scientist right now, sense experience can't be a source of knowledge.

The argument suggested by Descartes' and Unger's evil geniuses is this:

1. We can't be certain that our sense experience is not caused by an evil genius.
2. If we can't be certain that our sense experience is not caused by an evil genius, we can't be certain that what we sense is real.
3. If we can't be certain that what we sense is real, we can't acquire knowledge through sense experience.
4. Therefore, we can't acquire knowledge through sense experience.

An evil genius of the sort described by Descartes or Unger could exist. There is no contradiction involved in assuming that there is such a being. As a result, premise 1 seems to be true. And given Descartes' assumption that knowledge requires certainty, premise 2 also seems to be true. If we can't be certain that we are not deluded, we can't acquire knowledge through the use of our senses.

Cartesian Certainty

Even if there is an evil genius, Descartes believes that there is at least one thing that he knows, namely, that he exists. He writes,

> . . . I was persuaded that there was nothing in all the world, that there was no heaven, no earth, that there were no minds, nor any bodies: was I not then likewise persuaded that I did not exist? Not at all; of a surety I myself did exist since I persuaded myself of something. But there is some deceiver or other, very powerful and very cunning, who ever employs his ingenuity in deceiving me. Then without doubt I exist also if he deceives me, and let him deceive me as much as he will, he can never cause me to be nothing so long as I think that I am something.[26]

Descartes can't doubt that he thinks because doubting is a species of thinking. Any attempt to doubt that he's thinking proves that he's thinking because to doubt is to think. But he can't think unless he exists. So he's also certain that he exists. With this truth—I think, therefore I am—as a first principle, Descartes hoped to set our knowledge of the external world on as firm a foundation as our knowledge of mathematics.

The facts that he thinks and that he exists are not the only facts he knows, however. He also knows the contents of his own mind. For example, if Descartes is hungry, he knows that he is hungry. If Descartes is in pain, he knows that he is in pain. And if Descartes seems to see a tree, then he knows that he seems to see a tree.

This last bit of knowledge is important because it can serve as a basis for our knowledge of the external world. From the fact that you seem to see a tree, it doesn't follow that there is a tree. You might be dreaming, or you might be under the influence of an evil genius. But if there were a way to rule out these counterpossibilities, then you would know that there is a tree. What's needed, then, is a principle that will bridge the gap between appearance and reality.

Descartes claims to have such a principle—the principle of clarity and distinctness—which says that whatever is clearly and distinctly perceived is true. As he puts it, ". . . as often as I so restrain my will within the limits of my knowledge that it forms no judgment except on matters which are clearly and distinctly represented to it by the understanding, I can never be deceived."[27] This principle allows Descartes to deduce truths about the external world from truths about his mental states. The deductions go like this:

1. I clearly and distinctly seem to see a tree in front of me.

2. Whatever I clearly and distinctly perceive is true.

3. Therefore, there is a tree in front of me.

What we know here is very little, but what we are ignorant of is immense.

—Pierre-Simon
Laplace

The principle of clarity and distinctness closes the gap between the way the world appears and the way it really is. If Descartes can prove that the principle is true, he can defeat the skeptics.

Descartes attempts to establish this principle by establishing the existence of God. He is fully aware that God did not give him an infallible mind. But he is sure that God, being all-good, would not give him a mind that could not know the truth. So if he falls into error, it must be his fault, not God's.

> Whence then come my errors? They come from the sole fact that since the will is much wider in its range and compass than the understanding, I do not restrain it within the same bounds, but extend it also to things which I do not understand: and as the will is of itself indifferent to these, it easily falls into error and sin, and chooses the evil for the good, or the false for the true.[28]

Descartes believes that God gave humans free will. Unfortunately our will sometimes usurps our understanding and jumps to unwarranted conclusions. When it does, we deceive ourselves. But if our will followed our understanding—if we believed only what was sanctioned by the principle of clarity and distinctness—we would never believe anything that was false.

Descartes' argument for the principle of clarity and distinctness, then, goes as follows:

1. God exists and is no deceiver.

2. If God exists and is no deceiver, then whatever I clearly and distinctly perceive is true.

3. Therefore, whatever I clearly and distinctly perceive is true.

The first premise of this argument is problematic, for as we have seen, Descartes' ontological argument for the existence of God is not convincing. (He offers other arguments, but they are even less convincing than his ontological argument.) But whether or not these arguments succeed, many commentators believe that Descartes' defense of the principle of clarity and distinctness suffers from a more serious defect: circularity.

A circular argument assumes what it is trying to prove. Descartes is trying to prove the principle of clarity and distinctness. He claims that the truth of this principle follows from the existence of God. But he uses this principle to prove the existence of God. So Descartes seems to be caught in a circle: he can't know that God exists and is no deceiver unless he knows that what he clearly and distinctly perceives is true. But he can't know that what he clearly and distinctly perceives is true unless he knows that God exists and is no deceiver. This problem is known as the "problem of the Cartesian circle."

This problem is not unique to Descartes. It faces anyone who takes a foundationalist approach to knowledge. **Foundationalism** maintains (1) that there are basic beliefs, that is, beliefs whose justification does not depend on other beliefs, and (2) that the justification of all other beliefs depends, at least in part, on the basic beliefs. Foundationalists use what are known as "epistemic principles" to bridge the gap between basic beliefs and all other beliefs. Critics of foundationalism claim that these principles cannot be justified in a foundationalist framework. So foundationalism is a flawed approach to knowledge.

The problem with this criticism is that epistemic principles don't have to be known in order to be used. (If they did, only epistemologists or those who had studied epistemology could know anything.) The principle of clarity and distinctness says that whatever is clearly and distinctly perceived is true. Descartes need not know this principle in order to use it. If the principle is true, then whatever Descartes clearly and distinctly perceives is true, whether or not he consciously accepts the principle. The beliefs generated by the principle can then be used to justify the principle.[29]

The problem with Descartes' attempt to justify the principle of clarity and distinctness is not that it is circular but that it is inadequate. The conclusion of a deductive argument can only be as certain as its premises. If the premises are doubtful, then so is the conclusion. But it is doubtful that God exists. So we can't be certain that the principle of clarity and distinctness is true. And because we can't be certain that it's true, then, according to Descartes, we can't know that it's true.

Reasonable Doubt

Doubt is not a very agreeable state, but certainty is a ridiculous one.

—VOLTAIRE

The assumption that lies behind the first premise of both the dream argument and the evil genius argument is that knowledge requires certainty. But is that true? Does Descartes know that knowledge requires certainty? He does only if he's certain that knowledge requires certainty. But can he be certain of that? Consider these propositions: that the earth is inhabited, that cows produce milk, that water freezes at 32 degrees Fahrenheit, and so on. These are all propositions we would ordinarily claim to know, yet none of them is absolutely certain. In light of these counterexamples, can Descartes legitimately claim to know that knowledge requires certainty? It wouldn't seem so. For unless he is certain that knowledge requires certainty, he can't know that it does. And he can't be certain that knowledge requires certainty because the counterexamples cited above provide good reason for doubting that it does.

So if knowledge doesn't require certainty, what does it require? It does not require enough evidence to put the claim beyond any possibility of doubt but, rather, enough to put it beyond any reasonable doubt. There comes a point beyond which doubt, although possible, is no longer reasonable. It's possible, for example, that our minds are being controlled by aliens from outer space, but to reject the evidence of our senses on that basis would not be reasonable. To know a proposition, then, we don't have to establish it beyond a shadow of a doubt. We only have to establish it beyond a reasonable doubt. This is the standard of evidence used in courts of law to adjudicate matters of life and death. If we can stake our lives on it, we should be able to stake our knowledge on it.

The Empiricist Alternative

As we saw in Chapter 2, empiricists such as David Hume believe that only terms that stand for ideas derived from sense experience can refer to real objects. The mind at birth, they claim, is a tabula rasa—a blank slate—that contains only what has been inscribed on it by the senses. Concepts that represent sensations, such as hot/cold, light/dark, sweet/sour, smooth/ rough, and the like, are the intellectual atoms or "simple ideas" out of which all "complex ideas" are composed. The complex idea of a tomato, for example, is composed of the simple ideas of a particular shape, size, color, texture, and so on. If a term does not stand for a simple or complex idea, it is meaningless. As Hume puts it, "When we entertain any suspicion that a philosophical term is employed without any meaning or idea (as is but too frequent) we need but enquire, from what impression is that supposed idea derived? And if it be impossible to assign any, this will serve to confirm our suspicion."[30] So empiricists reject the two characteristic theses of rationalism: (1) that reason is a source of knowledge of the external world, and (2) that we have some sort of innate knowledge.

Using his theory of concept acquisition, Hume tries to show that many philosophical terms—terms that purportedly refer to something that cannot be sensed, like causation, liberty, and the self—are meaningless. He sums up his program this way:

> When we run over libraries, persuaded of these principles, what havoc must we make? If we take in our hand any volume; of divinity or school metaphysics, for instance; let us ask, *Does it contain any abstract reasoning concerning quantity or number?* No. *Does it contain any experimental reasoning concerning matter of fact and existence?* No. Commit it then to the flames: for it can contain nothing but sophistry and illusion.[31]

Empiricism, then, leads to skepticism about the existence of anything that cannot be sensed.

Although empiricists deny that reason is a source of knowledge of the external world, they admit that it can be used to discover logical truths. For example, if we have the concept of identity, reason can tell us that A is identical to A. Such truths are knowable a priori because they can be known prior to or independently of sense experience. We don't need to gather any data or conduct any experiments to confirm them. Reason alone is sufficient to establish their truth.

General observations drawn from particulars are the jewels of knowledge, comprehending great store in a little room.

—JOHN LOCKE

foundationalism
The theory of knowledge that maintains (1) that there are basic beliefs and (2) that the justification of all other beliefs depends on the basic beliefs.

Statements that are logical truths, or can be turned into logical truths by substituting synonyms for synonyms, are known as "analytic" statements. Thus the statement that all males are males is analytic because it's a logical truth. The statement that all bachelors are males is analytic because it can be turned into a logical truth by substituting "unmarried male" for "bachelor."

Nonanalytic statements are known as "synthetic" statements. The statement that all crows are black, for example, is synthetic because it is not a logical truth nor can it be turned into a logical truth by substituting synonyms for synonyms. The truth of such statements can only be known a posteriori, by means of sense experience.

For the empiricists, then, there are two types of statements—analytic and synthetic—and all analytic statements are knowable a priori while all synthetic statements are knowable a posteriori. As Hume puts it,

> All objects of human reason or enquiry may naturally be divided into two kinds, to wit, Relations of Ideas, and Matters of Fact. Of the first kind are the sciences of Geometry, Algebra, and Arithmetic; and in short, every affirmation which is either intuitively or demonstratively certain. . . . Matters of fact, which are the second objects of human reason, are not ascertained in the same manner; nor is our evidence of their truth, however great, of a like nature with the foregoing. The contrary of every matter of fact is still possible; because it can never imply a contradiction, and is conceived by the mind with the same facility and distinctness, as if ever so conformable to reality.[32]

Synthetic truths differ from analytic ones in that they give us knowledge of the external world. Analytic truths, because they are equivalent to logical truths, don't tell us anything about the world. To be told that all bachelors are males is not to be told whether the world contains any males or bachelors. So even if reason is the source of our knowledge of analytic truths, it isn't a source of knowledge of the external world.

Thought Probe

The Problem of Induction

Enumerative induction has the form "Every A that has been observed has been found to be F. Therefore, every A that ever will be observed will be found to be F." Hume realized that this form of inference assumes that the future will resemble the past. But what justifies our believing that? We can't provide a deductive argument for the claim that the future will resemble the past because there is no more fundamental claim from which it logically follows. Nor can we provide an inductive argument for that claim because such an argument would be circular: it would assume what it is trying to prove. So there appears to be no way to justify enumerative induction. The belief that the future will resemble the past is not something we arrived at through a process of inference. Rather, it is a bias that is built into our thinking. If the belief that the future will resemble the past must be accepted on faith, is science a religion? Does hypothetical deduction (inference to the best explanation) suffer from the same problem?

The Kantian Synthesis

Immanuel Kant noticed a problem with the empiricist's classification of statements. Some truths seem to be synthetic a priori. Consider, for example, the statements "Every event has a cause" and "From nothing, nothing comes." These statements seem to be synthetic because they are not true by definition, and they seem to be a priori because they can be known without being empirically confirmed. So, Kant concluded, there must be another source of knowledge besides reason and experience.

To discover this source of knowledge, Kant examined the method of inquiry used by mathematicians because, he thought, they, too, traffic in synthetic a priori truths. He found that what makes it possible for them to discover such truths is that they study the principles the mind uses to construct mathematical objects.

> The true method . . . was not to inspect what he discerned either in the figure, or in the bare concept of it, and from this, as it were, to read off its properties; but to bring out what was necessarily implied in the concepts that he had himself formed a-priori, and had put into the figure in the construction by which he presented it to himself.[33]

Mathematicians don't study physical circles or triangles because no physical objects have the properties they're interested in. No physical circle, for example, has all of its points exactly equidistant from the center, and no physical triangle has the sum of all of its interior angles exactly equal to two right angles. Instead, Kant claims, mathematicians study the principles governing concepts that they themselves have constructed.

Just as mathematical concepts are not read off from experience but read into it, so Kant thinks that certain metaphysical concepts like space, time, and causality are read into experience to make sense of it. What the senses present to the mind, in the words of William James, is a "blooming, buzzing, confusion." To make sense of this material, the mind gives it a structure by bringing it under certain concepts and placing it in certain categories. Without these concepts, intelligible experience would not be possible. Kant explains,

> The objective validity of the categories as a-priori concepts rests, therefore, on the fact that, so far as the form of thought is concerned, through them alone does experience become possible. They relate of necessity and a-priori to objects of experience, for the reason that only by means of them can any object whatsoever of experience be thought.[34]

The faculty of the mind that gives us knowledge of these concepts Kant calls the "understanding." Truths discovered by the understanding are synthetic because they are not logical truths and a priori because they apply to all possible experience. Synthetic a priori truths, then, describe those features of the world that are necessitated by our construction of it.

Kant describes his view that the mind constructs the objects of experience as a "Copernican Revolution" in philosophy. It was previously assumed that our knowledge must conform to objects. But, instead, Kant insists that objects must conform to our knowledge. So just as Copernicus was able to explain

The empiricist thinks he believes only what he sees, but he is much better at believing than at seeing.
—GEORGE SANTAYANA

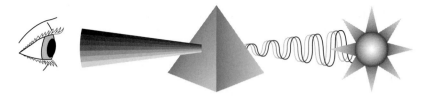

CONCEPTUALIZATION. According to Kant, all perception involves conceptualization.

The mind's eye   Conceptual scheme   Raw sense experience

the movements of the planets by rejecting the hypothesis that the sun moved around the spectator and replacing it with the hypothesis that the spectator moved around the sun, so Kant thinks he is able to explain the possibility of synthetic a priori truths by rejecting the hypothesis that our knowledge conforms to objects and replacing it with the hypothesis that objects conform to our knowledge.

Kant's theory of knowledge saves empiricism from skepticism by wedding it to rationalism. Empiricism holds that only concepts derived from experience have objective reality. But if this were the case, then concepts like space, time, and causality would not have objective reality because they are not derived from experience. Kant maintains, on the contrary, that these concepts, which are innate, do have objective reality because they make the experience of objects possible. They are a necessary condition of objective experience.

Kant is a precursor of present-day cognitive psychologists because he understands the mind on the model of an information-processing mechanism. Empiricists conceive of the mind as a passive receiver of information. Kant conceives of the mind as an active processor of it. But this view, too, seems to lead to a sort of skepticism. According to Kant, we are not directly aware of anything in the world. Everything we experience has been filtered through our conceptual scheme, which functions like a prism, taking the undifferentiated white light of experience and organizing it into identifiable objects (colors). So we know the world, not as it is in itself, but only as our conceptual scheme presents it to us.

The world as it is in itself Kant dubs the "noumena," and our experience of it, the "phenomena." We can never tell whether the phenomena accurately reflects the noumena because we can't get outside of our conceptual scheme and compare it with reality. We can never take off the conceptual spectacles through which we view the world. Consequently, we can never know the world as it is in itself.

Kant's view also seems to lead to a sort of relativism. Kant thought that every human being had to employ the categories he identified in order to have objective experience. But research by linguists, anthropologists, and social psychologists suggest that people in non-Western cultures categorize their experience differently than we do. It is still a matter of debate whether the differences are significant enough to justify the claim that they have different conceptual schemes, but in any event, it seems that Kant's goal of trying to prove that all human beings must use one particular conceptual scheme is doomed to failure. We can't establish the unique applicability of a conceptual scheme by comparing it to other conceptual schemes because any comparison requires standards, and any such standards would themselves be a part of a conceptual scheme. So there seems to be no non-question-begging way of establishing one conceptual scheme as the "correct" one.

Some conclude from this that truth is relative, that there is no one way the world is because people with different conceptual schemes live in different worlds. But such a conclusion is unwarranted because, from the fact that people represent the world to themselves in different ways, it doesn't follow that they live in different worlds.

Conceptual schemes can be viewed as maps. A territory can be mapped in many different ways, and each map, provided that it is an accurate one, can be considered true. Each science, for example, can be considered as a different map of reality. The map provided by biology may contain few of the concepts contained in the map provided by physics, just as a topographical map may contain very few of the symbols contained in a road map. But biology and physics can be maps of the same reality just as a topographical and a road map can be maps of the same territory, and both can be considered true. Whether you consult a biologist or a physicist will depend on what you want to do, just as whether you consult a topographical or a road map will depend on where you want to go. Different conceptual schemes, like different maps, are good for different things. So saying that there is no one correct conceptual scheme no more relativizes truth than saying there is no one correct map. What we must not forget is that, as mathematician Alfred Korzybski famously noted, "the map is not the territory."[35] People using different maps are not necessarily traversing different territories. Similarly, people using different conceptual schemes are not necessarily living in different worlds. The world is what it is and is not affected by our representations of it.

Facts are stubborn things; and whatever may be our wishes, our inclinations, or the dictates of our passions, they cannot alter the state of facts and evidence.

—John Quincy Adams

Thought Probe

Constructing Reality

Are scientific laws invented or discovered? The traditional view is that scientific laws exist "out there" in the world and that the job of the scientist is to discover them. Kant, however, claims that "the order and regularity of the appearance we entitle nature, we ourselves introduce."[36] For him, reality is a human construct. Which view do you think is correct? Why?

Summary

Parmenides and Zeno argue that we cannot acquire knowledge by means of our senses because we know the world is different from the way it appears. Everything seems to be constantly changing, but change is impossible. So our senses must not put us in touch with reality. Plato, too, thinks that what we sense is not fully real. The only real objects are ideas or forms because they are unchanging and the ultimate cause of everything.

Descartes held that knowledge requires certainty. But if this is so, we know very little that is derived from our senses. Descartes presents two powerful arguments that purport to show that our senses cannot give us knowledge of the external world. His dream argument asserts that we cannot have knowledge because, for all we know, we may be dreaming right now. His evil genius argument says that we cannot have knowledge because, for all we know, our experiences may be caused by an evil genius.

Descartes believes, however, that he can know at least two things: that he thinks and that he exists. He can't doubt that he thinks because the very act of doubting is thinking. He can't doubt that he exists because existence is a necessary condition of thinking. Beyond these two propositions, Descartes believes that we can also know (be certain of) propositions about the way things seem. We can know that we seem to have certain sensations, though we could be mistaken about their cause. What's more, Descartes thinks that we have a principle that guarantees that many of our sensations accurately reflect reality. It's the principle of clarity and distinctness: whatever is clearly and distinctly perceived is true. If this principle is true, Descartes can defeat the skeptic.

Descartes tries to establish the principle's truth by bringing in God. God exists and is no deceiver, Descartes says, and if this is so, then whatever we clearly and distinctly perceive is true. But Descartes' attempt to establish the principle is inadequate. It is not certain that God exists. So it is not certain that the principle of clarity and distinctness is true. Consequently, Descartes' bid to defeat the skeptic fails.

Skeptical doubts arise from the notion that knowledge requires certainty, as Descartes insists. But does it? We seem to know many things that aren't certain. This casts considerable doubt on Descartes' claim. We do seem to know things—but without certainty. But if knowledge doesn't require certainty, what does it require? It requires not that a proposition be beyond any possible doubt but that it be beyond any reasonable doubt.

Because empiricists believe that sense experience is our only source of knowledge of the external world, they believe that no synthetic propositions are knowable a priori. But Kant believes that some synthetic truths can be known a priori because they describe the concepts that we must use in order to make sense of the world.

Study Questions

1. What are the requirements for knowledge?
2. What are Parmenides' arguments for the impossibility of change?
3. What is Zeno's paradox of bisection?
4. What is Plato's allegory of the cave supposed to demonstrate?
5. What is Descartes' dream argument?
6. What is Descartes' evil genius argument?

7. How does Descartes close the gap between appearance and reality?

8. Why do empiricists believe that there are no synthetic a priori truths?

9. How does Kant explain the possibility of synthetic a priori truths?

Discussion Questions

1. The ultimate virtual reality machine would present a world so real that we couldn't tell that it was fake. Can you know that you're not plugged into an ultimate virtual reality machine right now? If not, what difference does it make?

2. Descartes assumes that we can be certain about our mental states. Is that true? Could you be mistaken about your mental states? Could you be mistaken about the fact that you're in pain, for example? If so, what does that imply for Descartes' program?

3. Can the epistemic principles Descartes uses to prove the existence of the external also be used to prove the existence of other minds? Why or why not?

4. Can you think of something that people take for granted that they should be more skeptical of?

5. Can Descartes know that knowledge requires certainty? If not, does his program go through?

6. Can we know beyond a reasonable doubt that the external world exists? Why or why not?

7. Mystics have long maintained that ordinary perception is distorted by our conceptual scheme. To get a pure, undistorted view of reality, they try to perceive the world directly, without the use of any concepts. Is such pure perception possible? Can it serve as a source of knowledge? Kant claimed that thought without concepts is blind. Do you agree?

Facing Reality
Perception and the External World

Scientists and laymen alike assume that sense experience gives us knowledge of the external world. Descartes called this assumption into doubt by showing that we couldn't always trust our senses. But contrary to what Descartes would have us believe, knowledge doesn't require certainty. So from the fact that our senses might not be trustworthy, it doesn't follow that they aren't trustworthy. Nevertheless we are justified in believing what our senses tell us about the external world only if we have a good reason for believing that they put us in touch with it.

Direct Realism

Common sense tells us that our senses put us in direct contact with reality. When we see a book, for example, it seems that we are directly aware of the book itself. This view is known as **direct realism:** "direct" because it assumes that nothing comes between our perception of the world and the world itself, "realism" because it assumes that there is an external world that is not affected by what we think about it. Philosophers have challenged both of these assumptions.

The most telling argument against direct realism is the argument from illusion. If we were directly aware of physical objects in perception, then they should appear to us as they really are. But the way things seem is often very different from the way they are. This has led many to conclude that we're not directly aware of the external world. British philosopher A. J. Ayer explains,

> Why may we not say that we are directly aware of material things? The answer is provided by what is known as the argument from illusion. This argument, as it is ordinarily stated, is based on the fact that material things may present different appearances to different observers, or to the same observer in different

THE BENT PENCIL. Illusions like the bent pencil suggest that we don't perceive the world directly.

conditions, and that the character of these appearances is to some extent causally determined by the state of the conditions and the observer. For instance, it is remarked that a coin which looks circular from one point of view may look elliptical from another; or that a stick which normally appears straight looks bent when it is seen in water; or that to people who take drugs such as Mescal, things appear to change their colors.[37]

Physical objects cannot possess incompatible properties. Nothing can be both circular and elliptical, bent and straight, or red and green at the same time. But one and the same object can appear to have such incompatible properties. So what appears to us — what we're directly aware of in perception — must not be physical objects themselves.

Consider Ayer's example of the stick placed in a glass of water. The problem that it poses for direct realism can be put in the form of an argument.

1. What we see is bent.
2. The stick is not bent.
3. So what we see is not the stick.

But if we don't see the stick, what do we see? Empiricists have traditionally claimed that what we see is a representation or an appearance or an idea of a stick. The technical term that is often used to refer to what we're directly aware of in perception is **sense data.** Bertrand Russell introduces that term this way:

> Let us give the name of 'sense data' to the things that are immediately known in sensation; such things as colours, sounds, smells, hardnesses, roughnesses, and so

direct realism The doctrine that perception puts us in direct contact with reality.

sense data The objects that are immediately known in sensation.

Facing Reality **561**

on. We shall give the name 'sensation' to the experience of being immediately aware of these things. Thus whenever we see a colour, we have a sensation of the colour, but the colour itself is a sense datum, not a sensation. The colour is that of which we are immediately aware and the awareness itself is the sensation.[38]

Sense data, then, are the content of our sensations. They are what is given to us in sense experience. We take sensory experience to be about physical objects, but that is not what is given to us. What is given are sense data.

According to those who believe in sense data, then, the process of perception has two parts. The first part—sensation—involves receiving data from the senses. The second part—perception—involves interpreting that data and bringing it under a concept. Some believe that these two parts are temporally distinct—that one actually happens before the other—while others believe that they are only logically distinct—that although the process happens all at once, these are two discriminable aspects of the process. In either case, however, we're not directly aware of physical objects.

Perception supposedly gives us knowledge of the external world. But if all we are directly aware of in perception is sense data, there's a problem: how do we know whether our sense data accurately represent the external world? We can't get outside of our sense data and compare them with the external world. All we can do is get more sense data. So how can we know what the external world is like in itself? Locke put the problem this way:

> 'Tis evident that the mind knows not things immediately, but only by the intervention of the ideas [sense data] it has of them. Our knowledge, therefore, is real only so far as there is conformity between our ideas and the reality of things. But what shall be here the criterion? How shall the mind when it perceives but its own ideas, know that they agree with things themselves?[39]

On the sense data theory, it seems that we're trapped behind a "veil of ideas." How, Locke asks, can we lift the veil and come to know things as they are in themselves? This is the problem of the external world.

Representative Realism

Knowledge is what we get when an observer, preferably a scientifically trained observer, provides us with a copy of reality that we can all recognize.
—CHRISTOPHER
LASCH

Locke believes that we can lift the veil of ideas by recognizing (1) that our sensations are caused by external objects and (2) that at least some of our ideas (sense data) resemble the qualities of those objects. This view is often referred to as **representative realism.** Like direct realism, it maintains that there is a world that exists independently of our minds, but unlike direct realism, it maintains that our knowledge of that world is indirect; it is mediated by our sense data.

In support of the first claim, Locke offers a number of considerations:

- "Those that want the organs of any sense never can have the ideas belonging to that sense."[40] For example, those who are blind from birth can never acquire the idea of color. Similarly, those who have never had certain sensations can never have the sense data associated with them. For example, those who have never tasted a pineapple can never know what a pineapple tastes like.

- "Sometimes I find that I cannot avoid having those ideas produced in my mind."[41] The sense data that we receive does not seem to be up to us. If we look at the sun, for example, we cannot help but see bright light.

- "Many of those ideas are produced in us with pain, which afterwards we remember without the least offense."[42] There seems to be a real difference between the ideas that come from outside and those that come from inside. The ones that seem to be generated by external objects have much more force and vivacity than those generated by internal objects such as memories.

- "Our senses in many cases bear witness to the truth of each other's report concerning the existence of sensible things without us."[43] The information that we receive from various senses is usually complementary. The thing that looks like a fire feels hot, for example.

The best explanation of these facts, says Locke, is that our sensations are produced by external objects. "Thus the certainty of things existing *in rerum natura*, when we have the testimony of our senses for it, is not only as great as our frame can attain to, but as our condition needs."[44] It's not absolutely certain that sense data are caused by external objects because it's logically possible that we're dreaming. But even if it's not true beyond a shadow of a doubt, it is true beyond a reasonable doubt because the hypothesis that sense data are caused by external objects provides a better explanation of the data than the hypothesis that we're dreaming.

Thought Probe

Hypothesizing the External World

Do you agree with Locke that the hypothesis of an external world provides the best explanation of our sense data? Compare that hypothesis and the dream hypothesis in terms of the criteria of adequacy. Which does better with regard to simplicity, scope, conservatism, and fruitfulness?

If successful, however, all Locke's argument shows is that our sensations are caused by external objects. By itself, it tells us nothing about the nature of those objects. Locke maintains, however, that further reflection on the nature of our sense data reveals that some actually resemble the qualities of external objects. Thus we can have knowledge of the external world because some of our sense data conform to the qualities of external objects.

External objects have the power of producing sense data. They have this power in virtue of possessing certain qualities. But not every sense datum resembles a quality in an external object. For example, if we dip one of our hands in a cold bucket of water and the other in a warm bucket of water, and

representative realism The doctrine that sensations are caused by external objects and that our sensations represent those objects.

then dip both of them into a lukewarm bucket of water, the lukewarm bucket of water will feel cold to one hand (the one that had been dipped in the warm water) and warm to the other (the one that had been dipped in the cold water). But the water in the bucket cannot be both warm and cold. So the sense data of warmth and coldness cannot resemble qualities possessed by the water. These sense data exist only in the mind, not in the water itself. Locke calls these qualities **secondary qualities.**

Even though the water does not possess the qualities of being warm or cold, it must possess qualities with the power to produce the sense data of warmth and coldness. Locke calls these qualities **primary qualities.** For Locke, they are the essential qualities of material objects, the qualities that material objects could not possibly do without. As he puts it, "Qualities thus considered in bodies are, first such as are utterly inseparable from the Body, in what estate whatsoever it be; and such as Sense constantly finds in every particle of Matter."[45] They include solidity, extension, figure, and mobility. Locke thought that these qualities really exist in objects because they can be sensed by more than one sense, and, unlike secondary qualities, they do not vary as the conditions of perception are varied.

To get a better idea of what Locke is getting at with this distinction, consider the qualities that physicists attribute to the basic building blocks of matter: subatomic particles. They are solid (insofar as they do not contain gaps like a sponge), they have extension (insofar as they occupy space), they have figure (insofar as they have a shape), and they have mobility (insofar as they are in motion). Modern physics also attributes a number of other qualities to them such as mass, charge, and spin. But notice that nowhere in this list are qualities such as color, taste, sound. Modern physicists agree with Locke that these qualities are not possessed by the subatomic particles themselves. Individual electrons, for example, do not have a particular color, taste, or sound. These secondary qualities come into existence only when groups of particles interact with our sense organs.

Locke's representative realism solves the problem of the external world by claiming that some of our sense data, namely, those corresponding to primary qualities, actually resemble qualities of material objects. So at least part of our sense experience gives us an accurate picture of how material objects are in themselves.

Phenomenalism

The idealist deals with facts as much as with reality. He merely sees them differently.

—Margaret Halsey

Bishop George Berkeley (1685–1753) agrees with Locke that we directly perceive sense data. But he disagrees that the best explanation of our sense data is that they are caused by material objects. In his view, sense data are caused by God. To see how Berkeley arrived at this view, we can begin with his criticism of Locke.

Berkeley rejected Locke's distinction between primary and secondary qualities because he believed that primary qualities are just as variable as secondary qualities.

... after the same manner as modern philosophers prove certain sensible qualities to have no existence in matter, or without the mind, the same thing may be likewise proved of all other sensible qualities whatsoever. Thus, for instance, it is said that heat and cold are affections only of the mind, and not at all patterns of real beings existing in the corporeal substances which excite them, for that the same body which appears cold to one hand seems warm to another. Now, why may we not as well argue that figure and extension are not patterns or resemblances of qualities existing in matter, because to the same eye at different stations, or eyes of a different texture at the same station, they appear various and cannot, therefore, be the images of anything settled and determinate without the mind?[46]

Just as what feels warm to one hand can feel cold to another, Berkeley claims that what looks round from one angle can look elliptical from another. Primary qualities can differ depending on the conditions of perception just as much as secondary qualities do. So there is no reason to think that they are not in the mind, too.

But more important than his rejection of the distinction between primary and secondary qualities is Berkeley's rejection of the existence of material objects. Berkeley thought that our sensations could not be caused by material objects because material objects could not exist. The notion of a material object, he thought, was a contradiction in terms. We know that there are no married bachelors or round squares because such notions are self-contradictory — they violate the law of noncontradiction and thus cannot possibly exist. Berkeley thought that the notion of a material object was similarly self-contradictory. Here's the thought experiment that he used to prove his point.

Thought Experiment

The Inconceivability of the Unconceived

But, say you, surely there is nothing easier than for me to imagine trees, for instance, in a park, or books existing in a closet, and nobody by to perceive them. I answer, you may so, there is no difficulty in it; but what is all this, I beseech you, more than framing in your mind certain ideas which you call books and trees, and at the same time omitting to frame the idea of any one that may perceive them? But do not you yourselves perceive or think of them all the while? This therefore is nothing to the purpose: it only shows you have the power of imagining or forming ideas in your mind; but it does not show that you can conceive it possible the objects of your thought may exist without the mind. To make out this, it is necessary that you conceive them existing unconceived or unthought of, which is a manifest repugnancy. When we do our utmost to conceive the existence of external bodies, we are all the while only contemplating our own ideas. But the mind taking no notice of itself, is deluded to think it can and does conceive bodies existing unthought of or without the mind, though at the same time they are apprehended by or exist in itself. A little attention will

secondary qualities Qualities that exist in the mind but not in material objects themselves.

primary qualities Qualities possessed by material objects.

discover to any one the truth and evidence of what is here said, and make it unnecessary to insist on any other proof against the existence of material substance.[47]

We ordinarily suppose not only that material objects cause our sensations but that they continue to exist when no one is thinking about them. But Berkeley claims that this cannot be the case because it's impossible to conceive of something's existing unconceived.

Try it yourself. Try thinking about an object that is not being thought about. Berkeley says you can't do it because the minute you think about it, it's no longer not being thought about. But material objects are supposed to be able to exist without anyone thinking about them. So if we cannot conceive an object's existing unconceived, Berkeley claims, material objects cannot exist.

Even though Berkeley doesn't believe that there are any material objects, he doesn't recommend that we stop talking about them. Instead, he proposes that we understand our talk about them in a new way. When we claim that a material object is present, what we mean is that we have experienced a certain pattern of sensations. For Berkeley, then, material objects are nothing but recurring patterns of sensations.

Berkeley uses the example of a cherry to make his point:

> I see this cherry, I feel it, I taste it, and I am sure *nothing* cannot be seen or felt or tasted; it is therefore *real*. Take away the sensation of softness, moisture, redness, tartness, and you take away the cherry. Since it is not a being distinct from sensations, a cherry, I say, is nothing but a congeries of sensible impressions, or ideas perceived by the various senses, which ideas are united into one thing (or have one name given them) by the mind because they are observed to attend each other. Thus, when the palate is affected with such a particular taste, the sight is affected with a red color, the touch with roundness, softness, etc. Hence, when I see and feel and taste in sundry certain manners, I am sure the cherry exists or is real, its reality being in my opinion nothing abstracted from those sensations. But if by the word "cherry" you mean an unknown nature distinct from all those sensible qualities, and by its "existence" something distinct from its being perceived, then, indeed, I own neither you nor I, nor anyone else, can be sure it exists.[48]

Whenever we have certain sensations, we believe that a cherry is present. We can be mistaken, however. If we have the sensation of reaching for the cherry and our hand passes right through it, we know it's not a real cherry. What determines whether a perceived object is real, then, is not whether it corresponds to a material object but whether the sensations associated with it fit a particular pattern.

The view that statements about physical objects are reducible to statements about sensations is known as **phenomenalism.** In this view, to say "There is a tree in front of me" is equivalent to saying "If I were to have reaching-out sensations, I would have hardness sensations; if I were to have kicking sensations, I would have pain-in-the-toe sensations; . . ." and so on for every pos-

Some philosophers produce interesting theories but they themselves are fairly dull. George Berkeley (1685–1753) was not one of those. He produced an entirely original and exasperating (to some) view of the world known as "idealism"—but he also was a fascinating character in his own right.

He was born in Kilkenny, Ireland, and educated at Trinity College in Dublin. He graduated at age nineteen, was given a fellowship there in 1707, and proceeded to produce his greatest works—all during his twenties. He wrote A *Treatise Concerning the Principles of Human Knowledge* in 1710 and *Three Dialogues between Hylas and Philonous* in 1713. In 1709 he published a work, not of philosophy, but of psychology—"An Essay Towards a New Theory of Vision." His theory of vision became the definitive view of the subject and remained so for almost two hundred years.

His passion was the promotion of education in the New World. He wanted to establish a college in Bermuda for the Christian education of the people of America, and the Crown had promised him the funds to do just that. But the money never came, and he spent three years in Rhode Island waiting for it. He bequeathed his library and estate in Rhode Island to Yale University, where one of the colleges is named after him. Berkeley, California, also got its name from this Irish philosopher who lived most of his life half a world away.

Berkeley returned to London in 1732, and in 1734 he was made Bishop of Cloyne. For most of the rest of his life he tended to his duties as a cleric, publishing mostly works benefiting his flock.

Berkeley's reputation as a philosophical idealist followed him through the years and caused controversy and consternation everywhere. Samuel Johnson, the most famous man of letters in the eighteenth century, ridiculed his theory. The story is told of a philosopher who argued so strenuously with Berkeley that he suffered a fit of apoplexy and died. The tale is probably false, but it is easy to imagine some learned folks becoming incensed with Berkeley's counterintuitive idealism—especially since he claimed that his view was just common sense.

---

sible action. Phenomenalism, then, is the reverse of behaviorism. Whereas behaviorism tries to reduce talk about mental states to talk about material objects, phenomenalism tries to reduce talk about material objects to talk about mental states. Twentieth-century empiricists, particularly logical positivists, found this view appealing because it provided an elegant solution to the problem of the external world. If material objects were nothing but patterns of sensations, then the problem of how we could know whether our sensations accurately represented the world could no longer arise. Phenomenalism closes the gap between appearance and reality by denying that the gap exists.

Sensations cannot exist without a mind to have them. Because Berkeley's objects are patterns of sensations, it follows that they cease to exist when no one is thinking about them. This view strikes many people as extremely odd because they believe that objects continue to exist whether or not they are in anyone's thoughts.

Suppose you leave a fire in a fireplace and come back a few hours later to find a heap of smoldering embers. Doesn't that prove that objects can exist without being observed? Not according to Berkeley. What you've experienced is just a typical pattern of fire sensations. There is no reason to suppose that in addition to the fire sensations there is also a material fire.

The classic philosophical conundrum—if a tree falls in the forest and no one is around to hear it, does it make a sound?—is often associated with

BISHOP BERKELEY
(1685–1753)

phenomenalism
The view that all talk of things is reducible to talk of sensations.

Berkeley. It is commonly believed that Berkeley would answer no to this question. But Berkeley would not respond to this question because it is based on an assumption that he rejects, namely, that objects can exist unperceived. If there were no one around to hear a tree fall, there would be no tree in the first place. So the question makes no sense.

Legend has it that when Samuel Johnson first heard Berkeley's theory he exclaimed, "I refute it thus!" and kicked a rock. But of course this doesn't refute Berkeley at all. Berkeley doesn't deny that usually when we have the sensation of kicking something that looks like a rock, we have the sensation of stubbing our toe. What he denies is that this recurrent pattern of sensation is best explained on the hypothesis that material objects exist. In his view, it is best explained on the assumption that God creates these sensations.

We do not produce our own sensations. What we sense is not up to us. So our sensations must be caused by something outside of us. According to Berkeley, that something is God. In his view, we are all telepathically linked to God, and God puts all of our sensations directly into our minds. Berkeley's God, then, functions just like Descartes' evil genius. But Berkeley does not consider his God to be evil, for he is not deluding us about the nature of reality; he is creating it.

Berkeley's view that God is the source of all of our sensations inspired Monsignor Ronald Knox to pen the following limerick:

There was a young man who said "God
Must think it exceedingly odd
If he finds that this tree
Continues to be
When there's no one about in the quad."

Reply:
Dear Sir: Your astonishment's odd
I am always about in the quad
And that's why the tree
Will continue to be
Since observed by
Yours faithfully,
God.[49]

According to Berkeley, things exist only as long as they are being thought about. That would seem to imply that things cease to exist when we stop thinking about them. But we are not the only beings that think about things. God does too. So things may continue to exist when we're not thinking about them as long as God is thinking about them.

Berkeley thought that his view refuted skepticism and proved the existence of God. It refuted skepticism by closing the gap between appearance and reality. In Berkeley's system, the question of whether our sensations accurately represent external objects does not arise because there are no external objects—objects are just collections of ideas. It proves the existence of God by showing that God is the best explanation of our sense experience.

Reality is that which refuses to go away when I stop believing in it.
—PHILLIP K. DICK

Although Berkeley thought that his system proved the existence of the Christian God, it does no such thing. In the first place, it gives us no reason for believing that the cause of our sensations is all-powerful, all-knowing, or all-good. Second, it gives us no reason for believing that our sensations are caused by one being. Maybe different kinds of sensations are caused by different kinds of spirits. So even if we accept a supernatural cause of our sensations, there is no need to identify it with the Christian God.

But must our sensations have a supernatural cause? If they can't be caused by material objects (because material objects cannot exist), it might seem that there is no other alternative. But Berkeley's rejection of material objects is questionable.

Berkeley claims that it's impossible for something to exist unconceived. This could mean one of two things: (a) that it's not possible to conceive *of* something that is unconceived or (b) that it's not possible to conceive *that* something exists unconceived. In the first case, our thought is directed on an object; in the second, a proposition. (a) is undoubtedly true. If something is being conceived (thought about) by someone, it cannot also be unconceived (not thought about). But (b) is false. You can believe the proposition that something exists unconceived without thereby thinking about any particular object. When you believe that something exists unconceived, the object of your belief — what your belief is about — is the proposition that something exists unconceived; not some individual thing. So believing that something exists unconceived is logically possible because it doesn't involve attributing both a property and its negation to anything. Consequently, the notion of a material object is not self-contradictory.

The question now becomes, Which is the better explanation of our sensations? That they are produced by God or by material objects? We have seen that, in general, natural explanations are preferable to supernatural ones because supernatural explanations usually raise more questions than they answer. Berkeley's theory raises a number of them. How is the mind link established? What sort of energy carries thoughts from God's mind to ours? Why does God choose the particular sensations he does? Why do some people get good sensations and others get bad ones? A theory that raises more questions than it answers, however, does not increase our understanding. Alan Goldman puts the point this way:

> . . . several other standard criteria for evaluating explanations disqualify appeals to the supernatural despite their seeming theoretical depth.
>
> First, such appeal does not really deepen our understanding . . . since we have no conception of the mechanism or the precise link between the supposed divine intention and their effects. This, coupled with the lack of predictive power, renders the appeal epistemically sterile. Not only would our understanding not be deepened by such an explanation, not only would no natural questions be answered, but many more would arise without possibility of answer.[50]

Berkeley's appeal to God as the cause of our sensations would be justified if it provided the best explanation of our sense experience. But it doesn't. It is inconsistent with established views about the cause of our sensations, and it is more complex than the materialist hypothesis in that it postulates supernatural beings. So Berkeley's theory lacks the virtues of conservatism and simplicity. It also lacks the virtue of fruitfulness. It has not successfully predicted any new phenomenon or solved any problems it was not intended to solve. The materialist theory, on the other hand, has innumerable successful predictions to its credit. Because Berkeley's theory does not provide the best explanation of perception, we're not justified in believing it.

But what if we remove God from Berkeley's theory? What if we simply say that objects are patterns of sensation and leave it at that? Explanation has to stop somewhere. If we take patterns of sensations as a brute fact without trying to explain where they come from, we could at least defeat the skeptic and simplify our theory of what exists. Unfortunately, phenomenalism can't even claim these benefits because material objects can't be reduced to patterns of sensations.

Consider the phenomenalist claim that to say that there is a tree in front of you is to say that "if you were to have reaching-out sensations, you would have hardness sensations; if you were to have kicking sensations, you would have pain-in-the-toe sensations; . . ." and so on for every possible action. From the fact that there is a tree in front of you, does it follow that if you had reaching-out sensations, you would have hardness sensations? No, because you might be on drugs; your nervous system might be wired wrong; you might be having a seizure, or the like. What you sense is determined by the state of your body at the time. If your body is in an abnormal state, your sensory patterns may also be abnormal. In order to make the sentence about sensations equivalent to the sentence about mental states, we would have to preface it with the statement "If your body were in a normal state. . . ." But now we no longer have a reduction because the statement about sensations contains a reference to bodies. Statements about material objects are not reducible to statements about sensations because we cannot translate all statements that refer to material objects into statements that refer only to sensations. So even a godless phenomenalism won't do.

It looks like the best explanation of perception is the one provided by science. There are material objects in the world. These material objects have certain intrinsic qualities identified by the physical sciences. When these objects interact with our sense organs, they produce certain sensations. To have knowledge of the external world, our sensations don't have to resemble the qualities of the objects that produce them. All we need to know is what properties produce what sensations in what circumstances. And science gives us that knowledge.

Summary

Direct realism claims that we perceive objects directly, without the intermediary of any ideas. The argument from illusion, however, suggests that we're not directly aware of the external world. Our perception of the external world seems to be mediated by our sensations.

Representative realism holds that our sensations are caused by material objects and that some of our sensations resemble the qualities of those material objects. The sensations that resemble the qualities of objects are known as primary qualities, whereas those that exist only in the mind are known as secondary qualities. All of our sensations can vary depending on the conditions under which they're produced, so it doesn't seem that the distinction between primary and secondary qualities is a viable one.

Berkeley not only rejects the distinction between primary and secondary qualities, he also rejects the notion that our sensations are caused by material objects. According to him, all that really exists are minds and their contents. Objects are just patterns of sensations. For them to exist, they must be perceived. To be is to be perceived. Berkeley tries to show that the whole idea of our sensations representing material objects is incoherent. The notion that material objects continue to exist when we're not thinking of them is incoherent, Berkeley says, because it's impossible to conceive of something's existing unconceived. He says that the best explanation of our recurrent patterns of sensations is not that material objects exist, but that God puts those sensations in our minds.

But there is nothing incoherent about the proposition that something exists unconceived. It is logically possible for matter to exist. Furthermore, the better (simpler, more conservative, more fruitful) explanation of our sensations is not that God produced them, but that material objects produced them.

Study Questions

1. What is direct realism?
2. What is the argument from illusion?
3. What is representative realism?
4. What is the distinction between primary and secondary qualities?
5. What is phenomenalism?
6. Why does Berkeley believe that sensations can't represent material objects?
7. Why does Berkeley believe that it's impossible for material objects to exist?

Discussion Questions

1. Do you think that the argument from illusion requires the postulation of sense data? Are there other ways of accounting for illusions?
2. Is there any difference between a perfect illusion and the real thing? If so, what?

3. Must a representative realist believe that some sense data actually resemble the qualities of material objects? Is it enough if the sense data just represent the qualities of material objects? Why or why not?

4. Can Berkeley's phenomenalism account for hallucinations? If all that exists are ideas, how could a hallucination be distinguished from an ordinary perception?

5. Is there some other plausible way to account for our sensations than by supposing that they're caused by material objects or God? If so, what would it be?

What Do You Know?

Knowing What Knowledge Is

So, it seems, we do know things — despite the best arguments of the skeptic to try to show that we do not. We can rightfully claim that we do indeed have knowledge.

But there is an underlying perplexity here. If we have knowledge, what exactly do we have? What, after all, is knowledge? The question is not about what particular propositions we know but, rather, what the definition of knowledge is. More precisely, the question is, What are the necessary and sufficient conditions for there being an instance of knowledge?

For hundreds of years, many philosophers thought that the answer to this question was obvious. Most nonphilosophers, if asked the question, would probably think it trivial — and that only a philosopher would seriously ask it. But a closer look reveals that the question — which concerns what has been called the "analysis of knowledge" — is both deep and important. As it turns out, the obvious answer is faulty, and coming up with a better answer has proved difficult. Philosophers have come to appreciate just how much depends on a suitable analysis of knowledge.

The issue here concerns propositional knowledge — knowledge that something is the case. (It does not concern other types of knowledge like, for example, knowledge of how to do something.) The "obvious" answer about what propositional knowledge is has been called the standard, or traditional, analysis of knowing. This standard account, or something much like it, was suggested in the writings of Plato[51] and has been echoed by other philosophers many times since. It says that propositional knowledge has three necessary and sufficient conditions. It holds that someone S knows a proposition p if and only if

1. p is true,
2. S believes that p is true, and
3. S is justified in believing that p is true.

Ignorance is the curse of God; knowledge is the wing wherewith we fly to heaven.

—WILLIAM SHAKESPEARE

The first two conditions mean that to know a proposition, we must believe it, and it also must be true. That is, knowledge requires true belief. Surely we can't know a proposition unless we believe it, and we certainly can't know it if it is not true. We can't know that bachelors are married because bachelors are not married. We just can't know what isn't so. And if we know that bachelors are unmarried, then we must believe that bachelors are unmarried. (Sometimes we might speak as though knowing does not require believing, as when we say, "I know you're standing in front of me, but I just can't believe it." But this is just a way of saying that we do know something but that it is nonetheless surprising or emotionally hard to accept.)

According to the standard account, even though true belief is necessary for knowledge, it alone is not sufficient for knowledge. Propositional knowledge requires more than true belief because we apparently can have true belief and still not have knowledge. Let's say that for no good reason you believe that, right at this moment, there are seven red BMWs parked side by side in a particular parking lot fifty miles away. Furthermore, let's suppose you're right—they really are parked there. You thus have a true belief. But do you then know that those cars are there? Not at all. On the standard account, if you have no reason for believing that they're there, you can't know that they are. Your true belief about their presence would be no better than a lucky guess, and lucky guesses can't be knowledge. Knowledge seems to require, not only that our beliefs be true, but that we have good reasons for—be justified in—believing them to be true. So, in the standard account, knowledge is justified true belief.

But something surprising happened that casts doubt on this very plausible view of knowledge. In 1963, philosopher Edmund Gettier used two simple thought experiments to suggest that there was a problem with the standard account.[52] Philosophers have been working ever since to propose new analyses of knowledge that repair or avoid the flaw in the standard account. This is one of the more striking instances in which thought experiments helped change the course of philosophy.

Gettier's thought experiments seemed to demonstrate that the standard analysis was inadequate by showing that someone could have a justified true belief that was not knowledge. They seemed to reveal, in other words, that the three conditions mentioned earlier were not jointly sufficient for knowledge.

Here's one of the thought experiments:

Thought Experiment

Gettier's Job Seekers

Suppose that Smith and Jones have applied for a certain job. And suppose that Smith has strong evidence for the following conjunctive proposition:

(d) Jones is the man who will get the job, and Jones has ten coins in his pocket.

Smith's evidence for (d) might be that the president of the company assured him that Jones would in the end be selected, and that he, Smith, had counted the coins in Jones's pocket ten minutes ago. Proposition (d) entails:

(e) The man who will get the job has ten coins in his pocket.

Let us suppose that Smith sees the entailment from (d) to (e), and accepts (e) on the grounds of (d), for which he has strong evidence. In this case, Smith is clearly justified in believing that (e) is true.

But imagine, further, that unknown to Smith, he himself, not Jones, will get the job. And, also, unknown to Smith, he himself has ten coins in his pocket. Proposition (e) is then true, though proposition (d), from which Smith inferred (e), is false. In our example, then, all of the following are true: (*i*) (e) is true, (*ii*) Smith believes that (e) is true, and (*iii*) Smith is justified in believing that (e) is true. But it is equally clear that Smith does not *know* that (e) is true; for (e) is true in virtue of the number of coins in Smith's pocket, while Smith does not know how many coins are in Smith's pocket, and bases his belief in (e) on a count of the coins in Jones's pocket, whom he falsely believes to be the man who will get the job.[53]

Man is not weak; knowledge is more than equivalent to force.
—SAMUEL JOHNSON

In the standard analysis, if someone has a justified true belief, then he should have knowledge. But in this thought experiment, Smith has a justified true belief yet clearly does not have knowledge. It is simply implausible to say that Smith knows (e) — even if he is justified in believing (e), and (e) is true. Some philosophers would say that Smith does not know (e) because his coming to believe a true proposition is accidental (like a lucky guess). Smith is right about (e), but his being right appears to be a mere coincidence. More precisely, Smith arrives at a true proposition on the basis of facts that are not relevant to the truth of the proposition. He reaches the truth, but his route is somehow illegitimate.

Gettier's other thought experiment is similar.

Thought Experiment

Gettier's Guy in Barcelona

Let us suppose that Smith has strong evidence for the following proposition:

(f) Jones owns a Ford.

. . . Let us imagine, now, that Smith has another friend, Brown, of whose whereabouts he is totally ignorant. Smith selects three place-names quite at random, and constructs the following three propositions:

(g) Either Jones owns a Ford, or Brown is in Boston;

(h) Either Jones owns a Ford, or Brown is in Barcelona;

(i) Either Jones owns a Ford, or Brown is in Brest-Litovsk.

. . . [Smith] proceeds to accept (g), (h), and (i) on the basis of (f). Smith has correctly inferred (g), (h), and (i) from a proposition for which he has strong evidence. Smith is therefore completely justified in believing each of these three propositions. Smith, of course, has no idea where Brown is.

But imagine now that two further conditions hold. First, Jones does *not* own a Ford, but is at present driving a rented car. And secondly, by the sheerest coincidence, and entirely unknown to Smith, the place mentioned in proposition (h) happens really to be the place where Brown is. If these two conditions hold, then Smith does *not* know that (h) is true, even though (*i*) (h) *is* true, (*ii*) Smith does believe that (h) is true, and (*iii*) Smith is justified in believing that (h) is true.[54]

This thought experiment has the same result as the other one. It appears to show that justified true belief is not sufficient for knowledge. Gettier's counterexamples seem to indicate that the traditional account is too broad—it includes too much. It bestows the title of knowledge on propositions that do not deserve it.

In the wake of Gettier's thought experiments and the subsequent improvements on them by other philosophers, it is clear that the view of knowledge that has been taken for granted for hundreds of years is inadequate. What, then, is the correct analysis of knowledge? This is the "Gettier problem."

Philosophers want a correct analysis of knowledge because, for one thing, they seek understanding for its own sake. But there is more hanging on the issue. A proper analysis of knowledge could help us decide in particular cases whether we do or do not have knowledge. Likewise it could show that the set of propositions that we know is much smaller (or larger) than we think. Here skepticism could once again arise. Given a certain account of knowledge, the skeptic could claim that the cases in which we may be said to have knowledge are few and far between. Also, with a particular account, we may find that our conceptions of how we come to know things (and therefore our views of ourselves) are radically transformed. Some have asserted, for example, that knowing is not a matter of having a justified true belief but rather of registering a belief in our minds the way a thermometer registers temperature. The world causes the registering, and knowledge is acquired. There is no need to drag in the traditional notion of justification. Could we accept such a view without radically altering our assessments of ourselves and of what we know?

Most philosophers who have addressed the Gettier problem have tried to revise the standard analysis so it won't be undone by Gettier-type thought experiments. Many have regarded the three conditions of the traditional account as necessary but have proposed some kind of fourth condition. Such revisions to the standard analysis are many and varied. Some philosophers, on the other hand, have tried more radical approaches. They have proposed replacing the standard analysis with something very different—like, for instance, an analysis that does away with the justification condition altogether.[55]

Each of these approaches is, of course, a theory about the correct answer to the question What is knowledge? Let's review some of the more noteworthy theories and assess whether any offer a better answer to the question.

The Defeasibility Theory

What exactly is the problem that the Gettier-type counterexamples bring to light? A straightforward way of diagnosing the difficulty is this: Someone has a justified true belief, but then lurking in the background is another piece of evidence that the person doesn't possess that undercuts the justification for that belief (and prevents knowledge). Put another way, the problem in such cases is that the person's justification is defeated by evidence that the person does not possess. That is, the person's justification is defeasible (capable of being made void).

So if this is a correct diagnosis, it would seem that the solution to the Gettier problem is to formulate a new definition of knowledge that takes this notion of defeasibility into account. In this analysis of knowledge, we would include the traditional three conditions but add a fourth regarding defeasibility. We would say that our knowledge requires having justified true belief—but also that if we were to come into possession of some additional evidence, this evidence would not defeat our justification. To have knowledge, our justification must be indefeasible. This solution, then, to the Gettier problem is the **defeasibility theory:** the doctrine that knowledge is undefeated justified true belief.

There are different ways to specify how this undefeated condition would work in an instance of knowledge. One straightforward notion is this: You would know a proposition only if it is true, you believe it to be true, you are justified in believing it to be true—and there is no other evidence (in the form of a true statement) that would defeat your justification if you came to possess that evidence. If there is just one true statement that, if you came to have it as additional evidence, would undermine your original justification, you could not be said to know.

At first glance this version of the defeasibility theory may seem to give us an analysis of knowledge that's a big improvement over the traditional account. But, alas, several thought experiments have revealed otherwise. Here's one of them.

Thought Experiment

Lehrer and Paxson's Demented Mrs. Grabit

Suppose I see a man walk into the library and remove a book from the library by concealing it beneath his coat. Since I am sure the man is Tom Grabit, whom I have often seen before when he attended my classes, I report that I know that Tom Grabit has removed the book. However, suppose further that Mrs. Grabit, the mother of Tom, has averred that on the day in question Tom was not in the library, indeed, was thousands of miles away, and that Tom's identical twin brother, John Grabit, was in the library. Imagine, moreover, that I am entirely ignorant of the fact that Mrs. Grabit has said these things. The statement that she has said these things would defeat any justification I have

defeasibility theory
The doctrine that knowledge is undefeated justified true belief.

for believing that Tom Grabit removed the book. Thus, I could not be said to [know] that Tom Grabit removed the book.

The preceding might be acceptable until we finish the story by adding that Mrs. Grabit is a compulsive and pathological liar, that John Grabit is a fiction of her demented mind, and that Tom Grabit took the book as I believed. Once this is added, it should be apparent that I did know that Tom Grabit removed the book.[56]

Do you see why this counterexample shows this version of the defeasibility theory to be unfounded? According to this defeasibility account, the observer in this case could not be said to know that Tom Grabit stole the book. The reason is that there is one piece of evidence (Mrs. Grabit's statement) that—had the observer come to possess this evidence—would have defeated the observer's original justification. All it takes is one bit of contrary evidence to destroy one's justification (and one's knowledge). But, in light of the additional information that Mrs. Grabit is a demented liar, it seems that the subject does know that Tom Grabit stole the book. Here, then, is an instance of defeated justified true belief that counts as knowledge. Surely this variation on the defeasibility theory is too strict—it says that we cannot have knowledge in cases in which we clearly do. So it must be wrong.

The Causal Theory

Some have assessed the problem in the Gettier-type counterexamples like this: It is just plain luck that the person's belief is true. The difficulty is that what made the belief true is not what caused the person to believe it. In Gettier's job seekers thought experiment, for instance, the true belief is "(e) The man who will get the job has ten coins in his pocket." What makes this belief true is the fact that Smith will get the job and he has ten coins in his pocket. But what caused Smith to believe (e) is that he had strong evidence for Jones's getting the job and having ten coins in his (Jones's) pocket. There seems to be no proper connection between Smith's true belief and the state of affairs that made the belief true. Alvin Goldman claimed that what's missing here is some kind of link between belief and truth, and a causal link fills the bill. He suggested, that for S to know p, the fact that p should cause S's belief that p. Thus we have the **causal theory:** the doctrine that knowledge is suitably caused true belief.[57]

Here "suitably caused" means produced by the state of affairs that makes the belief true. The causal theorist would say that you know that there is a book before you because the book itself—through your perception of the book—causes you to believe that there is a book before you. Jack knows that Jill is angry because her anger causes her to behave in an angry way, and her behavior causes Jack to believe that she is angry. Frank knows that Albany is the capital of New York because that fact causes, through Frank's memory, his belief that Albany is the capital of New York.

This theory is a dramatic departure from the standard account, for the causation requirement would replace the justification condition found in the traditional account. Knowing something, according to the causal theory, does not require being able to state your justification for your belief. Rather it requires being suitably causally connected to the object of your belief. This is not to deny that knowledge is sometimes based on inference, but when it is, the inference is part of the causal chain that produced that knowledge. In this way, the conversion of your true belief into knowledge can depend entirely on facts or items of which you are not even aware. This dependence on external factors is why the causal theory is sometimes called an "externalist theory." A theory like the standard account is called "internalist" because what changes true belief into knowledge depends on something—justification, in this case—that is part of the knower's mental life.

The causal theory easily accounts for the lack of knowledge in the Gettier (and many Gettier-type) cases. In both of Gettier's thought experiments, Smith's true beliefs are not caused by the states of affairs that make those beliefs true. This, says the causal theorist, is why Smith does not have knowledge.

But is suitably caused true belief really sufficient for knowledge? Consider the following thought experiment.

Thought Experiment

Goldman's Fake Barns

Henry is driving in the countryside with his son. For the boy's edification Henry identifies various objects on the landscape as they come into view. "That's a cow," says Henry. "That's a tractor," "That's a silo," "That's a barn," etc. Henry has no doubt about the identity of these objects; in particular, he has no doubt that the last-mentioned object is a barn, which indeed it is. Each of the identified objects has features characteristic of its type. Moreover, each object is fully in view, Henry has excellent eyesight, and he has enough time to look at them reasonably carefully, since there is little traffic.

Given this information, would we say that Henry knows that the object is a barn? Most of us would have little hesitation in saying this. Contrast our inclination here with the inclination we would have if we were given some additional information. Suppose that, unknown to Henry, the district he has just entered is full of papier-mâché facsimiles of barns. These facsimiles look from the road exactly like barns, but are really just facades, without back walls or interiors, quite incapable of being used as barns. Having just entered the district, Henry has not encountered any facsimiles; the object he sees is a genuine barn. But if the object on that site were a facsimile, Henry would mistake it for a barn. Given this new information, we would be strongly inclined to withdraw the claim that Henry knows the object is a barn.

Henry's belief that the object is a barn is caused by the presence of the barn; indeed, the causal process is a perceptual one. Nonetheless, we are not prepared to say, in the second version, that Henry knows.[58]

causal theory The doctrine that knowledge is suitably caused true belief.

A Barn Is Not a
Barn. . . .
Suppose there are
fake barns as well as
real barns in this coun-
tryside. (The visitor's
bureau has dotted
the countryside with
papier-mâché facsimi-
les of real barns.) Now
suppose Henry sees a
real barn. Does he
know that he sees a
real barn?

Henry seems to have a suitably caused true belief—yet he obviously does
not have knowledge. The right kind of causal connection seems to be there,
but that's not enough to ensure knowledge.

The Reliability Theory

In Goldman's fake barns thought experiment, why doesn't Henry know that
the object is a barn? Some have thought that the problem in such cases is
that the belief was acquired in an unreliable way. Henry doesn't know that
the object is a barn because, under the circumstances of facsimile barns dot-
ting the landscape, just looking while driving along is not a reliable way to
acquire the belief that a certain object is a barn. In this situation, Henry
would frequently believe that there was a barn when there wasn't one. His
belief would be produced in an unreliable fashion. This suggests an account of
knowledge that's an improvement over the causal theory. It is the **reliability
theory:** the doctrine that knowledge is reliably produced true belief. You
know p if p is true, you believe that p is true, and your belief is produced in a
reliable way.

The reliability theory does a good job, not only of accounting for lack of
knowledge in the preceding Gettier-type cases, but also in the original Gettier cases. A reliability theorist could say that in Gettier's job seekers thought
experiment, Smith arrived at the true belief (that the man who will get the
job has ten coins in his pocket) by unreliable means. The process was unreliable because it yielded true belief by pure accident. It was just luck that Smith

himself happened to have ten coins in his pocket. If not for this accident, Smith's belief would have been false. So Smith does not know, and the reliability theory explains why.

Like the causal theory, the reliability theory is externalist. What turns true belief into knowledge is the reliability of the process of producing belief. Some internal factor like the justification condition referred to in the standard account does not play a role. According to the causal theory, the knower may not even be aware of the belief-producing process. So here, too, knowing is a matter of registering truth, like a thermometer registering the temperature of a room. The important thing is that this registering be reliable.

But is such registering—such reliably produced true belief—knowledge? Let's pursue the thermometer analogy a little further in a thought experiment and see what it tells us.

Ignorance cannot be learned.

—GERARD DE NERVAL

Thought Experiment

Lehrer's Human Thermometer

Suppose a person, whom we shall name Mr. Truetemp, undergoes brain surgery by an experimental surgeon who invents a small device which is both a very accurate thermometer and a computational device capable of generating thoughts. The device, call it a tempucomp, is implanted in Truetemp's head so that the very tip of the device, no larger than the head of a pin, sits unnoticed on his scalp and acts as a sensor to transmit information about the temperature to the computational system in his brain. This device, in turn, sends a message to his brain causing him to think of the temperature recorded by the external sensor. Assume that the tempucomp is very reliable, and so his thoughts are correct temperature thoughts. All told, this is a reliable belief-forming process. Now imagine, finally, that he has no idea that the tempucomp has been inserted in his brain, is only slightly puzzled about why he thinks so obsessively about temperature, but never checks a thermometer to determine whether these thoughts about the temperature are correct. He accepts them unreflectively, another effect of the tempucomp. Thus, he thinks and accepts that the temperature is 104 degrees. It is. Does he know that it is? Surely not. He has no idea whether he or his thoughts about the temperature are reliable. What he accepts, that the temperature is 104 degrees, is correct, but he does not know that his thought is correct.[59]

How can Truetemp be said to know that the temperature is 104 degrees if he has no idea that his reliable belief-forming process even exists? He is in possession of correct information, but he has no idea if that information is correct. On the reliability account, having evidence regarding whether the information is correct is irrelevant. But this is implausible. In at least some cases, knowing seems to require more than just having correct information; it seems to require that we have some adequate indication that the information is correct. Without such indication, our having some true belief would be

reliability theory
The doctrine that knowledge is reliably produced true belief.

merely coincidental. Relative to whatever evidence we had, the belief would be no better than a lucky guess. But, as we have already observed, a lucky guess cannot be knowledge. The reliability theory may be able to account for many cases of knowledge, but it doesn't seem to account for them all.

The Explanationist Theory

Theories that are capable of giving more detailed explanations are automatically preferred.

—David Deutsch

Our list of failed theories grows longer. We have learned that several initially plausible approaches to the Gettier problem just won't do, and this is progress. What's more, in our investigation we have uncovered some clues that can point us toward a better theory.

First, we have learned a valuable lesson from the failure of the externalist theories. We have seen that knowledge requires not just true belief, but some adequate indication for the knower that the belief is true. The most plausible candidate for such indication is a kind of evidence indicating that a proposition is true. This evidence essentially amounts to justification, as expressed in the third condition of the standard account. The knower must have justification, and it must be the basis for the belief. So after touring the inadequacies of theories that jettison justification, we are back to realizing that we cannot do without it. Justified true belief, then, is indeed necessary for knowledge, though—as Gettier and others show—it is not sufficient. Any adequate theory of knowledge, then, must retain the three conditions of the standard account and add some qualification, a fourth condition.

The defeasibility theory does retain the three conditions and add a fourth, but we saw that the defeasibility addition was not up to the job. The theory, however, is based on an insight that seems entirely plausible. It is the notion that the central problem in the Gettier-type cases is that the believer's justification is undercut by evidence that the believer does not possess. If this is right, then what we need is a fourth condition stipulating that justification somehow not be undermined—a fourth condition that avoids the defects of the defeasibility addition. As several critics have noted, the difficulties for the defeasibility condition arise whenever one tries to specify how justification would be impaired under specific counterfactual conditions—that is, if the believer came to possess defeating evidence, if the believer came to have defeating evidence that wasn't misleading, or if some other complicated balance of defeating and nondefeating evidence were held by the believer. As we have seen, trying to pin down the right conditional arrangement is very difficult, as the failure of the defeasibility theory shows.

So how might we formulate a new theory that takes all this into account? The easy part is stipulating that this new approach must incorporate the three conditions of the standard account. The justification condition then must be internalist. The knower must have adequate indication that the belief is true—must be justified—and this justification must be the basis for the belief.

The harder part is formulating the fourth condition. How can we specify—without falling into the defeasibility trap—that justification should not be undermined? We could say that justification should not be undone by any other truths, even those to which the believer is oblivious. Or, to put it another way, the justifying evidence must not be undermined by the addition of any true proposition, including true propositions of which the believer is unaware. But this won't do because, as we have seen, one true proposition may contravene justification, whereas another may contravene that contravener and thus restore the justification.

Thus we need to take into account not just some true propositions, but all the relevant propositions, all the contraveners that are hidden to the believer. So a better suggestion is that knowledge requires justification that still stands after all the contraveners are sorted out. More specifically, it must be the case that for every true proposition that contravenes S's justification of p, there must be another true proposition that restores for S the justification of p. (Neither the contraveners nor the restorers are part of S's original justification.) When one's justifying evidence for a proposition fulfills this requirement, it is said to be truth-resistant—it resists the contravening of true propositions.[60]

According to this theory then, S knows p if (i) p is true, (ii) S believes that p is true, (iii) S is justified in believing that p is true (has justifying evidence that p is true and believes p on the basis of that evidence), and (iv) S's justification for p is truth-resistant. One way of saying this is that knowledge is justified true belief sustained by the collective totality of the justifying evidence. We know something when we have a justified true belief that is still justified even after all the evidence that we don't have is taken into account. This formulation then has no need for counterfactual conditions, the downfall of the defeasibility theory.

But there is an even more straightforward way to characterize this theory. When you have a justified true belief that is sustained by the collective totality of the justifying evidence, that belief provides the best explanation for the justifying evidence. If you have a justified true belief that there's a cat on the mat, and the collective totality of justifying evidence (some of which you are unaware of) sustains that belief, you know that there's a cat on the mat—for that belief is the best explanation for all the justifying evidence. The proposition that there is a cat on the mat is the best explanation for both your sensory experience of a cat on the mat and other justifying evidence that sustains your original justifying (sensory) evidence. If the totality of justifying evidence did not support that justified true belief, the belief would not be the best explanation for all the justifying evidence. You would not know. This is the **explanationist theory:** the doctrine that knowledge is justified true belief that provides the best explanation for the justifying evidence.

The question is, Does this theory handle the Gettier and Gettier-type counterexamples any better than the other theories? Let's test the theory on Gettier's guy in Barcelona thought experiment. Recall that Smith is justified in believing this false proposition: (f) Jones owns a Ford. And proposition (f) justifies Smith in believing (h) Either Jones owns a Ford, or Brown is in Barcelona.

As we saw before, Smith does not know (h). According to the explanationist theory, the reason for Smith's lack of knowledge is that (h) is not the

Knowledge is in the end based on acknowledgment.
—LUDWIG WITTGENSTEIN

explanationist theory
The doctrine that knowledge is justified true belief that provides the best explanation for the justifying evidence.

best explanation for all the justifying evidence. Smith is justified in believing that Jones owns a Ford, but this justification is contravened by further evidence—the true proposition that Jones does not own a Ford. Smith's justification is undermined, and there is no justifying evidence (no true proposition) to restore it. Yes, it is true that Brown is in Barcelona. But this true proposition does nothing to restore Smith's original justification (f). It is not part of the totality of justifying evidence. Clearly, (h) is not the best explanation for the totality of the justifying evidence. Smith does not know (h), and the explanationist theory explains why.

The theory has similar success in explaining the lack of knowledge in Gettier's other thought experiment, Gettier's job seekers.

Lehrer and Paxson's demented Mrs. Grabit is the thought experiment that tripped up a version of the defeasibility theory. Recall that Mrs. Grabit, Tom's demented mother, has declared that Tom's twin was in the library at the time of the theft but Tom was miles away. Here, the believer does know that Tom stole the book. Again, the explanationist theory accounts for knowledge in this case by pointing to the fact that the belief that Tom stole the book is the best explanation of the justifying evidence. The believer's visual evidence justifies his belief about Tom's theft, and adding the further evidence (demented Mrs. Grabit's claim, and the fact that it is mistaken) does not contravene the original justification.

By now, you can probably guess that the explanationist theory would also have no problem dealing with less complicated cases like Goldman's fake barns. Henry does not know that the object is a barn because his justification (based on his visual experience) is contravened by the further evidence that there are fake barns in the area and he therefore cannot visually distinguish true barns from barn facsimiles. Nothing restores the original justification. So taken altogether, the justifying evidence is not best explained by the belief that the object is a barn.

The explanationist theory can handle all of the Gettier-type counterexamples we have considered so far—plus, apparently, all of the many others we have not dealt with here. It withstands our toughest tests and, among all the theories we have considered, fits best with our strongest intuitions about knowing. It appears to give us, finally, the necessary and sufficient conditions for knowledge we need and thus offers a superior solution to the Gettier problem.

Summary

The traditional account of propositional knowledge says that there are three necessary and sufficient conditions for knowledge—a proposition must be true, one must believe that it is true, and one must be justified in believing that it is true. Philosopher Edmund Gettier and others, however, have produced thought experiments showing that one can have a justified true belief and still not know. So the traditional theory of knowledge is inadequate, and the challenge is to craft a better account.

One of the first attempts at another theory of knowledge was the defeasibility theory—the doctrine that knowledge is undefeated justified true belief.

It requires that our justification for a true belief not be defeated by additional evidence were we to acquire that evidence. But thought experiments reveal that undefeated justified true belief is not sufficient for knowledge.

The causal theory avoids the defeasibility problems. It's the doctrine that knowledge is suitably caused true belief. If what makes a belief true is also what causes the belief in us, we have knowledge, whether or not we have justification (in the usual sense) for that belief. The causal analysis fails, however, because it is possible to have suitably caused true belief and still not have knowledge. Also, it is possible to have knowledge without the proposed causal connection.

The reliability theory is an improvement over the causal theory. It's the doctrine that knowledge is reliably produced true belief. If your true belief arises from a reliable process, you have knowledge, even if you have no idea if the belief is well founded. But this is implausible because knowing seems to require more than just having correct information — it requires that we have some adequate indication that the information is correct.

The explanationist theory is the doctrine that knowledge is justified true belief that provides the best explanation for the justifying evidence. It requires justification in the traditional sense, but it stipulates that this justification be impervious to any other contravening evidence — that the totality of contravening and countercontravening evidence sustain the original justification. Another way to put this is that the true belief must be the best explanation for all the justifying evidence. This account fits well with our strongest intuitions about knowledge, and it can handle all the toughest Gettier and Gettier-type counterexamples. It is our best answer to the Gettier problem.

Study Questions

1. What is the standard account of knowledge?
2. What is Gettier's job seekers thought experiment? What does it reveal about the standard account of knowledge?
3. What is the defeasibility theory?
4. What is Lehrer and Paxson's demented Mrs. Grabit thought experiment? How does it attempt to undermine a version of the defeasibility theory?
5. What is the causal theory? Why is it called an externalist theory?
6. What is Goldman's fake barns thought experiment? How does it attempt to undermine the causal theory?
7. What is the reliability theory? Is it an externalist view?
8. How is the reliability theory an improvement over the causal theory?
9. What is Lehrer's human thermometer thought experiment? How does it attempt to undermine the reliability theory?
10. What is the explanationist theory? How does it explain the lack of knowledge in Gettier's thought experiments?

Discussion Questions

1. If the defeasibility theory is correct, is the scope of our knowledge (the extent of what we could rightfully claim to know) likely to be greater or lesser than what we normally assume?

2. If the causal theory is correct, how would this change the scope of our knowledge?

3. Suppose some weird surgeon secretly implants a device in your head that consistently gives you accurate beliefs regarding the terrain on Mars. You are not aware of this belief-forming process, but it is highly reliable. You thus have plenty of true beliefs about the Martian landscape—but do you know these propositions?

4. Suppose that every week, you suddenly believe that a certain five-digit number will be the big winner in the state lottery. You have no idea where these beliefs come from, but the numbers invariably win the weekly lottery. You never even check to see if the number does win; you just come to believe that it will. You regularly believe truly—but do you know?

5. How would the explanationist theory explain the lack of knowledge in Gettier's job seekers thought experiment?

Meditations on First Philosophy: Meditations I and IV

See Chapter 2 readings and the box "René Descartes: Father of Modern Philosophy" for biographical information. In this selection, Descartes argues for the principle of clarity and distinctness, which says that whatever one clearly and distinctly perceives is true.

Meditations on the First Philosophy in Which the Existence of God and the Distinction between Mind and Body Are Demonstrated.

Meditation I.

Of the things which may be brought within the sphere of the doubtful.

It is now some years since I detected how many were the false beliefs that I had from my earliest youth admitted as true, and how doubtful was everything I had since constructed on this basis; and from that time I was convinced that I must once for all seriously undertake to rid myself of all the opinions which I had formerly accepted, and commence to build anew from the foundation, if I wanted to establish any firm and permanent structure in the sciences. But as this enterprise appeared to be a very great one, I waited until I had attained an age so mature that I could not hope that at any later date I should be better fitted to execute my design. This reason caused me to delay so long that I should feel that I was doing wrong were I to occupy in deliberation the time that yet remains to me for action. Today, then, since very opportunely for the plan I have in view I have delivered my mind from every care [and am happily agitated by no passions] and since I have procured for myself an assured leisure in a peaceable retirement, I shall at last seriously and freely address myself to the general upheaval of all my former opinions.

Now for this object it is not necessary that I should show that all of these are false — I shall perhaps never arrive at this end. But inasmuch as reason already persuades me that I ought no less carefully to withhold my assent from matters which are not entirely certain and indubitable than from those which appear to me manifestly to be false, if I am able to find in each one some reason to doubt, this will suffice to justify my rejecting the whole. And for that end it will not be requisite that I should examine each in particular, which would be an endless undertaking; for owing to the fact that the destruction of the foundations of necessity brings with it the downfall of the rest of the edifice, I shall only in the first place attack those principles upon which all my former opinions rested.

All that up to the present time I have accepted as most true and certain I have learned either from the senses or through the senses; but it is sometimes proved to me that these senses are deceptive, and it is wiser not to trust entirely to any thing by which we have once been deceived.

But it may be that although the senses sometimes deceive us concerning things which are hardly perceptible, or very far away, there are yet many others to be met with as to which we cannot reasonably have any doubt, although we recognise them by their means. For example, there is the fact that I am here, seated by the fire, attired in a dressing gown, having this paper in my hands and other similar matters. And how could I deny that these hands and this body are mine, were it not perhaps that I compare myself to certain persons, devoid of sense, whose cerebella are so troubled and clouded by the violent vapours of black bile, that they constantly assure us that they think they are kings when they are really quite poor, or that they are clothed in purple when they are really without covering, or who imagine that they have an earthenware head or are nothing but pumpkins or are made of glass. But they are mad, and I should not be any the less insane were I to follow examples so extravagant.

At the same time I must remember that I am a man, and that consequently I am in the habit of sleeping, and in my dreams representing to myself the same things or sometimes even less probable things, than do those who are insane in their waking moments. How often has it happened to me that in the night I dreamt

From: René Descartes, *The Philosophical Works of Descartes,* ed. Elizabeth S. Haldane and G. R. T. Ross. (Cambridge: Cambridge University Press, 1931) 144–149, 171–179. Used with permission of the publisher. Notes have been omitted.

that I found myself in this particular place, that I was dressed and seated near the fire, whilst in reality I was lying undressed in bed! At this moment it does indeed seem to me that it is with eyes awake that I am looking at this paper; that this head which I move is not asleep, that it is deliberately and of set purpose that I extend my hand and perceive it; what happens in sleep does not appear so clear nor so distinct as does all this. But in thinking over this I remind myself that on many occasions I have in sleep been deceived by similar illusions, and in dwelling carefully on this reflection I see so manifestly that there are no certain indications by which we may clearly distinguish wakefulness from sleep that I am lost in astonishment. And my astonishment is such that it is almost capable of persuading me that I now dream.

Now let us assume that we are asleep and that all these particulars, e.g. that we open our eyes, shake our head, extend our hands, and so on, are but false delusions; and let us reflect that possibly neither our hands nor our whole body are such as they appear to us to be. At the same time we must at least confess that the things which are represented to us in sleep are like painted representations which can only have been formed as the counterparts of something real and true, and that in this way those general things at least, i.e. eyes, a head, hands, and a whole body, are not imaginary things, but things really existent. For, as a matter of fact, painters, even when they study with the greatest skill to represent sirens and satyrs by forms the most strange and extraordinary, cannot give them natures which are entirely new, but merely make a certain medley of the members of different animals; or if their imagination is extravagant enough to invent something so novel that nothing similar has ever before been seen, and that then their work represents a thing purely fictitious and absolutely false, it is certain all the same that the colours of which this is composed are necessarily real. And for the same reason, although these general things, to wit, [a body], eyes, a head, hands, and such like, may be imaginary, we are bound at the same time to confess that there are at least some other objects yet more simple and more universal, which are real and true; and of these just in the same way as with certain real colours, all these images of things which dwell in our thoughts, whether true and real or false and fantastic, are formed.

To such a class of things pertains corporeal nature in general, and its extension, the figure of extended things, their quantity or magnitude and number, as also the place in which they are, the time which measures their duration, and so on.

That is possibly why our reasoning is not unjust when we conclude from this that Physics, Astronomy, Medicine and all other sciences which have as their end the consideration of composite things, are very dubious and uncertain; but that Arithmetic, Geometry and other sciences of that kind which only treat of things that are very simple and very general, without taking great trouble to ascertain whether they are actually existent or not, contain some measure of certainty and an element of the indubitable. For whether I am awake or asleep, two and three together always form five, and the square can never have more than four sides, and it does not seem possible that truths so clear and apparent can be suspected of any falsity [or uncertainty].

Nevertheless I have long had fixed in my mind the belief that an all-powerful God existed by whom I have been created such as I am. But how do I know that He has not brought it to pass that there is no earth, no heaven, no extended body, no magnitude, no place, and that nevertheless [I possess the perceptions of all these things and that] they seem to me to exist just exactly as I now see them? And, besides, as I sometimes imagine that others deceive themselves in the things which they think they know best, how do I know that I am not deceived every time that I add two and three, or count the sides of a square, or judge of things yet simpler, if anything simpler can be imagined? But possibly God has not desired that I should be thus deceived, for He is said to be supremely good. If, however, it is contrary to His goodness to have made me such that I constantly deceive myself, it would also appear to be contrary to His goodness to permit me to be sometimes deceived, and nevertheless I cannot doubt that He does permit this.

There may indeed be those who would prefer to deny the existence of a God so powerful, rather than believe that all other things are uncertain. But let us not oppose them for the present, and grant that all that is here said of a God is a fable; nevertheless in whatever way they suppose that I have arrived at the state of being that I have reached—whether they attribute it to fate or to accident, or make out that it is by a continual succession of antecedents, or by some other method—since to err and deceive oneself is a defect, it is clear that the greater will be the probability of my being so imperfect as to deceive myself ever, as is the Author to whom they assign my origin the less powerful. To these reasons I have certainly nothing to reply, but at the end I feel constrained to confess that there is nothing in all that I formerly believed to be true, of which I cannot in some measure doubt, and that not merely through want of thought or through levity, but for reasons which are very powerful and maturely considered; so that henceforth I ought not the less carefully to refrain from giving credence to these opinions than to that which is manifestly false, if I desire to arrive at any certainty [in the sciences].

But it is not sufficient to have made these remarks, we must also be careful to keep them in mind. For these ancient and commonly held opinions still revert frequently to my mind, long and familiar custom having given them the right to occupy my mind against my inclination and rendered them almost masters of my belief; nor will I ever lose the habit of deferring to them or of placing my confidence in them, so long as I consider them as they really are, i.e. opinions in some measure doubtful, as I have just shown, and at the same time highly probable, so that there is much more reason to believe in than to deny them. That is why I consider that I shall not be acting amiss, if, taking of set purpose a contrary belief, I allow myself to be deceived, and for a certain time pretend that all these opinions are entirely false and imaginary, until at last, having thus balanced my former prejudices with my latter [so that they cannot divert my opinions more to one side than to the other], my judgment will no longer be dominated by bad usage or turned away from the right knowledge of the truth. For I am assured that there can be neither peril nor error in this course, and that I cannot at present yield too much to distrust, since I am not considering the question of action, but only of knowledge.

I shall then suppose, not that God who is supremely good and the fountain of truth, but some evil genius not less powerful than deceitful, has employed his whole energies in deceiving me; I shall consider that the heavens, the earth, colours, figures, sound, and all other external things are nought but the illusions and dreams of which this genius has availed himself in order to lay traps for my credulity; I shall consider myself as having no hands, no eyes, no flesh, no blood, nor any senses, yet falsely believing myself to possess all these things; I shall remain obstinately attached to this idea, and if by this means it is not in my power to arrive at the knowledge of any truth, I may at least do what is in my power [i.e. suspend my judgment], and with firm purpose avoid giving credence to any false thing, or being imposed upon by this arch deceiver, however powerful and deceptive he may be. But this task is a laborious one, and insensibly a certain lassitude leads me into the course of my ordinary life. And just as a captive who in sleep enjoys an imaginary liberty, when he begins to suspect that his liberty is but a dream, fears to awaken, and conspires with these agreeable illusions that the deception may be prolonged, so insensibly of my own accord I fall back into my former opinions, and I dread awakening from this slumber, lest the laborious wakefulness which would follow the tranquillity of this repose should have to be spent not in daylight, but in the excessive darkness of the difficulties which have just been discussed.

Meditation IV.

Of the True and the False.

I have been well accustomed these past days to detach my mind from my senses, and I have accurately observed that there are very few things that one knows with certainty respecting corporeal objects, that there are many more which are known to us respecting the human mind, and yet more still regarding God Himself; so that I shall now without any difficulty abstract my thoughts from the considerations of [sensible or] imaginable objects, and carry them to those which, being withdrawn from all contact with matter, are purely intelligible. And certainly the idea which I possess of the human mind inasmuch as it is a thinking thing, and not extended in length, width and depth, nor participating in anything pertaining to body, is incomparably more distinct than is the idea of any corporeal thing. And when I consider that I doubt, that is to say, that I am an incomplete and dependent being, the idea of a being that is complete and independent, that is of God, presents itself to my mind with so much distinctness and clearness—and from the fact alone that this idea is found in me, or that I who possess this idea exist, I conclude so certainly that God exists, and that my existence depends entirely on Him in every moment of my life—that I do not think that the human mind is capable of knowing anything with more evidence and certitude. And it seems to me that I now have before me a road which will lead us from the contemplation of the true God (in whom all the treasures of science and wisdom are contained) to the knowledge of the other objects of the universe.

For, first of all, I recognise it to be impossible that He should ever deceive me; for in all fraud and deception some imperfection is to be found, and although it may appear that the power of deception is a mark of subtilty or power, yet the desire to deceive without doubt testifies to malice or feebleness, and accordingly cannot be found in God.

In the next place I experienced in myself a certain capacity for judging which I have doubtless received from God, like all the other things that I possess; and as

He could not desire to deceive me, it is clear that He has not given me a faculty that will lead me to err if I use it aright.

And no doubt respecting this matter could remain, if it were not that the consequence would seem to follow that I can thus never be deceived; for if I hold all that I possess from God, and if He has not placed in me the capacity for error, it seems as though I could never fall into error. And it is true that when I think only of God [and direct my mind wholly to Him], I discover [in myself] no cause of error, or falsity; yet directly afterwards, when recurring to myself, experience shows me that I am nevertheless subject to an infinitude of errors, as to which, when we come to investigate them more closely, I notice that not only is there a real and positive idea of God or of a Being of supreme perfection present to my mind, but also, so to speak, a certain negative idea of nothing, that is, of that which is infinitely removed from any kind of perfection; and that I am in a sense something intermediate between God and nought, i.e. placed in such a manner between the supreme Being and non-being, that there is in truth nothing in me that can lead to error in so far as a sovereign Being has formed me; but that, as I in some degree participate likewise in nought or in non-being, i.e. in so far as I am not myself the supreme Being, and as I find myself subject to an infinitude of imperfections, I ought not to be astonished if I should fall into error. Thus do I recognise that error, in so far as it is such, is not a real thing depending on God, but simply a defect; and therefore, in order to fall into it, that I have no need to possess a special faculty given me by God for this very purpose, but that I fall into error from the fact that the power given me by God for the purpose of distinguishing truth from error is not infinite.

Nevertheless this does not quite satisfy me; for error is not a pure negation [i.e. is not the simple defect or want of some perfection which ought not to be mine], but it is a lack of some knowledge which it seems that I ought to possess. And on considering the nature of God it does not appear to me possible that He should have given me a faculty which is not perfect of its kind, that is, which is wanting in some perfection due to it. For if it is true that the more skilful the artizan, the more perfect is the work of his hands, what can have been produced by this supreme Creator of all things that is not in all its parts perfect? And certainly there is no doubt that God could have created me so that I could never have been subject to error; it is also certain that He ever wills what is best; is it then better that I should be subject to err than that I should not?

In considering this more attentively, it occurs to me in the first place that I should not be astonished if my intelligence is not capable of comprehending why God acts as He does; and that there is thus no reason to doubt of His existence from the fact that I may perhaps find many other things besides this as to which I am able to understand neither for what reason nor how God has produced them. For, in the first place, knowing that my nature is extremely feeble and limited, and that the nature of God is on the contrary immense, incomprehensible, and infinite, I have no further difficulty in recognising that there is an infinitude of matters in His power, the causes of which transcend my knowledge; and this reason suffices to convince me that the species of cause termed final, finds no useful employment in physical [or natural] things; for it does not appear to me that I can without temerity seek to investigate the [inscrutable] ends of God.

It further occurs to me that we should not consider one single creature separately, when we inquire as to whether the works of God are perfect, but should regard all his creations together. For the same thing which might possibly seem very imperfect with some semblance of reason if regarded by itself, is found to be very perfect if regarded as part of the whole universe; and although, since I resolved to doubt all things, I as yet have only known certainly my own existence and that of God, nevertheless since I have recognised the infinite power of God, I cannot deny that He may have produced many other things, or at least that He has the power of producing them, so that I may obtain a place as a part of a great universe.

Whereupon, regarding myself more closely, and considering what are my errors (for they alone testify to there being any imperfection in me), I answer that they depend on a combination of two causes, to wit, on the faculty of knowledge that rests in me, and on the power of choice or of free will—that is to say, of the understanding and at the same time of the will. For by the understanding alone I [neither assert nor deny anything, but] apprehend the ideas of things as to which I can form a judgment. But no error is properly speaking found in it, provided the word error is taken in its proper signification; and though there is possibly an infinitude of things in the world of which I have no idea in my understanding, we cannot for all that say that it is deprived of these ideas [as we might say of something which is required by its nature], but simply it does not possess these; because in truth there is no reason to prove that God should have given me a greater faculty of knowledge than He has given me; and however skilful a workman I represent Him to be, I should not for all that consider that He was bound to have placed in each of His works all the perfections which He may have been able to place in some. I likewise cannot complain that God has not given me a free choice or a will which is sufficient, ample and perfect, since as a matter of fact I am conscious of a will so extended as to be subject to no limits. And what seems to me very remarkable in this regard is that of all the qualities which I possess there is no one so perfect and so comprehensive that I do not very clearly recognise that it might be yet greater and more perfect. For, to take an example, if I consider the faculty of comprehension which I possess, I find that it is of very small extent and extremely limited, and at the same time I find the idea of another faculty much more ample and even infinite, and seeing that I can form the idea of it, I recognise from this very fact that it pertains to the nature of God. If in the same way I examine the memory, the imagination, or some other faculty, I do not find any which is not small and circumscribed, while in God it is immense [or infinite]. It is free-will alone or liberty of choice which I find to be so great in me that I can conceive no other idea to be more great; it is indeed the case that it is for the most part this will that causes me to know that in some manner I bear the image and similitude of God. For although the power of will is incomparably greater in God than in me, both by reason of the knowledge and the power which, conjoined with it, render it stronger and more efficacious, and by reason of its object, inasmuch as in God it extends to a great many things; it nevertheless does not seem to me greater if I consider it formally and precisely in itself: for the faculty of will consists alone in our having the power of choosing to do a thing or choosing not to do it (that is, to affirm or deny, to pursue or to shun it), or rather it consists alone in the fact that in order to affirm or deny, pursue or shun those things placed before us by the understanding, we act so that we are unconscious that any outside force constrains us in doing so. For in order that I should be free it is not necessary that I should be indifferent as to the choice of one or the other of two contraries; but contrariwise the more I lean to the one — whether I recognise clearly that the reasons of the good and true are to be found in it, or whether God so disposes my inward thought — the more freely do I choose and embrace it. And undoubtedly both divine grace and natural knowledge, far from diminishing my liberty, rather increase it and strengthen it. Hence this indifference which I feel, when I am not swayed to one side rather than to the other by lack of reason, is the

lowest grade of liberty, and rather evinces a lack or negation in knowledge than a perfection of will: for if I always recognised clearly what was true and good, I should never have trouble in deliberating as to what judgment or choice I should make, and then I should be entirely free without ever being indifferent.

From all this I recognise that the power of will which I have received from God is not of itself the source of my errors — for it is very ample and very perfect of its kind — any more than is the power of understanding; for since I understand nothing but by the power which God has given me for understanding, there is no doubt that all that I understand, I understand as I ought, and it is not possible that I err in this. Whence then come my errors? They come from the sole fact that since the will is much wider in its range and compass than the understanding, I do not restrain it within the same bounds, but extend it also to things which I do not understand: and as the will is of itself indifferent to these, it easily falls into error and sin, and chooses the evil for the good, or the false for the true.

For example, when I lately examined whether anything existed in the world, and found that from the very fact that I considered this question it followed very clearly that I myself existed, I could not prevent myself from believing that a thing I so clearly conceived was true: not that I found myself compelled to do so by some external cause, but simply because from great clearness in my mind there followed a great inclination of my will; and I believed this with so much the greater freedom or spontaneity as I possessed the less indifference towards it. Now, on the contrary, I not only know that I exist, inasmuch as I am a thinking thing, but a certain representation of corporeal nature is also presented to my mind; and it comes to pass that I doubt whether this thinking nature which is in me, or rather by which I am what I am, differs from this corporeal nature, or whether both are not simply the same thing; and I here suppose that I do not yet know any reason to persuade me to adopt the one belief rather than the other. From this it follows that I am entirely indifferent as to which of the two I affirm or deny, or even whether I abstain from forming any judgment in the matter.

And this indifference does not only extend to matters as to which the understanding has no knowledge, but also in general to all those which are not apprehended with perfect clearness at the moment when the will is deliberating upon them: for, however probable are the conjectures which render me disposed to form a judgment respecting anything, the simple knowledge that I have that those are conjectures alone and not certain and indubitable reasons, suffices to occasion me to judge the contrary. Of this I have had great experience of late when I set aside as false all that I had formerly held to be absolutely true, for the sole reason that I remarked that it might in some measure be doubted.

But if I abstain from giving my judgment on any thing when I do not perceive it with sufficient clearness and distinctness, it is plain that I act rightly and am not deceived. But if I determine to deny or affirm, I no longer make use as I should of my free will, and if I affirm what is not true, it is evident that I deceive myself; even though I judge according to truth, this comes about only by chance, and I do not escape the blame of misusing my freedom; for the light of nature teaches us that the knowledge of the understanding should always precede the determination of the will. And it is in the misuse of the free will that the privation which constitutes the characteristic nature of error is met with. Privation, I say, is found in the act, in so far as it proceeds from me, but it is not found in the faculty which I have received from God, nor even in the act in so far as it depends on Him.

For I have certainly no cause to complain that God has not given me an intelligence which is more powerful, or a natural light which is stronger than that which I have received from Him, since it is proper to the finite understanding not to comprehend a multitude of things, and it is proper to a created understanding to be finite; on the contrary, I have every reason to render thanks to God who owes me nothing and who has given me all the perfections I possess, and I should be far from charging Him with injustice, and with having deprived me of, or wrongfully withheld from me, these perfections which He has not bestowed upon me.

I have further no reason to complain that He has given me a will more ample than my understanding, for since the will consists only of one single element, and is so to speak indivisible, it appears that its nature is such that nothing can be abstracted from it [without destroying it]; and certainly the more comprehensive it is found to be, the more reason I have to render gratitude to the giver.

And, finally, I must also not complain that God concurs with me in forming the acts of the will, that is the judgment in which I go astray, because these acts are entirely true and good, inasmuch as they depend on God; and in a certain sense more perfection accrues to my nature from the fact that I can form them, than if I could not do so. As to the privation in which alone the formal reason of error or sin consists, it has no need of any concurrence from God, since it is not a thing [or an existence], and since it is not related to God as to a cause, but should be termed merely a negation [according to the significance given to these words in the Schools]. For in fact it is not an imperfection in God that He has given me the liberty to give or withhold my assent from certain things as to which He has not placed a clear and distinct knowledge in my understanding; but it is without doubt an imperfection in me not to make a good use of my freedom, and to give my judgment readily on matters which I only understand obscurely. I nevertheless perceive that God could easily have created me so that I never should err, although I still remained free, and endowed with a limited knowledge, viz. by giving to my understanding a clear and distinct intelligence of all things as to which I should ever have to deliberate; or simply by His engraving deeply in my memory the resolution never to form a judgment on anything without having a clear and distinct understanding of it, so that I could never forget it. And it is easy for me to understand that, in so far as I consider myself alone, and as if there were only myself in the world, I should have been much more perfect than I am, if God had created me so that I could never err. Nevertheless I cannot deny that in some sense it is a greater perfection in the whole universe that certain parts should not be exempt from error as others are than that all parts should be exactly similar. And I have no right to complain if God, having placed me in the world, has not called upon me to play a part that excels all others in distinction and perfection.

And further I have reason to be glad on the ground that if He has not given me the power of never going astray by the first means pointed out above, which depends on a clear and evident knowledge of all the things regarding which I can deliberate, He has at least left within my power the other means, which is firmly to adhere to the resolution never to give judgment on matters whose truth is not clearly known to me; for although I notice a certain weakness in my nature in that I cannot continually concentrate my mind on one single thought, I can yet, by attentive and frequently repeated meditation, impress it so forcibly on my memory that I shall never fail to recollect it whenever I have need of it, and thus acquire the habit of never going astray.

And inasmuch as it is in this that the greatest and principal perfection of man consists, it seems to me that I have not gained little by this day's Meditation, since I have discovered the source of falsity and error. And certainly there can be no other source than that which I have explained; for as often as I so restrain my will within the limits of my knowledge that it forms no judgment except on matters which are clearly and distinctly represented to it by the understanding, I can never be deceived; for every clear and distinct conception is without doubt something, and hence cannot derive its origin from what is nought, but must of necessity have God as its author—God, I say, who being supremely perfect, cannot be the cause of any error; and consequently we must conclude that such a conception [or such a judgment] is true. Nor have I only learned to-day what I should avoid in order that I may not err, but also how I should act in order to arrive at a knowledge of the truth; for without doubt I shall arrive at this end if I devote my attention sufficiently to those things which I perfectly understand; and if I separate from these that which I only understand confusedly and with obscurity. To these I shall henceforth diligently give heed.

Of the Principles of Human Knowledge

George Berkeley (1685–1753) founded the modern school of idealism, which maintains that to be is to be perceived: only that which one is aware of exists. At the age of twenty-five, Berkeley published *A Treatise Concerning the Principles of Human Knowledge*, which attempts to refute skepticism and atheism by denying the existence of matter. In 1713, he published *The Three Dialogues Between Hylas and Philonous*, which presents his views in a more popular dialogue format. He came to America in 1728 to found a missionary college in Bermuda. Although that project failed, he helped found both Yale and Columbia universities. In this selection from the *Principles*, he explains why he thinks it impossible for matter to exist.

It is evident to any one who takes a survey of the *objects* of human knowledge, that they are either ideas actually imprinted on the senses; or else such as are perceived by attending to the passions and operations of the mind; or, lastly, ideas formed by help of memory and imagination—either compounding, dividing, or barely representing those originally perceived in the aforesaid ways. By sight I have the ideas of light and colours, with their several degrees and variations. By touch I perceive hard and soft, heat and cold, motion and resistance, and of all these more and less either as to quantity or degree. Smelling furnishes me with odours; the palate with tastes; and hearing conveys sounds to the mind in all their variety of tone and composition. And as several of these are observed to accompany each other, they come to be marked by one name, and so to be reputed as one thing. Thus, for example, a certain colour, taste, smell, figure and consistence having been observed to go together, are accounted one distinct thing, signified by the name *apple*; other collections of ideas constitute a stone, a tree, a book, and the like sensible things—which as they are pleasing or disagreeable excite the passions of love, hatred, joy, grief, and so forth.

But, besides all that endless variety of ideas or objects of knowledge, there is likewise something which knows or perceives them, and exercises divers operations, as willing, imagining, remembering, about them. This perceiving, active being is what I call *mind, spirit, soul,* or *myself*. By which words I do not denote any one of my ideas, but a thing entirely distinct from them wherein they exist, or, which is the same thing, whereby they are perceived—for the existence of an idea consists in being perceived.

That neither our thoughts, nor passions, nor ideas formed by the imagination, exist without the mind, is what everybody will allow. And to me it is no less evident that the various sensations or ideas imprinted on the sense, however blended or combined together (that is, whatever objects they compose), cannot exist otherwise than in a mind perceiving them.—I think an intuitive knowledge may be obtained of this by any one that shall attend to what is meant by the term *exist* when applied to sensible things. The table I write on I say exists, that is, I see and feel it; and if I were out of my study I should say it existed—meaning thereby that if I was in my study I might perceive it, or that some other spirit actually does perceive it. There was an odour, that is, it was smelt; there was a sound, that is, it was heard; a colour or figure, and it was perceived by sight or touch. This is all that I can understand by these and the like expressions. For as to what is said of the absolute existence of unthinking things without any relation to their being perceived, that is to me perfectly unintelligible. Their *esse* is *percipi*, nor is it possible they should have any existence out of the minds or thinking things which perceive them.

It is indeed an opinion strangely prevailing amongst men, that houses, mountains, rivers, and in a word all sensible objects, have an existence, natural or real, distinct from their being perceived by the understanding. But, with how great an assurance and acquiescence

From: George Berkeley, *A Treatise Concerning the Principles of Human Knowledge* (Philadelphia: Lippincott, 1890). Notes have been omitted.

soever this principle may be entertained in the world, yet whoever shall find in his heart to call it in question may, if I mistake not, perceive it to involve a manifest contradiction. For, what are the forementioned objects but the things we perceive by sense? and what do we perceive besides our own ideas or sensations? and is it not plainly repugnant that any one of these, or any combination of them, should exist unperceived?

If we thoroughly examine this tenet it will, perhaps, be found at bottom to depend on the doctrine of *abstract ideas*. For can there be a nicer strain of abstraction than to distinguish the existence of sensible objects from their being perceived, so as to conceive them existing unperceived? Light and colours, heat and cold, extension and figures—in a word the things we see and feel—what are they but so many sensations, notions, ideas, or impressions on the sense? and is it possible to separate, even in thought, any of these from perception? For my part, I might as easily divide a thing from itself. I may, indeed, divide in my thoughts, or conceive apart from each other, those things which, perhaps, I never perceived by sense so divided. Thus, I imagine the trunk of a human body without the limbs, or conceive the smell of a rose without thinking on the rose itself. So far, I will not deny, I can abstract—if that may properly be called *abstraction* which extends only to the conceiving separately such objects as it is possible may really exist or be actually perceived asunder. But my conceiving or imagining power does not extend beyond the possibility of real existence or perception. Hence, as it is impossible for me to see or feel anything without an actual sensation of that thing, so is it impossible for me to conceive in my thoughts any sensible thing or object distinct from the sensation or perception of it. . . .

I shall farther add, that, after the same manner as modern philosophers prove certain sensible qualities to have no existence in Matter, or without the mind, the same thing may be likewise proved of all other sensible qualities whatsoever. Thus, for instance, it is said that heat and cold are affections only of the mind, and not at all patterns of real beings, existing in the corporeal substances which excite them, for that the same body which appears cold to one hand seems warm to another. Now, why may we not as well argue that figure and extension are not patterns or resemblances of qualities existing in Matter, because to the same eye at different stations, or eyes of a different texture at the same station, they appear various, and cannot therefore be the images of anything settled and determinate without the mind? Again, it is proved that sweetness is not really in the sapid thing, because the thing remaining

unaltered the sweetness is changed into bitter, as in case of a fever or otherwise vitiated palate. Is it not as reasonable to say that motion is not without the mind, since if the succession of ideas in the mind become swifter the motion, it is acknowledged, shall appear slower without any alteration in any external object?

In short, let any one consider those arguments which are thought manifestly to prove that colours and tastes exist only in the mind, and he shall find they may with equal force be brought to prove the same thing of extension, figure, and motion. Though it must be confessed this method of arguing does not so much prove that there is no extension or colour in an outward object, as that we do not know by sense which is the true extension or colour of the object. But the arguments foregoing plainly shew it to be impossible that any colour or extension at all, or other sensible quality whatsoever, should exist in an unthinking subject without the mind, or in truth, that there should be any such thing as an outward object. . . .

But, though we might possibly have all our sensations without them, yet perhaps it may be thought easier to conceive and explain the manner of their production, by supposing external bodies in their likeness rather than otherwise; and so it might be at least probable there are such things as bodies that excite their ideas in our minds. But neither can this be said; for, though we give the materialists their external bodies, they by their own confession are never the nearer knowing how our ideas are produced; since they own themselves unable to comprehend in what manner body can act upon spirit, or how it is possible it should imprint any idea in the mind. Hence it is evident the production of ideas or sensations in our minds, can be no reason why we should suppose Matter or corporeal substances, since that is acknowledged to remain equally inexplicable with or without this supposition. If therefore it were possible for bodies to exist without the mind, yet to hold they do so, must needs be a very precarious opinion; since it is to suppose, without any reason at all, that God has created innumerable beings that are entirely useless, and serve to no manner of purpose.

In short, if there were external bodies, it is impossible we should ever come to know it; and if there were not, we might have the very same reasons to think there were that we have now. Suppose—what no one can deny possible—an intelligence without the help of external bodies, to be affected with the same train of sensations or ideas that you are, imprinted in the same order and with like vividness in his mind. I ask whether that intelligence hath not all the reason to believe the existence of corporeal substances, represented by his ideas, and exciting them in his mind, that you can possibly have for believing the same thing? Of this there can be no question—which one consideration were enough to make any reasonable person suspect the strength of whatever arguments he may think himself to have, for the existence of bodies without the mind. . . .

But, say you, surely there is nothing easier than for me to imagine trees, for instance, in a park, or books existing in a closet, and nobody by to perceive them. I answer, you may so, there is no difficulty in it; but what is all this, I beseech you, more than framing in your mind certain ideas which you call books and trees, and at the same time omitting to frame the idea of any one that may perceive them? But do not you yourself perceive or think of them all the while? This therefore is nothing to the purpose: it only shews you have the power of imagining or forming ideas in your mind; but it does not shew that you can conceive it possible the objects of your thought may exist without the mind. To make out this, it is necessary that you conceive them existing unconceived or unthought of, which is a manifest repugnancy. When we do our utmost to conceive the existence of external bodies, we are all the while only contemplating our own ideas. But the mind taking no notice of itself, is deluded to think it can and does conceive bodies existing unthought of or without the mind, though at the same time they are apprehended by or exist in itself. A little attention will discover to any one the truth and evidence of what is here said, and make it unnecessary to insist on any other proofs against the existence of *material substance*.

Is Justified True Belief Knowledge?

Edmund L. Gettier (1927–) is a professor emeritus of philosophy at the University of Massachusetts at Amherst. In 1963, he made his reputation by publishing the following article, which offers a devastating challenge to the standard account of knowledge. In it, he offers counterexamples to show that one can have a justified true belief and still not know. This little paper generated an enormous response from philosophers, who devised alternative accounts of knowledge that they hoped would solve the "Gettier problem."

Various attempts have been made in recent years to state necessary and sufficient conditions for someone's knowing a given proposition. The attempts have often been such that they can be stated in a form similar to the following:

(a) S knows that P *IFF** (i) P is true,
  (ii) S believes that P is true, and
  (iii) S is justified in believing that P is true.

For example, Chisholm has held that the following gives the necessary and sufficient conditions for knowledge:

(b) S knows that P *IFF* (i) S accepts P,
  (ii) S has adequate evidence for P, and
  (iii) P is true.

Ayer has stated the necessary and sufficient conditions for knowledge as follows:

(c) S knows that P *IFF* (i) P is true,
  (ii) S is sure that P is true, and
  (iii) S has the right to be sure that P is true.

I shall argue that (a) is false in that the conditions stated therein do not constitute a *sufficient* condition for the truth of the proposition that S knows that P. The same argument will show that (b) and (c) fail if 'has adequate evidence for' or 'has the right to be sure that' is substituted for 'is justified in believing that' throughout.

I shall begin by noting two points. First, in that sense of 'justified' in which S's being justified in believing P is a necessary condition of S's knowing that P, it is possible for a person to be justified in believing a proposition that is in fact false. Secondly, for any proposition P, if S is justified in believing P, and P entails Q, and S deduces Q from P and accepts Q as a result of this deduction, then S is justified in believing Q. Keeping these two points in mind, I shall now present two cases in which the conditions stated in (a) are true for some proposition, though it is at the same time false that the person in question knows that proposition.

Case I:

Suppose that Smith and Jones have applied for a certain job. And suppose that Smith has strong evidence for the following conjunctive proposition:

(d) Jones is the man who will get the job, and Jones has ten coins in his pocket.

Smith's evidence for (d) might be that the president of the company assured him that Jones would in the end be selected, and that he, Smith, had counted coins in Jones's pocket ten minutes ago. Proposition (d) entails:

(e) The man who will get the job has ten coins in his pocket.

Let us suppose that Smith sees the entailment from (d) to (e), and accepts (e) on the grounds of (d), for which he has strong evidence. In this case, Smith is clearly justified in believing that (e) is true.

---

*IFF = if and only if.

From: Edmund L. Gettier, "Is Justified True Belief Knowledge?" *Analysis* 23 (June 1963): 121–123. Notes have been omitted.

But imagine, further, that unknown to Smith, he himself, not Jones, will get the job. And, also, unknown to Smith, he himself has ten coins in his pocket. Proposition (e) is then true, though proposition (d), from which Smith inferred (e), is false. In our example, then, all of the following are true: (*i*) (e) is true, (*ii*) Smith believes that (e) is true, and (*iii*) Smith is justified in believing that (e) is true. But it is equally clear that Smith does not *know* that (e) is true; for (e) is true in virtue of the number of coins in Smith's pocket, while Smith does not know how many coins are in Smith's pocket, and bases his belief in (e) on a count of the coins in Jones's pocket, whom he falsely believes to be the man who will get the job.

Case II:

Let us suppose that Smith has strong evidence for the following proposition:

(f) Jones owns a Ford.

Smith's evidence might be that Jones has at all times in the past within Smith's memory owned a car, and always a Ford, and that Jones has just offered Smith a ride while driving a Ford. Let us imagine, now, that Smith has another friend, Brown, of whose whereabouts he is totally ignorant. Smith selects three place-names quite at random, and constructs the following three propositions:

(g) Either Jones owns a Ford, or Brown is in Boston;

(h) Either Jones owns a Ford, or Brown is in Barcelona;

(i) Either Jones owns a Ford, or Brown is in Brest-Litovsk.

Each of these propositions is entailed by (f). Imagine that Smith realizes the entailment of each of these propositions he has constructed by (f), and proceeds to accept (g), (h), and (i) on the basis of (f). Smith has correctly inferred (g), (h), and (i) from a proposition for which he has strong evidence. Smith is therefore completely justified in believing each of these three propositions. Smith, of course, has no idea where Brown is.

But imagine now that two further conditions hold. First, Jones does *not* own a Ford, but is at present driving a rented car. And secondly, by the sheerest coincidence, and entirely unknown to Smith, the place mentioned in proposition (h) happens really to be the place where Brown is. If these two conditions hold then Smith does *not* know that (h) *is* true, even though (*i*) (h) *is* true, (*ii*) Smith does believe that (h) is true, and (*iii*) Smith is justified in believing that (h) is true.

These two examples show that definition (a) does not state a *sufficient* condition for someone's knowing a given proposition. The same cases, with appropriate changes, will suffice to show that neither definition (b) nor definition (c) do so either.

Why Don't You Just Wake Up?

Thomas D. Davis has taught philosophy at Michigan, Grinnell College, the University of Redlands, and De Anza College. He is the author of numerous short stories as well as two mystery novels with philosophical themes: *Suffer Little Children,* which received a Shamus Award from the Private Eye Writers of America for best first mystery of 1991, and *Murdered Sleep.* In this short story, Davis explores the implications of Descartes' dream argument.

I'm in the living room at home, and Dad's there, all serious, saying, "John, where's your mind these days—you've got to wake up," and I think I wake up, and I'm at my desk at home. I straighten up and yawn and pick up my history book, and just then Mom comes in, saying, "Johnny, you're just not concentrating—you've got to wake up," and I think I wake up, and I'm sitting in class. I look around, and Teresa's sitting next to me looking all upset, saying, "John, what's with you these days—why don't you just wake up," and I think I wake up, and I'm lying in bed in my dorm room.

It was all dreams within dreams within dreams, and what I thought was waking was just more dreaming. I am in my dorm bed and wonder who is going to come in next and wake me from this, only no one comes in, and the digital clock blinks slowly toward seven-thirty, and I guess this must be real.

It doesn't seem real, though. Nothing does these days. Everything that happens seems sort of vague somehow and out of focus and not all that important. I have trouble concentrating—taking things seriously—and everybody's on my case. That's the reason, I think, for all those dreams about dreaming and waking.

One reason, anyway. The other is that philosophy class and all that talk about Descartes and whether all reality could be a dream. That's not helping much either.

I'm late picking up Teresa again, and she's had to wait, and there won't be time for us to get coffee together. She gives me that exasperated look I see a lot these days, and we walk across campus without talking. Finally, she says:

"I don't know why I took that stupid philosophy class. I can't wait 'til it's over."

I know it's not really the class she's annoyed at. It's me and the way I've been lately. I know I should say something nice. But I'm feeling pushed and kind of cranky.

"I like the class," I say, to be contrary. "You do not."

"I do. It's kind of interesting."

"Interesting. Right. Like I really want to sit around all day wondering whether I'm dreaming everything in the world."

"Maybe you are."

"Sure." She shakes her head. "That's so stupid."

"Just because you say 'stupid' doesn't make it wrong. How do you know you aren't just dreaming this all up?"

She glares at me, but her eyes begin to dart the way they always do when she's thinking hard. She's not in the mood for this, but I've gotten her mad.

"Because . . . I know what dreams look like. They're all hazy. Not like the world looks now."

"You mean what you can see of it through the smog."

"Funny."

I know what she means, though. A few weeks back I would have said that being awake looked a lot different from dreaming. But the guy in class is right. That's just a matter of how things look. It doesn't prove how things are.

"Look," I say, "nobody's denying that what we call 'dreaming' looks different from what we call 'being awake.' But is it really different? Maybe 'being awake' is just a different kind of dream."

"Yeah, well, if I'm making all this up, how come we're talking about something I don't want to talk about?"

"Because you're not in control of this dream any more than you are your dreams at night. It's your unconscious doing it."

"This is so much bullsh. . . ."

"Why?"

From: Thomas D. Davis, "Why Don't You Just Wake Up?" *Philosophy* (New York: McGraw-Hill, 1993) 163–166.

"It's crazy. You're standing here trying to convince me that everything is my dream while you know you're real. That doesn't make any sense."

"Yeah, it does. I'm saying you can't know that I really exist, I can't know that you. . . ."

I stop suddenly, because something scary is happening. It's like a ripple moving through the whole world, coming from the horizon to my left, but moving fast as if the world is really much smaller than it appears. And where the ripple is, everything becomes elongated and out of focus. The ripple passes over Teresa, distorting her for a moment, like a fun house mirror. Then it's gone, and everything's back to normal.

"John, are you okay?" says Teresa, giving me a worried look. "You look white as a sheet."

"I don't know. I just got the weirdest feeling. I guess I'm okay."

"John, are you on something?"

"No. I told you. Really."

She looks at me for a moment and decides I'm telling the truth.

"Come on," she says, taking my hand. "The last thing you need right now is philosophy class. Let's go get something to eat and then sit in the sun for awhile. I bet you'll feel better."

"Hey, Ter, I'm sorry I'm being such a jerk. I . . ."

"Don't worry about it, John. It's okay. Come on."

Later I do feel better. I feel like things are almost back to normal. But my night is full of dreams within dreams, and the next day the world seems full of unreality once again. And then, at midday, the world ripples again.

I go to the university health service, and of course the doctor thinks it's drugs, and we go round and round on that until I insist that he test me and then he begins to believe I'm not lying. He becomes nicer then, and more concerned, and schedules some tests and an appointment with a specialist he'd like me to see, though he's "sure its nothing, just exhaustion."

Walking across campus, I see the world ripple again and suddenly I realize what it all looks like. It's like when you are watching a movie in class, and the movie screen ripples, distorting the image, and suddenly you're aware that it wasn't a world in front of you at all, but just an illusion on a not-very-large piece of material. I put my arm out to feel the ripple, only my arm ripples too because it's part of the movie.

I don't know what's happening, and I'm afraid. At night I keep myself from sleeping because the idea of dreaming is something I suddenly find disturbing. In the morning I'm exhausted, but I stumble off to class because I want something to divert my attention, but once there I have trouble paying attention. I guess the professor must have asked me something I didn't hear because I feel Teresa nudging me in the ribs, and hear her say, "Come on, John, wake up."

I look up then at the professor standing behind his lectern, and just above and in back of him a dark line seems to appear in the wall. It looks like the slow fissure of an earthquake, except that the edges fold back against the surface of the wall like the edges of torn paper, and I see that behind the tearing there is nothing at all, just darkness. Then I see that the tear isn't in the wall at all but in my field of vision because as it reaches the professor he begins to split apart and then the lectern and then the head of the student in the front row. On both sides of the tear the world distorts and folds and collapses. The fissure moves downward through the students and then, as I glance down, through my own body. No one is moving or screaming—they take no more notice than movie characters on a torn movie screen would. In a panic I reach out and touch Teresa, then watch as she and my hand distort, as everything, absolutely everything, falls away.

* * * * *

It is night. It's always night. A night without stars, without anything—just an infinite emptiness falling away on every side. And so I float, an invisible being in a nonexistent world.

How long have I been like this? I don't know. It feels like years, but that's just a feeling because there is nothing here by which to mark the time.

I try to remember how it was, but my memories are such pale things, and they grow more pale as time drags on.

I would pray, but there is nothing to pray to. And so I hope, for hope is all I have: that one day, as inexplicably as once I did, I will begin to dream the world again.

Suggestions for Further Reading

Audi, Robert. *Belief, Justification, and Knowledge*. Belmont, CA: Wadsworth, 1988.

Chisholm, Roderick M. *Theory of Knowledge*. Englewood Cliffs, NJ: Prentice-Hall, 1988.

Goldman, Alan H. *Empirical Knowledge*. Berkeley, CA: University of California Press, 1988.

Harman, Gilbert. *Thought*. Princeton, NJ: Princeton University Press, 1973.

Lehrer, Keith. *Knowledge*. Oxford: Clarendon Press, 1974.

Moser, Paul K. *Knowledge and Evidence*. Cambridge: Cambridge University Press, 1989.

Moser, Paul K., and Arnold vander Nat. *Human Knowledge: Classical and Contemporary Approaches*. New York: Oxford University Press, 1995.

Quine, W. V., and J. S. Ullian. *The Web of Belief*. New York: Random House, 1970.

Roth, Michael D., and Leon Galis, eds. *Knowing: Essays in the Analysis of Knowledge*. Lanham, MD: University Press of America, 1984.

Russell, Bertrand. *The Problems of Philosophy*. New York: Oxford University Press, 1912.

Unger, Peter. *Ignorance*. Oxford: Clarendon Press, 1975.

Notes

Chapter 1

1. Werner Heisenberg, *Physics and Beyond* (New York: Harper & Row, 1972) 210.
2. Francis Crick, *The Astonishing Hypothesis* (New York: Simon & Schuster, 1994) 3.
3. B. F. Skinner, *Beyond Freedom and Dignity* (New York: Bantam, 1971) 3ff.
4. Richard Dawkins, *The Selfish Gene* (Oxford: Oxford University Press, 1976) IX.
5. James McConnell, "Criminals Can Be Brainwashed—Now," *Psychology Today* 3 (1970) 14.
6. John Roach, "Delphic Oracle's Lips May Have Been Loosened by Gas Vapors," National Geographic News," August 14, 2001, www.nationalgeographic .com/news/2001/08/0814_delphicoracle.html. Retrieved August 1, 2005.
7. Plato, "The Apology," *The Dialogues of Plato*, trans. Benjamin Jowett (Oxford: Oxford University Press, 1892) 110.
8. Diogenes Laertius, The Lives of the Philosophers, ed. and trans. A. Robert Camonigri (Chicago: Henry Regnery Company, 1969) 78.
9. Plato, "Euthyphro," 5d–8b, trans. Lane Cooper, *Plato: The Collected Dialogues* (Princeton: Princeton University Press, 1973) 173–176.
10. Plato 176.
11. Jerry Fodor, *The Language of Thought* (Cambridge: Harvard University Press, 1979) 6–7.
12. Aristotle, "Metaphysics," book 4, 1008b, *Aristotle*, trans. Richard McKeon (New York: Random House, 1941) 742.
13. Aristotle 1006a, 737.
14. Arthur Conan Doyle, *A Study in Scarlet* (New York: P. F. Collier and Son, 1906) 29–30.
15. Ludwig F. Schlecht, "Classifying Fallacies Logically," *Teaching Philosophy* 14, no. 1 (1991): 53–64.
16. Edmund Husserl, *Ideas*, trans. Boyce Gibson (London: Allen and Unwin, 1952) 201.
17. Mary Anne Warren, "On the Moral and Legal Status of Abortion," *The Monist* 57 (1973) 43–61.
18. Warren 54–56.
19. John Locke, *An Essay Concerning Human Understanding* (Oxford: Oxford University Press, 1991) 335.
20. Locke 333.
21. Richard Swinburne, *The Coherence of Theism* (Oxford: Clarendon Press, 1977) 99.
22. Warren 57.
23. Warren 56–57.
24. National Institute of Neurological Disorders and Stroke Coma and Persistent Vegetative State Information Page, www.inds.nih.gov/disorders/coma/coma .htm. Retrieved August 1, 2005.
25. Antoni Gomila, "What Is a Thought Experiment?" *Metaphilosophy* 22 (1991) 88.
26. Daniel Callahan, "Abortion Decisions: Personal Morality," *Biomedical Ethics*, ed. Thomas A. Mappes and Jane S. Zembaty (New York: McGraw-Hill, 1991) 446.
27. Callahan 446.
28. Traveling backward in time would be possible if we didn't change the past or if the universe split into parallel worlds each time we traveled backward in time. Martin Gardner explains: "The basic idea is as simple as it is fantastic. Persons can travel to any point in the future of their universe, with no complications, but the moment they enter the past, the universe splits into two parallel worlds, each with its own time track. Along one track rolls the world as if no looping had occurred. Along the other track spins the newly created universe, its history permanently altered." Martin Gardner, *Time Travel and Other Mathematical Bewilderments* (New York: Freeman, 1988) 7.
29. Michael Tooley, "Abortion and Infanticide," *Intervention and Reflection*, ed. R. Munson (Wadsworth, 1983) 72.
30. Judith Jarvis Thomson, "A Defense of Abortion," *Rights, Restitution, and Risk: Essays in Moral Theory*, ed. William Parent (Cambridge: Harvard University Press, 1986) 2–3.
31. Jesper Hogstrom, "Dark Suckers," *Project Galactic Guide* (10 May 1992) online, Internet.

Chapter 2

1. René Descartes, *Discourse on the Method of Properly Conducting the Reason*, Part V, *The Philosophical Works of Descartes*, trans. E. S. Haldane and G. R. T. Ross (Cambridge: Cambridge University Press, 1973) 116.
2. Arthur Harkins, quoted in *The Tomorrow Makers* by Grant Fjermedal (New York: Macmillan, 1986) 220.

3. James S. Albus, quoted in *The Tomorrow Makers* by Grant Fjermedal (New York: Macmillan, 1986) 194.

4. Albus 195.

5. Gottfried Wilhelm von Leibniz, *Monadology and Other Philosophical Essays*, trans. Paul Schrecker and Anne Martin Schrecker (Indianapolis: Bobbs-Merrill, 1965) 17.

6. Verner Vinge, "What Is the Singularity?" http://www .ugcs.caltech.edu/~phoenix/vinge/vinge-sing.html. Retrieved August 1, 2005.

7. Shankara, *Crest-Jewel of Discrimination* (Hollywood: Vedanta Press, 1975) 110.

8. René Descartes, *Meditations on First Philosophy*, Meditation II, *The Philosophical Works of Descartes*, 149.

9. Descartes, Meditation I 145.

10. Descartes, Meditation I 145–146.

11. Descartes, Meditation I 147.

12. René Descartes, *Discourse on the Method of Rightly Conducting the Reason*, pt. 4, *The Philosophical Works of Descartes*, 101.

13. Adrian Thatcher, "Christian Theism and the Concept of a Person," *Persons and Personality*, ed. A. Peacocke and G. Gillett (Oxford: Basil Blackwell, 1987) 183–184.

14. Descartes, *Discourse*, pt. 4, 101.

15. Robert M. Young, "Animal Soul," *Encyclopedia of Philosophy* (New York: Macmillan, 1967) 122.

16. C.D. Broad, "Human Personality and Its Survival of Bodily Death," *Lectures on Psychical Research* (London: Routledge & Kegan Paul, 1962) 409.

17. Descartes, *Meditations*, Meditation VI 196.

18. Roger Sperry, quoted in *The Mechanics of Mind* by Colin Blakemore (Cambridge: Cambridge University Press, 1978) 159.

19. Princess Elizabeth, Letters to Descartes, May 6, 1643, in René Descartes, *Philosophical Writings*, trans. Elizabeth Anscombe and Peter Geach (Indianapolis: Bobbs-Merril, 1971) 274–275.

20. Descartes, "Passions of the Soul," sec. 31, *The Philosophical Works of Descartes* 345–346.

21. Colin Blakemore, *Mechanics of Mind* (Cambridge: Cambridge University Press, 1977) 3–4.

22. T. H. Huxley, *Method and Results* (New York: Appleton-Century-Crofts, 1893) 244.

23. Descartes, Meditation II 155.

24. David Hume, *Enquiries Concerning the Human Understanding and Concerning the Principles of Morals*, ed. L. A. Selby-Bigge (Oxford: Clarendon Press, 1972) 22.

25. Hume 365.

26. David Hume, *A Treatise of Human Nature* (London: Oxford University Press, 1973) 232–233, 234.

27. Rudolph Carnap, "The Elimination of Metaphysics Through Logical Analysis of Language," *Logical Positivism*, ed. A. J. Ayer (Glencoe, IL: Free Press, 1959) 60–81.

28. B. F. Skinner, *Beyond Freedom and Dignity* (New York: Bantam, 1971) 22.

29. Skinner 12.

30. Gilbert Ryle, *The Concept of Mind* (New York: Barnes & Noble, 1949) 16.

31. Hilary Putnam, "Brains and Behavior," *Readings in the Philosophy of Psychology*, ed. Ned Block (Cambridge, MA: Harvard University Press, 1980) 29.

32. Morton Hunt, *The Universe Within* (New York: Simon & Schuster, 1982) 51.

33. Hunt 62.

34. Blakemore 3–4.

35. Berry Beyerstein, *The Hundredth Monkey and Other Paradigms of the Paranormal*, ed. Kendrick Frazier (Amherst, NY: Prometheus Books, 1991) 45.

36. Thomas Nagel, "What Is It Like to Be a Bat?" *Readings in the Philosophy of Psychology* 161–163.

37. Jaegwon Kim, "Physicalism and the Multiple Realizability of Mental States," *Readings in the Philosophy of Psychology* 235.

38. John Lorber, quoted in Roger Lewin, "Is Your Brain Really Necessary?" *Science* 210 (December 1980) 1232.

39. Lorber 1232–1233.

40. Lorber 1233.

41. David Lewis, "Mad Pain and Martian Pain," *Readings in the Philosophy of Psychology* 216–217.

42. Hilary Putnam, "Philosophy and Our Mental Life," *Readings in the Philosophy of Psychology* 135–136.

43. Erik Baard, "Cyborg Liberation Front: Inside the Movement for Posthuman Rights," *Village Voice*, July 30–August 5, 2003.

44. John Searle, *The Rediscovery of the Mind* (Cambridge, MA: MIT Press, 1992) 65–68.

45. Michele Nicolosi, "Researchers Brainchild: Microchip Implants Boosting Mental Function," *The Orange County Register* (20 April 1997) online, Internet.

46. Larry Hauser, "Revenge of the Zombies," selected papers by Larry Hauser, online, Internet, 24 April 2002.

47. Marvin Minsky, quoted in "Where Evolution Left Off," *Andover Bulletin* (Spring 1995) 9.

48. Gerald Jay Sussman, quoted in *The Tomorrow Makers* by Grant Fjermedal (New York: Macmillan, 1986) 8.

49. "A Physicist Proposes a Theory of Eternal Life That Yields God," *Omni* (October 1994) 96.

50. Lewis 216.

51. Ned Block, "Troubles with Functionalism," *Readings in the Philosophy of Psychology* 276, 278.

52. John Markoff, "The Soul of the Ultimate Machine," *New York Times*, December 10, 2000.

53. Hilary Putnam, *Reason, Truth and History* (Cambridge: Cambridge University Press, 1981) 80.

54. Wired News, 06:43 AM, Mar. 19, 2002 PT, http://www.wired.com/news/medtech/0,1286,51163,00.html.

55. *The Matrix*. 35 mm, 136 min. Groucho II Film Partnership, Silver Pictures, Village Roadshow Productions, 1999.

56. Paul Churchland, *Matter and Consciousness* (Cambridge, MA: MIT Press, 1990) 39–40.

57. A. M. Turing, "Computing Machinery and Intelligence," *Minds and Machines*, ed. Alan Ross Anderson (Englewood Cliffs, NJ: Prentice-Hall, 1964) 5.

58. Turing 13.

59. John R. Searle, "Is the Brain's Mind a Computer Program?" *Scientific American* 262 (Jan. 1990) 26.

60. Farhad Manjoo, "Think Fast, Clever Robot," *Wired News*, 02:00 AM Oct. 13, 2001 PT http://www.wired.com/news/technology/0,1282,47548,00.html.

61. John R. Searle, *Minds, Brains and Science* (Cambridge, MA: Harvard University Press, 1984) 34.

62. Searle, "Is the Brain's Mind . . . ?" 28.

63. John R. Searle, "Minds, Brains, and Programs," *Behavioral and Brain Sciences* 3 (1980) 417–424.

64. Lewis White Beck and Robert L. Holmes, *Philosophic Inquiry* (Englewood Cliffs, NJ: Prentice-Hall, 1968) 180.

65. Searle, "Is the Brain's Mind . . . ?" 35.

66. Block 282.

67. Richard Rorty, "Mind-Body Identity, Privacy, and Categories," *Review of Metaphysics* (1965–66) 28–29.

68. Rorty 30–31.

69. Churchland 45–46.

70. Searle, *The Rediscovery of the Mind* 47.

71. Frank Jackson, "Epiphenomenal Qualia," *Philosophical Quarterly* 32 (1982) 127.

72. David Lewis, "Knowing What It's Like," *The Nature of Mind*, ed. David M. Rosenthal (New York: Oxford University Press, 1991) 234.

73. Jojo Moyes, "Teenager Sees Color after Life in Black and White," *The Independent*, October 22, 1997.

74. David J. Chalmers, *The Conscious Mind* (Oxford: Oxford University Press, 1996) 94–95.

75. Nelson Goodman, *Languages of Art* (Indianapolis: Hackett, 1976) 50, 68, 70.

76. Dale Jacquette, *Philosophy of Mind* (Englewood Cliffs, NJ: Prentice-Hall, 1994) 102–103.

77. Hilary Putnam, *Representation and Reality* (Cambridge: MIT Press, 1988) 110.

78. Thomas Nagel, *The View From Nowhere* (Oxford: Oxford University Press, 1986) 53.

79. Janos Szentagothai, "The 'Brain-Mind' Relation: A Pseudoproblem?" *Mindwaves*, ed. Colin Blakemore and Susan Greenfield (Cambridge, MA: Basil Blackwell, 1987) 334.

80. Roger W. Sperry, "Changing Priorities," *Annual Review of Neuroscience* 4 (1981) 12.

81. W. V. Quine, *Pursuit of Truth* (Cambridge, MA: Harvard University Press, 1992) 14.

82. John Dupre, "The Solution to the Problem of the Freedom of the Will," *Philosophical Perspectives*, 10 (1995): 390.

83. B. J. Baars and K. McGovern, "Cognitive Views of Consciousness: What Are the Facts? How Can We Explain Them?" ed. M. Velmans, *The Science of Consciousness: Psychological, Neurophysiological, and Clinical Reviews* (London: Routledge, 1996) 75.

84. Jay Dixit, "New! Improved! And Still 100 Percent Fake," *Washington Post*, 19 May 2002: BO1.

85. Dixit.

86. Lewis Baxter et al., "Caudate Glucose Metabolic Rate Changes with Both Drug and Behavior Therapy for Obsessive-Compulsive Disorder," *Archives of General Psychiatry* 49 (Sept. 1992): 681–689.

87. A. R. Peacocke, *Theology for a Scientific Age: Being and Becoming—Natural and Divine* (Cambridge, MA: Basil Blackwell, 1990) 156, 158.

88. Roger W. Sperry, "A Modified Concept of Consciousness," *Psychological Review* 76 (1969) 534.

89. Duncan Graham-Rowe, "Steering at the Speed of Thought," *New Scientist* 179 (July 26, 2003): 14–15.

90. Jerry Fodor, "Making Mind Matter More," *Philosophical Topics* 17 (Spring 1989) 77.

Chapter 3

1. This example adapted from Daniel Kolak and Raymond Martin in *The Experience of Philosophy* (Belmont, CA: Wadsworth, 1993) 149.

2. William James, "The Dilemma of Determinism," *The Will to Believe and Other Essays in Popular Philosophy* (Cambridge, MA: Harvard University Press, 1979) 117–118.

3. Samuel Butler, *Erewhon* (New York: Lancer Books, 1968) 131–132.

4. Margot Slade, "The Devil Made Me Do It," *Morning Call* [Allentown, PA] (29 May 1994) A8.

5. Clarence Darrow, *Attorney for the Damned* (New York: Simon & Schuster, 1957) 64–65.

6. John Steinbeck, *The Grapes of Wrath* (New York: Viking Press, 1939) 32.

7. William James, "The Dilemma of Determinism," quoted in Martin Gardner, *The Whys of a Philosophical Scrivener* (New York: Quill, 1983) 104.

8. Pierre-Simon Laplace, *A Philosophical Essay on Probabilities,* trans. F. W. Truscott and F. L. Emory (New York: Dover, 1951) 4.

9. Baron d'Holbach, "Of the System of Man's Free Agency," *The System of Nature,* Chapter XI (1770), trans. H. D. Robinson. (Manchester: Clinamen Press Ltd., 2000).

10. Baruch Spinoza, Letter 58 (to G. H. Schuler) *The Ethics and Selected Letters,* ed. Seymour Feldman, trans. Samuel Shirley (Indianapolis: Hackett, 1982) 250.

11. Peter van Inwagen, *An Essay on Free Will* (Oxford: Clarendon Press, 1983) 16.

12. Boethius, *The Consolation of Philosophy,* book 5, trans. W. V. Cooper (London: J. M. Dent, 1902) 145, 147.

13. John Calvin, *Institutes of the Christian Religion,* trans. John Allen (Philadelphia: Presbyterian Board of Publication Book, 1813), book 3, chap. 21, sec. 5.

14. Somerset Maugham, in the play *Sheppey.*

15. Tom O' Connor, "Emerging Defenses to Crime," http://faculty.ncwc.edu/toconnor/405/405lect.02.htm.

16. B. F. Skinner, *Beyond Freedom and Dignity* (New York: Bantam, 1971) 18.

17. J. B. Watson, "What the Nursery Has to Say About Instincts," *Psychologies of 1925,* ed. C. Murchison (Worcester, MA: Clark University Press, 1926).

18. Morton Hunt, *The Universe Within* (New York: Simon & Schuster, 1982) 63.

19. Thomas J. Bouchard, Jr; David T. Lykken; Matthew McGue; Nancy Segal; Auke Tellegen, "Sources of Human Psychological Difference: The Minnesota Study of Twins Reared Apart," *Science* 250 (October 12, 1990) 223.

20. Paul Davies, "What Happened Before the Big Bang?" *God for the 21st Century,* ed. Russell Stannard (Philadelphia: Templeton Foundation Press, 2000) 15.

21. Martin Gardner, *The Whys of a Philosophical Scrivener* (New York: Quill, 1983) 109.

22. John H. Hick, *Death and Eternal Life* (San Francisco: Harper & Row, 1976) 119.

23. Patricia Smith Churchland, "Is Determinism Self-refuting?" *Mind* 40 (1981) 100–101.

24. Max Born, quoted in Arthur Eddington, *New Pathways in Science* (New York: Macmillan, 1935) 82.

25. Born quoted in Eddington 87.

26. James 118.

27. Richard Taylor, *Metaphysics* (Englewood Cliffs, NJ: Prentice-Hall, 1974) 51–52.

28. James, quoted in Gardner 104.

29. A. J. Ayer, "Freedom and Necessity," *Philosophical Essays* (London: Macmillan & Co., Ltd., 1954) 271.

30. Peter van Inwagen, *Metaphysics* (Boulder, CO: Westview, 2002) 202ff.

31. Thomas Hobbes, *The Questions Concerning Liberty, Necessity, and Chance,* 1656 (vol. V of collected works).

32. Hobbes.

33. John Locke, *An Essay Concerning Human Understanding,* book 2, chap. 21, sec. 9 (Oxford: Clarendon Press, 1991) 238.

34. Walter T. Stace, *Religion and the Modern Mind* (Philadelphia: Lippincott, 1952) 254–255.

35. Richard Taylor, *Metaphysics,* 2nd ed. (Englewood Cliffs, NJ: Prentice-Hall, 1974) 49–50.

36. Samuel Chavkin, *The Mind Stealers* (Boston: Houghton Mifflin, 1978) 146–148.

37. Taylor 50–51.

38. Harry G. Frankfurt, "Alternate Possibilities and Moral Responsibility," *Journal of Philosophy* 66 (Dec. 1969) 828–839.

39. Harry G. Frankfurt, "Freedom of the Will and the Concept of a Person," *Journal of Philosophy* 68 (Jan. 1971) 12.

40. Frankfurt, "Freedom of the Will" 19.

41. Michael Slote, "Understanding Free Will," *Journal of Philosophy* 77 (March 1980) 149.

42. Robert Kane, *The Significance of Free Will* (New York: Oxford University Press, 1996) 35.

43. Daniel Dennett, "I Could Not Have Done Otherwise: So What?" *Journal of Philosophy* 81 (October 1984) 553.

44. James, quoted in Gardner 104.

45. Psychologist David Rumelhart of the University of California at San Diego says of the figure, "I can make it do what I want it to do. That's a trivial example of willing to do one thing rather than another, but the phenomenon itself is anything but trivial. And it's one of the essential human experiences that I can't see any way to simulate on a machine." Quoted in Morton Hunt, *The Universe Within* (New York: Simon & Schuster, 1982) 357.

46. Carl Ginet, *On Action* (Cambridge: Cambridge University Press, 1990) 90.

47. Benjamin Libet, "Do We Have Free Will?" *Journal of Consciousness Studies* 6, no. 8–9 (1999): 51.

48. Vilaynur Ramachandran, quoted in Bob Holmes, "Irresistible Illusions," *New Scientist* 159 (1998): 35.

49. Anthony Jack and Phillip Robbins, "The Illusory Triumph of Machine over Mind," *Behavioral and Brain Sciences* 27 (2004): 17.

50. Thomas Reid, *Essays on the Active Powers of the Human Mind,* in *The Works of Thomas Reid,* 8th edition, ed. Sir William Hamilton (Hildesheim, Zurich, New York: Olms Verlag, 1983) 599.

51. Roderick Chisolm, "Human Freedom and the Self," *Free Will,* ed. G. Watson (New York: Oxford University Press) 24–35.

52. Daniel Dennett, *Freedom Evolves* (New York: Viking, 2003) 100.

53. Roderick Chisholm, "Agents, Causes, and Events: The Problem of Free Will," *Agents, Causes, and Events,* ed. Timothy O' Connor (New York: Oxford University Press, 1995) 95.

54. Timothy O'Connor, "Agent Causation," *Agents, Causes and Events,* ed. Timothy O'Connor (New York: Oxford University Press, 1995) 173–200.

55. Jean-Paul Sartre, *Being and Nothingness,* trans. Hazel E. Barnes (New York: Philosophical Library, 1956) 439–441.

56. Raymond Smullyan, "Is God a Taoist?" *The Tao Is Silent* (New York: Harper & Row, 1977) 107–108.

57. Galen Strawson, "Libertarianism, Action, and Self-Determination," *Agents, Causes and Events,* ed. Timothy O'Connor (New York: Oxford University Press, 1995) 16.

58. Robert Nozick, "Choice and Determinism," *Agents, Causes and Events,* ed. Timothy O'Connor (New York: Oxford University Press, 1995) 101–114.

59. Nozick 105.

60. Mark Balaguer, "A Coherent, Naturalistic, and Plausible Formulation of Libertarian Free Will," *Nous* 38 (Sept. 2004): 382.

61. Balaguer 387.

Chapter 4

1. The Bible, Revised Standard Version (RSV), 1 Cor. 15:36–44.

2. Laura McCallum, "Olson Admits She's Soliah," Minnesota Public Radio, July 9, 1999, http://news .minnesota,publicradio.org/features/199907/ 09_mccalluml_soliah.

3. John Locke, *An Essay Concerning Human Understanding,* book 2, chap. 27, sec. 5.

4. Locke, sec. 3.

5. Locke, sec. 5.

6. Locke, sec. 9.

7. Locke, sec. 14.

8. Eric T. Olson, *The Human Animal* (New York: Oxford University Press, 1997) 7–8, 9.

9. Olson, 17.

10. Bertrand Russell, "An Outline of Intellectual Rubbish," *Unpopular Essays* (New York: Simon & Schuster, 1950) 77–78.

11. "Luz-ers Are Winners," *Ask the Rabbi,* online, Internet, 24 April 2002.

12. Daniel Wikler, "Not Dead, Not Dying? Ethical Categories and Persistent Vegetative State," *Hastings Center Report* 18 (February/March 1988): 45.

13. "Raelian Leader: Cloning First Step to Immortality," CNN.com, December 29, 2002, http://archives.cnn .com/2002/HEALTH/12/28/human.cloning/index .html.

14. Locke, sec. 15.

15. Olson, 9–10.

16. Peter Unger, "The Survival of the Sentient," *Action and Freedom: Philosophical Perspectives* 14, ed. J. Tomberlin, (Malden, MA: Blackwell, 2000) 331.

17. David Hume, *A Treatise of Human Nature* (Oxford: Clarendon Press, 1973) 633–634.

18. G. W. von Leibniz, "Discourse on Metaphysics," *Leibniz Selections,* ed. Philip P. Wiener (New York: Charles Scribner's Sons, 1951) 340.

19. Locke, sec. 14.

20. Locke, book 2, chap. 27, sec. 13.

21. Immanuel Kant, *Critique of Pure Reason,* trans. Norman Kemp Smith (New York: St. Martin's Press, 1965), note to A363, 342.

22. The Bible, RSV, Matt. 26:26–28.

23. Kenneth Ring, *Life at Death* (New York: Coward, McCann & Geoghegan, 1980) 32.

24. Susan Blackmore, *Dying to Live* (Buffalo: Prometheus Books, 1993) 165–182.

25. John Hick, *Death and Eternal Life* (San Francisco: Harper & Row, 1976) 40–41.

26. Gardner 298.

27. Kai Nielsen, "The Faces of Immortality," *Death and Afterlife,* ed. Stephen T. Davis (New York: St. Martin's Press, 1989) 1–29.

28. Locke, book 2, chap. 27, sec. 19. By "consciousness" Locke means "self-consciousness," that is, knowledge of our thoughts and actions, both past and present. Because memory is the faculty that gives us knowledge of our past thoughts and actions, it is memory that gives us our sense of self.

29. "Victim Has Multiple Personalities," *Morning Call* [Allentown, PA] (17 Aug. 1990) A3.

30. Ellen Hale, "Inside the Divided Mind," *New York Times Magazine* (17 April 1983) 100–106.

31. Locke, sec. 22.

32. Thomas Reid, "Of Identity," in *Personal Identity,* ed. John Perry (Berkeley: University of California Press, 1975) 114–115.

33. Bishop Butler, "Of Personal Identity," in *Personal Identity,* ed. John Perry (Berkeley: University of California Press, 1975) 100.

34. Derek Parfit, *Reasons and Persons* (Oxford: Clarendon Press, 1984) 220.

35. Robert Uhlig, "Soul Catcher," *Electronic Telegraph* 430 (18 July 1996) online, Internet.

36. Hans Moravec, *Mind Children* (Cambridge: Harvard University Press, 1990) 115–116.

37. Moravec 116.

38. Bernard Williams, "Personal Identity and Individuation," *Problems of the Self* (Cambridge: Cambridge University Press, 1973) 6–8.

39. Williams 8.

40. Nicholas P. Spanos, "Past-Life Hypnotic Regression: A Critical View," *The Skeptical Inquirer* 12 (Winter 1987–88) 174–180.

41. *Star Trek: Next Generation Technical Manual* (New York: Pocket Books, 1991) 102ff.

42. "Quantum Teleportation," *IBM Research,* online, Internet, 24 April 2002.

43. Parfit, 200–201.

44. Sidney Shoemaker, *Self-Knowledge and Self-Identity* (Ithaca, NY: Cornell University Press, 1963) 23–24.

45. Lou Jacobson, "A Mind Is a Terrible Thing to Waste," *Lingua Franca* 7 (August 1997) 6.

46. R. W. Sperry, quoted in *Brain and Conscious Experience,* ed. J. C. Eccles (New York: Springer, 1966) 304.

47. Parfit 254.

48. Shoemaker 279.

49. I. Biran and A. Chaterjee, "Alien Hand Syndrome," *Archives of Neurology* 61 (February 2004): 292.

50. Robert Nozick, *Philosophical Explanations* (Cambridge, MA: Harvard University Press, 1981) 27–114.

51. Parfit 326.

52. Parfit 326.

53. Walpola Rahula, *What the Buddha Taught* (New York: Grove Weidenfeld, 1974) 51.

54. Rahula 42.

55. Immanuel Kant, *Prolegomena to Any Future Metaphysics,* trans. Lewis White Beck (New York: Bobbs-Merrill, 1950).

56. Ilya Prigogine, *From Being to Becoming* (New York: Freeman, 1980).

57. Marya Schechtman, *The Constitution of Selves* (Ithaca, NY: Cornell University Press, 1996) 94.

58. Owen Flanagan, *Varieties of Moral Personality* (Cambridge, MA: Harvard University Press, 1996) 67.

59. Daniel Dennett, "The Self as a Center of Narrative Gravity," *Self and Consciousness: Multiple Perspectives,* eds. F. Kessel, P. Cole, and D. Johnson (Hillsdale, NJ: Erlbaum, 1992) 103–115.

60. Elyn Saks, *Jekyll on Trial: Multiple Personality Disorder and Criminal Law* (New York: New York University Press, 1997) 99.

Chapter 5

1. Paige Mitchell, *Act of Love: The Killing of George Zygmanik* (New York: Knopf, 1976) 18.

2. Mitchell 8.

3. William Fleming, *Arts and Ideas* (New York: Holt, Rinehart & Winston, 1986) 451.

4. David Barash, *The Whisperings Within* (New York: Penguin, 1979) 11.

5. A. J. Ayer, *Language, Truth, and Logic* (London: Penguin, 1971) 107.

6. Brand Blanshard, "The New Subjectivism in Ethics," *A Modern Introduction to Philosophy,* ed. Paul Edwards and Arthur Pup (New York: Free Press, 1973) 339.

7. Ellen Goodman, *Morning Call* [Allentown, PA] 15 (June 1993) A11.

8. Ruth Benedict, *Patterns of Culture* (New York: Pelican, 1934) 257.

9. Solomon Asch, *Social Psychology* (Englewood Cliffs, NJ: Prentice-Hall, 1952) 378–379.

10. Orna Feldman, "Thou Shalt Not Raise Self-Indulgent Children," *Brown Alumni Monthly* (October 1994) 20.

11. Quoted in David Crary of the Associated Press, "Woman Jailed for Daughter's Circumcision," *Morning Call* [Allentown, PA] (9 January 1993) A32.

12. G. W. von Leibniz, "Discourse on Metaphysics," *Leibniz Selections,* ed. Philip P. Wiener (New York: Charles Scribner's Sons, 1951) 292.

13. St. Thomas Aquinas, *Summa Theologica,* pt. 1, ques. 25, article 3 (London: Burns, Oates, and Washbourne, 1920).

14. Albert Pike, *Morals and Dogma* (Charleston, 1871) 722.

15. John Hick, *Death and Eternal Life* (San Francisco: Harper & Row, 1976) 200–201.

16. Renford Bambrough, *Moral Skepticism and Moral Knowledge* (Atlantic Highlands, NJ: Humanities Press, Inc., 1979) 15.

17. Richard A. McCormick, "To Save or Let Die: The Dilemma of Modern Medicine," *Journal of the American Medical Association* 229 (July 8, 1974) 174.

18. McCormick, 175.

19. Joel Feinberg, "Psychological Egoism," *Moral Philosophy,* ed. George Sher (San Diego: Harcourt Brace Jovanovich, 1987) 11–12.

20. Joseph Butler, "Sermons," *Ethical Theories,* ed. A. I. Meldon (Englewood Cliffs, NJ: Prentice-Hall, 1967) 239.

21. Ayn Rand, "The Virtue of Selfishness," *The Virtue of Selfishness: A New Concept of Egoism* (New York: Signet Books, 1964) 27.

22. Rand 31.

23. John Stuart Mill, *Utilitarianism* (Indianapolis: Bobbs-Merrill, 1957) 408.

24. Mill 409.

25. H. J. McCloskey, "A Non-Utilitarian Approach to Punishment," *Inquiry* 8 (1965) 239–255.

26. Richard B. Brandt, *Ethical Theory* (Englewood Cliffs, NJ: Prentice-Hall, 1959) 387.

27. W. D. Ross, *The Right and the Good* (Oxford: Clarendon Press, 1930) 34–35.

28. William Godwin, *Enquiry Concerning Political Justice and Its Influence on Morals and Happiness,* ed. F. E. L. Priestley (Toronto: University of Toronto Press, 1946) 126–127.

29. A. C. Ewing, *Ethics* (New York: Free Press, 1953) 46.

30. Neale Duckworth, "Living and Dying with Peter Singer," *Psychology Today,* 32 (January 1999): 56.

31. Ewing 151

32. It's the automobile. Approximately 50,000 people die in traffic accidents every year.

33. Mill 22.

34. Robert Nozick, *Anarchy, State, and Utopia* (New York: Basic Books, 1974) 42–43.

35. Bernard Williams, "A Critique of Utilitarianism," *Right and Wrong,* ed. Christina Hoff-Sommers (New York: Harcourt Brace Jovanovich, 1986) 95.

36. Judith Jarvis Thomson, "The Trolley Problem," *Rights, Restitution, and Risk,* ed. William Parent (Cambridge: Harvard University Press, 1986) 94.

37. Thomson 95.

38. Immanuel Kant, *Groundwork of the Metaphysics of Morals,* trans. H. J. Paton (New York: Harper & Row, 1964) 61.

39. Kant, *Groundwork* 88.

40. Immanuel Kant, *The Metaphysical Elements of Justice,* trans. John Ladd (Indianapolis: Bobbs-Merrill, 1965) 99–107.

41. Kant, *Metaphysical Elements* 107

42. R. M. Hare, *Freedom and Reason* (London: Oxford University Press, 1970) 160–161.

43. W. D. Ross, *The Right and the Good* (Oxford: Clarendon Press, 1967) 17–18.

44. Kant, *Groundwork* 96.

45. Immanuel Kant, *Lectures on Ethics,* trans. Louis Infield (New York: Harper & Row, 1963) 239–240.

46. Jeremy Bentham, *Principles of Morals and Legislation* (New York: Hafner, 1948) 311.

47. C. D. Broad, *Five Types of Ethical Theory* (London: Routledge and Kegan Paul, 1956) 132.

48. John B. Judis, "Kant and Mill in Baghdad," *The American Prospect* 14 (2003): 12.

49. Ewing, 58.

50. Ross 19.

51. Ross 28.

52. Ross 31.

53. John Rawls, *A Theory of Justice* (Cambridge, MA: Harvard University Press, 1971) 11.

54. Rawls 43.

55. Rawls 4.

56. Rawls 252.

57. Nozick 160–161.

58. Karl Marx, *Critique of the Gotha Program* (London: Lawrence and Wishart, 1938) 14, 107.

59. David Morris, "Dutch Tolerance," *Building Economic Alternatives* (Spring 1990).

60. Morris.

61. Nozick 160.

62. Nozick 11.

63. Nozick 110.

64. Lawrence Kohlberg, "The Development of Children's Orientations Toward a Moral Order," *Vita Humana* 6 (1963): 19.

65. L. J. Walker, "Sex Differences in the Development of Moral Reasoning: A Critical Review," *Child Development* 53 (1984): 1330–1336. See also Theo Linda Dawson, "New Tools, New Insights: Kohlberg's Moral Judgment Stages Revisited," *International Journal of Behavioral Development* 26 (2002): 154–166.

66. This sentiment is expressed by many authors in *Individual and Communitarianism,* ed. Shlomo Avineri and Avner de-Shalit (Oxford: Oxford University Press, 1992).

67. William Styron, *Sophie's Choice* (New York: Random House, 1994) 562.

68. "Tsunami Mother's Terrible Choice," BBC News, December 31, 2004, http://news.bbc.co.uk/2/hi/asia-pacific/4137053.stm.

69. Hilary Putnam, *Realism with a Human Face* (Cambridge, MA: Harvard University Press, 1990) 138.

70. Michael Stocker, "The Schizophrenia of Modern Moral Theories," *Journal of Philosophy* 73.14 (1976) 462.

71. Stocker 462.

72. Arthur Murphy, *Theory of Practical Reason* (LaSalle, IL: Open Court, 1965) 126.

73. Tom Keogh, "Children without a Conscience," *New Age Journal* (Jan.–Feb. 1993) 53–54.

74. Kurt Baier, *The Moral Point of View* (New York: Random House, 1965), quoted in *Making Ethical Decisions,* ed. Norman Bowie (New York: McGraw-Hill, 1985) 26.

75. Aristotle, quoted in *The Philosophy of Aristotle*, ed. Renford Bambrough, trans. J. L. Creed and A. E. Wadman (New York: New American Library, 1963) 303.
76. Alasdair MacIntyre, *After Virtue* (Notre Dame, IN: University of Notre Dame Press, 1984) 219.
77. MacIntyre 205.
78. The Buddha, quoted in Walpola Rahula, *What the Buddha Taught* (New York: Grove Press, 1974) 92–93.
79. MacIntyre 223.
80. Michael Slote, *From Morality to Virtue* (Oxford: Oxford University Press, 1992).
81. *The Republic of Plato*, trans. F. M. Cornford (Oxford: Oxford University Press, 1941) 45.

Chapter 6
1. Haim Watzman, "Archaeology vs. the Bible," *The Chronicle of Higher Education* (21 January 2000) A19.
2. Herman Bavinck, *The Doctrine of God*, trans. William Hendricksen (Grand Rapids, MI: Eerdmans, 1951) 78–79.
3. St. Thomas Aquinas, *Summa Theologica* (London: Burns, Oates, and Washbourne, 1920) 25.
4. Lucretius, *On the Nature of Things*, trans. William Ellery Leonard, Internet Classes Archive, online, Internet, 24 April 2002.
5. David Hume, *Dialogues Concerning Natural Religion*, ed. Norman Kemp Smith (Indianapolis: Bobbs-Merrill, 1947) 180.
6. Hugh Ross, *The Creator and the Cosmos* (Colorado Springs: Navpress, 1995) 14.
7. Edward Tryon, "Is the Universe a Vacuum Fluctuation?" *Nature* 246 (1973) 396–397.
8. Tryon 397.
9. Paul Davies, *God and the New Physics* (New York: Simon & Schuster, 1983) 31–32.
10. Lee Smolin, *The Life of the Cosmos* (New York: Oxford University Press, 1997) 87–88.
11. Hume, *Dialogues* 143.
12. William Paley, *Natural Theology* (Whitefish, MT: Kessinger Publishing, 2003).
13. John Stuart Mill, "Three Essays on Religion," *Essays on Ethics, Religion and Society*, ed. J. M. Robson (Toronto: University of Toronto Press, 1969) 451.
14. Clarence Darrow, *The Story of My Life* (New York: Charles Scribner's Sons, 1932).
15. Hume, *Dialogues* 170–171.
16. G. S. Kirk, J. E. Raven, and M. Schofield, *The Presocratic Philosophers* (Cambridge: Cambridge University Press, 1983) 304.

17. Aristotle, *The Presocratic Philosophers* 304.
18. Richard Dawkins, *The Blind Watchmaker* (New York: Norton, 1987) 89.
19. Dawkins 90.
20. Michael J. Behe, *Darwin's Black Box: The Biochemical Challenge to Evolution* (New York: The Free Press, 1996) 39.
21. H. Allen Orr, "Darwin vs. Intelligent Design (Again)," *Boston Review* (Dec.–Jan. 1996–1997) online, Internet.
22. Niall Shanks and Karl H. Joplin, "Redundant Complexity: A Critical Analysis of Intelligent Design in Biochemistry," *Philosophy of Science* 66 (June 1999): 275.
23. Kathleen Hunt, "Transitional Vertebrate Fossils FAQ," *The Talk. Origins Archive*, online, Internet, 24 April 2002.
24. Stephen J. Gould, "Hooking Leviathan by Its Past," *Natural History*, May 1994: 8–15.
25. Joseph Boxhorn, "Observed Instances of Speciation," *The Talk. Origins Archive*, online, Internet, 24 April 2002.
26. http://www.rael.org/English/index.html.
27. Paul Davies, "The Anthropic Principle," *Science Digest* 191.10 (1983) 24.
29. Stephen Hawking, *A Brief History of Time* (New York: Bantam, 1988) 174.
25. Smolin 101–102.
30. Isaac Asimov and Duane Gish, "The Genesis War," *Science Digest* (Oct. 1981) 87.
31. Duane Gish, *Evolution—The Fossils Say No!* 40, quoted in Jeffrie G. Murphy, *Evolution, Morality and the Meaning of Life* (Totowa, NJ: Rowman and Littlefield, 1987) 136.
32. Plato, "Cratylus," trans. Benjamin Jowett, *Plato: The Collected Dialogues*, eds. Edith Hamilton and Huntington Cairns (Princeton, NJ: Princeton University Press, 1961) 426a (p. 460).
33. Bertrand Russell, "Cosmic Purpose," *Religion and Science* (New York: Henry Holt and Company, 1935) 233.
34. S. Jay Olshansky, Bruce A. Carnes, and Robert N. Butler, "If Humans Were Built to Last," *Scientific American* 284 (March 2001) 50–55.
35. Doron Nof and Nathan Paldor, "Are There Oceanographic Explanations for the Israelites' Crossing of the Red Sea?" *Bulletin of the American Meteorological Society* 73 (March 1992) 305.
36. Hume, *Dialogues* 116.
37. Hume, *Dialogues* 114–115.
38. David Hume, *Enquiries Concerning the Human Understanding*, ed. L. A. Selby-Bigge (Oxford: Clarendon

Press, 1902) *Christian Classics Ethereal Library*, online, Internet, 24 April 2002.

39. St. Augustine, *City of God*, trans. Phillip Schaff (New York: Christian Literature Publishing Co., 1890) Book XXI, Chapter 8 (p. 655).

40. Thomas Jefferson, quoted in Saul-Paul Sirag, "The Skeptics," *Future Science*, ed. John White and Stanley Krippner (Garden City, NJ: Doubleday, 1977) 535.

41. Nicholas Humphrey, *Leaps of Faith* (New York: Copernicus, 1996) 96–97.

42. Robby Berry, "The Fivefold Challenge," *Skeptical Review* 6.4 (1995) online, Internet, 24 April 2002.

43. Cited in Paul Kurtz, *The Transcendental Temptation* (Buffalo: Prometheus Books, 1991) 96.

44. Bertrand Russell, *Mysticism*. Quoted in Walter Kaufmann, *Critique of Philosophy and Religion* (Garden City, NY: Doubleday, 1961) 315.

45. Jack Hitt, *Wired* 7.11 (Nov. 1999) online, Internet.

46. A. Mandell, "Toward a Psychobiology of Transcendence: God in the Brain," *Psychobiology of Consciousness*, ed. J. Davidson and R. Davidson (New York: Plenum Press, 1980) 379–464.

47. R. E. L. Masters and Jean Houston, *The Varieties of Psychedelic Experience* (New York: Holt, Rinehart & Winston) 254.

48. C. D. Broad, *Religion, Philosophy, and Psychical Research* (New York: Harcourt, Brace, 1953) 198.

49. John Hick, *Death and Eternal Life* (San Francisco: Harper & Row, 1976) 324.

50. St. Anselm, "Prologium," *St. Anselm* (La Salle, IL: Open Court, 1958) 8.

51. Gaunilo, *The Many-Faced Argument*, ed. John Hick and Arthur Gill (New York: Macmillan, 1968).

52. René Descartes, Meditation V, *The Philosophical Works of Descartes*, trans. E. S. Haldane and G. R. T. Ross (Cambridge: Cambridge University Press, 1911) 182.

53. Paul Edwards, "The Existence of God," *A Modern Introduction to Philosophy* (New York: Free Press, 1973) 375.

54. Blaise Pascal, *Pensées* (1670) *Classical Library*, online, Internet, 24 April 2002.

55. Galen Strawson, quoted in the *Independent* (London: 24 June 1990).

56. Herb Silverman, "Silverman's Wager," *Free Inquiry* (Spring 2001) 17.

57. André Breton, *Surrealism and Painting* (New York: Harper & Row, 1972).

58. Robert C. Coburn, *The Strangeness of the Ordinary* (Savage, MD: Rowman and Littlefield, 1990) 137.

59. William Rowe, "The Problem of Evil and Some Varieties of Atheism," *American Philosophical Quarterly* 16 (Oct. 1979) 337.

60. Fyodor Dostoyevsky, *The Brothers Karamazov*, trans. Constance Garnett (New York: Random House, 1950) 287.

61 Mark Twain, *Letters from the Earth*, ed. Bernard DeVoto (Greenwich, CT: Fawcett, 1962) 24–25.

62. Alvin Plantinga, *The Nature of Necessity* (Oxford: Clarendon Press, 1974) 186.

63. John Stuart Mill, "Three Essays on Religion," *Essays on Ethics, Religion and Society*, ed. J. M. Robson (Toronto: Routledge and Kegan Paul, 1969) 385.

64. James A. Haught, "Why Would God Drown Children?" *Free Inquiry* 25 (April/May 2005): 14.

65. David A. Lieb, "Arkansas Governor Wants God Held Harmless," Associated Press, *The Morning Call*, 22 March, 1997: A13.

66. John Hick, *Death and Eternal Life* (San Francisco: Harper & Row, 1976) 158.

67. Hick 158–159.

68. Fyodor Dostoyevsky, *The Brothers Karamazov*, pt. 2, book 5, chap. 4, trans. Constance Garnett (New York: Modern Library, 1950) 289.

69. Hick 159.

70. Somerset Maugham, *A Writer's Notebook* (New York: Penguin, 1967) 147.

71. Hick 156.

72. Hick 300–301.

73. R. K. Tripathi, quoted in Hick 301.

74. Charles Fried, *Medical Experimentation: Personal Integrity and Social Policy* (New York: American Elsevier Publishing Co., 1974) 101.

75. Harold S. Kushner, *When Bad Things Happen to Good People* (New York: Avon, 1981) 129.

76. Kushner 134.

77. John Baillie, *And the Life Everlasting*, quoted in Castell and Borchert, *An Introduction to Modern Philosophy* (New York: Macmillan, 1983) 164.

78. Theodore Drange, *Nonbelief and Evil: Two Arguments for the Nonexistence of God* (Amherst, NY: Prometheus Books, 1998).

79. Thomas Paine, *The Age of Reason* (New Jersey: Citadel Press, 1974) 60.

80. Lanning, quoted in Carl Sagan, *The Demon Haunted World* (New York: Random House, 1995) 159–160.

81. Antony Flew, "Theology and Falsification," *Philosophical Essays*, ed. John Shosky (Lanham, MD: Rowman and Littlefield, 1998).

82. *American Heritage Dictionary of the English Language* (Boston: Houghton Mifflin, 1970) 471.

83. Søren Kierkegaard, *Concluding Unscientific Postscript,* trans. David F. Swenson (Princeton, NJ: Princeton University Press, 1941) 513.

84. Tertullian, *De Carne Christi,* trans. Peter Holmes, *Ante-Nicene Christian Library,* Vol. XV (Edinburgh: T&T Clark, 1870) Chapter 5 Verse 4.

85. Kierkegaard 189.

86. Kierkegaard 189.

87. Bertrand Russell, *Let the People Think* (London: William Clowes and Sons, 1941) 2.

88. Kierkegaard 182.

89. Søren Kierkegaard, *The Journals of Søren Kierkegaard,* trans. Alexander Dru (London: Oxford University Press, 1938) 355, entry 1021.

90. Kierkegaard, *Concluding* 181.

91. Kierkegaard, *Concluding* 181.

92. Bertrand Russell, "Will Religious Faith Cure Our Troubles?" *Human Society in Ethics and Politics* (New York: Simon & Schuster, 1955) 207.

93. W. K. Clifford, "The Ethics of Belief," *Philosophy and Contemporary Issues,* ed. J. Burr and M. Goldinger (New York: Macmillan, 1984) 142.

94. T. H. Huxley, *Science and Christian Tradition* (London: Macmillan, 1894) 310.

95. W. K. Clifford, *Lectures and Essays: Volume II, Essays and Reviews* (London: Macmillan, 1879) 163.

96. Clifford.

97. Clifford, "The Ethics of Belief," 142.

98. Brand Blanshard, *Reason and Belief* (New Haven, CT: Yale University Press, 1975) 401.

99. Blanshard, 408–409.

100. Blanshard, 409.

101. William James, "The Will to Believe," *Philosophy and Contemporary Issues,* ed. J. Burr and M. Goldinger (New York: Macmillan, 1984) 146–147.

102. James, 20.

103. James, 29–30.

104. James, 31.

105. Ludwig F. Schlecht, "Re-Reading 'The Will to Believe'," *Religious Studies* 33: 217–225.

106. Robert Nozick, *Philosophical Explanations* (Cambridge, MA: Harvard University Press, 1981) 586.

107. Nozick 586.

108. George Berkeley, *Three Dialogues Between Hylas and Philonous, Harvard Classics,* Vol. 37 (New York: P.F. Collier and Son, 1909–1914), Part III.

109. Jean-Paul Sartre, "Existentialism and Humanism," *The Humanities in Contemporary Life* (New York: Holt, Rinehart, and Winston, 1960) 425.

110. Hazel Barnes, "The Far Side of Despair," from *The Meaning of Life,* eds. Steven Sanders and David R. Cheney (Englewood Cliffs, NJ: Prentice Hall, 1980) 107.

111. Kurt Baier, "The Meaning of Life," from *The Meaning of Life,* eds. Steven Sanders and David R. Cheney (Englewood Cliffs, NJ: Prentice Hall, 1980) 52.

112. Coburn 128–130.

113. Teale, quoted in Carl Sagan, *The Demon Haunted World* (New York: Random House, 1995) 12.

Chapter 7

1. Bertrand Russell, *The Problems of Philosophy* (New York: Henry Holt & Co., 1912) 73.

2. Plato, "Meno," 98b, trans. W. K. C. Guthrie, *The Collected Works of Plato,* ed. Edith Hailton and Huntington Cairns (Princeton, NJ: Princeton University Press, 1961) 382.

3. Plato, "Meno," 98a 381.

4. Aristotle, "Metaphysics," 1011^b 25–28, trans. Richard McKeon, *The Basic Works of Aristotle* (New York: Random House, 1941) 749.

5. Brand Blanshard, *The Nature of Thought,* vol. 2 (New York: Allen and Unwin, 1955) 264.

6. Charles Sanders Pierce, "How to Make Our Ideas Clear," *Popular Science Monthly* 12 (January 1878) 286–302.

7. William James, *Essays in Pragmatism* (New York: Hafner, 1948) 170.

8. Plato, "Theatetus," in *Plato: The Collected Dialogues,* eds. Edith Hamilton and Huntington Cairns, trans. F. M. Cornford (Princeton, NJ: Princeton University Press, 1961) 152a (p. 856).

9. Plato, "Theatetus," 171a, trans. F. M. Conford, *The Collected Works of Plato* (Princeton, NJ: Princeton University Press, 1973) 876.

10. W. V. O. Quine, "On Empirically Equivalent Systems of the World," *Erkenntnis* 9 (1975) 327–328.

11. J. L. Austin, "Unfair to Facts," *Philosophical Papers,* ed. J. O. Urmson and W. O. Warnock (Oxford: Oxford University Press, 1979) 165.

12. Heraclitus, *Herekleitos and Diogenes,* trans. Guy Davenport (Grey Fox Press, San Francisco: 1979) 15.

13. Hereclitus 14.

14. The Buddha, quoted in Walpola Rahula, *What the Buddha Taught* (New York: Grove Press, 1974) 25–26.

15. *The Philosophers of Ancient Greece,* (Albany: State University of New York Press, 1981) 60–61.

16. Aristotle *Physics* 187a 2–3.

17. Gregory Vlastos, "Zeno of Elea," *The Encyclopedia of Philosophy,* vol. 8 (New York: Macmillan, 1967) 378.

18. Russell Ruthen, "Catching the Wave," *Scientific American* 266 (March 1992) 90.

19. Plato, *The Republic*, 514a–520a, trans. Benjamin Jowett (New York: The Colonial Press, 1901).

20. Nick Bostrom, "The Stimulation Argument: Why the Probability That You Are Living in a Matrix is Quite High," *London Times Higher Education Suppplement* 16 May, 2003, http://www.simulation-argument .com/matrix.html.

21. Plato, "Phaedo," *The Dialogues of Plato*, trans. Benjamin Jowett (New York: Random House, 1937) 100e (p. 484).

22. René Descartes, *Meditations on First Philosophy*, Meditation I, *The Philosophical Works of Descartes*, ed. E. S. Haldane and G. R. T. Ross (Cambridge: Cambridge University Press, 1973) 145.

23. Descartes 145–146.

24. Descartes 147.

25. Peter Unger, *Ignorance* (Oxford: Oxford University Press, 1975) 7–8.

26. Descartes 150.

27. Descartes 178.

28. Descartes 175–176.

29. James Van Cleve, "Foundationalism, Epistemic Principles, and the Cartesian Circle," *The Philosophical Review* 88 (1979) 55–91.

30. David Hume, *Enquiries Concerning the Human Understanding and Concerning of the Principles of Morals*, sec. II, para. 20, ed. L. A. Selby-Bigge (Oxford: Clarendon Press, 1972) 22.

31. Hume, *Enquiries*, sec. XII, pt. III, para. 132, p. 165.

32. Hume, *Enquiries*, sec. IV, pt. I, para. 20, p. 25.

33. Immanuel Kant, *Critique of Pure Reason*, trans. Norman Kemp Smith (New York: St. Martin's Press, 1929) Bxii–Bxv.

34. Kant, *Critique of Pure Reason*, A93–B126.

35. Alfred Korzybski, *Science and Sanity*, 4th ed. (Lakeville, CT: International Non-Artistotelian Library, 1933) 58.

36. Kant, *Critique of Pure Reason*, A125.

37. A. J. Ayer, "The Argument from Illusion," *Perception and the External World*, ed. R. J. Hirst (New York: Macmillan, 1965) 128.

38. Bertrand Russell, *The Problems of Philosophy* 17.

39. John Locke, *An Essay Concerning Human Understanding*, book 4, chap. 4, sec. 3, ed. Peter Nidditch (Oxford: Clarendon Press, 1975) 563.

40. Locke, book 4, chap. 11, sec. 4, 632.

41. Locke, sec. 5, 632.

42. Locke, sec. 6, 633.

43. Locke, sec. 7, 633.

44. Locke, sec. 8, 634.

45. Locke, book 2, chap. 8, sec. 9, 134.

46. George Berkeley, "A Treatise Concerning the Principles of Human Knowledge," para. 14 in *Principles, Dialogues, and Philosophical Correspondence*, ed. Colin Murray Turbayne (New York: Bobbs-Merrill, 1965) 28.

47. Berkeley (23) 32.

48. George Berkeley, "Three Dialogues Between Hylas and Philonous" in *George Berkeley: Principles, Dialogues, and Philosophical Correspondence*, ed. Colin Murray Turbayne (New York: Bobbs-Merrill Company, 1965) 196.

49. Cited in Martin Gardner, "Quantum Weirdness," *Discover* (Oct. 1982) 69.

50. Alan Goldman, *Empirical Knowledge* (Berkeley: University of California Press, 1988) 233–234.

51. Plato, "Meno," 98a, 98b; "Theatetus," 201c–210b.

52. Edmund L. Gettier, "Is Justified True Belief Knowledge?" *Analysis* 23 (1963) 121–123.

53. Gettier 121–122.

54. Gettier 122–123.

55. For a comprehensive review of recent attempts to analyze the concept of knowledge, see Robert K. Shope, *The Analysis of Knowing: A Decade of Research* (Princeton, NJ: Princeton University Press, 1983).

56. Keith Lehrer and Thomas D. Paxson, Jr., "Knowledge: Undefeated Justified True Belief," *Journal of Philosophy* 66.8 (1969) 225–237.

57 Alvin I. Goldman, "A Causal Theory of Knowing," *Journal of Philosophy* 64, 357–372.

58. Alvin I. Goldman, "Discrimination and Perceptual Knowledge," *Journal of Philosophy* 73 (1976) 771–791.

59. Keith Lehrer, *Theory of Knowledge* (Boulder, CO: Westview Press, 1990) 163–164.

60. This notion and much of the following material are suggested by Paul K. Moser, *Knowledge and Evidence* (Cambridge: Cambridge University Press, 1989) 242–266.

Credits

PHOTO CREDITS

Chapter 1

p. 1 © Jerry Uelsmann; p. 20 © Araldo de Luca/Corbis

Chapter 2

p. 65 © Jerry Uelsmann; p. 69 The Kobal Collection/20th Century Fox; p. 75 © Bettmann/Corbis; p. 84 © The Granger Collection, New York; p. 92 © Bettmann/Corbis; p. 97 © Bob Krist/Corbis; p. 102 © Warren Anatomical Museum, Harvard Medical School; p. 125 © Elliot & Fry/National Portrait Gallery; p. 152 M.C. Escher's "Waterfall" © 2002 Cordon Art B.V.—Baarn—Holland. All rights reserved.

Chapter 3

p. 179 © Jerry Uelsmann; p. 199 © Bettmann/Corbis; p. 205 © Michael Nicholson/Corbis; p. 212 © Bettmann/Corbis; p. 218 © The Granger Collection, New York; p. 225 © Bettmann/Corbis

Chapter 4

p. 247 © Jerry Uelsmann; p. 256 Ladd Company/Warner Bros/The Kobal Collection; p. 264 © Steve Wewerka/Getty; p. 266 © Scala/Art Resource; p. 274 © Bettmann/Corbis; p. 285 © 1988 Paramount/MP & TV Photo Archive; p. 294 © The Granger Collection, New York; p. 301 M.C. Escher's "Drawing Hands" © 2002 Cordon Art B.V.—Baarn—Holland. All rights reserved.

Chapter 5

p. 325 © Jerry Uelsmann; p. 354 © Bettmann/Corbis; p. 359 Royalty-Free/Corbis; p. 370 © Bettmann/Corbis; p. 400 © Bettmann/Corbis

Chapter 6

p. 433 © Jerry Uelsmann; p. 442 © Bettmann/Corbis; p. 448 © Bruce Iverson; p. 479 © Charles David Honl

Chapter 7

p. 529 © Jerry Uelsmann; p. 549 © J. R. Eyerman; p. 561 © Brian Moeskau/Moeskau Photography; p. 567 © Corbis; p. 580 © Paul Trummer

TEXT CREDITS

Definition for "faith" from *American Heritage Dictionary of the English Language.* Copyright © 1970 by Houghton Mifflin Company. Reprinted with the permission of Houghton Mifflin Company.

Excerpt from "The Man Who Lives in a Rainbow" from *Wired News* (March 19, 2002), *www.wired.com.* Copyright © 2002. Reprinted with permission.

Erik Baard, from "Cyborg Liberation Front: Inside the Movement for Posthuman Rights" from *The Village Voice* (July 30-August 5, 2003). Copyright © 2003. Reprinted with the permission of *The Village Voice.* This selection contains an excerpt from William Butler Yeats, "Sailing to Byzantium" from *The Poems of*

W. B. Yeats: A New Edition, edited by Richard J. Finneran. Copyright 1928 by The Macmillan Company, renewed © 1956 by Georgie Yeats. Reprinted with the permission of Scribner, an imprint of Simon & Schuster Adult Publishing Group.

Mark Balaguer, excerpt from "A Coherent, Naturalist, and Plausible Formulation of Libertarian Free Will" from *Nous* 38 (September 2004). Reprinted with the permission of Blackwell Publishers, Ltd.

I. Biran and A. Chatterjee, excerpt from "Alien Hand Syndrome" from *Archives of Neurology* 61 (February 2004). Copyright © 2004. Reprinted with the permission of the American Medical Association.

Terry Bisson, "They're Made of Meat" from *Omni* (April 1991). Reprinted with the permission of *Omni.*

Colin Blakemore, excerpt from *Mechanics of the Mind.* Copyright © 1977 by Cambridge University Press. Reprinted with the permission of Cambridge University Press.

Brand Blanshard, "The Philosophic Enterprise" from *The Owl of Minerva: Philosophers on Philosophy,* edited by Charles J. Bontempo and S. Jack Odell (New York: McGraw-Hill, 1975). Reprinted with the permission of the Yale University Office of Trusts & Estates.

Brand Blanshard, excerpt from *Reason and Belief.* Copyright © 1975 by Brand Blanshard. Reprinted with the permission of Yale University Press.

Ned Block, excerpts from "Troubles with Functionalism" from *Readings in the Philosophy of Psychology,* edited by Ned Block. Copyright © 1980 by Ned Block. Reprinted with the permission of Harvard University Press.

Nick Bostrom, excerpt from "The Simulation Argument: Why the Probability That You Are Living in a Matrix Is Quite High" from *New York Times Higher Education Supplement* (May 16, 2003). Copyright © 2003 by The New York Times Company. Reprinted with permission.

C.D. Broad, excerpt from "Human Personality and Its Survival of Bodily Death" from *Lectures on Psychical Research.* Copyright © 1962 by C.D. Broad. Reprinted with the permission of Routledge.

David J. Chalmers, "The Puzzle of Conscious Experience" from *Scientific American* 273, no. 6 (December 1995): 80-86. Copyright © 1995 by David J. Chalmers. Reprinted with the permission of the author.

Patricia Smith Churchland, excerpt from "Is Determinism Self-refuting?" from *Mind* 40 (1981). Reprinted with the permission of Oxford University Press, Ltd.

Excerpt from "Raelian Leader: Cloning First Step to Immortality" from CNN.com (December 29, 2002). Reprinted with permission.

Robert C. Coburn, excerpt from *The Strangeness of the Ordinary.* Copyright © 1990 by Rowman & Littlefield Publishers, Inc. Reprinted with the permission of Rowman & Littlefield Publishers.

Thomas D. Davis, "Please Don't Tell Me How the Story Ends" and "Why Don't You Just Wake Up?" from *Philosophy, Third Edition.* Copyright © 1992 by McGraw-Hill, Inc. Reprinted with the permission of McGraw-Hill, Inc.

Gottfried Wilhelm von Leibniz, excerpt from "Discourse on Metaphysics" from *Leibniz Selections*, edited by Philip P. Wiener. Copyright 1951. Reprinted with the permission of Pearson Education, Inc., Upper Saddle River, NJ.

Lucretius, excerpt from *On the Nature of Things*, translated by William Ellery Leonard. Reprinted with the permission of JM Dent & Sons, Ltd./The Orion Publishing Group.

Alasdair MacIntyre, "The Virtues, The Unity of a Human Life and the Concept of a Tradition" from *After Virtue*. Copyright © 1984 by Alasdair MacIntyre. Reprinted with the permission of University of Notre Dame Press.

Farhad Manjoo, excerpt from "Think Fast, Clever Robot" from *Wired News* (October 13, 2001),. Reprinted with the permission of Wired News.

John Markoff, excerpt from "The Soul of the Ultimate Machine" from *The New York Times* (December 10, 2000). Copyright © 2000 by The New York Times Company. Reprinted with permission.

Michael Martin, excerpt from "The Miracle Sleuth" from *The Big Domino in the Sky*. Copyright © 1996 by Michael Martin. Reprinted with the permission of Prometheus Books.

James McConnell, excerpt from "Criminals Can Be Brainwashed Now" from *Psychology Today* 3 (January 1970). Copyright © 1970 by Sussex Publishers, Inc. Reprinted with permission.

JoJo Moyes, excerpt from "Teenager sees colour after life in black and white" from *The Independent* (October 22, 1997). Copyright © 1997 by Independent News & Media (UK) Ltd.. Reprinted with permission.

Michele Nicolosi, excerpt from "Researchers Brainchild: Microchip Implants Boosting Mental Function" from *The Orange County Register* (April 20, 1997). Copyright © 1997. Reprinted with the permission of *The Orange County Register*.

Doron Nof and Nathan Paldor, excerpt from "Are There Oceanographic Explanations for the Israelites' Crossing of the Red Sea?" from *The Bulletin of the American Meteorological Society* 73 (March 1992). Reprinted with the permission of the American Meteorological Society.

Robert Nozick, excerpt from *Philosophical Explanations*. Copyright © 1981 by Robert Nozick. Reprinted with the permission of Harvard University Press. Excerpts from *Anarchy, State, and Utopia*. Copyright © 1974 by Robert Nozick. Reprinted with the permission of Basic Books, a member of Perseus Books, L.L.C.

Tom O'Connor, excerpt from "Emerging Defenses to Crime" from *http://faculty.ncwc.edu/toconnor/405/default.html*. Reprinted with the permission of Thomas R. O'Connor, Ph.D.

S. Jay Olshansky, Bruce Carnes, and Robert N. Butler, excerpt from "If Humans Were Built to Last" from *Scientific American* 284 (March 2001). Copyright © 2001 by 2002 by Scientific American, Inc. Reprinted by permission. All rights reserved.

Eric Olson, excerpts from *The Human Animal*. Copyright © 1997 by Oxford University Press, Inc. Reprinted with the permission of Oxford University Press, Inc.

Derek Parfit, excerpts from *Reasons and Persons*. Reprinted with the permission of Oxford University Press, Ltd. "Divided Minds and the Nature of Persons" from *Mindwaves*, edited by C. Blakemore and S. Greenfield. Reprinted with the permission of Basil Blackwell, Ltd.

Plato, excerpts from "Euthyphro," translated by Lane Cooper, from *Plato: The Collected Dialogues*, edited by E. Hamilton and H. Cairns. Copyright © 1973 by Princeton University Press.. Reprinted with the permission of Princeton University Press.

Hilary Putnam, excerpt from *Reason, Truth and History*. Copyright © 1981 by Cambridge University Press. Reprinted with the permission of Cambridge University Press.

Raelian Movement, excerpt from *www.rael.org/english/index.html*. Reprinted with the permission of the USA Raelian Movement.

John Rawls, "The Original Position and Justification" from *A Theory of Justice*. Copyright © 1971 by the President and Fellows of Harvard College. Reprinted with the permission of The Belknap Press of Harvard University Press.

Richard Rorty, excerpt from "Mind-Body Identity, Privacy, and Categories" from *The Review of Metaphysics* (1965-1966). Reprinted with the permission of Catholic University of America..

W. D. Ross, excerpts from *The Right and the Good*. Reprinted with the permission of Oxford University Press, Ltd.

William Rowe, excerpt from "The Problem with Evil and Some Varieties of Atheism" from *American Philosophical Quarterly* 16 (October 1979). Reprinted with the permission of the publishers.

Gilbert Ryle, excerpt from *The Concept of Mind*. Copyright 1949 by Gilbert Ryle. Reprinted with the permission of International Thomson Publishing Services.

John Searle, excerpt from *The Rediscovery of the Mind*. Copyright © 1992 by the Massachusetts Institute of Technology. Reprinted with the permission of The MIT Press. "Is the Brain's Mind a Computer Program?" from *Scientific American* 262 (January 1990). Copyright © 1990 by Scientific American, Inc. Reprinted by permission. All rights reserved.

Sidney Shoemaker, excerpt from *Self-Knowledge and Self-Identity*. Copyright © 1963 by Cornell University, renewed 1991 by Sidney Shoemaker. Reprinted with the permission of Cornell University Press.

Herb Silverman, excerpt from "Silverman's Wager" from *Free Inquiry* (Spring 2001). Copyright © 2001 by the Council for Secular Humanism. Reprinted with permission.

Margot Slade, excerpt from "The Devil Made Me Do It" from *The New York Times* (August 2, 2002). Copyright © 2002 by The New York Times Company. Reprinted with permission.

Michael Slote, excerpt from "Understanding Free Will" from *Journal of Philosophy* 77 (March 1980). Reprinted with the permission of *The Journal of Philosophy*.

Lee Smolin, excerpts from *The Life of the Cosmos*. Copyright © 1997 by Lee Smolin. Reprinted with the permission of Oxford University Press, Inc.

Raymond Smullyan, excerpt from "Is God a Taoist?" from *The Tao Is Silent*. Copyright © 1977 by Raymond M. Smullyan. Reprinted with the permission of HarperCollins Publishers Inc.

Roger W. Sperry, excerpt from "Changing Priorities" from *Annual Review of Neuroscience* 4 (1981). Copyright © 1981. Reprinted with the permission of Annual Reviews, Inc. Excerpt from "A Modified Concept of Consciousness" from *Psychological Review* 76 (1969). Copyright © 1969 by the American Psychological Association. Reprinted with the permission of the American Psychological Association.

W.T. Stace, "The Problem of Free Will" from *Religion and the Modern Mind*. Copyright 1952 by W.T. Stace, renewed © 1980 by Blanche Stace. Reprinted with the permission of HarperCollins Publishers Inc. "Are Ethical Values Relative?" from *The Concept of Morals*. Copyright © 1937 by The Macmillan Company; copyright renewed 1965 by W.T. Stace. Reprinted with the permission of Scribner, an imprint of Simon & Schuster, Adult Publishing Group.

Michael Stocker, excerpt from "The Schizophrenia of Modern Moral Theories" from *Journal of Philosophy* 73.14 (1976). Reprinted with the permission of *The Journal of Philosophy*.

Richard Swinburne, excerpt from "The Vocation of a Natural Theologian" from *Philosophers Who Believe*, edited by Kelley James

Index

Page numbers in boldface refer to glossary terms.